1997 LECTURES
and
MEMOIRS

PROCEEDINGS OF THE BRITISH ACADEMY · 97

1997 LECTURES
and
MEMOIRS

Published for THE BRITISH ACADEMY
by OXFORD UNIVERSITY PRESS

Oxford University Press, Great Clarendon Street, Oxford OX2 6DP

Oxford New York
Athens Auckland Bangkok Bogota Bombay
Buenos Aires Calcutta Cape Town Dar es Salaam
Delhi Florence Hong Kong Istanbul Karachi
Kuala Lumpur Madras Madrid Melbourne
Mexico City Nairobi Paris Singapore
Taipei Tokyo Toronto Warsaw

and associated companies in
Berlin Ibadan

Published in the United States by
Oxford University Press Inc., New York

British Library Cataloguing in Publication Data
Data available

ISBN 0–19–726192–2
ISSN 0068–1202

Typeset by J&L Composition Ltd, Filey, North Yorkshire
Printed in Great Britain
on acid-free paper by
The Cromwell Press Limited
Trowbridge, Wilts

All the lectures in this volume have been refereed

The Academy is grateful to Professor F. M. L. Thompson, CBE, FBA
for his editorial work on this volume

Contents

Memoirs

Qumran: Founded for Scripture.
The Background and Significance of
the Dead Sea Scrolls

HARTMUT STEGEMANN

Georg-August-Universität Göttingen

ONCE UPON A TIME there was a beautiful young princess who—together with all her staff and all the animals within her palace—fell asleep for a long period of time. An angry fairy had put a curse on her to cause her to die by pricking her finger with a spindle. But afterwards, another more gracious fairy had turned her fate into a long sleep until one day a bold prince should enter her chamber and wake her. Meanwhile, her castle became surrounded by a great number of trees, interlaced with brambles and thorns, a hedge so thick that neither man nor beast could penetrate it.

There are several possible ways to identify the leading figure of this fairy tale with Qumran topics. There are three suitable candidates for an identification with Sleeping Beauty, namely the scrolls hidden in the caves, the often neglected reports by some ancient writers on the Essenes, and the ruins of Chirbet Qumran, lonely for almost a hundred generations. Each of these possible identifications also includes a well-known rescuing prince, even if none of those first heroes succeeded in becoming the decisive saviour of Sleeping Beauty.

Meanwhile, half a century of research since the discovery of the first Qumran scrolls has produced more than ten thousand manuscript editions, scholarly books, and learned articles on this subject. Nevertheless, many of the basic riddles of these unexpected findings are still unresolved. Some helpful suggestions in earlier stages of Qumran research are again overwhelmed by new thorns, and the younger generation of Qumran scholars seems to be occupied much more with mistaken results of earlier research than with

Proceedings of the British Academy, **97**, 1–14. © The British Academy 1998.
Read at the Academy 5 November 1997.

the genuine evidence from the scrolls. Another century of Qumran research will be needed to resolve all the riddles and to clear up several important oddities. But instead of lamentations let us see what is on the stage and in which directions the signposts at our present cross-roads point.

The first candidate for the role of the helpful prince of our fairy tale is clearly Muhammad edh-Dhib, 'the wolf'. This summer he died, aged about 67, as a poor refugee in Jordan. At the beginning of the year 1947 he was a bold Beduin boy aged seventeen who entered through a light-shaft in its ceiling a cave still blocked by stones in the rocky mountain slope of the Judaean Desert hills close to the Dead Sea. There he found many jars containing old scrolls. He belonged to the famous tribe of Ta'amireh Beduin who have lived for more than two millennia in that region between Bethlehem and the Dead Sea. According to 1 Maccabees 9: 58–73, support by this tribe—once called Odomera (9: 66)—enabled Jonathan and Simon, the Maccabees, in 157 BCE finally to defeat the Seleucid general Bacchides in the battle of Bethbasi— about two miles south-west of Bethlehem—and to free their country from its pagan rulers. In our days, the Ta'amireh discovered between 1947 and 1956 five of the eleven Qumran caves with most of the scrolls. After they had brought seven of them in the spring of 1947 to Kando, a Christian cobbler in Bethlehem, he sold four to the Syrian Metropolitan in Jerusalem, Mar Athanasius Samuel, and three others to a professor of archaeology at the Hebrew University in Jerusalem, the late Eliezer Lipa Sukenik, the father of the late Professor Yigael Yadin. These events caused the start of Qumran research, which became a breakthrough to a very new—otherwise impossible—modern understanding of ancient Judaism.

There is still a vivid debate on the relationship between the Qumran settlement and the scroll-caves surrounding it. Professor Norman Golb is of the opinion that Qumran was a government military post, while the scrolls were brought to its vicinity from Jerusalem. Pauline Donceel-Voûte argues that the settlement was a lonely villa without a library, wherever the scrolls may have come from and arrived there one day. Almost every year a new theory of this kind spreads all over the world. But already during his Qumran excavations from 1952 to 1958 the late Père Roland de Vaux had convincingly established the fact that the pottery in all the relevant caves was clearly manufactured within the Qumran settlement. Therefore, the scrolls too must once have belonged there. Indeed, the three 'scroll-caves' 7, 8, and 9 were really nothing else but the living-rooms of some people staying at Qumran. They were an integral part of the settlement, a fact that is ignored by almost all scholars.

The best explanation for the findings in all the other caves is still that of Père de Vaux. According to a report by Flavius Josephus, on 21 June 68 CE the Roman legio X Fretensis occupied the town of Jericho—about seven miles north of Qumran—and they destroyed the Qumran settlement a few days later. Meanwhile, the inhabitants had safeguarded all the contents of their library in the surrounding caves, finally putting the huge mass of remaining scrolls and documents in Cave 4, which is only 50 yards distant. This theory fits the evidence best and should no longer be doubted.

Initially, all the eleven scroll-caves together may have contained about 1000 scrolls and documents. Some of them decayed during the millennia without leaving any remnants. What today are called 'the Dead Sea Scrolls' are, indeed, just nine scrolls of which at least half of their former contents have survived, and only one of them—a scroll of the Book of Isaiah from Cave 1— is preserved almost completely. The remnants of all the other scrolls and documents, nearly 900 in number, are fragmentary. Often only one or two fragments of a formerly long scroll survived. The remains of about 200 scrolls are so poor that nobody is any longer able to identify their contents or to relate them to other known texts from the ancient past. Sometimes, it is even impossible to make out whether the square-script letters on such fragments once belonged to a Hebrew or to an Aramaic composition. Nevertheless, the remains of almost 700 scrolls and documents are still more or less decipherable. Often several copies of the same composition still exist, all of them fragmentary, but mutually completing one another. This kind of scholarly puzzle, which can only in part be tackled with infra-red photographs and which otherwise requires work on the originals of the scrolls in Jerusalem, still continues, while in some cases the results of such scholarly reconstructions are already published.

As a matter of fact, the present bad condition of most of the Qumran scrolls is only in part due to the climatic conditions in the caves where they were found. In March 1952, Père de Vaux and his staff discovered Cave 3, more than one mile north of Qumran. The famous Copper Scroll, with an inventory of sixty-three places containing rich treasures, was still well preserved hidden under rocks. On the other hand, the archaeologists found the sherds of about thirty-four jars scattered around, as well as many unwritten cover-sheets of former scrolls and the extremely fragmentary remains of about thirty manuscripts, usually only one or two fragments of each scroll, which had mostly fallen off their beginnings or their top- and bottom-edges. The remains of twenty of them are so poor that a textual identification is no longer possible. All the fragments from this cave fill just two pages in their final edition. How can this strange evidence be explained?

The mass of the former scrolls in Cave 3 must have disappeared already in the past. About 800 CE the Nestorian patriarch Timotheus I of Seleucia, today Baghdad, told his colleague Sergius of Elam in a letter that the dog of a hunting Arab had disappeared ten years before in a cave not very far from Jericho. When the Arab entered that cave, he found there plenty of old 'books'.

He informed the Jews in Jerusalem about his discovery, and many of them came and took the books home. There is no other Qumran cave that fits this description. Some of those Jewish inhabitants of Jerusalem at that time may have been Karaites. At least, the Karaites later on reported that many of their special teachings were due to some 'people of the cave', and from the genizah of the Karaite synagogue in Cairo, edited by Schechter in 1910, we know about half of the original text of the so-called Damascus Document, ten copies of which have now been found in different Qumran caves. In future, many more copies from former Qumran scrolls may become identified within the huge mass of medieval manuscripts from the Cairo Genizah, and also within the almost unexplored rich collection of the Karaite Firkovitch in St Petersburg. For the moment it may be sufficient to offer a plausible suggestion why no real scrolls could any longer be found in Cave 3 when scholars first came across this place in modern times.

A similar fate befell the scrolls in what were formerly four living and study rooms of the Qumran inhabitants at that southern edge of the marl terrace, which is today occupied by the ruins of the Qumran settlement. In 1955, the excavators still found in the ruins of those rooms the sherds of at least eight jars. But the poor remains of many scrolls written in Greek from Cave 7 fill just one page in the edition, while from Cave 8—apart from a phylactery and the mezuzah of the last inhabitant—only petty fragments of three scrolls could be rescued, from Cave 9 just one tiny fragment, from a fourth apartment nothing. Reports by Eusebius of Caesarea and Epiphanius of Salamis inform us that in the third century CE Origen could reproduce—as an additional column in the Psalter of his Hexapla—a Greek scroll which had been found, together with other Greek and Hebrew scrolls, in jars not far from Jericho shortly before in the year 217 CE. The only other Qumran cave with Greek and Hebrew manuscripts at the same time is Cave 4, which was not emptied until 1952. Therefore, Origen's additional text may very likely have come from Qumran's Cave 7. All the other scrolls from Caves 7, 8, and 9 seem to be lost for ever.

Furthermore, Caves 2 and 4 were entered some time in the Middle Ages by people who did not take away the scrolls which they found there, but destroyed most of them and scattered the remains on the floor, where they were rotted by humidity, or the wind blew them away. Also in better protected caves like Cave 1 and Cave 11 about half of the scrolls were glued by humidity or decayed in such a way that up to half of the former number of scrolls in those caves disappeared apart from some tiny fragments. Finally, the Beduin are said to have destroyed some scrolls in the early days, before they knew of their value. Some scrolls were hidden as illicit property in wet places and suffered from rain. Many fine fragments may be lost for ever, as they were acquired by tourists during the fifties and spread all over the world, and only very few of them have become known meanwhile to scholars or museums. You see,

Sleeping Beauty looks like the scattered remains of a very old mummy if we compare her today to the originally beautiful Dead Sea Scrolls' library at Qumran. But this is only a superficial impression. Everything will change at the moment when we recognise the contents of that evidence which finally survived in spite of so much loss.

All the Qumran scrolls were written within the period from the final decades of the third century BCE down to the destruction of Qumran in the year 68 CE. About 200 of them are usually designated as 'biblical manuscripts', but this large number includes thirty-six phylacteries or mezuzoth with only their traditional excerpts from Exodus and Deuteronomy. A scroll of the 'Pentateuch' contained only the 'Song of Moses', Deuteronomy 32, and some 'Psalter scrolls' only collections of some psalms. The twelve Minor Prophets were usually copied on one scroll, while on the other hand the books of the voluminous Pentateuch were generally distributed among several scrolls, sometimes two of them being written on a single scroll. The true number of biblical scrolls that contained the full text of at least one book is less than 140. But often the fragmentary state of preservation no longer allows us to state the former content of the whole scroll. On the other hand, sometimes different parts of the same scroll have been published separately from one another, as their contents appeared to belong to different books. Only after the full evidence has been published in the future will scholars be able to have a second look at such confusions.

The main profit we can gain from the biblical Qumran manuscripts is that we have now for the first time authentic evidence of those versions of the biblical books which were current in Palestine within the Second Temple period. The Masoretic Text of our Hebrew Bible is based on medieval manuscripts. The only 'Bible manuscript' before the Qumran discoveries was the so-called Nash Papyrus from the second or first century BCE with the text of the decalogue and of the Shema Israel. Only indirectly could early versions like the Septuagint or quotations by ancient authors help scholars to speculate on divergent readings behind them. Now we have at least fragmentary evidence of all books of the Hebrew Bible (except only for the book of Esther) which is about a millennium older than the Masoretic Text. The result is surprising. There are several scrolls which provide us with almost the same text that we already knew from the Middle Ages. But there are other scrolls which offer for the first time the divergent Hebrew text underlying the Septuagint. They demonstrate that the Greek translators used their Hebrew *Vorlage* less freely than is usually supposed. There are also scrolls of the Pentateuch with a text rather close to the so-called Samaritan version, which now turns out to be an old Palestinian form of text, which was only secondarily adopted by the Samaritans and slightly revised by them.

Some more evidence is exciting. There is a text of 1 Samuel which has not yet been finally published, and which is thought to be perhaps older than that of the masoretes. There are more than thirty copies of the Psalter which inform us that (*a*) the Psalter was already divided into its five traditional books in Qumran times, and that (*b*) books one to three—i.e., Psalms 1–89—were textually almost finally established at a time when the arrangement and contents of its final two books were still fluid. Whenever this period was during the third or second century BCE, this evidence at least refutes all still current assumptions that a final redaction of the whole Psalter, including also its opening Psalm 1, was completed as late as Maccabean times.

These are only a few examples of fresh approaches to our biblical text thanks to the Qumran discoveries. Within a few years from now, all the relevant evidence will be finally published. But Jewish and Christian Bible scholars will still need some decades of research to work out the manifold relationships between all these divergent manuscripts and the versions of the biblical books that have long been known, like the Masoretic Text or the Septuagint.

Another case of innovation resulting from the Qumran discoveries is the field of studies of apocalyptic. Since J. T. Milik published most of the Enoch evidence from Qumran's Cave 4 in 1976, everybody knows that the 'Astronomical Book' of the Enoch collection and its 'Book of the Watchers' are remarkably older than the biblical Book of Daniel, which was completed 164 BCE. Now we have copies of both Enoch apocalypses which are palaeographically dated about 200 BCE or into the beginning of the second century. The literary compositions themselves may come from the Persian period, or from the third century BCE at the latest. Nevertheless, current research in Jewish apocalyptic studies continues to be much more influenced by the later apocalyptic books of Daniel, of John in the New Testament, or of 4 Ezra than by those earlier Enoch sources.

Let me mention some other interesting findings. Before the Qumran discoveries, the Greek text of the Book of Tobit was our oldest version of it. Now we have four fragmentary manuscripts which demonstrate that this book was originally written in Aramaic. The Book of Jubilees was mainly known by Ethiopic manuscripts from the Middle Ages. Now we have at least fourteen fragmentary Hebrew copies of it which demonstrate inter alia that the author of this book still used the Tetragrammaton freely. This finding suggests that the Book of Jubilees may have been composed earlier than Ben Sira, who about 190 BCE totally avoided the Tetragrammaton. Nevertheless, almost all scholars continue to date the Book of Jubilees about the middle of the second century BCE.

Last but not least, the Qumran discoveries have provided us with about 120 literary works—or some fragments of them—which were previously quite unknown to modern scholarship. Only about forty of them were clearly composed by contemporaries of the inhabitants of Qumran, e.g., some rule-books, several pesharim, two midrashim, or hymns like the Hodayot. On the other hand, two thirds of these 'new' books seem to have been traditional to them, i.e., they may have been composed before the middle of the second century BCE in earlier Hellenistic times, or even in the Persian period. This kind of evidence includes some collections of prayers, liturgies, non-biblical psalms, the Songs of the Sabbath Sacrifice, the New Jerusalem composition, some calendrical works, even the text of the famous Temple Scroll or the first draft of the War Scroll. Those earlier centuries were at the same time the formative period for most of the books of the Hebrew Bible. Nevertheless, many Old Testament scholars still continue to regard all the new Qumran evidence as basically 'post-canonical' and without any bearing on their research. For them our Beauty is still sleeping. This is only a small selection from the broad field of innovation resulting from the Qumran discoveries, but enough to show its impact on previous interpretations and its challenges for further research.

My second identification of Sleeping Beauty includes some literary sources, especially the reports of Philo of Alexandria, of Flavius Josephus, and of Pliny the Elder on the Essenes. In this case, the saving prince of our fairy tale was the late Professor Eliezer Lipa Sukenik who bought his three scrolls in Bethlehem on 29 November and 22 December 1947. He also learned that those scrolls were found in a cave close to the north-western shores of the Dead Sea. After a glimpse also into the Serekh ha-Yachad scroll of the Syrian Metropolitan, which Sukenik had insufficient money to buy, he suggested in the first scholarly publication on the Dead Sea Scrolls (his 'Oṣar ha-Megilloth ha-Genuzoth [1948], written in Hebrew), that the scrolls might come from the Essenes, since according to Pliny the Elder 'the Essenes' had settled in just that region. This identification has been shared since then by most scholars. The problem is that it does not lead into the chamber of Sleeping Beauty, but only into the cellar of her castle.

Extremely rarely do we meet in the field of historical scholarship a contrast like that between the descriptions of the Essenes by Philo and Josephus on the one hand, and their understanding by Qumran scholars on the other. Philo and Josephus once agreed that the Essenes were a mighty group with more than 4,000 members, i.e., adult men who lived in their time in almost all towns and villages of Judaea. Compared to them the Pharisees had—according to Josephus—more than 6,000 members, only about half of them living in Judaea and most of the others in Galilee, while the élite Sadducees had at best a few hundred members. Therefore, the Essenes represented the most important of all the religious organisations in Judaea.

Both ancient authors also agree that the Essenes were regarded at that time as an unrivalled model of Jewish piety. Philo praised them in two long sections of his treatises, taking no notice of the Pharisees or of the Sadducees. Josephus not only mentions the Essenes frequently, but dedicates to their praise the long passage in paragraphs 119 to 161 in the second book of his description of the Jewish war, adding there just five short paragraphs (162–6) to describe also the Pharisees and the Sadducees, in spite of the fact that he himself was a Pharisee. Both Jewish writers of that time clearly shared the opinion that if you want to know the best of all Jews, you should look at this important group of the Essenes all over the country. Finally, the first Essene in history mentioned by Josephus was a man named Judah who taught his Essene students in the Jerusalem temple in the year 103 BCE, while any special settlement of the Essenes like that at the Dead Sea is mentioned neither by Josephus nor by Philo. The first time Josephus makes mention of the Essenes—together with the Pharisees and Sadducees as separate groups—is in a context where he depicts events about the middle of the second century BCE.

Qumran scholars who identify the Yachad, the religious organisation of the Dead Sea Scrolls, with the Essenes take a quite opposite view of them. They think of a small group of priests and laymen who—guided by the Teacher of Righteousness—left the temple in Jerusalem about the middle of the second century BCE because of a schism about the calendar and settled at Qumran, which became their headquarters. There they lived through more than two centuries in splendid isolation an ascetic, celibate life-style like monks. Only a few of them returned after some time to the towns and villages all over the country to marry and to continue a family life. This way, most Qumran scholars are accustomed to speculate, two kinds of Essenes came into being, the celibate main group in Qumran and several minor splinter-groups of married Essenes all over the country.

Indeed, according to Philo and Pliny the Elder all Essenes were unmarried, while Josephus seems to suggest that most of them never married, while some of them—'another order of the Essenes'—did so. The main problem is that in none of the many Dead Sea scrolls is there any hint of celibacy, while all rule-books from the Qumran caves—including Serekh ha-Yachad, the so-called 'Community Rule'—mention the idea of marriage as a matter of course. This fact is very important, as traditionally minded Judaism never could tolerate celibacy. The background is that, according to Genesis 1, God's first command to all mankind, who had just been created, was: 'Be fruitful, and multiply, and replenish the earth' (1. 28). It was impossible to follow this command other-wise than by marrying and begetting children. What God commanded to all mankind must be obeyed at least by Jews. All 'the people of the Dead Sea scrolls', as John Marco Allegro once called them, clearly did so. Were the 'people of the scrolls' not the unmarried Essenes as depicted by Philo, Josephus, and Pliny?

The solution is simple, but has not yet been accepted by most Qumran scholars. Every male Essene must marry at the age of twenty years. But he was prohibited from marrying more often than once in his life. If his wife died, if he divorced her, or if she turned out to be sterile, he could not marry a second wife after her or in addition to her. In Palestinian Judaism of that time girls were usually given in marriage aged about thirteen years. Every year they gave birth to a child. Because of these continual pregnancies in the early years of their lives they died at an average age of about twenty years, while their husbands so often became very old that the Qumran rule-books had to ordain that everybody must resign from all his offices at the age of sixty. This was the Essenes' regular pension age. Josephus was even of the opinion that 'most of them remain alive over a hundred years'. This statement is clearly exaggerated. On the other hand, Pharisees and other Jews used to marry at the age of about seventeen years. The result is that young Essenes remained unmarried for three to four years at an age when others were already husbands, and most adult Essenes were no longer married after their only wife died, or they had divorced her. This way no Essene was celibate, but at least eighty per cent of the Essenes were not yet married or no longer married.

This would have been the reality behind the ancient writers' praise of the Essenes as unmarried people in general, a Jewish group with more than 4,000 members who really lived according to the model of the Pythagoreans, while at the same time the Greek world was not able to present an equivalent to such an impressive school of philosophers who devoted their whole lives solely to study, not to women and taking care of children. The pure existence of the Essenes, as they depicted them, was an outstanding opportunity to demonstrate that the often insulted Jews were much better than the rest of the world. The Essenes offered the most brilliant example for this demonstration, even if the reality was slightly refined by Philo and Josephus.

The assertion of a lifelong celibacy of all Essenes is the only major discrepancy between 'the people of the Dead Sea scrolls' and the Essenes as depicted by the ancient Jewish writers. If they did not mention particularities like calendrical orientations or messianic hopes, which are important in the scrolls, this reserve was due to the supposed interests of their Hellenistic, partly even pagan readers. Sometimes scholars point to other more or less apparent discrepancies, but there is no need to discuss them here in detail. Cambridge University Press deserves thanks for having published in 1988 an extremely helpful book on *Josephus' description of the Essenes illustrated by the Dead Sea Scrolls* by Todd S. Beall, who also takes into account other authors like Philo. He convincingly concludes that none of the alleged 'discrepancies is serious enough to put into question the identification of' what he calls 'the Qumran community with Josephus' Essenes' (p. 129).

The best evidence for the identification of 'the people of the Dead Sea scrolls' with the Essenes is some findings in the Qumran manuscripts which clearly agree with peculiarities of the Essenes mentioned by Josephus, partly also by Philo, which at the same time distinguish them from the other Jewish organisations. The most impressive example is that both Josephus and the scrolls state that at least three years were needed to become a full member of the organisation—with a strict test at the end of every year of admittance.

To become a Pharisee demanded only basic knowledge of the most important prescriptions regarding ritual purity and giving the tithe and the promise to keep to them, while the Sadducees co-opted new members according to their own choice without any special entrance examination. Further Essene peculiarites of this kind were the daily assemblies of all full members of their local groups for their common prayers and for their common meals: no other groups shared those customs. Not only the sessions of their courts, but every kind of assembly must be presided over by a priest, while the Pharisees no longer kept to the traditional hierarchical order: in their group laymen could gain the very same privileges as the priests in the past. The Essenes immersed themselves in their ritual baths much more often and on more occasions than all other Jews of their time. Last but not least, only they had 'everything in common': the scrolls now demonstrate that this 'having in common' was related only to all property including labour and personal abilities, while the produce still belonged to the members like the inheritance—the 'nachalah'—of the country in the Torah: only the tithes of all produce—including even wages—must be delivered to the administrative authorities.

These many and basic peculiarities evidently demonstrate that 'the people of the scrolls' were none other than those Essenes who were described by Philo and Josephus, who lived in almost every village and town of Judaea including Jerusalem, and who were the most important religious organisation in this territory. But curiously, most scholars are still far from using those ancient reports on the Essenes as an important clue to a better understanding of the scrolls. This is best attested by the book of Todd S. Beall. The author discusses Josephus' description of the Essenes, sentence after sentence. For almost every detail he identifies and adduces at least one Qumran scholar who had commented on it during the decades of previous research. But significantly Beall could not adduce even one Qumran scholar who, during forty years of Qumran research, had commented on the number of 'more than 4000' Essenes (see pp. 48 and 120)—in spite of the fact that most scholars had always identified 'the people of the Dead Sea scrolls' with the Essenes.

There is only one explanation for this curious fact. Qumran scholars continue to start basically not from Philo and Josephus, who both mention this large number of Essenes, but from Pliny the Elder according to whom 'the Essenes' lived almost exclusively at a place close to the north-western shore of the Dead Sea (*Naturalis historia*, v. 15). There can no longer be any doubt that this information referred to no other place but Qumran. But it is impossible that more than 4,000 people—or at least most of them—lived there together through more than two centuries. Even if they had lived there in caves, tents, and huts, so many people could not gather for common worship and common meals within the Qumran buildings. Also there are about 1,200 graves in the Qumran cemeteries, a large number, but not sufficient for so many inhabitants for more than a century. In fact, Qumran scholars usually speculate on a number of only 150–200—or, as a maximum, of 300—people living there at the same time. Therefore, the real number of Essenes—including those in the towns and villages of the country—would never have exceeded 300 or even 500. The large numbers of Philo and Josephus must have been immoderately exaggerated and need no discussion. This is the impression one gains from earlier Qumran studies.

Indeed, from the very beginning of research on the Dead Sea Scrolls the special conditions of the Qumran settlement became the decisive criterion for all possible realities behind the findings, including the relevant idea of the Essenes. They were reduced to 'the Qumran community', to a small sectarian splinter-group of ancient Judaism, which would have had little importance for understanding the broader orientations of Judaism in late Second Temple times. A few years ago, a Jewish colleague did much research on one of the Qumran texts, 4QMMT, with a characteristic result: 'The two largest groups, the Sadducees and the Pharisees, represent the two main streams of ancient Judaism. . . . Somewhere between these two main groups stood the small, pietistic, zealous Qumran sect.' This is just the opposite of the idea of the Essenes propagated by their Jewish contemporaries, Philo and Josephus. It still needs much research and more developed suggestions before a final awakening of their highly interesting reports after a sleep of almost two millennia.

My third and final candidate for an identification with Sleeping Beauty is the Qumran settlement itself, including En Feshkha less than two miles south of it and once an integral part of the whole architectural ensemble. The prince is in this case Père Roland de Vaux who—together with his staff—dug and surveyed the whole area from 1952 to 1958. Today, Qumran is again a vivid site, now as a tourist attraction. Before the scrolls were discovered in the surrounding caves nobody was interested in these ruins, but since the last century the cemeteries had attracted the attention of some archaeologists as all the Qumran graves—except one—are orientated in a north-south-direction, which is strange compared to the other graves in Palestine. Thanks to the scrolls we now know that the dead in those graves face the Garden of Eden, the paradise, which according to Genesis 2 is situated around the sources of the rivers Euphrates and Tigris in what is today eastern Turkey, north of Qumran. This is a clear hint of the Essenes' belief in bodily resurrection at the end of days. Almost all the men who are buried there died at an age of twenty-five to thirty-five years. The exceptional grave at the western border of the main cemetery is that of a man who died aged about sixty, and who alone was buried facing the temple in Jerusalem.

When Père de Vaux excavated Qumran he found that at this place existed at first a small settlement in the late monarchical period, which was destroyed by the Babylonians in 587 BCE. The Qumran settlement, as we know it, was established at the same place—according to de Vaux—in the second century BCE and destroyed in the year 68 CE. Père de Vaux suggested that the Teacher of Righteousness came there with his adherents about the middle of the second century BCE. At first, they would have lived in tents or huts. But after some decades they started to build some small apartments, while the broader constructions were built only at the beginning of the first century BCE.

Today, this early theory is doubted by most scholars. The Qumran excavations revealed many coins. About 140 of them come from the time of Alexander Jannaeus (103–76 BCE), but only one from the time of his father John Hyrcanus, and not a single coin from the times of Jonathan and Simon, the Maccabees. This finding clearly demonstrates that the Qumran settlement was established no earlier than at the very end of the second century BCE, or in the early years of the first century BCE. At this time, the Teacher of Righteousness was no longer alive: he could never have paid a visit to this settlement or even stayed there. At this time all the rule-books of the Serekh ha-Yachad scroll had already been composed, as it is evidenced meanwhile by its oldest copy from the second century BCE: it was clearly not composed for the few inhabitants of Qumran, but for the Essenes all over the country, a fact that is also textually attested by three passages in the top part of column VI. Whatever the purpose behind the Qumran buildings may once have been, they never served as some kind of monastery for the Teacher and his adherents.

How many people lived at any one time at Qumran? The number of 1,200 graves in the cemeteries after about 170 years of settlement, combined with the fact that the men died there aged about thirty years on the average, suggests the conclusion that there was a local population of about fifty adult men. The same number results from the dimensions of the dining hall. For in the same room the common prayer services of all local members also took place, which were held according to the traditional temple ritual: all must prostrate themselves with outstretched arms. This way not more than ten rows with six men each could pray at the same time, i.e., sixty persons was the upper limit for Qumran inhabitants. This is at the very best one-and-a-half per cent of the more than 4,000 Essenes. Why did some of them start to stay there at all?

Furthermore, Qumran never served as the headquarters of the Essenes. In the scrolls several kinds of documents are mentioned which must have been available in the organisational centre, e.g. membership lists, the results of the new ranking every year, registers of the common property, administrative acts, decisions of the courts, or records of the past heroic deeds of some members of the Essenes. Not one document of this kind could be identified within the hundreds of scrolls and other written evidence from the Qumran caves. One can only speculate on the headquarters of the Essenes: perhaps it was in Jerusalem, but certainly never at Qumran.

What we need is a new approach to the archaeological Qumran evidence beyond the former view of Père de Vaux, which will at the same time explain the huge mass of related scrolls and the striking fact that only very rarely were two, or even three scrolls written by the same scribe: why are there several hundreds of different scribal hands during the time from about 100 BCE to 68 CE, when the Qumran settlement existed?

Let me tell you in short my own explanation. According to 1Q Serekh ha-Yachad, VI. 13–23 all new members of the group had to undergo a test at the end of each of at least three years before their final admittance. Not only was their behaviour during each year tested, but more importantly their progress in Bible knowledge, particularly in Torah knowledge. To get knowledge means in this case to learn by heart. According to another passage in the Serekh ha-Yachad, V, 23 f., this kind of test was repeated every year also for full members to establish their rank within the classes of priests, Levites, and laymen: the rank of everybody very much depended on his further progress in Bible knowledge. Last but not least, every full member of the Essenes must spend a third of every night together with the other Essenes in his town or village in studying the Torah: this implies at least three hours in the summer or almost five hours in the winter every night for the rest of his life.

This way, the Essenes had not only the best Bible knowledge of all Jews, but everybody also needed several scrolls for this kind of learning and study, scrolls with the five books of the Torah, scrolls with the books of some prophets, and a Psalter scroll. According to my calculations, the more than 4,000 Essenes needed at least about 50,000, perhaps up to 200,000, scrolls through the 170 years of Qumran's existence. In my opinion, they established this settlement half a century after their coming into existence as they had discovered a new way to tan leather with the ingredients of Dead Sea water, which produced a better quality of leather (most of the Qumran scrolls from the first century BCE onwards have a much better quality than the Qumran scrolls from the third and second centuries BCE) and enabled them to manufacture much more scroll leather than by the traditional methods.

This way, Qumran would have been founded for Scripture. The rough leather tannery was in En Feshkha, at that time immediately at the edge of the Dead Sea, as much water from there was needed for that process. At Qumran the fine leather preparation was installed, also a long room for manufacturing the scrolls by sewing together their single sheets; above this room was the scriptorium, where about ten to twelve scribes wrote at the same time guided by dictation, in the basement the central library with the master-scrolls and some others for study in the reading room. All the few further rooms and buildings at Qumran were just the equipment which the people working there needed for their daily lives. When Qumran was destroyed, this way of manufacturing scrolls ended—or continued at some other place which we do not know. But the end of Qumran was not at the same time the end of all the many Essenes, even if the Qumran findings cannot help us to detect their continued way of existence.

Please allow me a short final remark on how the Essenes once came into being. In the time of the rigid Hellenisation of Palestine by Antiochus IV and by the high priest Menelaus, thousands of Jews had left the country and settled in the surrounding territories of what are today Lebanon, Syria, Jordan, and Egypt. In those places of exile, they established several organisations like 'The New Covenant in the Land of Damascus', or the so-called Asidaioi perhaps in Jordan. About the middle of the second century the Teacher of Righteousness unified most of these groups—according to 4QPsalms[a], IV. 23 f. seven of them—and led them back to the Holy Land.

This was the constitution of the Essenes, 'the pious ones' as they were called by others, as an All-Israel Union, which the Essenes themselves designated as their Yachad. For political reasons a few, but important, groups refused to become members of this Yachad, mainly those priests who continued to serve at the temple in Jerusalem under the high priest Jonathan—from them the Sadducees later evolved—also the 'schismatic' Pharisees as a splinter-group of the former Asidaioi, and finally some members of the 'New Covenant in the Land of Damascus' who refused to return.

Nevertheless, this way the Essenes—guided by their Teacher of Righteousness—became the most important religious organisation in Judaea, not as progressive reformers, but as traditionally orientated Jews—remember that two thirds of all the new books from the Qumran caves may come from pre-Essenes times—no heretics, but the best of all Torah-orientated Jews of their time, not only according to Philo and Josephus, but likewise according to their own testimony in the scrolls. But if you look back at half a century of Qumran research you may agree that Sleeping Beauty has not yet woken completely, however we may identify her. The fairy tale continues.

Note. References are available from the author on request.

Life and Work in Shakespeare's Poems

COLIN BURROW
Gonville and Caius College, Cambridge

IN BORGES'S HAUNTING TALE CALLED 'Shakespeare's Memory' a Shakespearean scholar meets a man called Thorpe (a name which we will meet again later on) who claims to possess Shakespeare's memory, and who offers to pass it on to our hero. The scholar, a thorough German, thinks this will enable him to write his master work: a biography of Shakespeare, written with true inside knowledge, and so he accepts the offer of Shakespeare's memory. At first nothing happens; then odd sounds and half-glimpses of something almost forgotten begin to spring on him at unexpected moments. These sensual recollections become more frequent until they form a pervasive sense of guilt at some unremembered act. He finds, though, that Shakespeare's memory can tell him nothing specific about the content of Shakespeare's mental processes and nothing at all about Shakespeare's works. Despite this he is gradually dominated by his parasitic memory, until it begins to swamp his own recollections. Eventually, fearing madness, he dials a telephone number at random, and passes on Shakespeare's memory to its next, anonymous, host.[1]

Surely this is a tale with a moral for anyone attempting to write about Shakespeare's life and works: it suggests that the experience of being Shakespeare is irretrievable even to someone who possesses his memory.

---

[1] Jorge Luis Borges, *Obras Completas 1975–1985* (Buenos Aires, 1989), pp. 393–9. The tale contains what is either a delicious typo or an engaging deliberate Borgesian error: the scholar writes an article to prove that Sonnet 117 was written in the Armada year of 1588, and then discovers that Samuel Butler had suggested the same date for the poem in 1899. This clearly must be a reference to Sonnet 107 rather than 117, and suggests that one model for Borges' hero was the indefatigable Leslie Hotson, who dates 107 to 1588 (as Butler had done) in 'The Mortall Moone', repr. in *Shakespeare's Sonnets Dated and Other Essays* (London, 1949), pp. 4–21.

Proceedings of the British Academy, **97** 15–50. © The British Academy 1998.
Read at the Academy 21 October 1997.

Few of us, if we were honest about it, would wish to re-enact Shakespeare's life—to inhabit the anxieties of a first performance, or the even greater anxiety of the desperate last-minute revisions which might have occupied the night before a first performance, to feel the chill of touring performances outside, or to relive the possible infidelities of his love life. Fortunately my aim is not to retrieve Shakespeare's life and mind from his works. I have slightly rearranged the brief of the Chatterton lecture, and have decided not to discuss 'the life and works of a dead English poet', as the lecturer is supposed to, but to talk about life and work *in* Shakespeare's poems instead. This may keep at bay the insanity suffered by Borges's hero, as well as the pandemic of madness which strikes those who have attempted in real life to consider Shakespeare's poems as the key to his mind. Poor Delia Bacon was the first to drive herself into madness and destitution in her attempts to prove that Francis Bacon wrote Shakespeare, but her life has its fictional parallel in the zealous efforts of the hero of Oscar Wilde's 'The Portrait of Mr W. H.' to prove that the Sonnets were addressed to a boy player called Willie Hughes.[2] One of the most entertaining pieces of biographical madness is G. W. Phillips's *Sunlight in Shakespeare's Sonnets*,[3] which proves (how could so many readers have missed it?) that the Sonnets tell how Shakespeare was seduced by an aristocratic woman, whose illegitimate son by Shakespeare then went on to cuckold his father with Anne Hathaway. With sunlight (and what a terrible pun it is) like that who needs darkness? But there are darker biographical productions: the ingenious Martin Green infers from the lines 'Why didst thou promise such a beauteous day, | And make me travel forth without my cloak' (34. 1–2)[4] that Shakespeare had forgotten to wear a condom, which his father, a glover, sold under the counter, and so had contracted venereal disease from the young man. Green is undeterred by the facts that condoms are not recorded in England before 1660 and were never called 'cloaks'.[5] The end of this lecture will make a case for keeping something like life in play while reading Shakespeare's Sonnets, but it will be a slightly less sickly version of life.

    The chief aim of this lecture is to think about the Sonnets and the narrative poems as a group, and to relate them to some of the material realities from

---

[2] See S. Schoenbaum, *Shakespeare's Lives*, 2nd edn. (Oxford, 1991), pp. 385–94.

[3] (London, 1935).

[4] All quotations from the non-dramatic verse will be my own modernisations of the earliest quartos.

[5] Martin Green, *The Labyrinth of Shakespeare's Sonnets: An Examination of Sexual Elements in Shakespeare's Language* (London, 1974), pp. 16–24. Green speculates further (p. 24) that 'Conceivably, his observation as a child of the traffic in condoms which might have formed a significant portion of his father's business, and the resultant exposure to him of the horrors of venereal disease, may have imbued in Shakespeare both that fascination with, and revulsion over, sexual activities, which is so characteristic a feature of his works.' It is a great shame that 'conceivably' there is not a joke.

which they grew. I hope in the process to go some way towards explaining why scholars have worried for so long about the life that lies behind those enigmatic works, the Sonnets. This does not sound a radical aim. But actually Shakespeare's poems and Sonnets have rarely been considered together as a group and are even more rarely treated as a major part of Shakespeare's works. Indeed the poems and Sonnets tend to moulder at the back of collected editions of his work, and lurk unobtrusively in multiple volume editions: they are found in volume twenty of twenty one in the Boswell Variorum, in volume ten of ten in Malone, or, more remarkably, in volume seven of Rowe's six volume edition. The Sonnets first appeared in 1609, towards the end of Shakespeare's theatrical career, which might give some chronological basis to this positioning; but, if recent and rigorous stylometric tests are to be believed, several of the Sonnets are very likely to have been composed at the start of Shakespeare's career, and the whole sequence should be thought of as something approaching Shakespeare's life's work, receiving touches of the poet's pen until shortly before its publication.[6] The first printed work to bear Shakespeare's name was *Venus and Adonis* (1593). The second was *Lucrece* (1594). These facts give strong grounds for putting the poems at the front of our thinking about Shakespeare, and perhaps even at the front of collected editions of his works. It also should prompt us to ask why we do not think of Shakespeare as primarily a non-dramatic poet.

One reason for this is, of course, that he wrote quite a few pretty good plays. But there are other reasons. The narrative poems were extremely successful in their time. Eight editions of *Lucrece* and sixteen of *Venus and Adonis* survive from between 1593 and 1640 (and it is quite possible that other editions were printed and then eagerly read to pieces). *Venus and Adonis* was Shakespeare's most popular printed work. The very success of the narrative poems, oddly, made them peripheral to the Shakespearean canon: since they remained market-able commodities through the seventeenth century printers jealously guarded their right to reprint the copy. This may well explain why there was appar-ently no serious effort to include the poems in the first Folio of 1623. In the eighteenth-century editions which until very recently provided the models of editorial method and disposition the poems will very often be found in the supplementary volumes which contain *dubia* and *spuria*, somewhere among *Edward III* and *A Yorkshire Tragedy*. This is usually thought to be a conse-quence of the low critical esteem which the poems enjoyed. But it may be one of the more unlikely by-products of the copyright act of 1710. This act is chiefly famous for having granted, for the first time in English law, limited rights to authors to control and benefit from the printing of their works. But the same act also provided that printers who already owned the copyright on existing works

---

[6] See A. Kent Hieatt, Charles W. Hieatt, and Anne Lake Prescott, 'When did Shakespeare Write *Sonnets* 1609?', *Studies in Philology*, 88 (1991), 69–109.

would retain it for twenty-one years. This meant that if a printer could rapidly find and print old works to which no-one else had a valid claim, he might expect to enjoy the benefit of copyright for the majority of his working life.[7] This unique legal position may well have been the precipitating force behind a scramble for Shakespeare's poems at the end of the first decade of the eighteenth century. In 1709 Bernard Lintott produced a reprint of the narrative poems and the first quarto of Shakespeare's Sonnets; in 1710 Edmund Curll and E. Sanger printed a volume of the poems, edited by the shadowy George Gildon[8] which was designed to look like the seventh volume of Rowe's collected edition of the theatrical works. For copyright purposes it seems likely that Gildon's volume could count as a different work from Lintott's, since it presents a version of John Benson's re-ordered and partly bowdlerised version of the Sonnets, in which individual poems are combined together and given titles of a kind that makes them appear to resemble Cavalier epistles to a mistress. The dates at which Lintott's and Curll's volumes appeared are extremely significant, however, both for their proximity to each other and for their proximity to the 1710 copyright act.[9] It is not clear who, if anyone, owned the copyright to the Sonnets before this date, since their first publisher, Thomas Thorpe, is not known to have assigned it to anyone else; but it does appear from the subsequent printing history of the poems and Sonnets that Curll and Sanger's rights to the copy of Benson's reordered and re-titled version were respected.[10] There were two issues of

---

[7] See Marjorie Plant, *The English Book Trade: An Economic History of the Making and Sale of Books* (London, 1965), pp. 117–18 and Terry Belanger, 'Tonson, Wellington and the Shakespeare Copyrights', in R. W. Hunt, I. G. Phillips, and R. J. Roberts (eds.), *Studies in the Book Trade in Honour of Graham Pollard*, Oxford Bibliographical Society Publications, NS 18 (Oxford, 1975), pp. 195–209. Also of note is Giles E. Dawson, 'The Copyright of Shakespeare's Dramatic Works', in Charles T. Prouty (ed.), *Studies in Honour of A. H. R. Fairchild*, University of Missouri Studies, 21 No. 1 (Columbia, 1946), pp. 12–35.

[8] Gildon's name appears attached to the introduction in few extant copies (the remainder are signed 'S. N.'), but later editors attribute the work to him: so Thomas Evans, *Poems Written by Mr William Shakespeare* (London, n.d. [1775]), fol. ¶2ᵃ refers to 'Mr Gildon'. On Gildon see R. M. Alden, 'The 1710 and 1714 Texts of Shakespeare's Poems', *Modern Language Notes*, 31 (1916), 268–74. It is unclear whether or not Gildon was responsible for the significant revisions to the 1714 edition: Tonson paid £28 7s. to John Hughes, the editor of Spenser, in connection with the 1714 edition of Rowe, on which see Kathleen M. Lynch, *Jacob Tonson, Kit-Kat Publisher* (Knoxville, 1971), p. 131.

[9] The act was passed in 1709, but its provisions took effect from 1 April 1710. See Plant, op. cit., p. 118.

[10] It is possible that Humphrey Moseley acquired the copyright to Benson's text, or at least the unsold copies of it, in around 1655, since 'Poems Written by Mr William Shakespeare Gent.' figures in a catalogue of books for sale bound with the second part of James Howell's *Dodona's Grove*, which Moseley printed in 1650. See Harry Farr, 'Notes on Shakespeare's Printers and Publishers, with Special Reference to the Poems and *Hamlet*', *The Library*, 4th Series 3 (1923), 252. For a defence of Benson's methods, see Margreta de Grazia, 'The Scandal of Shakespeare's Sonnets', *Shakespeare Survey*, 46 (1993), 35–49, and Josephine Waters Bennett, 'Benson's Alleged Piracy of Shake-speares Sonnets and some of Jonson's Works', *Studies in Bibliography*, 21 (1968), 235–48.

Rowe's Shakespeare in 1714, one of which is said to be in eight volumes and is printed for that great collector of Shakespearean copyrights Jacob Tonson; the other includes the poems, and is said to be in nine volumes. The ninth volume is 'Printed by J. Darby . . . for E. Curll, K. Sanger and J. Pemberton. Sold by J. Tonson in the Strand'. The most probable explanation for the existence of these different versions is that by 1714 Tonson accepted *de facto* Curll and Sanger's ownership of the copyright of the poems and Sonnets, and came to some reciprocal arrangement with them as to the printing and selling of copies.

Subsequent high-profile editions of Shakespeare continued this tradition of shuffling the poems into supplements. When Pope's edition of the dramatic works appeared in 1725 it too was rapidly augmented by a supplementary volume of the poems, edited this time by George Sewell;[11] the presence of Pemberton's name on the title page of this volume marks a connection with the earlier consortium of printers. Title pages are not easy to interpret, but this evidence may indicate that a collected edition of Shakespeare's plays and poems could not be produced in the early eighteenth century without the collaboration of Curll, Sanger, or Pemberton. For copyright reasons as much as any other the non-dramatic verse had to shiver in a supplementary volume (and certainly by 1775 printers were recognising public demand for the poetical verse).[12] Tonson, otherwise an energetic pursuer of Shakespearean copyrights, simply failed to obtain the copyright of these works.

This may appear to be no more than bibliographical archaeology, but archaeology can sometimes reveal the foundations of our present attitudes. The majority of modern editions unthinkingly follow the precedent thus accidentally established. This is even true of Edmund Malone's revolutionary edition of the poems and Sonnets in 1780.[13] Malone returned the Sonnets to the order in which they appeared in 1609, and was the first to suggest that the

---

[11] The 1725 edition refers on its title page to 'Mr Shakespeare's miscellany poems'. Both Gildon and Sewell had been involved in producing miscellany poems: Gildon's 'Miscellany Poems upon various occasions' appeared in 1692; Sewell wrote the preface for Addison's 'Miscellanies in Verse and Prose' in 1725. They evidently thought that Shakespeare's poems could be presented to readers as contributions to this vogue. A reprint of 1728 of Sewell's edition is said to be printed for Tonson, who again appears to be manoeuvring for a stake in the poems.

[12] The 'Advertisement' to Thomas Evans's edition of *Poems Written by Mr William Shakespeare* (London, n.d. [1775]) states that 'several editions of the Poems of Shakespeare have been printed, but the eager desire to be possessed of the complete works of the noblest of poets, have rendered them scarce'.

[13] For a more sceptical account of Malone, see Margreta de Grazia, *Shakespeare Verbatim: The Reproduction of Authenticity and the 1790 Apparatus* (Oxford, 1991). De Grazia tells a convincing tale of how Malone transforms Shakespeare's works into historical documents, and how he denigrates the work of printers and players in order to elevate both Shakespeare's originary genius and his own editorial brilliance, but is less generous in her treatment of Malone than anyone who has attempted to edit the Sonnets must be.

first 126 of the Sonnets were addressed to a young man and that the remainder were directed to a mistress.[14] Malone's edition, despite its originality of editorial content, shows remarkable continuity with its predecessors: it is another supplementary volume, called a *Supplement to the Edition of Shakespeare's Plays Published in 1778 by Samuel Johnson and George Steevens*, in which the inferior labour of editing the non-dramatic verse was shuffled off onto a younger and less well-known man. The poems appeared annexed in this way partly because Steevens hated them: he famously stated that 'the strongest act of Parliament that could be framed, would fail to compel readers into their service'.[15] It is also more than likely that the analogy with Gildon and Sewell's volumes helped to determine the volume's marginal relation to the dramatic works: by 1780 a supplement was just where one put the non-dramatic verse. And editors, who are very good at being unthinking, have unthinkingly followed this august precedent, more or less to this day.[16]

What Malone also established was the idea that the narrative poems and the Sonnets had little in common and ought to be thought about in quite different ways. The Sonnets had a basis in autobiography; the narrative poems were mere genre pieces of antiquarian interest, which came well out of a comparison with Drayton and Daniel at their second best, but which seemed wearisome to an enlightened modern reader.[17] This aspect of Malone's work has scarcely been undone to this day. Editors and critics have often pointed out that Venus, when she persuades Adonis to breed, anticipates the 'procreation' Sonnets, and have diligently followed Malone in finding echoes of the dedication to *Lucrece* in Sonnet 26, but have done surprisingly little more to develop connections between the poems and Sonnets.[18] Some critics have sensed a recurrent interest in the perversities of sexual passion in all these poems, or

---

[14] *Supplement to the Edition of Shakespeare's Plays* (London, 1780), p. 579. On the after-shocks of this biographical reading, see Peter Stallybrass, 'Editing as Cultural Formation: The Sexing of Shakespeare's Sonnets', *Modern Language Quarterly*, 54 (1993), 91–103.

[15] Quoted in Hyder Edward Rollins (ed.), *The Sonnets*, A New Variorum Edition, 2 vols. (Philadelphia and London, 1944), ii, 337–8, from 'The Advertisement to the Plays of William Shakespeare' (1793).

[16] The Oxford Shakespeare embeds the poems in chronological position among the dramatic works. The effect of this is to invite readers to think of the Sonnets in conjunction with *Troilus and Cressida* and *Measure for Measure*, and the narrative poems in the context of *Richard III* and the *Comedy of Errors*. This is misleading given the high likelihood that at least Sonnets 127–54 were written in the mid-1590s (on which see Hieatt, Hieatt, and Prescott, see above, n. 6), and that one of the most satisfying contexts in which to read them is provided by *Love's Labour's Lost*.

[17] Malone concludes that although the narrative poems 'appear to me superior to any pieces of the same kind produced by Daniel or Drayton', nonetheless Shakespeare's 'disposition was more inclined to the drama than to the other kinds of poetry; that his genius for the one appears to have been almost a gift from heaven, his abilities for the other, only the same as those of other mortals.' The poems, he claims, are marred by 'the wearisome circumlocution with which the tale in each of them is told', *Supplement* (London, 1780), p. 575.

[18] Ibid., p. 602.

have drawn attention to the ways in which both in the Sonnets and in the narrative poems lovers are forced into passivity as a price of their desire.[19] But through the majority of their critical life these two groups of poems have sat apart from one another in the critical mind: Jonathan Bate's *The Genius of Shakespeare* follows this fashion and plunders the Sonnets for biographical clues while all but ignoring the narrative poems.[20] The poems and Sonnets suffer a longstanding critical need to be viewed together and pulled nearer to the front of our view of Shakespeare.

* * *

But why not just take them, as Malone more or less did, and as tenaciously old-fashioned critics continue to do, as windows onto the life and mind of Shakespeare? The current critical climate is not hospitable to readings of this sort, and for good reasons. Many critics writing today would hold a version of a materialist and historicist thesis about human identity. This has three main prongs. The first is that personhood is not the same thing now as it was *c*.1600. The second is that personhood is both a material and a relational phenomenon: that is, you are what you are by virtue of how you stand in relation to other people, by virtue of what you possess and of what and how you earn. These material circumstances change through time so much that it makes no sense to speak of one's having the same experiences as Shakespeare. The third prong is that texts and minds do not mix: writers leave material textual traces behind, which echo other texts and other voices, which refract their social circumstances, and which are recorded by the quirky means of the early modern printing house. And the printing house was a place of messy labour:

> Two men are requisite about the presse, one to take, to gather, and order the sheetes, or leaves; thother to beate on the fourme which is on the presse, and to distribute or bray the ynke on the stone or block: which could not serve the turne by reason of the great travaile required therein, if they did not drawe the presse one after the other, and by turnes . . . The ynke is made of the smoke or sweat of oyle, which must be beaten, and distributed, because of the thicknes . . .[21]

---

[19] See Heather Dubrow, *Captive Victors: Shakespeare's Narrative Poems and Sonnets* (Ithaca and London, 1987); Jonathan Bate, 'Sexual Perversity in *Venus and Adonis*', *The Yearbook of English Studies*, 23 (1993), 80–92. For some suggestive links between attitudes to descriptive language in *Venus and Adonis* and the Sonnets, see Pauline Kiernan, 'Death by Rhetorical Trope: Poetry Metamorphosed in *Venus and Adonis* and the Sonnets', *Review of English Studies*, 184 (1995), 475–501.

[20] Jonathan Bate, *The Genius of Shakespeare* (London, 1997), pp. 34–64.

[21] Louis Le Roy, trans. R[obert] A[shley], *Of the Interchangeable Course, or Variety of Things in the Whole World* (London, 1594), fol. 22^r. (Usage of 'i' and 'j' and 'u' and 'v' have been modernised). The manufacture of printing ink from boiling linseed oil is described by Steve Wood, *The History of Printing Ink*, British Printing Society Jubilee Series of Monographs, 1 (London, 1994), pp. 2–3 and John Moxon, *Mechanick Exercises on the Whole Art of Printing*, ed. Herbert Davis and Harry Carter, 2nd edn. (London, 1962), pp. 82–6.

Here's work indeed: even the ink is made of sweat. And this is how Shakespeare's poems as artefacts were made. Critics in the materialist school would argue that texts are so thoroughly a material and social a production that they cannot be thought of as the work of one great genius, let alone as a key to unlock the heart of a single man.[22] To read Shakespeare now one should think about work—how Shakespeare was paid, about the labour of a compositor—and the material relics which result. One should look at typographical oddities in the early quartos, and how they complicate the concept of a single authorising genius. Rather than seeing the poems as transcriptions of life one should dwell on gems, jewels, and splodges of ink: acknowledge that you live in a material world.

This position has generated a large body of subtle work, and has shifted our focus on the literature of early modern England from the self and its demands, towards the many ways in which objects and material relations shape human needs and designs. A recent collection of essays called *Subject and Object in Renaissance Culture* is founded on the belief that personal identity in the Renaissance was rooted in a dialectical relation between agents and material objects: its varied essays suggest that in this period people established their identity through money, clothes, paper, ink, and the physical form of the book.[23] This movement has made us sceptical, if the New Criticism had not already achieved this, about any claims that poems relate simply to lives and minds. The materialist outlook also speaks directly to Shakespeare's period, in which material metaphors and aids were often invoked in discussions of how minds worked. Thomas Wright's discussion of memory in *The Passions of the Mind* is representative: 'for although true friends have always a secret cabinet in their memories to talk in their minds with them whom they love although absent, yet except the memory be revived by some external object oblivion entereth'.[24] Pictures and love tokens—material objects—help the memory, which is itself figured as a material space, a 'secret cabinet'.

---

[22] The mastermind of this movement is of course Jerome McGann, whose *A Critique of Modern Textual Criticism* (Chicago and London, 1983) has generated considerable interest in the sociology of text production. Analogous work on the Sonnets includes Randall McLeod (as Random Clod), 'Information Upon Information', *Text: Transactions of the Society for Textual Scholarship*, 5 (1991), 241–78, and Randall McLeod, 'Unemending Shakespeare's Sonnet 111', *Studies in English Literature*, 21 (1981), 75–96. See also Margreta de Grazia and Peter Stallybrass, 'The Materiality of the Shakespearean Text', *Shakespeare Quarterly*, 44 (1993), 255–83. The interest in the material realities of the Elizabethan print shop also, of course, owes much to D. F. McKenzie's detailed analysis of the erratic work-patterns of early modern compositors in 'Printers of the Mind: Some Notes on Bibliographical Theories and Printing House Practices', *Studies in Bibliography*, 22 (1969), 1–75.

[23] Margreta de Grazia, Maureen Quilligan, and Peter Stallybrass (eds.), *Subject and Object in Renaissance Culture* (Cambridge, 1996).

[24] William Webster Newbold (ed.), *The Passions of the Mind in General* (New York and London, 1986), p. 200.

But the materialist thesis also has its limitations. In its harder forms it finds it difficult to explain the reception history of the poems, particularly of the Sonnets, in the late eighteenth century and after, except by appealing to a rather wearied view of a romantic *Weltanschauung* which turns poems into autobiographical documents whether they will or nill. Is Borges interested in Shakespeare's memory simply because he was aware of generations of post-romantic biographic criticism? Did Edward Dowden talk insistently about Shakespeare's life ('I wish . . . to attain to some central principles of life in him which animate and control the rest') or his mind ('There is something higher and more wonderful than St Peter's, or the last judgement—namely the mind which flung these creations into the world') simply because he was smoking the fag end of Romanticism?[25] This seems unlikely. Earlier readers may be responding to some feature of the texts beyond those put there by their projective imaginations. There is, after all, in Shakespeare's poems a marked tendency to renounce material aids to mental functions, and a marked tendency to talk about the mind, that inner cabinet to which Wright alludes, as something which is interestingly unrevealed. The Sonnets which describe absences often stress the power of Shakespeare's memory rather than objects to recall the beloved:

> Since I left you, mine eye is in my mind,
> And that which governs me to go about
> Doth part his function, and is partly blind,
> Seems seeing, but effectually is out:
> For it no form delivers to the heart   5
> Of bird, of flower, or shape which it doth latch;
> Of his quick objects hath the mind no part,
> Nor his own vision holds what it doth catch:
> For if it see the rud'st or gentlest sight,
> The most sweet-favour or deformèd'st creature,   10
> The mountain, or the sea, the day, or night,
> The crow, or dove, it shapes them to your feature.
>   Incapable of more, replete with you,
>   My most true mind thus makes mine eye untrue.   (113)

To state the painfully obvious, Shakespeare does not here say that it is only by weeping into the handkerchief which his friend has given him that he is able to recall what his friend looks like. The memory is so strong that it turns everything into a cue, and in the process turns the world and its visual objects into representations of the friend. Shakespeare's memory, that record which is presented as being so incomparably vivid that it breaks the connection between

---

[25] Edward Dowden, *Shakespeare: A Critical Study of his Mind and Art* (London, 1875), pp. 2 and 5.

mind and the material world, matters more here than material things. The poem presents us with what might be called a subjectivity effect, and it does so by showing that its author knows what he sees, and knows what the world sees, and knows that there is a disparity between what the world sees and what he sees. This disparity establishes the power of love as a transformative force which distinguishes the lover's experience from that of his readers: we see crows or doves; he sees his beloved.

Sonnet 113, with its mind sinking into the eye, is also one of several Sonnets which attach a peculiar—by which I mean idiosyncratically Shakespearean—emphasis to the word 'mind'. 'Mind' is an extraordinarily powerful word in the Sonnets: it can evoke the sinking of consciousness into itself in the absence of the beloved ('Since I left you, mine eye is in my mind'), or the alienness of strangers ('That I have frequent been with unknown minds' (117. 5)). It is often used in contexts where its precise sense is extremely hard to pin down: Sonnet 59 asks

> O that record could with a backward look,
> Even of five hundred courses of the sun,
> Show me your image in some antique book,
> Since mind at first in character was done,
> That I might see what the old world could say
> To this composèd wonder of your frame.   (59. 5–10)

The wishful transformation of the young man into an antiquity is odd enough, but even odder is the suggestion that images or printed characters can bear the stamp of mind. 'Mind' can mean 'disposition' or 'memory' in this period, but still the suggestion that somewhere back then people were making material images of 'mind' has the elusiveness which invites speculation about what mind is and about how it relates to printed matter. What gives the poem its teasing flavour is Shakespeare's responsiveness to the pliability of the word 'character' in the late sixteenth- and early seventeenth-centuries: its primary sense is 'writing' or 'print', but the noun can also mean 'idiosyncratically individual handwriting' (*OED* 4c, which aptly cites the Duke in *Measure* 4. 2. 192–3: 'Look you, sir, here is the hand and seal of the Duke. You know the character, I doubt not').[26] The growing interest in Theophrastus' *Characters* in the 1590s and early years of the seventeenth century may have helped to push the word towards its later senses of 'personal qualities or distinguishing attributes'.[27] The word occurs four times in different forms in the Sonnets, and on each occasion it is used in a way that is slightly different from the

---

[26] All quotations from the dramatic works are from Stanley Wells and Gary Taylor (eds.), *The Oxford Shakespeare* (Oxford, 1986).

[27] See J. W. Smeed, *The Theophrastan 'Character': A History of a Literary Genre* (Oxford, 1985), pp. 1–35.

usages in the dramatic verse.[28] When Shakespeare uses the verbal form of 'character' in the dramatic works to describe the operations of memory it tends to have a close connection with the processes of making a material record: Julia in *Two Gentlemen of Verona* addresses Lucetta as 'the table wherein all my thoughts | Are visibly charactered and engraved' (2. 7. 3–4), and Polonius, ever the technically correct schoolmarm, urges Laertes 'these few precepts in thy memory | See thou character' (*Hamlet* 1. 3. 58–9). The Sonnets tend to blur over the precise nature of the physical medium on which memories are charactered, leaving the word adrifting towards pure mental space: 'What's in the brain that ink may character | Which hath not figured to thee my true spirit?' begins Sonnet 108. The verb 'character' there does not bed thought down into print: it is raised towards an immaterial sense of 'body forth distinctively' by its proximity to 'spirit'. When the Sonnets describe records or emotions they often gently press the balance away from the materiality of table books and written texts towards the enigmatically mental: 'What's in the brain' becomes in itself a question and an object of enquiry for readers. This in turn can prompt the thought that there is something irretrievably private about mental realities, that memories and emotions can only be offered in the charactered form of print, and yet that the medium is their product rather than their master.

Here a pair of poems is particularly relevant. The first of them, Sonnet 77, has traditionally been thought (since Steevens in 1780) to have originally accompanied the gift of a blank commonplace book:

> Look what thy memory cannot contain,
> Commit to these waste blanks, and thou shalt find
> Those children nursed, delivered from thy brain,
> To take a new acquaintance of thy mind.
> These offices, so oft as thou wilt look,
> Shall profit thee, and much enrich thy book.   (77. 9–14)

On the face of it this poem offers much to materialistic critics: memory must be written down, and needs a material record. As critics are coming to recognise, the ways in which writers from this period recorded their thoughts in the physical form of a commonplace book have a profound effect on how they shaped their learning as they wrote, and on the ways in which they

---

[28] The other occurrences are 85. 3, 108. 1, 122. 2. 85. 3 is particularly obscure: 'My tongue-tied Muse in manners holds her still, | While comments of your praise, richly compiled, | Reserve their character with golden quill' is often emended to 'thy character', suggesting that the writings store away the distinguishing attributes of the young man. (On the 'their/thy' error in Q see n. 50 below). This emendation should be regarded with some suspicion, however, since it tallies so neatly with the view that the Sonnets are concerned with inner mental attributes. The unemended form suggests that the distinctive elegance of the writings is hoarded away like a hidden treasure.

conceptualised the workings of their minds.[29] But we should also notice here
that when memory *is* written down in a material form it becomes something
more than mere matter; it becomes alive, something, or even someone, that one
has to meet anew, like a new friend.[30] In the imagery of the Sonnets memory
more often accompanies the language of life than that of dead material; and as
a result the poems imply that there is something more vital to memory than
script, print, or matter.

The Sonnet which is often thought to be a companion poem to 77 is 122. It
considers what happens when one loses the externalised memory provided by a
commonplace book (which is presumably what 'thy tables' refers to in line 1):

> Thy gift, thy tables, are within my brain
> Full charactered with lasting memory,
> Which shall above that idle rank remain
> Beyond all date even to eternity;
> Or at the least so long as brain and heart   5
> Have faculty by nature to subsist,
> 'Till each to razed oblivion yield his part
> Of thee, thy record never can be missed.
> That poor retention could not so much hold,
> Nor need I tallies thy dear love to score,   10
> Therefore to give them from me was I bold
> To trust those tables that receive thee more.
>   To keep an adjunct to remember thee
>   Were to import forgetfulness in me.

John Benson in his edition of this poem sought to embed it in the life: he called
it 'Vpon the receit of a Table Booke from his Mistris',[31] assuming as he so
often does that the addressee of the poems is female. But what matters here is
less the material form of the lost book, than Shakespeare's memory, which
gives immortality to the young man as a fragile record could not. That memory
is again elusive, and it is again figured as at once a book ('those tables', l. 12)
and as something organic, persisting 'so long as brain and heart | Have faculty
by nature to subsist'. And again that transitional word 'charactered' is used to
keep the poem teetering on the boundary between the impersonality of the
scripted and the singularity of a mental disposition. The memory has not just
the impersonality of an inky record, but a flavour too of the distinctively
individual: it is 'charactered' in the sense that it is written in the table of
the brain; but the biological metaphors also allow that there is something (as

---

[29] See e.g. Anne Moss, *Printed Commonplace Books and the Structuring of Renaissance
Thought* (Oxford, 1996).
[30] On the frequent association between childbirth and poetic creation in this period, see
Katherine Eisaman Maus, 'A Womb of his Own: Male Renaissance Poets in the Female
Body', in James Grantham Turner (ed.), *Sexuality and Gender in Early Modern Europe:
Institutions, Texts, Images* (Cambridge, 1993), pp. 266–88.
[31] *Poems Written by Wil. Shake-speare Gent.* (London, 1640), sig. E6^r.

we would put it) 'characterising' about the unique privacy of the memory. What it means to call Shakespeare *early* modern is to recognise the weight given to the former of these definitions; but what it means to call Shakespeare early *modern* is to insist that he is easing the verb 'charactered' towards its later senses. The later part of the poem suggests that the poem envisages its own future life: ' 'Till each to razed oblivion yield his part | Of thee, thy record never can be missed' might hint that the friend and his (or conceivably her) poems will only live for as long as the poet is alive to remember them. That same phrase also though admits the far grander possibility that the poet's memory of the works lost with the commonplace book will live as long as this poem has readers: ' 'Till each' could mean 'until all people'. Either way memory is linked to life; and either way a scripted 'character' blends into a personal record. But also either way we never discover what was actually written on the mysterious missing table book.

These examples suggest why generations of readers have speculated about what was in Shakespeare's mind, and what lay hidden in his memory. The poems raise urgent questions about the ways in which scripted and printed characters can hold on to life. But the poems I have just been discussing also show why no-one has definitively answered these questions, why Borges's narrator finds Shakespeare's memory so lacking in biographical content, and why so many commentators have thought that they alone held the key to Shakespeare's Sonnets. These poems raise questions about mind and its relations to matter. They suggest that there is a mental realm of memory beyond and above material records, that things can 'live in your memory' (as Hamlet puts it) even when their material record is lost. But, crucially, they do not tell their readers what is in the private realm of memory, or what the lost commonplace book actually had in it. If we think of Shakespeare's presentation of mind as a materialist one we should see his materialism as heuristic: that is, material objects are invoked to hint at the existence of mental realities which resist material embodiment.

Another example will clarify this rather difficult point. *A Lover's Complaint*, a poem which until quite recently was regarded as peripheral to the canon,[32] begins with the destruction of material objects, and those objects are again enigmatic and personal to an equal degree. A young woman is

[32] For arguments for the poem's authenticity, see Kenneth Muir, ' "A Lover's Complaint": A Reconsideration', in Edward A. Bloom (ed.), *Shakespeare 1564–1964* (Providence, Rhode Island, 1964), pp. 154–66; reprinted in *Shakespeare the Professional and Related Studies* (London, 1973), 204–19; MacD. P. Jackson, *Shakespeare's ' A Lover's Complaint': Its Date and Authenticity*, University of Auckland Bulletin, 72, English Series, 13 (Auckland, 1965). John Kerrigan's edition of *The Sonnets and A Lover's Complaint* (Harmondsworth, 1986) returned the poem to where it belongs, after the Sonnet sequence. His *Motives of Woe: Shakespeare and 'Female Complaint'* (Oxford, 1991) presents the most critically convincing account of the poem's relation to its tradition.

'Tearing of papers, breaking rings a-twain' (6), and 'Cracked many a ring of poesied gold and bone' (45). The poem, though, refuses to reveal what was actually in the papers or what was posied on the rings. (Thomas Whythorne, the Elizabethan music-master whose insatiable and disastrous courtships of widows are recorded in his autobiography, relates how he gave a ring engraved with the words 'The eye doth find, the heart doth choose, and love doth bind till death doth loose' to one of his would-be inamoratas:[33] Shakespeare is deliberately less revealing). And this air of material enigmas is further developed later in the poem, when we seem, by virtue of eavesdropping on a conversation between two lovers, to have discovered something about the prior history of these objects. The female narrator tells how the young man who courted and ruined her received gems and 'deep-brained Sonnets' from the many women who wooed him, which he then passed on to her:

> '"And lo, behold these talents of their hair,
> With twisted metal amorously impleached,
> I have received from many a several fair,
> Their kind acceptance weepingly beseeched
> With the annexions of fair gems enriched,
> And deep-brained sonnets that did amplify
> Each stone's dear nature, worth and quality.

> '"The Diamond? Why, 'twas beautiful and hard,
> Whereto his invised properties did tend.   (204–12)

It has been suggested that these tokens are what we see the young woman destroying at the start of the poem.[34] But they are a little less transparent than that. Certainly the language of this part of the poem is obscure even by the standards of *A Lover's Complaint*. 'Annexions' is a coinage, and the significance of the diamond is so arcane that it prompts a phrase which still nobody is quite sure they understand: 'invised properties' probably means 'hidden qualities', but it even hides its hiddenness in impenetrable obscurity. Seeing these objects does not give access to the emotions behind a love affair in material form. It gives readers all the intimacy of eavesdroppers, and all the eavesdropper's sense of puzzlement: we see apparently significant objects and apparently significant exchanges, and yet the specific significance of these things in the lives of those we observe is withheld from us. This might lead us to say that in Shakespeare's poems objects do not reveal emotions; they encrypt them intriguingly, and start his readers on a quest for mind. An object is held up as something which offers a point of access to an experience, but the experience which it signifies, and whatever those mysterious 'deep-brained sonnets' actually relate, is withheld from us.

---

[33] Thomas Whythorne, *The Autobiography*, ed. James M. Osborn (London, 1962), p. 159.
[34] So John Kerrigan (see above, n. 32), p. 18.

I have so far suggested that an interest in the limitations of material vehicles for conveying mental realities is a strong unifying thread in Shakespeare's poetic *oeuvre*. This creates enigmas, which have encouraged critics in the past to speculate about Shakespeare's life and mind. The next section of this lecture attempts to trace the roots of this interest in the enigmas of personal experience back to *Venus and Adonis* and *Lucrece*. I will also attempt to offer an explanation for Shakespeare's curious desire simultaneously to proffer and withhold the workings of the mind. The explanation I will present is in its way a materialist one. I shall suggest that this feature of his works can be related to the very odd demands of the early modern book-buying public. Briefly put, many of those who bought poems in this period wanted to obtain private and occasional material—exchanges between lovers, communications between poets and their patrons—but they also wished to obtain this material in cheap printed form. They wanted the accessibility and the economy of print, whilst also wishing to obtain works with the cachet of private manuscripts. What I think Shakespeare does is to insist more strongly and more delicately than any other poet in the period that those private exchanges, private documents like commonplace books, and the even more private mental realities to which they bear witness, remain private even when they are published in material forms. I will also suggest that in the narrative poems Shakespeare is worrying about the risks of publishing and selling a poem, and about the kinds of work which poems can perform.

* * *

Venus and Adonis, as I have said, was the first printed work to which Shakespeare's name was attached, and *Lucrece* was the second. These simple facts can give cues as to how these poems should be read: they are the first efforts of a young poet to make a name in print. And, as such attempts often are, they are anxious even despite their florid accomplishment. *Lucrece*, as has recently been recognised, is rich in metaphors both of trading and of publication. These metaphors often overlap with the horror at sexual impurity which hangs over the whole poem: Lucrece's beauty is 'published' by Colatine at the start of the poem ('why is Colatine the publisher | Of that rich jewel he should keep unknown?' (33–4)) and his rash willingness to vulgarise the beauty of his wife is what initially provokes Tarquin to assault her. The link between publication and prostitution is quite common in Shakespeare's plays, and a page smirched by an alien hand is often associated with sexual impurity (think of Othello's 'Was this fair paper, this most goodly book | Made to write "whore" upon?').[35]

---

[35] *Othello* 4. 2. 73–4. On the association in Shakespeare, see Ann Thompson and John O. Thompson, *Shakespeare: Meaning and Metaphor* (Brighton, 1987), pp. 163–70 and 177–83.

Wendy Wall has related this link between publishing and be-whoring to fears among writers in the 1590s that publication effeminised: to print a poem for money, rather than to allow it to circulate in manuscript among a small coterie, was akin to selling it on the streets in a sort of printed version of pimping.[36] As Wall suggests, being read, being published, becoming a material object for sale, and being sexually violated are all elements in Shakespeare's *Lucrece*. But the poem does not simply yield its secret character to a print audience: it publicly proclaims itself to be called *Lucrece* on its title page; the more risqué title *The Rape of Lucrece* is privily concealed within the volume's running-titles (until the edition of 1616). Characters in the poem also resist being read, and retain for themselves something of the reserve of a poem written for private circulation; or to put that more strongly, they resist translation of mental impulse into material form. Lucrece herself fears that her rape will be published in her face:

> Yea, the illiterate, that know not how
> To cipher what is writ in learnèd books,
> Will quote my loathsome trespass in my looks.   (810–12)

The verb 'to cipher', meaning 'to interpret a coded writing' is peculiar to *Lucrece*. It occurs three times in the poem in this sense but nowhere else in Shakespeare's works, and its frequency in the poem suggests that minds are harder to read than Lucrece allows. Indeed her responses to her rape are so opaquely ciphered that no-one whom she encounters can read them. Lucrece's maid sees 'sorrow's livery' (1222) on her face, but is unable to interpret the reasons for her grief, and it proves impossible throughout the poem to read the mind's construction in the face. When the groom to whom Lucrece consigns her letter to her husband blushes, Lucrece assumes he does so because he sees her shame ciphered in her face. Actually, Shakespeare tells us, he blushes because he is a bashful fellow ('it was defect | Of spirit, life, and bold audacity' (1345–6)). Lucrece misreads others, and she does so because she mistakenly believes that her shame is published in her appearance. Physiognomy is not as reliable a guide to character in life as it is in the depiction of the sack of Troy, where Ajax and Ulysses' faces 'ciphered either's heart; | Their face their manners most expressly told' (1396–7). Tarquin has forced upon Lucrece a state of near-derangement in which she thinks all her thoughts and actions are made immediately legible to others. In fact her mind is hidden, and material

---

[36] Wendy Wall, *The Imprint of Gender: Authorship and Publication in the English Renaissance* (Ithaca and London, 1993), p. 69: 'So feminized, the book became an appropriate object of male desire: desirable in its own right in the marketplace of sonnet sellers and buyers.' Wall's account of *Lucrece* develops some elements explored in Nancy Vickers's influential ' "The Blazon of Sweet Beauty's Beast": Shakespeare's *Lucrece*' in Patricia Parker, Geoffrey Hartman, and David Quint (eds.), *Shakespeare and the Question of Theory* (New York and London, 1985), pp. 95–115.

objects—from physiognomic signals, to letters to her husband, to the tapestry representation of the sack of Troy onto which she projects her grief—cannot contain or reveal it. This she discovers as she moves from the company of the maid and the groom (who are the two characters in the poem whose real life equivalents were most likely to have been illiterate in early modern England) to adopt a writerly relation to an audience. As she tries to compose a letter to her husband she discovers the difficulty of publishing even so public a shame as a rape, or even of saying simply 'come home':

> Her maid is gone, and she prepares to write,
> First hovering o'er the paper with her quill.
> Conceit and grief an eager combat fight:
> What wit sets down is blotted straight with will.
> This is too curious good; this blunt and ill.
> Much like a press of people at a door
> Throng her inventions which shall go before.   (1296–1302)

She revises and re-revises her letter, and eventually opts for a cryptic expression which holds 'her grief, but not her grief's true quality'. The cabinet of her mind remains closed to those who observe her, and at the end of the poem it closes its doors altogether to prying eyes:

> Immaculate and spotless is my mind;
> That was not forced, that never was inclined
> To accesary yieldings, but still pure,
> Doth in her poisoned closet yet endure.   (1656–9)

Hidden away, her mind resists the kind of public and published stigma which she fears by hiding in its closet. This was the most symbolically private of solitary places for Elizabethans of more than middling rank, and the place in which private papers and hidden tokens of love resided, and from which printed poems were often said to have been liberated.[37]

---

[37] On the ways in which closets could be used to present a zone of private experience to a select audience, see Patricia Fumerton, *Cultural Aesthetics: Renaissance Literature and the Practice of Social Adornment* (Chicago and London, 1991). On p. 69 she writes 'The history of the Elizabethan self, in short was a history of fragmentation in which the subject lived in public view but always withheld for itself a "secret" room, cabinet, case, or other recess locked away (in full view) in one corner of the house.' Fumerton also makes suggestive relations between the private treasuring of miniatures and the coy semi-self-revelations of the Elizabethan sonnet, although she does not extend her observations to include Shakespeare. More recent work on the closet, such as Alan Stewart, 'The Early Modern Closet Discovered', *Representations*, 50 (1995), 76–100, has emphasised its role as a space for collaborative male labour. Closets and chambers in Shakespeare's poems, however, do tend to be places in which, as Angel Day puts it in *The English Secretorie* (London, 1592), p. 109, 'we do solitarie and alone shutte up our selves'. Nashe's preface to the unauthorised first Quarto of *Astrophil and Stella* (London, 1591) describes how poetry 'although it be oftentimes imprisoned in Ladyes casks, & the president bookes of such as cannot see without another mans spectacles, yet at length it breakes foorth in spight of his keepers, and useth some private penne (insteed of a picklock) to procure his violent enlargement'.

The most trenchant recent critique of *Lucrece* the poem is that by Ian Donaldson. He argues that the work is radically confused: sometimes its heroine appears to belong to a shame culture, in which her pollution by Tarquin matters because it will cause horror in those who see her and acquire a social stigma; at other times Shakespeare seems to represent pre-Republican Rome as a proto-Christian guilt culture, in which Lucrece's own perception of her moral weakness is the primary grounds of her misery.[38] The features of the poem which I have just been considering go some way towards countering this criticism. The poem delicately and quite deliberately suggests that Lucrece inhabits both these kinds of world. She thinks she lives in a shame culture in which all can see her violation published in her countenance; but guilt, her consciousness of what has been done to her and of what she feels about it, remains hidden within her. The poem refuses to publish her shame; indeed it keeps it in the closet, albeit a poisoned one. As Shakespeare never lets us forget, *Lucrece* is a chamber work: its main action, the rape, occurs within a private chamber, and readers are insistently reminded of the geography of the violation: the Argument plants the word: 'The same night he treacherously stealeth into her chamber'; it is then harped on throughout Tarquin's hesitant advance: 'The locks between her chamber and his will | Each one by him enforced retires his ward' (302–3); 'Now is he come unto the chamber door | That shuts him from the heaven of his thought' (338–8); until he arrives at Lucrece's inner sanctum: 'Into the chamber wickedly he stalks, | And gazeth on her yet unstainèd bed' (365–6). The first touch of Tarquin's hands on Lucrece create an inner privacy within her private chamber, as her veins shrink back into the private spaces of her body:

> They, must'ring to the quiet cabinet
> Where their dear governess and lady lies,
> Do tell her she is dreadfully beset,
> And fright her with confusion of their cries.   (442–5)

The dominant metaphor here, as so often in the poem, is of a city under siege; but the passage also places great emphasis on the domestic inner spaces of the citadel of that city. A cabinet, a closet, these hidden places of personal retreat, are where Lucrece habitually resides. The effect of the rape and its violation of her private spaces is to force her to generate more privacy and more privacy, until, at the end of her story, the mind hides from all eyes in its 'poisoned closet'.

The preoccupation of *Lucrece* with hidden spaces and private zones enables us to put the case against Wendy Wall's view of *Lucrece* a little more strongly: Wall occasionally overstates the commodity value of texts in

---

[38] Ian Donaldson, *The Rapes of Lucretia: A Myth and its Transformations* (Oxford, 1982), pp. 40–56.

the period and so can correspondingly underestimate what makes them critically intriguing to readers. The majority of those who bought verse in this
period are unlikely to have done so in order to feel as they picked up a new
collection of poems that they were enjoying complete material possession of a
person or a poem or an experience or mental state. They did not, as Wall can
suggest in her more enthusiastic moments, feel as though they were buying not
just *Lucrece* the book, but also Lucrece the woman. It is likely that many of
them bought poems in the hope of intimacy with elevated doings, but also in
the knowledge that what they bought would present them with only a glittering
carapace of greatness, which would leave them feeling more on the outside of
a charmed circle than ever. Many of those who bought the strange volume of
poems attributed to Shakespeare called *The Passionate Pilgrim* in 1599 are
likely to have done so in the hope that it would contain what Francis Meres in
the previous year had described as Shakespeare's 'sugred Sonnets among his
private friends'.[39] Purchasers of poems might wish to feel as though they were
just on the edges of an intimate circle of friends, not quite sure what private
allusions meant, not perhaps even quite sure who the poems were originally
for, but relishing them anyway. In the process of publishing Lucrece's story
Shakespeare plays to these expectations among his readership: he intimates
that material forms, faces, poems, tapestries, letters, will never completely
deliver the imprint of mind. Minds and material entities do not marry in
Shakespeare's verse or in life without impediments.

I have begun my account of Shakespeare's career as a poet with his second
published poem *Lucrece* because it sets the outlines of my case so clearly: that
Shakespeare's poems, to abuse a legal phrase, are poems of material non-
disclosures. Shakespeare's first poem, *Venus and Adonis*, however, has a similar,
though less explicit, plot of material vulgarisation and mental reservation. The
verbal mannerisms, distinctive vocabulary and sheer sexiness of *Venus and
Adonis* were immediately imitated by other poets. The poem determined the
public view of Shakespeare for the next decade: one of the ways in which *The
Passionate Pilgrim* volume of 1599 was designed to look as though it was by
Shakespeare was by its inclusion of sonnets about Venus and Adonis of a
richly erotic kind.[40] The frenzy of erotic writing to which *Venus and Adonis*
gave rise, though, has all but obscured its more anxious side. This is a poem,

---

[39] Francis Meres, *Palladis Tamia* (London, 1598), sigs. 2O1^v–2O2^r.

[40] For an account of the reception of *Venus and Adonis*, see Katherine Duncan-Jones, 'Much
Ado with Red and White: the Earliest Readers of Shakespeare's *Venus and Adonis* (1593)',
Review of English Studies, 176 (1993), 479–501. On *The Passionate Pilgrim*, see Arthur F.
Marotti, 'Shakespeare's Sonnets as Literary Property', in Elizabeth D. Harvey and Katharine
Eisaman Maus (eds.), *Soliciting Interpretation: Literary Theory and Seventeenth-Century
English Poetry* (Chicago and London, 1990), pp. 150–4, and C. H. Hobday, 'Shakespeare's
Venus and Adonis Sonnets', *Shakespeare Survey*, 26 (1973), 103–9.

like *Lucrece*, which worries about publication, and which, like many poems from the 1590s, is preoccupied with awkward questions about what kinds of work words can achieve. So far I have concentrated more on life and minds than on work; but *Venus and Adonis* is centrally preoccupied with what it is to labour in words. The dedication to the Earl of Southampton promises that Shakespeare will devote all 'idle hours' to the production of 'some graver labour', which presumably is a reference to *Lucrece*, which was printed in the next year. Shakespeare's way of describing his ambition has a hint of anxiety to it, as it just glancingly suggests that hours might still be 'idle' even when they are filled with the scribbling work of writing poetry.[41] The senses of 'idle' in this period extend from 'Not engaged in work, doing nothing, unemployed' (*OED* 4a), which might mark Shakespeare's use of it as glancingly a proud claim to the leisured ease of a gentleman; but the darker range of the word, 'vain, frivolous, trifling' (*OED* 2a), points a recognition that writing may achieve little. That association of words with vanity and material ineffective-ness shoots through the poem. Throughout *Venus and Adonis* words are trying in vain to work. Venus begs and beseeches and bullies Adonis to sleep with her—in vain. The poem confronts the active but ineffective eloquence of Venus with Adonis's zealous interest in what many Elizabethans would have thought of as 'real' work. Indeed Adonis has what could almost be called a bourgeois preoccupation with honest labour. For him the sun does not simply sink, but 'His day's hot task has ended in the west' (530). When his horse bolts in pursuit of a mare he solemnly declares that 'all my mind, my thought, my busy care, | Is how to get my palfrey from the mare' (383–4): for him mind and urgent labour are inseparable. Adonis, the hoarder, declares 'The night is spent' (717); Venus the eloquent spendthrift retorts 'Be prodigal' (755). The poem dramatises a clash not just between Venus's life of leisure and Adonis's life of active pursuit, but between someone who wants to work through words, and someone who thinks the only way to live is by material labour. The encounter between these two attitudes to labour can become wonderfully corporeal, as when the ever-active Adonis thinks that Venus has passed out, and assumes that the more frantically he works at it the better his chances of reviving the languishing goddess ('He wrings her nose, he strikes her on the cheeks, | He bends her fingers, holds her pulses hard. | He chafes her lips . . .' (474–6)). But it can also become a tangled debate about how words can bear on material realities. The one point at which the idle Venus thinks she is about to get through to the stubbornly laborious Adonis is when she taps in to his burgher mentality: she promises him 'increase' through reproduction, and presents herself as an object for sale:

---

[41] The classic studies of this area of anxiety are Richard Helgerson, *The Elizabethan Prodigals* (Berkeley and London, 1976) and the same author's account of the ways in which poets attempted to fashion poetical careers for themselves, *Self-Crowned Laureates: Spenser, Jonson, Milton and the Literary System* (Berkeley and London, 1983).

> To sell myself I can be well contented,
> So thou wilt buy, and pay, and use good dealing.
> Which purchase if thou make, for fear of slips,
> Set thy seal manual on my wax-red lips.   (513–6)

Nice goddesses, of course, do not sell themselves. Venus has trapped herself by accommodating her speech to the financial concerns of her audience. And once Adonis has kissed her she ups the price, like a genteel courtesan who pretends not to know the meaning of money: her 'vulture thought doth pitch the price so high | That she will draw his lips' rich treasure dry' (551–2). As she goes on to persuade Adonis to use his capital of beauty in procreation she meets her first real resistance. Adonis (finally) says 'You do it for increase — O strange excuse, | When reason is the bawd to lust's abuse' (791–2). 'Increase', as Adonis well knows, means both 'profit' (*OED* 4) and 'biological multi-plication, offspring' (*OED* 6: 'From fairest creatures we desire increase' as Sonnet 1 begins, at once urging marriage on the young man and stretching out a needy paw for reward). The pun here accuses Venus of taking payments for sex, and the way Venus is described after Adonis's rebuke hints at her metamorphosis into a fallen woman. When Adonis leaves her for the active business of the hunt her company becomes a throng of echoes, whom Shakespeare figures as servile barmen:

> For who hath she to spend the night withal
> But idle sounds resembling parasites,
> Like shrill-tongued tapsters answering every call?   (847–9)

These tapsters, like poor Francis in *1 Henry IV* who cries 'Anon, anon Sir' to every call, are the lowest sort of company. This is not a respectable joint. Venus, the goddess who does not even need to tread on the ground, has engaged her eloquence to achieve the simple goal of seduction, and then sinks to the status of Doll Tearsheet, selling herself in taverns. In a printed poem addressed to a noble patron, and a patron who was being persuaded to marry during the period of the poem's composition by the material means of financial penalties, this is a touching tale: it fuels Southampton's resistance to seduction, and invites a reward for doing so. But it also entertains the awkward sugges-tion that to put words too openly to work is to prostitute the muse.[42] This poem frisks lightly, but it also worries about the material efficacy of words, and the potential costs to an author of selling his works in public.

The poem, though, like *Lucrece*, is not simply a study in the materialities of work and print. It is also, like *Lucrece*, fascinated by the privacies of the mind. Adonis, as well as jealously hoarding his financial and sexual reserves,

---

[42] G. P. V. Akrigg, *Shakespeare and the Earl of Southampton* (London, 1968), pp. 31–3 and 195–6.

keenly preserves a little sanctum of mental space into which Venus's seductive eloquence can win no access:

> For know, my heart stands armèd in mine ear,
> And will not let a false sound enter there,
>
> Lest the deceiving harmony should run
> Into the quiet closure of my breast;
> And then my little heart were quite undone,
> In his bed-chamber to be barred of rest.   (779–84)

Adonis equates virginity with retaining a private retreat in 'the quiet closure of my breast', and when he finally escapes homeward from Venus's grasp it is presumably to his solitary bed-chamber. His retreat is reminiscent of Sonnet 48, in which the poet's love is hidden away as a secret treasure 'Within the gentle closure of my breast'. And this hidden intimacy is a state to which even Venus aspires: she too ends the poem retreating into a solitary chamber. Her eyes flee back from the sight of the dead Adonis, and the description of their flight is among the greatest passages in Shakespeare's non-dramatic verse:

> So at his bloody view her eyes are fled
> Into the deep-dark cabins of her head,
>
> Where they resign their office, and their light,
> To the disposing of her troubled brain,
> Who bids them still consort with ugly night,
> And never wound the heart with looks again,
> Who, like a king perplexèd in his throne,
> By their suggestion gives a deadly groan,
>
> Whereat each tributary subject quakes,
> As when the wind imprisoned in the ground,
> Struggling for passage, earth's foundation shakes,
> Which with cold terror doth men's minds confound.
> This mutiny each part doth so surprise
> That from their dark beds once more leap her eyes,
>
> And, being opened, threw unwilling light
> Upon the wide wound that the boar had trenched
> In his soft flank . . .   (1037–53)

What makes the passage so agile, so needful of its remarkable cross-stanzaic enjambement,[43] is its materialism, its rootedness in the material fact of battery and retreat, of guards excited by assault into entering the most secret inner reaches of the citadel. It takes us back to the landscape of *Lucrece*, in which

---

[43] The punctuation of Field's compositors generally follows stanzaic patterns. A full stop is routinely placed at the end of a stanza. Of the six exceptions to this rule, four are the result of the need to compress the line to fit the forme (lines 372, 432, 678, 1068), and two (lines 834 and 876) have no relation to the syntax. The comma which ends line 834 ('cry so,') is probably the result of eyeskip from the line above ('wo, wo,').

women flee into the depths of a secret chamber in order to escape an invading catastrophe. 'Cabin' is probably used in *OED* sense 3b: 'A small room, a bedroom, a boudoir', or it may have the same sense as 'cabinet': 'A small chamber or room; a private apartment, a boudoir' (*OED* 3). For Shakespeare those inner reaches were equated with areas of mental reservation. But the passage works by generating subjectivity from those material realities: it presents a woman whose perceptual apparatus is wrenched out of kilter with what is actually before her by the intensity of emotion. This is a privacy of the mind, and it is a form of subjectivity which owes its origins to the experience of being made to see the world in a uniquely separate way by suffering a distinctive pain. Venus, like Lucrece and like Adonis, is finally stung into solitude; at the end of the poem she hurries away 'In her light chariot' to Paphos 'where the queen | Means to immure herself and not be seen' (1192–4), and her eyes withdraw from the sight of the dead Adonis 'as the snail, whose tender horns being hit, | Shrinks backward in his shelly cave with pain' (1033–4). The snail, carrying a private bedroom on its back, is the perfect emblem of the wincing inwardness finally celebrated in this most adolescent of poems. *Venus and Adonis* offers its readers a deliciously public display of sexual desire, which, as the title-page boasts, one could buy as a material object 'at the signe of the white Greyhound in Paules Church-yard'; but at its end it shrinks back into the concealed cabinet of the mind.

* * *

The narrative poems, then, lightly touch on questions of what it is to publish, and on what sorts of emotional reality remain private even in printed works. I have also suggested that this interest is distinctively tuned to the market for poetry in the 1590s. I would like now to return to Shakespeare's Sonnets, and explore in a little more detail the ways in which the extraordinarily enigmatic volume in which they first appeared can be related to some of the qualities I have found in the narrative poems.

There has been a huge amount of debate about the Sonnets, about whether they were illicitly printed, or whether Shakespeare authorised their publication. There has been even more debate about who, in real life, the 'Mr W. H.' might be who is referred to in the printer's dedication to the volume (and Jonathan Bate and Katherine Duncan-Jones have shown this year that there is still life in the old battles betwen advocates of Henry Wriothesley, Earl of Southampton and William Herbert, Earl of Pembroke).[44] I am by conviction a sceptic: my only firm belief about the Sonnets is that there must be something pretty remarkable about the volume which contains them to have stimulated

[44] See Katherine Duncan-Jones (ed.), *Shakespeare's Sonnets* (London, 1997), pp. 53–64 and Jonathan Bate, *The Genius of Shakespeare* (London, 1997), pp. 45–54.

this amount of debate. I would therefore not want to say, as most editors do, that the balance of probabilities must lie with one side or the other in these debates. I would rather want to understand why both sides might have a case. And this leads me to my root conviction about the volume called *Shake-speares Sonnets*. It is a volume which gives off such radically conflicting signals about its relations to the life of its author that it could have been designed to do so. Moreover it could have been designed to operate more or less exactly on the borderline between the published and the privately concealed on which I have attempted to locate *Venus and Adonis* and *Lucrece*. These features of the volume become apparent if it is inspected as a material object, through the eyes of a notional seventeenth century book-buyer. Once this inspection is over it might be possible to draw some conclusions about how best to read the poems.

A potential buyer who picked up a copy of *Shake-speares Sonnets* from the stall of William Apsley or John Wright in 1609 would immediately have recognised that they were holding a different kind of work from either *Lucrece* or *Venus and Adonis*. The volume at first sight would look like a real work: it seems monumental, with its author's name not tucked away at the end of the dedication, but blazoned on the title page and used as a running title for each opening. The first page of the volume contains the printer's dedication, studded with lapidary full stops designed to give it the appearance of a carving on stone.[45] Scattered through the volume are poems which proclaim their status as perdurable works: (55) 'Not marble, nor the gilded monuments | Of princes shall outlive this pow'rful rhyme . . .'. Individual poems too, draw voraciously on the vocabulary of labour: the language of the law, 'charters', 'sessions', 'leases', 'pleas', weaves into the metaphorical texture of the poems, as does the exchange of capital and interest. The arts of the parfumier, the painter, the dyer are all welded together in a collection which both looks like a work and is uniquely accommodating of labour and its language.

A reader who looked more closely at the volume, however, might begin to notice features which qualified this initial impression of the monumental. The dedication, with its teasing use of those initials W. H., might remind its would-be purchaser of a tradition of erotic fictions which use their preliminary matter to hint that the characters in the fiction might have some bearing on real life. George Gascoigne's *Adventures of Master F. J.* is found in a volume prefixed by an epistle, supposedly from someone called H. W., but almost certainly by Gascoigne himself, which relates how its manuscript passed to him from someone called G. T. to his printer A. B.[46] The proliferation of initials in

---

[45] This account of the volume owes much to the intriguing thoughts of Katherine Duncan-Jones, 'What Are Shakespeare's Sonnets Called?', *Essays in Criticism*, 47 (1997), 1–12, although I believe that the volume also gives off quite contrary signals.

[46] *A Hundreth Sundrie Flowres bound up in one Small Poesie* (London, 1573), fo. 201.

F. J. invites its readers to apply them to real people, although it is fairly clear that they are inventions of the author.[47] Some sonnet sequences, notably Giles Fletcher's *Licia*, invite readers to apply the generic name of the woman to whom they are addressed to real people, whilst also deliberately not making such identifications explicit:

> It may bee I am so devoted to some one, into whose hands these may light by chance, that she may say, which thou now saiest (that surelie he is in love) which if she does, then have I the full recompense of my labour . . . If thou muse what my LICIA is, take her to be some *Diana*, at the least chaste, or some *Minerva*, no *Venus*, fairer farre; it may be shee is Learnings image, or under some heavenlie woonder, which the preciest may not mislike; perhaps under that name I have shadowed *Discipline*. It may be, I meane that kinde courtesie which I found at the Patronesse of these Poems.[48]

In Fletcher's preface the invitation to muse on the identity, allegorical or otherwise, of his mistress is left teasingly open. This is how erotic fictions make themselves spicily real in the period: they simultaneously invite and shrink from what early modern writers would have termed 'application' of works to life. 'W. H.' is as likely to be a late contributor to this tradition as he is to be a real life nobleman.[49] His presence at the threshold of the volume

---

[47] See Adrian Weiss, 'Shared Printing, Printer's Copy, and the Text(s) of Gascoigne's *A Hundreth Sundrie Flowres*', *Studies in Bibliography*, 45 (1992), 71–104. On Gascoigne's prefatory manoeuvres, see John Kerrigan, 'The Editor as Reader: Constructing Renaissance Texts', in James Raven, Helen Small, and Naomi Tadmor (eds.), *The Practice and Representation of Reading in England* (Cambridge, 1996), pp. 102–24. Another notable example of the deliberately suggestive use of initials is Alexander B. Grosart (ed.), *Willobie his Avisa; or the True Picture of a Modest Maid, and of a Chaste and Constant Wife (1594)* (Manchester, 1880), p. 8, in which 'Hadrian Dorrell', almost certainly a fictional character, claims of the name 'AVISA' that 'I think it to be fained name, like unto *Ovids Corrinna*' and that it may be an acronym for 'Amans Uxor Inviolata Semper Amanda'. He goes on, in a gesture typical of the efforts of early modern erotic writers at once to detach their work from reality and at the same time to embed themselves in the stuff of life: 'Yet I would not have *Auisa* to be thought a politike fiction, nor a truethlesse invention, for it may be, that I have at least heard of one in the west of England, in whom the substance of all this has been verefied . . . This forceth me to conjecture, that though the matter be handled poetically, yet there is something under these fained names and showes that hath been done truly.' The poem famously contains a character called W. S., a player who is also an unsuccessful lover. This led the indefatigable Arthur Acheson, in *Mistress Davenant and the Dark Lady of Shakespeare's Sonnets* (London, 1913), to argue that the 'Dark Lady' was the wife of an Oxford landlord. For a characteristically judicious discussion of *Willobie* and the Sonnets, see Hyder Edward Rollins, ed., *The Sonnets*, A New Variorum Edition, 2 vols. (Philadelphia and London, 1944), ii, 295–313. The analogy between the two volumes lies in their shared willingness both to invite and eschew application, rather than in any common shared allusion to facts in Shakespeare's life.

[48] Giles Fletcher, *The English Works*, ed. Lloyd E. Berry (Madison, Wisconsin, 1964), pp. 78–80.

[49] For the engaging suggestion that he owes his life to a misprint of 'W. SH.', see Donald Foster, 'Mr W. H., RIP', *PMLA*, 102 (1987), 42–54.

invites readers to scrutinise it for signs of life, whilst also providing an
assurance that whatever biographical traces the volume offers will be well
concealed. If we look at the monumental volume of *Shake-speares Sonnets* as a
physical object we can see that it provokes—deliberately or not—niggling
questions about the life to which it relates.

The volume might also reasonably prompt speculation about where the text
of the poems came from. It contains the odd line that does not rhyme (25.9), a
couplet that is repeated in two poems (36 and 96), a fifteen line Sonnet (99), a
Sonnet with a second line which repeats, unmetrically, a phrase from its first
line (146), a repeated error in which 'their' is printed for 'thy', an error which
mysteriously stops at Sonnet 128, at a point in the sequence when some
unusual spellings also begin to appear.[50] These features would be less pronounced to an early modern reading public, used to haphazard orthography and
accustomed to correcting and sometimes even rewriting printed texts as they
copied them into their own commonplace books;[51] but they might also qualify
the initial impression of the monumental. Whatever the origins of this volume

[50] Q confuses 'their' and 'thy' at 26. 12, 27. 10, 35. 8, 37. 7, 43. 11, 45. 12, 46. 3, 46. 8, 46.
13, 46. 14, 69. 5, 70. 6, 128. 11, 128. 14, and possibly also at 85. 3. As MacD. P. Jackson's
analysis of compositorial preferences in the Sonnets, 'Punctuation and the Compositors of
Shakespeare's *Sonnets*, 1609', *The Library*, 5th Series 30 (1975), 1–23, shows, the error is
usually made by compositor B, although 35. 8 and 37. 7 were set by compositor A. The most
probable explanation (offered by Malone) is that the copy contained two letter abbreviations
for the personal pronoun in which 'they' and 'thy' looked alike, but the absence of errors
after 128 is striking. The mistress is consistently addressed as 'thou', which may conceivably
have helped the compositor to unscramble difficult copy; but this would of course also make
instances of the possessive pronoun very high (around 2.1 instances per poem as against 1.5
instances per poem for the earlier part of the sequence, or 1.6 if one includes the occurrences
erroneously set as 'their') and so multiply the opportunity for error. This suggests that the
copy for the poems after 128 may have significantly differed in orthography from the early
part of the sequence. This is also suggested by some unique or unusual spellings: 'Broake' is
found only in 143. 2 and 152. 3; 'bouldness' is unique; 'ynough', 133. 3 occurs also in Q1 of
Troilus (also printed in 1609 by Eld, so this could be a compositorial quirk); 142. 14 'mai'st'
appears to be unique; 'wofull' occurs thirty-two times elsewhere in the canon and is usually
pre-1600. This hypothesis sits suggestively beside the recent claim on stylometric grounds
that Sonnets 126–54 are among the earliest poems in the sequence. See A. Kent Hieatt,
Charles W. Hieatt, and Anne Lake Prescott, 'When did Shakespeare Write *Sonnets* 1609?',
Studies in Philology, 88 (1991), 69–109. For the view that 'The 1609 edition represents not
that dream of a traditional textual editor, the author's final intention, but rather a set of poems
in various stages of composition', see Heather Dubrow ' "Incertainties now Crown Themselves Assur'd": The Politics of Plotting in Shakespeare's Sonnets', *Shakespeare Quarterly*,
47 (1996), 299. Marotti, 'Shakespeare's Sonnets as Literary Property' voices a similar
opinion about the miscellaneity of the Sonnet sequence.
[51] For scribal adaptations of some Sonnets, see John P. Cutts, 'Two Seventeenth Century
Versions of Shakespeare's Sonnet 116', *Shakespeare Studies*, 10 (1977), 9–16; Mary Hobbs,
'Shakespeare's Sonnet II—"A Sugred Sonnet"?', *Notes and Queries*, 224 (1979), 112–3;
R. H. A. Robbins, 'A Seventeenth Century Manuscript of Shakespeare's Sonnet 128', *Notes
and Queries*, 212 (1967), 137–8. For manuscript versions of individual Sonnets which may
reflect authorial variants, see Gary Taylor, 'Some Manuscripts of Shakespeare's Sonnets',
Bulletin of the John Rylands Library, 68 (1985), 210–46.

it does not have the appearance of a printed work which derives from a finely revised authorial fair copy (and here it will be clear that I am not as confident as Katherine Duncan-Jones that the volume is likely to have been authorised by Shakespeare: its physical appearance is more ambiguous than she allows).[52] It looks much more like the printed offshoot of a partially revised manuscript, which its author may have wished to keep private. A keen early modern collector of sonnet sequences might dig deep in his (or again, conceivably, her) memory when he brought the volume home: what other work, this person might ask, blazons its author's name on the running titles of each page? Most sonnet sequences have no running titles, or at most use the title of the fictional addressee at the top of each page. Most sonnet sequences have an authorial dedication, rather than one signed by the printer, and most sonnet sequences carefully dispose one or two complete poems onto each page, and add an ornamental border at the top and maybe at the bottom of each page.[53] *Shakespeares Sonnets* has none of these features, and to contemporary readers versed in the genre it would have looked unusual: Sonnets topped by the name of Shakespeare stagger across pages, their form broken by the printed page. Our Jacobean sonnet-buyer might recall that only one other printed sonnet sequence shares all these features, and that was the 1591 edition of *Sir P. S. His Astrophel and Stella*, an edition which was called in, and which is manifestly the printed offshoot of a manuscript which walked away from its rightful owner.[54] This unauthorised volume also blazons the unmistakable initials of Sir Philip Sidney over every page. As a physical object, the Quarto of *Shake-speares Sonnets* manages to look like a monumental achievement at

---

[52] See Appendix.

[53] Exceptions are rare: Barnabe Barnes' *Parthenophil and Pathenophe* (1593), sig. A2^v contains an epistle from the Printers: 'The Author though at the first unknowne, yet enforced to accorde to certaine of his friendes importunity herein, to publish them by their meanes, and for their sakes . . .'. The poems that follow are disposed chaotically across openings. The general pattern, especially marked in sequences such as Bartholomew Griffin's *Fidessa* (1596) and Richard Barnfield's *Cynthia* which were printed for Humphrey and Matthew Lownes, is to present one sonnet per page with ornamental borders at the top and bottom of each page.

[54] The case for attending to physical similarities between these two volumes has been persuasively made by Marotti, 'Shakespeare's Sonnets as Literary Property', pp. 154–5. For the converse and equally defensible view, that the resemblances to the 1591 edition of *Astrophil and Stella* should be interpreted as signs that Shakespeare's sequence is the summation of its genre, at once recalling and overgoing its origin, see Katherine Duncan-Jones, 'What Are Shakespeare's Sonnets Called?', *Essays in Criticism*, 47 (1997), 1–12. For discussion of the first quarto of *Astrophel and Stella*, see H. R. Woudhuysen, *Sir Philip Sidney and the Circulation of Manuscripts 1558–1640* (Oxford, 1996), pp. 365–84, J. A. Lavin, 'The First Two Printers of Sidney's *Astrophil and Stella*', *The Library*, 5th Series 26 (1971), 249–55, and McDonald P. Jackson, 'The Printer of the First Quarto of *Astrophil and Stella* (1591)', *Studies in Bibliography*, 31 (1978), 201–3. For various accounts of why the volume was called in, see William A. Ringler (ed.), *The Poems of Sir Philip Sidney* (Oxford, 1962), pp. 542–3, and Germaine Warkentin, 'Patrons and Profiteers: Thomas Newman and the "Violent Enlargement" of *Astrophil and Stella*', *Book Collector*, 34 (1985), 461–87.

the same time as appearing to be a product of miscellaneous processes: it looks at once like a monument and like a heavily revised manuscript copy hyped into print by an eager printer, who may or may not have liberated it from the author's private closet.

If our Jacobean reader stopped his physical appraisal of the volume and began to read it, he would find this elusive blend of the monumental and the messily quotidian replicated in the poetic structure of the volume. The poems which seem to claim the most for the immortalising power of monumental verse often also suggest that organic frailties play across their surface, turning a marble monument into a work which lives by virtue of being continually re-read, and recreated in the hearts of new lovers. Sonnet 18 ('Shall I compare thee to a summer's day') ends not just with promise of a poetic monument, but with a claim that its subject's future life is dependent on the continuation of biological life:

> Nor shall Death brag thou wand'rest in his shade,
> When in eternal lines to time thou grow'st.
> So long as men can breathe or eyes can see,
> So long lives this, and this gives life to thee.   (18. 11–14)

Sonnet 55 begins proudly declaiming that 'Not marble, nor the gilded monuments | Of princes shall outlive this pow'rful rhyme'. But the couplet confesses that what guarantees the survival of 'The living record of your memory' is the poem's continuing appeal to readers. This is what makes it live: 'So, till the judgement that yourself arise, | You live in this, and dwell in lovers' eyes'. Possessive apostrophes are not used in the Quarto: its 'louers' could correspond to either the modern singular possessive form or to the possessive plural. The young man's vitality comes either from the singular gaze of his lover, whose claim to immortalise his subject thus dwindles to a hyperbole exchanged between friends, or from the repeated rehearsal of his beauty by subsequent readers, in which case the hyperbole is warranted. These senses hint that the life of this monumental poem depends upon its being re-read, re-lived, inscribed in new lives. They also generate uncertainty as to whether the poem was designed to hide in a private communication between friends, charactered in the idiosyncratic hand of Shakespeare, or to be blazoned in print for eternity.

What makes the volume *Shake-speares Sonnets* unique is the extent to which its every element can be seen under the marmoreal aspect of a work or in the shifting light of life: its appearance, its dedication, its willingness to link monuments with the quotidian, all these features invite from its readers a deliberate interplay between reading the collection for the life as a private manuscript record of a secret love, and reading it as a monumental printed work. Recent scholarship enables us to add to these features a multiplicity of other structures within which to read the poems. There are moments when the sequences seem to take a chronological pattern, relating a narrative which it is tempting to associate with autobiography. When the poet writes

> Three winters cold
> Have from the forests shook three summers' pride,
> Three beauteous springs to yellow autumn turned
> In process of the seasons have I seen,
> Three April perfumes in three hot Junes burned,
> Since first I saw you fresh, which yet are green.   (104. 3–8)

it is right to bear in mind the convention that sonneteers live life in multiples of three.[55] But recent stylometric tests have shown that Sonnet 104 begins a mini-sequence of poems which show a higher incidence of 'late rare words' and a lower incidence of 'early rare words' than the group which precedes it.[56] Stylistic analysis prompts the teasing suggestion that three years actually might have passed in Shakespeare's life since he wrote Sonnet 103. An autobiographical frame is one of the narrative structures which a reader of the Sonnets needs to keep in play, but this sort of living sequencing has to be allowed to coexist with an awareness of scrupulously artful shapeliness. So Sonnet 49 appears to be out of place to many readers, since it occurs among a group of poems about travel and absence. It begins anticipating a future cata-strophe with 'Against that time (if ever that time come) | When I shall see thee frown on my defects'; in doing so it anticipates 63, with its fearful opening 'Against my love shall be as I am now, | With Time's injurious hand crushed and o'er-worn'. And it does so in a manner which is artful despite the Sonnet's apparent oddity of placement: the human body was believed to suffer a 'grand climacteric' at 63 (and this fact has often been invoked in relation to Sonnet 63),[57] but (and this point has not to my knowledge been made about the poem before) it also was believed to suffer a minor climacteric at 49. The two poems are consciously linked as crisis poems. The effect of jutting this numerological artistry, reminding us of the frailty of life, in among the horsey business and packing away of jewels with which Sonnets 48–51 are concerned, is to juxtapose a craftsman's control over the pattern of his poem with the daily shocks of living bustle. The combination of miscellaneity and apparent artfulness which

---

[55] Horace's declaration in *Epodes*, XI. 5–6 ('This third December since I ceased to desire Inachia is shaking the leaves from the trees') was imitated by Desportes and Ronsard, on which see Rollins, *The Sonnets*, A New Variorum Edition. There are signs this was not simply a convention, however: Daniel refers in the 1592 text of *Delia* (31. 6) to three years of courtship, but extends it to five in 1594.

[56] See Hieatt, Hieatt, and Prescott, 'When did Shakespeare write *Sonnets* 1609?' 91. 'Zone 3', of which 104 marks the start, is however a section of the sequence with a relatively low instance of rare words, and so firm conclusions about the dates of poems in this part of the sequence are difficult to draw.

[57] See René Graziani, 'The Numbering of Shakespeare's Sonnets: 12, 60, and 126', *Shakespeare Quarterly*, 35 (1984), 79–82, which notes that the 126 poems to the young man equal twice the number of the grand climacteric.

governs the structure of the Sonnets volume, and what appears to have been the extraordinarily extended period of its composition, go to make the poems uniquely demanding: they tempt their readers to identify characters, to turn them into a unified narrative, to read for the life, to fancy they see an artful pattern behind the whole; but the poems always retreat at the last moment from a full revelation either of life or of a full shaping design.[58]

Since the 1960s the editorial tradition of the Sonnets has been unhealthily divided. Editors influenced by the New Criticism have concentrated, often to brilliantly illuminating effect, on the verbal complexity of the poems, but have sometimes shrunk from the intricacies of bibliographical analysis and have tended to dismiss biographical interpretations as 'gossip' or 'chit-chat'.[59] Editors in the biographical school have put much energy into determining the occasions and addressees of the poems, and have laboured with the empiricist's belief that truths are always single and always determinable—*either* Southampton, *or* Pembroke. The time has come for this division to end. It will only end when critics and editors appreciate two things: firstly, that there are no empirically ascertainable certainties about the addressees or the origins of the Sonnets; secondly that that indeterminacy is a very important part of the reading experience of the poems. The Sonnets draw a large measure of their power from their willingness to suggest that they offer clues to lives and mental experiences which remain nonetheless irretrievable. And given that they are by the author of *Venus and Adonis* and *Lucrece*, those poems preoccupied by not quite publishing mental secrecies, this is what one would expect. When Sonnet 53 begins

> What is your substance, whereof are you made,
> That millions of strange shadows on you tend?
> Since every one hath, every one, one shade,
> And you, but one, can every shadow lend.

---

[58] On the miscellaneity of sonnet sequences, see Germaine Warkentin, ' "Love's Sweetest Part, Variety": Petrarch and the Curious Frame of the Renaissance Sonnet Sequence', *Renaissance and Reformation*, 11 (1975), 14–23. Carol Thomas Neely, 'The Structure of English Renaissance Sonnet Sequences', *ELH*, 45 (1978), 359 notes that 'The Italian model—fragmentary composition followed by careful selection and arrangement into a sequence—both justifies the expectation of structure in the sequence and predicts its loose elastic nature'. On the origins of the term 'sonnet sequence', see William T. Going, 'Gascoigne and the Term "Sonnet Sequence" ', *Notes and Queries*, 199 (1954), 189–91 and 'The Term "Sonnet Sequence" ', *Modern Language Notes*, 62 (1947), 400–2. For arguments that individual Sonnets suit their positions in the sequence see Graziani, 'The Numbering of Shakespeare's Sonnets'. This approach yields more convincing fruit than the root-and-branch numerology of Alastair Fowler, *Triumphal Forms: Structural Patterns in Elizabethan Poetry* (Cambridge, 1970), pp. 174–97.

[59] John Kerrigan, *The Sonnets and A Lover's Complaint*, p. 11 says that biographical criticism 'soon finds itself spinning off the text into vacuous literary chit-chat'. L. C. Knights begins his essay on the Sonnets of 1934 with the sally 'That there is so little genuine criticism in the terrifying number of books and essays on Shakespeare's Sonnets can only be partly accounted for by the superior attractiveness of gossip', repr. in Peter Jones (ed.), *Shakespeare: The Sonnets. A Casebook* (London, 1977), p. 74.

the words 'substance' and 'shadow' seem at first to belong to the register of metaphysics, as they do generally in the Sonnets. 'Substance' carries the primary senses 'essential nature' or 'That of which a physical thing consists; the material of which a body is formed and in virtue of which it possesses certain properties' (*OED* 6a), which is opposed to the shadow, or insubstantial image, of a thing. The proximity of the poem to 54, which is about artistic representation, suggests that 'shadow' could mean 'artistic representation' (*OED* 6b) as well as having the daemonic overtones which commentators have sometimes found in the poem: so 'what are you made of that you generate so many representations?'. But then why 'tend', a word which can be used of the activities of servants or underlings (and which is so used in 57: 'Being your slave, what should I do but tend | Upon the hours and times of your desire?')? Does this word suggest that a more material scene is obliquely imaged in the lines, in which a person of miraculous 'substance' in *OED* sense 16a ('Possessions, goods, estate; means, wealth') is tended on by 'shadows', in the sense of 'parasites or toadies' (*OED* 8a)? This material scene of a rich patron thronged by scroungers is fleetingly registered in the poem. But, as so often happens in the Sonnets, the suggested presence of a material scenario forces a flurry of metaphorical activity from the poet. The material import of 'substance' prompts the poet to erect a barrage of defensive metaphors so thick that they momentarily suggest supernatural influence, or that a horde of Platonic shadows clusters around the true form of the addressee's beauty.[60] A game has nearly been given away, and the best way to hide it is with ghostly suggestion.

This example suggests that one should read the Sonnets experimentally, inventing for them possible circumstances, embedding the poems in those circumstances, and listening to how they sound. They will evade succumbing to those circumstances because their power lies in their ability to suggest that they could live in almost infinitely multiple circumstances. This form of experimental embedding, though, enables the range and depth of the poems' language to emerge at its richest. And this is how their earliest readers might well have responded to Sonnet sequences, as they copied individual sonnets into their commonplace books, or slipped copies of poems under the doors of their mistresses' chambers.[61] The poems in the sequence in which they appear

---

[60] For a reading of another Sonnet which is alive to its material circumstances, see John Barrell, 'Editing Out: The Discourse of Patronage in Shakespeare's Twenty-Ninth Sonnet', in *Poetry, Language and Politics* (Manchester, 1988), pp. 18–43.

[61] Thomas Whythorne, *Autobiography*, p. 21 describes how he left a poem for a lady 'between the strings of a gittern'. Whythorne's autobiography is frequently invoked as evidence for the social deployment of verse in the period. It was probably composed in 1575, shortly after the publication of George Gascoigne's *Adventures of Master F. J.*, to which it has more than passing resemblances. Both narratives may have roots in reality, or the 'factual' account of Whythorne's life may have roots in fiction. Shakespeare's fellow Warwickshireman Michael Drayton gives no less equivocal evidence of the practical utility

in Q and preceded by their dedication to Mr W. H. have a quality which one might call situational ambiguity. That is, they suggest a multiplicity of additional possible senses if their readers are prepared to try them out, to see how they fit, in different narrative settings. Let us finally consider one very famous example, Sonnet 116:

> Let me not to the marriage of true minds
> Admit impediments; love is not love
> Which alters when it alteration finds,
> Or bends with the remover to remove.
> O no, it is an ever-fixèd mark,   5
> That looks on tempests and is never shaken;
> It is the star to every wandering barque,
> Whose worth's unknown, although his height be taken.
> Love's not Time's fool, though rosy lips and cheeks
> Within his bending sickle's compass come.   10
> Love alters not with his brief hours and weeks,
> But bears it out even to the edge of doom.
>   If this be error and upon me proved,
>   I never writ, nor no man ever loved.

The greatness of the poem lies in its willingness to allow temporal effects to play across the surface of its vision of love as an immutable force. It does not simply assert the immutability of love; it suggests that there are specific temporal circumstances which make it necessary to state that immutability. Several critics have been prompted to embed this poem in the life: Seymour-Smith in his note imagined that 'The situation seemed to be that the Friend, no doubt flattered at first by Shakespeare's "return" to him, was soon puzzled by his obviously changed attitude. No doubt he upbraided Shakespeare for this . . . in some such petulant terms as: "You no longer love me as you used to, because I am older", and so on.'[62] Helen Vendler, in a rigorously aesthetic reading of this Sonnet, also feels that its form of love derives from a dramatic setting: she sees it as an answer to a declaration by the friend that loves do just end.[63] These critics are doing what readers of the Sonnets are invited to do. I

---

of sonnet-writing when he ruefully acknowledged that a sonnet he wrote for a 'witlesse Gallant' succeeded in winning the mistress over, but the poems he writes to his Idea miserably fail to gain her affection, *Idea. In Sixty Three Sonnets* (1619), Sonnet 21. Drayton's suggestion that poets wrote poems for friends and patrons to use, though, may be one further expression of the sonneteer's traditional sense of the ineffectiveness of his own verse in winning a mistress over.

[62] Martin Seymour-Smith (ed.), *Shakespeare's Sonnets* (London, 1963), p. 169.

[63] Helen Vendler, *Ways into Shakespeare's Sonnets* The Hilda Hulme Memorial Lecture, 3 December 1990 (London, 1990), pp. 20–4. She too is prompted to imagine an actual conversation: 'The young man has, after all, said, "I did love you once, but now impediments have arisen through alteration and removes."'

do not think either of them are right, because I believe that the success of the poem, and indeed the success of all the Sonnets, depends on its refusal to offer sufficient grounds for applying it to any one circumstance. Its opening lines raise practical problems of stress, emphasis, and sense which invite exploration of embedding the poem in a variety of possible dramatic scenarios. Its opening line probably means chiefly 'I will not acknowledge that there are any barriers to love'. But how strong is the stress on 'me'? Strong enough to carry a hint of rebuke? And the echo of the Solemnization of Matrimony makes this a particularly strong claim, turning it into a churchly vow, taken at that critical moment when the couple are asked if there is any impediment to their marriage. Why at such a sacred moment use the word 'admit', and why that emphasis on 'alteration'? Could one imagine that the poem was written by someone who is nobly forgoing a lover rather than simply reaffirming his vows, that the marriage of true minds alluded to in the first line is not between the poet and his addressee, but between the addressee and another person? 'Admit' on this reading would not mean 'confess' but 'allow to enter' (*OED* 1). The first lines would mean 'Do not allow *me* [and that is where a reader might well let the iambic stress fall] to come between you and the person with whom you have such a perfect mental affinity: I love you so truly that I can keep on loving you forever even when I forgo you.' When set in this sort of imaginary life the poem takes on new resonances, some noble, some bitter—or it wins its nobility through and despite of bitterness: to say that love alters not where it alteration finds becomes a rebuke (you have altered; I have not); the heroic 'bears it out even to the edge of doom' becomes deliberately strained, an instance of the scarcely suppressed irony masquerading as masochism in which the Sonnets abound. A love emerges which is above circumstance; but that expression of love is strategically directed to someone who has betrayed that ideal, and so is embedded in circumstance. I would not wish to present this as a new or even as a true hypothesis about the poem; rather I use it as an example to suggest that the life, the literary vitality, of the poem depends on one's willingness to experiment with its relations to the surrounding sequence, to its author's life, to other possible lives.

The Sonnets have fascinated so many for so long because of their unique ability, inscribed in their physical form, their order, their vocabulary, to be both monumental works and suggestive fragments of life at once. The life from which they spring can never, of course, be recaptured, but that does not mean that we should give up the chase. We should perhaps, though, devote less energy to fruitless attempts to associate Shakespeare, sexually or otherwise, with members of the English nobility, and put more energy into imagining the kinds of dramatic microclimate—the occasions, the emotional and social structures—which gave these poems their first life. Even if we know that the content of Shakespeare's memory will always elude us, even if we know that his life will never be known by us as it was by him, to keep looking for these unfindable entities is a central criterion of a serious engagement with his poems. And, moreover, it is what his poems invite his readers to do.

Appendix: Were Shakespeare's Sonnets Really Authorised?

Katherine Duncan-Jones has argued in 'Was the 1609 *SHAKE-SPEARES SON-NETS* Really Unauthorized?', *Review of English Studies*, NS, 34 (1983), 151–71, and in her edition of *Shakespeare's Sonnets* (London, 1997), pp. 32–41, against the received opinion that Shakespeare's Sonnets were printed without their author's consent. Her case rests in part on a revisionary account of the career of Thomas Thorpe. She notes Thorpe's close relations with theatrical circles, his work for the super-scrupulous Ben Jonson over *Volpone* and *Sejanus*, and his role in producing high quality printed editions of theatrical texts throughout the early years of the seventeenth century. The range and distinction of Thorpe's productions leads Duncan-Jones to conclude that it is likely that the printer came by his copy through personal contact with Shakespeare, possibly with Jonson as an intermediary.

If this case is accepted in its totality it has significant critical and editorial consequences: the order, the spelling, even the odd loose end of the text in Q might be seen as deriving from a copy which had authorial sanction. Duncan-Jones couches her argument strongly in order to counter the many attacks which have been launched against Thorpe, and this means that evidence which could be regarded as running against her case is given relatively light treatment. She does not discuss the fact that Thorpe's first effort with William Apsley to register a piece of copy, 'a panegyric or congratulation for the concord of the kingdomes of great Britaine in the unitie of religion under king JAMES' on 23 June 1603, was cancelled because the work was already registered to 'Master Seaton', Edward Arber, ed., *A Transcript of the Stationers' Register*, 5 vols. (London and Birmingham, 1875–94), iii, 37. This could, of course, have been a simple mistake by a young printer, but it may be an indicator that Thorpe was not at the start of his career completely scrupulous in his quest for copy to print (obtaining copy without an author's consent in this period was not a crime; to print copy registered in the name of another printer, however, violated one of the key principles of the stationers' company). Nor does Duncan-Jones give a very full account of Thorpe's apparent piracy of the copy of Marlowe's *Lucan's First Book Translated* from Blount, as discussed by W. W. Greg, 'The Copyright of *Hero and Leander*', *The Library*, 4th Ser., 24 (1944), 165–74. This case too is difficult: Thorpe's subsequent close relation with Blount may imply that the printers collaborated over the volume and tried to generate excitement by making the copy appear to have been stolen (Blount assigned his rights to print *Sejanus* to Thorpe on 6 August 1605, Arber, iii, 297). Taken in conjunction with Thorpe's unlicensed printing of *The Odcombian Banquet*, however, which Duncan-Jones dismisses as a harmless caper, the episode of Marlowe's Lucan might indicate that Thorpe was capable of seeking copy from other printers as well as directly from authors' hands (*contra* Duncan-Jones's claim that the evidence 'points to Thorpe as a publisher who bought his copy directly from authors', pp. 160–1), and/or that he was willing to use preliminary matter to feed an audience's taste for the illicitly obtained. That Q has been seen as having been printed without its author's consent, and that its publisher's prefatory matter has fuelled speculation about the origins of the volume is not entirely surprising in view of Thorpe's earlier career.

Duncan-Jones provides strong evidence that Thorpe was careful about the typographical accuracy of the texts which he published, and this finding is partly what prompts her decision to follow the Quarto at several points in her edition when the majority of editors choose to emend. The examples of *Volpone* and *Sejanus* are striking; but there are counter-examples. The translation of Lucan by Sir Arthur Gorges is referred to by Duncan-Jones as a 'finely-printed text of a most distinguished translation' (p. 163). Here one must qualify her opinion: the volume is sumptuous in its appearance, but the quality of typesetting is relatively poor, with many pages showing clear compositorial errors. Here too questions about the origins of the copy are deliberately raised in the preliminary matter: the preface, purportedly by Gorges's son Carew who was then only ten, states that he stumbled on the poem 'in my fathers study, amongst many other of his Manuscripts' (sig. A3^v) and arranged with his schoolmaster to have it printed. This too is difficult evidence to assess, and might reasonably be seen as an effort on the part of the author to avoid the stigma of print. But this example does also show that relatively inaccurately printed works which are presented as having arrived in the printer's hands through intermediaries were part of Thorpe's stock-in-trade, as well as carefully prepared play-texts.

Thorpe otherwise only signed prefatory matter for volumes whose authors were dead (as in the case of Marlowe's Lucan, and the 1616 edition of John Healey's translation of *Epictetus Manuall*) or out of the country (as appears to have been the case with the 1610 edition of Healey's *Epictetus* and the same author's translation of *The Citie of God*). There are three works for which Thorpe may have composed anonymous preliminary matter, two of which are consistent with this pattern: Arthur Dent died in 1607, and Thorpe printed his *The Hand-Maid of Repentance* with an anonymous preface 'To the Christian Reader' in 1614. This was despite the fact that the copy was entered to John Wright, who published a substantial number of Dent's posthumous works, on 23 July 1614 (Arber iii, 551). The claim in the preface that the copy 'hath by Gods goodnes come unto my handes' (sig. A4^b) is either a piece of Pecksniffery or a suggestion that Wright informally allowed Thorpe to publish the copy. Jan van Oldenbarnveld was a Dutchman who had no discernible connection with the printing of *Barnevels Apology* for Thorpe in 1618, and the unsigned epistle to the reader suggests there was no relation of any kind between author and printer, since it presents 'Barneveltius' as a dotard. Theophilus Field's *A Christians Preparation* (1622) is the only work for which Thorpe may have composed an epistle for a living author whom he knew. Its 'Epistle to the Reader', signed 'Anonymous' (in Greek), is, however, the least likely of the three unattributed epistles to be Thorpe's, since its author claims friendship with Field, who was then the Bishop of Llandaff. Even this epistle, though, claims that the copy for the work which follows was originally only intended for the eyes of certain 'High and Honourable personages', and was only printed by the 'incessant importunity' of the anonymous author of the preface.

Given the extent of the plague in 1609 it is quite likely that Shakespeare was not in London at the time the Quarto was going through the press, and so one should hesitate before inferring from the presence of a signed dedication by Thorpe that the printer obtained the manuscript without its author's consent. Yet the analogy with other sonnet sequences, which usually only have dedications by their printers in cases where piracy is clear or suspected, and with the other works for which Thorpe produced signed preliminary matter, does admit the possibility that the Quarto may have been printed with less involvement from its author than Duncan-Jones implies.

These facts taken together do not comprise proof that Shakespeare's Sonnets were unauthorised (and even if it could be proven that Shakespeare authorised the publication this would not necessarily imply that the copy from which Eld's compositors worked was finally revised, or that Thorpe's Quarto presents a miraculous incarnation of authorial final intentions). But the evidence presented in this appendix does constitute grounds for regarding the case as 'not proven', as the Scots would say. Thorpe was quite capable of producing a volume printed with its author's consent which accurately reflected its copy. He was also quite capable of producing volumes which offered the excitement of unauthorised publication. The appearance of the Quarto of *Shake-speares Sonnets* leaves it open to readers to opt for either of these alternatives, or to teeter uncertainly between the two.

The Poetry of the Caroline Court

THOMAS N. CORNS

University of Wales, Bangor

I

MY SUBJECT IS THE WORK of those writers who have generally been called 'Cavalier poets'. It is a term that I resist, because it encourages the unhelpful practice of reading the literature of the late 1620s and the 1630s as it were backwards, from points of retrospection in 1642 or later. Paradoxically, it is a perspective which was encouraged among readers of the Civil War period as a positive recommendation of such poetry, while among later critics hindsight has supported an ethical criticism of a negative kind. Although in the seventeenth century it added a purposefulness and a heroism to the poets, since Dr Johnson it serves to incorporate them into the crises of the 1640s, not as witnesses but as accomplices in the early Stuart political disaster. The approach reached extreme expression in C. V. Wedgwood's influential *Poetry and Politics under the Stuarts*,[1] which directly or indirectly did something to set the agenda for even the best of recent accounts of these poets. Thus, Warren Chernaik finds himself drawn into an ethical discussion of Waller: 'This study . . . is an attempt not to rehabilitate Waller but to do him simple justice . . . .'.[2] Again, Kevin Sharpe's ground-breaking account of Carew, Davenant, and Townshend vindicates them (and simultaneously the Caroline court) by seeking to demonstrate that they did indeed whisper critical advice to their political masters, and that their masters were open to respectful dissent. He concludes, 'The equation of the court with sycophancy cannot stand; criticism, we have

---

[1] C. V. Wedgwood, *Poetry and Politics under the Stuarts* (Cambridge, 1960).
[2] Warren L. Chernaik, *The Poetry of Limitation: A Study of Edmund Waller* (New Haven and London, 1968), p. 14.

Proceedings of the British Academy, **97**, 51–73. © The British Academy 1998.
Read at the Academy 29 April 1997

now seen, was articulated insistently from *within* the court as well as from outside.'[3] Though he confutes the received position, he does so in terms which concede the primacy of the exculpation of the poetry of the 1620s and 1630s from the catastrophes of the 1640s. The fullest and most sensitive study, that of Earl Miner, in its periodisation has the work of Charles Cotton (d. 1687) as its *terminus ad quem*, and in so doing necessarily reads the poetry of the 1630s as ideologically and ethically continuous with that of the 1640s and after. Thus, Miner sets himself the agenda of describing 'conceptions of the self, of life, and the world . . . which one group, the Cavaliers, tended to set forth in terms of certain styles, certain recurring subjects, certain recurring approaches, and certain cultural assumptions'.[4]

That word 'Cavalier' certainly compounds the problem, and it ties twentieth-century misperceptions to those of the Civil War period. Before 1641, it had currency as a fashionable term for a fashionable phenomenon, 'a courtly gentleman, a gallant',[5] sometimes, I suspect, already with a pejorative edge. Sir John Suckling uses the word in that sense in the Dramatis Personae of *The Goblins* (?1637–1641).[6] But after 1641 it rapidly becomes the name for the stereotypical representation of the royalist activist, initially as a pejorative, thereafter as a word current with both sides. Thus William Lilly, writing in 1651 of what he had witnessed in 1641–2, 'all that took part or appeared for his Majestie [were termed] Cavaliers, few of the vulgar knowing the sence of the word *Cavalier*'. Indeed, with the word came, in parliamentarian propaganda, a wealth of association with hard-drinking, hard-living, rakehell womanising.[7] The hostile representation contains much that can be with facility nudged into a positive and rather gratifying self-fashioning. After the fiasco of the Bishops' Wars, an anonymous lampoon counselled Suckling:

> Since under *Mars* thou wert not borne,
> To *Venus* fly and thinke no scorne,
> Let it be my advice . . . .[8]

But after the Army Plot of 1641, in which he played a leading role, parliamentarian propaganda demonises him in altogether more attractive ways, as in the broadside *The Sucklington Faction, or Suckling's Roaring Boys*,[9] in which

---

[3] Kevin Sharpe, *Criticism and Compliment: The politics of literature in the England of Charles I* (Cambridge, 1987), p. 291.

[4] Earl Miner, *The Cavalier Mode from Jonson to Cotton* (Princeton, New Jersey, 1971), p. vii.

[5] *OED* s.v. 'Cavalier' sb. 2.

[6] *The Works of Sir John Suckling: The Plays*, edited by L. A. Beaurline (Oxford, 1971), p. 124: on the possible dating, see p. 274.

[7] See Thomas N. Corns, *Uncloistered Virtue: English Political Literature 1640–1660* (Oxford, 1992), pp. 3–7.

[8] 'Upon Sir John Suckling's hundred horse', lines 37–9, in *The Works of Sir John Suckling: the Non-dramatic Works*, edited by Thomas Clayton (Oxford, 1971), p. 205.

[9] Anon., *The Sucklington Faction, or Sucklings roaring boys* (London, 1641).

the 'cavalier' life seems not without its discreet charm. By the time of his death, in exile and in uncertain circumstances, the negative associations of cavalierism are set aside by Suckling's apologists, and he emerges as the epitome of all that is best in that cultural phenomenon:

> Thinke on a schollar without pride,
> A Souldier with much bloud un-dyed,
> A Statesman, yet noe whit ambitious,
> A Libertine, and yet not vitious,
> Thinke to the heigth, if man could bee,
> Or ere was perfect, this was hee . . . [10]

The dead Suckling could scarcely be responsible for how he was represented. But court poets of the 1630s saw in the 1640s the advantages of appropriating elements of the stereotype into the deflection of their own self-representation in more heroic directions. Thus, Herrick offers his blessing to 'His Cavalier,' 'the virtuous man' who can 'Saile against Rocks, and split them too; | I! and a world of Pikes passe through'.[11] Edmund Waller's 1645 collection, when he was already in exile for his part in the 'Waller Plot', concludes with a significant variant on the love lyric that characterises much of the volume, 'To Chloris upon a favour received':

> *Chloris*, since first our calme of peace
> Was frighted hence, this good we finde.
> Your favours with your feares increase,
> And growing mischiefs make you kinde:
> So the fayre tree which still preserves
> Her fruit and state whilst no wind blows,
> In stormes from that uprightnesse swerves,
> And the glad earth about her strowes
> With treasure from her yielding boughs.[12]

Waller as always is decorous, but the 'yielding boughs' approach explicitness; evidently times of war reverse the game of love, and his characteristic sighing and frustrated devotion give way to the soldier's rewards. In this he anticipates Richard Lovelace's characteristic posture in his first *Lucasta* (1649), in which an eroticised notion of warfare relates sexual value and achievement to die-hard royalism: 'I could not love thee (Deare) so much, | Lov'd I not Honour more.'[13]

Plainly most of the Lovelace oeuvre postdates 1640, and with Herrick's only volume, *Hesperides* (1648), it is difficult or impossible to determine when

---

[10] 'An Epitaph upon Sir John Suckling', tentatively attributed by Clayton to James Paulin, *Non-dramatic Works*, pp. 191–2, 341.
[11] 'His Cavalier', lines 7–9, *The Poetical Works of Robert Herrick*, edited by L. C. Martin (Oxford, 1956), p. 31.
[12] Edmund Waller, *Poems 1645* (Menston, 1971), p. 96.
[13] Richard Lovelace, 'To Lucasta, Going to the Warres', *Lucasta* (London, 1649), p. 3.

some of the poems were written, and all his pre-1640 material printed in
Hesperides necessarily assumes a rather changed ideological value in changed
circumstances; simple poems of celebration, for example, are suffused with
defiant nostalgia and a poignant sense of loss.

But in the case of Waller's poems, published while in exile, and in the case
of the dead poets Suckling (d. probably 1642) and Thomas Carew (d. 1640),
booksellers—most actively Thomas Walkley and the redoubtable Humphrey
Moseley—saw advantages in incorporating works produced during the personal rule into a movement, a royalist and indeed cavalier culture, displaced from
manuscript and performance into print by the diaspora of the royal court.
(Among the poets who concern me today, only William Davenant, with his
Madagascar collection of 1637, had published a volume before 1640.) Thus,
the printed collections bear a striking resemblance to each other, and increasingly their title-pages tie them to the royalist cause, incorporating them into the
rather desperate die-hard loyalism that, at the time of their writing, would
simply have been inappropriate. Thus, Moseley's edition of Waller has a
title-page alluding to his political life and, in his connections with Henry
Lawes, to his place in the royal court; Moseley's preface describes the poems
'going abroad . . . and like the present condition of the Author himselfe, they
are expos'd to the wide world, to travell, and try their fortunes'.[14] The title-page
of Walkley's first and second editions of Carew has his by-line 'One of the
Gentlemen of the Privie-Chamber, and Sewer in Ordinary to His Majesty.'[15]
Moseley's edition of 1651 styles him 'Sewer in Ordinary to His late Majesty'
and connects him with Henry Lawes, 'one of his late Majesties Private
Musick'.[16] Moseley (I presume) called his posthumous first edition of
Suckling's works *Fragmenta Aurea*, the golden fragments of a life broken in
the cause of the king. As Moseley tells the reader, Suckling 'liv'd only long
enough to see the Sun-set of that Majesty from whose auspicious beams he
derived his lustre, and with whose declining state his own loyal Fortunes were
obscured'.[17] Kevin Sharpe has sagely observed that from the early months of
the Long Parliament 'we can begin to trace the myths that have obscured the
story of the 1630s'.[18] Indeed so, and potently among them is the rewriting of
literary history that effects spurious continuities between the defiant and at
times rather mindless nostalgia of the 1640s and the poise, precision, and
optimism of the verse of the 1630s.

---

[14] 'An advertisement to the Reader', Waller, sig. A4^v.
[15] *The Poems of Thomas Carew with his Masque* Coelum Britannicum, edited by Rhodes
Dunlap (1949; Oxford, 1964), pp. 1, 111.
[16] Carew, pp. 118–19.
[17] 'The Stationer to the Reader', *Non-dramatic Works*, p. 6.
[18] Kevin Sharpe, *The Personal Rule of Charles I* (New Haven and London, 1992), p. 950.

II

Have you seen but a white lily grow,
   Before rude hands have touch'd it?
Have you marked but the fall o' the snow,
   Before the earth hath smutched it?
Have you felt the wool o' the beaver?
     Or swan's down ever?
Or have smelled o' the bud o' the briar?
     Or the nard i' the fire?
   Or have tasted the bag o' the bee?
O so white! O so soft! O so sweet is she![19]

The words are by Ben Jonson, the music is usually attributed to Robert Johnson, and the song was performed first on the public stage, as part of Wittipol's enticement of Mistress Fitzdottrel in *The Devil is an Ass*.[20] The text of the song recurs in the fourth part of 'A Celebration of Charis in Ten Lyric Pieces', with a new stanza at the beginning, first printed in the posthumously published *Underwood*.[21] Of itself, the poem illustrates a vital point about early Stuart literary culture: that the boundaries between literary contexts are porous; that lyric poetry and print culture negotiate a complex interrelationship with uncourtly, non-print, performance literary forms, like the theatre. The point is made again in Suckling's appropriation of the song, which also originates as a song in a play,[22] but it reappears in print, alongside his many other lyrics, undistinguished formally from them:

A Song to a Lute
Hast thou seen the Doun ith'air
   when wanton blasts have tost it;
Or the Ship on the sea,
   when ruder winds have crost it?
Hast thou markt the Crocodiles weeping.
   or the Foxes sleeping?
Or hast view'd the Peacock in his pride,
   or the Dove by his Bride,
   when he courts for his leachery?
Oh so fickle, oh so vain, oh so false, so false is she![23]

---

[19] *Ben Jonson*, edited by Ian Donaldson (Oxford and New York, 1985), pp. 314–15. Appendix A, below, contains a transcription by John Harper based on New York MS Drexel 4175, number 49. I am indebted to Professor Harper for his transcription, and to Dr Peter Flinn for preparing this and the other transcriptions in camera-ready form. I gratefully acknowledge the permission of the Music Division, the New York Public Library, Astor, Lenox and Tilden Foundations to publish this transcription. For a performance, Tragicomedia, *Orpheus I am*, EMI Classics CDC 7 543112 (1991), track 17, John Potter (tenor), Stephen Stubbs (archlute).

[20] Ben Jonson, *The Devil is an Ass*, edited by Peter Happé (Manchester and New York, 1994), II. vi. 104–13, pp. 121–2.

[21] Ben Jonson, pp. 310–19.

[22] *The Sad One*, IV. iv. 22–31, *Suckling, The Plays*, pp. 25, 250–1.

[23] Suckling, *Non-dramatic Works*, pp. 29–30. Appendix A shows the verse set against the music of MS Drexel 4175, a setting of Jonson's song.

The juxtaposition supports a number of points which can be generalised to much of the poetry of the Caroline court.

The poem is very dependent on its musical setting. In this case, almost certainly the poem is written to fit an extant song, and the work of the composer is antecedent to that of the poet. Moreover, the poem, which appears scarcely worth notice on the printed page, has a new charm and vitality in performance; the song moves towards a musical closure that matches the closure of its argument. Again, on the printed page, the poem seems metrically highly eccentric; the setting explains that eccentricity.

Secondly, like many other poems of the 1630s it actively seeks out and responds to another poem. Analogues are numerous. Thus, Suckling's 'Against Fruition I' is 'answered', *inter alios*, by Waller, in a detailed refutation which prints Suckling's points 'Con' against sex with his own points 'Pro'. It's hard to believe that either argument is seriously entertained. Suckling claims that sex can't be much good because it's a bit like ploughing and while, yes, the world needs workers, why should gentlemen toil to beget them when the lower classes can take of that 'homely' business: 'since there are enough | Born to the drudgery, what need we plough?'[24] Waller deconstructs the metaphor: literally, indeed, 'I need not plough since what the stooping Hinde | Gets of my pregnant Land, must all be mine', but the metaphorical ploughing, 'this nobler tillage', historically certainly falls to a gentleman's role.[25] Of course, in terms of cultural and social values Waller and Suckling can scarcely be separated. Sometimes even commendatory poems take argument with or respond to the works they commend. Davenant's 'Madagascar. A Poem written to Prince Rupert' has the potential to seem a shrewd criticism of Charles I's refusal to support the imperial venture; Suckling's 'To My Friend Will. Davenant; upon his Poem of *Madagascar*', congratulates him on his literary achievement while pointing up its remoteness from an external political reality:

> *Dav'nant*'s come
> From *Madagascar*, Fraught with Laurell home,
> And welcome (*Will*) for the first time, but prithee
> In thy next Voyage, bring the Gold too with thee.[26]

Sometimes the 'pro et contra' derive from the same poet, as in Carew's matched songs 'To my Mistris, I burning in love' and 'To her againe, she burning in a Feaver', and Milton's 'L'Allegro' and 'Il Penseroso' perhaps

---

[24] Suckling, 'Against Fruition [I]', lines 17–18, *Non-dramatic Works*, p. 37.

[25] Waller, *Poems 1645*, p. 87.

[26] 'To My Friend Will. Davenant; upon his Poem of *Madagascar*', in Sir William Davenant, *The Shorter Poems, and Songs from the Plays and Masques*, edited by A. M. Gibbs (Oxford, 1972), p. 7.

suggest themselves as further analogues.[27] We shall meet this dialogic mode again when we turn to consider poems of state. In the larger context, the 'debates' between contemporaries render the literary community of the Caroline court cohesive; they close the coterie; and they reflect a cultural milieu tolerant of civilised disagreement—within limitations.

But Suckling's response to Jonson is not within a generation but between generations, and—my third point—it reflects a larger concern among court poets of the 1630s to define their relationship to their great Jacobean precursors, Donne and more especially Jonson. Chernaik has written well on the later generation's qualified praise of their 'masculine strength',[28] and what the later poets carry forward is a narrow subset of their total repertoire. From Donne comes a plurality of lovers' voices and a range of situations; from Jonson comes the exquisite lyricism of his songs—songs like 'Have you seen but a white lily grow?'—and perhaps, too, some of the colloquial directness of his dramatic verse. What does not go forward to the court poetry of the 1630s is the opacity and concision of Jonson's epigrams (only Herrick writes a significant number of epigrams, and they are generally much more straightforward, syntactically, than Jonson's), and lost, too, is Donne's range of allusion. This narrowing down reflects, in part, a sense of audience—many court poems are socially functional addresses to powerful individuals; Davenant's New Year's Day gift poems to Henrietta Maria, out of simple politeness, must operate below a fairly low horizon of lexical and syntactical difficulty, for example. But clarity often is a prerequisite for performance poetry; song requires to be comprehensible to an aural reception.

Nor would the court poets of the 1630s have acknowledged much validity in Jonson's asseveration of the supremacy of the word in collaborative performance, his claim that 'the pen is more noble than the pencil'.[29] Just as Townshend, Carew, and Davenant could work with Jones, when Jonson could not, and accept his magisterial role as designer of court masque, so too the poets of the 1630s acknowledge their own, sometimes junior part, in the glittering accomplishments of the Caroline court culture. Richard Helgerson has described Caroline poets' sense of 'generational belatedness',[30] their sense of debt and inferiority to Donne and Jonson. But they have in ways that more than compensate a vivid awareness of their participation in a larger cultural formation which is characterised by its modernity, its innovation, its opulence, its royal sanction and its manifold accomplishments, in the vast Whitehall paintings of Rubens and

---

[27] Carew, pp. 34–5; *The Poems of John Milton*, edited by John Carey and Alastair Fowler (London and Harlow, 1968), pp. 130–46.

[28] Chernaik, *Waller*, p. 221.

[29] *Timber, or Discoveries*, in Donaldson, ed., *Ben Jonson*, p. 561.

[30] Richard Helgerson, *Self-Crowned Laureates: Spenser, Jonson, Milton and the Literary System* (Berkeley, Los Angeles, and London, 1983), p. 190.

the portraits of Van Dyck as well as in achievements of Inigo Jones—and court composers. They are part of a more than merely literary system.

Sir Roy Strong and Stephen Orgel have long since convinced cultural historians of the early Stuart period of the domination of the visual imagination in the realisation of images and representations of regal power.[31] But if masque constituted the defining genre of the epoch, the dominant cultural form on an everyday basis was surely music, perhaps pre-eminently music for dance and music for song. Both, of course, are important constituents of masque, but both have a daily role in the Jacobean and Caroline court. Charles played the viol; he had a large musical retinue as Prince of Wales and increased the musical complement of the king's household on his accession by merging his previous ensembles with James I's; he may well have composed music; and, most significantly perhaps, he advanced the finest composers of the 1620s and 1630s, among them Nicholas Lanier, who became Master of King's Musick in 1626, and Henry Lawes, who became a Gentleman of the Chapel Royal in the same year, and he rewarded them richly.[32] Lawes and Lanier, besides providing music for masques, produced and no doubt performed a copious amount of music for quotidian entertainment. Over 430 of Lawes's songs survive, and he set over forty poems by Carew and at least fourteen by Herrick, as well as poems by Suckling, Waller, and Lovelace.[33] Lanier and Lawes consolidated a transformation of English song, characterised by less obtrusive instrumentalism and a more declamatory singing style, approaching recitative. That renegotiation of the relationship of song to the rhythms of normal speech, begun by Thomas Campion, continued in ways that permitted the setting of poems while retaining the directness and clarity that characterises Caroline court poetry. Milton claimed in his sonnet to Lawes that he 'taught our English music how to span | Words with just note and accent . . .'.[34]

The revolution in English song permitted some singular achievements in the dialogue genre. Consider the following poem by Carew, set by Henry Lawes, 'A Pastorall Dialogue':

---

[31] See, for example, Stephen Orgel and Roy Strong, *Inigo Jones: The Theatre of the Stuart Court* (London and Berkeley, Los Angeles, 1973); Roy Strong, *Van Dyck: Charles I on Horseback* (London, 1972); Stephen Orgel, *The Jonsonian Masque* (Cambridge, Mass., 1965).

[32] Ian Spink, *English Song: Dowland to Purcell* (1974; London, 1986), p. 75; my discussion of Caroline song owes much to Spink, pp. 38–127. On the increase in the complement of the King's Musick and musicians' and composers' incomes, see Walter L. Woodfill, *Musicians in English Society from Elizabeth to Charles I* (New York, 1969), pp. 179–82; on Charles's household as Prince of Wales and on the mergers contingent on his accession, see Peter Holman, *Four and Twenty Fiddlers: The Violin at the English Court 1540–1690* (Oxford, 1993), especially chapters nine and ten.

[33] Spink, *English Song*, pp. 76, 94.

[34] John Milton, 'Sonnet XIII. To Mr H. Lawses, on his Airs,' line 2–3, in *Poems of John Milton*, p. 292; Spink, *English Song*, p. 76. It should be noted, however, that Campion explicitly sets himself a similar objective in the 'Preface' to his *Two Books of Ayres* (London, c.1614). I am indebted to Professor Harper for alerting me to the role of Campion in the transformation of English song.

A Pastorall Dialogue.

Shepherd, Nymph. Chorus.

Shep. This mossie bank they prest. *Ny.* That aged Oak
    Did canopie the happy payre
      All night from the dampe ayre.
Cho. Here let us sit and sing the words they spoke,
    Till the day breaking, their embraces broke.
      Shep.
See love, the blushes of the morne appeare,
    And now she hangs her pearlie store
      (Rob'd from the Easterne shore)
    I'th' Couslips bell, and Roses eare:
    Sweet, I must stay no longe here.
      Nymph.
Those streakes of doubtfull light, usher not day,
    But shew my sunne must set; no Morne
      Shall shine till thou returne,
    The yellow Planets, and the gray
    Dawne, shall attend thee on thy way.
      Shep.
If thine eyes guild my pathes, they may forbeare
    Their useless shine. *Nymph.* My teares will quite
      Extinguish their faint light.
She. Those drops will make their beames more cleare,
    Loves flames will shine in every teare.
      Cho.
They kist, and wept, and from their lips, and eyes,
    In a mixt dew, of brinie sweet,
      Their joyes, and sorrowes meet,
    But she cryes out. *Nymp.* Shepherd arise,
    The Sun betrayes us else to spies.
      Shep.
The winged houres flye fast, whilst we embrace,
    But when we want their help to meet,
      They move with leaden feet.
Nym. Then let us pinion *Time*, and chase
    The day for ever from this place.
      Shep.
Harke! *Ny.* Aye me stay! *She.* For ever.
      Ny. No, arise,
    Wee must be gone. *Shep.* My nest of spice.
    Nymph. My soule. *Shep.* My Paradise.
Cho. Neither could say farewell, but through their eyes
    Griefe, interrupted speach with teares supplyes.[35]

---

[35] Carew, *Poems*, pp. 45–6. Appendix B, below, contains a transcription by Sally Harper of *The Treasury of Musick: containing Ayres and Dialogues . . . composed by Mr Henry Lawes . . . and other Excellent Masters* (London, 1669), pp. 114–17. I am indebted to Dr Harper for her transcription. For a performance, Henry Lawes, *Sitting by the Streams*, The Consort of Musicke, director Anthony Rooley; track 5, Emma Kirkby and Mary Nichols (sopranos), Anthony Rooley (lute) (Hyperion CDA66135).

On the printed page, the poem seems merely to document the influence of French pastoralism in the Caroline court; in performance, its considerable structural ingenuity is apparent. The poem begins as if *in medias res*, as nymph and shepherd visit the scene of a lovers' tryst. Singing together, they frame a dialogue within the dialogue, in which they act out the roles of the unknown lovers whose lives they parallel and whose sensibility they assume. The narrative component of the embedded scene is carried by the second choric section, and the framing is completed by the third, which offers a musical closure to match the dramatic closure. The poem ends with grief's interruption of the lovers' speech, which chronologically anticipates the opening lines.

III

Carew's pastoral dialogue offers a useful transition into a consideration of gender-political implications of Caroline court poetry. Love poetry and especially love songs are very numerous in the oeuvres of court poets, and since many no doubt found their way into the repertoire of court musicians they must have been a major feature of the literary experience of the royal milieu. Carew's dialogue is typical of much of this material in its evasiveness about the nature of the relationship between the lovers and in its absence of any representation of a plausible external reality. In Donne's *Songs and Sonets*, there is often a sort of low-mimetic subject; lover speaks to lover in bedrooms and in bed; lovers sleep together; they sweat, they wake each other up, they feign sleep; they even pick fleas off each other.[36] But Charles I's decorous court is one purged of obtrusive sexual scandal. Sharpe well demonstrates that 'though it was almost impossible to enforce on the hundreds of individuals who made up the court the king's own strict codes of behaviour, Charles reacted firmly to public breaches of morality and decorum'.[37] Those who wanted to be part of his household at the least adopted, chameleon-like, a suitable coloration. As one male courtier observed: 'We keep all our virginities at court still, at least we lose them not avowedly.'[38]

I recall a sense of surprise when turning from Sharpe's account to reread Milton's *Defensio pro populo Anglicano* (1651), and his asseveration there that 'even in the theatre [Charles] kisses women wantonly, enfolds their waists and, to mention no more openly, plays with the breasts of maids and mothers'.[39]

---

[36] See, for example, 'The good-morrow', 'The sunne rising', 'The apparition', 'The flea', in *The Complete Poems of John Donne*, edited by C. A. Patrides (London and Melbourne, 1985), pp. 48–9, 53–4, 94–5, 47–8.

[37] Sharpe, *Personal Rule*, p. 212.

[38] Robert Reade, quoted by Sharpe, ibid.

[39] *The Complete Prose Works of John Milton*, edited by Don M. Wolfe *et al.* (New Haven and London, 1953–82), IV. i, 408.

Milton is characteristically very careful about accusations laid against Charles, so I wondered what he could have been thinking of. However, a glance at the typical female masquing costumes of the 1620s and 1630s and their extraordinary décolletage, explains how easily Milton may have been mistaken. Consider Inigo Jones's design for Henrietta Maria's costume as Chloris in Ben Jonson's *Chloridia* (1631); though it does mark some slight loss of confidence from Jones's earlier sketches.[40]

But Caroline masque defines the profoundly and explicitly eroticised version of married chastity which is at the centre of Caroline court culture. *Chloridia* ends with Chloris-Henrietta Maria commended to Charles in a song which celebrates her as,

> the queen of flowers,
> The sweetness of all showers,
> The ornament of bowers,
> The top of paramours.[41]

'Paramour' had long since developed its rather dubious connotations, and the *OED* cites this as its last occurrence in the sense of 'the object of chivalric admiration and attachment';[42] no doubt Jonson knew exactly how he was redefining sexual love in Caroline terms. Indeed, the closing gesture of *Chloridia* recurs frequently in the masques of the 1630s. Closing songs virtually tuck Charles and his queen up in bed, as in the closing lines of Carew's *Coelum Britannicum* (1634)[43] or William Davenant's *Temple of Love* (1638)[44] or his *Britannia Triumphans* (1638), in which the bedding of the royal pair offers a paradigm for the behaviour of 'each lady' and her 'lawful lover': 'Then all will haste to bed, but none to rise!'[45]

Of course court masque and court ritual are celebrations of royal power; but in the Caroline court that power is equated with sexual potency, and courtly ritual is redefined as fertility rite. Among the poems of state of the late 1620s and the 1630s royal panegyrics abound, and the royal pair are habitually celebrated as good breeders, as in Carew's 'New-yeares gift. To the King',[46] or Aurelian Townshend's 'Verse Epistle to Charles I',[47] or Waller's 'Of the Queen'.[48]

---

[40] Catalogued as items 181 and 180 in Orgel and Strong, *Inigo Jones*, pp. 439, 444, 445.

[41] Ben Jonson, *Chloridia*, lines 269–72, in Orgel and Strong, *Inigo Jones*, p. 270.

[42] *OED*, s.v. 'Paramour' sb. 2.c. and 3.

[43] Thomas Carew, *Coelum Britannicum*, lines 1126–38, in Orgel and Strong, *Inigo Jones*, p. 580.

[44] William Davenant, *The Temple of Love*, lines 511–19, in Orgel and Strong, *Inigo Jones*, p. 604.

[45] William Davenant, *Britannia Triumphans*, lines 627–44, in Orgel and Strong, *Inigo Jones*, p. 667.

[46] Carew, 'A New-yeares gift. To the King', especially lines 17–26, *Poems*, p. 90.

[47] Aurelian Townshend, 'Verse Epistle to Charles I: "'Tis but a while"', passim, in *The poems and masques of Aurelian Townshend*, edited by Cedric C. Brown (Reading, 1983), p. 50.

[48] Waller, 'Of the Queen', especially the penultimate verse paragraph, in *Poems 1645*, pp. 46–8.

The symbolic economy of the court postulates a polarity between regal sexuality and sexual anarchy. Though between the two terms there is tension, the latter only briefly and provisionally threatens the former. As the descent of masquers scatters the anti-masque, so too the libertine component in court poetry is made to lose to the royal alternative. Persistently, the status of obscene verse is that of a transient, unsustainable reverie. Herrick's 'Vine' ends as 'with the fancie I awook' and its status as a dream is explicitly acknowledged.[49] Many of his poems rehearse a sort of voyeuristic sexual sensibility of looking but not touching,[50] while he reiterates the status of his verse as separate from his life—perhaps from all decent life.[51] The gentry-class figures who people some of his pages act out in less opulent ways the married chastity of the royal pair; thus, he tells his brother, 'still thy wife, by chast intentions led, | Gives to thee each night a Maidenhead'.[52] Consummated licentiousness remains the province of the managerie of proletarians which inhabits the world of his epigrams, the Scobbles,[53] Luggses,[54] Groyneses,[55] and Dolls.[56] Again, Carew's 'A Rapture' is a fantasy set in 'Loves Elizium' that is remote from the values and imperatives of 'the world',[57] and it is balanced by poems moralising on the importance of sexual continence among women, warning against 'Snaring Poems . . . spred, | All to catch thy maiden-head'.[58] Carew makes the symbolic distinction clearest in 'To the Queene', which opposes 'wilde lust', whose only rule is *What ever pleaseth lawfull is*', with the 'sacred Lore' of Henrietta Maria, 'Which makes the rude Male satisfied | With one faire Female by his side', and forms 'loves pure Hermophradite'. Thus and only thus may bad sexuality be driven out by good, and 'the wilde | Satyr' reconciled to virtue.[59] It is in this context that those hundreds of court poems celebrating and advocating sexual love should be placed as reiterations of the highly charged eroticism of Caroline wedded chastity.

But the cult of Charles and Henrietta Maria also established the positive pole in that other binary opposition that finds expression in Caroline court

[49] Robert Herrick, 'The Vine', in *The Poetical Works of Robert Herrick*, edited by L. C. Martin (Oxford, 1956), pp. 16–17.
[50] For example, 'Delight in Disorder', 'Julia's Petticoat', 'Upon Julia's unlacing her self', 'Upon the Nipples of Julia's Breast', *Poetical Works*, pp. 28, 66, 157, 164.
[51] As in 'To his Book's end', *Poetical Works*, p. 335.
[52] Herrick, 'A Country life: To his Brother, M. Tho. Herrick', lines 41–2, *Poetical Works*, p. 35.
[53] Herrick, 'Upon Scobble. Epig.', *Poetical Works*, p. 44.
[54] Herrick, 'Upon Luggs. Epig.', *Poetical Works*, p. 79.
[55] Herrick, 'Upon Groynes. Epig.', *Poetical Works*, p. 106.
[56] Herrick, 'Upon Doll. Epig.', *Poetical Works*, p. 149.
[57] Carew, 'A Rapture', lines 2, 165, *Poems*, pp. 51–3.
[58] Carew, 'Good counsel to a young Maid', lines 11–12, *Poems*, p. 13.
[59] Carew, 'To the Queene', *Poems*, pp. 90–1.

poetry, the opposition between royal rule and its critics. Significantly, the positive values embrace not only the royal couple but also the culture that celebrates them. Again, Carew makes the point most clearly, both briefly in 'A New-yeares gift. To the King' and more extensively in 'In answer of an Elegiacall Letter upon the death of the King of Sweden from Aurelian Townshend, inviting me to write on that subject', which responds to Townshend's 'Elegy on the death of the King of Sweden: sent to Thomas Carew'.

The exchange, one of those civilised poetic dialogues we considered earlier, taken as a whole is in argument roughly homologous with Jonson's Jacobean entertainment, *Prince Henry's Barriers* (1610), which suggests that, indeed, Prince Henry can revive British chivalry, but for the time being there's much to be said in favour of James I's irenic policies:

> Nay, stay your valour; 'tis a wisdom high
> In princes to use fortune reverently.
> He that in deed of arms obeys his blood
> Doth often tempt his destiny beyond good.
> Look on this throne . . .[60]

Townshend's poem, which scarcely merits Carew's term 'shrill accents',[61] argues that Gustavus Adophus's death in triumph leaves a role and an opportunity for other 'Princes ambitious of renowne' to pick up 'His glorious gauntlets'.[62] Carew takes no issue with whether or not Charles I could assume that role. Rather, to a grim list of bloody triumphs in continental Europe he opposes a vision of the regal pair and the culture that celebrates them, of an England enjoying its '*Halcyon* dayes' under 'the blessed hand | Of our good King' and 'the Queene of Beautie'.

IV

The last poem I shall consider is another Carew song:

> *Boldness in love.*
> Marke how the bashfull morne, in vaine
> Courts the amorous Marigold,
> With sighing blasts, and weeping raine;
> Yet she refuses to unfold.
> But when the Planet of the day,
> Approacheth with his powerfull ray,

---

[60] Ben Jonson, '*The Speeches at Prince Henry's Barriers*', lines 396–400, in Orgel and Strong, *Inigo Jones*, p. 163.

[61] Carew, 'In answer of an Elegiacall Letter upon the death of the King of Sweden from Aurelian Townsend, inviting me to write on that subject', line 2, *Poems*, p. 74.

[62] Townshend, 'Elegy on the death of the King of Sweden: sent to Thomas Carew', lines 33, 35, *Poems and masques*, p. 48.

> Then she spreads, then she receives
> His warmer beames into her virgin leaves.
> So shalt thou thrive in love, fond Boy;
> If thy teares, and sighes discover
> Thy griefe, thou never shalt enjoy
> The just reward of a bold lover:
> But when with moving accents, thou
> Shalt constant faith, and service, vow,
> Thy *Celia* shall receive those charmes
> With open eares, and with unfolded armes.[63]

The poem illustrates well a number of the themes I have sought to develop. Most obviously, what seems trivial in print has a charm and a substance in performance. It rehearses, too, the cleaned-up sensuality of the Caroline court. The marigold 'spreads' herself to 'receive' the sun's beams, as Celia shall 'unfold' her arms. This is, obliquely, another celebration of married chastity—boldness wins the lady, but it is boldness in the assertion of vows of constancy and service. Again, there is a political dimension. The image of the sun-king abounds in early Stuart panegyric. Carew variously speaks of Charles's 'ruddie beame of Majestie',[64] while Prince of Wales, and his own sons are represented as growing 'From budding starres to Suns full blowne'.[65] Examples could with facility be multiplied. The regal connection points to word-play, on 'marigold' (often written 'marygold' in the early modern period[66]) and the royal Mary, Henrietta Maria. The sun's congress with the flower parallels the royal sun's congress with his queen, which once more is offered as a paradigm for the conduct of ordinary lovers, the 'fond Boy' and his Celia. Fittingly, one manuscript of the setting seems to attribute it to Charles I himself.[67]

After the outbreak of the First Civil War, when the masquing hall had fallen silent, the queen had gone to France, the royal art collections had been appropriated, soon to be dispersed, and what remained of the King's Musicke was but an echo of its former glory, the printed editions of the court poets were almost all that remained of the Caroline court, perhaps the first Renaissance English court to achieve a splendour to match Paris or Madrid. Those printed forms appeared as poignant documents to a recent past. But to appreciate them

---

[63] Carew, *Poems*, p. 42. Appendix C contains a transcription by John Harper of the setting in British Library, Additional MS 11608 f. 28. I am indebted to Professor Harper for the transcription. This transcription is published by permission of the British Library, which I gratefully acknowledge. For a performance, *Madrigals and Wedding Songs for Diana*, The Consort of Musicke, director Anthony Rooley; track 19, Emma Kirkby (soprano), Anthony Rooley (lute) (Hyperion CDA 66019).

[64] Carew, 'Upon the Kings sicknesse', line 30, *Poems*, p. 35.

[65] Carew, 'A New-yeares gift. To the king', line 26, *Poems*, p. 90.

[66] *OED*, 's.v. 'Marigold', Forms; see also 'mary-bud', s.v. 'Mary', 1.c.

[67] See Carew, *Poems*, pp. 291–2; BL Add. MS 11608 f. 28.

properly, we need to relocate them in the age of their creation, to see them as constituents of a larger formation which incorporated the purely literary into their larger context, a culture confident in and aware of its own accomplishment and modernity. They belong, not in the silent, monochrome world of 1640s print, but in the vivid, singing world of the 1630s, the world of Inigo Jones, Lawes and Lanier, Rubens and Van Dyck—and Carew and Suckling.

Note. This lecture was delivered at the British Academy on 29 April 1997. I am indebted to Gordon Campbell and John Harper for comment and advice on an earlier version.

Appendix A

Have you Seen the Bright Lily Grow?

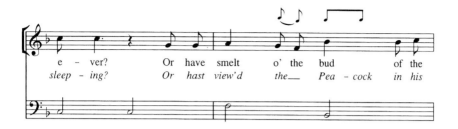

e - ver?   Or have smelt   o' the   bud   of the
sleep - ing?   Or   hast view'd   the___   Pea - cock   in his

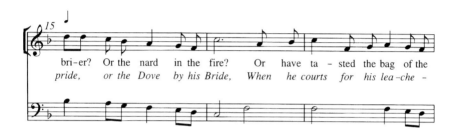

bri-er?   Or the nard   in the fire?   Or   have ta - sted   the bag of the
pride,   or the Dove   by his Bride,   When   he courts   for   his lea -che -

bee?   Oh,   so   white,   Oh,   so   soft,   Oh,   so
ry?   Oh   so   fick- le,   oh   so   vain,   oh   so

sweet   is   she,   so____ sweet   is   she!
false   is   she,   so____ false   is   she.]

Appendix B

A Dialogue

Shepherd and Nimph (two trebles or tenors)

Henry Lawes

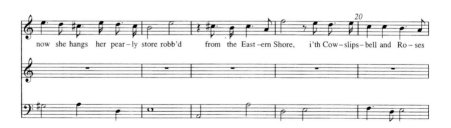

Appendix C

The Marigold

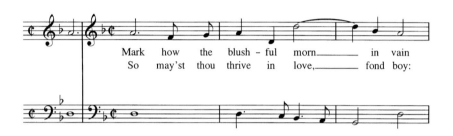

Mark how the blush – ful morn_____ in vain
So may'st thou thrive in love,_____ fond boy:

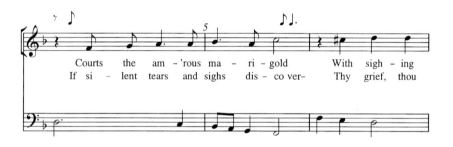

Courts the am – 'rous ma – ri – gold   With sigh – ing
If si – lent tears and sighs dis – co ver–   Thy grief, thou

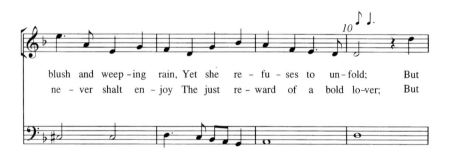

blush and weep – ing rain, Yet she re – fu – ses to un – fold;   But
ne – ver shalt en – joy The just re – ward of a bold lo – ver;   But

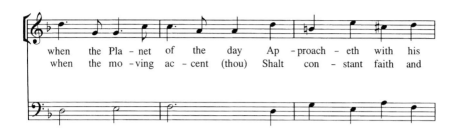

when   the Pla - net   of   the   day   Ap - proach - eth   with   his
when   the mo - ving   ac - cent   (thou)   Shalt   con - stant   faith   and

15

pow'r -   ful   ray,   Then   she spreads,   then   she   re - ceives
ser -   vice   vow,   Thy Ce - lia shall   re - ceive   those   charms,

His   warm - er   beams   in - to   her   vir - gin   leaves.
With   o - pen   ears,   and   with   un - fold - ed   arms.

The Winthrop Variation:
A Model of American Identity

SACVAN BERCOVITCH

Harvard University

IT IS A GREAT HONOUR to be here. I assume that I owe this privilege to the work I've done on New England Puritan rhetoric and its legacy to the American Way and I've taken the occasion, accordingly, to reconsider the premises behind my work. My concern is with method and approach, with the assumptions implicit in the ways I've tried to link literary and cultural analysis. But since this subject is a broad one—since moreover I'm uneasy with abstract speculation—I will limit my focus to a particular piece of rhetoric, John Winthrop's proclamation of the City upon a Hill. As all Americanists know, this piece of rhetoric comes from 'A Model of Christian Charity', the lay-sermon that Winthrop delivered in 1630 on board the flagship *Arabella*, on the Atlantic Ocean, setting out the terms of settlement for the new colony. Over the centuries his proclamation—'we shall be as a city upon a hill, the eyes of the world are upon us'—has established itself as a national icon in the United States. Indeed, the address itself may legitimately be called a cultural key-text. I speak not only of academic curricula but of established practice and creed. The procession of references and allusions to Winthrop's 'Model' runs more or less unbroken from colonial times to our own, and through all forms of discourse, from protest poetry to presidential orations. His projected City, beacon to the world, has become a commonplace, a cliché, a formulaic (and unfailingly effective) image of national purpose.

How and why did this happen? I mean to highlight the *problem* this involves by my title, 'A Model of American Identity'. The model American here stands for a transparently made-up concept of nationality; for a set of beliefs that has often been challenged and revised; for a vision of community

Proceedings of the British Academy, **97**, 75–94. © The British Academy 1998.
Read at the Academy 23 October 1997.

that has repeatedly been shown to falsify or conceal the actual course of history—and yet a concept, a set of beliefs, and a vision that have emerged over the course of history as a very entrenched, very coherent political and economic system, along with demonstrably very successful techniques of persuasion and incorporation. Those techniques derive from a variety of sources, among which the New England Puritan source has remained a constant connective. So the question is: what does that connective tell us about the cultural work of rhetoric? And more ambitiously: what are the advantages it offers as a model of literary and cultural criticism?

It's a question both of practice and of theory: on the one hand, a certain seventeenth-century text; on the other hand, a general approach to literary and cultural study. I would like to join the two by way of a familiar analogy. Theorists of all kinds have made the game of chess a standard trope for linking particulars and generalities. Chess, says Ludwig Wittgenstein, is how we think and speak. Chess, says William James, tells us how human beings, all of us, make choices; Georg Simmel claims that it's a mirror of all institutional structure, anywhere, any time. In poetry and fiction, from time immemorial, chess is the game of life.

Let me ask you, then, to think of chess as a model of literary and cultural studies.[1] And within this model, think of Winthrop's address, his 'Model of Christian Charity', as a test-case: a certain set of moves in a vast transatlantic chess game. I cannot assume that all of you will have read the text lately, but I think you'll find its contours familiar enough to follow my analysis. Basically Winthrop drew up the sort of social blueprint we might expect from a tough-minded Puritan idealist. His Model calls for a civic order compatible with a company of Christian believers: moral behaviour, legal decencies, economic reciprocity, proper deference in church and state, due regard for the spirit. All this, as I said, is couched in more or less familiar terms—and yet with a decisive turn in language and substance, a turn so sharp and compelling as to make it an abiding cultural legacy. Call it the Winthrop Variation.

Now, a variation in chess, like a variation in any other game, including the games of rhetoric, is a move that opens a new set of possibilities within the standard rules and regulations of play. It's a function in context. We say a variation is brilliant not because it transcends the game—not because it reaches to some higher realm beyond the rules—some world elsewhere of free play—but just the opposite. It's brilliant insofar as the variation stems

---

[1] I have outlined this approach in several essays, including 'Games of Chess: A Model of Literary and Cultural Studies', in Robert Newman, ed., *Centuries Ends, Narrative Means*, (Stanford, Stanford University Press, 1996), pp. 15–58. My notes to this essay (pp. 319–28) document the allusions in this lecture to chess history and to the various uses of the chess analogy. I am grateful to Peter Brown and Rosemary Lambeth for their hospitality and to thank Frank Kermode and Tony Tanner for their helpful remarks.

from, and thus leads us towards, a deeper sense of how the rules work. In this sense the variation is a model for analysing both the cultural work of the text and the literary fabric of culture.

Consider now the following proposition: 'America' is a rhetorical figure that designates a distinctive social-symbolic system as 'chess' designates a game with distinctive rules. To understand what a chess piece signifies is to engage in concrete and particular questions. For example: in what directions can the knight move? And under what circumstances? So too with America: it points to a dream of absolutes—freedom, opportunity, the good society—but we don't know what *these* abstractions signify unless we understand the function and context of the rhetorical pieces that make up this *particular* dream. This holds true as well for Winthrop's city on a hill. It may sound like a universal abstraction, but it turns out to be a universal with historical rules. It cannot stand, say, for a vision of tribal unity, like Jerusalem of old, or for a feudal ideal. *This* city comes down to us as a certain cultural artefact, an integral part of a national legacy, a key to the social-symbolic game through which the United States has usurped the meaning of America. As for the rules of that game, they involve the reciprocity between: (1) the norms of a certain way of life, associated with capitalism and modernisation; (2) an ambiguous territory, simultaneously confined to the United States, identified with the New World, and defined as boundless; (3) certain strategies of socialisation, rooted in the marketplace and ranging from religious multi-denominationalism to academic multi-culturalism; and finally, (4) certain symbolic structures, such as those inscribed in the City upon a Hill.

How and why did Winthrop's 'Model' become a key player in this game? What does this particular chess-piece signify? One answer is technical and practical, formulated from within the game as we now play it. The knight moves in such-and-such prescribed ways. The city on a hill radiates a certain specifically modern set of promises. Of course, there's plenty of room for ingenuity in expressing these promises: consider the complex negotiations potential in the reciprocities I just mentioned (territory, economy, forms of life) and of the extraordinary potential of language to convey that complexity. Like an effective strategy in chess, an effective social symbology opens up a variety of possible moves in any given situation. But they are rule-bound combinations, performed by rule-bound pieces. They apply to any chess match at any time or place.

This is the traditional application of the chess analogy. As a model for examining texts in context, it derives from the social sciences. The system dictates the moves. It's a view that depends on systematicity—which is to say, on a concept of the game from within, as an inherited set of rules. I would call this the short view of chess. And I've rehearsed its premises in order to contrast it with another, historically-oriented set of premises, what may properly be termed the long view of chess. For historically considered—as a game whose origins have not yet been recovered, and whose development spans some three thousand years and all corners of the globe—historically considered, chess is the most unstable of systems, the game of chance and change par excellence. Of all games, it's the one most susceptible to the vicissitudes of time and place. That long view is what I mean to convey: chess in all its bewildering trans-national, inter-cultural, multi-linguistic diversity: *the* game of chess, as distinct from just modern chess—chess, that is, as a model of linguistic and cultural *volatility*.

This use of the analogy is counter-conventional, perhaps counter-intuitive, but I hope you can entertain it for an hour. It's the best image I've found (particularly in its reversal of the traditional, systemic image of chess) for expressing the approach I took to the matter of New England. The particular advantage of studying 'America' for me was its transparently fictive quality and the relatively recent period of its creation. What fascinated me was the extraordinary prospect this offered for explaining the process of cultural formation. To study the history of the rhetoric of America is not to see the power of a tried-and-tested system. It is to watch step by surprising step the growth of a modern, text-based symbolic system-in-the-making.

How could we pose the question of the knight's function in these terms? Well, we would have to begin at the point before the knight came into play, in the territories of what would become the United States before the United States became America. Imagine chess, then, as a game with knights, bishops, rooks, and queens, in which there were once no knights on the chess board; in which for that matter there was once no chess board; and in which rooks and bishops had many other names and shapes, designating an astonishing variety of functions. That's the long view, chess historicised. As for the queen, it's pertinent to my argument to note that she entered the game rather late in time and that she was declared (what we now know her to be) the dominant figure on the board only in the 1490s, the Columbus era, somewhere in Isabella's Spain.

In sum, the value for me of the chess-analogy is that, without at all denying the importance of the rules—indeed, while highlighting their importance (for to speak of chess is *ipso facto* to invoke rules and regulations)—the long view of the game nonetheless sets the main emphasis on agency and process. For my purposes, chess is a model of the shifting sands of culture on which we build our houses of rhetorical absolutes.[2]

---

[2] It may be well to note that this is not a polemic against universalism. My concerns are limited to literary-historical issues, and I'm well aware that such limits themselves suggest, if only by contrast, a realm of experience that lies outside the scope of games altogether—a dimension of the universal which may be foundation in some pre-ludic sense, and which may even be said to influence the play of text and context.

The question of the knight here is a problem in symbolic transformation. Consider first the current scene, the game as we know it. 'American', understood as a figure of identity, is the great modern instance of the rhetoric of nationality. Its range of moves is emblazoned in its official logo, 'out of many, one'; and the effectiveness of its strategies is documented in the processes by which such risky catchwords as 'individualism', 'independence', 'revolution', and, nowadays, 'subversion' have been made a summons to conformity. And yet, only three hundred ago, 'American' meant a heathen savage or else the hemisphere at large, North and South. Like the game of chess as we now play it, the current figure of 'America' represents a dramatic transformation of meanings which, however, has drawn perforce on many earlier models of meaning. One of these, a persistent and influential one, is the model of Christian charity.

I have in mind both the general model and Winthrop's distinctive variation on it. In either case it involves both literary and cultural issues—the rules of expression that Winthrop had at his disposal in 1630, and the rules for authority and control (legal, social, economic) with which he had to contend. I treat these forms sequentially in the course of my talk, but I hope it will become clear that each is a function of the other.

The literary rules for Christian charity may be briefly summarised. We might call it the incarnation-game. The model of Christian charity is Christ. The participants agree upon a common game-plan: namely, a double reality, material and spiritual, which is paradoxically one. The goal of play is to make the paradox visible, while at the same time to maintain the qualitative difference between material and spiritual realities, as between Caesar and God, death and life. Broadly speaking, two kinds of moves are allowed. These are usually described as horizontal (in and of this world) and vertical (connecting heaven and earth). No doubt this description took hold because the linear-vertical intersection is a picture of the cross. Let me alter the picture somewhat to fit the game of chess. Think of two different chess pieces: first, the bishop, which moves only in a diagonal direction—let's say, the line that connects heaven and earth; and then, the rook, which moves only in straight-linear directions (lateral or up-and-down)—let's say, directions in and of this world, denoting varieties of social ranks. Augustine called these worldly directions the realm of linear time (as opposed to the view of eternity granted to those bound by charity in Christ), and following that tradition I will speak of the rook's move as linear. Linear, then, rather than horizontal; and diagonal rather than vertical. It's the picture of an angle, not a cross; or of the cross at an angle. I hope this slight change will seem neither cumbersome nor offensive.

The first point to make is the obvious one: the chess analogy reminds us that we are dealing with entirely conventional terms. The difference between linear and vertical is as standard in the game of rhetoric as the difference in chess between rook and bishop. The linear move is a form of indirect representation, by simile or by analogy: for example, the rich, like the elect, are few in number; or, Charles I is king of England as God is king of heaven. Representation here is oblique, metonymic; it assumes a basic disparity between the two parts of the comparison. We are confined, you recall, to the City of Man. Charles, we know, is not really God: We understand a priori that the rich are not *actually* the elect. They are *like* them—figurally *like*, as opposed to essentially *alike*.

The diagonal move has something like the contrary intent. It is a form of direct representation, as by *figura* or synecdoche: for example, Moses is a type of Christ; or, the true believer is an image of God's people. Here we are to understand that the true believer *is* one of God's people—is actually and substantially chosen by God. The point of this move is to bridge the apparent gap between the City of Man and the City of God. Whether or not Moses appears to you or me to be *like Christ*, he and Christ are essentially alike. Moses re-presents Christ literally *and* spiritually, both historically and under the aspect of eternity.

What's striking about Winthrop's address—what makes for the remarkable variation I spoke of—is the way he connects both kinds of move. He introduces the indirect form of representation first, through the image of hierarchy. His address opens with a picture of rich and poor, king and ministers. As God (he explains) has ordained variety and difference throughout creation, so it is the 'glory of princes to have many officers'. The analogy tells us that order is pervasive and absolute and at the same time it reminds us of the chasm separating earthly from divine power—'the condition of mankind', as Winthrop puts it, as distinct from that of the kingdom of heaven. Next comes direct figural connection: 'We are all one in Christ', Winthrop intones, 'members of one body', 'knit together in love'.[3] Here the picture he offers is one of essential equality. The community he portrays partakes of the spirit (reflects it in a glass, darkly) and so transcends all worldly hierarchies, along with every limit of time, office, and place.

Of course, these two images—the community as social network, the community as one in Christ—are not contradictory. Indeed, they often appear as complementary forms of speech, secular and sacred. In current literary discourse we have come to designate these forms as metonymy and metaphor. In the tradition that Winthrop inherited, the designations were analogy and type. For him the word 'model' could denote either a replica, as in an architect's design, which represents but is not itself the building, or else a perfected pattern of what we see—a kind of ideal mirror-reflection—as

---

[3] John Winthrop, 'A Model of Christian Charity', in Stewart Mitchell, ed., *Winthrop Papers* (Boston, 1931), ii, pp. 282–95.

Christ's life re-presents the believer's journey to God. In the first case, the case of metonymy or replica, a given society may be said to represent the divine order, but only as a figure of speech. In the second case, the case of metaphor or ideal reflection, representation signals a unity between the figure and the substance. The divine is re-presented (presented again) in a historical presence. Through grace, the believer, however imperfect, may be said in some sense really and truly to embody the ideal.

Figural representation, then, or actual re-presentation: the 'or' makes all the difference in the world. More precisely, it marks the difference between this world and the next. The representation by analogy, the replica, speaks of what's material, social, transient, like material wealth. The re-presentation of the ideal directs us away from that realm to the realm of the spirit. And yet the two kinds of speech are as close as 'like' and 'alike'. They are complementary pieces in the same game, like rook and bishop. They work together on the premise that their functions are distinct. In order to make all this as clear as possible, Church authorities from Augustine through Aquinas elevated that distinction (representation *or* re-presentation) into a central tenet of Christian hermeneutics. By that rule Luther denied the Pope's right to stand in for Christ. The Holy Roman Empire, he charged, was a replica of the true church, an analogy or trope, not a re-presentation of it. Indeed, the very fact that the Church of Rome claimed to *re*-present the true church made it a *false* replica. It pretended to powers it did not have in order (said Luther) to usurp the realm of the spirit for its own worldly ambitions. By that rule, too, Milton justified regicide by appealing directly to Christ, the true mirror-reflection of God as king—as Charles I (in his view) was emphatically not. It's not too much to say that the hermeneutics of like-versus-alike became a battle-ground of theological and social change. Understandably, the Reformers were charged with blasphemy—appropriately they called themselves *Protest*ants, Dissenters— but so far as they were concerned, they had come to fulfill the exegetical law, not to break it.

What, then, shall we say of Winthrop's apparent confusion? Representation and re-presentation, trope and type, metonymy and metaphor, blur and shift in his Model. It almost seems like a sleight of hand. His image of Christian charity moves in two directions at once. He identifies this particular community first as a hierarchy in the form of a colonial venture authorised by royal patent, and then (as it were in the same breath) as a spiritual unity *in imitatio Christ*. And then, having set out his basic lines of play—having established his terms of transformation—he proceeds to apply the concept of Christian charity in both senses at once. From either perspective, he asserts, we arrive at the same literal-spiritual end. On the one hand Christian charity *here* represents a contractual agreement. It entails matters of credit and debt, trade and exchange. As political scientists have long recognised, Winthrop's

Model is a landmark in modern contract theory.[4] On the other hand, however, and with equal force, his Model re-presents the charity of Christ, God's free love for the elect. Here, in New England, says Winthrop, social order is to be established in all its aspects—business transactions, legalities, social relations—under the aegis of the Gospel, 'according to the example of our Saviour'. He does not mean by this that the social is to be subsumed in the theological, as it is under certain forms of theocracy. Civil structures here retain their own separate sphere of power. But neither does he mean that these two aspects of colonial life are merely different parts of the same venture, co-existent, as they are in other colonies. Rather they are somehow conflated in this model; in some sense the political sphere and the spiritual are made interchangeable.

Somehow, in some sense: familiarity has dulled the force of Winthrop's innovation. We need the chess analogy to appreciate its scope and sheer daring. Imagine the argument I just outlined as a game in process. The different rhetorical terms are different pieces on a board. Those pieces are traditional, rule-bound. The rook, which can move only in a linear direction, is the worldly, colonial venture. The bishop, which can move only in a diagonal direction, is the christic ideal. Winthrop moves the piece horizontally, and says: 'My rook goes here'; and then, in his next turn, he moves the same piece diagonally, and says: 'My bishop goes there'; and then, as the game proceeds, he actually renames the piece, calls it alternately his rook-bishop or bishop-rook, and moves it consistently in what by all convention is a strange new linear-diagonal pattern.

How can we explain this behaviour? We cannot call his move a blunder—a 'monumental slippage', as one scholar has charged[5]—since Winthrop was a qualified professional at the game. Nor can we consider it to be a technical mistake, due to distraction or absent-mindedness, since the fact is that Winthrop won. His variation took hold. He won not only the match but the game. His strategy inspired many similar variations. It led to America's City upon a Hill. Here is his famous end-game:

> Thus stands the case between God and us: We are entered into a covenant with Him . . . [and if He] shall please to hear us . . . then hath He sealed our commission . . . but if we shall neglect the observation of these articles . . . [and] fall to embrace this present world . . . seeking great things for ourselves and our posterity, the Lord will surely break out in wrath against us.
> . . .

---

[4] Scott Michaelsen, 'John Winthrop's "Modell" Company and the Company Way', *Early American Literature*, 27 (1992), 85–100. In this broad survey of the legal literature, Michaelsen discusses Winthrop's address as a pioneering document in contract theory; Winthrop, he shows, was in this respect 'more pointedly modern than his colleagues'.

[5] Michaelsen, 'Winthrop's "Modell"', p. 88.

Now the only way to avoid this shipwreck . . . is to follow the counsel of Micah . . . we must be knit together in this work as one man. . . . We must delight in each other, make others' conditions our own, rejoice together, mourn together, labor and suffer together—always having before our eyes our . . . community as members of the same body. . . . [Thus] God will delight to dwell among us, as His own people . . . and we shall see much more of His wisdom, power, goodness, and truth than formerly. . . . For we must consider that we shall be as a city upon a hill. The eyes of all people are upon us; so that if we shall deal falsely with our God . . . we shall be made a story and a by-word through the world.

And to shut up this discourse with that exhortation of Moses . . . in his last farewell to Israel, Deut. 30: Beloved, there is now set before us life and death. . . . [If] we will not obey we shall surely perish out of the good land [which] we pass over this vast sea to possess it.

This City is neither a poetic conceit nor a religious commonplace. Rather it stands somewhere in between, an unusual piece of rhetoric that mixes traditionally distinct forms—direct and indirect, re-presentation and representation. Its political analogue is the body politic. But its scriptural origin is the Sermon on the Mount (the Beatitudes), where Christ speaks to the believers ('the salt of the earth') individually and universally. The believer shines as a city upon a hill, a living image of the church spiritual. And as a representation of the universal spiritual church, the city has a further, historical meaning. It is a figure in sacred history, signifying Jerusalem, the holy city, and by extension, the end-time New Jerusalem. And this prefiguration refers in turn back to Moses' so-called 'farewell exhortation'—his final advice to the Israelites (Deut. 30) as they prepare to enter Canaan—for by the rules of this game, the promised land is a figure or type of heaven.[6]

This sweeping configuration, sanctioned by the Church Fathers, by standard practice, and by the Geneva Bible, Winthrop turns into a means of legitimating a particular economic and social order. His address, it cannot be overemphasised, concerns the establishment of a society. He invokes the ideal in order to authorise secular forms. But he does not thereby collapse the distinction between type and analogy. That is the crucial point to observe about Winthrop's game-plan. He uses the combination of rhetorical moves, linear and diagonal, to instate a *tension* between them. His City refers to the figural Jerusalem which cannot fail. And it recalls the old, terrestrial, literal Jerusalem, which did fail, once and for all. Winthrop's City on a Hill signifies both of these—not one or the other, promise or threat, but a wilful conjunction of the two—figural and literal held together in a state of conditionality.

Again, it requires the chess analogy to convey the boldness of Winthrop's

[6] See the gloss to Deuteronomy 30: 18–20 and to Matthew 5: 14–6 in Lloyd E. Berry, ed., *The Geneva Bible* (facsimile of the 1560 Edition) (Madison, University of Wisconsin Press, 1969).

variation. Consider the following scenario: (1) a form of chess that allows for only linear or else diagonal moves; (2) a particular match where one of the players perceives that he *may* win if he can move a certain piece in a direction which is both diagonal and linear, as in fact the knight's move is in modern chess (it can be pictured as a move at a 45-degree angle); and (3) that he succeeds by negotiating a special set of conditions. 'Let's try an experiment', he proposes. 'If I win the game, then we'll agree that this new-fangled move was valid, a legitimate variation in play. If I lose, we'll declare the move to have been illegal, and the piece I used will simply revert to its former linear *or* diagonal status.' Does this sound far-fetched? Let me point out that the history of chess includes a variety of such instances—for example, the dramatic moment, during a period of revolutionary upheavals, when the caste-bound Indian foot-soldier or pawn was permitted to become a queen upon reaching the eighth rank (the opposite end of the board)—on the condition that the pawn *did* reach the eighth rank.[7]

Of course, Winthrop's variation goes one long step further than that. The pawn retains a singular concrete identity at any given time—either pawn or else queen. The goal, we might say, is upward mobility, but basically the game-plan remains class-bound. It is assumed that in principle, as a rule, pawns will remain pawns. Winthrop's move challenges that structure—and even (by indirections) the principle behind it. His emphasis is on provisionality and potential. Indeed, we can say with hindsight that that's precisely the radical crux of his strategy. It was Winthrop's *intention* to blur the line between bishop and rook. His linear-diagonal knight is fundamentally, by definition, contingent. It is founded upon the *if* in 'if I win'. Its context is a game in process. The terms are not win or lose—all or nothing—but rather win *and* lose, all *and* nothing. And those terms, be it noted, shift the very objectives of the match. I spoke earlier of the incarnation-game, but the paradoxes of incarnation deal with heaven and earth. Winthrop's provisional knight is an expression of permanent process—the process of the spirit made manifest in the process of colonisation; a colonial *way* (as in an 'errand into the

---

[7] I discuss these developments in 'Games of Chess'; here I limit myself to two examples of the volatility of chess (and its analogies) that are pertinent to the Winthrop variation. The first concerns the function of the bishop: see for example Thomas Middleton's *A Game of Chess* (1624), where, despite their opposing actions (as part of a battle of Good versus Evil), both sets of bishops, black and white, function as sinister and treacherous figures, revealing the relatively recent roots of the chess figure in continental Catholicism. The second concerns the notion of chess as the game of love—an analogy that runs from the first published treatise on chess (Luis de Lucena's *The Game of Love*, 1496) through the entire Petrarchan sonnet tradition (e.g., Henry, Earl of Surrey's sonnets of 1547). See in this regard Rowland Greene's discussion of the relation between Petrarchism and Renaissance colonisation, in *Post-Petrarchism: Origins and Innovations in the Western Lyric* (Princeton, Princeton University Press, 1991).

wilderness') that embodies the progress of the spirit. Provisonality here works
to fudge the distinctions that make for paradox. It transforms these instead into
the tensions distinctive to a particular New World venture: tensions in this
world between present and future, expectation and experience, migration and
possession—between the literal (linear) transition toward a new country and
the spiritual (diagonal) rights to its ownership. And the transition itself, so
conceived, effects a sea-change in identity—from the related-but-distinct concepts of settlers and saints to the mixed image (ambiguously contractual *and*
absolutist) of a company in covenant. What the City upon a Hill makes visible is
a far-reaching rhetoric of conditionality: in effect, a ritual of order-to-be that
potentially unites a group of colonists in the bonds of grace, and so grants them,
provisionally, the good land they have come to claim by prophecy and patent.

What circumstances prompted that move? How can we account for its
success? Historically, it can be shown that Winthrop's concept of potentiality
was his response to a desperate situation. The two-stranded model he advanced
was intended for a community confronting a double threat to order—a double
threat from within, stemming from religious dissent on the one hand and on the
other from worldly ambition. Winthrop's appeal to unity-in-love ('knit
together as one man') reminds us that the Puritans were militant sectarians,
and that their militancy posed clear dangers for the new colony. Predictably,
the history of the New England Way turned out to be a history of constant
theological debate. And it was also a history of steady economic growth.
Winthrop's appeal to hierarchy reminds us that the Massachusetts Bay
Company was a business venture. These religious zealots were entrepreneurs
intent on rising in the world. Their leaders were college-educated clergy,
merchants, and lawyers, like the Cambridge law graduate, John Winthrop,
grandson of a self-made businessman, and son of a nouveau-riche merchant
fallen on hard times. The statistics of the 1630 Great Migration are: 10 per cent
poor (servants), 10 per cent lower class (unskilled labourers), 1 per cent
aristocracy and riffraff combined, and the rest (79 per cent) 'middling':
artisans, tradesmen, shopkeepers, independent farmers. They came to the
New World at a time of severe economic depression in England, not only as
rebels against Anglican rituals, but equally as ambitious, mobile professionals
(thirty-something on the average), who had been enticed by the promises of a
chartered joint-stock corporation. As one historian has put it, quoting Winthrop's arguments in 1629 for migration, they were seeking profits in the
wilderness. That's the context for Winthrop's opening insistence on deference.
Behind his tough strictures on social distinctions—as also behind his later
eloquent appeal for mutuality—lie his well-grounded anxieties about governing a colony of middle-class dissidents. In the address itself he makes it plain,
grimly, that the immigrants he was appealing to were company-men keen for

'improvement', eager for 'substance', 'seeking great things in this present world', 'for [them]selves and [their] posterity'.[8]

By what authority could Winthrop impose control on this turbulent community? The answer may be gleaned in antiquarian fashion from the first gloss on his address, the headnote composed by Winthrop's son sometime in the mid-1630s:

> Written on board the *Arabella*, on the Atlantic Ocean, by the Honourable John Winthrop, Esquire, in his passage (with the great company of religious people, of which Christian tribes he was the brave leader and famous governor), from the Island of Great Britain to New England in North America.

The key words are 'company', 'Honourable', and 'Esquire'. I refer in general to the well-documented transition in the fifteenth and sixteenth centuries (the Tudor–Stuart Period) from medieval to modern systems of organisation. In particular, I think of that aspect of the transition which is signalled by Winthrop's claim to leadership. 'Company' is a pun on worldly and religious business, but its primary meaning lies in the entrepreneurial profile I outlined earlier. 'Company' for these emigrants meant above all a Company Incorporated, a group of businessmen, bureaucrats, and speculators, many of them Puritans, whose governing board had just voted to invest Winthrop, 'as [a] Justice of the Peace', with 'authority [in the new settlement] as in England'.[9]

Now, the Justice of the Peace is the office designated by 'Honourable' and 'Esquire', and it had taken on a dramatic new importance during the Tudor period. Previously, the chief law enforcer had been the sheriff, who controlled the courts of common law in the medieval village jurisdiction, technically known as the tourn. It was an authoritarian form of control, of course, but it was based largely on local tradition—customs and codes handed down orally from one generation to another—in effect, a medley of Anglo-Saxon, Latin, and Norman-French precedents, locally applied according to village or tourn memory, in more or less consensual ways, within relatively autonomous because relatively insulated communities.

The transition I mentioned from Medieval to Renaissance England might be described legally as a movement from tourn to corporation, and from sheriff to justice of the peace. That movement followed upon profound and lasting cultural changes—economic upheavals, class realignments, demographic shifts, and technological and scientific revolutions. It issued in the centralisation of authority under crown and court. By 1588, when Winthrop was born, a new

---

[8] John Frederick Martin, *Profits in the Wilderness: Entrepreneurship and the Founding of New England Towns in the Seventeenth Century* (Chapel Hill, University of North Carolina Press, 1991); Winthrop, 'Perticular Considerations in the J:W' and 'Generall considerations for the plantation', in Mitchell, ed., *Winthrop Papers*, ii, pp. 106–11, 121–4.

[9] Mitchell, ed., *Winthrop Papers*, ii, p. 282 n.

system of law was in place. I quote here from the standard legal history of the period:

> In the courts held by the Justices [of the Peace] was vested all the common law jurisdiction of the country, civil and criminal. Royal justice had won a complete victory of the older [feudal and communal] local courts. But [in 1500] there was still left to the old courts and the old officials—[that is,] to the tourn and the sheriff—certain police duties and criminal jurisdiction. Royal justice won its final victory when [under the Tudors] it practically absorbed this last remnant of their jurisdiction.[10]

In practice, this process of absorption entailed a centrally-regulated network of judicial redistrictings—now termed counties, boroughs, corporations, and companies. These were administered by court-appointed justices of the peace, who thus effectually became the watch-dogs of an emergent modern social apparatus, a nation-state in which the law was relatively codified and statutory, and the monarch was titular head of the church.

Among other things, this vast reorganisation was remarkable for two sweeping ironies. The first has to do with cultural contrasts. The process of centralisation reveals that the allegedly static, homogeneous world of the medieval tourn was actually a configuration of relatively independent communities, whereas the highly regulated modern world of boroughs, companies, and corporations was the product of upheaval and fragmentation. The second irony pertains directly to Winthrop's model. In late-sixteenth and early-seventeenth-century England, the agents of centralisation often turned their jurisdictions into centres of dissent. For the fact is that justices of the peace characteristically came from the class that also characteristically produced the Puritans, who then proceeded to turn their delegated powers against the central authorities. The Court-appointed leaders of Dissenting strongholds (such as the region of East Anglia, from which Winthrop came, along with most passengers of the *Arabella* fleet) used their new-won powers to rally their constituencies against the powers of the Crown.

They drew support in doing so from a widespread movement of disaffected rural gentry. The conflict itself, Country versus Court, need not concern us here. Suffice it to say that the Country outlook reflected an alternative set of strategies within the same vast process of modernisation I've just described; that it was directed largely against the growing importance of London; and that it often expressed itself in the rhetoric of arcadia. Squirearchy appears in these writings as a pastoral ideal, an oasis of virtue, benevolence, and peace in a desert of aristocratic corruption and urban chaos. To some extent Puritan spokesmen endorsed this rhetoric, but they also made a distinct and lasting contribution of their own. Perhaps because they had more at stake than others

---

[10] W. S. Holdworth, *A History of English Law* (London, 1903–9), i, p. 123.

in defying the Anglican establishment, they turned to a sharper, more vivid alternative to Court authority: namely, the authority of the national past. Their civic appeals, a large and unduly neglected archive—declarations of order, parliamentary speeches, political homilies, and, most remarkably, a long procession of lay-sermons by local dignitaries, especially JPs—lead us as it were beyond utopia into nostalgia. Considered together, they provide a kind of pastoral route into the legendary realm of Old England; the golden days of sheriff and tourn; a richly-elaborated fantasy of the harmonious and independent life of the medieval village.[11]

I believe we may trace the myth of the Middle Ages to these documents. They carry in embryo the dream-visions of Morris, Ruskin, and Tennyson—a longing for some quasi-feudal stability and spiritual kinship in a world of change. This is not the place to discuss either their language or their legacy, but one point is worth remarking, in view of the ironies I just mentioned. In rebelling against national authority, the English Puritans reinforced a new, implicitly modernising, emphatically Protestant model of nationalism. Their appeal to the past eventually extended from medieval to antiquarian fable and lore—from sheriff and tourn to Robin Hood, King Arthur, Alfred the Great, Druid legends—and so helped provide a secular myth of origins for the modern English state, and what was to be its far-flung empire, reaching in the New World from the tropical Bahamas to Canada's Dominion of the North.

This is precisely what Winthrop's model works *not* to accomplish. Considered as an example of cultural transformation, its most conspicuous aspect is the absence either of the pastoral dream or of medievalist nostalgia. The city on a hill is if anything more distant from the Good Country Life and Arthurian England than it is from seventeenth-century London. It's not that Winthrop shied away from the conflict between real and ideal. Quite the contrary: he magnifies this by substituting Christ for the sheriff. Apparently, however, he considered it inadequate or inappropriate to turn for corporate standards to antiquated feudal ways. And the reason, I've suggested, lay in his peculiar problem of authority. It may be well here to supplement my earlier sketch of those unruly Puritan emigrants with a contrast between them and the

---

[11] See Lawrence Stone, *The Crisis of the Aristocracy, 1558–1641* (Oxford, Oxford University Press, 1965); Peter Zagorin, *The Court and the Country: The Beginning of the English Revolution* (London, Methuen, 1968); and Conrad Russell, *The Crisis of Parliaments: English History, 1509–1660* (Oxford, Oxford University Press, 1971). The lay-sermons I refer to are found in the bibliographies to these and other major historical works of the period, such as Roger Lockyer, *Tudor and Stuart Britain, 1471–1714* (New York, St. Martin's Press, 1964); in legal compendia, such as Carl Stephenson and Frederick George Marcham, eds., *Sources of English Constitutional Law* (New York, Harper, 1937); in collections of sermons and parliamentary addresses; and in archives of Dissenting regions such as East Anglia which includes the county of Suffolk.

general population, drawn from the most recent detailed study of the Great Migration:

> [The] emigrants . . . [came from] places where commercial activity . . . [and] religious dissent combined to loosen the ties of traditional authority. . . . [In] England as a whole, [for example,] farmers outnumbered craftsmen by more than seven to one; [whereas] among the prospective colonists artisans were nearly twice as numerous as farmers. . . . [Moreover,] these farmers, who comprised 16% of the population, were 'relatively prosperous', 'literate', and 'independent'. . . . [As for the artisans, they] usually practiced skilled trades that placed them on the middle rungs of the economic ladder.[12]

In other words: the English country in 1630 was composed of diverse elements, many of them traditional, most of them steeped in residual habits of life. It would have been historically appropriate as well as ideologically expedient for the magistrates to appeal to the ideals of a common past. It would also have been rhetorically sound, an innovation within the traditional boundaries of Christian hermeneutics. The rhetorical connection between sheriff and Justice of the Peace spans space and time, real and ideal; but as a model of identity it remains in and of this world. It is a linear move, confined to the story of England.

The medievalist fantasy was an ingenious variation, but it could not accommodate the circumstances of the *Arabella* emigrants. Winthrop was responding to a special problem in religious and social cohesion, one that required (as Perry Miller noted) an ideal commensurate with the Protestant Ethic. Winthrop's variation is a dramatic move in that direction. It consecrates the secular tenets embodied in his delegated function as JP, while at the same time legitimating the separatist leanings—the tendencies towards independence, political as well as theological[13]—implicit in his religious company's

---

[12] Virginia DeJohn Anderson, *New England's Generation: The Great Migration and the Formation of Society and Culture in the Seventeenth Century* (Cambridge, 1991), pp. 31–2.

[13] I refer here to the resistance on the part of all Puritans to the doctrine of the divine right of kings. (See for example T. H. Breen, *The Character of the Good Ruler: A Study of Puritan Political Ideas in New England, 1630–1730* (New York: Norton 1970), p. 37). Winthrop invokes this doctrine at the start of his address, but he proceeds to submerge it within the higher rights of covenant. That is, he uses his office as JP to negotiate on behalf of his 'great company of religious people', directly with God as King. Winthrop's modernity in this regard is remarkable. Three brief annotations must suffice here. (1) The main convenantal concerns are financial ('giving, lending, and forgiving') as befits a 'venture for gain-sake', as the Massachusetts Bay Company officially described itself. (2) The main objection that Winthrop anticipates concerns self-interest; the questions he frames are mainly addressed to the self-interested individual ('a man and his family'), rather than to members of different classes or ranks; and his answers are mainly geared towards doctrines of industry and self-help (for 'he is worse than infidel', Winthrop points out, 'who through his own sloth . . . shall neglect to provide'). (3) These answers carefully blend Old and New Testament precedents; and it turns out to be a blend that balances private enterprise and communal welfare, where welfare combines voluntarism, mutual aid, and price and trade regulations.

dissent. And much more than that. In this double process of consecration and legitimation—contract and covenant, rook and bishop, entwined—Winthrop invents a new history for the colony, replacing its secular past, medieval and renaissance alike, with the progress of the church.[14] As he outlines the course of Christian Charity, his narrative runs not from England to New England, but from Eden ('man in the estate of innocency') to the Israelite 'household of faith', to Christian believers 'in the apostles' time' and climactically, in this time, to the covenanted 'community of peril'.

I want to focus on this last image for a moment, because it is Winthrop's dominant figure for the New England venture. 'Community of peril'—the very antithesis of the benign, harmonious vision of the tourn—is a fit correlative for Winthrop's strategy of probation. It also establishes a distinctive ancestry for his imperilled City upon a Hill. 'Christ', Winthrop explains, gave

> a general rule (Math. 7: 22). 'Whatsoever ye would that men should do to you, do ye the same to them.' . . . [That] rule must we observe in case of community of peril. Hence it was that in the primitive church they had all things in common. . . . Likewise in the return of our captivity, Nehemiah exhorts the Jews to liberality in remitting their debts to their brethren. . . . [This] is to be observed [as well] . . . in the latter stories of the churches.

I have omitted a key phrase from this passage in order to stress once more what Winthrop excludes from his genealogy: not just family and friends, sheriff and tourn, but English history altogether. In its place, as New England antiquities, Winthrop offers a procession of communities of peril: the Israelites returning from Babylon to Jerusalem; 'the primitive church' in flight from Roman persecution; and the 'latter-day' Reformers re-establishing the 'true religion' (as the formulaic Calvinist phrase had it) after the 'long night of Papal captivity'. This is no random gathering of *exempla*. It is the official outline of Protestant apocalyptica: the figural continuity from the Old Testament to the New and thence (along the lines of sacred history) to the prophecies of the 'latter-days'—what Winthrop calls the 'latter stories of the churches', meaning the Protestant Reformation.

---

[14] This new identity more than any other factor explains the conspicuous absence in the Winthrop compact of the usual language of royal prerogative—the traditional homage to colonial hierarchy that marks every other compact of the time, including English Puritan compacts, from Plymouth to Bermuda. A convenient contrast is the *Mayflower* document. In terms of my chess analogy, the Pilgrims conceived of their venture along standard linear-or-diagonal lines. They believed that they were on their way to heaven through the wilderness of this world (now shifting from Amsterdam to Virginia, or as it turned out, accidentally, to Plymouth); and as their compact makes clear, they 'convenanted' strictly in the then-legal sense of the term, as 'loyal subjects of our dread soveriegn Lord, King James', united in a 'civil body'. See (William Bradford, *Of Plymouth Plantation, 1620–1647*, ed. Samuel Eliot Morrison (New York, 1952), p. 52).

Now I turn to the phrase I left out, Winthrop's solitary reference to actual historical origins:

> That rule must we observe in case of community of peril [as] did some of our forefathers in times of persecution here in England and so did many of the faithful [elsewhere in Europe] in other [Protestant] churches, whereof we keep an honourable remembrance of them [in] latter [day] stories of the [martyrs.]

'Here in England' may be read as a transitional phrase, a gesture toward the old rules of the game. After all, Winthrop's identity as an imperial magistrate, theirs as colonial subjects, required the *Arabella* passengers to think of England as home. By all common sense criteria, they were Englishmen and -women. But we have textual grounds for reading the phrase in quite the reverse sense, as a move on Winthrop's part towards absorbing England, too, into his variation, as a figure for a corrupt Old World. I don't say he intended this. It was a move intended by a nascent social symbology—that is, by the new game rules latent in Winthrop's innovation. But latency also implies agency. To give credit where credit is due, we must note that Winthrop mentions only some 'forefathers', and these few only to elicit memories of religious persecution. They were Protestant saints hounded by the benighted Church of Rome—martyred in England, Winthrop stresses, as the saints had been martyred in pagan Babylon and Rome.

Now, some of these Reformation heroes may really have been related to some of the company then present, but that is not Winthrop's point. His genealogy is a model of spiritual descent; it identifies him as the 'brave leader' of 'Christian tribes' fleeing what he had called a year before, in journals and letters, 'a land of destruction', ripe for some 'catastrophe and punishing plagues from heaven'.[15] In that figural perspective, his phrase 'here in England', spoken in passage to a New World, is a wonderfully revealing moment of the dynamics of rhetorical change. It speaks by negation to the enormous visionary shift underway in Winthrop's model. What is displaced is both fantasy (a medieval utopia) and fact (familial, communal, and geographical origins). What comes into place, once the error is noted and emended, is broadly modern: a community written into existence by contract and consent, through a declaration of principles and rules that bend religious tradition to legitimate a venture in colonial enterprise.

'We must consider that we shall be as a city upon a hill': the imperative ('must consider') centres upon a perfectionist future (prefigured by the image of

---

[15] John Winthrop, 'Conclusions for the Plantation in New England', in vol. 2 of *Old South Leaflets* (Boston, n.d.), no. 50, p. 6; and Winthrop, quoted in Steven Foster, *The Long Argument: English Puritanism and the Shaping of New England Culture* (Chapel Hill, 1991), p. 109.

Moses at Canaan's frontier). In this case, however, perfectionism means self-doubt: the dream of 'we shall be' also entails the threat of being made 'a story and by-word through the world'. And vice-versa: the threat entails the dream of what 'we *shall* be'. Part of the brilliance of Winthrop's transvaluation is the fact that his double-edged rhetoric of peril has it both ways. Its conditional tense defines the community as secular, experimental, and fallible; and that same conditional tense is the premise of spiritual transformation. It is as though (1) an accurate replica might yield an ideal mirror-reflection; and (2) the force of that possibility were not a guarantee of perfection but instead the excitement of living in the 'might be'. If we keep discipline, says Winthrop, we will be a beacon to the world; if not, we will become a by-word for failure. The 'we' is circumscribed by a double 'if'. What we *are* at any time is beacon and by-word. That *and* is a formula for permanent anxiety. And anxiety is Winthrop's formula for empowerment. In game-terms, it is the conditional link that allows for the simultaneity of linear *and* diagonal identity. The 'if' that doubly circumscribes the 'we' affirms that we are already chosen because we are *now* under probation. By that symbolic logic, Winthrop already grants the emigrants, before reaching harbour, the territorial rights to the 'Canaanites'' 'good land', which they, the emigrants, have 'pass[ed] over this vast sea to possess'. By that emphasis on peril, he already releases them, *as emigrants and colonists*, from the burdens of their secular past, much as Moses had released *his* people from Egyptian bondage. And by thus liberating them from history, he establishes an unmediated correspondence between political goals and universal principles. What makes his model perfectionist also specifies perfectionism as modern and entrepreneurial.[16]

This is not to exaggerate Winthrop's achievement. I began by alluding to

[16] It seems pertinent here to recall, however briefly, the failure of alternative models of settlement. I have in mind the rhetorics of Latin-America, from Las Casas' christic savagism through Simon Bolivar's Hispanic Confederacy, Jose Marti's 'half-breed' *nostra America*, and Jose Vasconcelo's *raca cosmica*—a magic-realist tradition of disjunctions; a procession of model Americas that keep dissolving under the pressure of the contradictory visions— Aztec antiquities, Roman Catholicism, an 'Atlantean race', Iberian aristocracy, mestizo myths, the liberal Enlightenment. I don't claim that a successful rhetorical formula would have changed all that. My point is that the history of the Americas, North and South, demonstrates the persisting need in modern secular communities for some form of spiritual cohesion; that the game of Latin-American identity never developed a set of rules adequate to that end; that that essentially *literary* failure (what Vasconcelos termed 'the anarchy and solitude of Iberian-American emblems') has had significant practical consequences. By contrast, Winthrop's text highlights the astonishingly resilient rhetorics developed in the United States for connecting culture and society, moral and economic imperatives, and for containing the threat of multiple identities (including most recently Latino-Hispanic identities) within the boundaries of the city upon a hill. References above are to: Jose Marti, 'Our America' (1891) in *The America of Jose Marti* (New York, Methuen, 1953), pp. 138–51; Jose Vasconcelos, the *Cosmic Race: The Mission of the Ibero-American Race* (1925), transl. Didier T. Laen (Berkeley, University of California Press, 1979), pp. 1–38.

contemporary uses of his lay-sermon (from, say, Kennedy through Reagan to Clinton)[17] as a ritual of founding, a cultural totem designed both to infuse hope and to establish law and order. But I have assumed throughout that Winthrop's strategies were transitional, not a creation it its own right but a variation. Its sources lie in the rules and regulations of an Old World game: the Bible, the Church Fathers, and the Protestant Reformation. These are the lines along which Winthrop's new-fangled rook-bishop moves. Even when it arrives, hypothetically, at its special destination, 'New England in the North America', it occupies essentially an Old World position: Winthrop has European Protestants in mind when he says that 'the eyes of all people are on us'. It would be another forty years before the colonists would have an indigenous myth of their own—their own legends of a golden age of tribal patriarchs, rivalling the medieval tourn and ancient Rome and even the primitive churches, and located wholly within the 'American strand'.[18] And it would be another seventy years before the identity 'American' would be applied symbolically, exclusively, to white Protestant colonists, and specifically to those 'commissioned' by New England's God. Another generation or two, that is, had to elapse before Winthrop's rhetorical piece could claim a proper place for itself, its own sacred-secular New World Square. And of course a century would have to elapse *after that* before Winthrop's provisional knight could have a proper set of royalty to defend—a group of Founding Fathers, constructed according to Enlightenment rules of power, and eliciting liberal forms of failure and success, every pawn a king potentially.

Still, let us not underestimate Winthrop's achievement. He does say 'all people', as though 'the people' at large were the authorising constituency, and as though all of history were at stake. More important is the geographical shift that follows from his emphasis on process. By the logic of conditionality,

[17] References are to Ronald Reagan's televised debate summation in Fall, 1984, to John F. Kennedy's farewell address as Senator from Massachusetts, and to William Clinton's Second Inaugural, where the Philander Smith College Choir sang 'City on a Hill' (followed by Maya Angelou's poem on 'America's New Beginnings').

[18] Cotton Mather, *Magnalia Christi Americana; or The Ecclesiastical History of New England* (1702), ed. Thomas Robbins (Hartford: Peter Andrus, 1853), i, 25. The opening of Mather's epic (i, 25–7) is an example both of continuities and of the variations which the rhetoric elicited: The City on the Hill takes the form here of the doubled candelabra, symbol of New Israel; England expands to mean Europe, the Old World whose epic counterpart is fallen Troy; the American wilderness, by extension, assumes the epic grandeur of a New Rome and New Canaan combined; and the genealogy of the Newness follows the lines of descent established by Winthrop: from Eden (the golden age) to Israel (the seven candlesticks) to early Christianity (the *upright* children of Abraham) to the Reformation and thence, climactically, to Puritan America, 'specimen' of New Jerusalem. The key strategic move here comes in the provisional, volatile threat that closes the invocation: 'But we must therewithal ask your prayers that these golden candlesticks may not be quickly removed out of this place.'

Winthrop re-focuses the objective upon the meaning of the New World. *There* is the place of crisis and trial. That is where the spirit may be made visible: diagonally, through the regeneration of individuals; and linearly, through the community's secular-moral growth—in Winthrop's words, a covenant to develop here in this world, in this land, in 'wisdom, power, goodness, and truth'. The City on a Hill is the first ideal to take the fate of the New World as its condition of failure and success. And it is the first New World ideal to invest the very concept of newness with spiritual meaning grounded in a specific, then-emergent, now-dominant way of life. In that double thrust of Winthrop's image lies the explanation—the how and the why—for its continuing usefulness to the culture. As a rhetorical figure, it derives from two traditions that proved inadequate as the ideological framework for modern nationalisms: kingship and Christianity. Winthrop varied both those traditions to accommodate a modern venture, and in the course of variation he opened the prospect for something new under the sun, the America-game.

By now the rules of that game are not only familiar but dominant. Increasingly, they have come to seem natural, even universal. The chess analogy, historicised, offers a point of resistance to that tendency, at least in the area of literary and cultural studies.

Beyond Class?[1]
Social Structures and Social Perceptions in Modern England

DAVID CANNADINE

Institute of Historical Research, University of London

GEORGE ORWELL ONCE FAMOUSLY DESCRIBED England as 'the most class-ridden country under the sun'—a remark of such global reach in its comparative implications that it seems unlikely ever to be subjected to appropriately cosmic testing, let alone empirical verification.[2] Nevertheless, there are many people in England today, and also many living abroad, who are inclined to accept Orwell's remark as being broadly correct. But what did Orwell mean, and what do most people mean, when they think of English society in this way? After all, the extremes of wealth and poverty in England are no greater than in other nations: compared with the United States, the English rich are not as rich, nor the English poor as poor. In many measurable ways—economic, social, and political—England is *not* a uniquely inegalitarian society. But what *is* different, and here Orwell was surely right, is that the English, unlike the Americans, constantly think and talk about these inequalities, and they do so very largely in class terms.[3] Yet they do not think and talk about these class terms

---

[1] J. Alt, 'Beyond Class: The Decline of Industrial Labor and Leisure', *Teleos*, xxviii (1976), 55–80; P. Joyce, *Visions of the People: Industrial England and the Question of Class, 1848–1914* (Cambridge, 1991), pp. 1–2, 23; R. J. Morris, 'Class' in J. Cannon (ed.), *The Oxford Companion to British History* (Oxford, 1997), p. 217: 'Social class has lost its privileged position in the narrative of British social history'.
[2] G. Orwell, *The Lion and the Unicorn: Socialism and the English Genius* (Harmondsworth, 1982), p. 152. The essay was originally published in 1941.
[3] P. Gottschalk and T. M. Smeeding, 'Cross-National Comparisons of Earnings and Income Inequality', *Journal of Economic Literature*, xxxv (1997), 633–87; M. J. Burke, *The Conundrum of Class: Public Discourse on the Social Order in America* (Chicago, 1995).

Proceedings of the British Academy, **97**, 95–118. © The British Academy 1998.
Read at the Academy 24 April 1997.

rigorously or consistently, either as categories into which people are put, themselves included, or as models of English society as whole. They are very aware of class, and very conscious of class—but in very un-self-aware, very un-self-conscious ways.[4]

This is well borne out in Orwell's rather confused and uncertain account of England's social structure set out in his wartime essay: *The Lion and the Unicorn*. In one guise, wearing his venerable Tory hat, he saw it in hierarchical terms, as a traditional, layered, society of exceptional complexity, 'bound together by an invisible chain'. In another, and as befitted the offspring of an imperial and professional family, he envisaged England as divided between the upper, middle, and lower classes, with the middle class being much the most important. From yet a third perspective, that of the socialist revolutionary, he believed that English society was riven by one deep, fundamental cleavage, between 'the rich', the 'moneyed classes' and the 'ruling class' on one side, and 'the poor', the 'common people', and the 'mass of the people' on the other—those whom he hoped would soon rise up and overthrow their masters.[5] For someone who was so sensitive towards (and guilty about) the many nuances of social status and distinctions of social identity, these are curiously—but significantly—discrepant ways of seeing and describing what was, after all, the same single, unitary social world.[6]

Orwell's contradictory account of England as being simultaneously a hierarchical, a triadic, and a polarised society provides an appropriate starting point for the study of social structures and social perceptions from the eighteenth to the twentieth century. For the best way of reconciling these contradictions is to suggest that he was depicting and describing an England of shifting social perceptions and multiple social identities which helpfully, if inadvertently, anticipate the post-modern world we inhabit today. But our post-modern world is also a post-Marxist world, from which the once-appealing master narrative of class formation, class conflict, class consciousness, and class dominance, a narrative which effortlessly elided social structures, social

---

[4] For a sampling of recent works on the subject, see: P. Saunders, *Unequal But Fair? A Study of Class Barriers in Britain* (London, 1996); R. Marris, *How to Save the Underclass* (London, 1996); D. J. Lee and B. S. Turner (eds.), *Conflicts About Class* (London, 1996); Lord Bauer, *Class on the Brain: The Cost of a British Obsession* (London, 1997); S. Brook, *Class: Knowing Your Place in Modern Britain* (London, 1997); A. Adonis and S. Pollard, *A Class Act: The Myth of Britain's Classless Society* (London, 1997).
[5] Orwell, *Wigan Pier*, pp. 40–5, 48–9, 51–3, 55–6, 66–7, 70, 77–8, 81–3, 102, 106, 109.
[6] It is surely not coincidence that these are the same three ways of envisioning the social order as had been followed by an anonymous citizen of Montpellier in 1768. See R. Darnton, 'A Bourgeois Puts His World in Order' in idem, *The Great Cat Massacre and Other Episodes in French Cultural History* (New York, 1985), pp. 107–43. Indeed, it may well be that what is unusual about twentieth-century England is that all three models of social description remain plausibly available and widely used to a greater extent than anywhere else in western society. Perhaps this is what Orwell meant—or should have meant.

perceptions and social (and political) action, has long since been dethroned.[7] 'Class dismissed' is the mode and the mood in which history is now being written, not just in England, but throughout the west, and there have been considerable gains as a result, among them the recognition that social structures, social perceptions and social (and political) actions cannot be thus easily and effortlessly elided any more.[8]

To the extent that this means the history of modern England can no longer be built around the grand, heroic Marxist simplicities of class-formation, class-consciousness and class-conflict, as the essential means whereby these structures, perceptions and actions are connected, animated, unified, and realised, this seems both convincing and correct. But this should not mean, and does not mean, that all that remains are the random incoherence and 'chaotic authenticity' of past events.[9] Put more positively, we are left with the recognition that social structures, social perceptions, and social (and political) actions are interconnected in much more nuanced and contingent ways than it was once fashionable to suppose, and that (as Orwell unintentionally made plain half a century ago) social perceptions and social identities are multiple rather than single.[10] In the course of this lecture, I hope to borrow from and build on these insights, so as to sketch out, in a necessarily schematic and simplified way, a general approach to the study of social structures and social perceptions in modern England which tries to rise to the most pressing challenge facing historians today: the re-instatement of master narrative, but a master narrative built around multiple rather than single identities.

Here are two final points by way of preliminary. The first is to note that if we take the long view of England's social structure from the early eighteenth century to the late twentieth, one of its most conspicuous features has been its slow rate of change. At a very abstract level, we can borrow Lord Runciman's

---

[7] For valuable summaries of these developments, see: R. Price, 'Historiography, Narrative and the Nineteenth Century', *Journal of British Studies*, xxxv (1996), 220–56; J. Thompson, 'After the Fall: Class and Political Language in Britain, 1780–1900', *Historical Journal*, xxxix (1996), 785–806; C. Kent, 'Victorian Social History: Post-Thompson, Post-Foucault, Post-Modern', *Victorian Studies*, xl (1996), 97–134.

[8] For two excellent wide-ranging surveys, see A. Knight, 'Revisionism and Revolution: Mexico Compared to England and France', *Past & Present*, no. 134 (1992), 158–79; T. C. W. Blanning (ed.), *The Rise and Fall of the French Revolution* (London, 1996). For three recent attempts to write about 'great' revolutions, which stress contingency and accident rather than long term social trends and class formation, see C. Russell, *The Causes of the English Civil War* (Oxford, 1990); S. Schama, *Citizens: A Chronicle of the French Revolution* (London, 1989); O. Figes, *A People's Tragedy: The Russian Revolution, 1891–1924* (London, 1997).

[9] Schama, *Citizens*, p. xvi.

[10] J. Harris, *Private Lives, Public Spirit: A Social History of Britain, 1870–1914* (Oxford, 1993), p. 8; D. Tanner, *Political Change and the Labour Party, 1900–18*, (Cambridge, 1990), pp. 10–16.

recent typology, and agree that over this span of three hundred years, English society has been characterised by four broad systactic categories: by a small elite; by a larger group of managers, businessmen and professionals; by the general body of workers; and by a deprived and impoverished underclass.[11] In their occupational categories and relative proportions, these systacts have remained very much the same across the last three centuries of English history, whatever else may have been changing, and this general analysis gets ample statistical validation at the hands of W. D. Rubinstein, N. F. R. Crafts, and Peter Lindert and Jeffrey Williamson, who have recently been examining England's wealth and occupational structure from 1688 to the twentieth century.[12] Of course, these historians have been working with different data and different categories of social taxonomy, but their basic message is essentially the same.

Indeed, it has been the establishment of this long-durational picture of the slowly changing pattern of wealth and occupational distribution which has done most in recent years to subvert the Marxist or *Marxisant* belief that the historical process was driven inexorably forward by the economically-determined dynamic of class formation, class consciousness and class conflict. For it now seems generally accepted that social groups tied directly to what was only a gradually changing mode of production could not have come into being, struggled, risen and fallen in this simple, adversarial, apocalyptic manner.[13] More precisely, if economic and social structures have evolved in modern England at such a leisurely pace, then it is small wonder that efforts to depict the aristocracy as having been overthrown between 1832–46 were unconvincing; that the middle classes were always described as rising, but never arrived anywhere; and that the working class was no more 'made' in the first third of the nineteenth century than it was 're-made' during the last

---

[11] W. G. Runciman, *A Treatise on Social Theory*, vol. ii, *Substantive Social Theory* (Cambridge, 1989), p. 108.

[12] W. D. Rubinstein, *Men of Property: The Very Wealthy in Britain Since the Industrial Revolution* (London, 1981); P. H. Lindert, 'English Occupations, 1670–1811', *Journal of Economic History*, xl (1980), 685–712; idem, 'Unequal English Wealth since 1670', *Journal of Political Economy*, xciv (1986), 1127–62; P. H. Lindert and J. G. Williamson, 'Revising England's Social Tables, 1688–1812', *Explorations in Economic History*, xix (1982), 385–408; idem, 'Reinterpreting Britain's Social Tables, 1688–1913', *Explorations in Economic History*, xx (1983), 94–109; N. F. R. Crafts, *British Economic Growth During the Industrial Revolution* (Oxford, 1985), pp. 1–8, 48–70.

[13] W. Reddy, *Money and Liberty in Europe: A Critique of Historical Understanding* (New York, 1987); W. H. Sewell, jr., 'How Classes Are Made: Critical Reflections on E. P. Thompson's Theory of Working-Class Formation', in H. J. Kaye and K. McClelland (eds.), *E. P. Thompson: Critical Perspectives* (Philadelphia, 1990), pp. 50–77; P. Curry, 'Towards a Post-Marxist Social History: Thompson, Clark and Beyond', in A. Wilson (ed.), *Rethinking Social History: English Society 1570–1920 and Its Interpretation* (Manchester, 1993), pp. 158–200.

quarter. This is not, it now seems, the way in which things in the English past have happened.[14]

But we also need to remember—and this is the second and final preliminary remark—that contemporaries did not understand or visualise their society, their social structure, and their place within it in the sort of sophisticated analytical and descriptive categories recently provided by Lord Runciman or by Professor Crafts—a point well borne out by the fact that none of Orwell's three impressionistic models of English society can be easily reconciled with the four rigorous systacts of Runciman's version. Still less did they (and do they) envisage their world in those complex, contradictory, disputed and increasingly arcane taxonomies so beloved of many British sociologsts.[15] These were not (and are not) the conventional concepts or vernacular categories of English social self-understanding—concepts and categories which were less quantified and more varied, but which, nevertheless, provided people with the necessary and adequate means to understand their social world, to situate themselves within it, and to navigate their way through it.[16] It is with these commonplace social perceptions and multiple social identities—to all of which the word class is these days most frequently and ubiquitously applied—that I am concerned. What were (and are) they, and when, how and why have they altered (or not altered) during the last three centuries?

* * *

My starting point is one of provocative but (I hope) plausible simplicity: namely that during the past three hundred years, there have been only three basic descriptions of England's social structure that have been generally available to the population at large, to pundits and pamphleteers, and to the politicians. Moreover, the models in question are precisely those which George

[14] M. Taylor, 'The Beginnings of Modern British Social History?', *History Workshop Journal*, no. 43 (1997), 155–76; R. I. McKibbin, *The Ideologies of Class: Social Relations in Britain, 1880–1950* (Oxford, 1990); A. J. Reid, 'Class and Organisation', *Historical Journal*, xxx (1987), 225–38; idem, *Social Classes and Social Relations in Britain, 1850–1914* (Cambridge, 1995).

[15] G. Marshall, H. Newby, D. Rose, and C. Vogler, *Social Class in Modern Britain* (London, 1988); G. Marshall and J. Goldthorpe, 'The Promising Future of Class Analysis', *Sociology*, xxvi (1992), 381–400; R. E. Pahl, 'Does Class Analysis without Class Theory Have Promising Future?: A Reply to Goldthorpe and Marshall', *Sociology*, xvii (1993), 253–8. For some valuable comments (and criticisms) of British sociologists' continued obsession with class, see S. Ringen, 'The Open Society and the Closed Mind', *Times Literary Supplement*, 24 January 1997, p. 6.

[16] I must stress that this lecture is concerned with England, rather than with the United Kingdom, the British Isles, or the greater Britain beyond the seas. For a broader 'British' treatment of what is here discussed as an 'English' subject, and for fuller documentation and development of the arguments, see D. Cannadine, *Class in Britain* (London, 1998).

Orwell had outlined for inter-war England: the hierarchical view of society as a seamless web; the triadic version with upper, middle, and lower collective groups; and the adversarial picture of society polarised between 'us' and 'them'. Indeed, the continued co-existence of these three models may be traced back at least to the late medieval period, when English society was varyingly viewed as an integrated hierarchy, or as the three estates of warriors, priests and workers, or as divided between landowners and peasants.[17] More than half a millennium on, little seems to have altered. When A. H. Halsey recently set out to revise his justly influential book on social structures and social change in twentieth-century Britain, he felt obliged to choose between 'the vulgar Marxist theory of two classes at war', 'the simplification of three social strata of social classes', and 'the vulgar liberal conception of a continuous hierarchy of prestige or status'.[18] As this suggests, the language in which these three 'vulgar' or 'simplified' versions of our social structure and social identities have been articulated may have evolved and developed across the centuries, but in their essential form, the models themselves have remained remarkably constant and unchanging.

The hierarchical picture of English society, which derived from the Elizabethan notion of a 'great chain of being' and its medieval precursors, took it for granted that each individual had an allotted place in the divinely pre-ordained order of things. From the monarch, via the five grades of peerage, the baronetcy, and the gentry, then on to the differentially-ranked professions, and finally reaching down to the yeoman and agricultural labourers and the poor beneath, this unbroken line of close, personalised connection descended. Here was the social fabric understood as a seamless web of infinite, individualistic gradations, where obedience, subordination and deference were the natural attitudes and essential values which underlay the whole structure.[19] Throughout the eighteenth, nineteenth, and much of

---

[17] T. E. Powell, 'The "Three Orders" of Society in Anglo-Saxon England', *Anglo-Saxon England*, xxiii (1994), 103–32; G. Duby, *The Three Orders: Feudal Society Imagined* (Chicago, 1980); R. H. Hilton, *Class Conflict and the Crisis of Feudalism: Essays in Medieval Social History* (London, 1985), pp. 114–19, 122–3, 152–5, 164, 217–25, 246–52; D. A. L. Morgan, 'The Individual Style of the English Gentleman', in M. Jones (ed.), *Gentry and Lesser Nobility in Late Medieval Europe* (Gloucester, 1986), pp. 16–17; M. H. Keen, *English Society in the Later Middle Ages, 1348–1500* (London, 1990), pp. 1–24; D. Crouch, *The Image of Aristocracy in Britain, 1000–1300* (London, 1992), pp. 15–38, 41–4, 344–7. See also the very suggestive essays in R. Horrox (ed.), *Fifteenth-Century Attitudes: Perceptions of Society in Late Medieval England* (Cambridge, 1994), by G. L. Harriss, K. Mertes, R. Horrox, D. M. Palliser, and M. Bailey.

[18] A. H. Halsey, *Change in British Society* (4th edn., Oxford, 1995), p. 144.

[19] E. M. W. Tillyard, *The Elizabethan World Picture* (London, 1943); A. O. Lovejoy, *The Great Chain of Being: A Study in the History of an Idea* (Cambridge, Mass., 1936); W. F. Bynum, 'The Great Chain of Being After Forty Years', *History of Science*, xiii (1975), 1–28; D. Cressey, 'Describing the Social Order of Elizabethan and Stuart England', *Literature and History*, iii (1976), 29–44.

the twentieth centuries, this providentially-ordained view survived and flourished as the most popular and resonant way of envisaging the social structure and social identities of England. Every major politician, from Pitt to Salisbury, believed that it was their prime task to preserve this ranked, stable, social order, and as late as the 1950s, Winston Churchill still envisaged the English social world in these traditional, hierarchical terms.[20]

The second way of conceiving English society and English social identities was in three collective groups: not the medieval estates of warriors, priests, and workers, but as upper, middling, and lower. As Keith Wrightson has persuasively argued, this alternative vision of the people gradually developed during the seventeenth century, and by the eighteenth century, this triadic model was widely used. In 1776, it received its famous and more rigorous formulation at the hands of Adam Smith, who in *The Wealth of Nations* divided British society into what he called the three great and constituent 'orders': those who lived on rents, those who lived by profits, and those who earned wages in exchange for their labour.[21] Ever since, this three-stage model has furnished an exceptionally appealing guide to English society, especially for those who placed themselves in the middle — sometimes in the confident belief that their numbers were increasing and their circumstances improving, sometimes out of fear that their position was getting worse. 'I am always hearing', Harold Macmillan once observed as Prime Minister, 'about the middle classes. What is it they really want?' Since the early eighteenth century, this question has been regularly posed and sometimes answered. Either way, it presumes this same triadic, collective view of English society.[22]

[20] J. C. D. Clark, *English Society, 1688–1832: Ideology, Social Structure and Political Practice During the Ancien Regime* (Cambridge, 1985), pp. 93–118, 216–35; G. F. A. Best, *Mid-Victorian Britain, 1851–75* (London, 1971), pp. xv–xvi; F. M. L. Thompson, *The Rise of Respectable Society: A Social History of Victorian Britain, 1830–1900* (London, 1988), pp. 152–3, 173–4, 177, 181–2, 193–6, 360–1; P. Addison, *Churchill on the Home Front, 1900–1955* (London, 1992), pp. 47, 211, 311–15; I. Berlin, 'Mr Churchill in 1940', in H. Hardy and R. Hausheer (eds.), *Isaiah Berlin: The Proper Study of Mankind: An Anthology of Essays* (London, 1997), pp. 609, 612, 619, 621, 625.

[21] K. Wrightson, 'Estates, Degrees and Sorts: Changing Perceptions of Society in Tudor and Stuart England', in P. Corfield (ed.), *Language, History and Class* (Oxford, 1991), pp. 30–52; idem, ' "Sorts of People" in Tudor and Stuart England', in J. Barry and C. Brooks (eds.), *The Middling Sort of People: Culture, Society and Politics in England, 1550–1800* (Basingstoke, 1994), pp. 28–51; idem, 'The Social Order of Early Modern England: Three Approaches', in L. Bonfield *et al.* (eds.), *The World We Have Gained: Histories of Population and Social Structure: Essays Presented to Peter Laslett on His Seventieth Birthday* (Oxford, 1986), pp. 178–84; A. Smith, *An Inquiry into the Nature and Causes of the Wealth of Nations* (ed. R. H. Campbell and A. S. Skinner, with W. B. Todd, 2 vols., Oxford, 1976), vol. i, p. 265; vol. ii, pp. 423, 714.

[22] A. Briggs, 'Middle-Class Consciousness in English Politics, 1780–1846', *Past & Present*, no. 9 (1956), 65–74; D. Wahrman, *Imagining the Middle Class: The Political Representation of Class in Britain, c. 1780–1840* (Cambridge, 1995); A. Horne, *Harold Macmillan*, vol. ii, *1957–1986* (New York, 1989), p. 62.

The third version of the social order posits a simple, fundamental fissure between two large and antagonistic groups. This was how many contemporaries had come to envisage and understand the Civil War, when hierarchy collapsed and the English social fabric was rent in twain.[23] And although it was subsequently stitched together again, gaps and fissures remained. By the eighteenth century, it was commonplace to see society as divided between the great, the quality, the nobs, the gentry on the one side, and the poor, the rabble, the mob, the lower orders, or 'the people' on the other.[24] During the early nineteenth century, Cobbett depicted a nation polarised between 'the People' and 'the Thing', and it was this same manichean social vision which lay behind the agitation and the debates surrounding the Great Reform Bill and Chartism. The struggle between the bourgeoisie and the proletariat, or capital and labour, which Marx and Engels mistakenly tried to universalise, was but another version of the same dichotomous model, albeit the most elaborate and influential.[25] And as Patrick Joyce and Richard Hoggart have argued, the idea that England is split between a virtuous and downtrodden 'us' and a corrupt, self-seeking 'them' has resonated widely since Cobbett's time, well on into twentieth-century popular culture and popular politics.[26]

Of course, none of these vernacular visions and identities amount to what the late Ernest Gellner would have called 'real social knowledge'.[27] The hierarchical view was originally elaborated to do better justice to a late-medieval society which was more complex and diverse than that depicted by the three medieval orders of warriors, clergy, and workers. But the idea that *everybody*—whatever their income, occupation, or status or location—could

---

[23] D. Underdown, *Revel, Riot and Rebellion: Popular Politics and Culture in England, 1603–1660* (Oxford, 1985), p. 40, where he describes the Civil War as the result of 'two quite different constellations of social, political and cultural forces': 'on the one side stood those who had put their trust in the traditional conception of the harmonious, vertically-integrated society . . . On the other stood those . . . who wished to emphasise the moral and cultural distinctions which marked them off from their poorer, less disciplined neighbours.'

[24] Corfield, 'Class by Name and Number', in idem (ed.), *Language, History and Class*, pp. 117–18; Wrightson, ' "Sorts of People" ', pp. 34–40; N. Rogers, *Whigs and Cities: Popular Politics in the Age of Walpole and Pitt* (Oxford, 1989), p. 340; K. Wilson, *The Sense of the People: Politics, Culture and Imperialism, 1715–1785* (Cambridge, 1995), p. 287.

[25] For an early discussion of Marx as a special case of a more general formulation of social analysis, see R. Dahrendorf, *Class and Class Conflict in Industrial Society* (London, 1959), pp. 136–7, 245. I am also much indebted to an unpublished paper by G. Stedman Jones, 'The Rise and Fall of "Class Struggle": Middle Class and Bourgeoisie, 1789–1850'.

[26] Joyce, *Visions of the People*, pp. 56–65, 68–84, 245–55, 294–309; R. Hoggart, *The Uses of Literacy* (London, 1957), pp. 62–6. Ironically, but unsurprisingly, it was often socially superior renegades from 'them' who provided the leadership and social vision for the socially inferior 'us': see J. Belchem and J. Epstein, 'The Nineteenth-Century Gentleman Leader Revisited', *Social History*, xxii (1997), 174–93.

[27] E. Gellner, 'Knowledge of Nature and Society', in M. Teich, R. Porter, and B. Gustaffsson (eds.), *Nature and Society in Historical Context* (Cambridge, 1997), pp. 9–17.

be precisely placed in one single, all-embracing great chain of being was never wholly convincing. And if this was true for the fifteenth or sixteenth century, then how much more true was it two or three hundred years later, by which time society had become even more complex?[28] By the same token, and as the earlier abandonment of the three original medieval estates suggested, it was no less of an over-simplification to suppose that everyone could be shoehorned into three collective categories of landowners, capitalists, and labourers — categories which failed to recognise the increasing diversity of the economy, and which mistakenly presupposed that occupation was the single master key to social descriptions and social identities.[29] As for the notion that there was one single, great manachean divide: even the few examples presented here suggest that the line was drawn by different people at different times for different purposes; and in any case, whatever the gloomy prognostications that have been and still are sometimes made about the imminent likelihood of the fabric of English society being torn asunder, the fact is that this has not actually happened at any time during the last three hundred years.

In short, these three versions of the social structure might best be characterised as over-simplified rhetorical constructions — as *imagined* versions of the social order, or as what George Eliot memorably described as 'picture writing of the mind'.[30] Consider, in this regard, Mr Gladstone. In one guise, he was an 'out and out inequalitarian', with an 'hierarchical cast of mind', who saw the supreme task of political management as to maintain an orderly, ranked society where everyone knew their place. In another, he was the proud product of the Liverpool middle classes, and one part of him always accepted their triadic view of society. From yet a third perspective, he came to see the nation as split between 'the classes' and 'the masses', in one stark, great divide.[31] Or consider John Major, who in this context, if perhaps no other, may be spoken of in the same breath as the Grand Old Man himself. As the head of a government which defended hereditary peers in the House of Lords and insisted that the taxpayer should finance a new royal yacht, he

[28] For an incisive critique of hierarchy as being a way of seeing society, rather than 'real social knowledge', see P. N. Furbank, *Unholy Pleasure: The Idea of Social Class* (Oxford, 1985), pp. 75–83.

[29] Smith, *Wealth of Nations*, vol. ii, pp. 181–2; N. T. Phillipson, 'Adam Smith as Civic Moralist' in I. Hont and M. Ignatieff, *Wealth and Virtue: The Shaping of Political Economy in the Scottish Enlightenment* (Cambridge, 1983), p. 191; R. A. Houston, *Social Change in the Age of Enlightenment: Edinburgh, 1660–1760* (Oxford, 1984), pp. 19–20; R. Porter, *English Society in the Eighteenth Century* (Harmondsworth, 1990 edn.), pp. 53–4.

[30] G. Watson, *The English Ideology* (London, 1973), p. 181; M. C. Finn, *After Chartism: Class and Nation in English Radical Politics, 1848–1874* (Cambridge, 1993), p. 11.

[31] H. C. G. Matthew, *Gladstone, 1809–1874* (Oxford, 1986), pp. 3–5, 26, 29, 34–5, 53, 122–3, 130, 210; R. Jenkins, *Gladstone* (London, 1995), pp. ix, 406, 426; P. F. Clarke, *A Question of Leadership: Gladstone to Thatcher* (London, 1991), pp. 34–5; J. P. Parry, *The Rise and Fall of Liberal Government in Victorian England* (London, 1993), pp. 249, 296, 302.

emerged as a true conservative believer in the traditional, hierarchical social order. As the politician who talked of 'middle England' in terms of cricket grounds and old ladies pedalling to Holy Communion, he envisaged society in tripartite terms. From a third perspective, he saw England as deeply divided, with the Tories on the side of 'the people' against entrenched elites, as with the 'Citizen's Charter' and jibes about 'New Labour, old school tie'.[32] The phraseology may be new: but the three models of English society which they articulate have been around for a long time.

* * *

But so what? It bears repeating that if we are to understand popular perceptions of the English social structure during the past three hundred years, we need to recognise the continued co-existence of these three very different ways of seeing and simplifying what was—and what is—in fact the same single society. Indeed, as the examples of George Orwell, Mr Gladstone, and John Major suggest, these three models do not just generally co-exist at a popular and political level: they specifically co-habit inside individual people's heads. Yet they are very different, indeed discrepant, visions. The hierarchical picture sees society as a seamless web, regards people as individuals, and ranks them more according to status and prestige than occupation or income. The triadic version places people in collective groups, defines these collectivities largely in terms of their relation to the means of production (sometimes following Adam Smith, or sometimes following Karl Marx), assumes a certain degree of conflict over the surplus arising from their different economic activities, and gives most attention to those situated in 'the middle'. And the dichotomous formulation, which envisages society as being in a state of perpetual tension between the 'haves' (varyingly defined) and the 'have nots' (ditto) is based on a mixture of economic, social, political, and sometimes cultural criteria. Thus regarded, these three descriptions are not only extreme over-simplifications of complex social structures and protean social identities: they scarcely amount to what Gordon Marshall calls 'a rigorously consistent interpretation of the world'.[33]

On the contrary, they are, in their purest form, discrepant to the point of irreconcilability. For there is a substantial difference between seeing English society as an individualistic and providentially-ordained great chain of being; or as dominated by the middle class rather than by the aristocracy above or the workers beneath; or as adversarially polarised between two homogeneous

---

[32] P. Junor, *The Major Enigma* (London, 1993), pp. 53–4, 60, 85, 112–14, 146–7, 176–7, 254; H. Young, 'The Prime Minister', in D. Kavanagh and A. Seldon (eds.), *The Major Effect* (London, 1994), p. 22; W. Rees-Mogg, 'Class politics is below the salt', *The Times*, 14 October 1996; R. Harris, 'And is there honey still for Tory tea?', *The Sunday Times*, 23 February 1997.
[33] Marshall *et al.*, *Social Class in Modern Britain*, p. 187.

collectivities. Throughout his long career, Gladstone was never fully able to reconcile the fact that he was a conservative believer in the established order, a liberal embodiment of middle class views, and a crusading populist on the side of the ordinary people against the 'upper ten'. And it is these same contradictions in social perceptions and social philosophies which fissure the Tory Party today: is it neo-conservative hierarchical, or neo-liberal triadic, or neo-populist dichotomous in its view of English society?[34] One of the more remarkable aspects of the Conservative Party during the twentieth century (at least before 1 May 1997) has been its capacity to extend its social vision, to great electoral advantage, without the accompanying contradictions becoming too debilitatingly apparent: beginning with the traditional, landed hierarchical view; augmenting this with the middle-class triadic version; and more recently adding the populist confrontationalist approach.[35] Whether these very different social visions can be reconciled indefinitely, only time will tell.

These three vernacular views of English society and social identities have been abiding, resonant, and (at least conceptually) incompatible. One indication of this is that many historians of modern England, who have ostensibly been depicting national society as a whole, have in practice been doing little more than replicate one or other of these mutually-exclusive contemporary accounts. Consider the eighteenth century by way of illustration. Those who learn about Hanoverian England from the writings of Messrs Laslett, Perkin, Cannon, and Clark would see it as hierarchical, dominated by the traditional elite, from which the rest of society descended in ordered and stable ranks.[36] But those who learn about it from Messrs Holmes, Borsay, Brewer, and Langford would derive a very different version: in which the dominant and driving force was the middle class, the 'polite and commercial people', by comparison with whom neither the aristocracy, nor the working population, counted for anything like so much.[37] And there is yet a third manner in which

---

[34] For an early discussion of the contradictions between neo-conservatives and neo-liberals, see F. A. Hayek, *The Constitution of Liberty* (Chicago, 1960), pp. 402–3. For a more recent critique, see J. Gray, 'The Strange Death of Tory England', *Dissent* (fall 1995), pp. 447–52.

[35] A. Adonis, 'The Transformation of the Conservative Party in the 1980s', in A. Adonis and T. Hames (eds.), *A Conservative Revolution? The Thatcher–Reagan Decade in Perspective* (Manchester, 1994), pp. 145–67.

[36] H. J. Perkin, *The Origins of Modern English Society, 1780–1880* (London, 1969), pp. 17–37; P. Laslett, *The World We Have Lost* (2nd edn., London, 1971), pp. 23–54; J. A. Cannon, *Aristocratic Century: The Peerage in Eighteenth-Century England* (Cambridge, 1984); J. C. D. Clark, *English Society, 1688–1832: Ideology, Social Structure and Political Practice During the Ancien Regime* (Cambridge, 1985).

[37] G. Holmes, *Augustan England: Professions, State and Society, 1680–1730* (London, 1982); J. Brewer, *The Sinews of Power: War, Money, and the English State, 1688–1783* (London, 1988); idem, *The Pleasures of the Imagination: English Culture in the Eighteenth Century* (London, 1997); P. Borsay, *The English Urban Renaissance: Culture and Society in the Provincial Town, 1660–1700* (Oxford, 1989); P. Langford, *A Polite and Commercial People: England, 1727–1783* (Oxford, 1989); idem, *Public Life and the Propertied Englishman, 1689–1798* (Oxford, 1991).

eighteenth-century English society has been depicted: for Donald Coleman, there was one great divide, between those he called the 'gentlemen' and those he termed the 'players'; for E. P. Thompson, there was another, between the 'patricians' and the 'plebs', who were the direct descendants of the landlords and peasants of the late medieval period.[38]

The close correspondence between these three mutually-exclusive historical interpretations of English society, and the three mutually-exclusive contemporary social perceptions is as noteworthy as it is unrecognised and unremarked upon—and it is a correspondence, incidentally, which could be as easily demonstrated for the nineteenth and twentieth centuries as for the eighteenth. What conclusions might be drawn from this? One is that it is cause neither for surprise nor dismay that historians' social descriptions should so closely mimic contemporary social descriptions. (Although it is, perhaps, cause for mild regret that they seem so unaware that this is what they have been—and still are— doing.) Another is that when Peter Laslett tells us that eighteenth-century society is traditional, rural, and hierarchical, when Paul Langford asserts that it is modernising, urban, and middle class, and when E. P. Thompson says there is a great divide between the landowning *banditti* and the rest of the population, we should recognise that we are being given historical descriptions of Hanoverian society which are every bit as partial and discrepant as those of the contemporaries which they unselfconsciously echo and perpetuate.[39]

But how did contemporaries manage then, and how have historians managed since, to maintain these mutually-exclusive descriptions of what was, after all, the same single, unitary, and functioning society? Part of the answer is that although in the abstract these were different models, based on different criteria, in practice, it was—and it is—easy to move from one to another and

---

[38] D. C. Coleman, 'Gentlemen and Players', *Economic History Review*, 2nd ser., xxvi (1973), 92–116; E. P. Thompson, 'Patrician Society, Plebeian Culture', *Journal of Social History*, vii (1974), 382–405; idem, 'Eighteenth-Century English Society: Class Struggle Without Class?', *Social History*, iii (1978), 133–65; P. King, 'Edward Thompson's Contribution to Eighteenth-Century Studies: The Patrician-Plebeian Model Re-Examined', *Social History*, xxi (1996), 215–28.

[39] For a recent, and (inevitably) inconclusive attempt to discuss the relative merits of these three historical interpretations, see D. Hay and N. Rogers, *Eighteenth-Century English Society: Shuttles and Swords* (Oxford, 1997), pp. 17–36, 188–208. For an even more inconclusive debate on the popularity and appropriateness of the hierarchical and three stage models as the more 'accurate' guide to Hanoverian England, see the following exchange between J. M. Innes and J. C. D. Clark. Innes: 'I would happily wager that a thousand contemporary references will be found characterising eighteenth-century England as a "commerical society" to every one characterising it as landed, aristocratic, noble hierarchical or the like.' Clark: 'I happily accept: but, alas, Innes has not yet named the stake.' It cannot be said that such exchanges seriously advance the cause of historical understanding. J. M. Innes, 'Jonathan Clark, Social History, and England's "Ancien Regime"', *Past & Present*, no. 115 (1987), 181; J. C. D. Clark, 'On Hitting the Buffers: The Historiography of England's Ancien Regime: A Response', *Past & Present*, no. 117 (1987), 206, n. 34.

back again.[40] Especially if they were at the top of it, those with a traditional, individualistic view of society were also inclined to draw a single line between gentlemen like themselves, and every one else beneath them: from the hierarchical to the dichotomous model was an easy and frequent step. Those who belonged to the 'middling sorts' might instead rank themselves hierarchically, according to the prestige of their professions or public office. Alternatively, they might embrace the dichotomous model, in which case they could either conflate themselves with their betters as prosperous property owners, or join with their inferiors in attacking patrician privilege. And those of inferior status and income might see society as divided between themselves and everyone else who was better off, or as divided into workers, employees, and aristocracy, or as linked by an all encompassing chain of connection which threaded its way from the bottom to the top. Once again, it was possible to move from the dichotomous to the triadic to the hierarchical model with relative ease and plausibility.

Although these three visions and versions of English society in their purest forms have been conceptually discrete and taxonomically irreconcilable, it has often been possible in practice for contemporaries (and even, sometimes, historians[41]) to adjust and rearrange the categories, so as to meld and merge these models, moving backwards and forwards from one to the other. But this was (and is) also because the *language* in which these different visions of society were (and are) articulated drew often (and increasingly) on the same vocabulary. We tend to think that in England, as in France, Germany, or Spain, different models of social structures were expressed in different social vocabularies: that the hierarchical was articulated in terms of rank, order and station; that the triadic was expressed in terms of 'sorts' or classes; and that the dichotomous had its own terms, ranging from 'patricians' and 'plebs' to 'us' and 'them'. To some extent, this was (and is) no doubt so.[42] But there were other languages of social description which were more broadly applied, to such an extent that similar words employed in different contexts were actually referring to different models of society. For much of the time, rank and order and degree were used to refer not only to hierarchy, but also to the three-stage or the two-stage model of English social structure. And from the third quarter

---

[40] For some suggestive hints, see D. Wahrman, review of Langford, *Public Life and the Propertied Englishman*, in *Social History*, xvii (1992), 500–1; E. H. Gould, 'American Independence and Britain's Counter Revolution', *Past & Present*, no. 154 (1997), 134, n. 92.
[41] E.g. J. C. D. Clark, who employs both the hierarchical and (sometimes) the dichotomous model in describing eighteenth-century society: Clark, *English Society*, pp. 43, 90; King, 'Edward Thompson's Contribution to Eighteenth-Century Studies', *Social History*, xxi (1996), 221.
[42] P. Burke, 'The Language of Orders in Early Modern Europe' in M. L. Bush (ed.), *Social Orders and Social Classes in Europe since 1500: Studies in Social Stratification* (London, 1992), pp. 1–12.

of the eighteenth century onwards, all three models of society were increasingly articulated in another common language: and that, of course, was the language of class.

Self-evidently, it is impossible to provide satisfactory proof of the interchangeability of the language of social description, and of the increasing pervasiveness of the language of class across these different models of social structure, within the confines of a single lecture. But here are three examples which at least bear this proposition out. The first is Dr Johnson's *Dictionary* in which he offers alternative definitions of class. One is class as 'a rank or order of persons': as a synonym for individualistic hierarchy. The other is class as 'a set of beings or things, arranged under some common denomination', which implies collective categories, possibly three, possibly two.[43] The second example is that when, in his speech in the 'Don Pacifico' debate, Lord Palmerston talked of 'every class in society', he was not referring to the three-stage model of upper, middle, and lower: he was using class as a synonym for individual rank or station. To the extent that he saw mid-Victorian Britain as a 'viable class society', it was in hierarchical terms rather than triadic or polarised collectivities.[44] And the third is a recent speech of Tony Blair's, where he remarked that in 1900, England possessed 'a class structure in which the upper, middle and lower *ranks* were sharply delineated', remarks which remind us, that even today, when using the triadic model, the language of ranks and the language of class remain easily and essentially interchangeable.[45]

Thus far, then, I have sought to make three arguments: first that three models of social structures and social identities have been remarkably pervasive and enduring in England over the last three centuries; second, that although these models were conceptually very different, in practice contemporaries have easily moved from one to another; and third, that they have often, but not always, been articulated in the same words, sometimes the vocabulary of ranks and orders, sometimes and increasingly the language of class. Thus regarded, class may best be understood as the modern shorthand term for all three of the vernacular versions and visions of English society. In our post-Marxist world, class may have fallen, may even be dead, as the grand

---

[43] Corfield, 'Class by Name and Number', pp. 102, 114.

[44] Perkin, *Modern English Society*, pp. 408–9. As George Watson (*English Ideology*, p. 180) notes, 'much of the profusion of class terms and class discussion in the mid and late Victorian era becomes more intelligible and informative if it is seen as based on a general assumption [i.e. model] of rank and hierarchy'. By agreeable coincidence, Halsey, *Change in British Society*, pp. 200–1, prints a passport signed by Lord Palmerston in 1851, and rightly noted that it describes 'social hierarchy from Her Majesty down through the Viscount to Mr Holroyd, and thence to sons and daughters, and finally a man and maid servant'. This was how Palmerston, and most mid-Victorians, saw their nation.

[45] A. Blair, *New Britain: My Vision of a Young Country* (London, 1996), pp. 45, 65, 237, 298.

narrative of 'the history of all hitherto existing human society'. But in our post-
modern world, class as social descriptions and social identities, class as
hierarchy or as upper-middle-lower or as 'us' and 'them', class as ways of
seeing society and seeing ourselves, is still very much alive. Why else, indeed,
has John Major's notion of trying to make England into a 'classless society' —
an ambition predicated on the continued, if ill-defined, existence of class—
resonated so powerfully during the 1990s?[46]

The fact that Marxism is thought to be dead does not, should not, indeed
cannot, mean that class is dead—at least in England. But to clear these matters
out of the way is merely to bring several other problems more sharply into
focus. First: if it is the case that these three visions of English society have
remained largely unchanged across the centuries, and that they have often been
articulated in the same language, then where does that leave the argument, so
beloved of historians a generation ago, and of sociologists to this day, that the
crucial historical development, associated with the industrial revolution, was
the fundamental and irreversible shift from individual status to collective class?
Second: if the *same* vocabulary has often been used to describe *different* models
of English society, then what are the implications for the currently fashionable
claim that it is language which is the essential variable in constituting social
structures and social identities? Third: how, in the light of the answers to these
questions, might we better understand and begin to explain the ebb and flow of
these three visions of English society across the centuries? How, in short, might
we set about historicising—or, rather, re-historicising—class?

* * *

I begin by addressing the first question. It used to be believed by many
historians, and it is still proclaimed by many sociologists, that the crucial
(and crucially-connected) social and linguistic developments in modern
England took place at the time of the industrial revolution: the change from
an individualist hierarchy of ranks to a collective society of classes, in which
the language of status based on prestige was appropriately superseded by the
language of class based on income.[47] But from a post-modern perspective,

---

[46] K. Marx and F. Engels, *Manifesto of the Communist Party*, in K. Marx and F. Engels,
Collected Works, vol. vi (New York, 1976), p. 482; R. J. Morris, *Class and Class Con-
sciousness in the Industrial Revolution, 1780–1850* (London, 1979), p. 10; Junor, *The Major
Enigma*, pp. 202, 253–4; S. Hasler, 'Britannia rules—but she's enslaved to class', *The
Sunday Times*, 22 December 1991.

[47] Perkin, *Origins of Modern English Society*, pp. 176–217; A. Briggs, 'The Language of
"Class" in Nineteenth-Century England', in M. W. Flinn and T. C. Smout (eds.), *Essays in
Social History* (Oxford, 1974), pp. 154–77; Halsey, *Change in British Society*, pp. 57–9; S.
Edgell, *Class* (London, 1993), p. 1; A. Marwick, *Class: Image and Reality in Britain, France
and the USA since 1930* (London, 1980), p. 16, and p. 359: 'class, I have argued, had its
origins in the Industrial Revolution'.

there are two powerful objections to this venerable interpretation. The first is that the old, traditional hierarchies of status were *not* vanquished, and new middle and working classes, with a strong sense of collective identity and consciousness, were *not* coming into being. Among historians, this account of the years from the 1780s to the 1830s has been out of fashion for the best part of two decades, and there seems no prospect of its being revived in its old Marxist or *Marxisant* guise.[48] The second objection is that before, during and after the industrial revolution, all three models of English society were available, and remained available, and all three of them were expressed both in the language of ranks and in the language of class.[49] Taken together, these insights mortally undermine the old master narrative in which, thanks to the sudden economic change, the old English social hierarchy based on prestige was replaced by new social groups based on income, and at just the time that it was supposed the language of class was coming into being to describe them.

But if (to turn to my second question) different models of English society were and are regularly articulated in the same vocabulary (be it ranks or, increasingly, classes), where does this leave the by now very familiar argument that social identities are primarily the constructs of language? During the last two decades, the claim that language is the key to the creation of social identity, that our social vocabularies and our social fabric 'mutually prop each other up', has passed from fertile and suggestive hypothesis to self-evident and revealed truth without receiving much by way of convincing empirical verification.[50] But if the same social vocabularies have been used, and are still being used, to refer to very different models of society, then

[48] In which context it is worth recalling these remarks of E. P. Thompson, 'The Making of Ruling Class', *Dissent* (summer 1993), 380: ' "Class" was perhaps overworked in the 1960s and 1970s, and it had become merely boring. It is a concept long past its sell-by date'. For a work which wholly dismisses and disregards the concept of class, see F. M. L. Thompson (ed.), *The Cambridge Social History of Britain, 1750–1950* (3 vols., Cambridge, 1990). See also P. Addison, 'Dismantling the Class War', *London Review of Books*, 25 July 1991, pp. 12–13; G. Crossick, 'Consensus, Order and the Social History of Modern Britain', *Historical Journal*, xxv (1992), 945–51; T. Koditschek, 'A Tale of Two Thompsons', *Radical History Review*, no. 56 (1993), 68–84. In all these cases, class was being used (or not being used) to denote social identities which were collective, rather than hierarchical.

[49] For one study of early twentieth-century England which recognises the continued existence of all three models of society, see B. Waites, *A Class Society at War: England, 1914–1918* (Leamington Spa, 1987). For a recent impressionistic account which, like Orwell, uses all three models in a familiar, confused and un-self-aware way, see J. Cooper, *Class: A View from Middle England* (London, 1993 edn.), esp. pp. 11–14, 17, 149, 242, 318.

[50] Q. R. D. Skinner, 'Language and Social Change' in J. Tully (ed.), *Meaning and Context: Quentin Skinner and His Critics* (Cambridge, 1988), p. 132; G. Stedman Jones, *Languages of Class: Studies in English Working-Class History, 1832–1982* (Cambridge, 1983); R. Q. Gray, 'The Deconstructing of the English Working Class', *Social History*, xi (1986), 363–72; D. Mayfield and S. Thorne, 'Social History and its Discontents: Gareth Stedman Jones and the Politics of Language', *Social History*, xvii (1992), 165–88; J. Lawrence and M. Taylor, 'The Poverty of Protest: Gareth Stedman Jones and the Politics of Language—A Reply', *Social History*, xviii (1993), 1–16.

clearly the connection between the social vocabularies and the social identities is much more complex and contingent than has generally been realised. The difficulty for those devoted to the 'linguistic turn' is that they have often been so narrowly preoccupied with language that they have failed to notice that the same vocabulary may be describing very different models of social structure and thus implying very different social identities. This means that it is almost impossible to infer from the language itself which model of society is being referred to, and which social identities are being described. Here is a simple illustration. When people in England talk of 'the class system', and of their place within it, do they mean class as hierarchy, or as upper-middle-lower, or as 'us' and 'them'? The words themselves do not and cannot tell us.[51]

I now turn to my more positive and more extended comments about the ways in which the appeal of these visions of English society has waxed and waned across the centuries. If we accept that the language of class is often being used to describe the traditional, layered social order, this may enable us to recognise one of the most important but under-studied subjects in modern English history, and that is hierarchy. The belief that society was hierarchically constructed was not only central to the eighteenth and the nineteenth centuries: it has also been more important in our own century than has generally been recognised. The functioning hierarchy of aristocratic rulers and great estates may have declined, but hierarchical attitudes and perceptions have survived with remarkable tenacity during the last hundred years, with articulate defenders from W. H. Mallock and Lord Hugh Cecil to Maurice Cowling and Michael Portillo, and articulate critics, among whom R. H. Tawney was probably the most powerful.[52] At the same time, the image of England as a hierarchical society was successfully reasserted towards the close of the nineteenth century: in the proliferation of royal and civic ceremonial, which reaffirmed by display

---

[51] For the dangers inherent in such 'very literal reading of language', see D. Wahrman, 'The New Political History: A Review Essay', *Social History*, xxi (1996), 345. See also S. O. Rose, 'Respectable Men, Disorderly Others: The Language of Gender and the Lancashire Weavers' Strike of 1878 in Britain', *Gender and History*, v (1993), 393; M. W. Steinberg, 'Culturally Speaking: Finding a Commons Between Post-Structuralism and the Thompsonian Perspective', *Social History*, xxi (1996), 194–201.

[52] W. H. Mallock, *Aristocracy and Evolution* (London, 1898), p. 49; idem, *Memoirs of Life and Literature* (London, 1920), pp. 1–16, 197; Lord Hugh Cecil, *Liberty and Authority* (London, 1910), p. 56; idem, *Natural Instinct the Basis for Social Institutions* (London, 1926), pp. 14–15; M. Cowling, 'The Present Position', in idem (ed.), *Conservative Essays* (London, 1978), pp. 10–11; M. Portillo, speech delivered on 14 January 1994, quoting Shakespeare, *Troilus and Cressida*, Act 1, Scene iii, 'O, when degree is shak'd'. This passage, stressing order, hierarchy, and subordination, is discussed by Tillyard, *Elizabethan World Picture*, pp. 7–8. It is printed in K. Baker (ed.), *The Faber Book of Conservatism* (London, 1993), pp. 19–20, and is approvingly quoted by Lord Lawson in his foreword to Bauer, *Class on the Brain*. For R. H. Tawney's critique of the continued existence of hierarchy and hierarchical attitudes in inter-war Britain, see *Equality* (London, 1931), pp. 25–8, 31, 38–9, 50, 87–8, 97, 123.

the view that society was carefully layered; in the expansion and consolidation of the British Empire, where complex rules and rituals of precedence reached their zenith, especially in India; and in the re-structuring and extension of the honours system, with many new levels and divisions tied to different social strata. And as God was succeeded by Darwin, a new authority was found to legitimate this ranked, unequal social hierarchy. Divine providence might no longer sustain the view that society was best envisaged and understood as a great chain of being. But the new theory of secular evolution could—and did.[53]

One does not have to go to India to discover *Homo Hierarchicus*: he has been alive and well and living in England.[54] Perhaps the fact that England has, during the last three hundred years, endured only one military defeat, while avoiding invasion, occupation, civil war, and revolution helps explain why many people still insist on seeing it—some with approval, others with dismay—as the most hierarchical society in the western world.[55] Yet the fact is that hierarchy as a way of seeing things and as a way of doing things has been all but ignored as a serious subject in the modern period: by historians of the right because they incline to take its continued existence for granted; by historians of the left, and by sociologists, because they take its disappearance, sometime during the nineteenth century, no less for granted.[56] But if one looks

[53] D. Cannadine, *Aspects of Aristocracy: Grandeur and Decline in Modern Britain* (London, 1994), pp. 78–80, 88–90; B. Cohn, 'Representing Authority in Victorian India', in E. J. Hobsbawm and T. Ranger (eds.), *The Invention of Tradition* (Cambridge, 1983), pp. 165–210; Harris, *Private Lives, Public Spirit*, pp. 6, 234–5; Marwick, *Class: Image and Reality*, p. 30; W. D. Rubinstein, 'The Evolution of the British Honours System since the Mid Nineteenth-Century', in idem, *Elites and the Wealthy in Modern British History: Essays in Social and Economic History* (New York, 1987), pp. 222–61; S. R. Szreter, *Fertility, Class and Gender in Britain, 1860–1940* (Cambridge, 1996), pp. 165–73.

[54] L. Dumont, *Homo Hierarchcus: The Caste System and Its Implications* (Chicago, 1991); R. Burghart, 'Hierarchical Models of the Hindu Social System', *Man*, xiii (1978), 519–36; A. Appadurai, 'Is Homo Hierarchicus?', *American Anthropologist*, xiii (1986), 754–61.

[55] Consider these remarks of Pierre Laroque, describing the social order at the time of the Coronation of Queen Elizabeth II: 'Great Britain brings us into the presence of an old country very attached to her traditions. The British social hierarchy is to a large extent one of the products of these traditions. It is an accepted hierarchy which is widely recognised and has never been seriously debated. The majority of the population even show a real attachment to this social hierarchy. As a result there has never been deep class antagonism in Great Britain.' Quoted in A. Marwick, *British Society since 1945* (Harmondsworth, 1982), p. 257.

[56] For two suggestive and stimulating uses of hierarchy as a way of understanding the past, see G. Clark, *Symbols of Excellence: Precious metals as Expressions of Status* (Cambridge, 1986), esp. pp. 9–11, 27–30, 65–7, 104–5; J. Goody, *Cooking, Cuisine and Class: A Study in Comparative Sociology* (Cambridge, 1982), esp. pp. vii, 99–11, 133–53. For one rare attempt to treat hierarchy as a continuous and important theme in the history of our nation, see R. Strong, *The Story of Britain* (London, 1996), pp. 79–83, 205, 210, 259, 333, 335, 431–41, 489, 502–3, 527, 538, 568. It is surely not coincidence that Sir Roy Strong trained as a student of Tudor and Stuart portraiture and pageantry—portraits and pageants explicitly designed to celebrate, proclaim, and reinforce a hierarchical view of the world. For a rare example of a sociologist trying to deal with popular perceptions of our society as hierarchical, see D. Lockwood, 'Sources of Variation in Working-Class Images of Society', *The Sociological Review*, NS xiv (1966), 249–67.

at the history of social perceptions and social identities in modern England from the standpoint of Tudor times, there is clearly a question which cries out to be addressed and answered: whatever happened to the Elizabethan world picture? E. M. W. Tillyard himself provided his own speculative answer, which deserves to be followed up: 'we shall err grieviously . . . if we imagine that the Elizabethan habit of mind [i.e. seeing the world hierarchically] is done with once and for all. If we are sincere with ourselves, we must know that we have that habit in our own bosoms somewhere'.[57]

This survival of hierarchical perceptions needs to be given at least as much attention by historians as the more commonplace analyses of modern English society built around contemporaries' three-fold or two-fold models of collective identities. But this is not just a matter of recovering and giving appropriate attention to the most pervasive perception of English society, important although that undoubtedly is. For it bears repeating that throughout the last three hundred years, all three ways of seeing society have been available, and during much of the time, people have easily moved back and forth from one of them to another. But these models have not always co-existed peacefully. Despite their easy vernacular and linguistic accommodation, their deeper and more fundamentally irreconcilable incompatibilities were pregnant with confrontational political implications. At certain times, and in certain circumstances, these models became explicitly politicised and adversarially inflected, as different people sought to defend society as they saw it, or to change it for an alternative model: those who wanted to proclaim hierarchy against its critics and detractors; those who wanted to assert the importance of the middle class vis-à-vis those above and below; and those who occupied one or other side of what was seen as a great social (and political) divide.

The evidence for the ebb and flow in the resonance of these different social perceptions is clear. For most of the eighteenth century, with a slight interruption during the 1760s, the hierarchical view seems to have been the commonest, though there is ample evidence of its relatively peaceful co-existence with the other two models.[58] But from the 1780s to the 1840s, many people came to see English society in terms of three warring collectivities, or believed a great gulf had opened up between the rich and the poor, or thought that hierarchy urgently needed defending. During the mid-Victorian period, the hierarchical view was successfully reasserted, and the triadic and dichotomous pictures of society were generally much less popular. Then again, from the 1880s to the 1910s, there were those who hoped (or feared) that society was becoming divided between the people and the peers, or between employers and workers. During

---

[57] Tillyard, *Elizabethan World Picture*, pp. 101–2.
[58] J. Brewer, *Party Ideology and Popular Politics at the Accession of George III* (Cambridge, 1976), pp. 139–272; N. Rogers, 'The Middling Sort in Eighteenth-Century Politics', in Barry and Brooks, *The Middling Sort of People*, pp. 159–80.

the inter-war years, it seemed as though the conflict between capital and labour reached its peak in 1926, but the alternative vision, of an ordered, integrated, hierarchy was strongly articulated, most famously by Stanley Baldwin.[59] From 1945 to 1980, many people believed there was one fundamental division in society, between the middle and working classes, or capital and labour, which was institutionalised in the two great political parties, or between the Establishment and the non-Establishment, or U and non-U speakers. But there were also those who lamented that society was less hierarchical than it had been, while others despaired that it was more hierarchical than it ought to be.[60]

It bears repeating that all these views of English society were excessively simplistic. But there can be no doubt that at particular times, these competing social visions and politicised social identities have been very appealing. How was it, then, that different ways of envisioning English society, which for the most part peacefully co-existed and merged and melded into one another in the popular imagination, were sometimes proclaimed and asserted in this strident, competitive and confrontational manner? If we look at the issue this way round, then this should enable us to establish more plausible and more flexible connections between social structures and social perceptions than those rather rigid and one way links posited by the Marxists in one direction, or the followers of the 'linguistic turn' in another. For it is not that changes in social structures lead directly to changes in social perceptions, as in traditional accounts focusing on the making of class consciousness. Nor is it that social perceptions directly constitute and create social structures, as those who stress the constitutive power of 'the language of class' believe. Rather, it is that we need to understand how, when and why different social models (often expressed in similar language) have appealed to different people at different times by offering them the most resonant and appealing accounts of the world they think they inhabit—or of the world they think they want to inhabit.

Part of the answer to this question will clearly be to do with discontent: not in the sense that discontent is the direct expression of, or results in fundamental changes in, the social structure, which has not been the case in England during the last three hundred years; but rather in the sense that it is discontent which causes people to see the same social structure in an alternative light, as dissatisfaction means they discover new friends and make new enemies, as

<hr />

[59] D. Cannadine, 'Politics, Propaganda and Art: The Case of Two "Worcestershire Lads"', *Midland History*, iv (1977), 97–123; P. Williamson, 'The Doctrinal Politics of Stanley Baldwin', in M. Bentley (ed.), *Public and Private Doctrines: Essays in British History Presented to Maurice Cowling* (Cambridge, 1993), pp. 184–98.

[60] N. Mitford, 'The English Aristocracy', *Encounter*, Sept. 1955, pp. 5–11; A. S. C. Ross, 'U and Non-U: An Essay in Sociological Linguistics', *Encounter*, Nov. 1955, pp. 11–20; H. Thomas (ed.), *The Establishment* (London, 1959); P. Worsthorne, 'Class and Conflict in British Foreign Policy', *Foreign Affairs*, xxxvii (1959), 419–31.

riots and protests project and render credible a dramatically different vision of their society from that of elaborately staged and carefully ranked official processions, and as the three or two stage models of society thus come to make more sense to them than the traditional hierarchical picture. But if this is right, then it also means we ought often to be looking at the way in which social description sometimes becomes explicitly politicised, and at the part played by politicians in the creation and articulation of social identities, and in the process whereby one version and vision of society becomes, for a time, more appealing than the alternatives.[61] For many politicians, from Wilkes to Cobbett, Cobden to Gladstone, Lloyd George to Stanley Baldwin, Margaret Thatcher to John Major, one of the most important things they wanted and needed to accomplish was to persuade people to see their society (and their place within it) differently, which in practice has meant moving them from one model of social description to another.

Consider, in this light, these examples. When Wilkes invoked 'the common people' against the Hanoverian establishment, when Cobbett inveighed on behalf of the majority against 'old corruption', when the Whigs feared in the 1820s that the social fabric was being rent in twain, when the Anti-Corn Law Leaguers described themselves as a 'middle-class set of agitators' railing against aristocratic tyranny',[62] when Disraeli feared there were 'two nations' between whom no bond of sympathy or understanding existed, when the great Lord Salisbury lamented the 'disintegration' of hierarchy, when Lloyd George attacked 'the peers' in the name of 'the people', when Stanley Baldwin commended traditional rural and factory communities, when Harold Nicolson worried in 1945 that 'class feeling' was very strong, when Arthur Scargill claimed the miners were the advanced guard of the proletarian revolution,[63] and when John Major evoked 'middle England', many people did come (and have come) to believe that these arresting but over-simplified descriptions were genuine, truthful accounts of how Engish society actually was, or was becoming. In fact, of course, they were no such thing: they were not objective descriptions of contemporary society, and nor were they evidence that old social formations were dying or new social formations coming into existence. They were merely evidence that politicians were, in Lady Thatcher's words, 'trying to change the way we look at things', and this is an aspect of political

---

[61] K. Wilson, 'Whiggery Assailed and Triumphant: Popular Radicalism in Hanoverian England', *Journal of British Studies*, xxxiv (1995), 126.

[62] E. A. Wasson, 'The Great Whigs and Parliamentary Reform, 1809–1830', *Journal of British Studies*, xxiv (1985), 457; E. Royle and J. Walvin, *English Radicals and Reformers, 1760–1848* (Brighton, 1982), pp. 175–6; N. McCord, *The Anti Corn Law League, 1838–1846* (London, 1958), p. 127; G. M. Trevelyan, *The Life of John Bright* (London, 1913), p. 141.

[63] M. Crick, *Scargill and the Miners* (Harmondsworth, 1985), pp. 28–31; P. F. Clarke, *Hope and Glory: Britain, 1900–1990* (London, 1996), pp. 378–9.

behaviour and social perceptions which needs much more attention than it has thus far generally received. The more democratic Britain has become, the more party politics has been concerned with the creation, articulation and transformation of social identities, rather than merely being the direct reflection and unmediated expression of pre-existing social identities.[64]

* * *

This remark of Margaret Thatcher's leads conveniently to my conclusion, since I have been concerned throughout this lecture with the ways in which 'we look at things', and with the processes by which the ways in which 'we look at things' are changed. I have argued that these questions were not convincingly addressed by the old-style historians of class, any more than by the new-style historians of language. The first approach was in error in claiming the economically-determined creation of self-conscious classes leads directly to, and can be demonstrated by the existence of, the new language of class. The second approach is no less in error in supposing that language directly constitutes social perceptions and thus social identities. I have argued, on the contrary, that throughout modern English history, there have always been three different models of the social structure and social identities on offer, of which hierarchy has been both the most important and the most neglected. In theory these models and these identities are mutually exclusive, but in practice they are usually melded and merged one into the other, in part because they shared a common vocabulary, of which the language of class eventually became the most common of all. But at other times, these three models and identities become politicised, mutually-exclusive and confrontationally inflected, and it is the historian's task to find out when, how, and why this happened, and to construct from these answers the more detailed master narrative of the ebb and flow of multiple social identities that has been briefly sketched in here.

It has recently been argued that landscape is what culture does to nature: investing what would otherwise be regarded as the wilderness with shape and significance, meaning and identity.[65] Of course, this cultural activity is partly a matter of doing and making the landscape itself: of planting the trees, diverting the rivers, cutting the grass. But it is also the process whereby these trees, rivers, and grass become invested with the meanings and identities they bear, and that process is as much a matter of perception and politics, language and

---

[64] M. Thatcher, *The Revival of Britain* (London, 1989), p. 98; J. Lawrence, 'Class and Gender in the Making of Urban Toryism, 1880–1914', *English Historical Review*, cviii (1993), 629–52; D. Jarvis, 'British Conservatism and Class Politics in the 1920s', *English Historical Review*, cxi (1996), 59–84.
[65] S. Schama, *Landscape and Memory* (New York, 1995), pp. 10–18.

rhetoric, sentiment and association, as it is a result of the conscious and conspicuous acts of landscaping themselves. By the same token, it can also be argued that in England, class is what culture does to inequality and social structure: investing what are otherwise anonymous indivduals and unfathomable collectivities with shape and significance, meanings and identities, by moulding our perceptions of the social worlds in which we live and the social structures to which we belong. As with landscape, this is partly a matter of the social structure itself, which does change and evolve in terms of numbers, location, occupation, and so on—albeit relatively slowly. But like landscape again, it is also a matter of language, human agency and politics. Just as the meaning of landscape can be disputed, so perceptions of the social structure can be contested and changed: though only in terms of three basic models, which often employ a common vocabulary, sometimes of ranks, more usually of class.

The way people see themselves in society, the way people see the society to which they belong, and the way these things interconnect, contradict, diverge, and change over time: these are exceptionally complex issues, which have only recently surfaced on the agenda of historical inquiry.[66] But when Jonathan Dimbleby tells us the Prince of Wales 'yearns for lost hierarchies', when Alan Bennett writes of 'the conventional three-tier account of social divisions', and when John Kenneth Galbraith opines that the great divide in the world today is not between labour and capital, but between rich and poor, we ought at least to be able to recognise these familiar formulations for what they are: not original interpretations, but the latest variants of social descriptions going back three hundred years and more; and not complete, objective accounts of how society is, but partial, subjective visions of society as they want or choose to see it.[67] As these examples serve to remind us, we need to think more carefully and more self-consciously about how we think about ourselves as social individuals, social beings, and social groups, about how our forebears thought about themselves, and about how our successors might think about themselves. Like sex, class does not take place entirely inside our own heads: but for more reasons than one, that is probably the best place to begin thinking about it and looking for it.[68]

---

[66] In which regard, it is worth noting Lord Runciman's observation (*London Review of Books*, 10 March 1994, p. 5) that 'in twentieth as in fifteenth-century England, there are systematically observable inequalities of economic, ideological and political power, *to which the contemporary rhetoric relates in all sorts of still understudied ways*'. (My italics).

[67] J. Dimbleby, *The Prince of Wales: A Biography* (London, 1994), p. 523; A. Bennett, *Writing Home* (London, 1994), p. 33; J. K. Galbraith, *The Good Society: The Humane Agenda* (London, 1996), pp. 6–9. For a recent account of contemporary English society which uses all three models, see R. Seitz, *Over Here* (London, 1998), pp. 93–134.

[68] This is the argument advanced in Furbank, *Unholy Pleasure*; idem, 'Sartre's Absent Whippet', *London Review of Books*, 24 February 1994, pp. 26–7.

I end, as I began, with just such a head: another individual observer describing the social order of England more than half a century ago. But this is not George Orwell, it is someone else; and it is not the nation as whole, but one particular town. Nevertheless, the similarities in social perceptions are striking, and instructive. For once again, the same three models of society co-exist: comfortably yet contradictorily, compatibly but confusingly. One way of seeing it was as a civic procession, hierarchically structured from the Mayor, via carefully-ranked local figures and organisations, to the humblest labourer. A second vision divides it into upper, middle, and lower collective groups, with the observer emphatically in the centre of things. Yet a third picture is of the town riven by one great gulf, between those who had a regular income, and a lifestyle to match, and those who did not. The correspondence between these descriptions and perceptions of English society and those of George Orwell, or Mr Gladstone, or John Major, or countless millions of ordinary people across the last three centuries, is virtually exact. But to which town do these descriptions relate? And to whom are we indebted for them? The place was Grantham, and the author of these remarks was Margaret Thatcher.[69]

---

[69] M. Thatcher, *The Downing Street Years* (London, 1993), p. 10; idem, *The Path to Power* (London, 1995), pp. 5, 19, 23–4, 47, 546. For a more extended analysis of Thatcher's social visions, see Cannadine, *Class in Britain*, pp. 171–80.

Social Intelligence and the Emergence of Roles and Rules

ESTHER GOODY

University of Cambridge

I. Introduction[1]

THE INVITATION TO PRESENT THE 1997 Radcliffe-Brown Memorial Lecture has been a welcome opportunity to think again about some of the work of Professor A. R. Radcliffe-Brown. The questions which originally brought me to Cambridge to work with Meyer Fortes were, in those days, seen as in the domain of 'personality and culture'. However it was neither personality nor culture *per se* that interested me, but rather the ways in which social structure and culture together shaped individual behaviour in patterned ways. Radcliffe-Brown's ideas were among those I found most exciting. His various papers on 'joking relations' address such issues directly: there is something about living in strongly patrilineal societies which is associated with patterns of joking and disrespect towards men of the mother's lineage.[2]

---

[1] I wish to acknowledge the contributions of most helpful discussions with those who read earlier drafts of this paper, particularly Susan Drucker Brown, Paul Sant Cassia, and Rachel Goody. Robert Hinde's thoughtful comments on a draft of an earlier paper have led me to rethink certain issues and hopefully to be more explicit about these (E. N. Goody forthcoming).
[2] When I proposed this title for the Radcliffe-Brown Memorial Lecture I had forgotten that Meyer Fortes' last publication, appearing shortly after his death, was entitled *Rules and the emergence of society* (1983). In this work he sees the central importance of rules for human societies as anchored in the emergence of the role of 'father', which he suggests was the first truly social role. While Fortes directs attention to different proximate mechanisms than those explored in the present paper, he firmly links the emergence of human society to the creation of roles and rules. Although I read this monograph when it first appeared, it was his ideas about fatherhood which then absorbed me. When working out the themes for this lecture I

Proceedings of the British Academy, **97**, 119–147. © The British Academy 1998.
Read at the Academy 25 February 1997.

In the paper 'On Joking Relationships' Radcliffe-Brown wrote 'The joking relationship is a particular combination of friendliness and antagonism.' And 'The show of hostility, the perpetual disrespect, is a continual expression of that social disjunction which is an essential part of the whole structural situation [exogamous patrilineages], but over which, without destroying or even weakening it, there is provided the social conjunction of friendliness and mutual aid' (1952*b*: 90, 95). What sort of processes underlie this association? What is it about living in a patrilineal society that shapes aggression and joking towards matrikin?

One sort of intellectual history of social anthropology would chart the debates which developed from these papers on joking relations (Homans and Schneider's *Marriage, authority and final causes* (1955); Needham's *Structure and Sentiment* (1962); Jack Goody's paper on 'Mother's Brother and Sister's son in West Africa' (1969). Indeed some critics have doubted the very 'reality' of patrilineages as significant features of African societies. The issues involved are too complex to pursue here. In this paper I shall be concerned with societies in which the actors themselves describe their behaviour in terms of patrilineal descent; for present purposes we can set aside discussions among anthropologists about their own analytic categories. While it is vital to preserve the important distinction between actors' concepts and analytic concepts, the relation between them may need to be understood differently in the context of roles and rules as emergent forms. It is to this dynamic that my main remarks are addressed.[3]

Here I want rather to keep to the underlying questions Radcliffe-Brown raises about the nature of the links between the patterning of individual interactions and society-level forms like patrilineages. The interesting puzzles are: *How* are such peculiarly individual behaviours as aggression and joking— expressions of subjective feelings—shaped by sociocultural forms? *How* does it happen that certain sociocultural forms seem to very often shape individual subjective feelings in such similar, strongly patterned ways in different societies? And *what* have these puzzles to do with 'social intelligence'?

We may initially define social intelligence as the cognitive modelling of the contingencies of social interaction. To partially anticipate the argument, such cognitive modelling goes on in each individual head—but perforce makes use of sociocultural schemata, representations of 'how the world is'

---

had forgotten his identification of the dynamic relationship between roles and rules in the emergence of 'society'. Thus it is that we absorb ideas from our teachers and make them so integral to our thinking that we forget their origin! This paper, then, is a tribute to Meyer Fortes as well as to Radcliffe-Brown.

[3] This is a subject for a different paper.

in a particular society. This shifts our problem from the level of 'social structure' and 'learned routines' for privileged aggression and joking, down to the level of how the reciprocal cognitive modelling of certain sorts of interaction might come to be (i) patterned and (ii) shared within a society. This is a theoretical approach that works 'from the bottom up'—begins with individual behaviour and seeks to identify how this shapes higher-level processes and forms.

Overview

There are three elements to the account presented in this paper; taken together they offer a way of seeing certain structures—roles and rules which character-ise all known societies—as emergent from social interaction.

The first element is what has come to be called 'social intelligence', both primate social intelligence and its elaboration in human social intelligence. The most robust difference between sub-human primates and *Homo sapiens sapiens* is our use of spoken language. Clearly human social intelligence today is profoundly shaped by language. Given the long period during which spoken language may well have emerged, it is likely that the transition to hominid social intelligence would have been powerfully driven by increasing language skills.

The next element to look at is the nature of spoken language. There has recently been a shift from the analysis of language as formal structures, to studying how language is actually used in conversation. This is forcing us to see spoken language as the dynamic continual negotiation of conversational meanings between speakers. Monkeys and apes apparently do not make use of *joint attention* to construct external shared signs.[4] During the slow emergence of spoken language, humans must have become skilled at jointly establishing shared meanings. It may indeed have been this skill which made possible a lexicon of 'words', and gradually led to the emergence of grammar and syntax, and conventions for pragmatic meaning. Using spoken language—langua-ging—is a joint activity between speakers: conversation, dialogue, is the basic form of spoken language—not lexicon, grammar, or syntax.

The third element is the powerful interaction between the dialogic use of spoken language and the dyadic nature of social roles. In dialogue speakers reciprocally interpret and shape closure on intentions and meanings. They are able to do this largely through sharing knowledge and expectations about what the other is likely to mean. Dyadic roles are sociocultural frames for beha-

---

[4] Dorothy Cheney's 1997 Tanner Lectures *The evolution of mind and language* and discus-sion during the following seminar, 10–12 March 1997, University of Cambridge.

viour, and partly defined by expectations of mutual rights and obligations. Role partners hold each other accountable for role-specified behaviour. When role behaviour matches expectations, this enacts—and recreates—the roles themselves. When role behaviour does not fit expectations, deviations are sanctioned in an attempt to restore the balance. In both dialogue and role behaviour very similar procedures seem to be used to reciprocally shape joint closure on meanings and intentions. In learning how to use language we learn both how to make meaning in conversation, and how to use language procedures to construct and enact dyadic roles. The joking relations between mother's brother and sister's son so brilliantly described by Radcliffe-Brown are an example of this dynamic between role dyads and spoken dialogue.

This can be seen as a 'possible scenario' for the relationship between human social intelligence and the emergence of institutionally patterned forms like joking relations.

II. Primate Social Intelligence

Nicholas Humphrey's seminal observation was that the vaunted intelligence of higher primates cannot have been a response to challenges of technical mastery of the ecological environment or of tool use, but rather is a new sort of 'social intelligence' through which primates manage their social interdependence *with other primates* (1976). Primates are challenged by the increasing demands of cognitively modelling the possible contingent responses of others to their own goal-directed actions.[5] Humphrey uses the analogy of two people playing chess. As primates become more skilled at cognitively modelling others' possible alternative responses, they develop related skills for using this modelling of others' actions to manage social relations themselves.[6] Some of the most striking ethology concerns the modelling by monkeys and apes of others' responses in order to act deceptively—outwitting competitors for food for instance. The classic work here has been Byrne and Whiten's edited book

---

[5] Humphrey's original paper (1976) has been subject to many readings, scholars focusing on different aspects as these relate to their own theoretical concerns. This is hardly surprising with such a rich new vein to explore. It is too early for a useful debate about which lines are more productive; indeed it is to be hoped that these several themes will turn out to be linked in significant ways.

[6] In a theoretical discussion of primate social intelligence I termed this cognitive modelling **anticipatory interactive planning (AIP)** (Introduction to E. N. Goody (ed.), *Social intelligence and interaction* (1995)). Perhaps beguiled by the appropriateness of the initials, I failed to realise that this would, incorrectly, be taken to mean that such cognitive modelling was intentional and conscious (see for instance paper by Drew in *Social intelligence and interaction*). However the implications of the initials of the more appropriate alternative **anticipatory interactive modelling (AIM)** are not much better.

Machiavellian Intelligence in which contributors document field observations of social interactions reflecting the capacity for cognitively modelling of other individuals' responses (1988).

Ever since reading Humphrey's paper I have been fascinated by the implications of such a social intelligence for better understanding human social life. For it is clear that social intelligence is about how we attribute intentions and beliefs to others in order to better anticipate their responses. Indeed, there is a large literature documenting such attributions and resulting behaviour.[7]

But while recent work increasingly shows higher primates to be skilled at social intelligence, there remains the dramatic gap between such primates and our own hominid line. The sharing of some 98% of DNA with the higher apes suggests that a great genetic disjunction is unlikely; gradual adaptation of some emergent feature is more likely. Then how did this 'hominid transition' occur?

The editors of *Machiavellian Intelligence* consider both improved adaptations to ecological challenge and the gradual increase in tool-related skills, suggesting that they no doubt contributed to advances in hominid species. However they conclude that the most significant ratchet was almost certainly progressively augmented social/Machiavellian intelligence itself. As apes become more skilled at anticipating other apes' intentions, it was the most socially intelligent creatures who survived to reproduce. Their more socially intelligent offspring would have been even more difficult to deceive and anticipate, thus the next generation would have to be even *more* socially intelligent to succeed. The selective advantage of deception became a ratchet leading to continuously higher elaboration of social intelligence.

While such a dynamic is indeed persuasive, there is for those studying human societies a curious 'dark hole'. In neither the first volume of *Machiavellian Intelligence* (1988) nor its successor (Whiten and Byrne (eds.), forthcoming) is there a direct consideration of the role of spoken language for hominid social intelligence (apart from my own paper). Yet spoken language remains the single robust difference between apes and modern *Homo sapiens*. The argument seems to be that developed spoken language was relatively late in Hominid evolution (Paul Mellars (1996), cites the date of around 40,000 BP) and with 'culture' this is taken to mark the effective arrival of *Homo sapiens sapiens*. Thus spoken language is seen as the consequence of becoming fully human, and cannot have played any significant role in the emergence of hominids themselves.

---

[7] The 'attribution theory' of social psychology is an elaborate and systematic exploration of the role of attributing goals and intentions to social actors in determining patterns of interaction: Heider (1958), Thibault and Kelley (1959), Kelley (1979), etc., and more recently most of the papers in Fletcher and Fitness (eds.), *Knowledge structures in close relationships* (1996). See also E. N. Goody (1978a).

III. The 'Origin' of Spoken Language

From the 1860s there was a long period during which considering possibilities for the origin of human language was thought dangerously speculative and in any case of little scholarly interest.[8] Very much as with the edited volumes of Whiten and Byrne, and Michael Carrither's *Why humans have culture* (1992), language was treated as something that 'just happened', proved useful, and is certainly definitively human. However, in the past few years a number of important works have appeared that address the question of what form hominid proto-language might have taken.[9] This is not the place to discuss hypothetical early language, and related debates. What is important for an evolutionary perspective on hominid social intelligence is that with this recent work we may, indeed we must, begin to consider how hominid social intelligence would have been altered by this new tool for thinking—and acting with.

Any such project must be at least roughly anchored in time, although there is probably no dating scheme which will be undisputed. If one adopts the gradualist stance, then we can follow that of William Foley's discussion of the emergence of language in the hominid line in *Anthropological Linguistics* (1997). While these particular estimates may well be modified, there is clearly a real possibility that the emergence of spoken language was a slow process extending over many millennia.

IV. Using Language

The use of language has been studied in two broad traditions: the *product tradition* and the *action tradition* (Clark, 1996). The product tradition developed from the linguistic study of sentences, words, and speech sounds—the 'products' of language use. It has been strongly influenced by the work of Noam Chomsky on generative grammars (e.g., 1957). Sentences have a syntactic structure; words have a phonological and morphemic structure; segments have a phonetic structure; and words have lexical meanings; language use is determined by rules. However theories of language structure cannot be extended to actual discourse because they deliberately exclude any systematic treatment of speakers, listeners, time and circumstances of speaking. They also exclude all communicative acts not included in formal spoken language. In the *product* tradition each speaker is treated as an isolated

---

[8] The parallel constraints from archaeology and linguistics are briefly discussed in E. N. Goody 'Social intelligence and language: another Rubicon?' (forthcoming).

[9] See for instance: Bickerton (1990), Donald (1991), Lieberman (1991), Dunbar (1993). See also discussion in E. N. Goody (forthcoming).

Table 1. Emergence of spoken language: rough dates.

Homo habilis	Established early proto-language	from 2 million years
Homo erectus	Developing language	from 1.5 million years
Archaic *Homo sapiens*	Complex language	from 0.3 million years
Fully modern humans	Fully developed languages	from 0.05 million years

Based on: W. Foley, *Anthropological Linguistics*

individual seeking to communicate by following rules of grammar, which are 'hard-wired' in our brains. The product tradition studies language as if it were a complex 'physical' artefact—as immobile as a stone axe.

The *action tradition* joins two lines of thinking—the philosophies of Austin, Grice, and Searle, with the related fields of sociolinguistics (Sacks, Schegloff, Brown, and Levinson) and ethnomethodology (Goffman, Garfinkel, Heritage). In this tradition the concern has been not with frozen products of speech, but with understanding how people use language to construct meaning. It would be difficult to exaggerate the implications of this new concern with how meanings are constructed in use, both for linguistics itself, and for our understanding of social intelligence and social processes and forms. Here it is only possible to indicate a few central themes. For this I draw heavily on Herb Clark's recent incisive theoretical overview of the principles and dyadic procedures for *using* language, although it builds on a growing corpus of empirical and theoretical work by other scholars.[10]

Early work in the action tradition sought to widen definitions of using language, as in Austin's definition of 'speech acts' as 'what is actually accomplished by speaking in certain ways'. This led to efforts to open out the notion of 'context' since this clearly plays a central role in 'meaning'. And this in turn required new methods of studying language use through transcripts of natural conversation. Once the object of study was natural conversation it became clear that the major 'context' for each speaker is the other speaker's words. Dialogue, not formal text, was the actual mode of using language. Using language is a *joint activity* between speakers. Indeed Clark argues that it is the 'jointness of activity' which is prior, with discourse being the special case in which joint activity employs spoken language.[11]

---

[10] There are too many to list, but central works have been Austin (1962), Grice (e.g., 1957), Sacks, Schegloff, and Jefferson (1974), Brown and Levinson (1978/1987), Garfinkel (1967), Heritage (1990/91). Several chapters especially those by Drew, Good, Streeck, Brown, and Levinson on *Social intelligence and interaction*, ed. E. Goody (1995) either describe or imply these same themes.

[11] One of the implications of the material analysed in the present paper is that the emergence of spoken language may have both depended on and substantially enhanced the hominid capacity for joint attention and joint activity. Thus while for modern humans dialogue may be a 'special case' of joint activity, it may be that the 'work' of achieving joint closure on lexical meanings and the 'rules' of proto-grammar progressively enhanced hominid abilities for joint activity.

Joint activities have quite different properties from individual activities. Like playing chess or playing a piano duet, participants each act individually; but in order to 'do' chess or 'do' a duet, they must intricately *coordinate* their actions. Conversations are 'open-ended'. They are rarely scripted, and neither person knows at the start how the conversation will proceed or end. However joint actions still embody individual actions, but these are *participatory* actions in that they are coordinated. But how is this coordination achieved in conversation?

In formal terms the criterion for participatory joint actions is that each participant must *both* **intend** to do her own part and **believe** that the other intends to do his.

This still leaves both participants with what Schelling calls a *coordination problem* (1960, cited in Clark (1996), and also Levinson (1995)). 'Two people have a coordination problem whenever they have common interests, or goals, and each person's actions depend on the action of the other' (Clark 1996: 62). Schelling's ingenious experimental work was based on presenting separately to two people unknown to each other a coordination problem in the form of a game, and told that 'to win' both must select the same 'solution'. For instance: you are each told to meet the other somewhere in New York on Wednesday. Where will you meet and at what time? A majority picked the Information Booth at Grand Central Station and almost everyone picked 12 noon.

Schelling's work showed that people are quite successful at solving coordination problems by coordinating their predictions of what they would do with predictions of what the other would probably do in order to identify the one course of action that their expectations of each other can converge on. This coordination of expectations is achieved by using clues from knowledge about the background information the participants share. Clark following Lewis (1969) calls such a clue a *coordination device*. For instance, in one of Schelling's games when two people were asked to independently choose the same face of a coin 86% chose heads—here the coordination device was probably the mutual knowledge of the phrase 'heads or tails' where 'heads' comes first.

Clark follows Lewis in arguing that language use is really people solving coordination problems in jointly arriving at shared meanings. Much of his book is devoted to showing how the tool of spoken language, together with non-verbal communication, is used by alternately speaking participants in discourse to coordinate shared meanings. He writes: 'Utterances have traditionally been treated as autonomous acts by speakers, but that isn't right. Although speakers may assume the major responsibility, they cannot present utterances without the coordination of their addressees. . . . Getting what we say attended to and identified is just as much a joint action as getting them understood.' (Ibid. 253).

Table 2a. Levels of coordinating meaning between two speakers.

Speaker A's actions	Speaker B's actions
1 A is executing *behaviour t* for B	B is attending to *behaviour t* from A
2 A is presenting *signal s* to B	B is identifying *signal s* from A
3 A is signalling the proposition *that p* for B	B is recognising the proposition *that p* from A
4 A is proposing joint project *w* to B	B is considering A's proposal of *w*

The following invented example (after Clark 1996: 151–3) indicates the nesting reciprocality of the joint negotiation of meaning in dialogue.

To give the formal model content we can add the actions and speech from an example which Clark uses elsewhere: Speaker A gestures towards a chair and says to Speaker B 'sit down'. Action and speech are represented in bold letters in the second version of the table.

Table 2b. Levels of coordinating action and speech between two speakers.

Speaker A's actions	Speaker B's actions
1 A is executing a *behaviour* for B **A gestures towards chair**	B is attending to the *behaviour* from A **B looks at chair**
2 A is presenting *signal* to B **A says 'sit down' to B**	B is identifying *signal* from A **B hears and understands A say 'sit down'**
3 A is signalling a proposition for B **A signals a polite request to B**	B is recognising the proposition from A **B recognises A's polite request**
4 A is proposing joint project to B **A is proposing that B sit and be comfortable**	B is considering A's proposal **B is considering A's proposal that she sit and be comfortable**

Note we must start with A's initiating act of gaining B's attention (1). Each level is a prerequisite for the next. Joint attention of both speakers to the chair is a prerequisite for B to understand the 'topic' of the dialogue. The spoken signal 'sit down' confirms that the chair is where she should sit and describes the action; B must understand the words if she is to participate jointly with A in the dialogue. The third stage is the 'translation' of the words 'sit down' into the speech act—a polite request, not an order or a question. If the speech act had been recognised as an order or a question, B would be considering a very different proposed joint project with A at stage 4.

One of the most interesting sections of Clark's book concerns the ways in which language is used at each of these stages to confirm the correctness of the exchange. This is 'working on the coordination problem'. 'It is a fundamental principle of intentional action that people look for evidence that they have done what they intended to do.' (Ibid. 222). 'The participants in a joint action try to establish the mutual belief that they have succeeded well enough' for example, 'in reaching closure on the joint act of signaling and recognizing.' (Ibid. 226–7).

Thus dialogue involves two 'tracks'. Track 1 concerns talk about the topic of conversation; these are locutionary acts conveying lexical meaning: [A] 'It was, uh, it was a lovely day'. Track 2 uses language to comment on this; it is a metacommunicative act. When a speaker presents a signal on Track 1 she is also tacitly asking 'Do you understand me?' on Track 2. Thus if [B] responds 'yes' it operates on both Track 1, ratifying the assertion that it was a lovely day; and on Track 2, answering the tacit question—'Do you understand me?' Where there are problems with joint closure on meaning there are several different types of procedures for clarification, expansion, and repairing mistaken signals or recognition. A surprising amount of natural conversation is devoted to seeking and securing joint closure—to identifying the cues which permit solutions to the never-ending 'coordination problems' of dialogue.

In short, using language is not only about conveying lexical information, but in order to achieve this between *two* speakers a great deal of talk is about confirming that signals have been correctly identified and recognised, that both speakers have the same understanding of their joint conversational project. And as conversation unfolds through time, coordination problems continue, as do procedures for achieving joint closure on intended meanings.

V. Using Language and Social Intelligence

What does this *action view* of using language contribute to an understanding of the significance of human social intelligence for the emergence of roles and rules?

Contrast between ape and human social intelligence

Ape social intelligence has been characterised as driven by competitive individual attempts to deceive other apes. This view certainly ignores apes' use of the ability to model each other's contingent responses to achieve joint goals—cooperation. However the emphasis on such a Machiavellian social intelligence does reflect the essentially ego-centered nature of non-verbal communication. Primate 'mind reading' is 'all in the mind'. Each creature must cognitively model what she supposes to be the intentions of others. There are of course many cues—of hesitation, facial expression, gesture—indeed it must be the reading of these cues, combined with past experience, which underlies ape social intelligence.

Two new things happen with the emergence of spoken language. First, language is a 'tool' for doing cognitive modelling with *learned and shared* meanings and language structures. The number of shared meanings in contemporary lexicons is vast. Foley suggests that as proto-language developed there would have been recurrent cognitive overload as lexicon, then proto-grammar and then full grammar became increasingly complex (1997, chapter X). New cognitive structures and the external artifacts of grammatical structures must have evolved to manage such overloads. When we include the language-based schemata, scripts and communicative genre like politeness and narrative, it is clear that human languages are extremely powerful tools for cognitive modelling.

In addition, when we speak we hear what we say, at the same time that it is heard by our addressee. Because both speak the same language — we use a common lexicon, grammar and syntax — each speaker/hearer is using the same languaging tools to communicate intentions; both speak and hear the same signals. The cognitive modelling in each head uses similar signs, schemata, cognitive strategies for the process of jointly constructing meanings. Thus these are also tools for managing the coordination of meanings. There appears to be no evidence that apes devote joint attention to communicating *about* communication — metacommunication. It may well be that if there was a long period during which hominid proto-language emerged, the main cognitive 'work' during this phase was the joining of primate intersubjectivity to cognitive and social procedures for the sharing of links between referent and sign. Some time during the hominid trajectory, probably gradually, vocal communication became the object — and the product — of *jointly coordinated* activity. The contrast with ape ego-centric communicative acts is marked and profound.

VI. Dialogue

A simple but powerful corollary of this view is that it is conversation that is the fundamental basis of spoken language, not the formal properties of language, nor yet text (or even narrative). The paradigmatic form of conversation is dialogue — the speaking together of two people. In terms of social intelligence, dialogue mediates the processes of conveying and attributing intentions between actors. And as we have seen the meanings in conversation are jointly created in dialogue.

Structural coupling and the negotiation of conversational meaning

There is a generic mode of mutually interdependent interaction between organism and environment which Maturana and Verela (1987) have termed 'structural coupling'. The environment may be physical, chemical, or another organism. In this mode the behaviour of each shapes that of the other through extended reciprocal interdependence. It is impossible to understand the behaviour of either member without studying them in interaction through time. A particularly clear example would be that of mother–infant interactions in which the infant's close attention is responded to by subtle maternal cues which further shape infant attention and behaviour. (See Trevarthen 1979; Bruner 1978.) The body of literature deriving from Bowlby's (1969) work on attachment behaviour can also be seen in these terms.

We have seen that conversation is a joint activity in which shared meanings are shaped in interaction; it would seem that conversational dialogue is a peculiarly human mode of structural coupling. The speech of neither party alone constitutes the conversation; it is their joint, reciprocally unfolding speech through which meaning emerges. Where two individuals interact closely over time the dynamic of structural coupling can be seen as shaping their relationship. Each partner anticipates certain patterns of behaviour from the other, and adapts to these; thus behaviour of each is shaped by adaptations of and to the other. The role of dialogue in this co-adaptation is complex; it operates at the level of lexical meanings, speech acts, and coordination of meanings, as well as at the level of coordinating joint actions. Through dialogue partners develop a more-or-less explicit objectification of their relationship.

Dyadic roles

Clark has been particularly concerned to specify what it is that permits participants in conversation to understand each other and gain closure on joint meanings. He uses the term 'grounding' to cover the several kinds of shared information and experience that permit meaningful conversation. A large component of 'grounding' is shared experience and shared 'culture' that make it possible for participants to roughly predict what the other is likely to mean by what s/he says. While natural conversations among acquaintances tend to have a potentially very open form, certain kinds of dialogue such as greetings, politeness forms, and questions are highly predictable, with precisely specified scripts. However probably most conversations fall somewhere between these two extremes of openness and closure. These are often embedded in ongoing relationships which tend to be socioculturally framed—by family ties, work settings, friends, professional encounters with doctors, teachers, shop assistants, and so on. These are often 'role relationships' in the sense that they are instrumentally defined (at least in part), with the behaviour of each member of the role dyad seen by actors as reciprocally symbiotic in relation to the other.

At the time when anthropologists enter a community to study it, they find certain role dyads that are culturally specified, enduring dyadic relations. As such they are socioculturally constructed 'artefacts' — 'things in the world'. Like spoken language itself, while roles are 'things in the world', they must be learned by each individual member of a community. Though certain roles can be formally taught (occupational roles for instance), many, such as kin roles and friendship roles, are learned through observation and informal practice.

Where do roles 'come from'?

Ethologists recognise a few roles in primate societies: dominant/subordinate males, mother/son and mother/daughter roles, males who act as lookouts for the group (see de Waal 1982; Hinde (ed.) 1983). These roles are based on patterned reciprocal behaviour—the consequence of structural coupling. Individuals move into and out of such roles. They can be said to exist independently of particular individuals who may fill them at a given time. Dominance hierarchies are a clear case. Again, to the extent that within a band all mothers and daughters respond to ecological, biological, and social constraints (like maternal rank) in much the same ways, the 'mother–daughter' roles will be similar.

What might be the effect of spoken language on primate role dynamics? At the level of structural coupling, dialogue mediates interpersonal behaviour. Dialogue is itself a powerful mode of structural coupling, requiring the continual negotiation of joint meanings. At the same time, intentions, beliefs, wishes, and control are explicitly expressed verbally. These new kinds of information must make the cognitive modelling of own and other's social interdependence more effective. And since languaging is a mode of acting as well as speaking, languaging becomes a mode for securing *joint action* as well as for negotiating meanings.

Names and roles

Spoken languages, however, are not dyadic creations. Creating a shared lexicon, establishing conventions for linking words, distinguishing between names and actions, embedding clauses—these likely stages in the emergence of proto-language involve communities of speakers all 'doing languaging' with each other (see Hutchins and Hazlehurst 1995). This also means finding ways of referring to others. Names and kin terms (often used as names) are found in all human societies thus far studied. Indeed Robin Fox has suggested

that kin terms are among the very few human universals (1980). The everyday
use of kin terms has two powerful effects on social life. Because kin terms are
inherently dyadic, their use locates members of the community with respect to
other members. But even with a very simple kin terminology, dyads are linked
to other dyads. Mothers link to sons and to daughters; daughters link to sons,
and to other daughters; mothers link to husband/fathers; mother's mothers link
to daughter's daughters, and so on.

Further, once there is a term 'mother' or 'father' then these become names
of roles as well as for individual mothers and fathers. Rights and obligations
may then be recognised as applying not only to separate individual members of
structurally coupled dyads, but may become similar for all who hold these
roles. When spoken language permitted the naming of roles, expectations
generated in dyadic relations could be applied to all community members
acting in these roles. And of course in many small-scale societies kin terms
are used for categories of relative, what anthropologists call a classificatory
terminology; in many patrilineal societies all of the men in a patrilineage of the
father's generation are 'fathers'.

Three mechanisms may have led to such generalising of roles within a
community. First, whatever sociocognitive procedure had emerged for the
creation of shared lexical items would presumably also give rise to shared
meanings for role terms (Hutchins and Hazlehurst 1995). Second, individuals
move through kin roles occupying sequentially, and later simultaneously, child
roles, sibling roles, parent roles, spouse roles, parent's sibling roles, and parent's
parent roles. Thus nearly all members of the community come to share experience of all the kin roles. Eventually virtually everyone has acted as child to
parent, sibling to sibling, mother/father to child, husband/wife to wife/husband,
child to parent's sibling, parent's sibling to sibling's child, parent's parent to
child's child. Finally, the use of kin terms for reference and address within the
community places individuals within a network of kin roles vis-à-vis other
members of the community. This requires individual members of role dyads
to place themselves in relation to other dyads: brother to a sister who is also
mother of a child, that is a mother's brother; mother of a daughter who is wife to
a husband, that is a mother-in-law, etc. G. H. Mead (1967) pointed out that
hearing ourselves speaking permits us to take the roles of others vis-à-vis
ourselves, and see ourselves through others' eyes. This is very close to what
psychologists call 'decentering' — being able to understand a problem not just
from our own position, 'in the centre', but also from the point of view of another
actor. Thus sons gain an understanding of what it is to be a father; and fathers'
treatment of their sons draws on their own experience as sons. This capacity for
decentering must be critical for the cognitive modelling of other people's role-
contingent responses to our actions.

In a community built of overlapping kin roles, then, individuals live in a socioculturally structured world. We need not invoke some abstract thing called 'society', or even 'social structure' that is independent of individuals. Nor fall back on a generic 'learning of roles'. Individuals' experience of dyadic role interactions recreates these roles for all participants. And living in a sociocultural world of overlapping roles brought to life in everyday conversations and interactions knits together the experiences of each individual occupying several roles, and the sharing of these experiences with others in same and complementary roles.

Expectations, routines, 'rules', and accountability

The ethnomethodologist Howard Garfinkel (1967) was a cunning genius at using quasi-natural experiments to defamiliarise the familiar.[12] In one key study he asked his students to pick a time when they were doing ordinary things with a friend and simply respond to all of the friend's utterances with 'What do you mean?' [We can recognise this as Clark's Track 2 request for joint closure on meaning.] At first the friend would respond with an explanation, but as the question continued to be asked, responses became angry, and the conversation was often abruptly broken off with exclamations like 'What's wrong with you? You must be mad!' What is happening here? Garfinkel shows that everyday interactions generate implicit expectations of patterned reciprocities. Actors hold each other accountable for honouring these implicit expectations. When one actor violates these the other seeks to restore the familiar pattern, using progressively more focused and eventually antagonistic procedures. Garfinkel argues that it is the predictability of everyday interchanges that makes social interaction possible, and by continuing to conform to reciprocal expectations actors mutually construct a shared social world.

These responses to violation of implicit expectations are not necessarily on a conscious level. Heritage (1990/1) and Drew (1995) speak of 'routinized cognitive strategies'; they are also *shared* cognitive strategies, since the other's response tends to restore the expected pattern of behaviour. In a sense they are 'knowledge structures' in individual heads (see papers in Fletcher and Fitness (eds.) 1996). But they are also sociocultural artefacts since they are shaped by expectations linked to social roles.

Roles and 'rules'

In small-scale societies where role behaviour is publicly observable and roles replicated and shared, accountability for expected role behaviour takes more

---

[12] I am indebted to Paul Sant Cassia for this penetrating characterisation of Garfinkel's project.

explicit forms. In Gonja (northern Ghana) for instance, a woman whose husband fails to provide food may complain loudly, thus rendering him accountable to others—their children, her mother-in-law. Shaming him in this way may send him off to the farm, with no further sanction. If not, the mother-in-law may send food from her own fire, or rebuke her son directly (E. N. Goody, fieldnotes). Such actions may well make good the shortage of food. But they also serve to make explicit the norm that husbands are accountable for providing food for their families. John Haviland's (1977) ethnography of the Zinacantan Maya shows the power of gossip to assert norms and indeed he suggests that here gossip serves to select among implicit norms those appropriate for sanctioning behaviour in particular instances. In these examples we see 'rules' emerging from behaviour. Of course most societies also have formal institutions for holding actors accountable for rights and duties associated with roles: in Gonja these include the power of the head of a kin group over those under his authority, and the chief's court; and today of course local government courts. Radcliffe-Brown's paper on 'Social sanctions' (1952*d*) deals deftly with the domains of informal and formal sanctions.

VII. Emergent Roles and Rules: Mother's Brothers and Sister's Sons in African Patrilineal Societies

Starting from the view of social intelligence as the primate capacity to cognitively model others' contingent responses to goal-directed acts, I have explored some implications of the gradual attainment of spoken language for the emergence of roles and rules. It may be useful to see the structural coupling of role dyads as a basic mechanism through which speech-in-dialogue patterns interaction. And it must be axiomatic that the patterning of role dyadic interaction makes contingent responses more predictable, and thus the cognitive modelling of interaction, social intelligence, more efficient.

How can such a view contribute to an understanding of 'joking relations' between mother's brothers and sister's sons in patrilineal African societies?

First, what are the role dyads involved? Here we must consider the actors' view of the kin relationship in relation to lineage membership, siblingship, etc. Resources and affective ties are indicated in brackets.

There are two sorts of questions to be asked about the joking relationships between mother's brothers and sister's sons that have been reported for many African patrilineal societies: first, why are they characterised by snatching of property and 'privileged aggression'? And second, how is it that behaviour which seems so particularly personal has come to be patterned in similar ways,

Father/son [same patrilineage → jural authority; property;
socialisation affect, reciprocities of rearing]

mother/son (different patrilineage → nurturance; socialisation
affect; reciprocities of rearing)

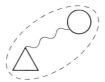

mother/mother's brother (same patrilineage → jural authority;
property rights; co-socialisation affect)

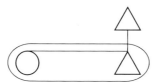

Mother's brother/sister's son (different patrilineage → No jural
authority; residual property rights; socialisation affect)

Note: → Stands for 'entails, leads to'

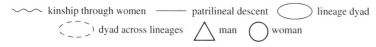

Figure 1.   Role dyads influencing mother's brother–sister's son joking relationship.

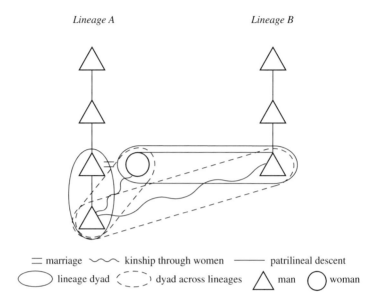

Father/son (same patrilineage → jural authority; property; socialisation affect, reciprocities of rearing)

Mother/son (different patrilineage → nurturance; socialisation affect; reciprocities of rearing)

Mother/mother's brother (same patrilineage → jural authority; property rights; co-socialisation affect)

Mother's brother/sister's son (different patrilineage → No jural authority; residual property rights; socialisation affect)

* → stands for 'entails, leads to'

Figure 2. Superimposed dyadic roles involved in mother's brother–sister's son relationship.

both within a single society and in many unrelated patrilineal societies? Both kinds of question require us to look at the whole complex of role dyads as a single network.

Why are these joking relationships characterised by snatching of the mother's brother's property?

Here we can follow the view developed by Jack Goody (1969) that in patri-lineal societies, snatching property from the mother's brother is an assertion of the rights which a youth would have had to his mother's lineage property *if she had been a man*. Due to the accident of birth which made his mother a woman, he is denied full rights to her lineage property which passes only through sons, not through daughters. But he is still a 'sister's child' and has other ritual and customary rights and duties with respect to her lineage kin. The fact that his mother's agnates *may not* refuse him the items he takes acknowledges, admits publicly, that he does have residual rights in their estate. In matrilineal societies where men do have rights to property through their mothers, youths do not 'snatch' property from their mother's brothers; they have direct jural rights to this property.

Why are these joking relationships characterised by 'joking' and privileged aggresion?

Radcliffe-Brown (1952*a,b,c*) refers to sister's sons' snatching of property and freedom to use verbal insults as 'privileged disrespect'/'hostility' and to the role dyad as a 'joking relationship'. Why should the joking and privileged aggression be so intimately linked?

There are two issues here. Why is it joking and aggression that are so closely related rather than some other behaviour? And why should such joking relationships be found between maternal uncle and nephew in patrilineal societies?

Joking and aggression

In northern Ghana Birifor boys often engage in play-fighting; not infrequently this switches into angry fighting which adults ignore unless weapons become involved. Birifor youths and men *need* to be skilled fighters. In the gangs of boys who spent their days looking after cattle, wrestling was used to establish an internal hierarchy, with the boy who could best all the others recognised as the 'chief'; this is striking in an 'egalitarian' society in which no chiefs were recognised (E. N. Goody 1993). Men are quick to take offence, and a man who is not ready to defend himself and others is generally despised. At large gatherings such as funerals and festivals adult men from the same patrilineage sit together by the path leading to their home village, their bows over their shoulders, ready in case a fight breaks out. An important elder of Baale village was killed in such a funeral fight last year. Fighting is real and dangerous.

The striking thing about formal joking relations is that neither partner is *permitted* to become angry. Usually the joking is relished, and joking partners and observers enter wholeheartedly into the spirit of the game. But in Gonja I have seen two joking partners shift suddenly from playful to angry fighting. At this point the bystanders quickly intervened. Some shouted even more outrageous insults, thus exaggerating the joking element; while several strong young men pulled the two apart, remonstrating—'Didn't they know they were joking partners?' 'What did they mean by allowing themselves to fight?' Significantly, a fight can easily polarise the men in a large gathering into opposing camps. What begins as a fight between two individuals can become a real battle. Institutionalisation of the joking relationship provides a mandatory mechanism for intervention in such a situation, and of switching back from an angry mode to the joking mode.

This dynamic was acted out one morning as I sat with some Gonja women. An old woman began teasing her granddaughter (of about five years) by pinching her. Finally the little girl began to cry, at which her mother and the other women shouted with laughter. A look of complete confusion came over the girl's face. But the women continued to laugh—gently, not in a taunting way. So the girl herself started to laugh. When I asked why the woman had pinched her own granddaughter, she explained that they were joking partners, and the girl had to be taught not to be angry, but to laugh instead. And indeed the women did not *allow* her to take offence; they laughed *with* her (not *at* her), and she soon joined in.

It would seem that there are potentially indistinct boundaries between play, playful aggression, and aggressive fighting. Where people are interdependent economically, politically, and ritually, and must live closely together, quarrels are inevitable. Were open fighting to result this could drastically disrupt social life. Joking relationships do not, of course, either prevent or ultimately settle quarrels. But they do provide a mechanism for redefining aggression as 'playful' and 'not serious'. Further, individuals in dyadic joking relations, joking partners, come to expect to relate to each other in playful, non-aggressive ways. And every joking episode recreates the joking idiom for actors and observers.

Why in patrilineal societies should the dyad 'mother's brother' and 'sister's son' be defined as a joking relationship?

Here it is useful to consider again the interaction among the full set of role dyads concerned in the mother's brother–sister's son joking relationship.

In patrilineal societies a youth and his father are members of the same jural group. Neither aggression nor joking are permitted, thinkable, from a son to his fathers. Bakhtin (1984) has argued that laughter is not allowed in authority relations; laughter here is subversive. There is little ambiguity about patterns of authority between generations within the patrilineage. However a youth and his mother's brothers do not belong to the same jural group. In terms of

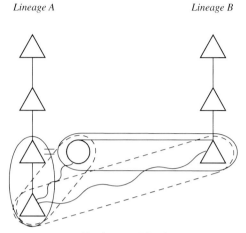

For key see Fig. 2.

Figure 3.   Superimposed dyadic roles involved in mother's brother–sister's son relationship.

generation difference, the mother's brother has authority over his sister's son. But he has no *formal, jural* authority over a member of a different patrilineage. Here there is ample room for ambiguity, as Radcliffe-Brown makes explicit. If we add to this the ambiguity inherent in the youth's submerged claims to the mother's brother's lineage property, then this dyad is one with a high level of potential friction. The contested claims of the sister's son to property, and of the mother's brother to authority, might easily lead to confrontation and an aggressive response, to a fight between the two which might quickly extend to the men of the two lineages. In Radcliffe-Brown's terms these are 'disjunctive' forces operating on the role dyad. He also writes eloquently of the expressions of 'conjunction' in friendliness and mutual aid. In the southern African patrilineal societies discussed in his papers conjunction is expressed through the mother's brother's assistance with the provision of a cow for bridewealth or for a sacrifice necessitated by sickness or misfortune. For the sister's son is still a 'child' of his mother's patrilineal ancestors, for whom he has to perform important ritual services, and on whom he depends in part for health and protection. Maternal patriclansfolk need their sisters' sons, and young men need their mother's male agnates. It is in this role dyad that behaviour is pre-emptively defined as a joking relation, within which the participants are simply not permitted, and do not permit themselves, to fight.

Roles and rules as emergent forms

The next question, of course, is how does friction between one set of individuals in a particular role dyad come to be managed in the same way by others in the same roles? In a way this is an impossible question to answer, since we cannot observe the process of institutionalisation as it happens. Perhaps the fundamental element is the efficacy of joking as a way of managing conflict. Here individual personality differences may well be critical. Some individuals are skilled at managing social relations and may use joking in an *ad hoc* way to handle conflict. However, joking is not a solitary form—it is pre-eminently dialogic; it takes two to joke. The response is as necessary as the initial remark. Indeed elaborate joking may extend through many exchanges of challenge and response. In Zincantan Maya society verbal humour includes both 'banter' (teasing, punning, playing with word meanings) and 'joking': 'Just crazy talk: both people answer each other in the same way' [translation of interview]. . . . 'Both parties to the exchange are consciously funny and/or insulting as they talk' (Haviland 1977: 189). Banter and joking occur in conversations, and are prominent in gossip. However with apparently one exception they are dyadic only in the sense that dialogue is. Joking associated with institutionalised roles appears to be limited to ritual entertainers in Cargo ceremonies. Haviland comments that some Zinecantans are known as unable to sustain a joking exchange—they just sit embarrassed, saying nothing. Others are proud of their skill at joining in joking with the Cargo ceremony musicians. It seems that where joking relations are not formally linked to role dyads individual differences in skill at joking are needed for participation.

However, where joking relations are formalised they often become a communicative genre with scripts for joking. There are slots for openings and retorts into which participants may put either standard forms or invented variations. Joking dialogue is a basic mode of dyadic interaction. In Gonja cross-cousins[13] (*kitcherpo*) are the most prominent of the prescriptively defined joking partners. They are expected to joke, often take great delight in doing so, and of course may not fight. Just *what* is considered funny is highly socioculturally constrained. In Gonja cross-sex joking tends to play with gender role incompetence (E. Goody 1978*b*). Here there is ample scope for veiled aggression, but it must be taken as hugely funny. A critical component then is the labelling of the role dynamic as 'joking'.

Once there are named joking relations in a given society they can be adapted to newly appearing problematic relations. This is a likely pattern underlying the emergence of joking in the textile industry of Daboya (Gonja). Here the counterpoised vectors of conjunction/disjunction operate in the role dyad of trader and weaver (who are usually of different ethnic origin). The

---

[13] 'Cross-cousin' is an anthropological term for the children of opposite sex siblings, children of a brother and sister. Children of same-sex siblings are termed 'parallel cousins'. In Gonja, as in many societies, the term is applied to classificatory relatives as well as to direct children of full siblings.

weavers depend on itinerant traders to buy their cloth, while the high quality of this cloth brings traders into this remote centre. Both weavers and traders seek a profitable deal. The joking dialogue genre is often used to manage these conflicting interests. The roles of traders and weavers are named, but not typified as a joking relationship; joking is not prescriptive. Rather, both partners appear to draw on the 'rules' of prescriptive joking relationships to contain their quite aggressive bargaining without jeopardising the long-term trading ties on which both depend. This is a *de facto* joking relationship. It is quite different from the prescriptive joking which is often found between members of neighbouring ethnic groups. Here close proximity (often with intermarriage) requires cooperation and engenders pressures for conjunction; competition— for land, grazing and water, and marriageable women—fuels disjunctive forces (Radcliffe-Brown 1952*b*, 1952*c*). Joking is not left to individual initiative, but enjoined on all members of each group. Existing prescriptive joking relations within the society would be readily adapted to manage the inevitable interpersonal tensions between groups in such a situation.

The emergence of a joking relationship

This ethnography and analysis can be seen as sketching a possible trajectory for the emergence of a dyadic joking role relationship, with a progression from individual behaviour to institutionalised roles and rules. Individual joking may (or may not) lead to idiosyncratic dyadic joking; this may (or may not) lead to systematic *de facto* dyadic joking in roles characterised by both conjunction and disjunction; systematic dyadic joking may (or may not) lead to the 'typification' and labelling of the roles as a 'joking relationship'; this typification of the joking relationship may (or may not) lead to the emergence of a rule which requires joking and forbids fighting between members of the role dyad. It is almost certainly misleading to place the emergence of a rule last, since the emergence of rules is also a gradual process. Even with the appearance of patterned joking in a single dyad the partners would implicitly hold each other accountable for responding in the expected joking fashion. The explicitness of the rule and the mode of managing accountability (informal and formal sanctions) move from the private to the public sphere along the trajectory.

VIII. Conclusions: Languaging, Accountability, Dyadic Roles and Social Intelligence

Haviland (1977) gives a brilliant account of the emergence of rules in the activity of Zinacantec gossip about the behaviour of absent individuals. In

Individual joking to manage conflict may →

Idiosyncratic dyadic joking may →

Systematic dyadic joking in a role dyad entailing ambivalent structured conflict may →

'Typification' and labelling of 'joking role relationship' may →

'Rule' prescribing joking relationship in typified role dyad.

Note: → stands for 'entails, leads to'

Figure 4.   Emergence of avunculate joking relations in patrilineal African societies

talking, gossiping, about others' behaviour it is described, typified, and evaluated. Haviland insists that gossip is 'all about rules'—but that these rules are shared but malleable, morally loaded and yet manipulated in terms of relations between gossip and audience (especially ibid. 148–70). He speaks of the 'dialogue' between gossip and interlocutor. The latter's responses are integral to the emergence of a gossip account: to identification of the object, to description of the events concerned, and to the evaluation of the object's actions. In gossip rules emerge as explicit in particular contexts. The wide participation in the gossip which makes behaviour accountable to these morally weighted rules must shape people's own future choices of how to act. It is striking that in Haviland's gossip texts the rules are virtually always framed in terms of social roles: 'old men', holders of Cargo offices, wives and husbands, fathers and sons, suitors and the girls they court. Thus it is pre-eminently rules concerning role behaviour which are affirmed and shaped by gossip.

In both gossip and joking relations humans *use* language to employ lexical meanings and socioculturally constructed language genre in the management of social interaction. Like monkeys and apes, humans seek to understand the intentions of those they live closely with, and to predict the likely interpretations of their actions by others. We might term this basic social intelligence. But only humans have the tool of spoken language with which to communicate shared meanings and to negotiate these in dialogue. This new tool, as I have tried to show, fundamentally changes the nature of human social intelligence because the components of cognitive modelling of others' intentions are both in individual heads and shared among members of the language community. Human intelligence has become social in an entirely new sense; the components for cognitive modelling are social products—lexicon, grammar, communicative genre, roles, and rules.

The language tool would seem to have been gradually constructed over the millennia in communities of speakers *through the use of the language tool itself* (Foley 1997). How was this possible? There are some clues. First, there is a striking contrast between the capacities of monkeys and apes for joint attention to communicative meaning[14] and the central role of joint attention in both the child's learning to talk and the use of language in dialogue. Joint attention appears to be necessary to establish shared lexical meanings (e.g. Hutchins and Hazlehurst 1995) which was probably the basis of early proto-language (Foley 1997). It would seem that a major change in mechanisms for joint attention occurred early in the emergence of spoken language. Perhaps this was mediated by cooperation in the production and use of tools. Perhaps the 'work' of establishing the shared meanings of early proto-language enhanced mechanisms for joint attention, which were also used for cooperation in tool use and production. Perhaps the joint attention involved in skills of early language and tool use supported each other.

Next, Foley's model of possible stages in the development of spoken language notes the likely recurrence of cognitive overload as vocabularies expanded, strings of words in an utterance became longer, modifiers were attached to nouns and to verbs, and so on (Foley 1997, ch. 2). Cognitive overload could have led both to increasing brain size and complexity, and to the emergence of *de facto* shared rules for word order and hierarchical structures of grammar. Note, however, that such increasing complexity would make even greater demands on joint attention to the using of language.

Finally, analysis of how meaning is constructed in everyday conversation shows this to be a continuously emergent joint process between speakers. Meaning is not simply coded in the lexical content of words. It is shaped, negotiated, and redefined through the dialogue they make together. Clark's analysis emphasises the primacy of joint closure by speakers on what each means and intends to mean. Levinson's (1995) view is very similar. Both Clark and Levinson stress that arriving at joint closure is far more difficult than it seems, since typically a great many possible alternative meanings exist. The importance of joint closure on conversational meaning is expressed in Grice's insistence that a speaker's meaning is only accomplished when what he intends to communicate is recognised by the addressee. '*Signaling and recognizing in communicative acts are participatory acts*' [in Clark's sense that participatory acts are individual contributions which together constitute the whole act]. 'The

---

[14] Dorothy Cheney in her Tanner Lectures on *The evolution of mind and language* and participants in the following seminar agreed that neither monkeys or apes are good at *joint* attention (Clare Hall, Cambridge, March 1997). Monkeys can follow another's gaze but have difficulty in pointing to the object of gaze. Chimpanzees have been observed to both follow another's gaze and point at object of joint gaze. But these are language-trained chimps living with humans. Some participants raised the question of how much of this kind of skill is taught by humans. There appears to be no evidence at all that in the wild monkeys or apes focus attention jointly on determining the meaning of signs.

joint act of one person signaling another and the second recognizing what the first meant is what I will call a *communicative act*' (italics in the original, Clark 1996: 130). But it is the speaker's intention, as well as the lexical meaning which must be recognised. The difficulty for the speaker of making sure that his intention is recognised is expressed in the continual Track 2 messages 'Do you understand?' (see above). Simple everyday conversation requires constant work at joint closure on understanding of each others' intentions. Again close joint attention is the prerequisite for using spoken language. This mutual attention is a prerequisite of the communicative act, itself only possible through the joint contribution of the participatory acts of both speakers.

Such a view of the emergence of spoken language entails a paradox. While early proto-language may have consisted simply of 'words', as it developed proto-grammar would have emerged, and finally complex grammar and pho-nemes. As language developed it became increasingly complex, increasingly rule-bound. The new resources of grammar etc. should have made it much easier to express meaning clearly in conversation, particularly as they became routinised and cognitively expressed. Yet even with these resources, today the making and understanding of meaning in conversation is extremely compli-cated. It still requires close joint attention and synchronisation of the indivi-dual participatory communicative acts which permit joint closure on the understanding of mutual intentions. It is as if the sociocognitive procedures for securing mutual closure on intentions in dialogue have become increa-sinlgy finely tuned to exploit the additional information made available by larger vocabularies and more complex grammar. Spoken language, roles and rules are sociocultural products, used as tools for thinking and acting with. First writing, and now computers have stretched the domain of dialogue far beyond face-to-face interaction. But we still have 'conversations' in letters and e-mail with kin, friends and colleagues—and with our computers.

IX. Coda

Although Radcliffe-Brown's papers on Joking Relations were written between 1924 and 1949, they are full of insights which still invite exploration through recent theoretical perspectives. His identification of the power of formal joking as a means to constrain relationships raises questions concerning the dyadic nature of humour. This fits well into the action perspective of language as the joint product of dialogue between speakers. For language is used in dyads and social roles are enacted in dyads. Other questions posed by Radcliffe-Brown's ideas include:

How is the cognitive ability to model alternative roles related to the human capacity for 'pretending' and for pretend role play?

The 'decentering' of individual perspectives in dyadic roles is mediated by spoken language. Recent work on autism suggests that there is a particularly human capacity to 'pretend' that things are other than they are; to imagine counter-factual situations (Leslie 1987). Whatever the cognitive deficit of autistic children is, it is associated with difficulty with pretending. Empirically, children in Ghana as well as in the West learn adult roles through pretend play (E. N. Goody 1993). It is as though when the playing of a variety of social roles is combined with the capacity to mentally model others' contingent actions, a cognitive schema is created for 'pretending'. It would be interesting to know whether autistic children also have problems with role play, and how their use of language is related to decentering.

Are joking relations still being created in modern 'global' society?

'Telling a joke' to a western audience is very different from the taunting challenge questions exchanged between Gonja joking partners. Under what conditions does humour reside in the 'story' and when in playing on the expectations of dyadic roles? For ironically, it could be argued that dyadic relationships are increasingly coming to characterise our own societies. The institutions of industry and of the state have become massive and remote from individual experience. We are each left mainly with dyadic roles—of family, neighbours, service relationships, and work. Mediating structures such as the patrilineages and age grades of traditional small-scale societies are largely absent. Will the dialogue skills which enabled us to evolve early language—and early society—still be able to help us adapt dyadic roles to a global world?

References

Austin, J. L. (1962), *How to do things with words* (Oxford).

Bakhtin, M. M. (1984), *Rabelais and his world* (Indiana UP).

Bickerton, D. (1990), *Language and species* (Chicago, Ill.).

Bowlby, J. (1969), *Attachment and Loss: Vol 1. Attachment* (Harmondsworth, England).

Brown, P. (1995), 'Politeness strategies and the attribution of intentions: the case of Tzeltal irony', in E. N. Goody (ed.), *Social intelligence and interaction* (Cambridge).

Brown, P. and Levinson, S. C. (1987 [1978]), *Politeness: some universals in language usage* (Cambridge).

Bruner, J. S. (1978), 'From communication to language: a psychological perspective', in I. Markova (ed.), *The social context of language* (Chichester).

Byrne, R. and Whiten, A. (1988) (eds.), *Machiavellian intelligence: Social expertise and the evolution of intellect in monkeys, apes and humans* (Oxford).

Carrithers, M. (1992), *Why humans have cultures: Explaining anthropology and social diversity* (Oxford).

Cheney, D. (1997) *The evolution of mind and language*, Tanner Lectures, Clare Hall, University of Cambridge. Forthcoming.

Chomsky, N. (1957), *Syntactic structures* (The Hague).

Clark, H. H. (1996), *Using language* (Cambridge).

Donald, M. (1991), *The origins of modern mind: three stages in the evolution of culture and cognition* (Cambridge, Mass.).

Drew, P. (1995), 'Interaction sequences and anticipatory interactive planning', in E. N. Goody (ed.), *Social intelligence and interaction* (Cambridge).

Dunbar, R. I. M. (1993), 'Coevolution of neocortical size, group size and language in humans', *Behavioural and Brain Sciences*, 16: 681–735.

Fletcher, G. O. and Fitness, J. (1996) (eds.), *Knowledge structures in close relationships* (Mahwah, NJ).

Foley, W. (1997), *Anthropological linguistics* (Oxford).

Fortes, M. (1983), *Rules and the emergence of society*, Occasional paper No. 39 (Royal Anthropological Institute, London).

Fox, R. (1980), *The red lamp of incest* (London).

Garfinkel, H. (1967), *Studies in ethnomethodology* (Englewood Cliffs, NJ).

Goffman, E. (1959), *The presentation of self in everyday life* (New York).

Good, D. (1995), 'Where does foresight end and hindsight begin?' in E. N. Goody (ed.), *Social intelligence and interaction* (Cambridge).

Goody, E. N. (1978*a*), 'Introduction', in E. N. Goody (ed.), *Questions and politeness: strategies in social interaction* (Cambridge).

—— (1978*b*) 'Towards a theory of questions', in E. N. Goody (ed.), *Questions and politeness: strategies in social interaction* (Cambridge).

—— (1993), 'Informal learning of adult roles in Baale', in M. Fieloux and J. Lombard with J-M. Kambou-Ferrands (eds.), *Images d'Afrique et Sciences sociales: Les pays lobi, birifor et dagara.* (Paris).

—— (ed.) (1995), *Social intelligence and interaction: Expressions and implications of the social bias in human intelligence* (Cambridge).

—— (forthcoming), 'Social intelligence and language: another Rubicon?' in A. Whiten and R. Byrne (eds.), *Machiavellian intelligence II* (Cambridge).

Goody, J. (1969), 'The mother's brother and the sister's son in West Africa', in *Comparative studies in kinship* (Stanford, Calif.).

Grice, H. P. (1957), 'Meaning', *Philosophical Review*, 66: 377–88.

Haviland, J. B. (1977), *Gossip, reputation, and knowledge in Zinacantan* (Chicago).

Heider, F. (1958), *The psychology of interpersonal relations* (New York).

Heritage, J. (1984), *Garfinkel and ethnomethodology* (Cambridge).

—— (1990/91), 'Intention, meaning and strategy: observations on constraints in interactional analysis', *Research in language and Social Interaction*, 24: 311–22.

Hinde, R. A. (1983) (ed.), *Primate social relationships* (Oxford).

Homans, G. C. and Schneider, D. M. (1955), *Marriage, authority and final causes* (Glencoe, Ill.).

Humphrey, N. K. (1976), 'The social function of intellect', in P. P. G. Bateson and R. A. Hine (eds.), *Growing points in ethology* (Cambridge).

Hutchins, E. and Hazlehurst, B (1995), 'How to invent a shared lexicon: the emergence of shared form-meaning mappings in interaction', in E. N. Goody (ed.), *Social intelligence and interaction* (Cambridge).

Kelley, H. H. (1979), *Interpersonal relationships: their structure and process* (Hillsdale, NJ).

Lieberman, P. (1991), *Uniquely human: the evolution of speech, thought and selfless behaviour* (Cambridge, Mass.).

Leslie, A. M. (1987), 'Pretence and representation in infancy: the origins of "theory of mind"', *Psychological Review*, 94: 412–26.

Levinson, S. C. (1995), 'Interactional biases in human thinking', in E. N. Goody (ed.), *Social intelligence and interaction* (Cambridge).

Lewis, D. K. (1969), *Convention: a philosophical study* (Cambridge, Mass.).

Maturana, H. and Varela, F. J. (1987), *The tree of knowledge: the biological roots of human understanding* (Boston).

Mead, G. H. (1967 [1934]), *Mind, self and society* (Chicago).

Mellars, P. (1996), 'Symbolism, language and the Neanderthal mind', in P. Mellars and K. Gibsom (eds.), *Modelling the early human mind* (Exeter).

Needham, R. (1962), *Structure and sentiment* (Chicago).

Thibault, J. W. and Kelley, H. H. (1959), *The social psychology of groups* (New York).

Radcliffe-Brown, A. R. (1952*a*), 'The mother's brother in South Africa', in *Structure and function in primitive society*, pp. 15–31 (London).

Radcliffe-Brown, A. R. (1952*b*), 'On joking relationships', in *Structure and function in primitive society*, pp. 90–104 (London).

Radcliffe-Brown, A. R. (1952*c*), 'A further note on joking relationships', in *Structure and function in primitive society*, pp. 105–16 (London).

Radcliffe-Brown, A. R. (1952*d*), 'Social sanctions', in *Structure and function in primitive society*, pp. 203–11 (London).

Sacks, H., Schegloff, E. A., and Jefferson, G. (1974), 'A simplest systematics for the organization of turn-taking in conversation', *Language*, 50: 696–735.

Schelling, T. (1960), *The strategy of conflict* (Cambridge, Mass.).

Steeck, J. (1995) 'On projection', in E. N. Goody (ed.), *Social intelligence and interaction* (Cambridge).

Trevarthen, C. B. (1979), 'Communication and cooperation in early infancy: a description of primary intersubjectivity', in M. von Cronach, K. Foppa, W. Lepinies and D. Ploog (eds.), *Human ethology: claims and limits of a new discipline* (Cambridge).

de Waal, F. (1982), *Chimpanzee politics* (Baltimore, Johns Hopkins).

Whiten, A. and Byrne, R. (eds.), (forthcoming), *Machiavelliann intelligence II* (Cambridge).

INAUGURAL BRITISH ACADEMY LECTURE

Plagiarism

CHRISTOPHER RICKS
Boston University
Fellow of the Academy

WHEN THE PRESIDENT—the previous President—of the British Academy invited me to give this lecture, I took up the terms in which he had written, and proposed the subject of plagiarism: 'It relates to "scholarly debate"; it has "general public interest"; and I even like the dark thought that it's something "the Academy exists to promote" . . .'. Judge then of my pleasure when, in his Presidential Address for 1997, the President announced that the lecture would be 'on "Plagiarism", not a subject which the Academy exists to promote, but one in which we all have an interest'.[1]

'SIR,—I am concerned to see your able correspondent W. H. throwing away his valuable time on so threadbare a topic as Plagiarism': Thomas De Quincey, or probably he,[2] in 1827. 'Of plagiarism, little new can be written': Hillel Schwartz, *The Culture of the Copy* (1996).[3]

The news this very day (10 February 1998) in *The Times* is of a student's going to the High Court

> to try to force Cambridge University to award him a degree after he was accused of cheating. Kamran Beg is believed to be the first student to challenge the university in court over allegations that he plagiarised part of an essay in his postgraduate finance degree at Trinity College. Mr Beg's

[1] I am grateful to the friends who commented on a draft: Kenneth Haynes, Marcia Karp, Michael Prince, Lisa Rodensky, and Christopher Wilkins.
[2] To the Editor of the *Saturday Evening Post*, 3 November 1827; *New Essays by De Quincey* (1966), ed. Stuart M. Tave, p. 181.
[3] Hillel Schwartz, *The Culture of the Copy* (1996), p. 311.

Proceedings of the British Academy, **97**, 149–168. © The British Academy 1998.
Read at the Academy 10 February 1998.

solicitor denied his client acted dishonestly and said he had inadvertently omitted attributions or footnotes to passages he had quoted.

Plagiarism is perennial. And annual. 1997 saw the publication here of Neal Bowers's pained book, *Words for the Taking*, the words of which were taken up in many a long review. Subtitled 'The hunt for a plagiarist', it told how some of Bowers's published poems were re-published by another, a pathological tinkerer who had many a name and a squalid criminal record. To Bowers may be added other continuing attentions. In almost every issue, *Private Eye* takes pleasure in exposing plagiarisms, and not only as the regular feature 'Just Fancy That!'. The *Sunday Telegraph* of 3 August 1997 carried a column by Jenny McCartney on the romance novelist Janet Dailey, her plagiarism and psychological problems. A very recent film, *Good Will Hunting*, currently triumphant in the cinemas of Boston Massachusetts (where the film is set), shows in an early scene the hero securing a woman's tender notice by accusing his rival of being about to plagiarise, and the closing words of the film are the retort of rueful friendship, 'He stole my line!'

So much is plagiarism in the air that when the *New Yorker* (22–29 December 1997) printed a cartoon about it (by Joseph Farris), I saw or imagined the cartoon's own doubleness: in a bookstore where there can be seen a section headed HISTORY, a man browses in the section headed PLAGIARISM. Books that are plagiarisms, I take it; but those shelves could as well consist by now of books on PLAGIARISM.

I choose this subject because it combines the enduring and the current, with a further twist: I shall argue that this dishonesty is too often exculpated by dishonesties, by evasive banter and by slippery history.

Definition, first. The *Oxford English Dictionary* rules:

> **plagiarism** The wrongful appropriation, or purloining, and publication as one's own, of the ideas, or the expression of the ideas (literary, artistic, musical, mechanical, etc.) of another.

Notice 'wrongful', as constitutive within the definition, and add, constitutive too, that—as Peter Shaw has put it (into italics)—'Throughout history the act of using the work of another *with an intent to deceive* has been branded as plagiarism.'[4]

Marcel Lafollette, in *Stealing into Print: Fraud, Plagiarism, and Misconduct in Scientific Publishing* (1992), has said of plagiarism that 'Its definition is simple'.[5] If he is, as I believe, right, why does Peter Shaw grant—too concessively—that 'There will always remain certain gray areas resistant to definition'? Because it is easy, even for someone as morally alert as Shaw, to

[4] 'Plagiary', *The American Scholar* (Summer 1982), p. 327.
[5] Marcel C. Lafollette, *Stealing into Print: Fraud, Plagiarism, and Misconduct in Scientific Publishing* (1992), p. 49.

let one thing slide into another. That the supporting evidence for the accusation of plagiarism may on occasion be elusive, insufficient, or uncertain, is not the same as thinking that the definition of plagiarism is uncertain. The gray areas may remain resistant to adjudication without being resistant to definition. It may be perfectly clear what constitutes plagiarism ('using the work of another *with an intent to deceive*') without its being clear that what faces us is truly a case of this. In his lasting book of 1928, *Literary Ethics*, H. M. Paull admits what we should all admit on occasion, 'the difficulty of deciding what is plagiarism and what is legitimate borrowing',[6] but the difficulty of deciding is not the same as the difficulty of defining. That it may in some cases be very hard to make this accusation—like many another accusation—stick, does not entail there being about the accusation anything loose.

Far from there being, as it suits some people to maintain, insuperable problems of definition, there aren't even any superable problems. The morality of the matter, which asks of us that we be against deceit and dishonesty, is clear, and is clearly defined. Those of us who believe, as to plagiarism, that nothing is more important than *not making excuses* should be more than usually careful not to permit the easy excusing that slides in with the misguided concession that the world has never been able to decide what it means by plagiarism.

One of the most adroit of the exculpators, Professor James Kincaid, wrote of plagiarism in the *New Yorker* in 1997 (20 January): 'As for defining it, we leave that to the officials—in this example, Northwestern University.' Quizzing Northwestern's sentence on the responsibilities of 'a conscientious writer', Kincaid asked: 'But how do I distinguish what I have "learned from others" from what I am "personally contributing"? If I subtract everything I have learned from others (including Mother?), what is left?'[7] These are good questions—essential questions for anyone whose profession is teaching—but only if they are genuinely questions, only if jesting Kincaid were to stay for an answer. For him, though, they are rhetorical questions, inviting abdication. Distinctions the conscientious making of which is crucial are guyed as naive nullities.

Kincaid on occasion has recourse to putting the word *original* within quotation marks, 'original', though not exactly quoting it. He does the same with 'plagiarism'. This is the usual intimation that a particular concept is a coercion by power, acquiesced in by naivety. The hermeneutics of suspicion avails itself of this punctuation of suspicion. Some of us at least, it implies, are aware that this concept—like every other concept—is implicatedly problematic; aware, too, that it is moreover not problematic at all, being nothing more than a construction, as they say, imposed by the powers that be or that were.

[6] H. M. Paull, *Literary Ethics* (1928), p. 126.
[7] *New Yorker*, 20 Jan. 1997, pp. 93–7.

Not plagiarism, then (something that people mistakenly suppose they understand); rather, 'plagiarism'. But the prophylaxis of quotation marks has itself come under suspicion lately, so the new thing is to announce that one both may be and may not be availing oneself of the nicety.

> I do not put the word 'plagiarism' in quotation marks most of the time, but perhaps those quotation marks should be imagined. . . . I have been interested, then, in cultural distinctions between legitimate and illegitimate forms of appropriation. For this reason, I may have used the term 'plagiarism' to describe a wider range of transgressive appropriations than perhaps the word ordinarily signifies.[8]

Laura J. Rosenthal, in *Playwrights and Plagiarists in Early Modern England: Gender, Authorship, Literary Property* (1996). But what may perhaps be more widely transgressive is assuredly narrower in one way: in that it eschews moral considerations. For what could be less morally open to scrutiny than the transgressive? Professor Rosenthal tells us that her purpose is 'to question differences between plagiarism, imitation, adaptation, repetition, and originality'. But rhetorical questioning leads to the required answer: that there is no difference between these things other than that power uses the opprobrious term, plagiarism, when the work emanates from those whom power dislikes. Appropriation of appropriations, saith the Preacher, appropriation of appropriations, all is appropriation.

The objection to such arguments is not that they are strongly political but that they are weakly, wizenedly, political. Professor Rosenthal's book is itself animated by a political fervour that is clearly and duly moral, but her undertaking then requires her to write as if a political reading—in her case, a reading à la Foucault—had to extirpate from a discussion of plagiarism all moral considerations. What would have to be in moral terms a matter of honesty or dishonesty (plagiarism being dishonest) is replaced—not complemented—by a matter of power, necessity, the tyrant's plea. The 'cultural distinctions between legitimate and illegitimate forms of appropriation' become a matter of nothing but 'the cultural location of the text and the position of the author',[9] instead of being among several aspects each of them germane. Rosenthal is convincing on particular injustices and prejudices, but her setting does an injustice to politics, in that the room it leaves for conscience is in the animating of the inquiry, not within the inquiry proper.

The consequence of an investigative determination that 'denaturalizes the distinction between imitation and plagiarism'[10] is that the prefix de- becomes a

---

[8] Laura J. Rosenthal, *Playwrights and Plagiarists in Early Modern England: Gender, Authorship, Literary Property* (1996), p. 10.
[9] *Playwrights and Plagiarists in Early Modern England*, p. 13.
[10] Ibid.

virus, working to demean and to degrade moral thought. That no moral position is natural does not of itself entail that moral positions are nothing but the insistences of power. Moral agreements, though not natural, may be valuable, indispensable, worthy of the respect that they have earned. That plagiarism may valuably be seen under the aspect of politics, and that politics may in turn be valuably seen under the aspect of power at the time, need not and should not issue in the denial that plagiarism asks to be seen too under the aspect of ethics. The extirpation of ethical or moral considerations by such political history is a sad loss, to political history among other needful things.

Plagiarism is a dishonesty. This can be swept to one side, leaving not the dishonest but the culturally conditioned and exclusively power-ruled illegitimate. Or it can be swept to the other side, leaving not the dishonest but— assimilating plagiarism now to copyright—the illegal.

It is natural to move to infringement of copyright when thinking of plagiarism, but crucial that one should be aware of moving. For as Paul Goldstein says in *Copyright's Highway* (1994): 'Plagiarism, which many people commonly think has to do with copyright, is not in fact a legal doctrine.'[11] In a review-article on Goldstein's book and two others (*Times Literary Supplement*, 4 July 1997), James Boyle, a professor of law, pondered 'Problems of defining the limits of copyright in the age of the Internet—and of pop-music parody'. His thoughts on intellectual property are germane to plagiarism, since intellectual property may be seen not only under a legal aspect but under a moral one. Boyle observes that 'there is considerably more dispute about the desirability, role and extent of intellectual property—even among defenders of the free market—than there was about the desirability of private property in general', and he concludes with the justified asseveration that 'intellectual-property law has become the boundary line, or perhaps the hinge, between art and commerce, between "free speech" and economic monopoly, between public culture and private property'.

The subtlety and tenacity of Boyle's thinking discredit James Kincaid's condescension to the law, setting it right; some of us, Kincaid is confident, have learnt from recent literary theory the complexities of intellectual property: 'Still, the law lumbers on as if nothing more complicated than cattle rustling were involved.'[12]

Far from lumbering, intellectual-property law is limber, well aware of the complications. But, to moral considerations the law must always offer a handshake at arm's length. For although the law is a moral matter, being distinguishable from but not distinct from justice, the law acknowledges that there is a moral world elsewhere. A pity, then, that the legal-eyed Alexander

[11] Paul Goldstein, *Copyright's Highway* (1994), p. 12.
[12] Kincaid, *New Yorker*, 20 Jan. 1997, p. 97.

Lindey, in *Plagiarism and Originality* (1952), on occasion grants too much to
the legal. 'Since any discussion of plagiarism is, from a realistic standpoint,
meaningless without reference to the legal consequences, I've devoted quite a
bit of space to court cases.'[13] Granted, legal consequences have a remarkable
realism, reality even, but it is misleading to speak as if opprobrium or disap-
proval, such as should be incurred by plagiarism, are from a realistic standpoint
meaningless. Again, Lindey writes, truly, that 'Plagiarism and infringement are
not the same thing, though they overlap', but he goes on at once to infringe the
moral sphere: 'Plagiarism covers a wider field; infringement involves more
serious consequences.'[14] It would be wrong to acquiesce in this implication
that the legal is of its nature more serious than the moral. That gambling debts
may be legally irrecoverable but are honour-bound was and is a social reality of
entire seriousness. The consequences of dishonourable behaviour have been,
and fortunately still sometimes are, no less serious than legal proceedings.

Lindey's momentary lapse has its literary counterpart, when Donald Davie
writes that 'the hymn-writer did not have copyright in his work as other authors
did; and so plagiarism is a concept that does not apply'.[15] But plagiarism is
distinguishable from infringement of copyright, and if it were *tout court* the
case—which I doubt—that plagiarism is a concept that does not apply to
hymns, this would have to be a consequence of something other than the
hymn-writer's not owning copyright. The same slide can be seen, not this
time in a lawyer or a critic but in a literary theorist. In *Hot Property: The Stakes
and Claims of Literary Originality* (1994), Françoise Meltzer sometimes lets her
attention slip. 'A good example of how originality and, therefore, plagiarism are
governed more by the character of the community than by immutable notions of
right and wrong is to be seen in the U.S. Copyright form.'[16] The legal rights and
wrongs may be manifest in the copyright form, but there are other rights and
wrongs. So it is a pity that in her firm account of the accusation of plagiarism
levelled at Paul Celan, plagiarism from Yvan Goll, Meltzer should assimilate the
moral question of plagiarism to the legal question of copyright.

> So was the widow Goll right about the most notorious of her charges? That
> is, did the phrase 'black milk' belong to her husband? The answer, of course,
> must be no. First, for a simple reason: even the American copyright form
> states that one cannot protect 'titles, names and short phrases'. It is impos-
> sible to claim the invention of so few words.[17]

[13] Alexander Lindey, *Plagiarism and Originality* (1952), p. xiii.

[14] *Plagiarism and Originality*, p. 2.

[15] *The Eighteenth-Century Hymn in England* (1993), p. 18.

[16] Françoise Meltzer, *Hot Property: The Stakes and Claims of Literary Originality* (1994),
p. 73.

[17] *Hot Property*, p. 74. Meltzer goes on: 'Moreover, Goll's poem was published in New
York in 1942, at a time (as Felstiner points out) when Celan was in a Rumanian labor camp
and "hardly likely to have seen it".'

This is muddled, muddied. That no one can legally protect short phrases is perfectly compatible with someone's justifiably claiming to have created a short phrase, and this is in turn compatible with someone else's being guilty of plagiarising a short phrase. 'Black milk' — 'schwarze Milch' — may be insufficiently remarkable as a short phrase for the charge of plagiarism to be substantiable, but there are equally short phrases which it would be worse than imprudent for me, say, to accommodate in a poem of mine without acknowledgement or allusion. T. S. Eliot offers many: 'maculate giraffe', 'sapient sutlers', 'beneficent spider', 'forgetful snow'. One could grant that none of these could be copyright while at the same time believing that the appearance of them outside Eliot might form the prima facie basis of a plagiarism charge.

To the exculpations of plagiarism that rest upon a limiting of the necessary judgment to legal judgment (breach of copyright then being the only breach that we need ponder), there have been added the exculpations that seek to call, as a witness for the defence, history. Simply: plagiarism is a recent construction in need of demystifying. For a reminder that the construction industry is booming, see *The Construction of Authorship* (1994), in a very up-to-date series called 'Post-Contemporary Interventions'.[18]

This recency claim has at once to deal with an unwelcome witness for the prosecution. Call Marcus Valerius Martialis. Martial's testimony is perfectly clear, is not at all recent, and is notarised in seven poems about plagiarism. Added to which, there is the further inconvenience, for the revisionist historian of plagiarism, that it is to Martial that we owe the very application to literary deception of the word *plagiarius*, the abductor of the child or slave of another.

> Th'art out, vile Plagiary, that dost think
> A Poet may be made at th'rate of Ink,
> And cheap-priz'd Paper; none e'er purchas'd yet
> Six or ten Penniworth of Fame or Wit:
> Get Verse unpublish'd, new-stamp'd Fancies look,
> Which th'only Father of the Virgin Book
> Knows, and keeps seal'd in his close Desk within,
> Not slubber'd yet by any ruffer Chin;
> A Book, once known, ne'r quits the Author; If
> Any lies yet unpolish'd, any stiff,
> Wanting it's Bosses, and it's Cover, do
> Get that; I've such and can be secret too.
>> He that repeats stoln Verse, and for Fame looks,
>> Must purchase Silence too as well as Books.[19]

The half-dozen other epigrams by Martial take an equally though differently sardonic tack in their contemptuous rebuking of the dishonesty of the plagiarist.

---

[18] Martha Woodmansee and Peter Jaszi (eds.), *The Construction of Authorship* (1994).
[19] Epigrams i. 66; this translation by William Cartwright was published 1651.

Since copyright is in hock to the cash-nexus and is a relatively recent invention, it would suit a certain political slant if plagiarism were a recent invention too. But what about Martial? He may get reluctantly acknowledged, but will then find himself labelled a distinctly unusual case. Revisionism knows that there is some wresting to be done, some wrestling, the Newest Laocoon. Thomas Mallon, in *Stolen Words* (1989), his study—in detail—of some central plagiarism cases, noticed that 'scholars will tie themselves up in knots exonerating Coleridge. In one book Thomas McFarland sees his thefts as being not plagiarism but "a mode of composition—composition by mosaic organization".'[20]

But then the older historians of plagiarism were sometimes off guard. H. M. Paull, for instance, after substantiating the stigma of plagiarism in classical times and thereafter, slips into misrepresenting the history that he himself tells. 'All this shows that such practices now needed an apology'; 'But perhaps the best proof that direct plagiarism was becoming discredited . . .':[21] yet Paull had shown that such practices had always needed an apology, that plagiarism had always been discredited. What, then, moved him to put such a gloss upon the history he had given? His progressivism. For Paull was committed, as his closing pages announce, to the conviction that 'on the whole there has been a distinct progress towards an unattainable ideal: unattainable whilst human nature remains unchanged. Forgery, piracy, and plagiarism, the three most considerable literary crimes, have sensibly diminished.'[22] The closing words of his book are 'contribute to the advancement of the 'race'. Paull's liberal progressivism is the fitting converse, obverse, of the prelapsarian revisionism which claims that, until the invention of the author, *circa* some time like the seventeenth century, there was no such thing as plagiarism and the deploring of it. In pious times, ere Authors did begin, before to plagiarise was made a sin . . .

Exculpations, then, have long been at work. Harold Ogden White, *Plagiarism and Imitation During the English Renaissance: A Study in Critical Distinctions* (1935), opened with a fervid denunciation of 'modern critics' for imposing the concept of plagiarism upon the past;[23] but despite his insistence that 'Englishmen from 1500–1625' were 'without any feeling analogous to the modern attitude toward plagiarism', his book is full of indictments of plagiarism, from classical and Renaissance times, that are entirely at one with what he deplores as the modern attitude toward plagiarism.[24] How does White effect

---

[20] Thomas Mallon, *Stolen Words* (1989), pp. 32–3.
[21] *Literary Ethics*, p. 110.
[22] *Literary Ethics*, p. 332.
[23] Harold Ogden White, in *Plagiarism and Imitation During the English Renaissance: A Study in Critical Distinctions* (1935), p. 202.
[24] See also Schwartz, *The Culture of the Copy*, p. 311.

this? By the simple expedient of substituting for the word plagiarism the word piracy.

> When the poetaster Bathyllus piratically claimed the authorship of an anonymously issued poem of Virgil's—so runs the apocryphal anecdote—Virgil retorted: 'I made the verses, another has stolen the honour.' But Martial's protest at the piracies of which he had been the victim is probably the most famous in all literature, because in it he first used the word *plagiarius*, literally 'kidnaper', for a literary thief.[25]

White quotes Florio on fellow-writers: 'What doe they but translate? perhaps, usurpe? at least, collect? if with acknowledgment, it is well; if by stealth, it is too bad.'[26] Is this not the deploring of plagiarism? As so often, a distinction kicked out of the door comes back in through the window. Call all plagiarisms piracy and you have rendered plagiarism non-existent. White certainly shows that imitation was greatly valued in classical times and in the Renaissance, but he does not show that there was no distinction then between imitation and plagiarism, no disapprobation of plagiarism, for he himself reports such disapprobation of unacknowledged, secret, or furtive borrowings. For Donne, White says, and substantiates, 'borrowed matter is to be thankfully acknowledged, not ungratefully purloined by stealth'.[27]

Thomas Mallon acknowledges, as everyone must, that something happened in the seventeenth century, but is it true that 'our basic sense of plagiarism came to be born'—*born*, that exactly—'in the seventeenth century'?[28] Printing had changed something, yes—but 'it was printing, of course, that changed everything'?[29] Everything? Not the nub dishonesty, the claiming credit for a poem someone else has written.

In *Crimes of Writing* (1991), a book that oddly does no more than mention plagiarism, Susan Stewart has a passing comment: 'plagiarism of course arises as a problem at the same time that other issues of writing's authenticity come to the fore'.[30] But 'problem' there has to cover a lot of ground; it is not the case that condemnation of plagiarism arose as late as the new commodification would like to believe. We are assured by Stewart that in medieval times there was no such thing as plagiarism (reprehensible), and yet the assurance, from Giles Constable, does waver rather: 'the term plagiarism should indeed probably'—indeed probably—'be dropped in reference to the Middle Ages, since it expresses a concept of literary individualism and property that is distinctly modern'.[31] And Martial, was he distinctly modern? He lacked a distinctly

---

[25] *Plagiarism and Imitation During the English Renaissance*, pp. 15–16.
[26] *Plagiarism and Imitation During the English Renaissance*, pp. 168–9.
[27] *Plagiarism and Imitation During the English Renaissance*, p. 128.
[28] *Stolen Words*, p. xii.
[29] *Stolen Words*, p. 4.
[30] *Crimes of Writing* (1991), p. 24.
[31] *Crimes of Writing*, p. 30, quoting Constable.

modern concept of literary property, no doubt, but he certainly had—and named—the concept of plagiarism.

As with other prelapsarian history, as with any telling of the Fall itself, the moment is elusive, contested, often gets pushed further back. Brean Hammond, in *Professional Imaginative Writing in England, 1670–1740* (1997), makes a good case for dating the 'originality' debate earlier than usual, retrieving it from the eighteenth century: 'there is, I would contend, an earlier cultural formation, that of dramatic writing in the 1670s and 1680s, wherein the problematic nature of borrowing from earlier works was already under heated negotiation'.[32] But why stop there, when it comes to negotiating the problematic nature of borrowing? Best, moreover, for Hammond to tread carefully on this 'original composition' ground, since there have been heavy investments in the eighteenth-century allocation. So Hammond prudently claims less than he might and should: 'In this period therefore, earlier than is sometimes supposed . . . there was the *beginning* of an *attempt* to define "originality" in writing and the *ur-conception* of proprietary authorship' (italics supplied).[33]

Stephen Orgel makes a similar move in his influential article on 'The Renaissance Artist as Plagiarist'. He claims that the charge of plagiarism did not appear significantly until after the Renaissance. One may grant a premise of his, as to 'different ages', without granting the elisions and assimilations that accompany it. Was Inigo Jones a plagiarist?

> Jones's practice may legitimately raise certain questions about the validity, function, philosophic implications of imitation; but such questions will also be profoundly time-bound. Different ages give very different answers to the basic question of what, exactly, it is that art imitates: for example, nature, or other art, or the action of the mind. Modern critics grow uncomfortable when it proves to be imitating other art too closely.[34]

Yes, such questions will be time-bound. But what exactly is Orgel's dissent from modern critics here? 'Imitating other art too closely' might be a matter of the servile, the inability to add anything at all—but then on this the modern critic would be at one with the ancient and the Renaissance critic. Or 'imitating other art too closely' ought to apply, given that Orgel's context is plagiarism ('The Renaissance Artist as Plagiarist'), to plagiarism. But here too the modern critic is not shown by Orgel to be at odds with the ancient and the Renaissance

---

[32] Brean Hammond, *Professional Imaginative Writing in England, 1670–1740* (1997), p. 83.
[33] *Professional Imaginative Writing in England, 1670–1740*, p. 21, my italics. This 'ur-conception' is later joined by 'prehistory', convenient to the historian, and by 'gestation': 'there is a prehistory to the conception of originality, at least in English culture, that suggests a longer gestation period than either [Martha] Woodmansee or [Mark] Rose allow' (p. 43).
[34] Stephen Orgel, 'The Renaissance Artist as Plagiarist', *ELH: A Journal of English Literary History*, 48 (1981), 479.

critic. Such modern critics as equate even very close imitation with plagiarism are unthinking, yes; but that the accusation of plagiarism is often foolishly and ignorantly levelled has no bearing on whether it can be, and could be back then, responsibly and justly levelled. There was, Orgel concedes, 'a long history of discomfort with Jonsonian borrowing';[35] nevertheless, if Jonson's borrowings were scarcely ever deplored as plagiarism (it was Jonson who did the deploring, launching in *The Poetaster* the missile 'plagiary' in English: 'Why? the ditt' is all borrowed; 'tis Horace's: hang him plagiary'), this need not be because the concept of plagiarism was scarcely present to people's minds but because the distinction between the furtively dishonest (plagiarism) and the openly honourable (imitation) existed and was well understood, with Jonson then judged to be practising not the unhappy former but the happy latter.

But Orgel needs a more dramatic history, a moment to identify, cultural history being one long identification parade. 'By the time Dryden was writing *Of Dramatic Poesy*, however, Jonson's borrowings required a defense': 'He invades authors like a monarch, and what would be theft in other poets, is only victory in him.' Orgel says of Dryden's aphorism: 'This was written only forty-five years after [Inigo] Jones's praise of Jonsonian "translation", and thirty years after Jonson's death. In that short time translation, imitation, borrowing, have become "learned plagiary", "robbery", "theft".'[36]

Now it may well be that the elapsing of the half-century brought about an exacerbation that ministered to ill-judgement in accusations of plagiarism; that it often became an easy, unjust, and uncomprehending charge. But this is not the same as maintaining that what had earlier been understood as translation and imitation, without reference even to the possibility of the accusation of plagiarism, was succeeded by a world in which the honourable terms 'have become' replaced by opprobious terms understood as posited of just the same practices, now without reference even to the possibility of praiseworthy translation and imitation. It is, to me, impossible to credit Orgel's insistence that 'The question of the morality of literary imitation, then, starts to appear significantly in England only after the Renaissance, and on the whole in reaction to it.'[37] Many of Orgel's most telling instances tell a story that is not the one he retails. Thomas Browne sees in plagiarism a great human failing, 'the age-old desire "to plume themselves with others' feathers"'. Orgel remarks: 'It is a vice, as Brown continually laments, that has always been with us: plagiarism is the Original Sin of literature.'[38]

It is when, à propos of plagiarism, Orgel turns to allusion that the gaps in the argument yawn. 'We might want to argue that there is a vast difference

---

[35] Orgel, p. 482.
[36] Orgel, pp. 482–3.
[37] Orgel, p. 484.
[38] Orgel, p. 483.

between adopting the role of a classic poet and copying his words, but is there? The adoption of roles by Renaissance poets involved a good deal of direct imitation and allusion.'[39] Well, we might admit that there is not a *vast* difference between adopting a role and (without acknowledgement, since Orgel is discussing plagiarism) copying out words, while still believing that there is a crucial difference. And is not allusion incompatible with plagiarism? 'So, to stay for the moment with simple cases, how would a Renaissance audience have responded to blatant plagiarism? Sometimes, obviously, simply as an allusion: a great deal of Renaissance art offered its patrons precisely the pleasures of recognition.'[40] Hearing 'Come my Celia', did the Renaissance reader 'condemn Jonson for plagiarizing Catullus? or did he, on the contrary, admire a particularly witty adaptation of the art of the past to the designs of the present?'

The latter, for sure. But this is because the Renaissance audience well understood that what it was responding to here, what 'Renaissance art offered' here, was *not* 'blatant plagiarism', was not plagiarism. Allusion, plainly; and the defence that the poet is alluding is one that, should it be made good, must exculpate the poet. That the defence is sometimes unconvincing is a different story. Thomas Mallon is right, I should judge, not to accept the defence of Laurence Sterne that maintains that those moments of his are never plagiarisms but always allusions. But allusion has to be the contrary (Orgel's 'on the contrary') of plagiarism, since allusion is posited upon our calling the earlier work into play, whereas the one thing that plagiarism hopes is that the earlier work will not enter our heads. T. S. Eliot said, in an interview in August 1961:

> In one of my early poems ['Cousin Nancy'] I used, without quotation marks, the line 'the army of unalterable law . . .' from a poem by George Meredith, and this critic accused me of having shamelessly plagiarised, pinched, pilfered that line. Whereas, of course, the whole point was that the reader should recognise where it came from and contrast it with the spirit and meaning of my own poem.[41]

The fame of Meredith's line, and the conclusive placing of it by both poets, leave me in no doubt that Eliot tells the truth here; but even those who suppose him being wise after the unfortunate event would grant that, if credited, allusion is a defence that must stanch the accusation of plagiarism. And one reason why plagiarism in, for instance, scientific research is importantly different is that it is not at all clear there what it would mean to claim that one was not plagiarising but alluding to (as against, say, referring to) earlier work.

That such-and-such wording, being an allusion, is not plagiarism, would

---

[39] Orgel, p. 479.
[40] Orgel, p. 480.
[41] *Yorkshire Post*; *The Bed Post* (1962), Kenneth Young (ed.), pp. 43–4.

not have to mean that there could not be any infringement of copyright. Paul Goldstein begins *Copyright's Highway* with the copyright conflict in 1990 when the rap group 2 Live Crew issued their derisive parody of the Roy Orbison/William Dees hit, 'Oh, Pretty Woman'. Parody, being allusive, cannot be plagiaristic, but it may still violate someone's rights—among them, copyright. The lawyer, though, needs to be sensitive to the judgments germane to literary allusion. Alexander Lindey, whose book on *Plagiarism and Originality* I value, ends up on one occasion agreeing amiably to overlook (as an authorial inadvertence) a moment that, contrariwise, solicits the reader's advertence:

> A reviewer of Evelyn Waugh's *Scott-King's Modern Europe* praised the following excerpt as a 'burst of stylish writing':
>
>> He was older, it might have been written, than the rocks on which he sat; older, anyway, than his stall in chapel; he had died many times, had Scott-King, had dived deep, had trafficked for strange webs with Eastern merchants. And all this had been but the sound of lyres and flutes to him.
>
> 'Stylish, indeed!' cried a reader with a long memory. The passage, he said, was obviously a paraphrase of the celebrated description of La Gioconda in the chapter on Leonardo in Walter Pater's *The Renaissance*:
>
>> She is older than the rocks among which she sits . . . she has been dead many times, and learned the secrets of the grave; and has been a diver in deep seas . . . and trafficked for strange webs with Eastern merchants . . . and all this has been to her but as the sound of lyres and flutes.
>
> John K. Hutchens, the book critic who published this intelligence, did not take it too seriously. It was the sort of thing, he felt, that could have happened to anybody. He was right.[42]

Oh no he wasn't right. Nor is Mr Lindey. Waugh was not covertly plagiarising, but this is because he was overtly alluding. Not waiving but waving.

An honest misunderstanding, this, on Lindey's part. It is the insufficient honesty with which the particular dishonesty that is plagiarism is so often treated that is the increasingly sad business. Samuel Johnson wrote of plagiarism as 'one of the most reproachful, though, perhaps, not the most atrocious of literary crimes'.[43] The reproach has to be for dishonesty, and yet how remarkably unreproached plagiarism usually goes.

The dishonesty is furthermore a point of dishonour. For honour is doubly at issue: the plagiarist hopes to gain honour from a dishonourable practice. 'His honour rooted in dishonour stood'. Peter Shaw, in his essay 'Plagiary', showed how kid-gloved the handling or fingering of plagiarism often is; he limned the psychology or psychopathology of plagiarism, including the embarrassment

---

[42] *Plagiarism and Originality*, p. 51.
[43] *The Adventurer* No. 95, 2 October 1753.

that so often overcomes those who find themselves faced by its two-facedness. His plea for responsible reproof strikes me as compelling, but it has not slowed down the manufacture of excuses. The usual dealings with this double-dealing are less than ever honest.

Yet then this, too, has a long history. William Walsh opened his entry on plagiarism, in his *Handy-Book of Literary Curiosities* (1909), with a question inviting the answer No: 'Is plagiarism a crime?' He duly arrived at the conclusion from which he had started: 'On the whole, as between the plagiarist and his accuser, we prefer the plagiarist. We have more sympathy for the man in the pillory than for the rabble that pelt him.' Even the case of Neal Bowers (that notable recent victim of one David Jones) incited in reviewers a need to dissociate themselves from his moral urgings. Mark Ford, in the *London Review of Books* (21 August 1997), expressed sympathy with Bowers in some ways (his plight 'considerably intensified by the difficulties he experienced trying to persuade others to take these thefts as seriously as he did'), and yet Ford is moved to mock Bowers ('Bowers assumes the mantle of heroic vigilante defending the integrity of poetry against potentially overwhelming forces of evil'), and proffers an insufficiently vigilant argument: 'It's hard to be as appalled by Jones's poetic kleptomania as Bowers insists one ought to be. This is perhaps partly because the two poems stolen from the 1992 issue of *Poetry* are not in themselves mind-blowingly original.' But a judgement on how appalled we should be by the conduct of the plagiarist (and Jones's continuing behaviour was diversely appalling) need not be commensurate with the degree of originality in the poems dishonestly laid claim to. The calculated indecorum of Ford's phrase 'not in themselves mind-blowingly original' gives vent to something, something that is not the same as finding Bowers's book tonally imperfect. Again, one might concur with James Campbell, in his review of Bowers (*Times Literary Supplement*, 28 February 1997), as to failures of tone in Bowers's wounded account ('a sanctimoniousness about his way of telling' the story, Campbell finds) while still judging it unjust of Campbell to deprecate the fact that 'Bowers frowns at colleagues who dare to smile when they hear about it'. As well Bowers might, I should have said. But then this too is continuous with the long history of casting as priggish those who, with a straight face, deplore plagiarism. For one of the touching moments in Bowers's book tells of how he too used to reach for evasive levity, giving his students what he called his 'thou-shalt-not-steal-spiel', 'mocking myself', staging 'my wise guy presentation'.

If I now refer to the demoralising of plagiarism, I refer to such discussion of it as evacuates morals as well as morale. One form of this might be politics as impervious to individual conscience, with plagiarism 'a cultural category defining the borders between texts and policing the accumulation of cultural capital'.[44] (Policing, in the mode, being a much scarier thing than theft.) Another form might be the genial throwing up of hands, as when a discussion of plagiarism glides from cake-recipes to cooked books and then to not living by bread alone:

> To an equally folk-anonymous tradition [as a recipe] belonged Dr. Martin Luther King, Jr., who in his Boston University thesis quietly integrated a few lines from theologian Paul Tillich and fifty sentences from another's thesis even as he would smoothly merge the rhetoric of evangelical preachers to emerge with his own voice in Montgomery.[45]

Even as? There is a lot of smooth merging going on there. As who should say, *Relax.* '—sure they are unsure. When a young historian, shown to have plagiarized his first book, becomes a Program Officer at the National Endowment for the Humanities, is a high school girl to blame for reworking a magazine piece on who was to blame for Pearl Harbor?'[46] Yes, she may well be. How many wrongs exactly *does* it take to make a right?

The essay that I take as most thoroughly colluding with the greatest number of wrongs is one from which I quoted earlier, that by James Kincaid in the *New Yorker* (20 January 1997). His title was 'Purloined Letters' (once more unto this breach), and his subtitle was 'Are we too quick to denounce plagiarism?' (No, this question does not expect the answer No.) Reviewing Neal Bowers's book, Kincaid speaks roundly ('no doubt about it') and then proceeds to get round it. To follow the moves, one needs an extended quotation.

> Sumner/Compton/Jones [Bowers's plagiarist] is a cheat, no doubt about it; and now and then we run across other cases of plagiarism that shut before they are open. For instance, one of my own students turned in a paper on 'Great Expectations' which was an exact copy of Dorothy Van Ghent's essay—an essay so celebrated that I recognized it right off and, at the first opportunity, raised the issue with my student. 'Shit!' she said. 'I paid seventy-five dollars for that.' It did seem a cruel turn of the screw to have term-paper companies selling plagiarized essays for students to plagiarize; but ethics are ethics, I told my student.
>
> I could speak loftily on the subject because the ethical issues in her case were so clear-cut. They aren't always.[47]

The exculpatory bonhomie is unremittingly at play and at work. There is the reassuring assurance that Van Ghent's essay was so celebrated that Kincaid really isn't seeking any credit for recognising it right off. There is the

---

[44] Laura J. Rosenthal, *Playwrights and Plagiarists in Early Modern England*, p. 3.
[45] Schwartz, *The Culture of the Copy*, p. 313.
[46] *The Culture of the Copy*, p. 314. Another shady business is the use by politicians of ghost-writers; as for 'the most famous political plagiarist of our time', Senator Joseph Biden, see Thomas Mallon's acute pages (*Stolen Words*, pp. 127–30).
[47] Kincaid, *New Yorker*, 20 Jan. 1997, p. 94.

unmisgiving little thrill of ' "Shit!" she said' (Tina Brown's *New Yorker*
wouldn't be printing a stuffed shirt)—Kincaid is a robust man from a robust
university where the women students are robust and no professor would take
amiss their being so. There is the syntactical *plaisanterie* of 'but ethics are
ethics, I told my student'. And then, at the move into the next paragraph, there
is the endearingly disparaging adverb 'loftily', disparaging oneself in the
nicest possible way and making it clear that, even in the most clear-cut
case, to take a moral tone would be a lapse: 'I could speak loftily on the
subject because . . .' Not that we have been given the chance to hear Kincaid
speak loftily on the subject; rather, 'ethics are ethics' came across, as it was
meant to, as calculatedly mock-pompous. A low move, 'loftily'.

I find this repellent, and not only professionally (professorially), in its
combination of failure of nerve with nerve. 'The ethical issues in her case
were so clear-cut': and was there any clear-cut dealing with the ethical issues?
Nothing is said of what the exposure of her dishonesty meant to and for the
forthright swearer; anyway, she deserves a jokey sympathy ($75? 'It did seem
a cruel turn of the screw . . .'). But then it is clear just where Kincaid's
sympathies are. Apparently all those who are not naive are now aware that
building an accusation of plagiarism is akin to 'building legal castles on what
literary theory warns is the quicksand of language'. 'But, no doubt because
there's so much uncertainty around, fervent denunciations of plagiarists are
popular: out-and-out plagiarists are criminals who safeguard the idea of
originality they threaten, giving us conscience-clearing villains to hiss. They
copy; we don't.' Fervent denunciations of plagiarists are popular? Not in the
higher intellectual world, they aren't; there, every conceivable excuse, and
many inconceivable ones, will be made for them. True, plagiarists are not
criminals (or very seldom are)—they are dishonest, dishonourable, and sometimes sick, people. Kincaid, relishing the problematics of it all, ducks and
weaves: 'Even educators may be learning how not just to punish but to employ
plagiarism'—really? . . . and then at once the dodge: 'how not just to punish
but to employ plagiarism, or something very like it'. Ah. 'Copying or imitating,
they say, is vital to gaining initial entry into a discourse.' Not even the arrival of
our comfy old friend 'discourse' quite sets my mind at rest. Need no attempt be
made to distinguish the dishonesty that is plagiarism from responsible kinds of
copying or imitating? 'What all of this suggests is that we might try to entertain
the idea that plagiarism, and even originality, are relative concepts.' True,
anciently true, in one way. Even Edward Young, who is usually blamed these
days for having, in his *Conjectures on Original Composition* (1759), set the
world on a grievously wrong course, declared himself 'content with what all
must allow, that some Compositions are more so [original] than others'.[48] But

[48] Edward Young, *Conjectures on Original Composition* (1759), p. 7.

not true, Kincaid's point, insofar as it insinuates that disapprobation need not constitute any part of the malpractice that has for centuries been called plagiarism. Kincaid has his thumb in the sliding scales. 'Plagiarism is best understood not as a sharply defined operation, like beheading, but as a whole range of activities, more like cooking, which varies from deliberate poisoning to the school cafeteria to mother's own.'[49] Maybe so, but whether 'sharply' defined or not, plagiarism is, and has always been, defined pejoratively.

Amoral jocularity about dishonesty is, in my judgement, immoral. Kincaid tells us not to 'get ourselves in a tizzy'. This demotic moment is the successor to 'but ethics are ethics, I told my student', and it serves the same end as that mock-pomposity: the evacuation of responsibility and of honesty. Demoralisation.

In an essay that has been widely cited, 'Two Extravagant Teachings', Neil Hertz subjected to scrutiny and to mockery the Cornell University pamphlet on plagiarism. He wrote of its 'ill-assured moral exhortation',[50] its symptomatic rhetoric. Some of his criticisms strike home—yes, there are lapses of tone, and even gouts of feeling within the admonishments that lend themselves to Hertz's Freudian detections. Even perhaps to his aligning a teacher's anxiety about the young's plagiarism with parental anxiety about the young's masturbation. But there is something wrong with the way in which a concern with the plaintiff's, the teacher's, psyche leaves no room at all for concern with the defendant's, the plagiarist's, conduct. It is the teachers alone who are to be morally judged. What, asks Professor Hertz, of the authorities' motivation?

> We might attribute it to justifiable moral indignation, the righteous contempt of the honest for the dishonest, but that wouldn't quite account for either the intensity of this rhetoric or its peculiar figuration—or for the strong fascination that student plagiarism generally seems to hold for academics.[51]

The phrasing is prejudicial: 'indignation' contaminated by 'righteous', and 'righteous' contaminated by the likelihood of self-righteousness, with 'fascination' contaminated by prurience. Not, as might be supposed at least sometimes to be the case, a principled dislike of dishonesty, and the exercise of an essential professional responsibility when it comes to judging (often with lifelong consequences) a student's writing.

About any such matter, yes, there can be impurity of motive in the moral insistence; but shouldn't educators in the American world of Hertz (and of me), where the selling of term-papers is big business and is a threat to education, be against plagiarism? Not if Hertz's line of talk were to be followed (whatever his own practice as a teacher), for he moves on to deprecate the 'uneasiness' in teachers 'that produces the ritual condemnation

---

[49] Kincaid, *New Yorker*, 20 Jan. 1997, p. 97.
[50] Neil Hertz, *The End of the Line* (1985), p. 144.
[51] *The End of the Line*, p. 149.

of student plagiarists when they are unlucky enough to be caught'. 'Ritual condemnation': this minimises or even extirpates moral responsibility, as does 'unlucky', and as does the ensuing reference to 'such a scapegoating'. Scapegoats are, by definition, innocent, they bear the burden of imputed unjust guilt; a dishonest student, or colleague, or novelist, is something else. But Hertz's exculpatory term 'scapegoating' has caught on, and is put to use, with due acknowledgement, by a later critic when for his own reasons he needs to put in a good word for Pecksniff, Pecksniff who stole Martin Chuzzlewit's architectural plans.[52] All is forgiven. But not to those who make scapegoats of plagiarists.

And the future? More of the same, I fear; and in the immediate future, next month to be precise, there will be a new book by Robert Scholes, *The Rise and Fall of English* (1998). He, too, knows, in the matter of plagiarism, that it is the plaintiff, not the defendant, who is the real enemy:

> In the academy the introduction to intertextuality received by most students takes the form of a stern warning against plagiarism. In a culture organized around property, patents, and copyrights, plagiarism has become a sin, occasionally a crime. In other cultures, or in certain contexts within our own, this sin does not exist.[53]

Not a sin, agreed, and not a crime, but that might be thought to leave plenty of room for plagiarism to be (and not just to have 'become', in what passes here for history and for anthropology) morally wrong, and for exculpations of it to be morally wrong too. 'A stern warning against plagiarism': how relaxedly we accede to the assurance that education should be made of less stern stuff.

In her weighing of plagiarism, 'The Wasp Credited with the Honeycomb' (*Theophrastus Such*), George Eliot first granted imaginatively the ways in which it is true that creation is re-creation, true that we are all indeed in debt to the world that went before and the world that is around, and then went on indeflectibly:

> I protest against the use of these majestic conceptions to do the dirty work of unscrupulosity and justify the non-payment of debts which cannot be defined or enforced by the law.

> Surely the acknowledgement of a mental debt which will not be immediately detected, and may never be asserted, is a case in which the traditional susceptibility to 'debts of honour' would be suitably transferred.

I think it an honour to teach at a university which has returned, in the courts, to the costly fight against term-paper fraud that it began twenty-five years ago, when a victory was duly secured; on 19 October 1997,

---

[52] Gerhard Joseph, 'Charles Dickens, International Copyright, and the Discretionary Silence of *Martin Chuzzlewit*', in *The Construction of Authorship*, ed. Woodmansee and Jaszi, p. 268.
[53] Robert Scholes, *The Rise and Fall of English* (1998), to be published 9 March 1998, pp. 98–9.

Boston University filed suit in U.S. District Court against eight online companies that sell term papers to students in Massachusetts. The University charges that accepting orders and distributing fraudulent term papers by phone, wire, and mail are acts of wire and mail fraud and violate the Massachusetts law prohibiting such sales and other laws.

But let me end by proposing one stubborn consideration that has, ever since Martial, ministered to these dishonourable exculpations. This is simply but crucially that Martial's inspired figure of speech, *plagiarius*, the thief, has itself had a distortive effect. For it must be conceded, not as bespeaking leniency for the crime of theft but as distinguishing one form of theft from most others, that it is importantly not the case that what the plagiarist does exactly is steal your poem. William Walsh in his *Handy-Book of Literary Curiosities* (1909): 'For although we are pleased to say, in our metaphorical language, that a plagiarist shines in stolen plumes, not a plume is really lost by the fowl who originally grew them.'

The *New Yorker* illustration to Kincaid's article showed a rectangle of print (some lines from the article itself), at pocket height, that had been cut away from a man's clothes and is clutched by the pickpocket, no longer the rightful owner's. But the illustration inadvertently brought home that the invocation of the pickpocket (by Coleridge, by Poe, by many others), or of the thief, both is and is not apt. And in being in some respects unapt, it then ministers to special pleading. For it is scarcely ever the case that the rightful owner actually loses possession of, or credit for, his or her creation. Martin Amis did not wrongfully lose credit for his novel; Jacob Epstein wrongfully gained credit for 'his'.

True, every now and then there will be a case which really does constitute theft, and is contrastively helpful for that very reason: a work claimed by X, published by X, not ever credited to its rightful author. Anne Fadiman, in her essay on Bowers's book in *Civilization* (February/March 1997), tells the touching story of how her mother's work was taken by John Hersey: 'The only time she ever saw her dispatches in print was inside a cover that said BY JOHN HERSEY'. But this is best judged to be piracy. Fadiman says: 'after your words—unlike your VCR—are stolen, you still own them. Or do you?' No, her mother didn't, never had been allowed to. But Glyn Jones still possessed, and still possessed credit for, the passage of prose of which Hugh MacDiarmid possessed himself for his poem 'Perfect'. Neal Bowers tells how a bronze cast that carried a poem of his called 'Art Thief' (mourning the theft of a work of sculpture from the site) was itself then stolen. Stolen. But the plagiarising of a poem is not characteristically its being lost to its originator.

What then, if anything, is stolen? We often say 'the credit', but even here there is almost always something misleading, the definite article. The plagiarist does not take the credit, he takes credit, credit to which he is not entitled. This is often despicable and always reprehensible, but it cannot be reprehended in quite the terms in which theft ordinarily is. To concede this is not to concede anything else, and is not to make any excuse for the wrongful, rather to make clear what the wrong is.

There is no chance of our ever giving up the vivid figure of speech which thought in terms of theft, but we should be aware that the very terms in which we speak (we are all guilty . . . —how delicious) play a part in contributing to the disingenuous discourse through which plagiarism steals.

Being Responsible and Being a Victim of Circumstance[1]

TONY HONORÉ
Fellow of the Academy

IT IS AN HONOUR to give the Maccabaean lecture in Jurisprudence, and to celebrate Cromwell's decision, taken in 1655 on sound legal advice, to allow the return of the Jews to England, the more so given my personal debt to a great Jewish lawyer and philosopher, Herbert Hart. The Maccabaean lecturer ought in decency to address, at a theoretical level, some puzzle that worries philosophers, lawyers, and ordinary people. In what follows I wrestle with a problem of this sort: the relation between treating people as responsible and treating them as victims of their circumstances.

It may be helpful at the outset to outline the argument that follows. I take a wide view of what it is to be responsible, while conceding that the term is often used more narrowly. We can be responsible even when we are not morally to blame or legally liable for our actions. We can be responsible for unintended aspects or outcomes of our conduct and for actions performed when we are not fully capable of acting rationally or when our freedom is restricted. Moreover this wide conception of responsibility is to be welcomed and defended against attempts to undermine it. Moral blame and legal liability, especially criminal liability, are narrower notions. When they are present their force is or should be mitigated when the person in question, though responsible, was not fully capable of acting rationally or their freedom to choose was distorted by their

[1] I am grateful to Andrew Ashworth, Tom Bingham, Edwin Cameron, Jean Floud, Roger Hood, John Gardner, Tom Nagel, Joseph Raz, Stephen Shute and, not least, Bernard Williams, all of whom read a draft of this lecture and gave me, without prejudice, the benefit of their reactions.

Proceedings of the British Academy, **97**, 169–187. © The British Academy 1998.
Read at the Academy 17 February 1998.

circumstances. To that extent we can properly treat people both as responsible and as victims of circumstance.

So much by way of introduction. Of the various ways of looking at human conduct, two seem at first sight difficult, if not impossible, to reconcile. We think of human behaviour as something for which, except in rare cases, the person whose conduct is in question—the agent, to use a convenient term—is responsible.[2] Agents are responsible because the conduct is theirs. They have intervened in the world and changed it. Their behaviour is the cause of that change.

At times, however, we think of human conduct differently: as the outcome of factors that cause and so explain it. These include genetic make-up, upbringing, environment, temperament, and the pressures to which we are all subject. Let us call them 'circumstances', and note that in this sense circumstances include internal factors (how one is constituted) as well as external ones, past and present. Circumstances can be seen as responsible, or partly responsible, for what we do. We are, up to a point, trapped by them. But they are responsible only in a weak sense. People can be called to account, but these background factors cannot be. So, when circumstances are said to be responsible for behaviour, the word is used in the sense in which any cause is responsible for its consequences—the short-circuit is responsible for the fire it brings about.

These different ways of looking at conduct are familiar outside the law. They also feature within it, especially in criminal law and procedure. In general criminal law treats adults as responsible and so liable to sanctions for the offences they commit. But sometimes it holds that they are not liable, are guilty of a lesser offence, or should be punished less severely than normal offenders. One ground for this—not the only one[3]—is that, when they acted, they were not (or not fully) capable of making a rational decision. By a rational decision is meant one that relates the conduct to the agent's general aims, though it may not conform to law or social mores. Those who are not capable of deciding rationally in this sense are regarded as not to blame, or less to blame than they would otherwise have been.

Why capacity and blame should be related in this way is not at first sight obvious: I shall return to the puzzle later on. But the link is a powerful one, and it fits the retributive notion that punishment should not be disproportionate to blame.[4] In English law the link between capacity, blame, and punishment underlies several features of the criminal process: the defence of insanity,

---

[2] The term 'agent' is used because our concern will be more with positive action than with failure to act, though this will be touched on briefly.

[3] I leave on one side for the moment social and moral deprivation, but return to it at the end of the lecture.

[4] A. Ashworth, *Sentencing and Criminal Justice* (2nd edn. 1995), ch. 4 (proportionality). Several other notions—deterrence, incapacitation, stigmatisation—enter into the rationale of punishment but I concentrate in this lecture on retribution, which is certainly one element in it.

the law relating to 'abnormality of mind' (resulting in 'diminished responsibility'),[5] the treatment of infanticide as less serious than murder,[6] and many matters that are routinely put forward in mitigation (that the offence was prompted by domestic tension, emotional stress, financial pressures, addiction to alcohol or drugs).[7] These latter factors are stressed both in pleas in mitigation and in the pre-sentence reports that are available to judges and presumably influence them in sentencing. They are thought to impair rational judgement and to affect self-control and other aspects of rationality such as cognition. Short-term factors can also be seen as affecting a person's capacity for self-control. Provocation in the form of physical aggression or grossly insulting behaviour can reduce liability from murder to manslaughter if it results in a temporary loss of self-control, and otherwise may be a mitigating factor that affects the sentence imposed. In all these cases the agent's ability to behave sensibly is taken to be impaired. The agent is in a broad sense responsible, since the conduct is in some respects intentional and so, at least in our culture, invites approval or criticism. But criminal liability is excluded or its impact reduced.

The incidents of the criminal process mentioned enter the law at different points and have different effects. The law is reluctant to accept impaired capacity as a complete defence to a criminal charge; it is much readier to treat it as relevant to sentencing. Yet these are all instances of 'responsible but . . .' and it makes for clarity to think of them as cases in which the agent is in a broad sense responsible but not, or not fully, to blame. If responsibility and capacity-linked-to-blame are treated as separate in this way,[8] the term 'diminished responsibility' can be seen as a shorthand way of referring to cases where an agent is responsible but not wholly to blame. There are no degrees of responsibility, but rather degrees of capacity to control one's behaviour. If so, a person who is in a broad sense responsible for conduct may be more or less exposed to criminal liability or moral censure on that account.

Though the examples given come from English law, there are parallels in most, perhaps all, other systems. Nor is there anything peculiar to the law

---

[5] Homicide Act 1957 s. 2.

[6] Infanticide Act 1938 s. 1 (1).

[7] Many other matters can be relied on in mitigation, such as the offender's youth, contrition and co-operation with the authorities e.g. by pleading guilty: A. Ashworth, *Sentencing and Criminal Justice*, pp. 133–49; Halsbury's *Laws of England* 11.2 paras. 1189–91; D. A. Thomas, *Principles of Sentencing* (2nd edn. 1979), pp. 194–222. Sometimes it is not clear (illness, homelessness, unemployment) whether the factors relied on are meant to account for the offence or to show that the offender is so disadvantaged already that punishment will merely add to existing handicap. I am concerned at this point with the factors that bear on the convicted person's deciding to act as they did, on which see J. Shapland, *Between Conviction and Sentence. The Process of Mitigation* (1981).

[8] For the argument that responsibility, unlike blame, need not depend on choices being open see B. Williams, *Making Sense of Humanity* (1995), pp. 17–19.

about viewing human conduct in the light of the agent's capacity for self-control and rational decision. In everyday life similar factors are thought to exclude or reduce blame for the bad things that people do to others and to themselves.[9]

An awkward question then presents itself. How can people both be responsible for what they do and at the same time be caused to act as they do by circumstances that impair their self-control? Must we, to be consistent, choose between these perspectives? If we can properly combine them, as in practice we do in ordinary life and in the law, when is it appropriate to look on people as victims of circumstance?

I think we may properly combine these ways of assessing our own and other people's conduct. But how far it is wise to do so depends on how far we think it desirable to press the search for the causes of and remedies for things that go wrong in our society. 'The choice of stance is up to us.'[10] An example will show what is meant. When someone has been disabled in a road accident it is proper, depending on the context, to pick out as the cause of their disability the medical condition that affects them, the accident that caused the medical condition, the driver's misjudgement, the disrepair of the road that brought about the accident, or the shortage of funds that led to the road's disrepair. Any of these can properly be cited as the cause of the victim's disability. No error of fact or logic is committed by selecting one rather than the other. The choice between them depends on the aim of the inquiry. Is its focus medical science, an insurance policy covering accidental injury, a lawsuit for negligence, a study of road safety, or an investigation of local authority finance? What is picked out as the cause depends on how far back and for what purpose we want to trace the causal process.

In much the same way, surely, people can in principle be both responsible agents and victims of circumstance. They can both be the authors of the good or harm that their actions bring about and be caused to act as they do. The question is not which view is exclusively correct but which it is better to adopt when we assess people's behaviour in everyday life and the law. The answer must be that in general we do well, indeed we are impelled (for reasons which I

---

[9] On the comparison between mitigation in court and the judgements we make in everyday life see Shapland, *Mitigation*, ch. 3.

[10] D. M. Mackay, 'The Use of Behavioural Language to Refer to Mechanical Processes', *Brit. Jour. Phil. Sci.* (1962), pp. 89–103. I agree with D. C. Dennett, 'Mechanism and Responsibility', in *Essays on Freedom of Action* (ed. T. Honderich 1973), pp. 159–74 that the choice of stance (e.g. intentional rather than physical) should not be endowed with a premature moral dimension. The initial question is whether we regard agents as people, not how we judge them morally or legally.

hope to make clear), to treat ourselves and others as responsible agents. But the argument for welcoming this conclusion is not that our behaviour is uncaused—something that we cannot know and which, if true, would be a surprise—but that to treat people as responsible promotes individual and social well-being. It does this in two ways. It helps to preserve social order by encouraging good and discouraging bad behaviour. At the same time it makes possible a sense of personal character and identity that is valuable for its own sake. But there is a proper place, which it is important to try to define, for the 'victim of circumstance' perspective.

Responsibility

To see how this can be the case, let us turn first to the notion of responsibility,[11] which, as mentioned, is here taken in a broad sense and does not necessarily import legal liability or moral blame, though it is a condition of both.

There are three sources of human responsibility. The primary one is responsibility for one's own conduct. Then there is the responsibility for other people, things[12] and events[13] that we choose to take on. Lastly, there is the responsibility that society thrusts on us, either informally or through the law, for example responsibility to one's family and community.

If these three sources are kept in mind, some false ideas can be nailed at the outset. One is that we are responsible only for our own behaviour; a second that we are responsible only when we are to blame; a third that we are responsible only when we choose to be. None of these is true. Being responsible for our own behaviour is the prime example of responsibility but not the only one. A person can be both responsible and legally liable for something they have not done. An employer can, for example, be vicariously liable for the act of an employee. Nor is this a legal quirk. People can be morally responsible

---

[11] H. L. A. Hart 'Varieties of Responsibility', *Law Quarterly Review*, 83 (1967), pp. 263–4 argued that the primary sense of responsibility was that of answering a charge. I am not sure about this, but in any case the underlying idea is embodied in the Greek *aitios*, being the cause of something (B. Williams, *Shame and Necessity* (1993), pp. 52–4), with the corollary of having to answer for it, not necessarily before a court. This combination yields the notion of responsibility for one's own (in some aspect intentional) conduct. This notion is in turn capable of extension by analogy to the second and third sources of responsibility mentioned in the text, where these elements are not all present, for example because the person responsible has to answer for the conduct of some other person of which he or she is not the cause.

[12] D. C. Dennett, *Elbow Room* (1984), p. 85: 'I *take* responsibility for anything I make and then inflict upon the general public.' It is not in fact necessary to have made it. The seller of something manufactured by another is responsible for inflicting it on the public.

[13] This may seem surprising, but insurers typically make themselves responsible for paying for losses caused by events such as shipwrecks.

for the behaviour of others.[14] Parents can, for example, be morally responsible
for the way in which their children behave even when they are not legally liable
for it. In that case the person who is morally responsible should act somewhat as
if the responsibility were legal. If the children have broken the neighbour's
window they should pay for the damage. This is one of the many ways in which
morality, as conceived in western culture, follows the legal model.

As these examples show, we can be responsible for the behaviour of others
without necessarily being to blame. The employer or parent is sometimes but
not always to blame for the employee or child's behaviour. The same is true of
our own behaviour. We can be responsible for what we do by sheer accident,
like unavoidably tripping someone. If we do this, though not to blame, we
incur at least a moral obligation. An apology is called for and the person who
has been tripped must be helped up and if necessary taken for treatment.

Thirdly, when people are responsible it is not always because they have
chosen to be responsible. Sometimes they have not chosen to be responsible
because they have not chosen do the thing for which they are held responsible.[15]
When they are responsible for their own doings this is usually because they have
chosen to act as they did. But at times they have no real choice. Someone who is
forced to hand over money by a mugger is responsible for handing it over. It may
well have been the right thing to do, though the victim had no real option. And at
times our convictions leave us with no real option. In such cases not only are we
responsible for what we do but we want, like Luther, to be seen to be responsible:
'Here I stand. I can do no other'.[16] But even those who choose to act as they do do
not necessarily choose to be responsible for what they do. When they are morally
or legally responsible for failing to act, failing, for example, to help a friend in
need or to pay income tax, they may have chosen not to help or not to pay but they
have not chosen to be responsible for the default. Social or legal norms required
them to act. Their duty arose from friendship or membership of the community,
and though they may have chosen to befriend someone or to belong to a certain
community, they do not choose what friendship or citizenship requires.

Responsibility is not confined, then, either in law or morals, to responsibility for one's own conduct or for one's fault or for situations in which one

[14] 'Morality' here refers to that type of ethical thought according to which behaviour should
be guided by something analogous to law (J. Feinberg, *Doing and Deserving* (1984), at pp.
30–7) in that moral reasoning issues in practical conclusions in the form of obligations (B.
Williams in *World, Mind and Ethics. Essay on the Ethical Philosophy of Bernard Williams*
ed. J. E. J. Altham and R. Harrison (1995), at p. 204). Morality in this sense is alien to Greek
thought, since classical Greece had no lawyers (i.e. to whom law was a distinct intellectual
discipline), just as Rome had no original philosophers. Nietzsche, *On the Genealogy of
Morals* (1887, trans. W. Kaufmann and R. J. Hollingdale, 1967), p. 64 put the point about the
relation between legal and moral guilt, duty, etc. in a typically provocative way.
[15] Williams, *Humanity*, (1995), p. 4.
[16] Words attributed to Luther at Worms in 1521: *Hier stehe ich. Ich kann nicht anders. Gott
helfe mich.*

has chosen to be responsible. It has a wider significance. That we should think of ourselves as responsible agents, as taking on responsibility for other people and things, and as having it thrust on us, is what makes possible a shared sense of one's identity and character and of that of others. It makes possible a life in common in which people relate to one another as individuals, each with distinctive traits, virtues, and shortcomings, and with a personal history that is largely made up of what they have done, of their achievements and failures.[17]

To grasp what is involved in being responsible, a good start is to think of the ways in which we take on responsibility.[18] Most of them involve assuming control of some situation or purporting to control it. The manager of a business, the leader of a political party, the head of a school takes on a role by virtue of which they are responsible for the business, the party, or the school. If it does well they gain credit and are commended for its success; if badly, they incur discredit and may be blamed for its shortcomings. People also take on transient responsibilities, divorced from any sustained role, say for arranging a meeting or seeing that a friend's children get to school on time. When they promise that something is the case, for example that the car they are lending is in good condition, they make themselves responsible for its condition. If the children get to school on time, if the car is sound, they gain credit; if not, they incur discredit.

The credit or discredit that comes from taking on responsibilities need not have legal implications. The business manager may not be legally liable for the losses the business incurs. The party leader is not legally liable for the party's failure to be re-elected. Nor need the credit or blame be moral. Though moral virtues may help to ensure success, success may also be due, or partly due, to natural ability or luck—by which I mean events that are unforeseen and often unforeseeable.[19] The market moves in the business manager's favour, the political opposition is bankrupt. The manager or leader then gets credit for success, but not moral credit. The same is true of failure, which can come about through moral failings, but also from want of skill or bad luck, or a

---

[17] 'A conception of personal identity according to which each of us is . . . a being essentially related to others by ties of recognition and concern': M. Nussbaum, 'Aristotle, nature and ethics', in Altham and Harrison (eds.), *World, Mind and Ethics*, at p. 109. The theme was developed, and acquired the label 'outcome responsibility' in H. L. A. Hart and T. Honoré, *Causation in the Law* (2nd edn. 1985), intro. lxxx–lxxxi; T. Honoré, 'Responsibility and Luck. The Moral Basis of Strict Liability', *Law Quarterly Review*, 104 (1988), pp. 537–45; and 'The Morality of Tort Law. Questions and Answers', in D. G. Owen (ed.) *Philosophical Foundations of Tort Law* (1995), pp. 81 f.

[18] Something wider than taking on a role, on which see Hart, 'Varieties', pp. 347–8. One can take on responsibility, for example, for the truth of some assertion.

[19] This refers to luck as to external circumstances and to how our actions turn out. There can also be good and bad luck in the way in which we are constituted, our inclinations, capacities and temperament: T. Nagel, *Mortal Questions* (1979), pp. 28, 32–3. Though for some people 'luck averages out in the long run' (Dennett, *Elbow Room*, p. 95) it can have an unexpected and unwelcome impact on a particular action for which the agent is responsible.

combination of these. In this connection the word 'blame' can be misleading. Some forms of blame carry no moral or legal baggage. People are blamed for actions that exhibit want of skill, bad judgement, or inattention: a footballer for not scoring when he had an open goal, a politician for advocating a policy that lost votes, a motorist for overlooking a convenient short cut.

Much the same is true when, instead of people taking on responsibility, society thrusts it on them by requiring them to do something. Here also they gain credit for fulfilling the obligations they owe to their family and friends and to the community, and discredit if they fail to fulfil them. The credit is often slight, even minimal, but requirements like that of compulsory military service can lead to one's being ordered to the battle front. Duty may then require something close to heroism.

Societies and individuals could not have devised these ways of taking on responsibility or of thrusting it on others unless they first understood what it was for people to be responsible for their actions.[20] This primary responsibility, unlike responsibility for what people take on, attaches automatically and with the feature already noted, that they gain credit for getting things right, but incur blame for getting them wrong.

Our responsibility for what we do is certainly connected with the control we have over our conduct. But though our conduct must have an intentional aspect, what we do includes its unintended aspects[21] or consequences.[22] If Oedipus (intentionally) kills a man in a quarrel and that man turns out to be his father, he has killed his father. If while driving (intentionally) I accidentally run someone over and the injured person dies as a result, I have killed that person. Though in the main we control our conduct, to succeed in what we set out to do depends partly on other people and on luck.[23] To act is to some extent to take a chance,[24] to mortgage one's credit,[25] since we decide what to do in

---

[20] Including responsibility for our actions in taking on responsibilities for other people and events.

[21] Williams, *Shame*, at p. 69 (Oedipus)

[22] This is to adopt the idea of action as an intervention in the world which is in some aspect intentional. The limit of our intervention is set by later interventions, so that the consequences that form part of our action do not extend indefinitely. The theme is developed in Hart and Honoré, *Causation*, at pp. 68–81 and Honoré, 'Causation and Remoteness of Damage', *Intern. Encycl. Comp. Law*, 11 (1971), ch. 7. For a more restricted view of action in the context of criminal law, see Maurach/Zipf, *Strafrecht* (6 edn.) *Allg. Teil* I (1983), pp. 198–96.

[23] T. Nagel, *Mortal Questions*, at pp. 25–6.

[24] Because 'how things turn out determines what [the agent] has done': Nagel, *Mortal Questions*, pp. 29–30.

[25] I developed this theme in 'Responsibility and Luck. The Moral Basis of Strict Liability', *Law Quarterly Review*, 104 (1988), pp. 530–53. The argument is that when we act we bet on things turning out right, not only in the spectacular cases (such as Chamberlain signing the Munich agreement) where the agent knows in advance that he will be judged according to how things turn out, but in general. See also Dennett, *Elbow Room*, p. 165 ('when people get caught in wrong deeds, their gambles wise or foolish have simply lost').

conditions of incomplete certainty. Moreover the difference in this respect between being responsible for what we do ourselves and taking on responsibility for other people or things is a matter of degree. A competent motorist setting out from Oxford to Glasgow will probably arrive safely. Still, something turns on the road conditions, the reactions of other drivers, and sheer luck.[26] When we act we intervene in the world, and since, unlike the objects of scientific experiment, we are not insulated from our environment, to act is to interact with other people and things. Inevitably there is some risk that what we decide to do will go wrong. It is no accident that a person who is risk-averse tends to be inactive.

Responsibility, then, whether it attaches automatically or is voluntarily taken on or is imposed by society, involves a combination of actual or assumed control and risk. To be responsible is to take the credit and discredit arising from something that is in a sense ours, either because it is our conduct (and conduct invites self-assessment or assessment by others), or because we have made it ours by taking on responsibility for it or have had it thrust on us. 'We' is to be understood broadly. Groups and organisations such as businesses and states can be responsible as well as individuals. But it is central to responsibility that it exposes the individual or group to risk. Some thinkers have indeed argued that criminal liability[27] and moral blame[28] should never depend on luck. That is a possible, though in my view mistaken, view. But the issue it raises is not one about responsibility but about the consequences attaching to it. It may be that people, though responsible for doing harm, should not be made criminally liable or morally blamed for it unless they intended or foresaw the harm. But it would not follow that no one can be morally responsible as a result of bad luck. For that to be true we should have to adopt a narrowly effort-based view of human action, according to which what someone does is always identified with what they try to do, and never constituted by its unintended outcome. Or we might opt for a selfish conception of morality, so that, for example, a relative could not be responsible for bringing up an orphaned child since the death of the child's parents was, from the relative's point of view, an unexpected piece of bad luck. It would be no part of that morality to fix people with responsibility for those who unexpectedly suffered

---

[26] But careful foresight can reduce the role of luck in what a person does: Dennett, *Elbow Room*, pp. 92–9.

[27] A. Ashworth, 'Belief, Intent and Criminal Liability', in J. Eekelaar and J. Bell (eds.), *Oxford Essays in Jurisprudence* (Third Series, 1987), pp. 1–31; 'Taking the Consequences', in S. Shute, J. Gardner, and J. Horder (eds.), *Action and Value in Criminal Law* (1993), pp. 107–24, criticised by R. A. Duff, *Intention, Agency and Criminal Liability* (1990), ch. 6; 'Acting, Trying and Criminal Liability', in *Action and Value in Criminal Law*, pp. 75–106.

[28] B. Williams, 'Moral Luck', *Proc. Aristotelian Soc. S.V.* 50 (1976); *Humanity*, ch. 21; Nagel, 'Moral Luck' in *Mortal Questions*, ch. 3.

misfortune. Spouses could not take one another for better or worse. Could there be such a morality? I am unsure, but, if there were, many would prefer not to be part of the society in which it prevailed.

Responsibility, then, involves taking risks. But why should we welcome the fact that we live in a society in which we are responsible for our conduct and take on or have thrust on us a wide range of responsibilities for people and things?[29] The prime reason can hardly be that the system of responsibility enables us to decide when people can be morally blamed for things that go wrong or when legal sanctions can be imposed on them. These are important but secondary aspects of the institution. They back up its primary function, which is to promote both self-respect and individual and social well-being. Being responsible serves as an incentive to aim at and succeed in doing things that are regarded as valuable. In that way people gain credit for success in worthwhile activities (achievements) and avoid the discredit that attaches to failure in worthwhile activities (botches) and to success in nefarious ones (misdeeds). If they were not responsible for what they did the movements involved would be those of their bodies, but the achievements, botches, and misdeeds would not be theirs. They would not be actions, since actions have an intentional aspect, and there can be no intention without a person to do the intending.[30] Their behaviour would be the outcome of circumstances to which it would be pointless to attach credit or discredit.

Only by being responsible for what we do and take on can we be motivated to get things right.[31] But responsibility for our actions comes with a price tag. Not everything that is socially approved is morally admirable. Nonconformists and rebels have their value. The institution of being responsible works best when the motive of securing approval is combined, and if necessary over-ridden, by a willingness to take responsibility for unpopular, mistaken or wrong actions. Though the motive of seeking credit and avoiding discredit is essential to the working of responsibility, it does not follow that we are responsible only for those actions which, if successful, redound to our credit in the eyes of others. Other values that relate closely to our sense of identity, in particular self-respect and concern for autonomy, impel us to accept responsibility even for actions which seem to others (and perhaps in retrospect to ourselves) to be wrong. This is true even as regards those aspects and consequences of our conduct that we did not intend.

---

[29] Dennett, *Elbow Room*, at pp. 153–72 has a good discussion of why it is 'rational for us to [esteem free will and] covet responsibility' (p. 155) and why a well-designed society should provide for 'some measure of arbitrariness and wise risk taking' (p. 164). The value he attaches to free-will, as opposed to freedom, seems however misplaced (below n. 39).

[30] This remains true even if the notion of a person possessing in a self a 'locus of self-control' (Dennett, *Elbow Room*, at p. 81) is in some sense a construct. It is a necessary construct if we are to embrace the intentional stance and the idea of responsibility.

[31] Dennett, *Elbow Room*, at p. 165.

Though actions, as noted, must have an intentional aspect[32]—they must under some description have been intended—they commonly have unintended aspects as well. We do one thing meaning to do another, or meaning to do it but not foreseeing the outcome. It is then important to our sense of ourselves as persons to accept responsibility for what was not intended or foreseen. Consider the testimony of Vaclav Havel,[33] former dissident, now president of the Czech republic. When detained for the first time he wrote and signed what he thought was a cleverly phrased letter to the Public Prosecutor asking to be released from detention. In doing so he came, without meaning to, dangerously close to saying what the authorities wanted to hear. They released him and then exploited the letter to discredit him. It was only five years later, when detained again, that Havel stopped trying to explain away his mistake and came to accept full responsibility for what he had done. 'The mistake lay', he puts it, 'in an unconscious effort to localise the essential cause of my failure somewhere "outside" in "circumstances", "conditions" "external factors or influences"'. Redress lay in 'assuming full responsibility here for one's elsewhere, today for one's own yesterday', so that 'the "I" achieves continuity and identity with the self'.

The style of Havel's explanation is metaphysical, but the underlying idea is clear. Our identity and integrity depend on our taking responsibility for the way in which we act or have in the past acted even in its unintended aspects.[34] The same is true by analogy of states. To accept responsibility for the unintended consequences of state action or default (e.g. the deaths in the Irish famine of 1845, the Armenian deportations of 1915 onwards, the concentration camps of the Boer War) can for a nation be the condition of self-respect and of reconciliation with the unintended victims of government action.

It may be objected that to treat people as responsible for what they do even in its unintended aspects is to ask too much of them. But to do so is not in itself to attach to them moral blame or legal sanction. It means basically that the person or group in question must accept what has happened as their doing and so as open to assessment, favourable or unfavourable. If what happened was bad, they will have a moral obligation to try to put it right, for example to acknowledge it and apologise, even though they were not morally to blame. That may be the whole extent of the obligation arising from their

---

[32] Perhaps there can be sub-intentional actions: B. O'Shaughnessy, *The Will. A Dual Aspect Theory* (1980), ch. 10.

[33] V. Havel, *Letters to Olga* (translated P. Wilson 1988), nos. 138, 139.

[34] Cf. 'The mature agent . . . will recognize his relation to his acts in their undeliberated, and also in their unforeseen and unintended aspects . . . he will be able to acknowledge more generally that he can be as responsible for some things that he did not intend much as he is for things that he did intend, and in ways that have nothing to do with the law of negligence': Williams, *Humanity*, p. 32, cf. *Shame*, ch. 3.

responsibility—which is not to underrate the importance of apologising when an apology is due.[35]

Is even this too much to expect? Remember that people do not have the option of claiming responsibility when things turn out well and disclaiming it when they turn out badly. The principle involved is that of taking the rough with the smooth. More precisely, those who control a situation from which they may derive either benefit or detriment are entitled to the benefit that in the upshot accrues from it but must take the risk of any corresponding detriment. This principle has been developed mainly in legal contexts, such as sales, property transfers and vicarious liability. For that reason philosophers do not usually regard it, or at any rate mention it, as an aspect of justice. It looks, however, very like a species of distributive justice, since the distribution of burdens is the counterpart of the distribution of benefits.[36] But however it is classified, its moral force can hardly be denied.[37]

Is it an objection to this wide view of responsibility that being responsible for one's conduct, with its concomitant credit and discredit, is in the interest only of those who attract more credit than discredit overall? And what of the inade-quates, so prominent in the criminal process, who persistently go astray? What of the deviants who pursue anti-social aims? To draw up a balance sheet is a complicated matter. People cannot be sure in advance whether their activities are likely to yield a positive balance. And even those who incur more discredit than credit gain protection against the harm that others might otherwise do them from the fact that the others will be held responsible for their actions. Moreover those who are inadequate or deviant should and for the most part do wish to be held responsible for their actions. They wish their autonomy to be affirmed rather than denied. Their sense of themselves as persons, even inadequate persons, is largely built up from their consciousness of what they have done. Their actions, though they reflect their background and make-up, progressively determine their character both in their own eyes and those of others. Being responsible for them is crucial to their sense of identity as persons who develop and change over time. If their behaviour could not be attributed to them in this way, they would have to conceive of themselves as attenuated beings: objects to which things happen.[38]

---

[35] The importance of acknowledging that one has hurt someone, even unintentionally, is captured in eastern Christianity by the practice of asking for forgiveness for sins 'voluntary and involuntary'.

[36] See Honoré, *Morality*, at pp. 83–5.

[37] Though we need not be morally to blame in order to be responsible the 'taking the rough with the smooth' principle provides an argument in favour of our acknowledging responsibility for our actions.

[38] Nagel, *Mortal Questions*, at p. 36, says that 'the self which acts and is the object of moral judgment is threatened with dissolution by the absorption of its acts and impulses into the class of events'. This seems to me true also of the pre-moral self; the threat is to peoples' identity, not merely to how they are judged.

If they were not prepared to treat themselves as the authors of their conduct they could not even minimally aspire to dignity, pride, or self-confidence. Since those who are inadequate or deviant need these attributes as much as, or more than, others, it must be important both to them and to the rest of us to treat them as far as possible as responsible agents, while making allowances for their special difficulties.

Determinism and Freedom[39]

Though to hold people responsible for their behaviour may make for individual and social well-being, is it open to us to do this if their behaviour is determined by their circumstances? It is sometimes said that determinism, if true, is irrelevant to the moral and legal responsibility of human agents.[40] But can this be the case, given that intelligent people have been and are concerned to show that the things that go wrong in our society are better tackled by eliminating the causes of wrongdoing than by punishing, censuring, or isolating the wrongdoers?

To avoid a superficial discussion of a complex issue, I assume that it makes sense to treat people as the authors of and hence responsible for their actions. I leave open whether this is because they or their decisions cause their actions or because some non-causal relationship between them and what they do makes this a coherent view.

The worry remains that, though it may make sense to treat people as responsible for their conduct, if human actions are caused by circumstances, people are not *really* responsible for what they do. However beneficial it may be to treat them as if they were, to do so is to resort to a salutary lie. And salutary lies stop being salutary when the deception is revealed. Are people's actions in fact caused by their heredity, make-up, and external circumstances? No one can be sure. Though valuable work has been done by psychologists,

---

[39] This brief discussion of a very complex topic is concerned with the hypothetical impact of determinism on our freedom—a matter of degree, since we can be more or less free—not our hypothetical freewill, which either exists or doesn't (Williams *Humanity*, pp. 3–8). There is no need therefore to take sides in the argument between compatibilists and incompatibilists, except to the extent that in my view determinism, if it turns out to be true, is compatible with human responsibility. The question is whether, if our actions are caused by our circumstances, this means that we are so much less free than we commonly suppose that it would be inappropriate to treat us as responsible for them.

[40] P. F. Strawson 'Freedom and Resentment': *Proc. Brit. Acad.* 48 (1962), pp. 1–25 ('practically inconceivable' that it would make a difference); G. Strawson, *Freedom and Belief* (1986), ch. 2; 'Consciousness, Free Will and the Unimportance of Determinism', *Inquiry*, 32 (1989), p. 3; S. J. Morse 'Diminished Capacity', in *Action and Value in Criminal Law*, at p. 239.

neurologists, and sociologists the precise regularities involved, if they exist, await discovery. But it seems to make sense in each individual case to ask what reasons, conscious or unconscious, induced someone to act as they did. A person who gives up regular employment for freelance work can tell us the reasons that led to the decision (that they wanted more free time), or, if the reasons were partly unconscious (that they could not get their own way in the office), a colleague may be able to do so. At any rate it seems plausible to assume that some reason or reasons determined the decision to make a change. It is true that 'determined' is here used in a very weak sense. When we think of a reason as explaining a decision we assume merely that it can, along with other unspecified conditions, on occasion determine a decision of that sort, not that it invariably does so, or even that it regularly does so in the absence of counteracting factors. The regularity we have in mind is far removed from the sort of regularity we suppose to exist when purely physical sequences are in question. Even so, we tend to assume that *something* determines people's decisions. That nothing determined them would imply that they were not merely unpredictable but inexplicable: a belief that would be truly alarming.[41]

Should this disturb us? It seems that even 'strong psychophysical explanations' bordering on psychological laws are compatible with the notions of choice, decision, action, and intention to which we are committed when we treat people as responsible.[42] To suppose, as a working hypothesis, that our actions are determined does not make it implausible or illogical to treat ourselves as the authors of our actions when we judge ourselves and others as social beings. How far back it is rational to go in tracing causes depends on the purpose for which we want to get at the cause of something that has gone wrong. This must also apply to the causes of human conduct. It is rational to treat people as the authors of their actions in the context of a system of responsibility that seems valuable both for individuals and for society as a whole. To treat human action as a stopping point beyond which causal inquiries are not ordinarily pursued is sensible and indeed indispensable.[43] Perhaps we can dimly imagine an alternative world in which people were regarded as mere automata. In that world to treat people as the authors of their actions would be a bad way of explaining events. As things are, what (if anything) determines people's decisions includes their make-up, preferences and ideals, so that the hypothesis that their decisions are determined hardly makes them victims of circumstance.

[41] Hume, *Enquiries*, s. VIII part i, puts this well.
[42] Williams, *Humanity* p. 8 cf. Hart, *Punishment and Responsibility. Essays in the Philosophy of Law* (1968), p. 28 n. 1.
[43] Voluntary actions in particular are often treated as natural stopping-points when causal explanations are sought: Hart and Honoré, *Causation*, at pp. 41–4. But obviously there may be contexts in which it is sensible to pursue the inquiry further.

All the same, worries about freedom remain. One of these concerns manipulation. Could someone who discovered the psychological laws underlying human choice and knew enough about our make-up manipulate us into making the choices that suited him? Perhaps, up to a point. Advertisers influence us by conscious argument and unconscious conditioning. What if those who discovered the psychological laws underlying human choice were funded by an unscrupulous advertising agency? That would be alarming, but we have ways of defending ourselves. If our decisions are determined, this only means that when we decide to do something we regard some reason or reasons as sufficient to induce us on that occasion to reach the decision we in fact reach. It does not follow that the same reasons would be sufficient to induce another person to reach the same decision in similar circumstances or to induce us to decide the same way on another occasion. Human beings are so complex that psychological generalisation from particular instances is a good deal more precarious than physical generalisation. The underlying psychological laws, if they exist, must be extremely complex.

Moreover to predict with confidence how a person will behave would remain difficult because people can be secretive about the details of their make-up and preferences. One aspect of the difficulty facing a knowledgeable manipulator is that any causal laws that may govern human choice are not likely to remain secret for long. Once they are made public the person who has to decide what to do has the option of falsifying any prediction based on the laws.[44] So the hypothetical laws will constantly need to be revised. In practice, then, the danger of our being manipulated to a greater extent than we are already, should rigorous psychological laws one day be discovered, must be slight.

Victims of circumstance

This leaves open the question of when, if ever, it is in order to treat responsible agents in morals and in criminal law as victims of circumstance. Before imposing sanctions or attaching blame law and morality require something more than that the person concerned is responsible for what they have done. One further requirement common to both, as we have seen, is that in the circumstances the agent had the capacity to reach a rational decision about what to do. When this capacity is present blame for bad behaviour is appropriate and criminal liability may, depending on the state of the law, be imposed. But, though capacity has often to be treated in criminal law as an all or nothing

---

[44] Dennett, *Mechanism*, at p. 184 ('as an Intentional system I have an epistemic horizon that keeps my own future as an Intentional system indeterminate').

matter, since an offender must be found guilty or not guilty, in real life our ability to decide rationally is a matter of degree. So different degrees of blame, punishment, and censure correspond to the extent to which the agent's capacity is impaired.

This implies that criminal law and morality treat agents as victims of circumstance insofar as circumstances impair their capacity to reach a rational decision. When a person suffering from impaired capacity behaves badly this is taken into account in fixing the extent of criminal liability or moral censure even though it is not possible to prove that the impaired capacity was the cause of the bad behaviour. Capacity is taken into account on the retributive principle that punishment should not be disproportionate to blame. This principle acts as a constraint on the extent to which it is permissible to punish offenders in order to deter others, to promote the general welfare or to mark the community's abhorrence of what someone has done. To apply this principle courts need to be able, at least roughly, to measure desert. One way in which they do it is by making desert depend, among other factors, on capacity. Other things being equal, the less the defendant's capacity for rational decision the less punishment the defendant deserves. Why should this be so?

To take account of capacity makes sense only if we start from a model of rational decision and behaviour. The model is that of the agent who knows or can discover the circumstances in which he or she has to reach a decision and the option or options that are available, and can think sensibly how to choose between them. This is not the way in which even the most rational person normally decides what to do. It describes rather how they can set about deciding what to do if they want to and are prepared to make the effort. It represents what is in general open to the agent rather than any process that the agent has actually gone through on the relevant occasion.

The notion of capacity involved here is that of a general capacity to do this or that, including a capacity to reason and to conform to norms. But this does not imply a capacity to have behaved differently on the occasion for which the agent is being criminally prosecuted or morally censured. The point is one that I made as long ago as 1964;[45] Dennett has developed it further.[46] When we say that someone can do something (has the capacity to do it) we use 'can' in a general, not a particular sense: we mean that the person will in general succeed in doing it if they try. To assert that someone could have acted differently on a given occasion does not mean that given the precise circumstances including the impulses to which the agent was then subject that person could have done something different. It is rather that doing something different was not ruled out by the agent's general capacities. It is after all perfectly familiar that we

---

[45] 'Can and Can't', *Mind*, 73 (1964), pp. 463–79.
[46] *Elbow Room*, at pp. 144–52.

fail, say, on a particular occasion to jump a six-foot ditch, and not for want of trying, though we know perfectly well that we can jump it, perhaps because we have done so before.

This general sense of 'can' is the sense, I believe, in which capacity is and should be understood in criminal law. Those who are under the age of criminal responsibility or who are exempt on the ground of insanity are exempt because they do not *in general* sufficiently understand what causes what or what options are open to them. They do not *in general* possess the balance of judgement that is needed for making sensible decisions, though they may be able to do particular things quite competently. The criminal law has of course to draw firm lines based on age or recognised mental disease, but the relation of capacity to age or mental disability is in reality a matter of degree. Criminal justice recognises this to the extent that it is practicable to do so without endlessly prolonging investigation and trial. It commonly fixes different minimum ages on the one hand for criminal responsibility in general and on the other for liability to certain types of punishment such as imprisonment. It draws distinctions between the mental incapacity (insanity) that excludes criminal liability altogether and lesser incapacities arising from, say, abnormality of mind that reduce the gravity of the offence. It caters for temporary mental disturbances such as underlie provocation as a defence to murder and those milder upsets such as domestic stress that can be adduced in mitigation of punishment.

It is not easy to say why impaired capacity should lead to agents being treated as to some extent victims of circumstance. Why are they less at fault and less to be punished or censured than those of full capacity? To hold that they are seems to undermine responsibility as an institution that is outcome oriented: one that works by motivating success and stigmatising failure. The link between capacity, fault, and punishment works against these aims, since people with impaired capacity are often more likely to offend and to do harm than those whose capacity is normal. The mentally disturbed are likely to be more dangerous to their neighbours than the mentally normal. Why, if they offend, are they to be punished or censured less than those of full capacity, who are in general less likely to do bad things? Why is it that, though such people can, with due safeguards, be rendered harmless by confinement in institutions, they cannot be blamed for what they have done, at least not to the full extent?

It seems inescapable that this is one of the ways in which regard for justice prevents us from rewarding success and penalising failure to the full extent that a goal-oriented outlook would suggest. But why exactly should law and morality, as a matter of justice, pay attention to people's capacity to control their conduct?

It is remarkably difficult to find a satisfactory answer. The best I can do is to suggest the analogy of a handicap. If life in community is to be looked on as something like a competition, in which those with impaired capacities find it more difficult to get things right, it seems fair that they should be punished or censured less when they get them wrong. They start the race from behind or have already fallen behind so that, if they stumble, any punishment should take account of the handicap they already bear.[47] For, to the extent that they are punished, the punishment may well operate as an additional handicap, so that next time round (say when they come out of gaol) they start from still further behind. It is as if the horse carrying the heaviest weight was obliged to carry a still heavier weight. It may be that this way of looking at behaviour, in the context of fair competition, explains why, given the competitive model of society which responsibility presupposes, capacity is taken into account when punishment and censure are in issue. It is this that unites fault in the sense of getting something wrong and fault in the sense of being legally or morally to blame.

If this is the link between responsibility and capacity, consequences for penal policy follow that go beyond the allowance for impaired capacity that is already built into the legal system. For if account is taken of the extent to which people are handicapped by impaired capacity to control their behaviour, should the system not also take account of the extent to which they are handicapped by social or moral deprivation.[48] People can be fully rational and yet live in miserable conditions; they can belong to a subculture or underclass largely cut off from and hostile to the rest of society.

To put it more precisely, people's circumstances can be such that their range of choice is limited and within that range they are subject to pressure to make wrong choices. They can have 'scarcely more capacity for free choice than the person under duress'.[49] Their freedom, both positive and negative, is impaired. It is not poverty as such but this combination of restricted options and pressure to make wrong choices that can be seen as a serious handicap in the race of life. Those who suffer from it, like the incapable, are to some extent victims of circumstance.

But it is important not to succumb to the temptation of treating the restricted freedom of the socially and morally deprived as relieving them of responsibility.[50] For they, like the rest of us, benefit from the system of

---

[47] The idea of reformatories for young offenders rested on this notion.

[48] J. Floud, 'Sociology and the Theory of Responsibility: "Social Background" as an Excuse for Crime', in *The Science of Society and The Unity of Mankind* (ed. R. Fletcher, 1974), pp. 204–21 and *Psychological Medicine*, 5 no. 3 (1975), pp. 227–38 sketches the idea of 'social abnormality' as a conceivable defence in criminal law. I am arguing not for this, but for a candid recognition of social and moral handicap as a mitigating factor relevant to punishment.

[49] A. Ashworth, *Principles of Criminal Law* (2nd edn. 1995), p. 245.

[50] S. J. Morse, 'Culpability and Control' *University of Pennsylvania Law Rev.* 142 (1994), 1587, 1652–4.

responsibility that gives others an incentive to treat them well and to abstain from harming them. Even more important, their self-respect and sense of identity, limited though it may be, depends on their being held responsible for their conduct. To preserve their integrity we and they must refuse to treat what they do as merely the outcome of pressure exerted by others or of the narrow range of options open to them. To hold them responsible is to respect them as people. For this reason social and moral deprivation should be seen not as a hitherto unrecognised defence to a criminal charge, or as excusing wrong-doing, but rather as a matter to be taken into account in assessing moral guilt and in sentencing. The criminal process, against which the deprived are relatively defenceless, should acknowledge that in the race of life they start far back and that punishment, particularly imprisonment, is likely to set them further back. Probably judges do to some extent take account of social and moral deprivation, so understood. But it would be healthy to recognise this openly.

Society has to punish, because that is the only way of keeping deviance within manageable bounds. But in some ways those who are tried and convicted are like military conscripts chosen by ballot. The lot falls on them, but it could have fallen on others who committed similar offences without being caught, or who were caught but had the intelligence and resource to conduct a sophisticated defence. Once we are alive to the role of chance in the criminal process, it seems proper to take account of the fact that some of those prosecuted, though responsible for what they did, are handi-capped by incapacity or deprivation, and can easily be set on a downward spiral from which recovery is unlikely.

What is Labour-Market Flexibility? What is it Good for?

ROBERT M. SOLOW

Massachusetts Institute of Technology
Fellow of the Academy

THE EARLIEST KEYNES LECTURES tended to be on Keynesian subjects, either Keynes himself or the parts of economics on which he was a major influence. More recently that habit of piety has weakened or disappeared. I intend to go back to it, but not in the sense that I will be concerned with what Keynes or later Keynesians thought about this or that. The connection is more abstract. The macroeconomic role of the labour market is at the very centre of all that current talk about high and persistent European unemployment and its sharp contrast with the recent experience of the United States. The macroeconomic role of the labour market is also at the heart of one version—more or less the standard version—of Keynesian economics.

One legacy of *The General Theory*—much disputed—is the notion that the true source of excessive unemployment need not be some flaw in the labour market itself. In another standard version of the story, however, a lower nominal wage would correspond to higher employment, with the main chain of causation running through a lower price level, higher real money stock, lower interest rate, and higher aggregate real expenditure. In that story a higher nominal money stock would work just the same, without the need for deflation. From this angle, nevertheless, it looks as if nominal-wage-rigidity is the root of the problem. But other arguments, to be found in the *General Theory* itself, in Christopher Dow's Keynes Lecture of a few years ago, and in more recent work by Frank Hahn and myself, claim that full nominal wage flexibility would bring with it enough other problems to make it a non-solution to the

Proceedings of the British Academy, **97**, 189–211. © The British Academy 1998.
Read at the Academy 30 October 1997.

problem of unemployment. It is certainly not progress to *define* complete wage-flexibility as the achievement at every instant of a nominal wage at which employment will be 'full' and then to declare that wage-flexibility is the solution to the problem of excessive unemployment.

All this will remind you of your youth, assuming that you are not young any more. It is not the trail that I want to follow. I propose to start from the other end. Measured unemployment has been very high in Europe for more than a decade, as compared both with the period before 1975 and with the United States currently. Almost uniformly, in public discussion of what is after all a high-visibility issue, the blame for this failure falls on 'rigidities in the labour market'. That response has already achieved the status of a reflex, exhibited by any central banker you might care to ask. The same knee-jerk reaction appears also as the conclusion of the OECD Jobs Study (though it might more appropriately be described as the assumption of the OECD Jobs Study). My plan is to start from that end and work backwards to something more precise and more analytical. It is only fair to say that there has been some serious good sense written on this topic; an excellent example is the 1995 pamphlet by G. Alogoskoufis, C. Bean, *et al.*, *Unemployment: Choices for Europe*, published by the Centre for Economic Policy Research in London. I want to mention also an interesting article by Stephen Nickell in the Summer 1997 *Journal of Economic Perspectives*.

My first observation is that 'labour-market rigidity' is never defined very precisely or directly in this context, but only by the enumeration of tell-tale symptoms. Thus a labour market is inflexible if the level of unemployment-insurance benefits is too high or their duration is too long, or if there are too many restrictions on the freedom of employers to fire and to hire, or if the permissible hours of work are too tightly regulated, or if excessively generous compensation for overtime work is mandated, or if trade unions have too much power to protect incumbent workers against competition and to control the flow of work at the site of production, or perhaps if statutory health and safety regulations are too stringent. It seems clear that those who point to labour-market rigidity as the source of high unemployment have something other than simple nominal or real wage rigidity in mind, or so I shall assume.

This sort of definition by example is far from satisfactory. Not that the examples are irrelevant: each of the restrictions I have mentioned certainly contributes its mite to labour-market rigidity in the very broad sense that it limits the possible responses to any exogenous change in circumstances. Nevertheless there are (at least) two important reasons to look for something more systematic.

Every one of these regulations or restrictions was intended to promote a desirable social purpose. Some may do so ineffectively or inefficiently. That is worth knowing; but the fact remains that wholesale elimination of these 'rigidities' is neither desirable nor feasible. They might be modified or traded off against one another; but to do that intelligently already presupposes some sort of yardstick. One needs to form some idea of how much a particular regulation contributes to overall labour-market rigidity; in other words, one needs some roughly quantifiable measure of rigidity. Such a measure would serve other purposes as well: comparisons from time to time and place to place, for example, require a way of talking about the overall degree of rigidity.

The second reason is more parochial, but still important. If 'labour-market rigidity' is to be more than a slogan, it needs to be incorporated into macroeconomic model-building, into the normal way we think about the determination of wages and employment in modern market economies. The catalogue of restrictions might be—and has been—studied one at a time from this point of view. But it is too hard to take account of them all at once. The analytical foundations of policy in this field would be strengthened if there were a useful summary indicator of labour-market rigidity that could function as an input into careful thinking about the macroeconomics of the labour market.

My candidate for this summary indicator is the location of the 'Beveridge curve' in whatever economy we are discussing. The Beveridge curve is the (negatively sloped) relation between the vacancy rate (the number of unfilled jobs expressed as a proportion of the labour force) and the unemployment rate (the number of unemployed job-seekers expressed as a proportion of the labour force). One can usually find such a curve in national data, if the data exist. It has negative slope for the commonsense reason that jobs are easier to fill, and the vacancy rate therefore lower, the more unemployed workers there are for employers to choose among. (This property can of course be derived from more primitive assumptions.) It is named after Sir William Beveridge, whose famous wartime report *Full Employment in a Free Society* defined 'full employment' to be a state of affairs in which the number of unfilled jobs equals the number of unemployed workers; this definition picks out the intersection of the Beveridge curve and a 45-degree line from the origin, when the unemployment rate is measured on one axis and the vacancy rate on the other.

A perfectly flexible labour market would then be one that interposes no obstacle to the frictionless matching of an unfilled job and an unemployed worker with the appropriate skills. In that case vacancies and unemployment could never coexist. The Beveridge curve would coincide with the axes of the diagram; there could be vacancies with no unemployment or there could be unemployment with no vacancies. Of course no real labour market could be perfectly flexible in that sense. Labour-market rigidities (including skill mismatches now) are precisely what allows vacancies and unemployment to coexist, and the more rigidities there are, the further the Beveridge curve diverges from the limiting case, the further from the zero–zero point it is located.

One can test this interpretation against the list of symptoms I mentioned earlier. Generous unemployment insurance benefits allow unemployed workers to reject vacant jobs in the hope of finding something better; the 'something better' might include not working for a while. Restrictions on hiring obviously make it harder to match a vacancy with an unemployed worker. Restrictions on firing are more subtle; they may inhibit the creation of vacancies, but they also induce employers to be pickier because a bad match is costlier to undo. In fact anything that limits the employer's control over performance is likely to shift the Beveridge curve adversely because adjustment to bad hires will be more difficult. Just thinking in terms of the Beveridge curve makes it easier to extend the list of effective labour-market rigidities. For instance, anything— statute, union rule, regulation or custom—that limits the geographical, industrial, or occupational mobility of workers, indeed anything that leads to segmentation of the labour market, is bound to shift the Beveridge curve adversely, because vacancies in one segment cannot be matched with unemployed workers in another. Obviously I have been ignoring genuine heterogeneity by tacitly including all workers and all jobs in one labour market. The real situation is more complicated but does not have to be dealt with in this sort of informal exposition.

Wage inflexibilities, including a high reservation wage, may also push the Beveridge curve away from the origin by preventing hires that could have been made if the wage were more flexible. I would like to leave it at that for now, because a complete theory of the labour market is not needed for the simpler point I am trying to make now: a good way to summarise the degree of rigidity in any national market is to see how far its Beveridge curve is from the limiting, unachievable case of perfect flexibility.

The theory of the Beveridge curve is in pretty good shape. (The best discussion is by Olivier Blanchard and Peter Diamond in 'The Beveridge Curve', *Brookings Papers on Economic Activity*, 1989, No. 1, pp. 1–60 and 74–6; they have a handful of other papers, including a brief introduction in 'The Flow Approach to Labor Markets', *American Economic Review (Papers and Proceedings)*, v. 82 (May 1992), 354–9.) The real problem is empirical. The very concept of a count of job vacancies is vague around the edges, and the same can be said of a count of unemployed workers. Employers can be more or less serious about filling a job, just as people can be more or less serious about finding a job. But national unemployment counts exist almost everywhere, whereas vacancy statistics are quite rare.

In the United States, official vacancy statistics were collected only for a brief interval in the 1960s. Instead the custom is to use a privately-collected time series of the volume of help-wanted advertising in newspapers. This is obviously an imperfect surrogate; for example, a vacancy may be advertised several times or not at all, and in any case the role of the newspaper as an advertising medium has been changing. But it is a lot better than nothing. In Europe the availability of vacancy statistics differs from country to country, and there are occasional changes in definitions and methods. But there is enough to get on with.

The sort of labour-market model encouraged by the use of the Beveridge curve allows one to talk of labour-market flexibility as distinct from simple wage-flexibility. I have taken that opportunity for a couple of reasons. Those who talk about the need for more flexibility in European labour markets are presumably not just asking for more wage-flexibility; if they were, they could say so directly. Besides, the macroeconomics of wages is a very long story, going back at least to Pigou's *Theory of Unemployment*; there is nothing to be gained by bringing it up here. There is, however, one relevant empirical point that I would like to underline.

There was a time, in the early and middle 1980s, when the 'wage-gap hypothesis' was a leading candidate explanation for what was even then seen as unusually high unemployment for Europe. (The main reference is *The Economics of Worldwide Stagflation*, 1985, by Michael Bruno and Jeffrey Sachs.) The hypothesis was that real wages in Europe had outrun labour productivity. Among the consequences were low profitability, low investment, and a lot of unemployment. It is easy to see how this could have happened. Real wages typically move with labour productivity. An unexpected productivity slowdown began some time around 1970 (and continues still, though no longer unexpected); slow adaptation to this change could account for the opening of a wage-gap if real wages continued to reflect inertia induced by older expectations. One common extension was the idea that in Europe real wages were sticky; in the US nominal wages were sticky so the real wage could be 'inflated down'.

To say that the real wage has outrun the productivity of labour is to say that the share of wages in aggregate output has risen; and in fact the profit share in the major Continental economies was unusually low from about 1975 to the early 1980s.

Beginning in the early 1980s, however, there was a remarkable distributional shift to profits. The wage share in Europe began to fall, and may not yet have stopped falling. By now the wage share on the Continent is substantially lower than in North America. The wage-gap has disappeared, more than disappeared so to say, but the unemployment lingers on. The significance of this fact is that one cannot build a really convincing story about current unemployment that rests primarily on wage-rigidity that holds the economy-wide real wage at too high a level. The dynamics do not fit.

It is worth a reminder that the unemployment rate in the UK climbed to very high levels in the years 1981–7 and has since receded, not to where it was in the 1970s but to a figure substantially lower than in France and Germany. During this period the profit share fluctuated around an essentially horizontal trend; here too the profit share has been rising in the 1990s, but it is still ever so slightly lower than in the mid-1980s. There is no particular comfort for the wage-gap story here either.

The Beveridge curves provide a somewhat heterodox perspective on the role of labour-market rigidities. (Here and elsewhere I am deeply indebted to Professor James Medoff of Harvard for his pioneering empirical work and his generosity in helping out with data and analysis. The data plotted in the European Beveridge-curve diagrams are all extracted from official sources. The figures are not really comparable from country to country, not even the unemployment rates. They are useful primarily for comparisons over time for each country separately.) I begin with the US (Fig. 1) because it is the natural benchmark for comparison with France, Germany, and the UK.

The diagram plots the 'vacancy rate' vertically and the unemployment rate horizontally, on an annual basis. Remember that the 'vacancy rate' is really an index of help-wanted advertising normalised by the labour force. It would be possible to doctor the data: the unemployment rate could be corrected for demographic changes, as George Perry suggested long ago; and the help-wanted index could be keyed to the brief period when vacancies were actually measured, and could be adjusted for the change in the importance of newspapers as an advertising medium, as Katharine Abraham showed a decade ago. I have omitted such refinements because it is only the qualitative picture that matters for now.

That qualitative picture stands out clearly. From 1958 through 1971, the US seemed to move along a well-defined Beveridge curve. During 1972–4 the curve shifted adversely, and settled for 1975–86 about three percentage points of unemployment to the right of its earlier location. Then, in 1987 and 1988, the curve seemed to return to its initial position, and has remained there for the past decade. One can interpret this as saying that the US experienced an episode of acute labour-market rigidity between the early 1970s and the early 1980s, and has now reverted to form. (Blanchard and Diamond, in the 1989 paper already cited, produce a monthly Beveridge curve for a different period, 1952–88, using slightly different data. The general evolution is entirely consistent with what I have just described.) Does this make sense?

I can invent a libretto to go along with that melody. The story line includes the pronounced productivity slowdown, leading first to an unrealistic reservation wage, and then to an eventual adjustment to reality. One could also make something of increasing segmentation of the labour market as older manufacturing industries decayed, and the economic structure shifted in favour of the service sector and the Sunbelt. I called this a libretto precisely to underline the

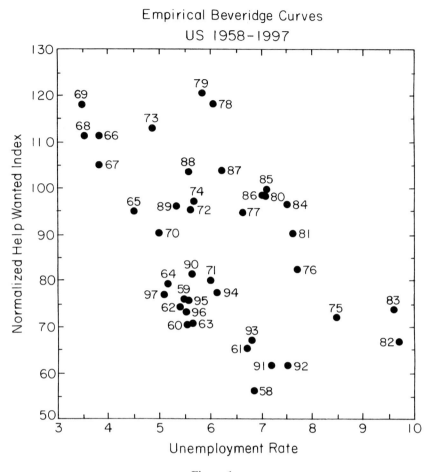

Figure 1.

lightweight character of the exercise. One can always invent a plausible story to cover a single episode; in this case the episode lasted for forty years, at least, and had three acts. It is worth noting, however, that the sorts of scenery emphasised in the usual verion of the European opera do not seem to have been on stage in the US.

The picture in the UK (Fig. 2) as shown in the second diagram, is more complicated. Perhaps bemused by what happened in the US, I am inclined to push my luck and suggest an analogous, though not quite similar, evolution here. A determined reader of tea leaves could certainly see an initial Beveridge curve for the years 1964–72. Beginning in 1973, during a period of mostly rising unemployment, the whole curve seems to migrate to the right, settling down from 1983 to 1987, and then moving leftward again to what looks like a

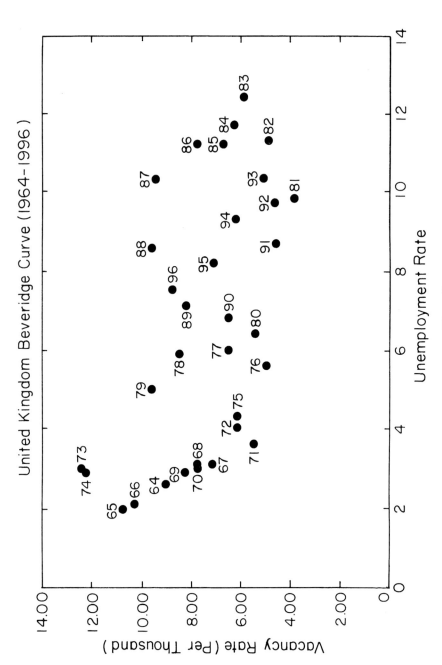

Figure 2.

stable position—at least temporarily—in the 1990s. The initial rightward shift spans almost nine percentage points of unemployment at the extreme; and the reversion to the left takes about four percentage points back. A vacancy rate that would have corresponded to three per cent unemployment in the 1960s is accompanied by roughly eight per cent unemployment in the 1990s. This is obviously a much bigger change than can be inferred in the US.

There is, however, an underlying similarity in timing. In both cases the adverse shift of the Beveridge curve begins around 1972 or 1973. The temptation is strong to identify it in the UK, as in the US, with the slow adjustment of wages to the productivity slowdown that began in those years. (It might once have been thought that the first OPEC oil shock was the source of the maladjustment of wages, or even of the productivity slowdown itself. But that idea has lost whatever plausibility it ever had, if only because the later fall in the real price of oil had no corresponding effect. In any case, the rightward shift of the Beveridge curve seems to have begun a bit too early to be explained in that way.)

The leftward migration of the Beveridge curve also dates from 1987 in both countries. That coincidence might offer a hint as to the underlying cause. But I would prefer to leave that inference to others who know more than I do about the timing of institutional, political, and other changes in the UK and US labour markets that might account for the stories told by the two Beveridge-curve diagrams. Apart from these similarities in timing, there are drastic differences. The two most noticeable are, first, that the adverse shift in the UK was larger and more drawn out in time than the corresponding shift in the US, and, second, that the UK Beveridge curve has reverted only about halfway back to its initial favourable location, whereas in the US the 1960s and the 1990s seem to look alike. It will take a knowledgeable combination of formal analysis and local anecdote to account for those differences. My immediate interest lies elsewhere, and especially in the contrast with the corresponding developments in France and Germany.

For that we can look at the third and fourth Beveridge-curve diagrams (Figs. 3 and 4), which are in fact very much like each other and very different from the preceding ones for the US and the UK. In both France and Germany there is a suggestion of a vertical portion of the curve at the extreme left. This is what one would expect to see if there were a minimal level of frictional unemployment necessary for the labour market to function at all; it would reflect entry and exit from the labour force, turnover from one job to another, and so on. The diagrams make it look as if that minimal unemployment rate were just under three per cent in France, achieved in the late 1960s and early 1970s, and one per cent in Germany, achieved at exactly the same time.

Then the picture gets more interesting. Something may have happened beginning in 1975, in both countries. But the simple configuration of the data

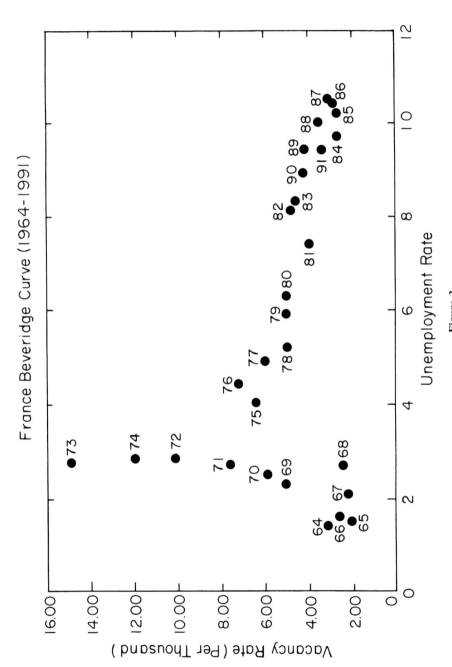

Figure 3.

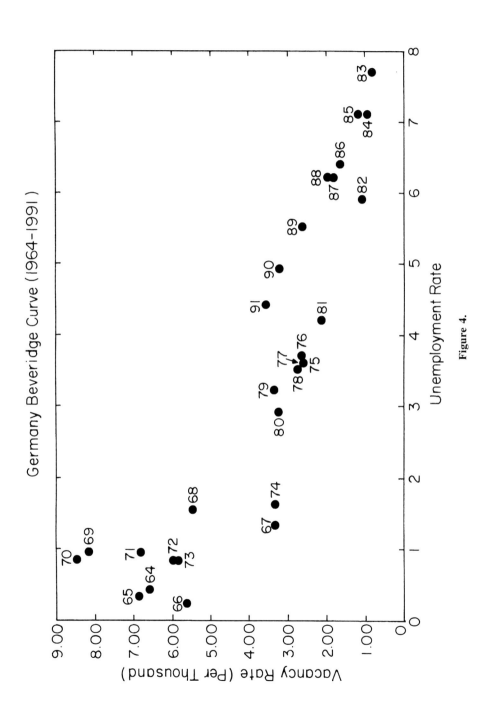

Figure 4.

allows two interpretations. One is that there was a small rightward shift of the Beveridge curve in both countries, amounting to about one percentage point of unemployment in France and fractionally more in Germany. The other is that there was no shift at all, and the whole twenty-eight-year period traces out a single, more or less stable, Beveridge curve. In practice, this is a distinction without a difference, because the adverse shift, if there was one, was so small.

In the case of France, moreover, the years 1964–9 are anomalous. The eye could make a case that a significant shift separates the years before and after 1970. But that would seem to have little to do with the period of endemic high unemployment in the 1980s and 1990s.

Unfortunately the interval described in these graphs ends in 1991, because the later data are for various reasons incomparable with the earlier observations. So we cannot look at the 1990s through this particular lens. However the small reductions in unemployment that took place in France between 1986 and 1990 and in Germany between 1983 and 1991 do seem to be traversing much the same Beveridge curve as was traced out in the opposite direction in France between 1980 and 1986 and in Germany between 1983 and 1991. In saying this I am taking account of the normal presumption that evolving data would trace out counter-clockwise loops around the curve representing stationary equilibrium positions.

I have said that these observations are open to slightly different interpretations. But I also have to claim that the main message transmitted by the Beveridge curves transcends these alternatives. That message goes squarely against the cliché that high and persistent European unemployment is entirely or mainly a matter of 'labour-market rigidities'. It is precisely in France and Germany, where unemployment has been higher and more persistent, that there is no sign of a big adverse shift in the Beveridge curve. It is precisely in the US and the UK, where unemployment has been at least more variable and, in the case of the US, lower, that one can detect a substantial adverse shift, followed by a favourable one.

To the extent that the location of the Beveridge curve is a reasonable summary for the degree of labour-market rigidity, the large continental economies do not seem to have suffered from noticeably more rigid labour markets during the high-unemployment 1980s than they did in the low-unemployment 1970s. In fact what stands out from the pictures for France and Germany is the depressed level of the vacancy variable. It is a pity not to have comparable data for the last five years.

In the case of Germany, where the data now include the Ostländer, one can at least say that there is no indication of a rebound in vacancies. The case of France is even less clear. There is a new series of 'new job vacancies' and it has risen smartly since 1991; but this sounds like a measure of 'job creation' and it is impossible to interpret it in isolation from information about job destruction and pre-existing vacancies. It is a reasonable judgement that the major difference between France and Germany now and in the early 1970s is that the demand for labour is now much weaker. It is not reasonable to blame that large increase in unemployment on *worsened* labour-market rigidity.

I think that the evidence just presented is very strong, but probably not conclusive. That is because the location of the Beveridge curve cannot be a complete summary of the degree of labour-market rigidity at a given time and place. In particular, one of the factors underlying the generation of vacancies is the intensity of job-creation through the appearance of new firms and the expansion or transformation of old ones. It is certainly possible that job creation could be inhibited by apprehensiveness about the working of the labour market. As an example, limitations on their ability to discharge workers if sales expectations are disappointed would surely make employers less eager to create vacancies and hire workers. (Whether this mechanism is quantitatively important is another matter.) In principle this side-effect could be seen as an adverse shift in the Beveridge curve. But one must allow for the possibility that the same effect could be confounded with a movement along the Beveridge curve in the data for France and Germany.

To explore this possibility, I turn to an altogether different kind of evidence. A year or two ago the research branch of the McKinsey consulting firm (it is called the McKinsey Global Institute) conducted an extensive study of economic performance in France and Germany. A handful of academic economists (of whom I was one) participated in that study as an active advisory committee; but the part of the work that I need to emphasise here was done mainly by McKinsey's own people, each contributing experience and expertise in a particular industry. This part of the study consisted of six detailed industrial case studies, each comparing the performance of a particular industry in France and Germany with the same industry in whatever country was the world champion in productivity, usually the US but Japan in one instance and the Netherlands in another. The industries studied were automobiles, housebuilding, telecommunications, retail trade, consumer banking, and computer software.

The notion of 'economic performance' is not self-explanatory. In the McKinsey study a national industry got good grades for high productivity—compared with the benchmark—and for high employment. It is important that in most cases the two go together. The country with the highest productivity in any particular industry is usually the country that has created the most jobs in that industry, and this is true even in industries like telecommunications where it cannot be thought that the benchmark country has drained jobs from others. No economist will be surprised at this finding; it is worth mentioning only because political opinion in Europe often seems to embrace a refined version of the old Luddite fallacy.

These remarks are just by way of introduction. The relevant and important part of the McKinsey case studies is that in each instance the team tried to think explicitly about causality. If a particular industry in France or Germany has been deficient in productivity or in job creation, *why* has it not done better? What factors in the institutional environment and what features of economic policy have caused the shortfall in productivity and in job creation? This part of the analysis was generally not mechanical or even quantitative; it relied on the experience and judgement of the consultants and their informants in each industry, but the advisory committee was able to insist that these judgements be backed up by concrete detail. We would not have tolerated arguments that violated economic logic. This is not the way I am used to arriving at conclusions. But I have to say that I found the process enlightening. The case I am trying to make can only benefit from finding that altogether different approaches lead in a common direction.

In the course of this and earlier studies, the McKinsey group has worked out a standard protocol for characterising causal influences on a given industry in a given place. It is a sort of vertical checklist, beginning with the macroeconomic environment and descending through externally imposed product-market regulations and institutions, through the constraints and costs that stem from the organisation of the labour and capital markets, including the incentives and limitations that arise from pressures on corporate governance, to the intensity of competition and the degree of exposure to industrial best practice, and ending with details of the production process and the organisation of functions and tasks. In the end, each of these potential causal factors is classified as being important, merely secondary, or not significant at all in distinguishing the productivity and job-creation performance of this national industry from the corresponding benchmark. I want to report on these conclusions.

I will describe the conclusions case by case, before summarising the overall message. In the automobile industry, the only mature manufacturing industry among the six, Japan is the benchmark. Comparing France and Germany with Japan, the group finds that restrictive work rules are a factor of only secondary importance, and differences in labour costs are negligible. The important causal factors come from the limited exposure of the European industry to competition, and from inferior management of operations.

In housebuilding, it is found that labour-market factors are essentially insignificant in explaining the productivity shortfall of France and Germany compared with the Netherlands. Differences in product regulations and in internal organisation are far more important. Germany does have higher labour costs than the other countries, including France, and these might be a secondary factor if benchmark productivity were achieved.

In the telecommunications sector, the conclusion is that restrictive work rules are a secondary causal factor in productivity comparisons. The important causal factors are elsewhere. Independent of productivity differences, the French and German industries generate less output and employment than they might. This surely has nothing to do with the labour market and everything to do with competitive intensity, pricing, and marketing effort.

In consumer banking, the European productivity shortfall has little or nothing to do with the labour market, and much more to do with forces arising in product markets and in internal management. Nor does the labour market have a significant effect on the output of consumer-banking services, conditional on productivity. Differences in job-creation arise elsewhere.

In retailing the productivity differences are small, but the underlying facts are more complicated. An important part of the picture is that high minimum wages in France and Germany induce stores to avoid high-service, high-employment formats. Thus the European industry does not provide the large number of low-wage jobs that it does in the US.

In the software industry, labour-market flexibility is an insignificant factor. All the action in job-creation is in product markets and scale effects.

I have compressed a detailed and sophisticated report by McKinsey into a couple of slogans. But I have to summarise even those. There are a few contexts in which labour-market factors are a significant influence on the number and kind of jobs created. But the bottom line is clearly that these case studies strongly confirm the inadequacy (to put it mildly) of the standard litany that places the blame for low employment in Europe squarely on the inflexibilities of the labour market. It turns out that practised observers of the industrial scene, when they come down to careful, structured evaluation, do not classify labour-market rigidities as an important causal factor in the failure of (at least) these six industries to create more jobs. One might guess—naively, I think—that the observers in question, consultants and business insiders, might normally be disposed to single out the labour market for criticism. The fact that they do not do so lends a little more weight to the conclusion.

This kind of evidence reinforces the interpretation of the Beveridge curves suggested earlier. The likelihood is that France and Germany have moved to high-unemployment regimes by sliding *along* their Beveridge curves, and not as victims of adverse shifts in their Beveridge curves. The implied weakness in job creation is most likely the result of excessive and anti-competitive product-market regulation, restrictive macroeconomic policy, especially monetary policy, and inadequate discipline from the capital markets. This is quite different from the conventional picture.

None of this is to deny that European labour markets are in fact highly regulated and spotted with rigidities. Even if these deviations from a pure spot market are not the main source of the long spell of high unemployment, they may still be a source of real cost to the European economy. Anything that limits the ability of firms to adapt to changed circumstances is a possible source of inefficiency. So one might prescribe an attempt to achieve greater labour-market flexibility even if this were not expected to have any durable effect on the level of unemployment. There are some qualifications, however.

Flexibility also entails some costs of its own, and they are worth mentioning because they seem to be neglected in current debates, despite their obviousness. A job provides not only a regular wage but also some security of income. It is not far-fetched to simplify by imagining each job to be characterised by its wage and by some measure of its permanence, like its expected duration. Jobs have many other relevant characteristics as well, ranging from safety to sociablity, but I would like to focus on security. Employees clearly value both aspects of a job (as who should know better than tenured academics). On the other side of the labour market, both aspects of a job represent costs to employers. The provision of job security is costly precisely because it limits the employer's freedom of action in adapting to exogenous changes in the market environment. One would expect both parties to an employment contract to be willing on some terms to trade off wages against security. One can see this happening in collective bargaining, with further by-play among differently situated workers on that side of the bargain. (Frank Hahn and I have made a first stab at modelling this situation; see pages 95–101 of our *Critical Essay*.)

One obstacle to this line of thought is that it is hard to contract for job security *per se*. The relevant characteristic of a job is its *ex ante* expected duration, not its *ex post* actual duration. It is almost impossible to say whether any concrete act of 'downsizing' represents (*a*) the occurrence of a contingency whose possibility was foreseen in the original explicit or implicit contract, or (*b*) an attempt on the part of the firm to shift risk to its employees in violation of the explicit or implicit contract. Whichever is true, the firm will always plead necessity and the workers will resent the *ex post* application of a rule, whether or not it was contemplated *ex ante*.

There are no doubt sophisticated ways to achieve incentive compatibility in this context. In actual fact, however, one imagines that employment contracts try to meet this difficulty by imposing inefficient limitations on the firm's flexibility (for instance by regulating outsourcing). To repeal many or all of such arrangements suddenly by legislation amounts to a shift of risk from a firm to its employees. This is not self-evidently a reasonable thing to do. Workers are almost certainly more risk-averse than the firms that employ them, since they have practically no opportunity for diversification and no possibility to claim compensation through the tax system for a capital loss on job-specific human capital.

The welfare economics of job security is a complicated subject that deserves more analysis than it has had, and surely more than I have tried to provide here. I introduced the subject only to make a point about economic policy. If pure unadulterated labour-market reform is unlikely to create a substantial increase in employment, then the main reason for doing it is the anticipated gain in productive efficiency, however large that may be. But if we respect the wage earner's desire for job security, and it seems at least as respectable as anyone's desire for fast cars or fat-free desserts, then an improvement in productive efficiency gained that way is not a Pareto-improvement. More labour-market flexibility may still be worth having—and I think it is— but then the losers have a claim in equity to some compensation. The trick is to find a form of compensation that does not cancel the initial gain in labour-market flexibility. Some forms of job-protection, like those described in the insider–outsider literature, provide job security for incumbent workers at the expense of the excumbents. That is not what we are after. But a bit of ingenuity might get somewhere. I call attention to the fact that this is a far cry from your basic European central banker's folk-theorem.

Discussion

Charles Bean, *London School of Economics*

Like Apple Pie and Motherhood, it seems that labour-market 'flexibility' must be a desirable feature of an economy. Yet too often the argument that greater labour-market flexibility is required to tackle Europe's unemployment problem is accepted uncritically. Professor Solow—whom I had the very great honour to study under in my youth—makes some telling and pertinent criticisms of this conventional wisdom. I have much sympathy with his general line of argument that the role of labour-market institutions has been overplayed in the public debate and that of product-market imperfections underplayed. However, I would not want to downplay the role of the labour market quite as much as he does.

Bob first argues that excessively high real wages cannot be the problem in Europe since the wage share has been falling during the last fifteen years or so. Unfortunately this does not imply that factors leading to excessive 'wage push', such as over-generous unemployment benefits, are not the cause of the unemployment problem. In the very short-run it is probably true that excessive wage pressure shows up as an increased wage share. However, as firms cut back on employment the marginal and average product of labour will rise so pushing the wage share back down; in fact with a Cobb-Douglas production technology one would observe no change in the wage share at all. Furthermore the resulting decline in profitability will discourage investment, thus reducing the demand for labour below what it would otherwise be (this is a process to which my co-discussant, Bob Rowthorn, has also drawn attention). The fall in labour demand, and consequent rise in unemployment, will then lead to a fall in equilibrium wages. Indeed, if there are constant returns to scale in labour and capital together, the equilibrium real wage in the long-run will be determined *entirely* by the state of technical knowledge and the user cost of capital (determined largely in the global capital market); wage-push factors thus show up in higher unemployment, but not in either a higher wage share or a higher real wage. I conclude that one can learn little about the causes of unemployment by looking at the movements in these latter variables alone.

Bob then goes on to argue that the Beveridge Curve linking unemployment and vacancies is a useful indicator, and that a reduction in labour-market flexibility should show up as an outward shift of the Beveridge Curve; this is not obviously the case in France and Germany. Now I agree that it is a useful weapon to add to the diagnostic armoury, but it is only half the story and needs to be used carefully. Figure 5 outlines a simple model of the joint determination of unemployment and vacancies (the exposition follows the work of Christopher Pissarides and his co-authors). The number of successful job matches will be increasing in both the number of firms looking for workers and the number of unemployed workers looking for jobs. Hence the pairs of unemployment and vacancies consistent with a constant unemployment rate can be represented by the downward sloping line, UV; above (below) the UV line unemployment will be falling (rising). This is the Beveridge Curve. However, there is a second line, VS (for Vacancy Supply), that tells us how many vacancies firms open at any given unemployment rate, and thus also where along the Beveridge Curve the economy is located. This VS schedule embodies within it both the factors determining labour demand (technology, firing cost, . . .) and wage determination (unemployment benefits, . . .), and is

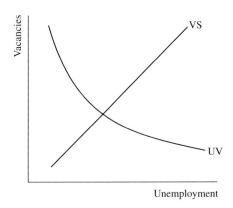

Figure 5.

upward-sloping because high unemployment implies a low level of wage pressure and thus a high propensity of firms to open vacancies.

We can use this apparatus to study the effects of various labour-market institutions and policies. Let me start by noting that increased labour-market 'flexibility' is usually taken to cover a whole raft of policies, including reduced impediments to hiring and especially firing, measures to increase the mobility of labour across both regions and occupations, eliminating restrictions on working time, union bashing, less generous unemployment benefits and lower minimum wages. The effect of each of these is, however, very different and cannot all be collapsed into a simple statement that increased (reduced) flexibility shifts the Beveridge Curve in (out). Thus, an increased mismatch between the skills of the labour force and the needs of firms will indeed just shift UV out as Bob suggests. However, anything that increases wage pressure such as higher minimum wages or aggressive union behaviour will shift VS down. And an increase in the generosity of unemployment benefits would shift both UV out (because it makes the unemployed more choosy about which jobs to accept) and VS down (because it makes the employed more willing to push for higher wages). Consequently the German and French experience is in my view entirely consistent with the roots of the unemployment problem lying within the labour market.

However, Bob supplements his use of the Beveridge Curve with the lessons of the McKinsey comparative study of economic performance. This sort of 'checklist' methodology is somewhat alien to economists, and I have to say that I can understand why, as I find it somewhat difficult to draw out the policy implications. I have already noted that in the long-run real wages are pegged down by the state of technology and the required return on capital, not by labour-market institutions which in general equilibrium only affect unemployment. I thus do not find it altogether surprising that when firms are asked about the most important factor inhibiting job creation that product market and internal management factors might be primary and labour market factors only secondary. However, it might be very difficult for policy to do anything about the primary factors (although I hasten to add that I am all in favour of product market de-regulation in Europe), while the general equilibrium consequences of changes to labour-market institutions may still be quantitatively important. Furthermore even if increased labour-market rigidity is not the *cause* of Europe's higher unemployment, nevertheless labour-market reforms may still be desirable. Put simply, the macroeconomic environment deteriorated in the 70s and 80s because of the productivity slowdown, the oil price shocks and the subsequent disinflation, and Europe's labour-market institutions were simply less well suited to handling this deterioration in the environment than the United States.

Finally let me agree wholeheartedly with a point that Bob makes in relation to the political feasiblity of reform. Most of the rigidities that people say need to be removed or moderated are not accidents of the system, but play a role either in offsetting market failures (mandated severance pay compensates workers who otherwise bear most of the costs of job destruction) or more usually transferring rents (minimum wages may harm the job prospects of the unemployed—although even this is open to debate—but raise the wages of those in work at the cost of shareholders). Reform is difficult because there will always be losers, and in practice it may be difficult to compensate them. Reform will be politically easier to sustain when there are fewer losers, and it will thus be easier to enact reform in a booming economy where jobs are plentiful than in a depressed one. The focus on fiscal consolidation in the run up to monetary union, and the possible future immobilisation of fiscal policy under the Stability Pact, has in my view made it much harder to push through reform than necessary. It would have been far better if the governments of Europe had embarked on labour-market reform *before* setting out on the road to a Single Currency.

Robert Rowthorn

It is always a pleasure to hear a lecture by Robert Solow. He has an unrivalled ability to strip away the extraneous details of any problem and focus on the core issues. This lecture is no exception. Within the space of an hour he has elegantly demolished the conventional wisdom which now dominates European economic thinking. He argues that neither high wages nor rigid labour market practices are the primary cause of the present high unemployment in continental Europe, as exemplified by France and Germany. He concedes that lower wages and more flexible labour markets might help to reduce unemployment, but he regards these as palliatives which do not address the central problem. In his view, the 'weakness in job creation is most likely the result of excess and anti-competitive product-market regulation, restrictive macroeconomic policy, especially monetary policy, and inadequate discipline from capital markets'. With some qualifications, I agree with this unfashionable view, and I am pleased to hear it so well presented by such an eminent economist.

In support of his position Solow presents three pieces of evidence: (1) the relationship between wages, productivity and profits over the past thirty years; (2) the relationship between unemployment and vacancies; and (3) the results of a McKinsey study of industrial performance to which he contributed. Let us take these in reverse order. The McKinsey study found that, in five of the six industries examined, labour-market considerations are not a major factor behind Europe's poor employment record. The one exception is retail distribution where minimum wage laws inhibit the growth of low-wage jobs on the American pattern. These findings strongly support Solow's views regarding the secondary contribution of working practices to European unemployment. However, their implications for the wages are less clear.

Most of the industries covered by McKinsey pay comparatively high wages even in the USA, and minimum wage laws are of minor relevance to them. It is striking that in the one industry where low-paid employment is important in the USA, the McKinsey study found that minimum wages did inhibit such employment in Europe. If the study had covered a wider range of industries, this finding would probably have been more common. In a cross-section analysis of the OECD countries, Andrew Glyn has identified an inverse relationship between employment and wage dispersion. The employment rate is in general highest in countries with the greatest wage dispersion, in part because very low pay at the bottom end of the earnings spectrum encourages low-productivity employment in labour-intensive sectors. This suggests the following interpretation of modern experience. In most OECD countries the overall demand for labour has been inadequate. In the USA, and to some extent the UK, the response has been to deregulate labour markets, allowing wages to fall and forcing workers to accept whatever job is available. The result has been a proliferation of low-paid jobs mainly in the service sector. In continental Europe this has not been allowed to happen and the wage floor has been maintained, with the consequence that inadequate demand for labour is reflected in overt unemployment. Thus, increased wage dispersion in the USA and higher unemployment in continental Europe are two sides of the same coin. They are the outcome of different responses to a common overall shortage of demand for labour. Opinions may differ as to which response is better.

An important part of Solow's lecture concerns the relationship between vacancies and unemployment, as summarised by the so-called Beveridge curve. He shares the conventional view that the position of this curve is a reflection of labour market rigidity, and that an outward shift in the curve indicates increased rigidity. I agree in principle, but I also think that some caution is required. As Solow himself points out, in the case of the UK there was a huge outward shift in the Beveridge curve between 1975 and 1983, when unemployment increased from four per cent to almost thirteen per cent with no significant change in vacancies. Most of the increase occurred after 1980 when the Thatcher government was in power and busy attacking the unions and dismantling protective legislation. It is difficult to believe that rigidity actually increased during this period, certainly not on a scale sufficient to explain the outward shift in the curve. An alternative explanation is that the economy suffered from pre-existing rigidities which were only exposed when it suffered the shock of a severe crisis. For example, during the period in question, the UK experienced an industrial collapse which destroyed millions of jobs in manufacturing, mining, and construction. Traditional industrial areas were severely affected by these losses and the knock on effect on local service activities. The effect was to create a large pool of unemployed workers, who were geographically concentrated, lacking the skills required for other jobs, and reluctant to move. Most of these workers were not able to take advantage of the new opportunities created by the economic boom of the late 1980s, with the result that unemployment remained fairly high despite a pronounced shortage of labour in some areas. This outward shift in the Beveridge curve cannot be ascribed to increased labour market rigidity, but to pre-existing rigidities which inhibited labour mobility and the retraining of workers following a major, regionally and industrially specific, shock. The same is probably true on a less dramatic scale in the USA. It is interesting that large shocks during this period do not seem to have shifted the Beveridge curve in France and Germany. It may be that labour mobility or retraining possibilities were greater in those countries, or the shocks less regionally specific, or regional job creation programmes more effective. Whatever the reason, Solow is right to point out the difference, and to insist on the fact that France and Germany have been sliding along their Beveridge curves, with the implication that what is really at fault is an overall lack of demand for labour in these countries.

This brings me to my final point which concerns wages and profitability. I think that Solow understates the significance of wages for employment. The conventional theory of the Beveridge curve tells us that an increase in real wages may simultaneously reduce the number of vacancies and the number of people in employment, thereby causing the economy to slide down the Beveridge curve. The observed behaviour of unemployment and vacancies in France and Germany is therefore theoretically consistent with the fact that wages are too high. However, this is probably too static an interpretation. The dynamic issue is the effect of wages on profitability, and thereby on investment and future employment. It is here that the wage gap literature, of which Solow is so critical, is relevant. Profits were squeezed during the 1970s because of worker militancy and the failure of wages to absorb the full cost of higher oil and commodity prices. Firms increased prices to protect their profit margins, but this led to accelerating inflation in many countries, and governments eventually responded by raising interest rates and provoking an economic crisis. Real profits fell still further as capacity utilisation declined, and the result was a collapse in investment. In the ensuing recovery, profits were partially restored and investment picked up, but the recovery was not sufficiently strong or prolonged to compensate for the previous shortfall in investment. The situation has been made worse by the restrictive policies applied during the run up to EMU. As a result of these events, most Continental economies are now much too small to provide employment at reasonable pay for those desiring work.

I have not the time to analyse in detail why European investment has been so low, and I shall content myself with the following observations. For much of the past quarter century European economies have been characterised by excess capacity as a result of government anti-inflationary policies, and many of them experienced a decade of low profitability in the 1970s and 1980s. There has been a widespread recovery in profits, but they remain quite low in Germany, especially when compared to the opportunity cost of capital. For example, the net business profit rate in Germany averaged 13.5 per cent over the period 1969–73 as compared to a long-term real interest rate on government bonds of 2.0 per cent. For the period 1989–93 the corresponding figures were 10.8 per cent and 3.7 per cent. Thus the gap between net profits and interest fell from 11.5 per cent to 7.1 per cent. I do not have the equivalent figures for other Continental countries, but the figures on profit shares in manufacturing suggest that net profits have recovered to their pre-Oil Shock levels in most of them. However, long-term real interest rates have been very high for many years, and much of the time firms have been operating with excess capacity, both of which have served to depress investment and prevent countries from making good their long-standing shortage of capital stock. To produce a substantial reduction in continental unemployment requires a period of above average investment and growth. To achieve such a combination requires both expansionary demand policies and a prolonged period of above average profits.

The above observations suggest that wages may still be a factor behind unemployment in Europe through their effect on profits and investment. If wages were lower, profits would be higher and there might be more investment, and ultimately more jobs. Moreover, the *fear* of wage inflation causes governments to adopt restrictive policies that create unemployment and inhibit investment. It may be that such a fear is mistaken, because in the medium term more investment might reduce inflation by increasing productivity and thereby offsetting the inflationary effect of higher wages. If this is the case, governments should be willing to accept a transitory period of higher inflation before new capital stock comes on stream. Of course, to advocate such an approach is hopeless at the moment, because policy makers are still dominated by an inflation phobia which makes them unwilling to risk even a temporary acceleration in inflation as the price of more investment and more jobs. However, if high unemployment continues, political pressures may eventually force the authorities to rethink and start to experiment with more expansionary policies.

To sum up. I agree with the basic thrust of Robert Solow's argument that labour market rigidities are not the primary cause of high unemployment in Europe, but I would give more of a role to wages and the wage-profits nexus than he does. However, this is a minor qualification and I strongly welcome his lucid and stimulating contribution.

ERIC BIRLEY

Eric Barff Birley
1906–1995

HE PREFERRED TO BE KNOWN as Eric Birley. In fact he insisted that he be called Eric by everybody, including students. The family name Barff was not used by him, and the second initial was often omitted after the Second World War. He was born on 12 January 1906 at Swinton in Lancashire, the youngest of four sons, with two younger sisters. His parents were J. Harold Birley and Edith Gladys Fernandes Lewis. His father, to whom he was very close, died in 1940, his mother not till 1976, aged 96. Harold Birley was an Alderman in Manchester. He came from a textile manufacturing family, the family firm being Charles Macintosh. The original Charles Macintosh had discovered how to use rubber to make waterproof fabrics, gone into partnership with Birley Bros., who owned a mill, and given a new word to the English language. Hugh Birley, Eric Birley's great-grandfather, was second-in-command of the Manchester and Salford Yeomanry at Peterloo; he later became Borough Reeve of Manchester.

Birley went to preparatory school at Bakewell, where an early interest in archaeology was kindled from visiting prehistoric caves in the Peak District. He was intended for Rugby, but his brother Robin, who was due to be head boy at Clifton, persuaded him to try harder for Clifton, where he went with a scholarship. There he came under the influence of Norman Whatley as headmaster, who had been a friend of G. L. Cheesman, who wrote a basic work on *The Auxilia of the Roman Imperial Army*, published in 1914. Cheesman was killed in the First World War, and Norman Whatley presented Birley with his notes, including the texts of all the inscriptions relating to the *auxilia* then known. (The *auxilia* were the non-citizen troops of Rome, organised into *alae* and *cohortes*.) Birley also dated to this time his interest in the legions. Whatley is said to have predicted that his tutors at Oxford might find he would

Proceedings of the British Academy, **97**, 215–232. © The British Academy 1998.

spend too much time studying the Roman army and too little time doing anything else.[1]

His first interest then was the Roman army, to which he added at Oxford, in his own words, 'the fascination of epigraphy . . . and the attractiveness of Roman nomenclature, hence also the study of prosopography'.[2] He went to Brasenose College. His later actions as Master of Hatfield College in the University of Durham were to be greatly influenced by his experiences at Brasenose, and he cherished the distinction of being made an Honorary Fellow of Brasenose in 1987. His tutor in ancient history, Michael Holroyd, compelled him to learn German for his very first essay: Birley recalls that the first word he learnt was *Schlacht*.[3] Birley's knowledge of written and spoken German was to play a significant part in building up his wide acquaintance with scholars abroad, one of his most distinguishing characteristics, and with his military interests led directly to the form of his war-time service. He was to make regular visits abroad in the years before the Second World War, beginning in 1926, looking at pottery but also exploring military sites in Germany, Austria, and Switzerland, including those on the Rhine–Danube frontier, the closest parallel to Hadrian's Wall.

His first excavation was at Bainbridge in Wensleydale in 1926. Under the influence of R. G. Collingwood he soon became involved in excavation on Hadrian's Wall, initially at Birdoswald in 1927. Here he was to work with and revere F. G. Simpson. It was on the Wall in 1928 that he learned he had achieved a Double First in Greats.

He observed sites in the city of London for the Society of Antiquaries of London in 1928–9, meeting there Mortimer Wheeler and J. A. Stanfield, the latter being important for the development of his interest in Samian ware. His report on work at the Midland Bank site in Princes Street was his first archaeological report.[4]

The year 1929 was to be significant. He was at Birdoswald alongside Ian Richmond, who was co-director with Simpson, when the two inscriptions were discovered that were to form the basis of thinking about the Wall from then on, virtually unchallenged for forty years and still with influence today. There was an element of drama here, for Collingwood, visiting the excavation, was placed before a mock-altar and photographed, standing on a Roman stone-slabbed floor. When the slabs were raised and cleaned it was discovered that Collingwood had been standing on a worn inscription, face-up, the 'altar' on another, face-down. The two inscriptions, one of AD 205–8 and the other of AD 296–306, attested

---

[1] Arthur Moyes, *Hatfield 1846–1996* (Durham, 1996), p. 205.
[2] E. Birley, *The Roman Army: papers 1929–86* (Amsterdam, 1988), p. vii.
[3] E. Birley, *Überlegungen zur Geschichte des römischen Heeres* (Heidelberg, 1987), p. 1.
[4] E. Birley, 'Report on recent Excavations in London. I The Midland Bank site, Princes Street, E.C.', *Ant. J.* 9 (1929), 219–28.

reconstruction in a Wall fort. It was already accepted, mainly on the basis of J. P. Gibson's and F. G. Simpson's work at Poltross Burn milecastle, that there were three periods of occupation on Hadrian's Wall, with a fourth in the forts alone. The first was assumed to end in disaster in AD 180, the second somewhere after AD 270, with no clear historical context. The new inscriptions from Birdoswald prompted Birley, after discussion with Collingwood, to put forward new dates for the end of periods I and II. He first published these in *Archaeologia Aeliana* for 1930; the inscriptions and pottery from Birdoswald, the supporting evidence for these views, were published by him later that same year.[5] These new dates were closer to the construction work attested by the inscriptions. They were *c.* AD 195, later refined to AD 197, for the end of period I, and *c.* AD 295, later refined to AD 296, for the end of period II. Most importantly, the notion of destruction occasioned by disaster was transferred to these dates. Simpson's third period could also be lengthened to AD 368, later AD 367, for the whole of the Wall, not just the forts. In subsequent thought the effects of 'disasters' in AD 197 and AD 296 were extended to the whole of Roman Britain, and it tended to be assumed that structural periods on individual sites would correspond to the 'four Wall periods' even if the evidence from them was insufficient for or contradictory to such a possibility. Collingwood accepted these ideas wholeheartedly; he had stressed the significance of AD 197 in 1930, and was the first to refine the end of period I to AD 197, in 1931.[6] Richmond hesitated a little. In the Birdoswald report, in his discussion of the structures, Richmond does not decide between AD 181 and AD 196–7.[7] Thereafter all three expounded the views initially put forward by Birley. The influence of Collingwood, Birley, and Richmond, the latter two at the beginning of their academic careers, greatly assisted in the general acceptance of these views, and the dating of the Wall periods put forward was not seriously challenged till the late 1960s, by Birley's own pupils as it happened.[8] The debate was thus re-opened, and continues.

Also in 1929 Birley took a step of significance for his immediate and long-term future. With the Chesters estate on the market, he purchased Vindolanda,

[5] E. Birley, 'Excavations on Hadrian's Wall west of Newcastle upon Tyne in 1929', *Arch. Ael.*, 4th ser., 7 (1930), 143–74: the crucial section is 164–74; (with I. A. Richmond), 'Excavations on Hadrian's Wall in the Birdoswald–Pike Hill Sector, 1929': part II 'The pottery' (175–98), part III 'The inscriptions' (198–202), *Cumb. & West.*, 2nd ser., 30 (1930), 169–205.
[6] R. G. Collingwood, *The Archaeology of Roman Britain* (Oxford, 1930), p. 85; 'Ten Years' Work on Hadrian's Wall 1920–30', *Cumb. & West*, 2nd ser., 31 (1931), 87–110 especially 106.
[7] I. A. Richmond (with E. Birley), 'Excavations on Hadrian's Wall in the Birdoswald–Pike Hill Sector, 1929', part I 'Birdoswald Fort', 173.
[8] These early challenges are summarised in: D. J. Breeze and B. Dobson, 'Hadrian's Wall: some problems, part IV: The three destructions of Hadrian's Wall', *Britannia*, 3 (1972), 200–8 with references; J. P. Gillam, 'The frontier after Hadrian—a history of the problem', *Arch. Ael.*, 5th ser., 2 (1974), 1–15.

with an eye to its potential for excavation, and almost as an afterthought decided to live near the site in what had been the home of Anthony Hedley, the site's first excavator. He remained here till he finally moved to Durham.

In 1930 Simpson resigned his directorship of the Durham University Excavation Committee, so it could be given to Birley. In 1931, on Michael Holroyd's suggestion to Sir James Knott, Birley was appointed lecturer at Armstrong College, Newscastle, then part of the University of Durham. (That same year he was elected a Fellow of the Society of Antiquaries of London.) He grew a moustache to try and look older than his students. In 1935 Ian Richmond had to return to Britain and give up his Directorship of the British School at Rome, and at Birley's suggestion a second lectureship was created in the Durham division of the university, to which Birley moved, Richmond being appointed to the Newcastle post. Apart from the observation on behalf of the Society of Antiquaries of London referred to above and war service Birley's only employment was in the service of the University of Durham, from which he retired in 1971; he and Durham were imperishably linked.

There are many aspects to these pre-war years. Pride of place should naturally go to his marriage in 1934 to Margaret Isobel Goodlet, his pupil from 1931 onwards. She was to be known to generations of students as Peggy. The honeymoon was in Germany. Robin was born in a Corbridge nursing home in 1935, Tony at Chesterholm in 1937. Robin was named after Colling-wood, Tony after Anthony Hedley, the antiquarian and excavator of Vindo-landa who had lived at Chesterholm. There were important friendships formed, C. E. (Tom Brown) Stevens, his best man, Ronald Syme, whom he first met in 1929 and always admired, John Charlton, Percy Hedley, Ian Richmond, and Mortimer Wheeler, whom he first met at the London Museum in 1929. These extended to the Continent; he met Kurt Stade, assistant to the doyen of frontier studies, Ernst Fabricius, in 1929 at Birdoswald.

In his development as a scholar, there are three important aspects, his excavations, his publications, and his students. His publications in both the local journals, *Archaeologia Aeliana* of the Society of Antiquaries of Newcastle upon Tyne and the *Transactions of the Antiquarian and Archaeological Society of Cumberland and Westmorland*, began in 1930; he wrote regularly in both for 30 years, as can be traced in the published bibliography of his writing from 1928 to 1974.[9] They include his work on the Wall itself, Vindolanda, and Housesteads. Most notable at the last-named site was his work on the civil settlement, virtually unparalleled till Robin Birley began to explore the one at Vindolanda. A section of the fourth report in 1935 was devoted to civil settlements of Hadrian's Wall, and drew instructive comparisons with the Saalburg, an important site in Germany.[10]

[9] A full bibliography of his work 1928–74 was published in *Britannia* 6 (1975), xi–xxviii, to which a general reference is given.
[10] *Arch. Ael.*, 4th ser., 12 (1935), 205–26, reprinted in E. Birley, *Roman Britain and the Roman Army* (Kendal, 1953), pp. 69–86.

His guide to Housesteads, published in 1936, with a second edition in 1952, was not replaced till 1989. In 1936–7 he dug at Birrens, in Roman Scotland though an outpost fort of Hadrian's Wall. His interest in the problems of Scotland had emerged in lively debates with Sir George Macdonald in the pre-war years over in particular the dating of the Roman withdrawal from Scotland in the first century AD, although there were also differences, long unresolved, over the respective chronologies of Hadrian's Wall and the Antonine Wall, and Birley's assertion that Birrens went on into the third century. The Birley contributions, with T. D. Pryce, appeared in the *Journal for Roman Studies*, and were based largely on the evidence of Samian ware.[11] More recent work has tended to support Birley's earlier dating of the withdrawal from Scotland, but not the occupation of Birrens in the third century, and shed fresh light on the respective chronologies of the two Walls, without solving all the problems.[12]

In 1935 he had turned his attention to Corbridge, writing the guide and reinterpreting the pre-First World War excavations in the light of Birdoswald 1929. A third edition in 1954 took account of more recent work, and it was only replaced in 1989. In 1936 he began a co-operation with Ian Richmond on excavating the site, concentrating himself on the finds. This was to continue till 1973, John Gillam replacing Richmond as director of excavations on Richmond's translation to Oxford in 1957. In 1939 he dug with Richmond at Carzield in Scotland.

His publications in these pre-war years show a wide range of interests. The full bibliography of his work 1928–74 (see above n. 9) may be consulted. Where he is not responsible as director for reporting on the structures, his preference was clearly for inscriptions and for pottery. He ranged widely with his studies of inscriptions, though still within Roman Britain. A particular concern was with the units stationed on the Wall, culminating in his paper in 1939,[13] 'The Beaumont inscription, the Notitia Dignitatum, and the garrison of Hadrian's Wall', originally intended for the Congress of Roman Frontier Studies that he was planning, to be linked with the 1940 Pilgrimage, aborted by war. His work on pottery shows an early interest in the red-gloss ware known as Samian, with its stamps and decoration, the latter often identifying a particular potter's work. He had

[11] E. Birley (with T. D. Pryce), 'The First Roman Occupation of Scotland', *Journ. Rom. Stud.* 25 (1935), 59–80; 'The Fate of Agricola's Northern Conquests', *Journ. Rom. Stud.* 28 (1938), 141–52.

[12] B. R. Hartley, 'The Roman occupations of Scotland: the evidence of samian ware', *Britannia* 3 (1972), 1–55 (the early withdrawal; the chronology of the two Walls); A. S. Hobley, 'The Numismatic Evidence for the Post-Agricolan Abandonment of the Northern Frontier in Northern Scotland', *Britannia*, 20 (1989), 69–74; Anne S. Robertson, *Birrens (Blatobulgium)* (Edinburgh, 1975), p. 286.

[13] *CW*, 2nd ser., 39 (1939), 190–226.

also a considerable interest in coarse pottery, including again stamped wares, *mortaria* and *amphorae*. Finally, his paper in 1932 on the Roman fort at Brougham[14] was to set a pattern in the methodical survey of all known evidence for sites, particularly that from antiquaries, reproduced in numerous papers for *CW*, in *Research on Hadrian's Wall* and in his paper on the Hinterland of Hadrian's Wall referred to below.

In all of this is missing more general work on the Roman army. He himself attributes this to preoccupation with the problems of work on and near the Wall.[15] It is noteworthy, however, that his first published work, in 1928,[16] was on the legionary title *Gemina*, still a crucial contribution, and that his review and discussion of volume XVI of the *Corpus Inscriptionum Latinarum*, on diplomas, certificates of citizenship for auxiliary soldiers, in 1938,[17] aroused considerable interest, making his reputation on the Continent. Finally, a major paper on the origins of legionary centurions, of enduring value, arguing that they followed largely the recruitment of the legions, and the centurionate was not artifically restricted to men from Italy, was to be published in Budapest in 1941, as part of a *Denkschrift*.[18]

Birley's attitude to his pupils was distinctive from the beginning. He gave them freely of his time, his library, and his collected materials. Not uncommonly he was content to resign to them the further methodical pursuit of a topic in which he was interested. He was dealing with small numbers, thirty-four students before the Second World War. Yet out of them came John Gillam, later Reader in the University of Newcastle upon Tyne, who was to establish himself as an expert in Roman coarse pottery as well as in Wall and frontier studies, George Jobey, later Professor in the University of Newcastle upon Tyne, who was to be a 'one-man Royal Commission' for native settlement in the Roman and pre-Roman period in Northumberland, Kenneth Steer, who after a notable doctoral thesis on Roman Durham became eventually Secretary of the Royal Commission of Ancient and Historical Monuments of Scotland, Peter Wenham, with a long association with St John's College, York, and excavations in York, and Ronald (G. R.) Watson, whose doctoral thesis on Roman Military Book-keeping led eventually to his book *The Roman Soldier* (London 1969). Maurice Callendar's doctoral thesis was on Roman *amphorae*, a typical development by a pupil of a Birley interest.

---

[14] *CW*, 2nd ser., 32 (1932), 124–39.
[15] E. Birley, *The Roman Army: papers 1929–86* (Amsterdam, 1988), p. vii.
[16] *Journ. Rom. Stud.* 18 (1928), 56–60=*Army: papers*, pp. 311–15.
[17] *Journ. Rom. Stud.* 28 (1938), 224–29.
[18] 'The origins of legionary centurions', *Laureae Aquincenses Memoriae Valentini Kuzsinszky dicatae*, ii (Budapest, 1941), pp. 47–62, repr. in *Roman Britain and the Roman Army* (Kendal, 1953), pp. 104–24, and in *Army: papers*, pp. 189–205.

There are a number of interesting features of Birley's output before the Second World War. It reposed of course on the methodical assembling of data, in notebooks, card indexes, and files, on all his many interests. Many of his books he had rebound with interleaving, and they were meticulously annotated. There is no attempt at this stage, and little at any time, to produce a monograph. His publications were mainly articles, with a few reviews each year. They appear predominantly in the two local journals already referred to, the reviews often in the *Proceedings* of the Society of Antiquaries of Newcastle upon Tyne, and the *Durham University Journal*. *The Antiquaries Journal* carried some of the reviews, and the controversy with Sir George Macdonald featured in *The Journal of Roman Studies*, but otherwise there is little in national journals. *Archaeologia Cambrensis* received offerings in 1936, and *Proceedings* of the Society of Antiquaries of Scotland and the *Dumfriesshire and Galloway Natural History and Antiquarian Society Transactions* had a small amount of material relating to excavations in Scotland.

On the eve of war Birley was already known as an authority on Hadrian's Wall, with a considerable record of excavation. He was a noted epigraphist, largely writing on British material, with a number of pottery specialisms. His interest in the Roman army was well evidenced for the units on Hadrian's Wall, but his wider interests had hardly appeared, except in one review and a not yet published paper which was to appear in an unlikely place under wartime conditions.

War came suddenly and strangely to him. He was attending a congress in archaeology in Berlin in August 1939, where he made new acquaintances. He was summoned back by a telegram apparently from Peggy but in reality from the War Office. He was a Territorial officer, and his interest in military matters and his command of German had been registered at the time of the Munich crisis. He left in such haste that he left his pyjamas behind with the Nesselhaufs (Herbert Nesselhauf was author of CIL XVI, notably reviewed by Birley, and had become a personal friend). Frau Nesselhauf preserved them for him till after the war. Birley was to spend the entire war with British Military Intelligence. He was a careful observer of the Official Secrets Act, and information on his work is sparse. It was concerned with the study of the careers of German officers, and attempting to discover the reasoning behind their promotions, and with the strength, distribution, and movements of German divisions. He headed the Military Intelligence Research Section and ended the war as Chief of the German Military Document Section with the rank of Lieutenant-Colonel. In *The Code Breakers*, cited by A. Moyes in his history of Hatfield,[19] Robert M. Slusser, an American army officer who worked in the Military Intelligence Research Section, speaks of Birley's

---

[19] Moyes, *Hatfield*, p. 206.

contribution to Anglo-American intelligence in the Second World War as of fundamental importance, and notes that he had access to the Ultra decodes from the very beginning of the war. Milton Shulman in an article in the *Evening Standard* (24 November 1995), who worked under him, opined 'that Eric Birley was pre-eminent among those who gave our commanders the information needed to defeat Hitler'. This was with special reference to D-Day. He quotes Birley as writing to him: 'My main help was that I had been used to reading German views on the Roman army. And that I suppose put me on the right wavelength. I came across sufficient captured German army documents to make me realise that they were far more valuable than MI6 reports, most of which were nonsense or works of fiction.' Birley first went to America in mid 1943 to prepare for D-Day. By the time hostilities in Europe ended Birley was able to assemble at Camp Ritchie, Maryland, 300 tons of German military documents, including the records of the *Heerespersonalamt*, and a cageful of more than a hundred German officers and NCOs. He was able to check then or some other time that his estimate of German divisions in 1940, shortly before the fall of France had been correct at 130 (actually 128 plus two *Waffen-SS* divisions), as compared to the French estimate of 80. To complete his military experiences the lectures he gave on Roman history and archaeology at Featherstone Park to prisoners of war, some later to become noted archaeologists, among them Professor D. Hafemann, should be mentioned. There is a description of him sitting by the Rhine with his opposite number in German military intelligence, watching the barges go by. After five or so he accurately predicted the number of the next barge, having cracked the system of numbering and the sequence. The story is not irrelevant—as Arnoldo Momigliano, the distinguished ancient historian, once observed of him, Eric Birley could reconstruct history from a pair of used railway tickets.[20] He did in fact crack the London Transport numbering system from collecting bus tickets when he was at the War Office. He was a great observer of patterns, whether in figured Samian, where he could link up a newly found piece at Corbridge with others found in the pre-First World War excavations and on widely separated parts of the site by memory alone, or in Roman and German military careers.

He received the MBE in 1943, the Order of Polonia Restituta in 1944 from the Free Polish Government, and the Legion of Merit from the President of the United States in 1947. An unwelcome legacy from his wartime experience was the wrecking of his eyesight. He had always had very low blood pressure, and the pressure of work in the War office clearly exacerbated it. At one point he had a collapsed lung. He had also lost years from his academic career, but he had acquired new insights into the way that armies worked, in selection of officers and deployment of units.

[20] J. Wilkes, obituary in *Independent*, 26 October 1995.

On his return to Durham Birley took on responsibilities enough for three or four men. He had been promoted Reader in Archaeology and Roman Frontier Studies in 1943. To this he joined in 1947 the post of Vice-Master of Hatfield College in the University of Durham. This was no ordinary appointment. The Durham colleges do no teaching but are responsible for the final selection of their students, and each has its own ethos. Hatfield had existed since 1846, but under wartime conditions had lost its own Master and its buildings, sharing both with University College. Its separate existence was threatened. There was a vigorous rally of its old students at the celebrations of the centenary of the college in 1946, and Birley's appointment as Vice-Master was in part a response to it. He worked towards the re-establishment of the college on an independent basis, and was appointed Master in 1949. From then till 1956 he continued with the energetic re-creation of the college, being in effect its second founder. He introduced moral tutors on the lines of Brasenose. He also followed the methods of his Brasenose College Principal in gathering to his College the best of sportsmen, albeit those who were quite capable of obtaining good degrees. Birley spent these years fighting vigorously on behalf of Hatfield, often with the Warden of the Durham Colleges, Sir James Duff, as well as with the difficulties of inadequate accommodation and catering facilities, accentuated in the immediate post-war years. His Vice-Master, Professor Fisher, wrote that 'The current fortunes of Hatfield reflect his devotion and sagacity, his sound appreciation of financial and academic exigencies, and his steady pursuit of an ideal and the development of a distinctive College ethos.'[21] The choice to give up the mastership and go on as professor to concentrate on archaeological work and teaching was a hard one.

Academically he broke new ground. He continued old interests, pottery, particularly Samian and mortarium stamps and surveys of the evidence for forts in *CW*, but also began a series of papers on general aspects of the history of Roman Britain and on the organisation of the Roman Army. They would have graced any national or international journal, but he chose to publish them in *Durham University Journal*. Their quality was extraordinary, and as he himself notes they were from the starting-point of epigraphic or literary evidence; the archaeological influence was indirect.[22] Notable were papers on Britain under Nero, under the Flavians, and after Agricola, but of equal or greater significance were the papers on the Roman army, particularly the equestrian officers, who commanded the auxiliary regiments and supplied the majority of legionary tribunes. Birley was able to show that these officers fell into three main groups, men in their late teens or early twenties, men in their thirties, and older men. Those in their thirties were the largest group,

---

[21] Moyes, *Hatfield*, p. 235.
[22] E. Birley, *Roman Britain and the Roman Army* (Kendal, 1953), p. vii.

normally commissioned after serving as municipal magistrates. Initial selection
and promotion were discussed, and the *ab epistulis*, the man in charge of the
emperor's correspondence, had an important input. Most important of all,
equestrian officers were civilians except when in post, and would revert to
civilian life if not offered a further appointment. A further article on equestrian
officers discussed how geographical origins might be teased out by prosopographical methods, making the point that the conclusions of Alfred von
Domaszewski in his *Rangordnung des römischen Heeres* (Bonn, 1908) were
too sweeping. His interest in names comes out clearly. The papers are best read
in his collection, *Roman Britain and the Roman Army*, referred to below.

So far he had dealt with the centurionate and the equestrian officers. He
extended his interest in initial selection and promotion to the senatorial officers
in his British Academy lecture, published in 1954, on 'Senators in the emperor's
service'.[23] Here again he laid emphasis on the early selection of men of talent, as
shown by which of the four colleges they were assigned to within the viginti-
virate, the twenty junior magistracies that began the senatorial career. Their
subsequent careers bore out or showed modifications of that initial judgement.
The themes of selection and promotion, of social and geographical origin, are
repeated, and show the insights garnered from the *Heerespersonalamt*.

A year earlier he had taken a significant step, in publishing a number of
his articles in *Roman Britain and the Roman Army* (Kendal, 1953). This was
on the urging of several of his friends, notably Herbert Nesselhauf and H. G.
Pflaum, and made available his papers to a far wider audience. It was to be
through his papers, not through any monograph, that he made his impact.
Hans Georg Pflaum was to be a valued friend, who applied in his study of
the procurators the seeking of patterns in individual careers arranged on a
chronological basis with the evidence fully detailed, an approach that naturally appealed to a number of Birley pupils. Birley was to include his review
of Pflaum in his major collection of papers on the Roman army, cited
below.[24]

A year earlier still Birley had set out to the Congress of Greek and Latin
Epigraphy in Paris in 1952 a programme of desirable work on the epigraphy of
the Roman army, emphasising the way the army worked, the prosopographical
approach, the importance of geographical and social origins, and recruiting.
Much of it he was to carry out through his pupils, as M. Speidel 'the Elder',
himself a leading Roman army scholar, points out.[25]

His archaeological programme had changed significantly. While still

[23] *Proc. Brit. Acad.* 39 (1954), 197–214=*Army: papers*, pp. 75–92.
[24] *Army: papers*, pp. 165–72.
[25] *Actes du deuxième congrès int. d'épigraphie grecque et latine, Paris 1952* (Paris,
1953), 226–38=*Army: papers*, pp. 3–11. M. Speidel, *Roman Army Studies*, ii (Stuttgart,
1992), p. 13.

keeping up an interest in Samian and mortarium stamps he gave up excavation, except for his continuing link with the Corbridge training courses. His last excavation otherwise was a small one at Brough under Stainmore in 1954. He contributed to Wall studies the editing of the Handbook to the Centenary Pilgrimage in 1949 (Kendal, 1949), which although intended as a daily guide to pilgrims gave him some opportunity to discuss sites and give some general conclusions. It was no substitute for a book on the Wall.

The major venture of 1949 was the creation of the Congress of Roman Frontier Studies, a gathering of international scholars interested in these topics. It was a project which he had hoped to realise in 1940, and he set it up by dint of much correspondence. Here his earlier contacts with Continental scholars were of great importance; Birley already knew everyone concerned. He edited the transactions in 1952 (*The Congress of Roman Frontier Studies, 1949*, Durham, 1952). It was arranged to coincide with the Pilgrimage, and Congresses were to be held in Britain alongside the Pilgrimages in 1959, 1969, 1979, and 1989 in addition to those abroad. This brainchild of Birley's has led to seventeen Congresses so far, and their value has lain not simply in the volumes of papers produced but in the opportunity offered for scholars to meet and discuss informally with others working on the different frontiers of the Empire. Birley in 1974 became Honorary Life President of the Congress, an honour richly deserved.

Birley's energy seemed inexhaustible in these years. For eight years, 1948/9–1956/7, he edited the Transactions of the Cumberland and Westmorland Society, and continued his magisterial surveys of the evidence for Roman forts in its area of interest. In 1956, as already mentioned, he had to choose between Hatfield and archaeology, and followed archaeology, with a chair in archaeology. It was a year of illness also, as his body rebelled against overwork. During his years at Hatfield he had carried on the work of the department of archaeology in a hut above the tennis court. But now he transferred his activities to the Old Fulling Mill, so often visible in the foreground on the river bank on photographs of the west end of Durham Cathedral. As Geza Alföldy put it, it became 'the headquarters of the Roman army'.[26] His teaching method had long been established. He simply gave freely of his time, his library, open to all including undergraduates, and his materials. He did not favour a first degree in archaeology, so was content to teach undergraduates following other courses, chiefly though not exclusively in Modern History and in Classics. Numbers were still small, so he was free to teach them virtually on a one-to-one basis. They were encouraged to do research, but all equally enjoyed his attention and support. Room was found for research students in strange places, a desk in

---

[26] G. Alföldy, *Laudatio auf Eric Birley* in: E. Birley, *Überlegungen zur Geschichte des römischen Heeres* (Heidelberg, 1987), p. 13.

the master's office at Hatfield, later in every nook and cranny of the Mill. He acquired some colleagues. John Gillam was shared with the Newcastle division of the university from 1948, till John Mann was appointed to a full-time post in Roman archaeology in Durham in 1957. He had already been impressed by Birley's writing and meeting him at Corbridge. In 1955 Rosemary Cramp introduced Anglo-Saxon archaeology to the department, and in 1966 Dennis Harding the Iron Age. Rosemary Cramp was to succeed Birley as head of department, expand the department considerably, and introduce a first degree in archaeology. She has spoken feelingly of Birley's courtesy and generosity to her, allowing her first choice of rooms in the Old Fulling Mill. The department that Birley founded has gone on from strength to strength.

Birley drew his pupils, formal and informal, from many sources. Examples only can be given here, mainly illustrating the way in which Birley handed on topics in which he had an interest to his pupils for the fuller treatment for which he himself lacked time. From modern history Brenda Heywood did a major Ph.D. project on the Vallum, unhappily still unpublished, presented in 1954. In 1955 Brian Dobson, from Hatfield, which made for a double tie, presented a thesis on the *primipilares*, the senior centurions of the Roman army, noted as needing attention by Birley in his paper to the Congress of Epigraphy. The thesis was long after published as *Die Primipilares* (Köln, 1978). He was also to be given the task on Birley's recommendation of re-editing the text of Domaszewski's *Rangordnung* of 1908, published in Koln in 1967, Domaszewski being the great Roman army scholar to whom Birley was the natural successor. Michael Jarrett, also a modern historian from Hatfield, produced a doctoral thesis in 1958 on Roman municipal aristocracies in the West. He went to University College Cardiff, eventually as professor, and published the second edition of *The Roman Frontier in Wales* (Cardiff, 1969) and *Maryport, Cumbria* (Kendal, 1976), a fort he first studied for a BA thesis at Birley's suggestion. David Breeze, a modern historian, was one of the last to follow this path, producing a doctoral thesis in 1970 on the soldiers below the rank of centurion in the Roman army. Of his many publications may be singled out *The Northern Frontiers of Roman Britain* (London, 1982) and *Roman Scotland* (London, 1996). With Brian Dobson he published *Hadrian's Wall*, an account of its history now in its third edition (1987).

Roy Davies came from classics to make himself an operational papyrolo-gist and wrote on peace-time routine in the Roman army, his doctoral thesis of 1967. He died tragically early in 1977; a selection of his papers was published by Breeze and Maxfield, both Birley pupils, in 1989.[27] Birley also drew in students following other honours courses; Iain MacIvor, a Hatfield man when

---

[27] Roy Davies, *Service in the Roman Army*, David Breeze and Valerie Maxfield, (eds.) (Edinburgh, 1989).

Birley was master, ended up as a consequence as Chief Inspector of Ancient Monuments in Scotland, a post in which he was succeeded by David Breeze. Graduates came from other universities. Valerie Maxfield came from Leicester to take the diploma in archaeology, later re-assessed as of MA status, and went on to do a doctoral dissertation on the *dona militaria* of the Roman army in 1972, published as *The Military Decorations of the Roman Army* in 1981. Other doctoral theses in these years were on Roman Cavalry (S. H. Bartle, 1961), the Later Roman Army (J. Hepworth, 1963), and Mauretania Caesariensis (R. I. Lawless, 1969). J. E. H. Spaul contributed a M.Litt. on Mauretania Tingitana.

Most archaeologists found their way to Corbridge till the training courses closed down in 1973. There often Birley introduced himself to them. John Mann has already been referred to, and John Wilkes came from University College London via Corbridge to submit a doctoral thesis on Dalmatia in 1962. He is now Professor at the London Institute of Archaeology, and wrote a book on *Dalmatia* (London, 1969), based on this thesis. Norman McCord from the Newcastle division became a regular site supervisor at Corbridge and developed an interest in aerial photography alongside his continuing basic interest in history which brought him a chair.

Honours students taking archaeology as a subsidiary course, and graduates of other universities drawn to Durham, often via Corbridge, do not begin to exhaust the number of people influenced by Birley. He took an interest in all scholars, often inviting them to Durham for visits. Margaret Roxan was so invited, for ten days, and given unlimited time. She received much stimulus and support, in effect supervision, in correspondence in completing her doctoral thesis on the *auxilia* of the Iberian Peninsula, a topic suggested by Birley. She was to become the logical successor to Herbert Nesselhauf in the study of Roman Military Diplomas. The late Hubert Devijver recalled in a letter the impact of an invitation to Durham for a fortnight in response to a request for advice. 'I learnt more in that fortnight than one can learn in years of self-study.' His great work was to be a prosopography of the equestrian officers of the Roman army, a Birley interest since he acquired Cheesman's papers. Geza Alföldy, now Professor of Ancient History in the University of Heidelberg, was reached first through correspondence, then a meeting, then a welcome to England 'as a son'. The same pattern is there: the steady, friendly criticism, the careful reading through of articles in typescript. The adjectives are typical: approachable, unassuming. The breadth of Birley's correspondence was enormous, his contacts with scholars, particularly the young, uncountable. This often formed the subject matter of the epigraphy seminars he introduced into the department for post-graduates and interested undergraduates. His pupils, in the widest sense, expressed their appreciation of him in publishing *Britain and Rome*, edited by Michael Jarrett and Brian Dobson (Kendal, 1966), containing thirteen papers, to be presented to him on his sixtieth birthday. He was honoured similarly by dinners on his seventieth and eightieth birthdays by his pupils and friends.

His outreach was not confined to academics. Reference has already been made to his support of the local societies with his writing and editing. This was also exemplified by his continuing willingness to drive for miles on winter nights to talk to every form of society all over northern England and southern Scotland, refusing even travel expenses. He taught adult education classes also, and afforded a warm welcome to local amateur archaeologists; the department was always open to them.

These 'pupils', a title claimed by many who had no formal instruction from him, formed a distinctive 'Birley-school'. They were trained in a particular way, to seek out the basic evidence, and they found kinship with one another in a shared teaching and a shared affection for their teacher, which often led to co-operation in publications, as David Breeze has noted. They have been accused of arrogance, but would argue this only means that they were taught to look at the evidence for a hypothesis, not at the reputation of the scholar advancing it.

Turning back to his activity and publications after his professorship in 1956, an increasing interest in the writing of antiquaries and the history of research is clear, alongside his other interests. Thus his inaugural lecture in 1958 looked at the history of archaeology in the north of England, with a warm tribute to F. G. Simpson, and the interesting comment that 'my own first academic interest is in Roman history—more particularly in the history and organisation of the Roman army—and that for me archaeology has always been a diversion, and not the real string to my bow'.[28] In a burst of activity regarding his Wall interests he produced the fourth Horsley memorial lecture, on John Horsley and John Hodgson[29] and a paper on the Hinterland of Hadrian's Wall,[30] drawing on his files and his already published profiles of forts in the C and W area. The year 1958 saw also the publication of *Central Gaulish Potters*, prepared by Grace Simpson in the Department of Archaeology with his support.

1959 was again a year of the Hadrian's Wall Pilgrimage. Birley was to preside over it as President both of the Society of Antiquaries of Newcastle upon Tyne and as President of the Antiquarian and Archaeological Society of Cumberland and Westmorland. An unfortunate accident limited his activity. The Handbook for the Pilgrimage also had to be postponed, and appeared in 1961 as *Research on Hadrian's Wall* (Kendal, 1961). This characteristically

---

[28] E. Birley, *Archaeology in the North of England* (Durham, 1958), p. 19.
[29] Horsley lecture: *Arch. Ael.*, 4th ser., 36 (1958), 1–46.
[30] *Dur. NAAST*, 11 (1958), 45–63.

was not Birley's view of Hadrian's Wall but a magisterial compilation of all that could be extracted from antiquaries and other earlier research on the Wall. As such it cannot be superseded.

He rounded off his contributions on the Wall with a guide to Chesters, in 1959, not replaced till 1990, and a survey of excavation at Corbridge, 1906–58.[31] His contributions to the two local journals dry up in the 1960s for the first time since the 1930s. He became President of the Architectural and Archaeological Society of Durham and Northumberland in 1959, thus serving all three local societies as President.

Notable papers on the Roman army continued. In 1955 he had reflected on 'Hadrianic Frontier Policy'[32] at a Frontier Congress. In 1958 he published 'Beförderungen und Versetzungen in römischen Heere', concerned with senatorial and equestrian officers, and in 1965 he published the second part of the article, dealing with the centurionate, 'Promotions and Transfers in the Roman army II: the Centurionate'.[33] Again it was the theme of promotion and transfer and the reasons behind them. In 1966 in *'Alae* and *Cohortes Milliariae'*[34] he established that these larger auxiliary units came into being at a particular time, and those promoted to command them had distinctive careers. In 1969 a paper on 'Septimius Severus and the Roman army'[35] analysed this emperor's distinctive contribution, and he covered twenty years of frontier research in the 1969 Frontier Congress volume, which he helped to edit, published in Cardiff in 1974.[36]

One disappointment of these years needs perhaps to be chronicled, as a fact, not in criticism of any individual. Richard Wright had been chosen by R. G. Collingwood to take on the burden of *Roman Inscriptions of Britain.* During the war years in particular he and Sir Ian Richmond grew close together. Richmond rightly received special praise when Wright drew his great labour to a conclusion in 1965. It was frustrating to Birley that it had not proved possible to involve him to a significant extent, and a loss to scholarship

---

[31] *Arch Ael.*, 4th ser., 37 (1959), 1–31.

[32] *Carnuntina: Vorträge beim internationalen Kongress der Altertumsforscher Carnuntum 1955, Römische Forschungen in Niederösterreich Band III* (Graz-Koln, 1956), pp. 25–33= *Army: papers*, pp. 12–20.

[33] 'Beförderungen und Versetzungen in römischen Heere', *Carnuntum-Jahrbuch* (1957), 3–20=*Army: papers*, pp. 93–114 (in translation as 'Promotions and Transfers in the Roman army: senatorial and equestrian officers'); 'Promotions and Transfers in the Roman army II: the Centurionate', *Carnuntum-Jahrbuch* (1963/64), 21–33=*Army: papers*, pp. 206–20.

[34] *Corolla Memoriae Erich Swoboda Dedicata* (Graz, 1966), pp. 54–67=*Army: papers*, pp. 349–64.

[35] *Epigraphische Studien*, 8 (Dusseldorf, 1969), 63–82=*Army: papers*, pp. 21–40.

[36] 'Twenty years of *Limesforschung*', in Eric Birley, Brian Dobson, and Michael Jarrett, (eds.), *Roman Frontier Studies 1969, Eighth International Congress of Limesforshung* (Cardiff, 1974), pp. 1–4.

that his knowledge of the Roman army and administration could not be fully utilised. His review published in 1966 reflects that loss and that frustration.[37]

Birley had always valued teaching as his major activity, and to give it up on retirement in 1971 was a wrench. His great web of correspondence continued, though there was necessarily some diminution of energy. Notable among his later publications, which continued to flow, were contributions to the massive *Aufstieg und Niedergang der römischen Welt*. One of these was on the religion of the Roman army, reviewing work since that of Domaszewski, in 1978. It was reprinted along with other army papers, including the early ones already reprinted in *Roman Britain and the Roman Army*, in *The Roman Army: Papers 1929–86* (Amsterdam, 1988). Other contributions included a major paper on the Deities of Roman Britain (1973) and one on Law in Roman Britain (1980).[38]

It is impossible to follow these later publications in detail, though the publication of *The Roman Army: Papers 1929–86* is noteworthy as representing Birley's own judgement on which of his army papers deserved a wider audience. Twenty-six of the forty-five papers were published after his retirement, and he continued writing till 1993. No bibliography of his post-1974 works has yet been published. Some of those reprinted in 1988 were given to the *Bonner Historia-Augusta Colloquium*, a regular meeting of scholars interested in the problems of the *Historia Augusta*, a collection of biographies, of Roman emperors. Others who came were his friends Ronald Syme, H.-G. Pflaum, J. F. Gilliam, and H. von Petrikovits. Birley attended these meetings from 1965 to 1986. Pflaum used to show him the proofs of *L'année épigraphique* on these occasions.

A major preoccupation in retirement was the Vindolanda Trust, founded in 1970. This was to explore the civil settlement at Vindolanda under the direction of Robin Birley, his elder son. There were two major results that can be identified. Vindolanda developed into a major Wall site, from being simply the consolidated remains exposed by Eric Birley between the wars. This was made possible not only by the structures of the civil settlement and the fort walls being exposed and displayed, but by the wealth of associated finds. Unusual oxygen-excluding conditions led to the preservation of much that is normally lost, leather, textiles, wood. Above all, a whole category of documents were added to the written record. These were wooden tablets inscribed in ink, yielding a mass of information on the official and unofficial activities of officers and men, with information on the development of hand-

---

[37] *Journ. Rom. Stud.* 56 (1966), 226–31.

[38] 'The Religion of the Roman Army 1895–1977', *Aufstieg und Niedergang der römischen Welt*, ii. 16, 2 (1978), pp. 1506–41=*Army: papers*, pp. 397–432; 'The Deities of Roman Britain', *ANRW*, ii. 18, 1 (1986), pp. 3–112; 'Law in Roman Britain', *ANRW*, ii. 13 (1980), pp. 609–25.

writing and of the Latin language. Eric Birley as Chairman of the Trust from its inception to his death in 1995 took a close and eager interest in all these developments.

Honours came in these years. He had been made a Fellow of the British Academy in 1969, shortly before his retirement. His Fellowship of the Society of Antiquaries of London went back into his earliest years, to 1931. He had been a Vice-President of the Society for the Promotion of Roman Studies since 1951. His honorary Fellowship of Brasenose came in 1987. He became an honorary Fellow of the Society of Antiquaries of Scotland in 1980. In 1970 he became an honorary Dr Phil. of the University of Freiburg, in 1971 an honorary D.Litt. of the University of Leicester, and in 1986 Dr *honoris causa* of the University of Heidelberg. This last was particularly appropriate, as he was recognised as the spiritual heir of Alfred von Domaszewski, doyen of Roman army studies, who spent so much time at Heidelberg. He received a moving tribute from Professor Geza Alföldy on that occasion, who claimed for Heidelberg the honour of belonging to the Birley-school.[39]

His reputation was always greater abroad than in this country, partly because archaeology and epigraphy are not an integrated discipline in Britain. He figured little on the national scene; he was not a political animal, and his chosen channels of publication were such that a reader of national journals only would hardly know his work. He was a man of the Roman Military North, extending into Scotland and Wales, with his heart ever in the north-west. Abroad it was a different matter, and there he always found it easier to relax. He never gave any priority to publication; he thought of teaching as his main job. Tony Birley has pointed out that Michael Holroyd, Birley's tutor at Oxford, only published one paper. Birley of course published far more, and articles of lasting significance, but his basic attitude was the same. Much that was important was hidden away in its place of original publication. He was able to support and stimulate much more effective and original work than he could ever have undertaken himself, even though given the time he could probably have done it better. His pupils, and again the term must be used in its widest sense, were always conscious of their debt to him. Often materials and thinking were handed on for others to complete and put their individual mark on. The nearest he came to writing a monograph was perhaps *The Fasti of Roman Britain*, a study of the major officers and officials of Roman Britain, which he worked on for years but finally handed over to his son Tony as a project in progress in 1965. It was published, with Tony's distinctive marks upon it, in Oxford in 1981.

He had a long and happy marriage. His sons inevitably lost time with him

---

[39] G. Alföldy, *Laudatio*, p. 16. He expanded on this *Laudatio* in his obituary of Birley, *Saalburg Jahrbuch*, 48 (1995), 140–4.

because of the war years, but he was always there for them, and they have enjoyed distinguished careers under his sage counsel. His grandchildren were ever a delight to him. He listed his recreations in *Who's Who* as archaeology, significant for the amount of time he put in working and also for his attitude to archaeology. When not working he delighted in a quiet game of dominoes with a few close friends in Corbridge. Essentially he was a shy man, with difficulty in expressing his emotions, who found dogs easier to get on with than humans. He enjoyed composing light verse, publishing *Fifty-one Ballades* in 1980, some dating back to the pre-war years; on the Frontier Congress in 1969 he had composed limericks.

Peggy is crippled with arthritis, and he devotedly cared for her in the various homes they occupied after he left Hatfield. Illness weighed heavily on him in the last years, particularly the increasing loss of sight. He died in his bed in Carvoran, their last married home; his ashes are buried at Vindolanda.

Eric Birley played a major part in the study of Roman Britain, particularly Hadrian's Wall, and of the Roman army, through his own work and that of his 'pupils'. In the University of Durham he founded a department of archaeology that continues to play a distinguished role, and he was the second founder of Hatfield College. He was the founder of the International Congress of Roman Frontier Studies. In Roman army studies he was recognised as the successor to Alfred von Domaszewski, as the foremost scholar of his time, with papers of enduring influence. But with all the enormous importance of the writing, it is as an outstanding teacher of all with whom he came into contact that he will be remembered. It has been pointed out that he taught under the shadow of Durham Cathedral, where is the tomb of the Venerable Bede. Birley, like Bede, also a European scholar, made it his delight 'to learn or to teach or to write'.

May the last words on him be those of the late Hubert Devijver on behalf of all Eric Birley pupils: 'The sight of E. B. with his pipe, and always in the company of his faithful dog, will stay with me, forever.'

BRIAN DOBSON
University of Durham

Note. I should like to acknowledge the considerable help given to me in compiling this obituary by Professor A. R. Birley, Dr R. E. Birley, Professor D. J. Breeze, and Professor J. Wilkes, who read and commented on earlier drafts, and by Professor G. Alföldy, the late Professor H. Devijver, Emeritus Professor J. C. Mann, and Dr M. Roxan.

THOMAS BURROW

Thomas Burrow
1909–1986

THOMAS BURROW, Boden Professor of Sanskrit in the University of Oxford 1944–76, uniquely made an original and in many respects decisive contribution to both Indo-Aryan and Dravidian philology.[1] As research student and fellow at Christ's College, Cambridge, in the 1930s, he described, from recently deciphered administrative documents in Kharoshti script, the version of the Gandhari Prakrit language that was in use in Chinese Turkestan c. AD 300. His translation of the documents followed in 1940. While employed in the Department of Oriental Printed Books and Manuscripts, British Museum, 1937–44, he began to establish a systematic comparative historical philology of the Dravidian languages which, coupled with his equally pioneering descriptions of individual tribal languages, led to the magnificent *Dravidian etymological dictionary* (with M. B. Emeneau; 1961, rev. edn. 1984). At Oxford, he began a series of Sanskrit lexical, grammatical, and phonological studies which culminated in *The Sanskrit language* (in the series The Great Languages; 1955, rev. edn. 1973) and *The problem of shwa in Sanskrit* (1979) and on which, despite failing eyesight, he was actively engaged until his sudden death in 1986 aged 76.

Born on 29 June 1909, he was educated at Queen Elizabeth Grammar School, Kirkby Lonsdale, and Christ's College, Cambridge, where he read for the Classical Tripos until specialisation in Comparative Philology led him to study Indology under the tuition of E. J. Rapson, principal co-editor of the administrative documents from the kingdom of Shan-shan in Chinese

[1] I gratefully acknowledge bibliographical and biographical assistance from E. Tucker and G. R. Hart of Oxford. T. H. Barrett (SOAS) and R. Salomon (University of Washington, Seattle) kindly provided bibliographical data with reference to Niya Prakrit.

Proceedings of the British Academy, **97**, 235–254 © The British Academy 1998.

Turkestan.[2] He was awarded First Class Honours in both parts of the Oriental Languages Tripos and studied for a year in London at the School of Oriental [and African] Studies, working on the Kharoshti script and Prakrit language of those documents and benefiting there from H. W. Bailey's expertise in dealing with the Iranian and other extraneous elements involved.

The results of this work appeared in articles from 1934, followed by *The language of the Kharoṣṭhi documents from Chinese Turkestan* (CUP, 1937), for which he had been awarded the Ph.D. degree of the University of Cambridge, and eventually by *A translation of the Kharoṣṭhi documents from Chinese Turkestan*, published by the Royal Asiatic Society (London, 1940, in the Forlong Fund series). Unique as is the survival of an ancient Indo-Aryan administrative archive, the purely Sinological relevance of its actual content has inhibited any serious attempt, from the Indological side, to improve upon these as yet provisional treatments of form and content. John Brough's description of the kingdom[3] has, however, confirmed Burrow's readings and interpretation of some key passages. A Chinese rendering has been published on the basis of Burrow's translation; and his work has provided some 800 lexical attestations of the language for R. L. Turner's *Comparative dictionary of the Indo-Aryan languages* (London, 1966).

The morphology and syntax of these Prakrit documents were shown to have reached a stage of development that is scarcely attested in the other Indo-Aryan languages within India before the second millennium AD. Developments such as the loss of distinction between nominative and accusative, and the formation of a new synthetic preterite tense, could not have been suspected on the basis of literary texts in Gandhari Prakrit, which substantially retain the syntax of the sub-continent.

Oskar von Hinüber did not consider it appropriate to include the grammar of the dialect in his survey of recent research on the early Middle Indo-Aryan languages.[4] It may be, however, that in spite of von Hinüber's view of the changes as 'Sonderentwicklungen, die durch Einflüsse aus zentralasiatischen Sprachen wie Sakisch oder Tocharisch erklärt werden können' (*Das ältere Mittelindisch im Überblick*, 67), Burrow's belief (*The language of the Khar. docs.,* vi) that 'There is no reason to impute this to the users of the language in

---

[2] *Kharoṣṭhi* inscriptions . . . discovered at the Niya, Endere, and Lou-lan sites 1906–7 (Oxford, 1920–9).

[3] 'Comments on third-century Shan-shan and the history of Buddhism', *BSOAS*, 28, 3 (1965), 582 ff. = *Coll. papers* (London, 1996), 276 ff. Burrow's materials were also used by the Japanese and Chinese historians Nagasawa Kazutoshi, Enoki Kazuo, Ma Yong, and Lin Meicun for their comments on the history of the kingdom, and by the last-named for his Chinese version of the documents and for his study of 'A new Kharoṣṭhī wooden tablet from China', *BSOAS*, 53, 2, (1990), 283 ff. (For references, see Brough, *BSOAS*, 33, 1 (1970), 39 = *Coll. papers*, 297, 351, and Lin, op. cit., 290 n.)

[4] *Das ältere Mittelindisch im Überblick* (Wien, 1986).

Central Asia, because with them it was a stereotyped official language, whereas the phenomena observed are those of normal linguistic change' represents the truth of the matter. The particularly striking formation of an active preterite from the passive participle is paralleled in Khotanese Saka, and there is at least partial collision of the direct cases in Tocharian. Since, however, both phenomena recur in the modern Dardic of the north-west, perhaps the decisive factor was an exposure to Iranian influence in Gandhara. This was the case with regard to lexical borrowing, as has recently been confirmed by Dieter Weber in *Languages and scripts of Central Asia*, ed. by Akiner and Sims-Williams (London, 1997), p. 31.

From 1938, Burrow was able to devote much of his time to Tamil and the other major Dravidian languages. Excused military service on grounds of impaired vision, and given custody of the South Asian books that had been evacuated from the British Museum, he proceeded avidly to study both texts and lexica. As noted by Emeneau, who worked with him at Oxford in 1956–7, one of his great assets was a prodigious and tenacious memory.

Like Turner in the field of the modern Indo-Aryan languages in 1914, Burrow had encountered a language family that had yet to be subjected to Neo-grammarian scrutiny, and where comparison with Tamil forms had consistently passed for historical linguistics. His 'Dravidian studies' (*BSOAS*, 1937–48 = *Collected papers on Dravidian linguistics*, Annamalainagar, 1968) examined the most basic sets of vocalic and consonantal correspondences in order to establish the actual direction and relative chronology of change.[5]

Building on the pioneer work of Gundert and Kittel, he also tackled the problem of identifying Dravidian loanwords in Sanskrit, a problem bedevilled by the pan-Indian tendency to adopt Sanskritised forms in lieu of or alongside inherited vocabulary, and by the impossibility of identifying with certainty the ultimate source of the bulk of the shared vocabulary. Some 500 lexical items were examined, together with considerations of methodology, in articles from 1945 onwards, and eventually incorporated in the Burrow–Emeneau *Dravidian etymological dictionary (DED)* (Oxford, 1961), and its *Supplement* (Oxford, 1968). There were some additions in 1970 and 1983, and numerous retractions in the revised edition (*DEDR* (Oxford, 1984), Appendix). The material has been used and evaluated in M. Mayrhofer, *Kurzgefasstes etymologisches*

---

[5] Bhadriraju Krishnamurti, 'Comparative Dravidian studies', in *Current trends in linguistics*, 5 (1969), 309 ff. includes a detailed account of Burrow's contribution: 'his lucid and definitive statements . . . constitute the beginning of a true comparative phonology for Dravidian'. He reviews Burrow's contribution to the question of Dravidian–Uralian affinity ('Drav. studies IV'). Otto Schrader had culled a common stock of 70 basic words connected with human physiology (30% of all such vocabulary in the Kannada dictionary): Burrow, from first-hand knowledge, found 72 words, retaining only 17 of Schrader's equations.

Wörterbuch des Altindischen (KEWA) (Heidelberg, 1956–76) and *Etymolo-gisches Wörterbuch des Altindoarischen (EWA)* (Heidelberg, 1986–).[6]

The retractions (in cases where the word was later deemed to be of Indo-Aryan or other extraneous origin) draw attention to the large measure of uncertainty that still remains, in the absence of any large-scale investigation of the shared vocabulary. One of them, Tamil *pacantu* (*DEDR* 4054 and App. 46) was evidently unmasked only at the last moment as the common Urdu word *pasand*. It was decided, for example, that Tamil *cūṭakam*, Gondi *sūṛa* 'bracelet' (App. 39) must stem from Prakrit *cūla(a)*, and not vice versa: but such questions might better have been left open. The original Prakrit, rather than Sanskrit provenance of Indo-Aryan loans in Dravidian was long over-looked, so that Telugu *mēna* and Tamil *maittuṉaṉ, macciṉaṉ* (designating a relation by marriage) had not been recognised as stages in the Sanskritisation, as well as in the assimilation, of a loan from Prakrit *mehuṇa* (< *maithuna*). Indeed the presentation in 1984 (*DEDR*, App. 53) still appears to misread the situation, by giving precedence to the mock-Sanskrit form *maittuṇa-*, although this is not known ever to have taken on the meaning that developed in Prakrit.

In 1949, M. B. Emeneau of the University of California at Berkeley, following his own extensive fieldwork on four non-literary Dravidian languages (Kota, Toda, Koḍagu, Kolami) had made the proposal that Burrow should collaborate with him on an etymological dictionary, which would facilitate research on Dravidian comparative linguistics by making available to other scholars Burrow's collections of material from literary sources, as well as Emeneau's unpublished vocabularies. Seeing, however, that the finer details of phonology, and eventually the rudiments of morphology, would only be worked out when all the available evidence was collected, Burrow also turned to fieldwork. Of this aspect of Burrow's work Emeneau wrote:

> In another phase of his Dravidian scholarship he was a pioneer. Up to 1940 the tribal languages of India had been investigated in the main by civil servants and missionaries, with the exception of my own professional work in the 30s on several languages that were easily accessible to investigation. Beginning in 1950, Burrow used a new operational method. He teamed up with the late Sri Sudhibhushan Bhattacharya of the Anthropological Survey of India . . ., whose collaboration was indispensable on all levels, but especially as inter-preter. In a succession of fieldtrips in the 50s and 60s in Central India, in country usually very inaccessible, they investigated a number of Dravidian tribal languages that had been previously only badly known or not even known at all. This resulted in joint publication of two books and numerous articles. This type of joint research has since then been normal. . . .[7]

---

[6] Cf. also notably Mayrhofer's reviews of *DED* in *Kratylos*, 6 (1961), 154 ff. and *DED(S)* in 13 (1968 [1969]), 208 ff.

[7] *IL*, 47 (1986), unpag.

For *The Parji language* (1953) and *The Pengo language* (1970), Burrow and Bhattacharya had recorded virtually unknown dialects from the hinterland of the Eastern Ghats, offering basic and interim grammar, vocabulary, and sets of texts, adequate for the immediate purpose of lexical comparison and for establishing the connection of Pengo with the Gondi group and the independent status of Parji within the Kolami–Gadba group. These and other publications and their fieldnotes cover Koṇḍa, Kui, Kuwi (of the Gondi group) to the north, Maṇḍa (allied to Pengo), Gadba to the east, and Kolami to the west.

The Burrow–Emeneau etymological dictionaries amply achieved their objective, so that in Dravidology 'there has hardly been an article or publication since 1961 which has not liberally drawn on the materials collected and organized in this work' (Bh. Krishnamurti). They are rather of the genre of comparative dictionaries, since the aim was to make Dravidian etymology possible by scrutinising and (so far as possible) verifying all the available lexical material and grouping like with like: there are over 5,500 lemmata, supported by data drawn from up to twenty-eight Dravidian languages and by the attestation of loans into ancient and modern Indo-Aryan. The cross-referencing (also to the *Comparative dictionary of the Indo-Aryan languages*) and indexing, including a compressed but highly useful index of English meanings, are all that one could wish for, and misprints are virtually unknown. Since the individual languages have sorely lacked dictionaries on historical principles, *DEDR* is an important tool for literary as well as linguistic research.

Meanwhile, Burrow was making a large and potentially equally important contribution to the historical phonology, morphology, and semantics of Sanskrit. The originality of his approach made his work both stimulating and often controversial: rightly so, for Sanskrit grammars and lexica had remained static for half a century, often reflecting an uneasy interim compromise between Indian traditional opinion and European philology. Two newly discovered languages, Hittite and Tocharian, had shown little sign of supporting the view of the Indo-European parent language that had been reconstructed in their absence, from the languages—such as Sanskrit—that had achieved the most sophisticated level of grammatical refinement. He introduced this new evidence, together with the 'laryngeal' theory, to a very large Anglophone audience, via the Philological Society ('"Shwa" in Sanskrit', *TPS*, 1949) and his book *The Sanskrit language* in Faber and Faber's widely read series The Great Languages (London, 1955, 1959, 1965, rev. edn. 1973).

In so doing he was one of the first Sanskritists to accept that there is Indo-Aryan support for the postulation of a 'consonantal shwa' (or 'laryngeal' *ḥ*) in the parent language, to whose influence had been ascribed *inter alia* the existence of radical long vowels and the voiceless (and some of the voiced) aspirate consonants, points which, though hardly proven or provable, remain standard doctrine.[8] He refused to accept the postulation of a 'vocalic shwa', and this view, unusual at the time, has since been firmly endorsed by Mayrhofer in 1981 and 1986.[9] It led him, however, with perfect consistency, to deny the strict identity of, for example, Sanskrit *pitŕ* and Greek πατήρ as manifesting such a vowel in the root syllable.

Virtually no scholar was then prepared to support this assault on one of the longest standing axioms of Indo-European Comparative Philology. Though Burrow repeated the thesis in *The Sanskrit language*, his prediction[10] that 'the rewriting of all our handbooks of IE comparative grammar . . . as far as ə is concerned is unavoidable, and this creation has become so pervasive in the theory of Indo-European that its removal entails the rewriting of a good deal besides' has quite failed to materialise. Kuryłowicz's systematic and equally innovative *L'apophonie en indo-européen* (Wrocław, 1956) retained shwa, as did his *Problèmes de linguistique indo-européenne* (Wrocław, 1977). Szemerényi's influential *Einführung in die vergleichende Sprachwissenschaft* (Darmstadt, 1970, rev. edn. 1990) still states that 'Schwa . . . ergibt sich aus morphologisch ganz klaren Entsprechungen wie skt. . . . *pitar-* . . . *a-di-ta*' and gives no credence to G.Av. *ptā* and Skt *-tta*, or indeed to Burrow and his move to treat the *-i-/-a-* of *pitŕ*/πατήρ as a secondary phenomenon as compared with the *-a-/-a-* of pairs such as *ślakṣṇá*/λαγνός.

Yet the consensus view, as now described by Mayrhofer, is not entirely convincing. Mayrhofer conceded only grudgingly that the proliferation of vocalic reflexes in Indo-Iranian is dialectal,[11] and, while denying the possibility of a single basic 'Murmelvokal' (*Idg. Gr.*, 1986, 122 and 177), has adopted instead three individual and unstable vocalic entities, variously labelled 'vokalische Kontinuanten' (p. 126), 'überkurzer Sprossvokal' (p. 138), and 'Fortsetzung' (p. 142) which all collided in Indo-

---

[8] M. Mayrhofer, *Indogermanische Grammatik (Idg. Gr.)*, I, 2 (Heidelberg, 1986), 121 ff.

[9] *Indogermanische Grammatik* 122 f., 177 'jener "Murmelvokal", der auf nicht ganz aufgeklärte Weise im ausgehenden 19. Jahrhundert an die Stelle der sonantischen Koeffizienten Ferdinand de Saussures gesetzt worden ist'. Cf. *idem*, 'Laryngalreflexe im Indo-Iranischen', *ZPSC*, 34 (1981), 429 = *Ausg. kl. Schr.*, II, 294.

[10] 1949, 61.

[11] His 'Laryngalreflexe', 436 mentions 'das . . . vielleicht auch durch Dialektunterschiede gestörte Material'; much reliance is placed on Pkt *āgamamīṇa*, Y.Av. *pita* (and O.Pers. *pitā*), despite older G.Av. *-əmna* and *(p)tā* (versus *fəδrōi/piθrē*, to which may be added *zą θā* in Y 44.3 *ząθā pàtā = pitā̆ janitā̆*, different from Y 43.5 *ząθa*, v.l. *ząθβa*, 'birth'; see *EWA*, s.v. *janitár*). Mayrhofer does not mention Burrow's understandable objection to the impression that this creates of derivation of the monosyllable *(p)tā* from a monosyllable (*pHtā) via the disyllable *pitā*. For Burrow, parallels for the otiose extension *-i-* seen in *pi-tŕ, sthi-tá*, etc. are provided e.g. by √*sā-, si-*, √*śā-s, śi-ṣ-*, and by Gk δολι-χός alongside Skt *dīr-gháḥ*, Hitt. *dalu-gaš*.

Iranian with the vowel *i.[12] Szemerényi, resisting both Burrow's and Mayrhofer's revised versions of the hypothesis, eventually (reviewing Burrow's *Problem of shwa in Sanskrit* in *Kratylos*, 28, 1983, 75) admitted the need for a comprehensive analysis of all instances where Skt -i- has hitherto been regarded as derived from shwa. Burrow, he declared, 'would obviously bring the best possible qualifications for such a difficult task', but the call came too late. Similar was the reaction of Hiersche in *OLZ*, 1982, 6, 595 ff.

The most strenuous objection that had been voiced by earlier reviewers concerned the precious identity of *pitṛ́* and πατήρ (Benveniste)[13] and of (*pṛṇ)imah* and (δάμν)αμες (Gonda):[14] these critics too made no mention of Av. *ptā* and (*friiạn)mahī* which, as far as Burrow was concerned, prove that the identity is illusory. Martinet[15] made explicit the critics' assumption that Burrow's notation *p-itā́*, *duh-itā́* (1949, 38 f.) implied an analysis π-ατήρ, θυγ-άτηρ with an unacceptable suffix *-ater. Burrow later acknowledged the fault, although his article in fact had gone on to explain the -i- as a root extension (p. 46: 'the root extended by suffixal *i*'), and to describe (p. 59) Gk. στ-α-τός in terms reminiscent of his view (p. 23) of Skt *darś-a-táḥ* as a post-Ablaut formation with multiple full-grade vowels (unlike the more primitive *sthi-táḥ* and *dṛṣ-ṭáḥ*). Burrow's ill-considered attempt to explain the phenomenon in terms of serial extensions, such as he envisaged in *hár-i, harí-t, hárit-a* and in √*śā-s-, ś-i-ṣ-* and √*sā-dh-, s-i-dh-*, also distressed the critics, though they might have seen that the gaucherie of this argumentation scarcely affects the main point at issue, i.e. that, whether they are to be explained on the basis of epenthesis or proliferation of existing suffixes, there is no need for a laryngeal explanation for the appearance of such medial vowels.

He might have strengthened the case for scepsis by questioning the generally held belief that Indian grammatical theory has any bearing on the matter. Like others, he referred to *tṝ-* and *san-* as 'so-called *seṭ*-roots' (p. 26), thus fostering the impression that the grammarians had actually envisaged '*tari-*' and '*sani-*' as alternative forms of the roots. Burrow's protest may have been tacitly influenced by the fact that Pāṇini speaks (7.2.10, 35) only of suffixes as being regularly prefixed with *i-* (*seṭ*), but exceptionally also unprefixed (*aniṭ*) in the case of so-called '*anudātta*'

---

[12] Mayrhofer had previously tended rather to contemplate the sonorisation of fricatives: *Nach hundert Jahren* (Heidelberg, 1981) (=*SbHAW*, 8, 1981), 18 f.

[13] *BSL*, LI (1955), 25: 'Je ne crois pas qu'aucun comparatiste sait (*sic*) tenté d'adopter cette vue extrême'. Precisely the word *pitṛ́* was and is a bad choice as a support for shwa: it seems likely that, as in the case of *mātṛ́* (*EWA*, s.v.), a childish word has been assigned grammatical gender (*pa-/mā-*) and declension (after the manner of *náp-t, náp-t-ṛ*?).

[14] *Lingua*, VI (1957), 289.

[15] *Word*, X (1956), 304 ff.

roots.[16] The twelfth-century commentary on *Dhātupāṭha* concurs, although itself participating in the eventual confusion: *pratyayasya seṭtve 'niṭtve ca, upacārād dhātos tathāvyapadeśaḥ* 'While it is the suffix that is *seṭ* or *aniṭ*, the terms may be loosely applied to the root' (Kṣīrasvāmin s.v. *bhū́*). Pāṇini's sources, enshrined in the *Dhātupāṭha*, were presumably concerned to identify a 'regular' *-a-/-i-* conjugation of verbs, so that the list of roots was subdivided first on the basis of strong and weak stems in the present system (*bháva-/ad-*), then on the basis of the strength of stems elsewhere (*bhaviṣyá-/dhakṣyá-*), and finally on the basis of the strength of personal endings (*dviṣṭé/dvéṣṭi*). Certainly, the result was that lists of strong verbs ('*udātta*') with *seṭ* conjugation and of weak verbs ('*anudātta*') with *aniṭ* conjugation) were prepared; but at no point was the *-i-* deemed to be integral to the root. The later tendency to talk of '*seṭ* roots' instead of '*udātta* roots' will reflect the fact that the term *udātta* had become meaningless, once Pāṇini had determined that *-i-* is integral, not to the conjugated tense stem, but to the suffix.

Burrow reinforced his attack on the vocalic shwa in an article in *Pratidā-nam*, 1968, and in *The problem of shwa in Sanskrit* (Oxford, 1979). In the latter, he compiled a more complete repertoire of instances of the reduced-grade vowel *-a-* in Sanskrit (*rā-*, *rá-tna*; *vidā-*, *vidá-tha*, and the like), which would rule out the notion of vocalic shwa (*-i-*) as a reduced grade.[17] He was by

---

[16] The traditional, merely mnemonic application of the terms '*udātta*' and '*anudātta*', '*anudāttet*' and '*udāttet*' used in the *Dhātupāṭha*, being consistently applicable only to consonant-final roots, is surely secondary. The terms *udātta* 'accented' and *anudātta* 'unaccented' have no bearing on the accentuation of the *seṭ/aniṭ* forms themselves, but seem intended to associate 'regular' *seṭ* future stems like *bhaviṣyá-* with such 'regular' root-accented present stems as *bháva-*; and to associate 'irregular' non-presents like (Sū.) *soṣya-* and (Gr.) *totsya-* with such 'irregular' root-unaccented presents as *sunóti, tudáti.* Thus *bháva-, bhaviṣyá-* is '*udātta* par excellence' and *sunó-, soṣya-* is '*anudātta* par excellence'. In the root-accented Classes I and IV, *udātta* verbs constitute respectively some 90% and 60% of the class and take precedence as the norm; but in classes such as V and VI, *anudātta* verbs, which yield only some 50% and 25% of the respective totals, are given precedence. (Sub-groups, vowel-ending or grammatically motivated, are another matter, being arranged according to notions of cyclic digression, the only principle of sequence that Palsule was able to detect: see *The Sanskrit Dhātupāṭhas*, Poona, 1961, 31; *udātta* verbs take precedence in Class VIII, in keeping with the ostensible strength of the root syllable.)

This classification, involving an extension of the concept of accentual strength, and reflecting a rather post-Vedic notion of regular *-a-/-i-* conjugation, presumably inspired the more sophisticated sub-classification of roots into *udāttet*, etc., where the terms correlate strength of stems with voice. The '*anudāttet*' weak stems, associated with strong middle-voice endings, take precedence in the more basic consonant-final *bhvādi* categories over '*udāttet*' strong stems with weak active endings (cf. *-nuté/-nóti* respectively); and '*svaritet*' serves to denote a combination of strong and weak stems.

[17] 'never before has the complete material been put together in such an impressive fashion': O. Szemerényi, *Kratylos*, 28 (1983), 73 f.

now willing to accept laryngeals only where directly attested in Hittite. He stressed the failure of Hittite to support the theory of laryngeal-induced lengthening: Hitt. *pahš-* 'protect' is virtually unique; Skt *dāntá* and *damayati* would seem to owe their vocalism to their disyllabic base (cf. Hitt. *damaš-*); and (in the absence of corresponding disyllabic bases) there is no evidence that *terH and *senH (Hitt. *tarh-* and *šanh-*) could yield anything but a *tārayati* (unattested in the relevant sense 'overcome') and *sānayati* (presupposed by a Vārttika). Burrow did, however, adopt the notion of a glottal fricative as a pointer to the mechanism that would serve both to lengthen Skt *-sūta, suvāná* over against *-suta, -svāná* and (provided one upheld Brugmann's Law) to preserve the short radical syllable in *janayati* as against *kārayati*. The suggestion has at least the merit of offering a convenient notation *jan'* for nasal long-sonant roots in Sanskrit, preferable to the shwa-based notation *JAN'* that has been adopted by Mayrhofer.

This length-generating and length-retarding factor, conceived (in deference to Saussure's theory of disyllabic bases) as the 'residual trace' of a vowel, was a laryngeal in all but name, and it appealed to no-one as an improvement upon the shwa hypothesis or the laryngeal hypothesis. In respect of the pure vowels, he had abandoned the proposition that a lengthening process must inevitably involve some pre-existing vocalic or consonantal trigger; but he drew no moral from this, nor did he observe that the Sanskrit grammarians' postulation of long-sonant roots on the one hand and of *set* suffixes on the other is an inadequate guide to the Avestan and Ṛgvedic material as a whole.

Burrow did not realise the extent to which the assumption of medial consonantal shwas, which he had accepted, is bound up with, or even dependent on, the postulation of vocalic shwa. Saussure believed that 'sonant coefficients' *A and *O (i.e. the eventually postulated laryngeal consonants) were necessary to explain vowel length in one particular category of root syllables; and that they yielded in isolation a single weak vowel (eventually labelled shwa and styled an allophone of zero). This belief presupposed the surprising assumption that in Indo-Iranian his coefficients *A and *O could collide with *i; it also assumed a link between the fictitious long-sonant roots (*kṝ-, pṝ-*, etc.) and the proliferating morpheme divider *-i-*, both features more obviously typical of Sanskrit than of the proto-Indo-Iranian one might have inferred from Av. *darəga, dugədar*, and *(p)tā*.[18]

To carry conviction it would have been necessary to widen the campaign. The general anxiety to uphold the equation στατός/*sthitá* reflected the feeling that it importantly substantiates the putative laryngeal explanation of the

---

[18] For the dependence of Saussure's proto-laryngeal on his proto-shwa, cf. Mayrhofer, *Nach hundert Jahren*, 23, n. 67, and 28, n. 79.

vocalism and of the aspiration of *sthā-*. Burrow did go so far as to deny (1979, 20) that an isolated equation like Skt *pā-s-*/Hitt. *pah-š-* has any bearing on the vocalism of Skt *sthā-*; but he might have strengthened his position by observing that there is no need to assume that the aspiration of *sthā-* reflects anything more than a purely Indo-Iranian tendency to avoid the ambiguity of unaspirated forms like *abhiṣṭi* ('aid' = 'Bei-stand': *EWA*).[19] In another instance where a significant laryngealist tenet rested on one dubious example, Burrow's scepticism was apparent, but unproductive: 'It is believed that one type of IE ʜ . . . affected a preceding surd differently, by voicing it, in Sanskrit *píbati* = O. Ir. *ibid* "drinks" . . . but this appears to be the only example' (1955, 71 f.; cf. 1979, 37).[20] With his commitment to Dravidian linguistics and to completing the revision of *DED*, however, he was in no position to mount the implied full-scale reappraisal required.[21]

He did not survive to take stock of the evidence which in 1986 Mayrhofer marshalled as irrefutable proof of the ubiquity of laryngeals. If Burrow was right, the main surviving relevance of laryngeals would be to the occasionally disyllabic *-ā-* of Indo-Iranian and other syllable-initial phenomena with which neither Saussure nor he was concerned, e.g. *bhā́s* = *bhá'as* (RV 6.10.4), *pā́nt* = *pa'ant* (9.65.28–30), and *vā́ta* 'wind' = *vá'ata* (9.97.52, etc.: *EWA* *vaHata-*, Hitt./huu̯ant-/).[22] Burrow's only relevant comment (1955, 238, on the disyllabic suffix in *téṣām*) does not address the main problem: but since Hittite offers no medial laryngeal in its version of *vā́ta*, he would have been undismayed.

His willingness in 1955 to accept the consonantal aspects of recent laryngeal theory (deriving Skt *tīr-ṇá, tirati* from *t^irH-* and *ráth(i)ya* from *$rotHiHo$*, and so forth), while denying the long-standing vocalic shwa, gave a doubly innovative aspect to his most widely read work *The Sanskrit language*. Appearing at a time when it was Comparative Philology more than anything else that drew students to Sanskrit, the book combined a detailed comparative historical phonology and morphology (primarily of Vedic) with a masterfully compact survey of its Indo-European prehistory and its subsequent debt to

---

[19] Mayrhofer, *Sanskrit und die Sprachen Alteuropas* (Göttingen, 1983), 433, considered a laryngeal the only possible explanation for Skt *path-*: but Av. *padəbiš* ('paths') reveals that there had been a need in Sanskrit to create a distinction between *pathíbhiḥ* ('paths') and *padbhíḥ* ('feet').

[20] Despite Mayrhofer (*Idg. Gr.*, ɪ, 2, 143, n.184), the possibility that an onomatopoeic *bib- (Latin *bibit*) has been influenced by *pō-, seems worth canvassing. (Unlike Pokorny, *IEW*, 1969, Mayrhofer cites O.Irish *ibid* as 2 pl. imperative.)

[21] 'Burrow gehört zweifellos zu jener Art von Forschern, die kühn Schneisen schlagen und anderen das Aufräumen überlassen': R. Hiersche, *OLZ*, 1982, 6, 597.

[22] For *vā́ta*, see notably 'Die Vertretung der idg. Laryngale im Lateinischen', *KZ*, 100, 1987, 97 n. = *Ausg. kl. Schr.*, ɪɪ, 421 n.); for *pā́nt* m. 'drink' (the stem *pā́nta* is required only for the neuter transposition *pā́nta*, still with disyllable, at 10.88.1 *háviṣ pā́ntam . . . ā́hutam*), see *EWA*, s.v. *PĀ²*.

Middle Indo-Aryan, Dravidian, and Munda. It was thus the first general treatment of Sanskrit that sought to exploit the Hittite evidence and the laryngeal theory, while offering new insights into the post-Vedic evolution of Sanskrit: but the format left him no room for manoeuvre in the matter of referencing, indexing, and cross-referencing. Martinet, in his sympathetic review, understood that Burrow had no choice but to make the book a repository for his theory of apophony (no-one having offered any attempt at refutation in the intervening seven years). He admired too 'by far the most lucid total presentation of laryngeal lore ever printed' and the 'amazingly simplified picture of IE nominal derivation': 'with all its one-sidedness, Burrow's huge black and white fresco may convey a more valid impression of what the nominal system of Indo-European may have been at a certain stage than more painstaking and roundabout expositions'.

Burrow's traditionalist view of Indo-European as a 'two-dimensional' (Martinet) amalgam of reconstructions was unpalatable to general linguists. Such reviewers found fault with both his conservatism and his originality, and certainly he had committed himself to a fair number of ill-considered or even inscrutable etymologies (e.g. *nákṣ-atra* and *sy-oná* respectively). Although now sadly out of print, the years, its reprintings, the Hindi translation of 1965, and constant citation in Anglophone circles have shown that it is a book that continues to meet a need for the general reader and for the budding specialist.

Even the revised and improved edition of 1973 could do little to update all of Burrow's many knot-cutting solutions, only occasionally idiosyncratic or ill-advised; and no-one has taken up the challenge to try and do better. It was suggested by one reviewer of the revised edition[23] that Burrow had simply ignored justified criticism of the original, but this is by no means the case. The problem was rather the pressure imposed upon him by his medium, which evoked from Edgerton (*JAOS*, 1956, 193) the comment: 'It is clear that he knows the literature well, and in some cases a negative attitude can be detected towards certain views which he does not think it necessary even to mention specifically. It often takes a rather well-read specialist to divine what he is doing in such silent polemics'.

Burrow's reaction to Edgerton's own comments is typical: in the case of simple oversights (and the occasional howler: Russian *zemlja* had been credited with an -*l*- suffix), amendments were duly made. One detects, however, no reaction to Edgerton's complaint that the exposition of one original hypothesis, postulating identity of the neuter ending -*am* with an athematic nominal

---

[23] R. Schmitt, *Kratylos*, 17 (1972 [1974]), 203. M. Leumann had objected in *Kratylos*, 1 (1956), 29 to Burrow's treatment of *kṣ*/κτ, etc.: in the one specific instance where Burrow had indeed erred, the correction was made. The **teks-tōn* that was also criticised was a veiled allusion to proposals of Kuiper and Szemerényi; an improved formulation was only later provided by Mayrhofer (see *Idg. Gr*, I, 2, 156).

derivative suffix *-m*, is seriously flawed. To justify this postulate, Burrow had invoked *yugmá* 'paired' (BRD *yugmá* 'paarig, geradezahlig'): but this is actually a late Vedic form *yugma* whose predominant implication is 'even-numbered'. As Edgerton observed, it seems to be a replacement for earlier *yugmán (ŚBr. yugmábhiḥ, R yugmāni*); and even this version seems to replace *yug-mánt*, antonym of *á-yuj* in TS. It is a serious criticism, but it by no means invalidates the argument, since it seems as easy to deduce the desired suffix *-m-* from *-m-an, -m-ant* as from thematic *-m-a*. A stimulating suggestion had been made, where none existed before; and even a complete rewriting of the three pages involved would have done nothing to satisfy those who would demand an entirely more sophisticated treatment of the origins of case and gender (noting that he had naively treated the masculine accusative *-am* as a quite unrelated pre-existing entity), or those for whom such unverifiable hypotheses have no place in such a book unless, like vocalic and consonantal shwa, they have been around for a lengthy period. On the other hand, it would not have been impossible to include in the new bibliographical note some laconic reference to other specific factual criticisms.[24]

Burrow's contribution to Indo-European reconstruction continued throughout his career, notably in his studies of anomalous sigmatic forms in Sanskrit ('The Sanskrit precative', *Asiatica*, 1954 and 'An archaic verbal termination in early Indo-Aryan', *IIJ*, 1957); the antecedents of the Sanskrit consonant group *kṣ* ('On the phonological history of Sanskrit *kṣam-* "earth", *ŕkṣa-* "bear" and *likṣa-* "nit"' and 'Sanskrit *kṣi-*: Greek φθίνω', *JAOS*, 1959); the development of retroflex consonants in Sanskrit ('Spontaneous cerebrals in Sanskrit' and 'A reconsideration of Fortunatov's law', *BSOAS*, 1971–2); and vowel-length based on original *-o-* ('A new look at Brugmann's law', *BSOAS*, 1975).

His rejection of vocalic shwa apparently owed much[25] to Meillet's observation in *BSL*, 1933, that a proliferation of sigmatic forms (where preterite endings with initial *t-* are involved) is common to the Sanskrit *-iṣ-* aorist and to the *-is-* preterites of Latin and Hittite. It was the preconception of vocalic shwa that had prevented Meillet from postulating a common Indo-European source for the *-is-* forms of Sanskrit (a mainstay of shwa theory), and those of Latin, Armenian, and Hittite. By identifying an Avestan correlate *tuyā̊* for the Vedic 3 sg. precative active *bhūyáḥ*, and by collecting instances of anomalous 3 sg. *-stha*, Burrow was able to link these with 3 sg. *-s* and *-sta* preterite endings

---

[24] Such a list would have remained eclectic: Burrow was under no obligation to endorse all of Thieme's hostile criticisms (*Language*, 1955, 428 ff. = *JBRS*, 58, 1972, 197 ff.), the more general of which are based on some fundamental misunderstanding of Burrow's formulations, always Pāṇini-wise brief and careful. One must, however, regret Burrow's failure to accept that a *syoná* 'soft, agreeable' is unacceptable as evidence of a suffix *-avana, -ona*; and that an *arí* 'devoted, trustworthy, pious', apparently from Sāyaṇa's '*yajamāna*' via BRD 'anhänglich' and MW 'faithful', is unduly eccentric (cf. Thieme, 1955, 433).

[25] Cf. Burrow, *TPS* (1949), 56 'certain formations in *-i-*' (a characteristically tacit reference); *Asiatica* (1954), 39; *IIJ* (1957), 74 f.

found in Hittite, and hence to show that not just the Sanskrit precative but the sigmatic aorist as a whole could be traced to an ending -*s* in the 3 sg. This is the acknowledged basis of Watkins's theory[26] that all 3 sg. endings developed from root extension, -*t*, -*i*, -*s*, -*u*. Like Burrow, Watkins has reduced the scope of vocalic shwa by several categories: the Hittite -*āi*- diphthongs and the Indo-Iranian middle endings *-*i* and *-*madhi*. Hence Watkins's retention of it elsewhere, thus separating the Sanskrit -*is*- aorist from the other sigmatic preterites and the Sanskrit suffix -*(i)man* from Celtic *-*(i)amon*,[27] can seem anomalous on occasion.

A significant contribution to the clarification of Indo-European phonology was made by Burrow's completion of Kretschmer and Brandenstein's use of Hittite and Tocharian evidence to solve the problems associated with certain Greek cognates (κτ χθ φθ) of Sanskrit *kṣ*. He brought several key Indo-Iranian forms (*ŕkṣa*, *kṣiyánti*, *kṣám*, *kṣātí*, *kṣiṇánti*) into line with the rest of the evidence by indicating that the Sanskrit reflex can derive not from *ks* but from *tś* and *ḍẕh*, and by suggesting a possible etymology (*dah*- 'burn' for *kṣā*- 'burn'). The phonological developments involved have since been clarified by Kuiper and Mayrhofer, who has acknowledged in particular Burrow's contribution (*JAOS*, 1959) to Hittite-based solutions for *kṣám* and *ŕkṣa*, while disposing of certain doubts that had been expressed by Kuiper.[28]

H. W. Bailey having demonstrated that many Sanskrit words with retroflex consonants have Iranian cognates with dentals, Burrow provided sufficient additional material to imply that for etymological purposes retroflexion can generally be ignored in the post-Vedic period. Following Mayrhofer, but deeming the whole process to be prehistoric, he inferred 'a process of fission' due to 'spontaneous cerebralization', although at least in the case of -*ṇ*- and -*ṣ*- it would seem wiser to suggest dialect mixture (i.e. adoption of regional *māṇava* and *abhilāṣa* to support semantic nuances distinct from *mānava* and *vilāsa*, *ullāsa*).[29]

His subsequent 'reconsideration' of that 'permanent issue of dispute', Fortunatov's Law, claimed 'to establish it beyond all reasonable doubt'. It revised the list of words to which the law might apply, i.e. those in which retroflexion could possibly be due to -*l*- rather than -*r*-. The article encouraged

---

[26] Cf. Watkins, *Idg. Gr.*, III (1969), 53 ff. Burrow's point (*apās* → *ápāt*) seems to be overlooked by Oettinger, *Stammbildung des hethitischen Verbums* (1979), 435 and Mayrhofer, *Idg. Gr.*, I, 2, 143 ('*a-pā-t* → *ápās*').

[27] *Idg. Gr.* 54.

[28] See Kuiper, *IIJ*, 10 (1967), 103 ff. and Mayrhofer, *AÖAW*, 119 (1982), 246 f. = *Ausg. kl. Schr.*, II, 261 f.; *Idg. Gr.*, I, 2, 153 f.

[29] The early Ṛgvedic instances (Mayrhofer, *Mélanges d'indianisme*, 1968, 509 ff.) seem to correlate strongly with cultural objects and commodities: *maṇí* '(amulet) jewel', *sthū́ṇā* '(monumental) pillar', etc., so that it is not only *viṇā* 'lute' (p. 511) that may be branded a borrowable 'Kulturwort'. The dialect involved at this period might be that of Iranian artisans or merchants, whose dentals would differ from Indo-Aryan post-dentals. The word *pāṇí*, rare as a simplex and denoting 'hoof' at 2.31.2, is arguably applied as a humorous vulgarism to Indra's hands at 4.21.9 ('Don't just sit there . . . '). If so, the vulgar implication was soon lost.

Collinge to deliver his verdict that the 'law' still ranks as a 'doubtful, but not incredible' proposition and 'a useful label'.[30] Its argument is, however, a victim of Burrow's surprisingly monolithic view of Prakrit. He felt obliged to withdraw his very plausible explanation of *abhilāṣa* (<*abhilāsa* lex.) on the grounds that 'in Prakrit all the sibilants have fallen together as *s*' (*BSOAS*, 1972, 543f.), as though only the standard literary medium would have any influence on Sanskrit. Since this is not the case, and since graphic *yaṣo* for *yaso* may also play a part, the argument rebounds and there is no real incentive to believe that RV *pāsyà*, VS *bhāṣ*-, etc., are likely to owe their retroflexion to a survival of -*ls*-. As all examples with -*ṇḍ*- had been withdrawn as inapplicable, the case rests (p. 536f.) on an alleged preponderance of instances of -*ṭ*-, -*ṭh*-, -*ḍh*- from **-l-*, as against -*t/ṭ*- and -*tt/ṭṭ*-, etc., from **-r-*. Since, however, the latter very clearly reflect semantic differentiation on the basis of dialect mixture in Middle Indo-Aryan, and the former are generally reminiscent of the categories of vocabulary for which he had sought to demonstrate early 'spontaneous cerebralization' (read 'early dialect mixture', with note 29, above?), it is not surprising that the approach, on the evidence of subsequent issues of Mayrhofer's etymological dictionary, has failed to carry conviction. One may regret Burrow's rejection of plausible Dravidian etymologies, as for *taṭa* and *kuṇi*, under its incentive.[31]

In respect of Brugmann's Law too, Burrow strove to reconcile nineteenth-century theory with twentieth-century understanding of Sanskrit. The article in *BSOAS*, 1975, which sought to establish a correlation between IE -*o*- vocalism and the appearance of -*ā*- in Sanskrit in all types of syllable, has been welcomed by Collinge[32] as 'a radical new treatment' and 'a courageous revival and a notable clarification': it encouraged him to believe that Sanskrit -*ā*- < *IE* -*o*- might have a phonetic explanation (viz., inherently greater duration of the back mid vowel). Mayrhofer quotes,[33] without discussion, Burrow's finding as 'indoiran. /ā/ < idg. */o/ auch in geschlossener Silbe'. It must, however, be

---

[30] *The laws of Indo-European* (Amsterdam/Philadelphia, 1985), 45.

[31] RV *jaṭhára*, with an implication of 'tubby' (*jáṭhala*), seems semantically a good match for *pāṇí* (above, n. 29). It is wrong to distance *taṭa* from Dravidian on the basis of a sense 'slope' (BRD, *KEWA*): appropriate is *DEDR* 3031 with *taṭa*- and the senses 'impediment, restraint (of water), embankment, dam'. *Mbh.* 1.32.3 *himavatas taṭe* refers to a Tīrtha at the back of beyond; *R* 4.12.16 *niṣpapāta . . . bhāskaro 'staṭād iva* refers to the bounds of the Ocean, the ends of the earth, as do *Megh.* 60 *prāleyādrer upataṭam* and *Kathās.* 26.26 *śabdapūritadiktaṭān*: the respective translations 'to the foot of' (Ganguli), 'over the top' (Shastri), 'near the skirt of' (Kale), 'filling the sides of heaven' (Tawney), show BRD's alleged sense 'slope' to be inapplicable, as indeed do van Buitenen's quaint 'mortifications on the slope of' and Lefeber's compromise 'from behind the slope of'. The new Pléiade transl. of *Kathās.* has, in the instance, rightly 'limites de l'espace'. The error may reflect misunderstanding of *kaṭi-taṭa*, etc., for which nothing implies 'sloping' (BRD 'abhängig'): rather 'bounds, contour' of hips, both slim (*Mbh.* 3.146.66) and ample (13.14.108).

[32] *The laws of Indo-European*, 16ff.

[33] *Idg. Gr.*, ɪ, 2, 147.

emphasised that Burrow had to concede that the development is again not uniform in all dialects. In fact, he made only a tacit assumption of Iranian involvement, as when (p. 63) he passed over Av. *'pāšna'* (Skt *párṣṇi*)[34] without comment, and (pp. 60, 63, 74, re **ou*, **or*, **oi*) posited 'a different treatment of IE *-o-* in such positions as between Sanskrit and Avestan', i.e. an Iranian absence of Vṛddhi that occurs also dialectally in Indo-Aryan (p. 70).

Burrow's conviction (p. 75) of the inadequacy of attempts to link Brugmann's Law with a small handful of morphological categories is noteworthy. Mayrhofer (*Idg. Gr.*, ɪ, 2, 148) cites two such categories, without prejudice, but also without stressing this aspect of Burrow's thesis. Though it is only to be expected that the distinctive weak grade that appears in *hūtá* would encourage distinctive strong grades in *āhavá, hávīman,* and Pāṇ. *hvāyayati,* and that *cakara* would be resistant to lengthening, in company with *cakartha* and in contrast with *cakāra,* Mayrhofer is in such cases compelled by Brugmann's shwa, if not by Brugmann's Law, to believe that post-consonantal laryngeals must still have been active here in early Indo-Iranian. A Brugmann-inspired desire to find a way of closing the radical syllable in *cakara* and *janayati* compelled Burrow to retain the theoretical laryngeal and, shortly afterwards in *The problem of shwa in Sanskrit,* to attempt a new explanation for the phenomenon. In this context too, as Collinge has shown (*The laws of Indo-European,* 17), Burrow's attempt at a compromise has weakened his important demonstration of the wide scope of the phenomenon in Sanskrit, so that his contribution to Brugmann's Law has had no more evident impact than his assault on Brugmann's shwa.

In 'The Proto-Indoaryans' (*JRAS*, 1973), he gave a critical survey of research on the early location and interaction of Iranians and Indo-Aryans, and this has remained an oft-quoted source in subsequent discussions. He offered a useful historical argument with which to counter the traditional late dating of the Zoroastrian Gathas. He coupled this with a plausible theory that the Iranians must have encountered the Indo-Aryans already established in the vicinity of Eastern Iran, and he sought to support this with the more dubious contention[35]

---

[34] Surely one may read Av. *pāšni (pāšn<aē>ibiia* in *Vid.* 8.70f.; *ñ<ā> ibiia* in most MSS at 2.31) versus derived *kasu-pāšna, zairi-pāšna*: cf. notably RV *-aṅgula,* Av. *-aṇura.*

[35] The counter-argument of Boyce (*History of Zoroastrianism,* ɪ, (Leiden, 1975), 55, with n. 211), that the Zoroastrian objection to Daēvas was spiritual and ethical (and not noticeably xenophobic), did not go far enough. Gnoli relied on her argument so far as the term Daēva is concerned; but Burrow's philological argument (*JRAS*, 1973, 130f.) in general lacks cogency. The authenticity of Av. *daēva* 'god' is not threatened by the coexistence of *baga,* any more than that of RV *devá* by *bhága* (which latter is in Vedic a divine epithet and not only, as Burrow stated, 'the name of a particular deity'); the suggestion that in all Avestan literature 'there is no sign of any such classification as that into Devas and Asuras' is hard to reconcile with the existence of a detailed pandemonium in *Vid.* 10 and of references to a plurality of Ahuras. The notion of a twofold wind, favourable and unfavourable, in Iranian corresponds to two antithetical Vātas in RV 2.39.5 (left and right) and 10.137.2 (to and fro), so that it suggests more a potential basis for fission into Yazata and Daēva than the merging of two ethnic rivals.

that the word Deva, together with many of the Deva names, Varuṇa, Indra, etc., was an innovation peculiar to the Indo-Aryans of the Near East and India, which the Iranians must have adopted. Both the historical and the ethnic conclusions were adopted as 'the best and most likely working hypothesis' by Gnoli in *Zoroaster's time and homeland* (Naples, 1980, 70). In Mallory's *In search of the Indo-Europeans* (London, 1989, 42f.), Burrow's conception of the eastward migration was used to supplement Ghirshman's account of the westward movement into Mitanni. Archaeological evidence to support or disprove Burrow's view of the early migrations is neither available nor very likely to emerge.

All the while, Burrow had been publishing semantic studies of Sanskrit vocabulary. These, though carefully evaluated in Mayrhofer's etymological dictionaries, are less well known than they should be, partly because of a sometimes exaggerated tendency to hypostatise the material in terms of new etymologies. With reference to the paper 'Sanskrit *gṝ/gur* "to welcome"' (*BSOAS*, 1957), for example, Gotō[36] found that Burrow, in seeking to establish this base as a separate labio-velar root distinct from a velar root *gṝ/gir* 'to proclaim, celebrate', was guilty of exaggerating the antiquity of the phono-logical and semantic developments which he postulated. Nevertheless, the contribution that the article makes to the morphology and semantics of *gir-*, *gur-*, and *jar-* is an important one.

In view of the vexatious absence of any collective reprint of Burrow's articles on Indo-Aryan topics, it must be useful to list here the main items of lexicography which appear under anonymous rubrics in the bibliography (omitting those concerned solely with Dravidian provenance and the many etymological notes in his reviews' of *KEWA* in *Kratylos*):

'Indo-Iranica' (*Siddha-Bhāratī*, 1951): *sphyá, sthūlá, √tṛp, Srughna, āhlādayati, lakṣita, keśa, bṛsī.*

'Sanskrit etymological notes' (*Sarūpa-Bhāratī*, 1954): *kaṭaka* 'hill-side', *kuhū̃, √kṣam, kharvá, gambhīrá, nava* 'sneezing', *niryūha, nánāndṛ, priyaṅgu, √bhaṇḍ, matyà, marica, lavaṇá, líṅga, lūma, ślakṣṇá, √śliṣ, śvábhra, √saj, sphuliṅga.*

'Sanskrit *kava-* and related words' (*IL*, 1955): *kumārá, komala, ákava, kavatnú, ku-, kad, kubjá, ákūpara.*

---

[36] *Die 'I. Präsensklasse' im Vedischen* (Wien, 1987), 150f., 155. Burrow's statements in *BSOAS* (1957), 140 and *The Skt lg.* (1973), 393f. do not make it clear whether he was influenced by Szemerényi's similar suggestion (made in a paper read to the Philological Society in London on 8 February 1952); nor did he seem concerned by the fact that the proposal is consistent with the standard theory (Szemerényi, Mayrhofer, etc.) of three 'tectal' series, rather than with Burrow's own view that instances of Skt *k, g, gh* for expected *ś*, etc., are not convincingly explained thereby (*The Skt lg.* (1973), 76f.).

'Nirvacanāni' (*AORI*, Madras, 1957): *anujīrṇa, arṇasāti, uśíj, śmasi, ví gṛṇīṣe, vārdala, siṣákti, kuluñcá.*

'Sanskrit lexicographical notes' (*Fel. vol. Belvalkar*, 1957): √*ard-, kaḍitra* 'parchment', *kuḍaka* 'child', *nāgara* 'anchor', *palitopama, práṣṭi, bukkā* 'fragrant powder', *vārdhrīṇasa.*

'Notes on some rare words in Sanskrit and their etymology' (*BSOAS*, 1970): *marīsa* (= *soḍha, dūsa*) 'milk', *upamārayati* 'submerges', *dūrśá* 'goatskin', *panú* 'nourishment', *mukaya* 'mule', *varvaṇā* 'an insect', *saṃplomnāya* 'having kneaded'.

'Six notes on Sanskrit etymology' (*S. K. De mem. vol.,* 1972): *alarka* 'mad dog', *āmiṣa, chamaṇḍa* 'orphan', *nindu* 'who bears dead children', *pariparin* 'adversary' *lakuṭa.*

'Two Saka loanwords in Manusmṛti' (*UAJ*, 1975): *hoḍha* 'stolen property', *hitā* 'dam'.

'Five notes on Sanskrit etymology' (*Brahmavidyā*, 1980–1): *nema* 'foundation', *mār(i)ṣa, raṅga, veṣṭa* 'resin', *hīra* 'diamond'.

'Some notes on Sanskrit etymology' (*Ṛtam*, 1979–83): *aráṇi, alají, alasāndra* (a pulse), *avaṭíṭa* 'flat-nosed', *aṣṭ(h)i.*

'Miscellaneous notes on Sanskrit etymology' (*Kuppuswami Sastri comm. vol.* II, 1985): *oja* 'odd', *keṇikā* 'tent', *kākiṇī* 'cowrie', *trapusa* 'sour', *nāgoda* 'belly armour', *praśala* 'cold', *bhukkhāṇa* 'nose-bag', *varuḍa* 'basket-maker', *vali, vellati.*

'Four contributions to Sanskrit etymology' (*Festschrift Hoenigswald,* 1987): *kṝ, chaṭā, pitta, biḍāla.*

'Two homonymous verbs in Sanskrit' (*Happening Ben Schwartz*, 1988): *javate* 'thinks', *smayate* 'smears'.

'Sanskrit *glauḥ* and related words' (unpublished): *gilāyu* 'tumour'; *grumuṣṭí* 'balled fist', *-gluntha, gilodya* 'bulb'; *gulma, gulphita, guluccha* (*guccha, gutsa*), *guḍa; gaḍu(la); guṇikā, gṛñjana, gắrjara.*

Just one early paper demonstrates the extent to which Thomas Burrow's devotion to the pressing needs of Indo-European and Dravidian historical linguistics represents a considerable loss in the field of the history of Sanskrit literature. In 'The date of Śyāmilaka's Pādatāḍitaka' (*JRAS*, 1946), Burrow succeeded in identifying the historical setting that had been used as the background for one of the few extant specimens of Sanskrit one-act farce: he found that it referred, for local colour, to Bhadrāyudha and Indradatta, two important figures in the consolidation and defence of the western marches of the Gupta empire in the fifth century. An early and instructive example of the narrative genre that features a mock-serious Court of Love was thereby localised in the empire's western capital.

Subsequent discussion[37] has suggested, however, that the references in the monologue are to AD 455/6, not to c.410, the date that Burrow had proposed and that was consequently adopted by the editors when the text came to be reissued in 1959. The play itself would be datable up to c.510, when the western provinces finally fell to the encroaching Gurjaras. Since Bhadrāyudha's activities must be associated with the reign, not of Candragupta II, but of Skandagupta, Burrow's date was certainly too early.

The new argument for 455/6 also has its flaws, however. As Burrow observed, the play describes an apparently very youthful Indradatta as a satellite ruler of the westernmost province: and it happens to be known that Indradatta's son was ruling by 455/6. Burrow had further noted that the wording of the description of Bhadrāyudha's conquests recurs in the Bhitari inscription, where, however, the topic is the prowess of Skandagupta himself. This is much more likely to imply that the historical records relating to 455/6 have been plagiarised at some subsequent date for the purposes of the farce than vice versa. As Schokker has noted, there is a reference to the god Skanda's epithet Gaṅgāsuta in the play; this, probably implicit in the Skandagupta inscription, is pointless in the new context.

Such manipulation of historical data may be linked with the fact that, unlike the locales that are directly named in other associated farces, the western capital appears anonymously as sārvabhaumanagara 'imperial city'. While the composition of the play indeed has 455/6 as terminus post quem, the destruction of Ujjain c.510 is thus not necessarily a secure terminus ante quem. As Burrow's argument indicates, the dramatist seems to have been attempting to reconstruct the apogee of the 'Gupta golden age' for its setting: Skandagupta's inscriptions suggest that already in 455/6 life in Ujjain no longer embodied the idyll of sophistication and romance that the genre demanded.

Few scholars can match Burrow's achievement in revolutionising Dravidology and in pursuing a radically new approach to Sanskrit historical linguistics, while at the same time conducting (until 1965 single-handed) what was without doubt the most demanding BA degree course in all of Sanskrit studies worldwide, as well as many wide-ranging research supervisions in the field of Vedic and classical Sanskrit literature, Tamil, and the history of ancient India. He is remembered with affection and gratitude as a teacher and scholar of the old school, immensely learned and surprisingly reticent. As at the sister universities, Cambridge and London, students of Sanskrit had in any case to be suitably qualified linguists and above all self-reliant; but others besides Burrow's own students found him approachable and sympathetic, helpful and tolerant. As a reviewer of books, he would supply, virtually by

---

[37] Dasharatha Sharma, JGJhaRI (1956–7), 20; G. H. Schokker, The Pādatāḍitaka of Śyā-milaka (The Hague, 1966), 23.

return of post, a masterly and appreciative digest of any argument, abstruse or otherwise; negative criticism was invariably restricted to correcting points of linguistic or historical fact.

He was keeper of the Indian Institute in Oxford until its demise; Vice-President of the International Association of Tamil Research from 1966; Fellow of the British Academy (elected in 1970), an Honorary Fellow of the School of Oriental and African Studies, and an Honorary Member of the Linguistic Society of India. He was awarded the decennial prize of the Dravidian Linguistics Association, and in 1979 an issue of the *Bulletin of the School of Oriental and African Studies* was devoted to Sanskrit, Middle Indo-Aryan, Iranian, and Dravidian studies composed in celebration of his seventieth birthday. His books were presented to Wolfson College Library, Oxford: some 160 having reference to Dravidian, 80 to Indo-Aryan languages, 220 to Sanskrit and Prakrit literature, and 300 to linguistics, history, etc. His interleaved and annotated copy of Monier Williams's *Sanskrit–English Dictionary* has been deposited in the Indian Institute Library.

J. C. WRIGHT

School of Oriental and African Studies
University of London

Appendix

In the bibliography published in *BSOAS*, 50, 2 (1987), 350ff., read:

(1935[1]): 'Tokharian elements in the Kharoṣṭhī documents from Chinese Turkestan'.

(1936[2]): 'The dialectical position of the Niya Prakrit'.

(1954[1]): *Asiatica* (Festschrift Weller).

(1957[3]): *Annals of the Oriental Research Institute*.

(1958): *BRMIC*, 9, 2 (1958) (lecture delivered at the Institute in Sept. 1957).

(1970[1]): *BSOAS*, 33, 1 (1970) (In honour of Sir Harold Bailey).

(1977[1]): 'Sanskrit *irā* "nourishment"' *SO*, 47 (Aalto fel. vol.).

(1977[2]): 'Some cases of alternation between *c* and *ś* in Sanskrit' ['between *c* and *s*' is surely a misprint in the published text: the two references to *c/s* alternation seem incidental to the topic].

(1985): 'Miscellaneous notes on Sanskrit etymology' (paper submitted *c*.1970: see *Die Sprache*, 31 (1985), 324).

(1987): *Festschrift for Henry Hoenigswald*, (Ars Linguistica, 15), 57–64.

There is a specious misprint in the listing in Dandekar, *Vedic bibliography*, v, 827 of the title of the article 1983[1] as 'A note on the Indo-Iranian root *kan-* "smell" and the etymology of Latin *canis* "dog" ': for "smell", read "small".

Add:

'The language of the Kharoṣṭhi [*sic*] documents from Chinese Turkestan'. Cambridge University Thesis, [1935]. (Since the subscript dots were appended in ink, it seems possible that Burrow had intended to leave Kharosthi without diacritics. Publ. 1937.)

'Two homonymous verbs in Sanskrit', in *A linguistic happening in memory of Ben Schwartz* (Bibliothèque des Cahiers de l'Institut Linguistique de Louvain), ed. Yoël L. Arbeitman (Louvain-la-Neuve: Peeters, 1988), 489–92.

'Sanskrit *glauḥ* and related words' (unpublished typescript).

Two other short and possibly incomplete typescript articles were found after Burrow's death but cannot at present be traced: 'The Sanskrit root *kharj-* "to scratch, to itch" and its derivatives' and 'Vedic *aditi-/Aditi-*'.

Obituaries:

'Professor Thomas Burrow: Sanskrit and Dravidian studies', *The Times*, 18 June, 1986.

M. B. Emeneau: 'Thomas Burrow', *IL*, 47 (1986), unpag.

Gillian R. Hart, 'Thomas Burrow', *BSOAS*, 50, 2 (1987), 346–57, with a list of Burrow's books, articles, reviews and notices compiled by G. R. Hart, E. Tucker and J. C. Wright.

The Thomas Burrow Memorial Lecture at the XV All India Conference of Dravidian Linguistics, 1987 was published in *IJDL*, 16, 1 (1987), as follows:

H. S. Ananthanarayana: 'Thomas Burrow's contribution to Sanskrit studies', pp. 1–21.

P. S. Subrahmaniam: 'The non-literary languages and their contribution to Dravidian comparative grammar', pp. 22–30.

B. Ramakrishna Reddy: 'Burrow's fieldwork and research on tribal Dravidian languages', pp. 31–43.

Bh. Krishnamurti: 'Professor Thomas Burrow (1909–1986)', pp. 44–8.

ALISTAIR CROMBIE

Alistair Cameron Crombie
1915–1996

ALISTAIR CAMERON CROMBIE, one of the most influential historians of science of his generation, died at his home in Oxford on 9 February 1996. He was born on 4 November 1915 in Brisbane, Australia, the second son of William David Crombie and Janet Wilmina (*neé* Macdonald), both of Scottish extraction. His grandparents had made the move from farms in Scotland to very remote properties in Queensland, where they raised sheep in truly pioneering circumstances. From the beginning they were heavily dependent on the vagaries of the weather, and there is one family story of how their fate on the original trek had hung in the balance, depending entirely on their success in locating a river, which they managed to do with very little time to spare. By the time Alistair Crombie was born, the sheep stations were prospering. After school at Geelong Grammar School, he began his university career at Trinity College, Melbourne University, as a medical student, and took his first degree there in zoology in 1938. Most of his adult life, however, was spent in England, and more than half of it in Oxford. Leaving Melbourne, he continued his studies at Jesus College, Cambridge, where he took his doctorate in 1942 with a dissertation on population dynamics—a fact that explains his lifelong interest in the history of Darwinism. In a survey of the history of insect ecology by H. G. Andrewaka and L. C. Birch, his zoological work from this period is said to have greatly stimulated other research on interspecific competition. Between 1941 and 1946 Crombie occupied a temporary research position with the Ministry of Agriculture and Fisheries, which entailed working in the Cambridge Zoological Laboratory. His scientific interests led him to follow informally the lectures of the philosopher C. D. Broad, whose book *The Mind and its Place in Nature* greatly influenced Crombie. He was also

Proceedings of the British Academy, **97**, 257–270. © The British Academy 1998.

inspired by a reading of R. C. Collingwood. Steadily he moved in the direction of the philosophy of science and from there to the history of science.

University College London

In 1946 Crombie was appointed lecturer at University College London. Institutionally, at least, UCL had long been the main centre in Britain for the teaching of the history and philosophy of science, although not at an undergraduate level. Abraham Wolf had been the main driving force, immediately after the First World War, and an M.Sc. degree in 'Principles, History and Method of Science' was established there as early as 1924. Following the end of the Second World War, the astrophysicist and writer on philosophy of science Herbert Dingle was made head of the department, and in 1946 Crombie was recruited as one of its staff of five. The way in which the subject was taught at that time can be easily judged through Wolf's writings and those of Charles Singer (who was at UCL for a brief period from 1919), and their successors. (Douglas McKie, Angus Armitage, Niels Heathcote, and Dingle himself were Crombie's colleagues.) Broadly speaking, the subject was seen as the narrative history of successful scientific ideas and invention, and was meant to answer to the needs, or at least the interests, of the science departments. This is not to say that standard scientific criteria of acceptability were always enough. There were various scientific subjects that Dingle, who was carrying on a running battle with the relativists, would not countenance as a proper object of study, but this did not affect Crombie's teaching. Cambridge experience (and he continued to live in Cambridge) had made him more comfortable with the methodologists than the chroniclers, but above all it led him to view his subject as essentially a branch of the humanities. He was at least one with his new colleagues when in 1947 he joined with them and others in setting up the British Society for the History of Science as well as its Philosophy of Science Group. The latter became an independent body, the British Society for the Philosophy of Science, and Crombie became in fact the first editor of The British Journal for the Philosophy of Science, but by degrees he was moving in the direction of history, albeit of a sort very different from that in vogue at UCL.

UCL's influence on this dual subject should not be underestimated. In the years between the wars more than a hundred higher degrees were taken in the department there. One of those who had taken the doctorate was Frank Sherwood Taylor, who after Robert Gunther's death in 1940 became for a decade curator of the 'Old Ashmolean Museum'[1] at Oxford. Oxford had seen a number of half-hearted attempts over the previous thirty years to launch courses and research in the history of science beyond classical (natural) philosophy—most actively in astronomy and medicine—and Sherwood Taylor tried yet again. Courses were offered (in 1947–8) by S. F. Mason (an assistant demonstrator, in the parlance of Oxford science) and also by Crombie, as a visiting lecturer. Thwarted in a number of ways, Taylor left for the directorship of the Kensington Science Museum, to be succeeded by Conrad Josten in 1950. Josten inherited the ambition to institute teaching courses, but as a director rather than as a teacher. (His quietly imperious style did not always achieve the desired result. On one occasion it led the museum technician to clean one of the two blackboards preserved religiously from the time of a visit by Einstein to Oxford in 1931.) As a result of an initiative by Josten and others, a lecturership in the history of science was created in 1953, and Crombie was the successful applicant. His task was to be that of establishing the history of science as a normal part of teaching and research for students of science, history and philosophy, but under the control of the Committee of the Museum.

By 1953 Crombie had been working for some years on a study of various aspects of medieval science, and he had written two important books in parallel, one a general text-book, the other a scholarly monograph. The first, *Augustine to Galileo: The History of Science A.D. 400–1650* (London, 1952, expanded and modified in small but important ways in 1959), filled a significant void.[2] Eventually translated into seven languages, over the next thirty years it became one of the world's most widely used text-books of history of science. His other early work, *Robert Grosseteste and the Origins of Experimental Science, 1100–1700* (Oxford, 1953), grew out of an essay he wrote for the seventh centenary of Grosseteste's death, an occasion for other studies, written by more experienced scholars but from more traditional points of view. While Crombie was primarily concerned with Grosseteste's scientific thought, and ignored many of the things that had made the great bishop seem so important to other historians, he touched on a number of much more general themes, analysing the whole question of continuity and change in the European scientific tradition from the middle ages to the seventeenth century. Crombie's

---

[1] This was the common name for the Museum of the History of Science, an institution that had grown out of a collection of early scientific instruments assembled by Lewis Evans that was housed in the old Ashmolean building in Broad Street. The name was used by Robert Gunther, the first curator of the museum, to the intense annoyance of Lewis's brother, the archaeologist Arthur Evans, whose affinities were with the Ashmolean institution.

[2] An interesting account of how he changed his stance between editions will be found in B. S. Eastwood, *Isis* (March 1992). For an almost complete bibliography of his writings, see J. D. North & J. J. Roche, *The Light of Nature. Essays in the History and Philosophy of Science Presented to A. C. Crombie* (Dordrecht, 1985), supplemented by his own *Styles of Scientific Thinking* (London, 1994), discussed below.

claim to be able to detect in Grosseteste's thought significant traces of the experimental philosophy that made the scientific revolution of the seventeenth century possible has since been the object of much criticism. He overstated his case, perhaps, but much of his argument can be retained, and there is no doubt that the parts that are unacceptable served an important catalytic purpose in the decades that followed. His work was at least utterly different in character from that produced in the milieu in which he had worked up to that time.

Oxford

Crombie moved to Oxford in 1954, after a year as visiting Professor at the University of Washington, Seattle—a diplomatic error on his part, since there was much good will towards his subject in the university, but also a sense that matters ought to be moving more quickly. Indeed, there had been for some years a sporadic discussion of the merits of establishing a 'science Greats' analogous to 'classical Greats' (Literae Humaniores) and to 'modern Greats' (a name occasionally given to the course in Philosophy, Politics, and Economics). I first learned of the ruffled feathers quite fortuitously at approximately the time of the Crombie appointment, when as an undergraduate I met a very taciturn physics professor, holed up in a corner at a party given by the wife of the Warden of Merton. This turned out to be Frederick Lindemann, soon to be made Viscount Cherwell, of whose name and reputation I then knew absolutely nothing. From near silence he was suddenly galvanised into speech when I mentioned a point in the history of physics. He produced a succession of sharp personal remarks that meant nothing to me, but I was intrigued at the idea that such a dull subject could produce such an animated response. Since I had just visited the 'Old Ashmolean' I was also amused at his judgement that the museum was living proof of the law of increasing entropy.[3] But what I recall most clearly was his insistence that the history and philosophy of science—of which he seemed to have no high opinion—were the property of the scientists. I later heard this said often in Oxford, and it represented one of the hurdles that Crombie would have to cross.[4]

[3] As I later discovered, he was wrong, for C. H. Josten had by this time turned the graph downwards, but the effects had not yet made themselves felt.
[4] The point was made strongly in a letter to *The Times* on 17 August 1956 by a certain I. Aucken, who suggested that no one with experience of the tedium and delight of science will surrender this work for the sake of writing about other people's work, and yet that no one who lacks the experience is 'competent to write history that is safe for serious students of science to treat seriously'. To unseat himself from the horns of his dilemma, he conceded that the musings of superannuated scientists might have a genuine value. Such rhetoric is now much harder to find. The correspondence from which this item comes (see the issues between 11 and 25 August) included contributions by Crombie as well as Toulmin, Marie Boas, Dingle, and others.

When Crombie arrived, Stephen Toulmin was university lecturer in philosophy of science (he was there between 1949 and 1955), but most philosophers still felt very wary of these subjects. The point was put very well in an eloquent radio talk by J. P. Corbett, late in 1956, when he said that it would be better to draw a veil of silence over the questions on the methods and foundations of science in the so-called logic papers of the Oxford schools, but that it was high time that those responsible for the Oxford curriculum recognise that science is a significant strand in the social process. (More recognition within philosophy came soon afterwards.) Both Toulmin and his successor Friedrich Waismann included a historical dimension in their teaching, but to all intents and purposes Crombie was building on very low foundations. As for the history faculty, there was then very little systematic interest within it, beyond an occasional excursion on the part of individuals who found themselves unable to ignore entirely the scientific aspect of past intellectual life; but those individuals tended to feel very strongly about their subjects—and Grosseteste is only one of many shared subjects that come to mind—and did not like intruders. In short, the battle lines with which Crombie would have to contend were drawn in many Oxford minds before he ever arrived on the scene, and perhaps it was his failure to understand them that gave him something of a reputation for high-handedness.

I first met him personally soon after he arrived. I was an undergraduate and he had been persuaded to teach a course on the Leibniz–Clarke Correspondence and parts of Newton's *Principia* for one of the papers in philosophy. Already he was in the thick of controversy that stemmed in large measure— but of course not entirely—from proprietorial imperatives. His services were being called for by people in different faculties, but in the tradition of Oxbridge democracy he regarded himself as the guardian not only of his own conscience but of his time. Josten, more familiar with a continental hierarchy, had other ideas, especially when it came to the facilities of the museum.

The Leibniz–Clarke class, held at first in a room in the Old Ashmolean building, helped to bring matters to a head, but it was memorable for quite different reasons. It was the beginning of what became an extremely influential seminar in the history of science generally, not so much by virtue of Crombie's own contributions but by his guidance and his ability to attract notable senior scholars, many of them visiting Oxford from elsewhere. When Josten decided that coexistence was not possible, the meetings moved to All Souls, where Crombie was a member of common room. After 1969, when he was made a fellow of Trinity, and until 1983 when he retired, it was held in Trinity, and for all of these years it was the centre of gravity of Oxford history of science, at least in the eyes of most of the world outside Oxford. The meetings were often very casual, but they were not trivial. They had a vital core that will not emerge from a mere scanning of lecture lists and committee minutes, and the vitality came in part from the expectations of those present. The fortunes of the sciences themselves were burgeoning, and Crombie's moderate imperialism was such that as he became a talking point so did his subject. And slowly a feeling was growing that here, running in harness with philosophy of science, was an important subject that did not need to cling to the coat-tails of the sciences, one that had something to say to people from many other quarters of the university.

This is not to overlook the scepticism that was being expressed by some scientists in the university, almost certainly a majority, whose charge was that they were being asked to accept a soft option. They could point to the fact that much of the British literature of the period was of a very indifferent quality. The best work of the first half of the century was done by amateurs of some stature, such as Thomas Heath, J. K. Fotheringham, Edmund Whittaker, and Joseph Needham, but there was much over which it would be kindest to draw a veil. In a statement made at an Oxford conference in 1961 that amounted to his vision of the subject at that time, Crombie was obviously very sensitive to this charge:

> It seems difficult to see how a prospective historian at least of modern science can become really confident of his technical mastery of his materials unless he has had some fairly advanced training . . . in, and experience of the actual *use of* the analytical disciplines of science or mathematics, as distinct from simply studying the historical sources.[5]

This sentiment was well received by his select and distinguished international audience, and yet, nearer home, it was one that some in the history faculty were beginning to view with suspicion. It is with wry amusement that one can look back on a slow transition that was beginning to take place from a situation where scientific knowledge was thought to be not absolutely necessary to one in which it would be absolutely unnecessary. This might have mattered less had the history faculty not bid fair to corner the market, and to dictate the ground rules of the game into which it had entered late, but fresh. From another quarter came others preaching sociological correctives to more traditional intellectual history. Oxford conservatism managed at first to keep the wilder excesses of this movement at arm's length, but it did eventually have its repercussions.

For Crombie on his arrival this was all in the future. From the first, his style showed how he had been much influenced by Alexandre Koyré—one of several notable early contributors to the Oxford seminar, and one who did

---

[5] He went on of course to say that this was not enough. See 'History and Philosophy of Science at Oxford', *History of Science*, 1 (1962), 57–61, at 58. The paper summarised a talk given at a conference he and R. Harré hosted in Oxford in 1961, the proceedings of which were published in *Scientific Change: Historical Studies in the Intellectual, Social & Technical Conditions for Scientific Discovery & Technical Invention* (London, 1963).

Crombie the honour of disagreeing with him in a constructive manner. Crombie learned much from Koyré's criticism of his arguments for the influence of medieval thought on early modern science, as presented in his *Robert Grosseteste*.[6] Koyré's characteristic historico-philosophical outlook was not uncommon on the continent at that time, and indeed, an influential work by the American scholar E. A. Burtt had been written in a rather similar style even earlier.[7] Crombie, like the majority of those who attended his regular seminars before the mid-1960s, followed suit, treating history and philosophy as natural partners.[8] This approach struck a chord in the small but loyal group that came fairly regularly from the science area. As matters turned out, the formula did not last long. Gradually new forces entered the equation, and Crombie's career bore all the marks of these.

The ambitions that had been responsible for the rapid growth of the history and philosophy of science as a joint enterprise in the 1950s, both in Britain and abroad, were fading in the face of high specialisation on the part of the very people who should have been teaching across a broad spectrum.[9] As a guarantee of his independence, Crombie had engineered the setting up of a committee for History and Philosophy of Science independent of the museum, and through it—and through the good offices of such figures as William Kneale, Gilbert Ryle, Maurice Bowra, John Austin, William Paton, Friedrich Waissmann, and his successor Rom Harré—he was eventually able to intro-duce the joint subject into various corners of the undergraduate curriculum of five different faculties, as well as into the tough B.Phil. course, and to institute a Diploma, conceived as preparatory to doctoral work. The very breadth of his vision, which also characterised much of his writing, was not politically advantageous. These were the years of the Two Cultures discussion, but Crombie soon learned how empty was so much that was said in favour of bridges between the two. Again, the proprietorial compulsions of certain senior colleagues stood in his way—it was harder to claim territory that was conceived to lie on both sides of the bridge—and the old allies drifted apart. There was also unease among certain graduate students, who wished to specialise rather than to be forcefully broadened. (History graduates, for example, would typically argue that to have added the history of seventeenth-century science

---

[6] A. Koyré, 'Les Origines de la science moderne', *Diogène*, Oct. 1956, no. 16, 3–31.

[7] E. A. Burtt, *The Metaphysical Foundations of Modern Physical Science: A Historical and Critical Essay*, 2nd edn. (London, 1932).

[8] Koyré's influence on him was significant, but it has to be said that in his later work on Galileo Crombie resolutely opposed many of Koyré's theses concerning the platonising rationalism of Galileo.

[9] This lamentable narrowness becomes serious in the context of undergraduate teaching. There is nothing like the school curriculum in regular history to force breadth on historians of science.

to their repertoire was broadening enough, without further involvement in the science itself or philosophy of science.)

Another problem was that Crombie's broad outlook did not always fit very comfortably with the needs of the honour schools, the key to Oxford academic politics. Lecturing was not his forte, and he did not think tutoring to be his function. The undergraduate courses set up for the historians and for students in the natural sciences were taught independently, and by very different types of tutor. The scientists, the historians and the philosophers all had different interests and expectations, as he well realised, but there was more at stake than the notion of a single unifying discipline. He could not find a formula that would hold the allegiance of all interested senior members of the university whose support he badly needed, let alone the uninterested—such as D. N. Chester, the Warden of Nuffield, who made a sharp attack in Congregation in which the strongest argument against the subject was that it was administratively very inconvenient. Had Crombie taken a narrower view of his subject, and retreated into a scholarly corner, he might have avoided the common complaint that he was empire-building. He was not a good judge of the impression his plans were making on his colleagues, or of their true intentions. When a few Diploma students made known their displeasure at the idea that they should study philosophy of science, the situation was seized upon by some of his colleagues to embarrass him. There were even those who claimed that he was part of a Catholic plot to infiltrate the curriculum. (Ernest Jacob was jovial but serious when he said this on one occasion within my hearing.) At the other extreme of academic crustiness there were those who complained that Crombie was being 'irrelevant' in ignoring the sociology of science—a bandwagon that was gathering momentum in the late 1960s. The era of the atom bomb produced a curious ambivalence—a certain reluctance to admire the scientific mentality that had produced it, combined with a feeling that at least something must be said about it. By a strange sort of logic, some managed to proceed to the thesis that scientific mentalities were not a proper object of study except through their external repercussions. Their inner workings were deemed socially irrelevant, and therefore the study of them somehow violated the canons of good history.

Crombie was bemused by much of what was happening around him, and was content with the focus he had created for research at an advanced (rather than an undergraduate) level, largely unaware that others had plans for the subject differing from his. He had created a focus for academic controversy of perhaps too many different sorts, and this eventually worked against him. By the time the Oxford chair in history of science was created and filled (1971–2), the number of graduate students pursuing the history of science at Oxford had grown to more than fifty—of course by no means all were working with him—and the number of science undergraduates reading the special subject annually had peaked at over thirty. Despite this, the part he had played in building up the subject counted for little in the eyes of a committee whose members had a more parochial view of the field than his, and in some instances harboured a measure of deep personal animosity. It was to the great surprise of many outsiders that he was passed over for the chair. The fact certainly took away much of his missionary fervour, but he continued to act as a magnet to scholars from elsewhere. He was known either personally or through his writings to a very large number of scholars, and this, and the fact that he had been so active internationally, meant that the subject in Oxford continued to be identified more closely with him than with any other single person.

Styles of Scientific Thinking. Galileo

As a historian of science, Crombie's central interest was in the methods and styles of scientific thinking and reasoning and their development within the intellectual context of medieval and early modern Europe. It was a theme to which he returned repeatedly, and he spent more than twenty years in expanding what began as an article on the subject into a monumental three-volume study: *Styles of Scientific Thinking in the European Tradition: The history of argument and explanation especially in the mathematical and biomedical sciences and arts.*[10] In this he made a detailed comparative analysis of the forms of scientific reasoning that were developed within European intellectual culture, beginning with the Greek search for the principles of nature and argument itself, and applied to an ever wider variety of subject-matters. He thought that those who are concerned with the history of European scientific thought as a whole were obliged to begin there, since this very phenomenon was one initiated by the ancient Greeks. He went on to develop his strongly Eurocentric thesis into a demonstration of the importance of six styles of reasoning that were a characteristically European production. The styles in question had often been studied by philosophers of science, but Crombie's historical work was new both in its comprehensiveness and its thoroughness. In it he makes his reader aware—often perhaps unconsciously—of how little was the attention paid by so many modern historical writers to either the content of science or to the principles either of nature or of argument.

His six styles are: *postulation*, as used in Greek mathematics and the mathematical arts; the *experimental strategy* in the search for principles; *hypothetical modelling*, with its use of analogy; *taxonomy*, as the logic of ordering agreement and difference, and as a tool in the search for natural affinities and systems; *probabilistic and statistical analysis*, as a guide to reasonable expectation; and finally, *historical derivation*. By this last, he refers

---

[10] London, 1994.

to the genetic method, the way of looking at ostensibly unlike things and deciding on the grounds of their common characteristics what common 'historical' sources they have—a method applicable in subjects as diverse as linguistics and biology, as geology and the history of science itself.

Crombie's thesis was not without its problems. Beginning with postulation and the ancient search for principles and methods, he could not sidestep Mesopotamian and Egyptian science, in other words, science that was in no sense European. His way with this difficulty was to stress the importance of systems of thought. 'There is nothing', he wrote, 'in any surviving text corresponding to a theorem or a proof, no theory of numbers or generalized algebra, nothing that might indicate even an inkling of such conceptions.' In short, he believed that in Mesopotamian and Egyptian astronomy, medicine, and other empirical subjects, 'a general theory, a generalized explanation, a conception of natural causation' was lacking. He claimed that these cultures paid excessive attention to superhuman beings whom they credited with responsibility for phenomena, beings with a fickle character out of keeping with the regularities that guided European science.

His second style of scientific thinking he illustrated with reference to the science he had spent most of his life studying, from the thirteenth century to the seventeenth, a period that saw the advent of a sophisticated logic of experimental argument in different forms. The period saw a vigorous continuation of ancient discussions, but there was also a dialogue between natural philosophy and new developments in the practical arts, a dialogue that was later reinforced by ancient texts, and finally transformed into the art of the rational experimenter. In view of Crombie's well-known researches into Galileo, it comes as no surprise to experience a crescendo at the end of the first volume and the beginning of the second, when Galileo comes on stage. This is a cue for philosophical strategy to be reviewed in the light of the debate on Copernicanism, the character of the book of nature, the distinction of primary and secondary qualities, and so forth. Galileo is in fact kept securely in his place, a bright beacon, but one with a historical meaning only in relation to a network of others—a list of which includes Averroes, Clavius, Kepler, Ramus, and the Collegio Romano, and later takes in the Royal Society, Boyle, Newton, and Fontenelle. Mechanics, painting and sculpture, and the science of music are all fitted into this 'style', although they surface again under the next, that of 'hypothetical modelling'.

The modelling of natural processes—which has attracted much attention among philosophers of science during the last thirty years—Crombie presents as a technique introduced into early modern science with the help of ancient and medieval theology and the medieval and Renaissance arts. His examples include the modelling of the senses, with the camera obscura and the eye, as discussed by Leonardo and others. But there are analogies both grander and deeper. There is that all-pervasive analogy between divine and human creation, and there is also what might be counted a second-order analogy, between making and knowing—and here Crombie has interesting things to say about the modelling of language, a historically important theme.

The taxonomic style gets the shortest treatment. Crombie follows its history from the Hippocratic writings to the eighteenth century, in fact to Michel Adanson and Buffon, who gave a refreshingly modern answer to the question of the reality of species. They were not essences, said Buffon, but a series of individuals defined by genetic continuity. Those are of the same species that have the power to reproduce their likeness. That of course leaves the question of explicating likeness, so that essentialists are not exactly forced into retirement. When this section of the book ends, however, Darwin is on the horizon, and the cruder forms of essentialism are becoming a backwater—for if individuals are the only reality, then variations give evidence that living organisms can change from generation to generation, and form new species.

Probabilistic styles of scientific thinking, fifth in the Crombie series, are styles that arise out of a need to formalise decision-taking in the face of uncertainty. They have their roots in Greek and medieval qualitative notions. Crombie starts from the Hippocratic writings once more, although he acknowledges that this style of reasoning was not well quantified or axiomatised until the sixteenth and seventeenth centuries. The names to conjure with now include Pascal and Huygens, Leibniz and Halley, Bayes, the Bernoullis and Maupertuis, d'Alembert and Laplace. From the need to gamble rationally—whether at cards or on a patient's life-expectancy—to the biology of populations is a long intellectual journey, or rather only the beginning of a longer one, and it passes through some extraordinarily rich territory. Fate, the will of God, divination, the presentiment and knowledge of future events, scientific determinism, mercantile insurance, the morality of gambling in relation to covert knowledge of certainties, and economic and demographic statistics: these are only a beginning. The core natural sciences are not perhaps at first conspicuous, but they are never far away. Chance and providence become changed into principles of least action, not only in physics but in the adaptive diversification of living things. Malthus, for example, having (as he believed) modelled his notorious argument on Newton, was at length taken over by Darwin and Wallace when they used statistical methods to analyse evolutionary change. Heisenberg, Schrödinger, and other moderns fell outside the terms of Crombie's history, but that they too can be brought into the picture must be in the mind of many a reader. This was not unexplored territory, but what Crombie achieved was its integration into the map of western science generally, something that had not been done in quite the same way before.

His last style was that of historical derivation, again traced by him to a characteristically Greek point of view, that the world is generated by a natural causal process that continues to operate. Taking a class of phenomena and trying to identify common properties or common causes, one is led to the construction of a common ancestor. Crombie had much to say of the ways in which the method was applied in the sixteenth century with great success to the phenomena of language, but even more about the seventeenth- and eighteenth-century writers, say from Francis Bacon to Monboddo, who used the method to elucidate the history of the human mind and its mastery over nature. It is not just a question of postulating a common source: one must also be in a position to put forward an account of divergence from that source. One of the best chapters concerns the 'history of nature'—the geological history of the Earth, the origin of fossils, the explanation of the diversity of living types, and ultimately the transformation of species. Crombie was most at home in the life sciences, and those passages dealing with evolution and its antecedents are a pleasure to read.

This sixth brought him round once more to his previous 'style', for the transformation of organisms through time might be done not only by an innate, inbuilt, principle, but also in the style of a Maupertuis or a Laplace, by the statistical accumulation of marginal advantages. And so to Malthus' argument and its consequences, to which both Darwin and Wallace acknowledged their debt for the statistical treatment of natural selection, the model of net marginal advantage to the biology of populations. This was the subject of Crombie's last chapter. As he wrote:

> Taking a principle from the social sciences, they tried to demonstrate in the style of theoretical physics that its operation must, by an automatic statistical necessity, bring about increasing order from unordered random variations. The accumulation of repeated survivals of inherited advantages and disadvantages at different rates must necessarily transform and diversify the successive generations of competing automata to fit their diverse opportunities in the economy of nature, so that the better adapted must multiply, evolve and inhabit the Earth.

This well-received three-volume distillation of his life's work and ideals revealed among other things Crombie's abiding interest in the history of theories of the senses—echoing his earlier work in biology—and in particular the physiology and epistemology of vision and hearing, and their relation to the visual and musical arts. These are subjects touched upon in his numerous other publications—for example in the three published volumes of his collected essays—but they run through another of Crombie's studies, one that occupied much of the last thirty years of his life. Awarded the Galileo Prize by the Domus Galileana in Pisa in 1964, for an essay on Galileo, Crombie soon became a leading authority on that crucially important figure. His Galileo interest made Oxford a natural place to set up the Harriot Seminar, something we did with the collaboration of several distinguished Harriot scholars and the financial support of Dr Cicely Tanner, in 1967.[11]

[11] Between 1990 and 1997 Harriot continued to be celebrated in Oxford through an annual lecture in Oriel College. The pattern of the original Oxford seminar is followed more or less at Durham and Cambridge.

Crombie worked for more than three decades on two other books, *Galileo's Arguments and Disputes in Natural Philosophy* and *Marin Mersenne: Science, Music and Language*. His final illness, a brain tumour, took him unawares, and they were not to be. The second of these works is effectively to be found dispersed through his published writings, and much of the former can also be found elsewhere, although a typescript survives, awaiting additions by a collaborator, Adriano Carrugo. All of these component writings are true to the ideals of his formative years, in that they treat of science as a rational and not merely a social activity. The Galileo book led along the way to much invigorating controversy, largely over priority in the discovery and interpretation of key documents concerning Galileo's intellectual development, so that Crombie's main theses are well known to Galilean experts.

Recognition

Alistair Crombie was much more than an author. He did much to organise his subject, nationally and internationally. Apart from editorship of the BJPS he was one of three joint founders (with Mary Hesse and Michael Hoskin) and for some years joint editor of the review *History of Science* (1962–   ). In 1964 he became President of the British Society for the History of Science, and from 1968 to 1971 President of the Académie Internationale d'Histoire des Sciences. He had what might be portrayed as a colonial attitude to protocol in continental affairs—although it was not for want of knowledge of what was required. I recall a British protest he led at the IUHPS meeting in Moscow in 1971 at the treatment meted out by the Soviets to a Czech colleague,[12] which had the result that all of us on the national committee had the distinction of being individually photographed by the KGB—an honour that Oxford never equalled.

Crombie was in the last resort neither an organiser nor an orator but a writer, one who influenced large numbers of people in Britain and abroad, most of whom never met him. Many who knew him remarked on his anxiety to appear more English than the English, but this was true only up to a certain point. His origins allowed him to place himself at a due zoological distance from the world as he observed it, so that in Britain he could play the Australian, in England the Celt, in Rome the Englishman, in Oxford the Cambridge man, and so forth. For one who irritated many a colleague by

[12] Josef Smolka, nominated secretary of the International Union of the History and Philosophy of Science, was refused entry, our Soviets hosts claiming that they held a letter from him saying that he did not wish to come. The letter presumably failed to mention his baggage, which was allowed entry, together with the key to his flat.

his way of 'playing hard tennis', as he used to express it, he had an enviably large circle of friends, nationally and internationally. He was a loyal friend to a large number of younger scholars, and if he found it hard to forgive a slight, that was not inconsistent with his resolute defence of basic moral principles. After retirement he took up a half-time appointment as Kennedy Professor at Smith College, Northampton, Massachusetts. He held other visiting professorships in the USA, Paris, Tokyo, and Konstanz, and lectured in many European countries as well as in Australia and India. He was made a Senior Fellow of the British Academy in 1990. Crombie was a member of the Academia Leopoldina (Halle) and of the Pontifical Academy of Sciences—an appointment that gave him great pleasure, for despite his mild anti-clericalism his catholicism meant much to him. He held honorary doctorates of the universities of Durham, Paris X-Nanterre, and Sassari. He received the Forschungspreis of the Alexander von Humboldt Foundation, which took him to Germany for long periods in his last two years; and shortly before his death he was awarded the prestigious *Premio europeo ' Dondi'* (jointly with his old friend Marshall Clagett) for his life's work.

Alistair Crombie took very great pleasure from overseeing the gardens of Trinity, and indeed chief among his recreations at his Boars Hill home was landscape gardening, which he and his wife Nancy (who died in 1993) put into practice there for over forty years. They are survived by four children and their families, now including six grandchildren, and are buried together at Ramsgill in Yorkshire, near the cottage where they spent many of their summers and the church where they were married in 1943.

J. D. NORTH
Fellow of the Academy

I. E. S. EDWARDS

Iorwerth Eiddon Stephen Edwards
1909–1996

IN MOST MATTERS Eiddon Edwards was a traditionalist, and particularly in the formalities of life and the use of the English language. Usage did not excuse slackness, and he could never accept that personal habits in behaviour, speech, and writing could be changed from what he had learned in school, university, and social life in the 1920s and 1930s. I am not at all sure that he would have approved of the 'Eiddon Edwards' at the start of this memoir. He was much more comfortable with the formality and impersonality of 'I. E. S. Edwards' or, latterly, 'Dr Edwards'. He did not appreciate being addressed as 'Eiddon'— his preferred Christian name—by anyone who had not been invited to do so. By preference, even with relatively close colleagues, he chose to use surnames in address. It was nothing to do with the fact that most people who attempted 'Eiddon' failed to pronounce it correctly.

The names Iorwerth and Eiddon proclaimed a Welsh connection, and for much of his life he maintained good contacts with family roots in farming communities in and around Llanidloes and Newtown, Montgomeryshire (he certainly would not have approved of Powys). From this part of Wales his father came, but Edwards himself was a Londoner, born in Highgate on 21 July 1909. His parents were Welsh-speakers, and the language was spoken at home, but not exclusively. The young Edwards, as he later claimed, spoke Welsh more than English in his early years; as he grew up, bilingualism in Welsh and English was not considered necessary, and he did not maintain his competency in Welsh.

His father, Edward Edwards, was a Persian scholar in the Department of Oriental Printed Books and Manuscripts in the British Museum; his mother, Ellen Jane Edwards (*née* Higgs), was an acclaimed soprano, performing professionally in oratorio and opera. From his father Edwards inherited a propensity for, and interest in, oriental languages which would in due time

Proceedings of the British Academy, **97**, 273–290. © The British Academy 1998.

determine the course of his own career. His mother's musical talents were perhaps less evident in his own cultural interests in later life. He was not a concert-goer, and showed little interest in music apart from an abiding love for the works of Gilbert and Sullivan. He did not in later life often attend the theatre, not greatly relishing the stuffy atmosphere of the houses. Things had been different in the 1930s, and he frequently invoked the lighter comedies and musical shows of his youth—Aldwych farces, for example— which he had undoubtedly enjoyed, and remembered with affection and some precision.

Remembering, in fact, was something which mattered considerably to Edwards, fuelling his talk and making him a remarkable conversationalist and raconteur. In company he was never short of a suitable anecdote to illustrate a point, and his witty retelling of significant—and not so significant—events in his past, usually related in an engaging self-deprecatory manner, made him a welcome guest at any gathering of Egyptologists, especially of younger scholars for whom Edwards could bring to life long-dead luminaries of the subject, rendering them a deal more human than their published works suggested. And the gathering need not have been Egyptological for him to monopolise the talk. One old friend, Lord Coggan (Archbishop of Canterbury 1974–80), writing of dinners he had with Edwards and another contemporary, says: 'He was a better talker than listener! He engaged in a flow of conversation, recollections, etc. which allowed only for intermittent contributions from the other two of the trio!'

At Merchant Taylors' School, which at that time was still situated in Charterhouse Square in the City of London, Edwards had the opportunity to take up the study of Hebrew in the sixth form. Lord Coggan recalls the time when he first met Edwards in 1926. Both were members of the Hebrew Class at Merchant Taylors', probably the only school in Britain with such a class at that time, an extraordinary experiment in the extension of classical studies, which sadly did not survive the subsequent headmastership of Spencer Leeson, who disapproved of such early specialisation. 'My main recollection of Eiddon is that he and I competed (at school and at Cambridge) for various scholarships(?) and prizes. He went to Caius, and I to St. John's in 1928.' When he had left school, in the summer before he went up to Cambridge with a Merchant Taylors' Exhibition and a college major scholarship, he was able to start elementary Arabic studies. He was, therefore, well prepared to undertake the Oriental Languages Tripos, in both parts of which he gained first classes in 1930 and 1931. With University prizes and scholarships he then embarked on postgraduate research in Arabic.

His years at Cambridge remained halcyon to him for the rest of his life. He was comfortable in his studies, and greatly appreciated the freedom which the University offered. There were also rewards in recognition of his academic abilities. He further received an annual allowance of £100 throughout his University years, from Alfred Chester Beatty, the mining-engineer and industrialist. Beatty had, by the late 1920s, already begun to acquire oriental manuscripts with the help of specialist advisers in the various fields. Edwards's father provided Beatty with advice in acquiring, and help in cataloguing, Persian and Arabic manuscripts, and through him the younger Edwards had met Chester Beatty. The latter, with characteristic benevolence, ensured that Edwards, throughout his time at Cambridge, was able to live without financial strain and to travel in Europe. Such was the purpose of the allowance.

It would be unworthy, I believe, to suggest that Chester Beatty saw in the younger Edwards a possible successor to his father, who could be an orientalist adviser in the future. Nevertheless, Edwards did not forget that early generosity, and, after the Second World War, was able in some measure to repay his benefactor in a number of practical ways: by arranging the mounting of manuscripts, by then housed in the Chester Beatty Library in Dublin, by conservation officers of the British Museum during their vacations; by enabling the young, but difficult, Rolf Ibscher, son of the great Papyruskonservator Hugo Ibscher, to tease out and mount the fragile pages of Coptic Manichaean codices in the workrooms of the Egyptian Department in the British Museum; by finding for Beatty young scholars capable of studying and publishing manuscripts in that great Dublin collection.

In retrospect it seems strange that Edwards with his interest and training in oriental languages, should have in 1934, by examination, entered the Department of Egyptian and Assyrian Antiquities in the British Museum as an Assistant Keeper on the Egyptian side. There was, it must be accepted, a degree of practical opportunism in this move. The time was not good for conventional academic appointments. Edwards's father was a long-standing servant of the Trustees of the British Museum, and understood the advantages of a permanent post in times of economic crisis. And Edwards himself was not without interest in the ancient Near East and Egypt. While he was at Merchant Taylors' he had taken an active part in the school's Archaeological Society. The 1920s was a time of great discoveries: Tutankhamun's tomb in 1922, and Leonard Woolley's remarkable excavations at Ur. The pages of the *Illustrated London News* fed the public interest, offering well-illustrated reports on a regular basis.

It was the Near East rather than Egypt which attracted the young Edwards principally. Through his father he was able to meet, and receive encouragement from, H. R. H. Hall, the jovial successor to Sir E. A. W. Budge as Keeper of the Department of Egyptian and Assyrian Antiquities, and C. J. Gadd, the unassuming but impressively learned Assyriologist in the Department. Sidney Smith, the other departmental Assyriologist, who would succeed Hall as Keeper in 1930, was absent, seconded in the mid-1920s to direct the Iraq

Antiquities Department. The interest and glamour of Tutankhamun, which were so to concern Edwards in later life, were distant and intangible; the wonders of Ur, on the other hand, came in part to the British Museum, and could be inspected at close quarters, and the excavators questioned. But Egypt was not wholly neglected. Edwards recalled a moderately disastrous lecture on the pyramids which he delivered to his schoolboy contemporaries. It was, as he said, completely derivative—how could it have been anything else!—but it serves as a first indication of an interest in those great monuments which would in due course play such an important part in his studies and publication.

It was no unusual thing for new Assistant Keepers to arrive in the British Museum with little expert knowledge in the areas in which they were to specialise. A good degree in an established discipline determined a candidate's academic abilities. Some interest in the appropriate field would help. Edwards was well qualified by scholarly record and interest; he already knew the Museum and the senior members of the department in which he was to spend the whole of his career, apart from the war years. In 1934 the Department had in theory two vacancies to fill. Edwards replaced S. R. K. Glanville, who had moved in 1933 to University College London to become Reader in Egyptology, and succeeding Sir Flinders Petrie as the Edwards Professor in 1935. The second vacancy was filled shortly after Edwards's appointment by Richard Barnett, a classical scholar, who moved laterally from the Department of Greek and Roman Antiquities. Like Edwards, Barnett was a child of the Museum, being the son of Lionel Barnett, the distinguished scholar of Indian languages, who was Keeper of Oriental Printed Books and Manuscripts. The careers of Edwards and Barnett marched in parallel for the next forty years, both in the end achieving the Keeperships of their parts of the old department when it was divided in 1955 into the new Departments of Egyptian and of Western Asiatic Antiquities. There was more than a small element of rivalry in the relationship between Edwards and Barnett, which in later years brought benefits to both of the new departments. It could be said that they enjoyed a close, but uneasy, relationship.

During his first years in the British Museum Edwards turned himself into an Egyptologist. He worked in an environment particularly conducive to the learning of a new discipline. The tradition of his department was rooted in publication, and its emphasis was linguistic. Stephen Glanville, his predecessor, who had himself entered the department as a classicist and neophyte Egyptologist in 1924, had set a particularly hard example to follow; he had shown just how much could be done from scratch in a few years, becoming a perceptive editor of hieratic texts, a demotist of exceptional ability, and a sensitive writer on ancient Egyptian works of art. Glanville's was a testing record, and he contributed more to Edwards's development as an Egyptologist than being a stimulus to achievement. Teaching Egyptian at University

College London, he could readily include Edwards in his classes, and indeed extend his tuition in an informal, but particularly agreeable manner after hours in the more relaxed environment of public house or restaurant. Edwards was an apt student; being already well accustomed to Semitic oriental languages, he was readily capable of tackling the special difficulties of the hieroglyphic script and the successive stages of the ancient Egyptian language. It was not, however, until after the Second World War that he seriously came to grips with the niceties of that language.

Within the department there was one other Egyptologist, Alan Shorter, whose fields of interest were Egyptian religion and funerary papyri. Shorter did not find it easy to work with Sidney Smith, his Keeper, and indirectly Edwards profited from this conflict of personalities. For matters Egyptological Smith came increasingly to rely on Edwards, providing him with opportunities to advance his Egyptological studies, to travel to see the great European collections, to take part in the excavations of the Egypt Exploration Society in the Sudan, at Amara and Sesebi (1937–8); he even organised classes in Coptic in his Keeper's residence in the British Museum. As ever, the Museum was a focus of interest for foreign Egyptologists, and Edwards had exceptional opportunities to meet many of the leading scholars from Europe and America. His position as the Egyptologist in the British Museum was confirmed after Shorter's tragically early death in 1938.

The principal scientific fruit of his pre-war years was epigraphic. *Hieroglyphic Texts from Egyptian Stelae, etc.*, Part VIII, was published in 1939. This series had lain in abeyance since Part VII, by H. R. H. Hall, had appeared in 1925. The early volumes (especially the first) had not been seen as reliable; the drawings of texts were of very variable accuracy. A radical change was made in the textual presentation in Edwards's volume. All the texts were reproduced in photographic plates, and also printed in hieroglyphic type in the body of the work. It was not an ideal method, especially as the best available hieroglyphic type (the Gardiner fount) was not used. Such presentation did not allow the editor to deal in a satisfactory way with the kinds of sign-variation and significant detail which good epigraphy demands. Yet, within the restrictions imposed by the method of publication, Edwards dealt more fully and more satisfactorily with the individual monuments (mostly of Eighteenth-Dynasty date) than any of his predecessors in the series.

Epigraphy, however, was not a discipline which Edwards could have practised with ease. From childhood he had suffered from poor eyesight, which had greatly restricted his participation in many activities, like team games. It did not, however, limit his scientific work until his last years. He was, for example, well able to read poorly preserved and badly written hieratic documents. Monumental texts, on the other hand, often require a degree of close inspection, especially in damaged areas, which he would have found difficult to provide, especially in the field.

The outbreak of war in September 1939 put an end to serious work on the collections of the British Museum, and Edwards was put in charge of the dismantling of the Egyptian Department, and the removal of many of the objects to relative safety in Boughton House in Northamptonshire, made available for the purpose by the Duke of Buccleuch. Edwards, as one of the few younger members of the Museum's staff still out of uniform, spent considerable periods of time on duty in the country. It was an unreal existence, in which it was difficult to pursue conventional scholarship. Some reading could be done, but few books were available, and there were irksome, but necessary, duties of care and inspection to be carried out.

The tedium of restricted country life, with little intellectual stimulation for the most part, was for Edwards relieved first of all by his provisional call-up for the army. It had been deferred since he was involved in work regarded as being of national importance. He left on mobilisation leave in London in February 1942, and shortly after received a summons from the Foreign Office, who offered him a wartime post at the British Embassy in Cairo. After due consideration he decided to accept the offer, and left for Egypt by sea from Gourock in the *Mary Slessor*. The remainder of the war he spent in the Near East, in Cairo, Baghdad, and Jerusalem, a period of particular importance for his career. He became well acquainted with those countries which were of importance as far as the collections of his Museum department were concerned. He had so far not passed much time in Egypt proper, and his period in Cairo—spent refreshing his Arabic and reading Arabic newspapers for intelligence purposes—gave him opportunities for travel within the country, and to become better informed about the sites and great monuments. In Egypt he was happily joined by his wife, Elizabeth (*née* Lisle) whom he had married in 1938.

Of the monuments that captured his attention in particular were the pyramids, and they provided him with a very suitable subject for study and research, especially as most of the major examples lay within easy driving distance of Cairo. Shortly before the War he had been approached by one of his British Museum colleagues on behalf of the publisher Allen Lane, with the suggestion that he might consider writing a King Penguin on the pyramids for them. At that time he was too busily occupied with learning as much as he could about the Egyptian language, and about ancient Egypt in general, to contemplate an extra commitment requiring specialisation in such a large subject. Now, some four years later, he wrote to Allen Lane to enquire whether anything had come of the suggestion. In consequence, he was then asked to produce a Pelican book on the pyramids himself. This time he accepted the offer. It was a momentous decision. Pyramids would form a dominant feature of Edwards's work for the rest of his career. For the general public interested in ancient Egypt, Edwards and the pyramids would be almost synonymous.

Writing to Alan Gardiner from Cairo in September 1943, Edwards reported his acceptance of the Penguin/Pelican offer, and continued:

> Since last summer I have read almost all the publications on pyramid excavations and I plan to finish the remainder very shortly [there were good Egyptological libraries in the French Institute and the Borchardt Institute]. I have also visited all the Pyramids, to which access was remotely possible, between Giza and Meidum, including the Bent Pyramid. It has been an arduous, and sometimes a little hazardous, job, particularly for one like myself who has a tendency to claustrophobia, but it was worth the effort.

Later in the same letter he describes the problems of gaining access to the chambers inside the Bent Pyramid at Dahshur:

> It was, in fact, only with considerable difficulty, and by lying completely prone, that I was able to push myself through the space available. Even then my difficulties were not over, because I still had to cross the pit at the entrance to the chamber. Eventually I succeeded by getting the ghafir [Antiquities Service guard] to stand in the pit while I put one foot on his shoulder and leapt across to the threshold of the room. These acrobatics in a place lacking in fresh air and full of bats, not to mention a difficult retreat in the event of need, was scarcely to my liking, but there was no alternative. In both pyramids at Dahshur, [the other being the northern 'Red' Pyramid] the most impressive feature was the magnificent corbel vaulting of all the chambers.
>
> I am probably boring you with too detailed an account of my experiences, but Pyramids have been my one recreation for over a year and writing about them is now one of my weaknesses.

The result of his wartime reading and physical inspection of the pyramids was published in 1947. *The Pyramids of Egypt*, was, like its fellow Pelicans, authoritative. It was also comprehensive. From the outset it was seen to be just what was needed—a work on the pyramids, which traced their history and architecture from the great brick *mastabas* of the early dynasties to the steeply-angled constructions of Napata and Meroe. The latter Edwards had seen during his pre-war visit to the Sudan. The book's content was made up essentially of descriptions of the individual monuments drawn from the best authorities, and confirmed by himself on the ground. The treatment was critical and systematic. He dealt also with the various theories of construction and interpretation of purpose. His judgements were sober, and only occasionally adventurous. Pyramidologists and their wild beliefs found little place in his book.

The success of *The Pyramids of Egypt* went far beyond what might have been expected. It was not an easy read, but it was a triumph of synthesis, and an almost unfailing source of detail for both specialist and general reader. It has remained in print up to the present, having been fully revised in 1961, 1985, and 1993, with many improved reprints in between. Taking advantage of the friendships he developed over the years with those field-workers who advanced pyramid studies by their excavations—in particular Professor W. B. Emery, Monsieur Jean-Philippe Lauer, Dr Dieter Arnold—he kept in touch with the latest archaeological developments. Throughout his subsequent career he pursued the pyramids, engaging in the many controversies which occurred from time to time, but ever keeping an open mind in a field prone to speculation and wild theorisation. Many of his occasional publications dealt with pyramid matters, and it was fitting that the volume presented to him in 1988 was entitled *Pyramid Studies and Other Essays*. Not surprisingly, in matters concerning the pyramids—a never-ending subject of enquiry and also of discovery—Edwards was always among the first to be consulted, and his sober, not to say unencouraging, responses often provided the necessary depressant for over-enthusiastic claims. The use of a small robot buggy in recent years to examine the unexplained shafts leading from the so-called Queen's Chamber in the Great Pyramid, provided him with an opportunity, on the one hand to encourage the technological success of the method of investigation, and, on the other hand, to question cautiously the somewhat extravagant claims of some of the investigating team.

Pyramids and the book did not wholly engross Edwards's spare time in Egypt. Egyptologically, Cairo was by no means dead. W. B. Emery, living in his house-boat on the Nile worked on his Early-Dynastic publications when his duties in Military Intelligence allowed; Jaroslav Černý, who in a very few years would become Edwards's closest professional colleague, worked in the Czech delegation; Bernard Grdseloff, a brilliant young scholar of very wide interests, looked after the Borchardt Institute; Herbert Fairman, most recent director of excavations for the Egypt Exploration Society, was also attached to the British Embassy; in the French Institute was Alexandre Piankoff, a specialist in royal funerary texts. These and others met from time to time at Groppi's and the Turf Club, exchanging ideas and abundant gossip. While he was in Cairo, Edwards was Egyptologically able to act with far greater freedom than would have been possible in the British Museum. For example, he found that in matters concerning the care and organisation of the ancient monuments in Egypt and associated affairs—of especial interest to the Oriental Secretary, Sir Walter Smart, and to Sir Robert Greg, recently retired as British Commissioner for the Egyptian Debt (later to be the President of the Egypt Exploration Society, 1949–53)—his opinion was sought and his judgement valued. It was so in the case of the possible establishment of a British School in Cairo. The idea was strongly backed by the British Embassy, and there was for a time the possibility that the Borchardt Institute, with its fine library and twin villas in Zamalek, might become the base. A long and detailed memorandum was prepared, and Edwards played a not insignificant part in promoting the idea through correspondence with colleagues in Britain.

In the end nothing came of the discussions, and the same was the case on several occasions subsequently when Edwards was again involved, particularly in 1950, when Sir Mortimer Wheeler, recently appointed Secretary of the British Academy, encouraged Edwards, as Treasurer of the Egypt Exploration Society, to enlarge the application for the annual grant to the Treasury to include a sum for the setting up of an institute in Cairo. Again a nucleus library was available, offered by the widow of Professor P. E. Newberry, who had died in 1949. The time was not ripe, and again nothing came of it. But Edwards had in his Cairo days, and in Baghdad and Jerusalem, learned much about negotiation, and the need always for the careful presentation of cases and the importance of diplomacy. In later life he practised his acquired skills with considerable success, although sometimes these skills could be misinterpreted.

Returning to the British Museum after the war, Edwards found himself the sole curatorial officer on the Egyptian side in his department. H. R. G. Bass, who had come to the Museum in 1939 after Shorter's death, had been seconded to the Admiralty in 1940, and he chose not to return after the war. For five years Edwards shouldered the increasing burden of Egyptian matters in a department, which, like the rest of the Museum, was struggling to rebuild itself, rehousing the collections and restoring scholarly contacts. The Egyptian galleries in the Museum had been damaged only superficially by bombing, and it was possible to reinstall the exhibition in the great Sculpture Gallery which had been reorganised with considerable improvements by Sidney Smith in the 1930s. It was a slow process, involving the moving of hundreds of stone monuments, some weighing many tons, with a small staff of masons, and inadequate resources. In the upper galleries changes could be made in the presentation of funerary materials and small objects, and a very creditable series of thematic displays was organised in a remarkably short time. Publicly, the Egyptian galleries were among the first fully to open in their entirety in the Museum. The preparation of the various exhibitions could only be undertaken after the hundreds of boxes had been returned from their last wartime billet, in subterranean quarries near Bath, unpacked, and their contents sorted into categories and stored. This last task, which had never previously been dealt with satisfactorily in the Egyptian collections, became a major preoccupation, and Edwards had little time beyond it and the exhibitions for serious scholarly work of a systematic kind.

An opportunity for escape from the daily round of museum business came in 1947, when he was awarded the Peet Memorial Travelling Scholarship by the University of Liverpool. It enabled Edwards to spend some months in Egypt, collecting material for the chapter he had undertaken to write on the Early Dynastic Period in Egypt for the recently planned new edition of the

Cambridge Ancient History. Coming so soon after the war, this welcome interlude allowed him to refresh old contacts, professional and diplomatic, in Egypt, to visit more ancient sites than was possible under war conditions, and to meet European and American colleagues, newly returned to their pre-war concessions in the country. His chapter was completed not long after his return to London, but various set-backs delayed the appearance of the revised *Cambridge Ancient History*, by which time he had himself succeeded Stephen Glanville as the Egyptological editor.

Edwards's efforts on behalf of the *Cambridge Ancient History* are now little known, although at the time any contributor, and not only those writing about Egypt, was soon made aware of the very high standards set by the editors, of whom Edwards as editor-in-chief was a determined upholder of verbal precision and conventional stylistic purity. The history itself could in a sense look after itself; that is, the individual contributors could, except in a few cases, be trusted to produce texts which would be up-to-date, comprehensive, and not too innovative. When Edwards joined C. J. Gadd and N. G. L. Hammond on the editorial team in 1958, the position of the new edition was somewhat chaotic. Some of the chosen contributors to the first two volumes had completed their chapters, but wanted to bring them up-to-date; most chapters were still to be submitted; some contributors had died, others were still to be chosen; some were yet undecided, many were just slow in producing. From 1961 chapters for the first two volumes began to be printed and issued as individual fascicles, and the completed volumes were published, each in two parts, between 1970 and 1975. For Parts 1 and 2 of Volume III, published in 1982 and 1991, Edwards continued to play a major editorial role. Throughout his long association with the *Cambridge Ancient History* Edwards sustained a remarkably tenacious engagement in his editorial duties. For the first two volumes he was editor-in-chief, and he must be given the greatest credit for the form of the volumes, and for maintaining, even if slowly at times, the momentum towards publication. Most editorial work is subject to criticism, and that for the *Cambridge Ancient History* was particularly so. Like all multi-authored works, the volumes, as they appeared, were criticised, often condescendingly, but often with some justice, especially over technical aspects, some of which concerned editorial decisions, such as the Bibliographies and form of footnotes. Many editors with less determination and sheer stamina than Edwards would have withdrawn long before the end. But here he displayed a pertinacity which characterised his commitment to many projects in his career, sometimes pursued, as some thought, beyond the point of advantage. Edwards was not, and would not have claimed to be, an historian in the strictest sense, but his careful approach to all scholarly matters ensured that his two chapters for the *Cambridge Ancient History*, 'The Early Dynastic Period in

Egypt' (Vol. I, 2) and 'Egypt from the Twenty-second to the Twenty-fourth Dynasty' (Vol. III, 1), presented the surviving evidence fairly and clearly.

Scholarship and its pursuit were serious matters for Edwards. As things were in the British Museum it was not easy in the post-war period to pursue a line of research with regularity, no matter how great one's commitment might be. With little professional support, he was for many years obliged to spend most of his time on the periphery of scholarship. There were, and would be, chances of escape to universities, but the Museum was, in a sense, in his blood, and he felt an abiding loyalty to that, often ungenerous, institution. In 1948 he had been encouraged to put his name forward for the Brunner Chair in Egyptology in the University of Liverpool, following the retirement of A. M. Blackman. Edwards explained his reluctance to do so in a letter to Alan Gardiner:

> I feel I am under an obligation to stay in the B.M., at least for some time. They have generously given me leave to spend the winter in Egypt, when it was most inconvenient for them to spare me, and it would be a shabby return on my part if I were to leave their service just now. I have therefore replied to the Vice-Chancellor briefly to that effect. It was a rather difficult decision to make because the chance of enjoying considerably greater leisure for study and research was not one to be lightly discarded, and, in addition, there was the undeniable attraction of a far more lucrative post, as you yourself pointed out. However, I feel sure that I have made the correct decision and the only possible one in the circumstances.

It is possible that, in addition to his genuine feeling for the Museum, he did not relish the idea of a move to Liverpool. The British Museum was in London and at the centre of things Egyptological. And there might be other opportunities in the future. One such came in 1951, when Jaroslav Černý resigned the Edwards Professorship at University College London to succeed Battiscombe Gunn at Oxford. Again Edwards was a strong candidate to succeed Černý. On this occasion, and with the knowledge that there were moves afoot to divide the Department of Egyptian and Assyrian Antiquities into two, he again agreed not to put himself forward as a candidate on the understanding that he should be promoted to the position of Deputy Keeper in the interim. In 1948 Sidney Smith had left the Museum to become Professor of Ancient Semitic Languages and Civilization in the School of Oriental and African Studies. His successor. C. J. Gadd, was due to retire in 1955, and that event would provide the occasion for the departmental division. So it happened. In 1955 Edwards became the first Keeper of Egyptian Antiquities, and Richard Barnett the first Keeper of Western Asiatic Antiquities.

In the winter of 1953–4 Edwards was invited to spend a semester in Brown University, Providence, Rhode Island, to teach in the recently established Egyptian Department of that university. It gave him his first serious experience of university teaching, and it was very much to his liking. He had, not long before his transatlantic visit, showed signs of nervous tension, and the complete change from the British Museum, and the different scene of New England proved to be very therapeutic for him. He also had the chance for the first time to get to know the great collections of Egyptian antiquities in American museums. It was an exceptionally happy experience, and he wrote: 'Perhaps the highest praise I can give the Americans is by saying that I have never been happier since my undergraduate days at Cambridge.' To the end of his life, his Cambridge years were remembered with particular pleasure, and it would have given him great satisfaction if he had been able to end his academic career in his own university. The Herbert Thompson Professorship, which had been founded in 1946, was held by Stephen Glanville, Edwards's first instructor in the ancient Egyptian language, and by now his closest Egyptological friend. Glanville had in 1954 become Provost of King's College, and he had intimated to Edwards his hope that when he resigned his professorship in a few years, Edwards would succeed him. Tragically, Glanville died unexpectedly in 1956, and in the ensuing search for a successor for the Herbert Thompson Chair, Edwards was not seriously approached. It was, probably rightly, thought that an approach would have placed Edwards in a very difficult position. Only a year had passed since the establishment of the independent Department of Egyptian Antiquities in the British Museum, and his own appointment as the first Keeper. If he, after such a short time in office, had left for Cambridge, the very future of the Department might have been in jeopardy.

Quite differently, and in the end much more satisfactorily, Edwards's becoming the first Keeper of Egyptian Antiquities gave him the senior status which was a matter of concern to him. It also allowed him to begin the process of establishing in the British Museum a centre of Egyptological studies. It was a slow process; but traditions of service to scholars and to the general public, characteristic of the Museum in general, were expanded beyond what had previously been possible. His acquaintance with a great many foreign Egyptologists, and his willingness to allow them easy access to unpublished materials, resulted in the steady increase in the scholarly exploitation of the Egyptian collections, and their consequent publication.

Edwards's capability to pursue his own scholarly interests was, as formerly, constricted by the demands of office. Nevertheless, with the encouragement of Černý, he embarked on the study of a group of unusual texts, written on long, narrow strips of papyrus in the Twenty-first and Twenty-second Dynasties (*c.*1069–715 BC). They were oracular amuletic decrees, as Edwards termed them, personally written for named individuals—women as well as men—to be carried in small tubular containers as amulets against a variety of dangers and hazards in life. They were issued by the priests in charge of various oracles, and they throw great light on the extent to which the ancient

Egyptians considered their lives to be governed, even interfered with, by a huge number of spirits and influences, mostly hostile.

Six of these texts were identified in the papyrus collection of the Egyptian Department, mostly by Jaroslav Černý in the late 1940s, while he was still at University College London. In 1949 a seventh example was acquired by the Museum, arousing Edwards's special attention, and proving to be the spur which stimulated his studying the whole group with the intention of publishing in due course a fourth series of *Hieratic Papyri in the British Museum.* To begin with it was to be a joint publication, and for years Edwards and Černý worked through these very difficult texts, written in crabbed, cursive, hieratic hands. As time passed, however, other examples turned up in various collections—in Turin, Paris, Cairo, New York, Chicago, Philadelphia, and one known only from photographs in Berlin. Some were identified by Černý, others by Edwards; they were alerted about others by helpful museum curators. Even after his move to Oxford in 1951, Černý would visit the British Museum almost weekly, and spend much time going through what had now become Edwards's personal work in progress. *Oracular amuletic decrees of the Late New Kingdom* appeared in 1960. Twenty-one texts were published, their transcriptions alone representing a work of major achievement. In the tradition of the series, commentaries were not extensive, but in all respects reflecting the great attention to detail and sober judgement which were characteristic of Edwards's scholarship. It was a publication of first-class importance, leading in 1962 to his election as Fellow of the British Academy.

He was a very regular attender at Section meetings of the Academy, being a lively contributor to discussions. On two occasions of some significance in the development of Academy activities, he served on the organising committees. In 1969 the British Academy and the Royal Society held their first joint symposium. The subject was 'The Impact of the Natural Sciences on Archaeology', and it was held to celebrate the twentieth anniversary of the discovery of radiocarbon dating. Edwards and Sir Mortimer Wheeler represented the Academy on the organising committee. He had first learned about the technique when he was in America, and had been introduced to Willard Libby, its discoverer. There was something a little bizarre in his being involved in such a scientific matter. His own competence in science was practically negligible. A former school friend, Sir Irvine Goulding, recalls that he had been asked by Edwards's father 'to give him some coaching in Maths for School Certificate. I can't remember why I was selected for the purpose, but the result was that Eiddon asked me for occasional calculations (mostly very elementary) to the end of his days.' In spite of his lack of confidence with numbers, Edwards recognised the significance of the carbon-14 process for dating in antiquity, and he had played a central role in setting up a Carbon-14 Committee, based on the Research Laboratory of the British Museum, which for many years screened the applications sent in by archaeologists for the testing of their samples. At the symposium Edwards himself contributed a paper, 'Absolute dating from Egyptian records, and comparison with carbon-14 dating'.

He again formed part of the Academy representation on the organising committee for a second joint symposium with the Royal Society. On that occasion the subject was 'The Place of Astronomy in the Ancient World', the subsequent volume of contributions being published under the same title in 1974.

During the 1960s at the British Museum, the infant Egyptian Department developed steadily towards a robust and active maturity. New permanent exhibitions were prepared in the upper galleries, and a fruitful programme of publications was developed. In particular, Edwards initiated a new series of catalogues of objects in the Egyptian collection. Until that time, scholarly publication had concentrated on written material, papyri, ostraca, and inscribed stone objects. By the time of his retirement in 1974, four volumes of other categories of antiquities had been published, and other volumes were in the process of preparation.

In 1962 the Arts Council of Great Britain, with the Royal Academy, sponsored an exhibition in Burlington House of Egyptian works of art drawn chiefly from museums in Cairo and Alexandria. The core items in '5000 Years of Egyptian Art' represented the first loan exhibition from Egypt to be shown in Great Britain. Edwards was the principal Egyptological organiser, and through his involvement he became acquainted with the Minister of Culture and National Guidance of the United Arab Republic (as Egypt was then termed), Dr Sarwat Okasha. In due course, the friendship which developed between Edwards and Okasha provided a solid basis of understanding during the long-drawn-out negotiations which led to the successful launching of the great Tutankhamun loan exhibition at the British Museum in 1972.

'The Treasures of Tutankhamun' marked the high point of Edwards's career in the British Museum. No exhibition, before or since in the Museum made such a mark on the British public, attracting throughout its nine months (from April to December) unprecedented crowds of visitors. Edwards spared no effort to ensure both the success of the exhibition as a public event, and also the maximising of receipts for the UNESCO fund for the preservation of the temples of Philae, a cause very close to his heart. In every aspect of the organising of the show, he took a central part: in the choice of objects, in securing their careful conservation where needed, in negotiating with Egyptian officials, in writing the catalogue, in the supervision of souvenirs for the shop, in the daily reception of special visitors to view the exhibition in advance of the public opening, in the multifarious activities that attended the show. It became an obsession with him throughout the year, and the resources of his department were strained to their limits.

It was undoubtedly his exhibition in almost every respect, although others connected with the Museum, including certain Trustees, were eager to claim credit for securing this loan to mark the fiftieth anniversary of the discovery of Tutankhamun's tomb. But the success was complete, spectacularly and financially. Yet Edwards was left with a sense that his efforts had not received the recognition they deserved, especially from the British Museum. He was, however, awarded the CMG in 1973 on the recommendation of the Cairo Embassy for his part in securing the notable improvement in relations between Great Britain and Egypt. He had previously, in 1968, been appointed CBE for his services to the Museum.

One consequence of his involvement with the London success was the invitation to help with the subsequent Tutankhamun exhibition, organised by Thomas Hoving, then Director of the Metropolitan Museum of Art, New York. Edwards had no part in choosing the objects, or the physical organising of the show in its progress to six places in the USA in 1976–7; but he wrote the catalogue entries for the exhibition and the texts for two lavishly produced volumes, *Tutankhamun: His Tomb and its Treasures*, and *Tutankhamun's Jewelry*. He was also much consulted by Hoving over a wide range of matters, from negotiations with the Egyptian authorities to the marketing of products associated with the exhibition. Throughout America 'The Treasures of Tutankhamun' was a great success, but Edwards was disappointed that the strong commercial emphasis, promoted by Hoving, failed to produce a financial return at all comparable with that of his exhibition in London. Monies from the six American showings were to be used for the rehabilitation of the Cairo Museum, in which it was planned that the Metropolitan Museum would play a major role. This task remains to be done.

After his retirement from the British Museum in 1974, Edwards devoted much time to participation in a series of joint committees of UNESCO and the Egyptian Ministry of Culture: for the saving of the monuments of Philae, 1973–80; for the reorganising of the Cairo Museum, 1985; for the planning of the proposed new National Museum in Cairo, 1985; for the protection of the monuments of Giza, 1990. Through his successful efforts on behalf of the Philae appeal during the London year of Tutankhamun, he had developed very good relations with the Under-Secretaries in charge of the Antiquities Service, Dr Mohammed Gamal ed-Din Mokhtar, and then Dr Ahmed Kadry. Edwards was seen to be a true friend of Egypt, and, perhaps more importantly, a safe pair of hands, who could be trusted to carry through difficult negotiations, and tiresome bureaucratic processes, with determination. Some of the joint committees deliberated, reached conclusions, but saw no subsequent action on their recommendations. The outstanding exception was the Philae committee for which Edwards acted as unofficial secretary, pushing matters forward and instituting imaginative initiatives.

The most interesting and important of these initiatives involved the recovery of the Gate of Diocletian, which lay forgotten in the Nile mud outside the coffer dam built around the principal monuments on Philae Island, to allow the pumping out of the water submerging the temples, and the subsequent dismantling of the buildings. At a reception at the British Embassy in Cairo in 1975, Edwards had met a group of Royal Naval Minehunters which had been engaged in helping to clear the Suez Canal and its approaches. In 1976, when Edwards realised that no provision had been made for the recovery of the Diocletian Gate, he remembered the Royal Naval divers. J. E. Thompson, Lieutenant-Commander RN (retired) has confirmed the sequence of events:

> Not only did Dr Edwards draw attention to the monument, but he also suggested that perhaps, bearing in mind the recent clearance of the Suez Canal, it may be that a request to the British Government for assistance in the underwater recovery might be greeted favourably and, that the Royal Navy, whose members had recently worked in conjunction with the Egyptian Navy in the successful clearance of the Suez Canal, could assist in the project.

From October 1976 until April 1977, British and Egyptian divers successfully raised the blocks of the gate, and visitors to Philae may now see, if they penetrate to the northern end of Agilkia Island—where the Philae temples have been re-erected—the rebuilt Diocletian Gate and associated quay. They form an unmarked memorial to Edwards's care and ingenuity.

On retirement Edwards was determined to return to a more active programme of scholarly research. In particular, he had plans for a comprehensive revision of the important series of Tomb Robberies texts of the Twentieth and Twenty-first Dynasties in the British Museum, some of which had been conserved and remounted during his Keepership. Unfortunately, the demands made on his time, by his involvement with UNESCO committees, the American exhibition, and other commitments, diverted him from the regular study of these papyrus documents, and finally, with the rapid deterioration in his eyesight, he was obliged to abandon his plans. It was, there can be no doubt, a sad decision to make, for he was deeply committed to scholarship, and was well aware that he had not fulfilled all that he had hoped to achieve. He was fortunate, however, in retaining throughout his last years his mental capacities, and, while his excellent memory became a little less reliable, he was still able to present papers, to make valuable contributions to academic discussions, and generally to be welcomed at international gatherings. His advice was widely sought—he was for many years a valued member of the Committee of Visitors for the Department of Egyptian Art in the Metropolitan Museum of Art—his judgement was valued, and his encouragement and support were enlisted in a wide range of matters. Over the years he was appointed a Member of the German Archaeological Institute and the Austrian Archaeological Institute; he was a Corresponding Member of the Fondation Égyptologique Reine Élisabeth (Brussels) and the Académie des Inscriptions et Belles-Lettres (Paris).

From 1962 until 1988 he was a Vice-President of the Egypt Exploration Society. An unfortunate dispute over constitutional and procedural changes in the Society led, sadly, to his resignation from the Vice-Presidentship. He had served the Society well in many capacities since he had first become a member of the Committee in 1936. As Treasurer (1949–61) he had brought to a satisfactory conclusion the negotiations to secure a government grant for the work of the Society initiated by his predecessor, Hugh Last, in 1946. At the outset the application for funds was made directly to the Treasury, and Edwards did not welcome the development arranged by Sir Mortimer Wheeler, by which the grant was channelled through the British Academy, and, shortly afterwards, administered wholly by the Academy. In the Society he also introduced new financial procedures which established the publications programme of the Society on a firm and prosperous basis.

Edwards always placed great emphasis on sound judgement, and in his own dealings, both scholarly and administrative, he took time to reach decisions, and then adhered tenaciously to what he had decided. Tenacity could lead to stubbornness, and an unwillingness to be swayed by others whose judgements he might not respect. There were times when a little flexibility might have led to a quicker solution to a problem. Principles were important to him, and he was rarely inclined willingly to compromise them. In general, however, he was kind and sympathetic, more understanding of human weakness than might have been expected of one who laid so much store on convention and proper practice. He was a social person, although not indiscriminately so, enjoying company, and very generous in hospitality. For many years Morden Lodge, the dower house of Morden Hall in South London, was the Edwards family home. Its large garden provided Edwards himself with a challenge and an escape from museum administration. Here, he and his wife Elizabeth welcomed and entertained many visiting scholars, especially during the eventful year of Tutankhamun.

There were two children of the marriage, and it was an exceptionally bitter blow when Philip, a young man of great charm, ability, and promise, died prematurely of leukaemia in 1968 during his second year at New College. It was a tragedy borne with remarkable fortitude by Elizabeth and Eiddon Edwards and their daughter Lucy. He rarely spoke of Philip in later years; his reticence in personal matters was characteristic. He did not readily understand how different the young people of the 1960s were from those of the 1920s; but he could appreciate that in the culture of post-war Britain, Philip was an outstanding example of all that was best. He also became more understanding as time passed, and enjoyed a very happy relationship with Lucy's daughters.

Although failing sight restricted his last years, Edwards never indulged in self-pity, or ceased to pursue activities in which he was interested. He continued to travel regularly from Deddington in north Oxfordshire, where the family had moved in 1980, to London. He also settled down and composed his autobiography, which is yet to be published. He died unexpectedly, but mercifully quickly, in London on 24 September 1996. He was 87. A memorial service, at which an address was given by Professor H. S. Smith, FBA, was held in St George's Church, Bloomsbury, on 1 November 1996.

T. G. H. JAMES
Fellow of the Academy

Note. I am especially indebted to Elizabeth Edwards for reading the draft of this memoir, checking details of her husband's life and career against his autobiography, and making many felicitous suggestions for the improvement of my text. I am further grateful to the Rt. Revd. and Rt. Hon. the Lord Coggan, PC, and Sir Irvine Goulding, contemporaries of Eiddon Edwards at Merchant Taylors' School, for providing information on his early years. J. E. Thompson, Lieutenant-Commander RN (retired) made contact at just the right moment to tell the story of the retrieval of the Diocletian Gate on Philae Island. He has kindly allowed me to include part of it in the memoir.

The autobiography completed by Edwards shortly before his death has not been used directly for this memoir. Its publication should take place in the near future.

Pyramid Studies and Other Essays, published in Edwards's honour by the Egypt Exploration Society in 1988, contains a bibliography (by Anthony Leahy) of his publications up to 1986.

EDMUND LEACH

Edmund Ronald Leach
1910–1989

1. Achievements

EDMUND LEACH was born in Lancashire, England, on 7 November 1910. He went to school at Marlborough College and later entered Clare College, Cambridge, as an Exhibitioner and read Mathematics and Mechanical Sciences, obtaining a First in the BA degree in 1932.

After some years of civilian life in China he returned to England and studied Social Anthropology under Bronislaw Malinowski and Raymond Firth at the London School of Economics. He was an active member of Malinowski's famous seminar. An abortive field trip to Kurdistan in 1938, frustrated by the Munich crisis,[1] was followed by a prolonged trip to Burma in 1939 in the course of which the Second World War broke out. From autumn 1939 to the summer of 1945 he served as an officer in the Burma Army. He saw much of Northern Burma, and he gained an unrivalled knowledge of its hill tribes, particularly the Kachin, on whom he was an undisputed authority.

He took his Ph.D. from the London School of Economics in 1947 where he also obtained his first teaching appointment. He carried out a survey in Sarawak and his report entitled *Social Science Research in Sarawak* (1950) set out the guidelines for subsequent investigations by a number of distinguished anthropologists (particularly Derek Freeman, William Geddes, Stephen Morris).

Edmund Leach relinquished a Readership at the LSE in 1953 in order to

---

[1] On the basis of this aborted field trip, Leach wrote *Social and Economic Organization of Rowanduz Kurds*, London School of Economics Monographs on Social Anthropology, no. 3, London, 1940.

Proceedings of the British Academy, **97**, 293–344. © The British Academy 1998.

return to Cambridge as Lecturer (1953–8). In 1954 he published *Political Systems of Highland Burma* which embodied some of the results of his work in Burma. A field trip to Ceylon in 1953, supplemented by another made in 1956, provided the information for a second work of distinction: *Pul Eliya, A Village in Ceylon* (1961). In due course he was promoted to Reader, and in 1972 the University honoured him by appointing him to a personal chair. His research and writing vigorously continued throughout his career, despite mounting administrative and other responsibilities.

His escalating academic recognition was sign-posted by his twice winning the Curl Essay Prize (1951, 1957). He also won the Rivers Memorial Medal (1958). He delivered the Malinowski Memorial Lecture (1959), the Henry Myers Lecture (1966), the Mason Memorial Lecture (1970), the Cantor Lectures at the Royal Society of Arts (1973), the Munro Lectures at the University of Edinburgh (1977), and the Huxley Memorial Lecture (1980). He spent a year in the United States in 1961 as a Fellow of the Center for Advanced Study in the Behavioral Sciences, Stanford, and a term at the Johns Hopkins University in 1976 as John Hinkley Visiting Professor.

In the United States, Edmund Leach delivered the Lewis Henry Morgan Lectures at the University of Rochester in 1975, the Hinkley Lectures at Johns Hopkins University in 1976, the Harvey Lecture Series, University of New Mexico (1983), and the Patten Foundation Lectures (1984–5) at Indiana University. I have most probably missed some other instances, but one might say that Leach accomplished a grand slam of distinguished lectures on both sides of the Atlantic Ocean.

He is the first and only anthropologist so far invited by the BBC to deliver the Reith Lectures (1967), *A Runaway World?*, which notably brought him to the attention of the general public.

Leach's wide-ranging substantial contributions to knowledge are attested by his impressive bibliography.[2] It is no exaggeration to say that in sheer versatility, originality, and range of writing he was and still is difficult to match among the anthropologists of the English-speaking world. His contributions have touched on kinship and social organisation; hill tribes and valley peoples; land tenure and peasant economy; caste and class; myth and ritual; binary thought, classification, and liminality; information theory, semiotics, and symbolic communication; art and aesthetics; ethology and archaeology; computer technology and model building; British structural-functional method and the structuralism of Lévi-Strauss; and Biblical materials and the myths of Classical Greece.

Altogether Leach was the author of some eight books, co-author of one,

---

[2] See *Edmund Leach. A Bibliography*. Royal Anthropological Institute of Great Britain and Ireland. Occasional Paper no. 42, 1990.

and editor of several essay collections. A hallmark of all his writings was a forceful, vigorous, direct, and clear prose, effective in exposition as in debate. He was a tireless reviewer of books in anthropology and a variety of cognate disciplines, and a prolific essayist not only in professional journals but also in publications for the general reading public such as *The Listener*, *New Society*, *New Scientist*, *The Spectator*, *Encounter*, *The Times Literary Supplement*, *New York Review of Books*, *London Review of Books*, and *New Republic*. He in fact wrote for and spoke to a much wider public and audience than the vast majority of social anthropologists, and positively sought to have a dialogue with specialists in other disciplines. All this added to his fame in mature years both as a notable spokesman for the discipline and as a commentator on general contemporary issues.

Apart from a distinguished academic career as a social anthropologist, Edmund Leach rendered noteworthy services to education, knowledge, and professional societies in general. In 1966, he succeeded Lord Annan as Provost of King's College, a college which counts in this century among its galaxy Lord Maynard Keynes, E. M. Forster, Lowes-Dickinson, Rupert Brooke, Arthur Waley, Pigou and Lord Kaldor. As Provost of King's until 1979, he also served as Fellow of Eton College. In addition to being Head of a famous College, he served at the highest levels in the administration of the University itself. His fellow anthropologists honoured him by electing him Chairman of the Association of Social Anthropologists (1966–70) and President of the Royal Anthropological Institute (1971–5). His gaining a wider academic recognition was signified by his election as President of the British Humanist Association (1970) and as a Fellow of the British Academy (1972). He was a member of the Social Sciences Research Council for a number of years beginning in 1968. He was elected Honorary Fellow of the London School of Economics (1974), Honorary Fellow of the School of Oriental and African Studies (1974), Honorary Fellow of Clare College (1986), and Foreign Honorary Member of the American Academy of Arts and Sciences (1968).

A high point of Leach's career was reached when he was knighted in 1975, and also elected a Trustee of the British Museum (1975–80). In 1976 the University of Chicago conferred on him the honorary degree of Doctor of Humane Letters, and Brandeis University honoured him in the same way.

This enumeration of achievements might unproblematically convey the idea that Leach by virtue of his own capacities, his social background, comfortable circumstances, public schooling and Cambridge education, and his considerable writings quite naturally ascended the ladder of achievement to become a much honoured member of the British Establishment.

The canonised Leach himself would not have settled for a hagiographic narrative, nor did he want himself to be considered as aspiring and conforming to the career of an honours list grandee. We have before us a complex person, subject to tensions and frustrations, blessed with a creative experimental and reflexive mind that was more concerned with restlessly probing rather than with consolidating knowledge. While he tested the presuppositions and limits of orthodoxy, he was deeply protective and conservationist about the institutions he valued.

2. Childhood and Youth

Leach's family home was located in Rochdale, Lancashire, and it was established by his grandfather Robert Leach, 'wealthy flannel manufacturer, a product of the English industrial revolution'.[3] Leach had a lively sense of his family background as a descendant of closely intermarried Rochdale mill owners. All four of his great grandfathers were mill owners who lived within four miles of one another, and they were all related by marriage. The changing fortunes of his extended family led to the dispersal of his own father and his nine brothers in search of their own fortunes in the far flung empire; six of them, including his father, regrouped to make their fortune in sugar in Argentina. Born last, Edmund was, unlike his older bilingual Anglo-Argentine brothers and sister and many cousins, solely brought up in Rochdale, the favoured child of his mother, Mildred.

From public school to coming of age in Cambridge

Mothered with singular affection and tolerance and encouragement, the youngest Leach would in any case have found Marlborough a trial, but life was made more difficult by the fact that being the twenty-first in a line of Leaches sent to that school, all of whom had automatically played in the cricket eleven, he was the odd man out. 'Much later, when I had made my way into the Upper Sixth, I was ruthlessly coached so that I could bring honour to the school by winning a mathematics scholarship to Clare College, Cambridge.'[4] He was quite unhappy at Marlborough.

But Cambridge proved to be 'a glorious experience'. He had won a Mathematics exhibition to Clare College where he went in 1929, and perhaps he was disappointed to find that he wasn't a real mathematician and changed to the Mechanical Sciences Tripos. While in the usual Oxbridge style claiming to

---

[3] Adam Kuper, 'An Interview with Edmund Leach', *Current Anthropology*, 4 (August–October 1986), 375.
[4] Ibid.

have 'spent a blissful two years of practical idleness', he must have studied conscientiously, knew he could get a First, and 'damned well got it'. But one can sense that the blissful Cambridge years were also a time of searching and questioning about art, music, sex, literature, films and theatre, politics, and morals. The privileged undergraduates of Cambridge largely selected from a limited range of private schools and sharing social class conventions were in the early thirties not blithely unconcerned with questions regarding sexual norms, gender relations, and morals in general. They felt stirrings of class injustices and conflict, and the forebodings caused by the Nazi movement in Germany.

One of the main issues which no doubt had great personal relevance for young people who in one way or another had been exposed to Victorian conventions and religious orthodoxy was where they stood in relation to organised religion. Of his own religious legacy Leach not entirely jokingly remarked: 'In practice I was brought up a hard-boiled Christian, and mud sticks if you throw enough.'[5] Though he had a distaste for organised religion (and doctrines such as papal infallibility) he at the same time wrestled with the question that civilised society necessarily depends on morals and ethics, which had their basis in human judgements of value, and in the case of religion, rested on faith.

The gathering of stormclouds

Leach's Cambridge years, 1929–32, were also the time of emerging rifts in the British class system. The General Strike of 1926 had already signalled a steep class divide. The Great Depression had epidemic global repercussions—very high unemployment, long lines of workers, their families living on the dole and queuing for everyday necessities. And menacing in this context was the rise of Hitler's party of National Socialism in Germany, its mobilisation of a youth movement, the spread of Nazi sentiments, the build up of armaments and the threat of aggrandising war. Leach had himself visited Germany in the summer of 1931 and had forebodings about the future.

In retrospect in 1986 Leach described the impact of these developments on Cambridge undergraduates and their mood as follows: 'the more intellectual among us were almost all of a radical, near communist, political persuasion. We were already coming to hate the social rigidities of the system in which we had been reared, the injustices of which were visible on every side. By comparison with the present generation of Cambridge undergraduates, we were very politicized. We had no use for compromise.'[6] It was in this environment that Leach's own socialist sympathies were crystallised.

[5] Rosemary Firth, 'A Cambridge Undergraduate: Some Early Letters from Edmund Leach', *Cambridge Anthropology. Special Issue: Sir Edmund Leach*, 13: 3 (1989–90), 10.
[6] In Edmund Leach, 'Glimpse of the Unmentionable in the History of British Social Anthropology', *Annual Review of Anthropology*, 13 (1984): 1–23; 9.

The Chinese interlude

The next phase was his trip to China and this adventure is well told by Stephen Hugh Jones. On graduation he went to China on a four year contract with the trading firm of John Swire and Sons (Butterfield and Swire), a move he put down to a combination of the family characteristic of wanderlust, his own love of travel, and his need for a job. He served in Hong Kong, Shanghai, Chungking, Tsingtao, and Peking and there acquired skills in business, financial dealings, and administration, activities he thoroughly enjoyed and which he used to such good effect in later years.

Leach was delighted by China; off duty from business, he spent his time exploring with fascination its cultural system, learning something of the language and collecting jade sculpture and ancient pottery. On holidays he travelled widely, travel which included climbing four of the five sacred mountains of the country.[7]

At the end of his assignment he had planned to travel home to England via Russia by way of the Trans-Siberian railway, but his plans were thwarted by political turmoil in Russia. By chance encounter in Peking he met Kilton Stewart, a psychiatrist and former Mormon missionary with an interest in anthropology who invited him to join an expedition to the island of Botel Tobago off the coast of Formosa to visit the Yami. The Yami, who at first sight, appeared to be 'real primitives' made an indelible impression upon him. Using his engineering training, Leach made meticulous drawings of their boats and technology and these were the subjects of his first anthropological publications.

3. Apprenticeship and the Second World War

Malinowski's seminar

Although he had read some of Malinowski's early writings as an undergraduate, Leach did not meet Malinowski until after his return from China in 1936. By that time Malinowski, famously established at the London School of Economics, had acquired a great reputation not only as the most exciting author of anthropological works but also as a great teacher.

Leach was introduced to Malinowski by Raymond Firth and he joined Malinowski's seminar at the London School of Economics in 1937. Malinowski obviously made an enormous impression on him, and in retrospect Leach eulogised him as one of his two 'supernatural beings' or 'deities', the

[7] Stephen Hugh-Jones, *Edmund Leach, 1910–1989.* (Privately printed for King's College, Cambridge 1989), pp. 10–11.

other being his mother's uncle, Sir Henry Howarth. In his own words, Leach was 'converted' to anthropology in 1937.[8] The extraordinary career of Malinowski has been recorded: notably his origins in Poland, his change of discipline from physics and mathematics to anthropology, his passage to England and training at the LSE, his fieldtrips to Melanesia, and his election to the first chair in Anthropology at LSE in 1927. Although an outsider, Malinowski had within a few years risen to preeminence in London, interacting with British anthropologists such as the Seligmans, Frazer, Haddon, Rivers, Marett, and Westermarck, and perhaps even more impressively, as time went on developed a large personal acquaintance with scholars in various other fields.[9] Aside from his influential connection with the International African Institute, Malinowski also participated in the work of the British Social Hygiene Council, and Mass Observation.

In addition to being an articulate propagandist for his own 'Functional School of Anthropology', Malinowski was an impresario adept at popularising and demonstrating the relevance of anthropology to other professional groups and to the public at large. These feats certainly must have impressed the members of his seminar in the late thirties, and set for at least some of them a pattern to follow. Edmund Leach, by his own activities later, suggests such an emulative response.

In his colourful way Leach has conveyed the euphoria and sense of special occasion he associated with the seminar group, focused on the charismatic Malinowski and enhanced by a coterie of about a dozen or so anthropologists most of whom were drawn from the British Commonwealth, the British Empire, and South Africa. They were a 'pretty exotic group' who were certainly not upholders of the colonial regime. And then there were some others as well from Europe and China.[10]

[8] See Leach, *Social Anthropology* (Fontana Paperbacks, 1982), pp. 7–8.

[9] 'In Britain alone he co-operated with or was influenced by a range of men including Richard Gregory, Havelock Ellis, A. H. Gardiner, Julian Huxley, C. K. Ogden, Cyril Burt, C. S. Myers, J. C. Flugel, W. Powys Mathers, G. H. L.-F, P. H. Rivers, J. H. Oldham—all of whom were interested from different angles in the wider implication of his science.' Raymond Firth, 'Introduction: Malinowski as Scientist and as Man', pp. 1–14, in Raymond Firth (ed.), *Man and Culture. An Evaluation of the World of Bronislaw Malinowski* (London, Routledge & Kegan Paul, 1957).

[10] S. J. Tambiah, 'Personal Accounts: Edmund Leach Situates Himself', *Cambridge Anthropology. Special Issue: Sir Edmund Leach*, 13: 3 (1989–90), 37. Leach explained that Malinowski's *Coral Gardens* had been published in 1935, Firth's *Tikopia* in 1936, and Bateson's *Naven* in 1937. Leach mentioned the following as being at various times members of Malinowski's seminar: Raymond Firth, Evans-Pritchard, Fei Tsiao Tung, Francis Hsu, Kenyatta, S. F. Nadel, Audrey Richards, Lucy Mair, Phyllis Kaberry, Ian Hogbin, William Stanner, I. Schapera. In this non-exhaustive listing one notes the absence of Radcliffe-Brown, whose career has a different trajectory, and who had recently arrived from Chicago to take up his Oxford chair. London and Oxford would develop into the two rival foci; but Malinowski did interact with Radcliffe-Brown. It would seem that Leach's own contemporaries included Phyllis Kaberry, Ian Hogbin, William Stanner, Nadel, Kenyatta, Fei Tsiao Tung, and Francis Hsu.

In the summer of 1938 Leach visited Iraq, planning to write a thesis on the Rowanduz Kurds. 'It came to nothing. After the Munich crisis and Chamberlain's gesticulations about "peace in our time" I was back in London with an aborted project. I spent the next academic year, 1938–39, working as Raymond Firth's research assistant, an extremely valuable experience from my point of view. Malinowski was on sabbatical leave at Yale (he never returned), but Meyer Fortes came back from West Africa at that time and taught me during the spring and summer semesters.'[11]

Burmese days (1939–45)

> Then, in the summer of 1939, the Firths left for Malaysia to conduct the research which produced, among other things, Raymond Firth's *Malay Fishermen* (1946), while I left for north-east Burma to undertake field research among the Kachin. The monograph that I had planned to write would not have had the quantitative detail which characterises Raymond Firth's book, but it was to be a socio-economic study of the same general kind. I hoped to display the organisation of the local community in terms of domestic production and the network of trading. Segmentary lineages and cross-cousin marriage didn't come into the story at all.[12]

There seems to have been an additional stimulus and agency in Leach's choice of Upper Burma for his fieldwork:

> In Malinowski's seminar he had met Noël (H. N. C.) Stevenson, a member of the Burma Frontier Service then home on study leave and whose book *The Economics of the Central Chin Tribes* Edmund later made us, his undergraduate students, all read. This link now came in useful. At Stevenson's suggestion, he set off for the village of Hpalang in the Kachin Hills of north-east Burma to carry out field research and to monitor the effects of Stevenson's social uplift project dubbed the 'Kachin regeneration scheme'.[13]

Leach arrived in Burma in August 1939, just about the time that Hitler had launched his awesome war. There was no going back to England this time

---

[11] *Current Anthropology*, 4, 376.

[12] Ibid.

[13] Hugh-Jones, *Edmund Leach*, p. 14. I can confirm that those of us who attended Leach's lectures on Economic Anthropology in the sixties were told to read H. N. C. Stevenson's *The Economics of the Great Central Chin Tribes* (1943). Stevenson's discussion of the Tefa system ('debt' and 'bond' slavery) provided Leach with material for making a striking contrast with the conceptions surrounding classical Greek chattel slavery, and his discussion of 'feasts of merit' and the activities of the 'feasters' club' with material for explicating the manner in which 'tangible perishables' (like food and livestock) were converted to 'intangible imperishables' (titles, reputation and relations of debt and power). Leach had anticipated Bourdieu's now famous concept of 'symbolic capital'.

round, and so Leach signed up with the Burma army and went into the field to Hpalang to conduct his research.

Leach conducted fieldwork in Hpalang for nine months in the years 1939–40, and he also contrived to get married in 1940 to Celia Joyce, daughter of Henry Stephen Guy Buckmaster. Thereafter he was called to serve in the Burma Army. He was stationed in Maymyo from October to December 1940, and during this training period he had the time to complete a draft of what he referred to as his 'functionalist' monograph on Hpalang. News of the fall of France reached the Leaches and thinking that all was lost, they quickly packed up and went to Maymyo, where their daughter Louisa was born on October 31 1941. Subsequently, they went to Schwebo, north of Mandalay. Mercifully the child also helped to save Celia's life because, as Edmund wrote, 'when the crunch came in Spring 1942, nursing mothers who were wives of white officers were flown out, the rest walked and mostly died'. Celia and infant were flown to Calcutta, and subsequently they took a boat from Bombay to England. Edmund did not see them again for three and a half years.

The Japanese invaded in 1941, and in 1942 in the midst of derailments caused by their advance, Leach lost all his papers—the draft monograph, notes, photographs, etc. In July 1942 while on sick leave in Calcutta he reconstructed the monograph on Hpalang from memory. But during his subsequent extensive travels in the Kachin Levies operation he was fated to lose that document too. But the memory of Hpalang was not lost for ever—for he would reconstruct Hpalang again and present a distilled portrait of this 'unstable Kachin *Gumsa* community' as chapter IV in his post-war classic *The Political Systems of Highland Burma*.

When the Japanese arrived at the end of 1941, Leach was assigned to an intelligence outfit run by H. N. C. Stevenson, the Frontier Service officer who had had some training in anthropology under Malinowski.

> I was supposed to hang around Hpalang (the base of my earlier fieldwork) with a radio set. My assistant lost his stores and the radio, and we had to head for home. It is a long story. I reached Kunming (capital of Yunnan Province) after many adventures and seven weeks of walking. I was then flown to Calcutta, very ill from dysentery. I tried hard to get back to regular soldiering, but my official unit had been disbanded, and, after a period of sick leave, I was ordered to report to Colonel Stevenson at a remote airfield in Assam. This was August 1942.[14]

Leach was sent back into Burma to create the Kachin Levies, but since Stevenson had met with an accident and was out of commission, a retired Australian Burma Military Police officer was put in formal charge of the Kachin Levies operation. Leach quarrelled with him, was reduced in rank

---

[14] The arduous retreat into China took its toll and it is surmised that his bothersome skin cancer on the head late in life was probably caused by the exposure to the sun.

from acting major to substantive second lieutenant, and was transferred to the Civil Affairs Service. 'Among other things the Civil Affairs Service had responsibility for the civil administration of "liberated" Burma as the British army moved back in. In this role I ended up as a staff major, deputy to the chief civil affairs officer at 14th Army Headquarters, an Establishment figure if ever there was one.'[15] The eminence he served under was General Slim and Leach had performed effectively in the civil administration of liberated Burma.

Leach would characterise his 'extraordinary series of war experiences' as a 'strange mixture of the absurd and the horrible'. But there was one benefit that he derived from it: 'I travelled very widely in the Kachin Hills and got to know a great variety of different sorts of "Kachin". This diversity provided the basis for my subsequent anthropological thinking.'[16] In fact his wide ranging recruiting trips and operations with the Kachin Levies had given him a panoramic and dynamic view of the connections between the varieties of hill tribes, and this knowledge would be the basis for a theoretical contribution of fundamental importance.

4. The Anthropologist at Work: Teacher and Theorist

The career start at LSE

Leach returned to England in the summer of 1945, supposedly on short leave, but after Hiroshima all return trips were cancelled, and he was demobilised in January 1946. Raymond Firth was now professor and head of department at the London School of Economics and 'between us we agreed that I should reread all the literature of the Kachin (and of other Burma frontier 'tribes'), going back to the beginning of the 19th century, and reassess it in the light of my "on the ground" experiences'. He completed the thesis in the spring of 1947.[17]

After completing the Ph.D., pursuant to a proposal made to the Colonial Office by Firth, Leach went in 1947 to the newly acquired Crown Colony of Sarawak to suggest what kinds of research should be done to collect more information about the inhabitants. He carried out a survey in Sarawak and his report entitled *Social Science Research in Sarawak* (1950) which was gratifyingly accepted by the government set out guidelines for subsequent investigations by a number of distinguished anthropologists: Derek Freeman who worked with the Iban, Bill Geddes with the Land Dayak, Stephen Morris with the Melanau, Ju-kang T'ien with the Kuching Chinese, and Tom Harrison with the Coastal Malays.

[15] *Current Anthropology* 27, no. 4 (August–October 1986) 377.
[16] Ibid.
[17] Ibid.

On his return from Borneo, Leach joined the staff at LSE as a lecturer, and one of his primary tasks was to be responsible for the teaching of 'primitive technology' then an integral part of undergraduate anthropology. 'But it soon appeared not only that his major interest was in social anthropology, but that with his usual devastating logic, he had concluded that what passed for primitive technology should properly be studied as examples of simple applied mechanics—or not at all. [This no doubt reflected his engineer's training.] So he turned to social anthropology completely, and also with his talent for administration, assumed responsibility for the general organization of under-graduate teaching in the department.'[18]

It was in this phase of his early career at LSE that he decided to resign his position in order to work full time for over a year on the book, *Political Systems of Highland Burma*.[19] He then rejoined the LSE in a new appointment as Reader.

We may note that while his doctoral thesis was about 'the hill tribes of Burma and Assam' and was oriented, following Firth's interests, in socio-economic interactions and agro-ecological adaptations and practices, the book in question, more closely focused on the Kachins (and their Shan neighbours), while using the same information plus a great amount of archival and historical sources, was of a different genre.

By this time Meyer Fortes had become head of the anthropology depart-ment at Cambridge, and Leach could not resist the offer of a lectureship there even if it meant a demotion in rank.

Leach in due course became settled in Cambridge, and his reputation began to soar. He became Reader in 1957, and the Department came to be seen as the arena for a titanic debate between Fortes and Leach which assumed mythological proportions especially in the common room talk of outsiders. It was at Cambridge that Leach would develop his reputation as 'critical rethinker of anthropology' and as one of the 'most original minds in modern social anthropology'.[20]

Early Cambridge years: forging a perspective

Leach's next fieldwork monograph, *Pul Eliya, a Village in Ceylon*[21] appeared in 1961. This same year, Leach has said, was 'a kind of watershed' in that he

---

[18] 'Obituaries. Professor Sir Edmund Leach. Critical Rethinker of Social Anthropology', *The Times*, Saturday, 7 January 1989.

[19] E. R. Leach, *Political Systems of Highland Burma: A Study of Kachin Social Structure*. London School of Economics Monographs on Social Anthropology, no. 44 (University of London, Athlone Press, 1954).

[20] These evaluations were made by Raymond Firth in a letter to the Department of Anthropology at the University of Chicago when Edmund Leach was proposed in 1976 as a candidate for an Honorary Degree, which was duly conferred on him.

[21] *Pul Eliya, a Village in Ceylon: A Study of Land Tenure and Kinship* (Cambridge University Press, 1961).

had brought out a book of essays, *Rethinking Anthropology*[22] 'which showed much more clearly than anything I had produced before just how far I had distanced myself from my teachers'.[23] This was also the same time—the academic year 1960–1—which Edmund and Celia Leach spent at the Center for Advanced Study in the Behavioral Sciences at Palo Alto, California—when he had a fruitful encounter and dialogue with Roman Jakobson and at the same time recovered a deeper consciousness of his own transformational bent *via* mathematics and engineering. Palo Alto had been a happy time. Leach's sense of intellectual excitement (which was also heightened by his attending Gregory Bateson's seminars on dolphin communication and ecological adaptation) was matched by Celia's responding to the California light, weather, flora, and landscape with intensified painting and pleasurable outdoor living.

The year 1961 was also when Leach published two essays which signalled his fascination with Lévi-Strauss's work on mythology. They were 'Golden Bough or Gilded Twig?'[24] and 'Lévi-Strauss in the Garden of Eden: An Examination of Some Recent Developments in the Analysis of Myth'.[25] This was the beginning of Leach's own increasing preoccupation with what he called 'the interface between art and religious mythology'.

The conjunction of all these influences, trends, different intellectual preoccupations and productions in the same year seems both unusual and improbable, and for orderly commentary we have to do some chronological sorting.

Leach did the field research in Ceylon (now Sri Lanka) on which *Pul Eliya* is based during the period June to December 1954, supplemented by a further brief visit in August 1956. He had from 1955 till 1957 begun to publish on his Ceylon materials,[26] and must have submitted his final monograph manuscript for publication before he went to Palo Alto in 1960, probably as early as 1957. *Pul Eliya* was theoretically primarily an argument mounted against the structural-functionalist approaches of Radcliffe-Brown and Meyer Fortes.

Rethinking Anthropology, although it came out in 1961, is actually a collection containing essays crafted over a period extending from 1953 to

---

[22] *Rethinking Anthropology*. London School of Economics Monographs on Social Anthropology, no. 22 (University of London, Athlone Press, 1961).

[23] Leach, 'Glimpses', p. 19.

[24] *Daedalus* (Journal of the American Academy of Arts and Sciences) 90, no. 2 (Spring 1961), 371–87.

[25] *Transactions of the New York Academy of Sciences*, series 2, 23, no. 4 (1961), 386–96.

[26] For example, 'Land Tenure in a Sinhalese Village, North Central Province, Ceylon'. Summary in *Man*, 55, article 178 (1955), 166–7; 'Structural Continuity in a Sinhalese Village (Ceylon Northern Dry Zone)', Proceedings of the Ninth Pacific Science Congress, 1957. It was also during this phase that he wrote 'Polyandry, Inheritance and the Definition of Marriage, with Particular Reference to Sinhalese Customary Law', *Man*, 55, Article 199 (1955), 182–6. Later reprinted in *Rethinking Anthropology*.

1961. The first essay was 'Cronos and Chronos', published in 1953[27] and the last was the capstone Malinowski Memorial Lecture (1959), which also provided the title for the collection. But the collection is given a unity by the fact that five of the six essays are concerned with issues relating to kinship and marriage. One central essay, 'The Structural Implications of Cross-Cousin Marriage', will be discussed later: it addresses the issue of representing Kachin marriage exchange and political hierarchy. Let me deal here with only two other essays pertaining to his call to his British colleagues to rethink anthropology, which included his urging the experimental trying out of new ideas even if they did not quite work out.[28]

An important essay contained in the collection is 'Jinghphaw Kinship Terminology', completed in Calcutta in 1943 during the war, and first published in a 1945 volume of the *Journal of the Royal Anthropological Institute* which actually did not appear in print until 1948. This essay was innovative in that Leach attempted to uncover the 'rules' that organised the 'superficially extremely complex' terminology, and his approach foreshadowed an approach (which he would progressively refine) that seeks out the 'structure of relations' in a mathematical- logical or algebraic sense. The rules constituted 'the ideal patterns of Jinghphaw society', and he underscored the point that 'any structural analysis of a kinship system is necessarily a discussion of ideal behaviour, not of normal behaviour'.

It is noteworthy that this mode of analysis was attempted many years before Leach encountered the writings of Lévi-Strauss, who in 1953 recognised Leach's essay as having some affinity with his own structuralist approach. This is relevant to considering the thesis—which Leach himself wished to establish—that his own predilection towards a mathematical-transformational approach, stemming from his earlier training in engineering, preceded as much as it later converged with features of Lévi-Strauss's structuralism. It was in regard to this matter of intellectual affinities and influences that Leach would draw attention to his felicitous meeting with Roman

---

[27] 'Cronus and Chronos', *Explorations* no. 1 (1953), 15–23. Its companion, 'Time and False Noses', appeared in *Explorations* no. 5 (1955), 30–5. They were combined under one heading in chapter 6 of *Rethinking Anthropology*.

[28] In doing so, I do not wish to detract from the seminal ideas concerning the definition of marriage and the relations between bridewealth and marriage stability among the Lakher and Kachin treated in the two remaining essays in the collection. I may also mention in this context another essay in a similar theoretical vein, published elsewhere, 'Concerning Trobriand Clans and the Kinship Category Tabu' (1958), relating kinship terminology to the dynamics of marriage, residence, and affinal payments, and attempting to solve a classical puzzle about Trobriand clans. It is also a contribution to the complex issues of interrelations between linguistic and social phenomena. This essay is published in Jack Goody (ed.), *The Development Cycle in Domestic Groups*, Cambridge Papers in Social Anthropology (Cambridge University Press, 1958).

Jakobson (and Halle) in 1960–1 at the Center for Advanced Study at Palo Alto. Leach was particularly taken with Jakobson's pattern of distinctive features in phonology—it rang bells of recognition that 'he had been there before'—and with Jakobson's search for linguistic universals. Leach had been initiated into linguistic theory, and he had begun to see that his 'deepest concerns were with what is now discussed under such grandiose labels as semiotics and cognitive science'.[29]

'Rethinking Anthropology' is the centre-piece in the collection which bears the same title. It was delivered with fanfare and expectation on 3 December 1959 as the first Malinowski Memorial Lecture at the London School of Economics, and Leach did not fail both to stimulate and to provoke his British audience. With characteristic ebullience Leach reminisced in later years that on this occasion he had not only denounced 'butterfly collecting' but also 'to the mystification of most of my audience, I referred to the significance of binary arithmetic and computer machine code as devices for modelling sociological process'.[30] The lecture exhorted anthropologists to break out of the straitjacket of viewing 'societies' and 'cultures' as plural empirical wholes and as concrete bounded entities capable of being labelled as types. Rather than labour at sketching particulars in detail (this by the way was the target and context for understanding Leach's earlier notorious remark that he was 'frequently bored by the facts' and 'cultural peculiarities'[31]) anthropologists should search for *general* patterns—whether similar or transformational—that may turn up in *any* kind of society. The patterns he was offering were relations between terms symbolised as mutually connected and variable in a 'topological' or 'algebraic' sense. Relationships between pairs of opposites was a case in point. In the field of kinship for example this pattern was explorable in the relations between 'incorporation' and 'alliance', as variably contrasted in different 'societies', such as Trobriand, Kachin, and Tallensi, in terms of 'blood and appearance' or 'controlled supernatural attack' versus unconscious 'uncontrolled mystical influence'.

This analytic and interpretive perspective became a dominant theme which Leach would restate, refine, and elaborate in many of his subsequent writings. We encounter for example a further explication of the notion of 'relational structures' in his BBC Reith Lectures, *A Runaway World?* (1968).

---

[29] Leach, 'Glimpses', p. 19.

[30] Ibid.

[31] *Political Systems* (1964), p. 227. 'I read the works of Professors Firth and Fortes not from an interest in the facts but so as to learn about the principles behind the facts' (ibid.). In fact, his extensive reviewing activity and his comparative essays show 'an unrivalled grasp of ethnographic detail' (Chris Fuller and Jonathan Parry, 'Petulant inconsistency? The intellectual achievement of Edmund Leach', *Anthropology Today*, 5(3) (June 1989), 11.)

The Cambridge Don as teacher

In their obituaries and reminiscences, Leach's students at Cambridge have affectionately described his large and powerful presence in strikingly similar ways.

He consciously did not present himself as a model of sartorial fashion or high table wit with elegant gestures, but he certainly possessed the skills of an actor and orator, who in responding to audiences gave his well organised, provocative, vibrant lectures, illustrated with slides and graphic figures drawn with chalk of multiple colours. In fact he took pride in displaying his practical skills, and his being a competent mechanic who was way ahead of other academics in using a personal photocopying machine (his students were eager recipients of the acid-smelling notes and queries he liberally distributed), and in the appreciation of the uses of a computer—which, in time becoming antiquated, challenged his electronic skills.[32]

To return to his relationship with and impact on students. They crowded to hear him, sensing that they were participants in the breaking of new ground. Equally encouraging of students thinking for themselves were Leach's conscientious and informal supervisions: students both undergraduate and postgraduate marvelled, were gratified, and frequently overwhelmed by the numerous pages of written comments on their essays and chapters which they received from such a busy man.[33]

Leach's relationship with and impact on his postgraduate students in part bears witness to the British virtue (much in evidence among established academics) of allowing them to develop and express their views, and of tolerating eccentricity within implicitly understood limits. Although he did not aspire to be the founder of a school, there were at least three cohorts of students who in their own right achieved high reputation and who regarded Leach as *a* (for some *the*) primary teacher and with admiration and affection. The first includes[34] Frederik Barth, Jean La Fontaine, Nur Yalman, Anthony Forge, Martin Southwold, and Ralph Bulmer, and the second and third Adam Kuper, Geoffrey Benjamin, Stephen Gudeman, Andrew Strathern, Marilyn Strathern, Ralph Grillo, Ray Abrahams, Jonathan Parry, C. J. Fuller, Alfred

---

[32] Leach, 'Glimpses', 9–10. 'I tend to think of social systems as machines for the ordering of social relations or as buildings that are likely to collapse if the stresses and strains of the roof structure are not properly in balance. When I was engaged in fieldwork I saw my problem as trying to understand "just how the system works" or "why it held together" ' (p. 10).

[33] A testimony to Leach's role as a supervisor, recognisable as authentic by other students as well, is provided by Ray Abrahams, 'Edmund Leach. Some Early Memories', *Cambridge Anthropology. Special Issue: Sir Edmund Leach*, 13: 3 (1989–90), 19–30.

[34] This listing is not complete, and I apologise to those who regard him in this light and have been missed out, owing to my ignorance.

Gell, Stephen Hugh-Jones, Christine Hugh-Jones, and Caroline Humphrey. 'Leach may not have created a school, but he certainly had many fiercely partisan students whose personal experience convinced them that they were working with one of the most exciting and creative intellectuals of his generation.'[35]

When I arrived in Cambridge in 1963 (to take up a Smuts Fellowship at the University and a Commonwealth Fellowship at St John's College) he already had the reputation of being the *enfant terrible* of the profession and stories circulated how he could be severe with shoddy work, sometimes had a scorching effect on this or that graduate student, had now and then explosive rows with some colleagues, and could be impatient with boring or stodgy seminar speakers, who might be treated to a disconcerting clinking of keys in his pocket, or in extreme moments, his turning away and reading a newspaper. It is in this state of demanding mind and stirred emotion, evoked by some writings he regarded as adversarial or incompetent that Leach wrote some of his most cutting and biting reviews, and forceful, even vitriolic, responses to those who ventured to take him on. British anthropologists who were more used to the thrust and parry of polemical review writing rather enjoyed and expected it of him, but many Americans mostly subject to the etiquette of sugar coated reference-writing, tended to approach Leach as an unyielding and aggressive defender of the faith, until he disarmed them with chuckling, even nonchalant, admissions of the vulnerability and impermanence of some of his past arguments.

One reason perhaps why students—who were his juniors—found Leach compellingly magnetic was that he never gave the impression that he was preaching a doctrine which they were obliged to accept. He did convey to them that he was on the attack, disputing orthodoxy and testing the limits of current knowledge. That may have been his hold on his audience, which listened attentively, even entranced, and went away encouraged to think for itself and to tackle the puzzles of the discipline on their own.

Leach reserved his greatest attention and affection for those doctoral students whose research particularly engaged him. As their supervisor and their friend he enthusiastically and conscientiously attended to their financial needs and communicated his assessments of their field research; he obviously enjoyed reviewing their field notes and texts in myths and rituals of the people being studied, and pondered their analyses and in turn offered his own analyses in an equal dialogue.

Many of his graduate students will enthusiastically testify to his ample and stimulating involvement in their fieldwork and thesis writing. At the same time it is crucial to recognise that Leach most definitely did not aspire to found a

---

[35] Fuller and Parry, 'Petulant inconsistency?'.

school with pliant disciples attached to him. He likewise baulked at others' efforts to monumentalise him. He fiercely rejected any effort by his former pupils (and other colleagues) to commemorate his career with a festschrift.[36] His position was that this genre of edited volumes containing disparate essays usually lacked coherence and never amounted to much as anthropology. In a curious way, such resistance also accorded with his own lack of enthusiasm for crafting a systematic totalising theoretical system, recapitulating his previous works and cumulatively built up piece by piece. In fact he readily acknow-ledged in informal exchanges with those with whom he was comfortable that he was aware of his inconsistencies. He would maintain that creative thinking was possible only if you were prepared to take the risks. Inconsistency did not worry him because he thought it was consistent with a Hegelian dialectical mode of thought. His impulsion was to 'experiment', 'probe', 'play' with new ideas, and push at the margins.

Theoretical positioning

There were two sets of contrasts, or 'oppositions' in the structuralist sense, that Edmund Leach frequently employed to characterise the theoretical impulsions and tensions in his writings. One was that he was simultaneously a structuralist and a functionalist; the other was that he was attracted to mathematical equations of relations and transformations (as a schoolboy preparing to enter Cambridge he had concentrated on mathematics) but that having been trained as an engineer he had pragmatic concerns in how designs were drawn, implemented, adapted to context and put to use. He once said that there was a tug of war within him between a pure mathematician manqué and an empiri-cist engineer manqué, who, however, recoils from counting. 'I feel that some-times I am on both sides of the fence.'[37]

The statement that he was simultaneously a structuralist and functionalist needs an extended gloss on what he meant by that self-definition. The follow-ing is a beginning. While rejecting the Radcliffe-Brownian (and Durkheimian) notion of 'function' as contribution of a component to the maintenance and integration of a social 'system' (itself viewed in organismic terms), and the Malinowskian notion of 'function' primarily in terms of serving individual 'biological' needs and, secondarily societal needs, Leach in various writings seems to have adopted the notion of function as connection between compo-nents, such that functional relations constituted an interconnected totality ('the total interconnectedness of things'). The 'interconnectedness' that

---

[36] Leach had scotched many attempts by his pupils and colleagues to do him honour in this way. I myself was the recipient of a quick and firm missive the moment a rumour reached him that I and certain others were contemplating a festschrift.

[37] Tambiah, 'Personal Accounts', p. 34.

Leach meant, however, comprised 'relational systems' in the sense that they were 'transformations' of one another.[38] This conception of functional relations thus rejects the Malinowskian notion of a cultural system as 'a unique self-sufficient functioning whole' and the Radcliffe-Brownian notion of 'whole societies', bounded and 'distinguishable as species types and classifiable as such in a kind of Linnaean taxonomy'. These were the perspectives he rejected first in his *Political Systems of Highland Burma* and even more explicitly and unforgettably as 'butterfly collecting' in his famous Malinowski Memorial Lecture in December 1959, urging the view that anthropologists ought to be searching for generalisations for which cultural and social boundaries were quite irrelevant or impossible to impose. This view of function derived from mathematics and not from biology or psychology as was the case with the followers of Radcliffe-Brown and Malinowski. 'Consequently, from my point of view there was no inconsistency between "functionalism" and "structuralism" (in its then novel continental sense)'.[39]

Leach progressively clarified that his 'structuralism'-cum-'functionalism' consisted in seeing 'relational systems' as 'transformations' of one another, that certain devices stemming from or assimilable to his mathematical and engineering training such as binary arithmetic, information theory, computer coding, could be deployed for perceiving patterns in classificatory thought, myth and ritual, and in social processes. More ambitiously, he saw the possibility of establishing 'cross cultural transcriptions' as the objective of his notion of the comparative method. These ideas gave an underlying unity and continuity to the way he would tackle many of the issues he undertook to investigate.

At the same time he also successfully exploited aspects of the 'functionalist' perspective he principally associated with Malinowski and Firth, and which dynamically focused on how individual actors (including groups) used and manipulated ideal categories and rules and norms of social conduct in contexts of action to further their interests and goals. Leach deployed this pragmatic instrumental or strategising perspective on many occasions—how mythological genealogical variants (in 'structuralist' terms variations on a theme) were manipulated by competing Kachin lineages to further their claims or more generally how myth variants were related to 'function and social change', how double descent systems might make sense if considered as networks through which different activities were channelled, or how an imposing, intricately carved, but densely populated Hindu temple façade whose details could not be distinguished by the worshipper was meant to convey a sense of

---

[38] See, for example, Leach's *A Runaway World?* This idea is elaborated in his later writings as we shall see.
[39] Leach, 'Glimpses', p. 19.

power and awe.[40] In this mood Leach would criticise on the one hand the formalism of some of the structural functionalists who reified social systems as organisations of social principles and, on the other, the non-contextualised abstract codes of some structuralist exercises divorced from social uses or lacking empirical grounding.

While remembering that Leach had many irons in the fire at any one time, I would risk a broad two-fold temporal division of his writings into those written and published from about 1940 to 1961, and those written from around 1962 (and especially after 1965) into the late 1980s. During the first phase he was primarily concerned with refining, extending and polemically criticising certain formulations surrounding kinship, segmentary descent structures and social organisation of 'tribal' societies made by the leading figures in British social anthropology—such as Radcliffe-Brown and Malinowski, who were his elders, and Meyer Fortes, Raymond Firth, Evans-Pritchard (who were senior to him), and Max Gluckman, Audrey Richards, Jack Goody and others who were his contemporaries. Of all these personages, Leach explicitly named on several occasions Malinowski and Firth as his teachers; less frequently, he also referred to Fortes as one of his teachers.[41]

One might say, to simplify and accent matters, that in his mind in the category of senior figures, Leach opposed Radcliffe-Brown, whose typing structural-functional organic systems he rejected and whom he personally disliked, and Malinowski, his charismatic teacher whom he liked, and whose ethnographic writing he admired much more than his theoretical contributions. At the next level, he positioned himself in contrastive relations to his part-teachers who were slightly older than him, namely Fortes and Firth. Though a participant in Malinowski's seminar, Fortes had gravitated towards Radcliffe-Brown, whose theoretical perspective he whole-heartedly espoused, and Leach saw Fortes as his sparring opponent and theoretical foil. Leach was benignly inclined toward Firth who was sponsor and friend and had initially taught him 'most of what I know about anthropology'.

While Leach repeatedly idolised his dead hero, Malinowski, it was also evident from his words and deeds, that initially he had imbibed much from his other teacher and friend and sponsor, Raymond Firth, who has outlived him. I would surmise that Firth's own dynamic treatment of the relation between normative rules and actor oriented usages first of all accorded with Leach's

---

[40] See Edmund R. Leach, 'The Gatekeepers of Heaven: Anthropological aspects of grandiose architecture', *Albuquerque Journal of Anthropological Research*, 39 (3) (Fall 1983), 243–64.

[41] In 'Glimpses', Leach states that 'Raymond Firth and Meyer Fortes were my teachers and closest associates throughout my academic career'. In *Custom, Law and Terrorist Violence* (Edinburgh at the University Press, 1977) Leach declares that he considered Malinowski 'the greatest and most original of all social anthropologists'.

own intuitions about how people acted, and secondly, provided fire power against the officialising doxa of Radcliffe-Brown and his followers.

I have mentioned certain British anthropologists who figured with varying significance in Leach's professional concerns in the first phase. There is another from across the channel in France whose writings as the leading French theorist increasingly became more and more important for Leach to take into account and come to terms with, but with whom he did not have a close personal relationship. This person was Claude Lévi-Strauss. Leach's intellectual engagement with and preoccupation with Lévi-Strauss's ideas in his own writings is a vital part of his biography. Admiration spiced with dissent, however, was not in this case a prescription that could bind the two in a relation of enduring 'alliance'.

5. The Political Systems of Highland Burma

Leach's first large work, *The Political Systems of Highland Burma*[42] is widely regarded as a landmark in political anthropology. It is a classic, still widely read and cited, and in the eyes of many arguably his best book. This master-piece already contains many of the issues he grappled with throughout his career: his critique of many of the orthodoxies of 'structural functionalism' à la Radcliffe-Brown; his admiring engagement with Lévi-Straussian 'structural-ism' as deployed in *The Elementary Structures of Kinship* and simultaneously his rejection of some of the substantive, methodological, and theoretical sub-missions in that book; and his attempt to straddle and combine some features of 'functionalist' empiricism and pragmatism with 'structuralist' rationalism and deductive formalism (an exercise with philosophical ramifications that engaged Leach more consciously in later years).

Leach has remarked that his first book, among other things, is 'organized as a kind of dialogue between the empiricism of Malinowski and the ration-alism of Lévi-Strauss and these two contrasted strands of my thinking should be apparent to the reader in all my later writings'.[43]

One of Leach's achievements in *Political Systems of Highland Burma* was to argue against the view that 'the boundaries of society and the boundaries of culture can be treated as coincident' and thereby powerfully to dissolve the older ethnographic fixation on tribes as bounded entities and wholes, and to unveil for our viewing a landscape of highland Burma as an open system of many lineages linked in circles of wife givers (*mayu*) and wife takers (*dama*),

[42] The London School of Economics and Political Science. London: G. Bell and Sons, Ltd., 1954. Reprinted with Introductory Note by the Author in 1964.
[43] Leach, *Social Anthropology*, p. 44.

communicating with one another diacritically through variations of dialect, dress, and other local differences, and capable of dynamically generating and as well as contesting tendencies towards extra-local hierarchical political formations. It was a model of an open-ended system, constrained but not determined by certain 'objective' conditions, and capable of an expanding multiplication as well as incorporation of new lineage segments. In this way he changed extant notions of tribes, ethnic identity, and repetitive equilibrium as timeless static ontological entities of anthropology. The book also proposed a stimulating view of the patterning of myth and ritual and their role in political action, and grappled in an exploratory way with the integrated use of historical materials in anthropological analysis.

In a separate essay, 'The Structural Implications of Matrilateral Cross-Cousin Marriage', published in 1951 some three years before *Political Systems*, Leach had already produced the first English language commentary on Lévi-Strauss's *The Elementary Structures of Kinship* especially as it bore on his Kachin materials.

In the above mentioned 1951 essay, Leach set out to demonstrate that the Kachin *Gumsa* type social order was not inherently unstable and threatened with break up by virtue of *internal intra-kinship* processes generated by the marriage rules towards greater and greater inequality and imbalances as Lévi-Strauss maintained; what has to be considered in a fuller analysis is how arrangements by which women travel 'down' and marriage goods move 'up' in compensation are interlocked with territorial sovereignty, land tenure, and patron client relations, so as to maintain in dynamic tension a stratified political system of the *Gumsa* type. Lévi-Strauss had been mistaken in thinking that women moved upwards hypergamously thus creating the demographic bottlenecks at the top.[44] Leach provides an elegant analysis of how the prescriptive marriage exchange among the Kachin is integrally linked up with and sustained by the wider political and economic circumstances, and here we see his version of structuralism and functionalism displayed at its best. It should be noted, however, that Leach appears to be asserting that the Gumsa system can be presented as stable and in equilibrium in terms of a 'model', but that in fact it was an 'unstable' form owing to various dynamic processes which are described in the book.

Vis-à-vis Lévi-Strauss's 'mechanistic' model deriving from kinship categories and marriage rules themselves taken as structuring the system, Leach was arguing that kinship structures per se should not be essentialised and reified as formal systems containing an exhaustive internal logic, but should be explicated in terms of how actors use and manipulate them within

---

[44] See ' "Kachin and Haka Chin"; A Rejoinder to Lévi-Strauss', *Man*, NS. 4 (2) (1969), 277–85.

the larger political economy, which, while providing directives and incentives to action, is also in turn constituted and changed by the dynamic strategising acts and normative ideological constructs of the actors.[45]

Leach's assertion in *Political Systems* was that events and behaviour on the ground are 'only seen as structured when they are ordered by means of verbal categories'.[46] The three categories of ideal political order that the Kachin themselves used in their political dialogues ('discourses' in modern jargon) were *gumlao* and *gumsa* which were respectively 'democratic egalitarian', and 'ranked-aristocratic' in their connotations and which gave conceptual gloss and a mental ordering to their own activities; the third, *shan*, pertained to the monarchical/feudal conceptual ordering of the neighbouring valley centred people.

In Leach's language gumlao and gumsa categories are 'transformations' of each other in the mathematical/structuralist sense. The Shan model is predicated on entirely different principles—for example, the Shan chief who is polygamous receives wives and concubines as 'tributes' from his petty chiefs and political subordinates and as wife-taker is superior to the givers thus reversing the Kachin *mayu-dama* (wife-giver–wife-taker) evaluation; and the building blocks of Shan monarchical polity are not segmentary descent lineages. A fundamental misunderstanding is generated when a Kachin chief gives a wife to a Shan prince: the former in his own terms as *mayu* is the ritual superior; the latter in accepting a tributary gift from a political subordinate is in his terms the superior overlord. Therefore the Shan model is not a transformation of the gumlao-gumsa dyad; individual gumsa Kachin chiefs may try to 'become' Shan by adopting Shan pretensions and claims, but such developments are subverted by the Kachin themselves whose basic valuations and practices resisted this kind of political subjection. As Parry and Fuller put it:

[45] This in my view is an instance and an occasion in which Leach's structural and functional perspectives meet and combine to illuminate, and come close to Pierre Bourdieu's theoretical ambition stated years later in formal terms in *Outline of a Theory of Practice* (Cambridge University Press, 1977. The original French text, entitled *Esquisse d'une théorie de la pratique, précédé de trois études d'ethnologie kabyle*, was published in 1972 by Librairie Droz S.A., Switzerland) to combine 'rules' with 'practices', to steer clear of 'mechanistic sociologism' and 'spontaneous voluntarism' and to track the relation between objective structures, the cognitive and motivating dispositions they shape (habitus), the strategies of action to realise practical aims, in social situations, and the final outcome as 'practices' ('regulated improvisations'), which recursively have a feedback effect on objective structures. (Whether in fact Bourdieu has actually realised this ambition is a debatable matter that need not concern us here.) Unlike Bourdieu who has attempted to produce a systematised theory of practice with an attendant set of concepts, Leach as I have remarked before was uninterested in such ambitious theorising, and implicitly illustrated the relation between semantics and pragmatics, structuralism and functionalism, cultural rules and individuals' manipulating to maximise their power and status by means of empirically oriented analyses.

[46] Introductory note to the 1964 reprint of *Political Systems*, p. x. Leach refers to Pareto's *Traité de Sociologie*, and to its English translation: Arthur Livingston (ed.), *The Mind and Society*, (New York, Dover Publications, 1963).

'Partly because a gumsa polity had a more precarious productive base, partly because a gumsa chief was liable to alienate his kinsmen by treating them like a Shan prince's subjects—which he could hardly afford to do since his wealth . . . was in people rather than land—the nearer such a polity got to the Shan model, the more likely it was overthrown by a "democratic" rebellion'.[47]

Leach's famous thesis of 'oscillating equilibrium' asserted that over a period of 150 years, which is the historical time span he has dealt with, the Kachin communities may be seen as oscillating between the gumlao-gumsa poles. He was later to explain that this oscillating model was influenced and adapted from 'Pareto's discussion of the alternating dominance of the "lions" and the "foxes" and his conception of a "moving equilibrium" '.[48] His concern with historical process over a large span of time had led him to transform and formalise the indigenous Kachin categories into his own construction of an 'as if' model, between whose poles could be situated particular Kachin communities in time and space. He repudiated those readings of his text that inferred that he was saying that Kachin communities mechanically and inevitably moved through an everlasting cyclical process, with the additional connotations of a historical determinism that such a view carried. There were two kinds of processes that he adduced to counter this reading. Over a span of time particular communities may stay put or move in different paces and directions, and there is no way in which all these circumstances could be aggregated or summed up as constituting one integral total moving equilibrium system, or a system moving unidirectionally.

Leach's explication of the gap between 'ideal categories' and 'actual behaviour', 'rule and practice' focused on how individual Kachin actors driven by self-interested power motives instrumentally manipulated the ambiguous meanings and contested the application of those categories to their on the ground situation. In this respect Leach had anticipated the current interest in 'agency'. And when wearing this hat, Leach would argue that 'to the individual himself [different social systems] present themselves as alternatives or inconsistencies in the scheme of values by which he orders his life. The overall process of structural change comes about through the manipulation of these alternatives as a means of social advancement. Every individual of a society, each in his own interest, endeavours to exploit the situation as he perceives it and in so doing the collectivity of individuals alters the structure of the society itself.'[49]

In an important review, published in 1958, Ernest Gellner charged Leach with holding a position that was an 'idealist error'[50] in so far as Leach

---

[47] Fuller and Parry, 'Petulant inconsistency?', p. 12.

[48] Introductory note to the 1964 reprint of *Political Systems*, lx.

[49] *Political Systems*, p. 8.

[50] Ernest Gellner, 'Time and Theory in Social Anthropology', *Mind*, 67, NS, no. 266 (April 1958).

emphasised verbalised thought categories as providing the phenomenological map for viewing and interpreting the world out there, but that the dynamic behaviour of actors and the untidy 'facts on the ground' did not bear a direct correspondence to the ideal categories which were manipulated for personal advancement in the power game. The persisting element in social relationships was a pattern structure of verbal concepts, open to diverse interpretations, rather than empirically observable and existing kin groups.

It may come as a surprise to many readers, including some of his disciples, that in fact while rejecting Gellner's attribution of 'error' Leach did accept and did again and again explicate in the later decades of his career his 'idealist' position, which he conjoined with his 'humanist' and 'empiricist' orientations. This idealist-humanist-empiricist position radically separated him from what he saw as Radcliffe-Brownian empiricism and quasi-rationalism which saw societies as 'concrete' systems held together by principles of kinship and descent, and theoretically capable of being represented on 'the method of science involving observation, classification and generalization', in short a natural science of society. According to Radcliffe-Brown, 'The fundamental problems' of a theoretical science must 'depend on the systematic comparison of a number of societies of sufficiently diverse types'.[51] Leach's objections are that aside from the myopia of structural-functionalists regarding the issue of 'the lack of fit between ideal categories and empirical discontinuities', their static classificatory types failed to see their societies 'as continuously adaptive sub-systems within an unbounded matrix'.[52] In other words, Leach came to underscore as part of his credo, what he already had perceived in *Political Systems*, that 'historical process' is open-ended and cannot be represented in causal determinative evolutionary terms.

6. Pul Eliya: The Challenge to Descent Group Theory

Leach introduces the monograph on Pul Eliya[53] as having two aspects, firstly as an addition to the already substantial literature relating to Ceylonese land tenure, and secondly, 'as an academic exercise designed to provide a critical test of certain features of the theory and method of British social anthropology, especially as it related to the general field of kinship theory'.

---

[51] See Edmund Leach, 'Social Anthropology: A Natural Science of Society?' Radcliffe-Brown Lecture, 1976. From the *Proceedings of the British Academy*, LXII (Oxford University Press, 1976), pp. 157–80. In this lecture Leach assembled in one place all the objections he had to the Radcliffe-Brown brand of structural functionalism.

[52] *Political Systems*, p. 16.

[53] E. R. Leach, *Pul Eliya, a Village in Ceylon: A Study in Land Tenure and Kinship* (Cambridge University Press, 1961), p. 1.

Whatever professional anthropologists may say in regard to its theoretical implications for kinship theory, there is no doubt at all that the monograph is a masterly, detailed, and unmatched account of the land tenure system prevailing in a village in the 'dry zone' North Central Province in the year 1954.

It is possible that those anthropologists who have studied people who practice shifting agriculture with hoe technology or pastoralism have for the most part little sense—although these systems have land tenure concepts and inheritance rules—of the almost obsessive concern for people of South Asia, who practice sedentary plough agriculture in fields of fixed size and position, with values oriented towards possession of land and its transmission, and all the well-being, status, and symbolic capital that goes with it.

Although there have been previous partial accounts by colonial public servants and recent Sri Lankan scholars of traditional irrigation technology and land tenure arrangements, Leach's study is the first full scale empirical study of the actual 'workings' of a particular agrarian and social system in all the details of its singular particularity. *Pul Eliya* is a case study that illuminates the previous academic treatises in unexpected ways.

This work did in fact stimulate a number of other field studies in Sri Lanka in which the relation between social structure and land tenure was a critical axis both for the people studied and for the anthropologists.[54]

Keeping in mind those many omnibus wide-ranging monographs, common to the field of anthropology which aim to touch on almost every aspect of the social and cultural life of single communities, Leach modestly and accurately says that his formal subject matter 'covers an extremely narrow field' namely 'the local land tenure system' and its relation to kinship. This narrow field in fact becomes an inexhaustible vista filled with ethnographic particulars that in my view constitutes one of the richest and analytically illuminating documentations of virtually all aspects of a 'peasant economy', both synchronically as it operated in 1954, and diachronically from 1890 or so to 1954. Land tenure is a canopy that covers much in the areas of production, distribution, consumption, and exchange.

Some wags have joked that because Leach lost all his Kachin field

---

[54] For example, Gananath Obeyesekere, *Land Tenure in Village Ceylon* (Cambridge University Press, 1967); Marguerite S. Robinson, *Political Structure in a Changing Sinhalese Village* (Cambridge University Press, 1975); Stanley J. Tambiah, 'The structure of kinship and its relationship to land possession in Pata Dumbara, Central Ceylon', *The Journal of the Royal Anthropological Institute*, 88, Part I (1958), 21–44; Stanley J. Tambiah, 'Kinship fact and fiction in relation to the Kandyan Sinhalese', *The Journal of the Royal Anthropological Institute*, 95, Part II (1965), 131–79; Stanley J. Tambiah, 'Polyandry in Ceylon—with special reference to the Laggala Region', in *Caste and Kin in Nepal, India, and Ceylon*, ed. Christoph von Fürer-Haimendorf (Bombay: Asia Publishing House, 1966), pp. 264–358; Nur Yalman's *Under the Bo Tree* (Berkeley, California: University of California Press, 1967) is contemporaneous with Leach's work, but of course both were in contact as teacher and student at Cambridge.

notes during the Second World War, he compensated by publishing all the information he collected in Pul Eliya. Leach genially admitted that there is something to this charge, but that there was a serious purpose behind his detailed documentation.

The resort to and handling of archival and contemporary first-hand information is truly amazing: cadastral surveys first done in 1890, and surveys later repeated; tax records from 1860–93; land title registrations, plot ownership and transmissions from 1890–1954; administration reports; court cases and litigation—all these backed by Leach's own complete mapping of the Old Field and the residential compounds (*gamgoda*), and all categories of other land owned and used, and a thorough compilation of genealogies and much else.

All this exhaustive and meticulously checked information is marshalled to cover the central aspects of economic life: landownership and its transmission through time; the maintenance of the irrigation system; cultivation operations and landlord–tenant–labourer arrangements; credit and debt relations; labour organisation and labour exchange, and sharing of rewards in different phases of a single cultivation season culminating in harvesting, threshing, and share distribution; forms of cultivation in compound gardens, and the fascinating system of shifting cultivation (*chena*) on dry land, according to the 'wheel pattern'. All these details are there not only to provide an understanding of the multiple dimensions of the economic life of the Pul Eliya people but also as ammunition for waging a theoretical campaign, ambitious and risky. The facts are marshalled and presented, as Leach warned, to the point of 'unreadability', because the validation of his theoretical assertions depended on the empirical *method* he had chosen to substantiate the assertions. Thus, *Pul Eliya* is for Leach an experiment in method which would generate the empirical data needed to confirm his assertions. This experiment in method he compared to the usual anthropological field work of his time in this way. From Malinowski onward, the so-called field study and case history took the form of the anthropologist's propounding a general hypothesis and then presenting his or her cases and examples *to illustrate the argument.* 'The technique of argument is still that of Frazer. Insight comes from the anthropologists' private intuition; the evidence is only put in by way of illustration.'[55]

Covering quantitatively and qualitatively everything of significance in a small universe in relation to a chosen topic cannot of course be done in a literal sense, but it is important for any serious reader of *Pul Eliya* to realise that Leach harnesses his uncompromising empiricism to a theoretical end, namely that the quantitative patterns formed by the data would in themselves constitute a 'social order' or 'social structure', akin to the quantitative rates of the 'normal' as opposed to the 'normative' invoked by Durkheim in *Suicide*. This

[55] Leach, *Pul Eliya*, p. 12.

would be a different representation of 'social structure' from that propounded and allegedly confirmed by resort to jural norms and 'mystical' concepts of solidarity by the leading British exponents of 'structural-functionalism'.

What is Leach's quarrel with this school of thought that 'emanated from Oxford'? During the period 1934–54 'the most important developments in anthropological work were concerned with the enlargement of our understanding of the nature and significance of unilineal descent groups'.[56] The chief contributors to this effort were Radcliffe-Brown, Evans-Pritchard, especially in his study of the Nuer (1940) and Fortes, notably in his summing up (1953).[57] By virtue of its success and also its biases, this body of descent group theory invited its antithesis.

Radcliffe-Brown 'consistently exaggerated the importance of unilineal as opposed to bilateral (cognatic) systems of succession and inheritance'. Though uncommon in Africa, the main site for theorising about unilineal descent groups (UDGs), cognatic systems are widely distributed throughout the world and far exceed in frequency other types, yet Radcliffe-Brown gave them little notice. A question that arises then is how his generalisations apply to societies in which unilineal descent is not a factor.

A main assertion of Radcliffe-Brown, further accented by Fortes (and ultimately deriving from their reading of Henry Maine's *Ancient Law*), was 'that in societies with a lineage structure the continuity of the society as a whole rests in the continuity of the system of lineages, each of which is a "corporation", the life-span of which is independent of the individual lives of its individual members'.[58] Although, as Weber made clear, there could be other bases or means of incorporation such as locality and ritual initiation, or other special interests, these theorists saw descent per se as the most effective basis of incorporation, especially because 'descent is fundamentally "a jural concept" (as Radcliffe-Brown argued)', and its significance was that it served 'as the connecting link between the external, that is the political and legal aspect of what we have called unilineal descent groups, and the internal or domestic aspect'.[59] Readers of *Pul Eliya* who come across Leach's barrage against theorists who consider kinship per se as 'a thing in itself' will find their clues to what he meant by this expression in the view that kinship, especially descent, is the very generative basis of jural status, succession and inheritance rights, placement and incorporation in descent groups, which by a further extrapolation from the internal domestic domain to the external domestic domain, also provides the grid for political and legal relations. In a society

[56] Ibid., p. 5.
[57] E. E. Evans-Pritchard. *The Nuer* (Oxford University Press, 1940), M. Fortes 'The Structure of Unilineal Descent Groups', *American Anthropologist*, 55 (1953), 17–41.
[58] Leach, *Pul Eliya*, p. 6.
[59] Fortes, 'Unilineal Descent Groups', p. 30.

like that found in Pul Eliya, where no unilineal descent principle prevails, 'it is locality rather than descent which forms the basis of corporate grouping'.[60] It is only after one has worked through the ethnography that this statement can be tested and understood.

There are other entailments to the UDG approach which Leach criticises as constructing a 'static' and 'equilibrium' view of society insulated from dynamics and change. 'If anthropologists come to look upon kinship as a parameter which can be studied in isolation they will always be led, by a series of logical steps, to think of human society as composed of equilibrium systems, structured according to ideal legal rules'.[61] In Leach's mind, and in terms of what would be a central concern and demonstration in Pul Eliya, the intrinsic equilibrium kinship model is particularly guilty of considering economic factors and activities to be of 'minor significance', and thus the study of social adaptation to changing circumstances is made impossible.

The insensitivity to economic activities and relations of production in general stemming from the emphasis on the lineage principle was also reflected by Radcliffe-Brown who constantly stressed the jural and 'legal aspects of kinship relations as manifested in *the rights of inheritance in contrast to the economic aspects manifested in work cooperation*' [emphasis added].[62] This last criticism, simply mentioned in one line in the introduction, would in fact become a central issue of exposition in the text: that while inheritance and transmission and possession of property over time is of vital concern to the Sinhalese peasantry, so is the organisation and cooperative relations of labour in the operations of cultivation and harvesting of rice, of tank fishing, and shifting agriculture (*chena*), and the rewarding of them through distribution of the product. The jural ties of kinship and inheritance stemming from 'descent' are quite different from labour cooperation directed by ties of affinity. Furthermore, the stress on patrilineal descent and organisa-tion leads to 'explaining away' the importance attached to *matrilateral and affinal kinship connections*.[63] Leach's thesis seems to be that if economic activities are a primary concern and basic to social life, and if changes in economic circumstances do engender changes in the kinship system, the latter cannot be regarded as 'intrinsic and autonomous', and the possibility is raised that economic relations might in this sense be 'prior' to kinship relations.

Leach is not bent on simply offering, in contrast to 'unilineal systems', the

---

[60] Leach, *Pul Eliya*, p. 7.
[61] Ibid., p. 7–8.
[62] Ibid., p. 6.
[63] Fortes is famous for his thesis of 'complementary filiation': in patrilineal systems with polygynous marriages each mother serves to internally distinguish the male siblings born of the same father; also marriage is an individual matter, and siblings will have different networks of affines through marriage.

Pul Eliya case as a 'bilateral system'. The distinction between non-unilineal and unilineal systems is not useful either: Pul Eliya does not belong to either type, and moreover, for some aspects of life in that village there is at work a notion of 'descent', and in others a contrasting notion of affinity. Similarly, Leach is not keen on distinguishing between 'jural' and 'economic' relationships where they are interactive and copresent. He would much rather be seen as offering the subversive agenda of persuading the unilineal descent group theorists to see in the Pul Eliya exposition reasons for loosening the primacy they accord in their accounts of unilineal societies to the structuring role of kinship per se, and permit other existential activities and contextual circumstances a creative and structuring role. 'Kinship as we meet in this book [*Pul Eliya*] is not "a thing in itself". The concepts of descent and affinity are expressions of property relations which endure through time. Marriage unifies; inheritance separates; property endures. A particular descent system simply reflects the total process of property succession as affected by the total pattern of inheritance and marriage. The classification of whole societies in terms of such a parameter can only be meaningful in an extremely crude sense.'[64] This is the polemical challenge posed in trenchant terms, and aimed directly at the kinship theory of Radcliffe-Brown and his followers.

What is the relation between 'custom' and the 'behaviour of individuals'? Repudiating 'the currently fashionable structuralist concept of social solidarity', which he dubs as a 'mysticism' invoked as an ultimate explanatory device and absolute virtue towards which all social activity is of necessity directed, Leach proposes a different way of thinking about the distinction between and relation between custom and individual behaviour, ideal model and statistical order, normative and normal. In a way the answer he searches for is an extension and elaboration of a perspective first broached in *Political Systems of Highland Burma*, in which he tried to probe the correspondence between 'ideal type thought categories' (such as gumsa and gumlao) and the 'empirical facts on the ground'. The thought categories he warned should not be equated with actual behavioural relations. But *Political Systems in Highland Burma*, though an advance, had, as Leach recognised, 'idealist' connotations, even 'idealist pitfalls'. *Pul Eliya* seeks to go further by incorporating a 'materialist' dimension, so to say, and the answers Leach proposes to the grand question can only be sensibly reviewed and judged after doing our homework of closely attending to the ethnography he presents.

That the people of Pul Eliya had 'ideal concepts' and normative formulations, which anthropologists have labelled as belonging to the domain of 'kinship' is readily admitted and documented by Leach. He agrees that kinship terminology classifies kin; that certain kinds of kin terms, specifying parent

[64] Leach, *Pul Eliya*, p. 11.

and child, siblings—especially older and younger brother—and cross-cousin and brother-in-law, may also be accompanied by formulaic norms of 'ideal' conduct, such as the famous 'right' of a man to claim a mother's brother's daughter; and that incest taboos may serve as constraints on most actors. All these and other kinship particulars, however, do not determine or predict actual conduct, because there is much cultural and social space 'outside their scope' which provides the context, circumstances, and interests which actors pursue to reach their goals.

It would be absurd to think that the perspective of individual actors making strategic choices to maximise their interests and goals makes these motivated acts somehow amoral or non-social because they have 'personal' or 'private' relevance. The rules that define a game are different from the strategies and moves the players can adopt in playing the game, and that again is different from the actual performance of the players, for players manipulate and play with different skills, and opportunities, and cope with unexpected contingencies and accidents. An entailment of the individual strategising perspective is that while actors may know what they individually are trying to attain, and may know what the results are for them, all the actors in a situation are not for the most part aware of the aggregate distributional patterns and outcomes of all their acts. This pattern of outcomes is what Leach called the 'statistical order' (and the 'curves', 'averages' and other measures that are used to calculate the 'normal').[65]

Leach's discussion of ideal models and actual behaviour, as especially displayed in his treatment of marriage patterns and their situational logic, anticipates and reminds one of Bourdieu's schema in *Outline of a Theory of Practice*[66] for linking 'objective structure' and 'subjective action'. Leach's grappling with the issue of the relation between 'ideal' *pavula* (kindred) and 'effective' *pavula*, of how both these structures interrelate, but in which it is the axis of affinity and *massina* (cross-cousin) alliance that supersedes in social life the role of formal male sibling ties, is another variant example of the same general issue. Moreover, the unpacking of the alleged solidarity of male siblings by filiation and as primary heirs to parental property, by revealing how their being competitors to that patrimony creates a social distance among them, further accentuated by distinctions of age, is an acute diagnosis of contradictory trends built into that building block of 'kinship principles' central to Africanist descent group theory, namely 'solidarity of the sibling group'.

But there are other revelations which surprise us in another way. The ideal formulation held that inherited *paraveni* field plots in the Old Field are so

---

[65] The neoclassical model of market under conditions of perfect competition is an extreme ideal formulation of this logic.

[66] P. Bourdieu, *Outline of a Theory of Practice* (Cambridge University Press, 1977).

precious for validating status that they ought not to be sold, especially to 'outsider' traders of the wrong *variga*, and even worse of alien 'race' (Muslims and Tamils). This formulation was utterly contravened by many of the titled and wealthiest farmers of the village. But there were circumstances and manipulations and strategies (including the unwillingness of locals to cultivate the plots as tenants or labourers to these 'outsiders') by which the plots returned to the ownership of the Pul Eliya *minissu*; and there were similar processes of conversion into citizenship of new owners or their children by means of marriage with Pul Eliya women, and transforming that property into 'heirlooms'. These processes demonstrate the routes by which actual gaps between ideal model and actual events are over time closed and retrospectively made to look as if the ideal norms have not been violated and have always been observed. In the case of the cooperating labour teams (*kayiya*) involved in the tasks of harvesting and threshing, whose membership is not obligatory on the basis of kinship, but open to choice, Leach finds that the total pattern of the teams (the statistical order) shows that the teams were bodies of kinsmen linked by affinal ties and *pavula* links. The outcomes thus affirm the Pul Eliya social structure as revealed by other outcomes in other formal situations.

There are other examples of how a master ethnographer meticulously engaged with micro-details, assembles his data according to a combined 'idealist cum empiricist' perspective (a self-ascription). But the most important documentation concerns the dialectical relation between ideal formulations and actual behaviour. Leach laboured to convince his readers that despite various events over time (especially from 1890–1954) among the people of Pul Eliya and their closest neighbours who consider themselves of the same variga (sub-caste/territorial corporation), events that had to do with changes in the ownership over plots and associated water rights (especially in the Old Field and old residential area), despite drastic changes in the economic status of individual families and their heirs (changes in regard to economic differentiation), and despite changes that made available new categories of land by virtue of governmental policy and legislation, etc., the people of Pul Eliya managed to maintain virtually unchanged the topographical layout of the 'tank-village' in terms of two fields and three *baga*, and of the notion of 'shares' subdivided into strips and their associated agrarian duties of tank and irrigation maintenance. This topographical system (a cultural agrarian model that was influenced by certain given 'natural' economic ecological factors) was existentially more salient and relatively rigid and frozen. But the social system of the locals, exemplified by their 'kinship system', though framed in terms of cultural ideal principles, was in fact much more flexible in its workings, and this 'adaptability' was primarily a response to changes in the ownership of prime land and water rights produced by inheritance, marriage, sales, and gifts.

But when the anthropologist tracks these flexible dynamic social relations (large areas of which are given shape as a dialectic between ideal kin and subcaste rules and actual behaviour), Leach discovers that these actual relations (aggregated as 'statistical orders') are themselves significantly related to the manner in which the actors are spatially situated as contemporaneous contiguous owners and neighbours, or as potential neighbours or combiners of plots through marriage. The agrarian system as such that requires that owners of neighbouring strips must cooperate to maintain irrigation, must get along to work the system of water sharing, and also the system of strip location and that tells people which physical combination of contiguous plots are worth possessing or acquiring—ultimately has a steering role to play in the social relations of people, and the actual patterns that 'debts of social obligation' and ties of amity assume on the ground. It is in this sense that 'locality rather than descent forms the basis of corporate grouping' in Pul Eliya.[67]

7. The Engagement with Structuralism

The year 1961 also saw the first attempts by Leach at structuralist analysis of myths influenced by certain Lévi-Straussian precedents. In 1955 Lévi-Strauss had published the essay 'The Structural Study of Myth'[68] containing his famous decoding of the Oedipus myth, and in 1958 he had published the even more important tour de force 'La Geste d'Asdiwal',[69] that—in due time, but not immediately—came to have a special recognition as an exemplar in British academic circles.

Leach responded to the stimulus of Lévi-Straussian structuralist myth analysis with two 1961 essays: 'Golden Bough or Gilded Twig?',[70] and 'Lévi-Strauss in the Garden of Eden: An Examination of some recent Developments in the Analysis of Myth'.[71] And in the following year, he published the remarkable essay, 'Genesis as Myth'.[72]

'Genesis as Myth', brief though it is, dealt with three stories from the first four chapters of Genesis—the story of the seven-day creation, the story of the

[67] Bourdieu, *Outline of a Theory of Practice*, p. 9.

[68] Lévi-Strauss, 'The Structural Study of Myth', *Journal of American Folklore*, 68 (270) (1955). A modified version was printed in his *Anthropologie Structurale* (Paris, 1958), the English version of which is *Structural Anthropology* (New York, 1963).

[69] Lévi-Strauss, 'La Geste d'Asdiwal', *Annuaire de l'E.P.H.E.* (Sciences Religieuses) (1958–59, Paris).

[70] *Daedalus*, 90 (2) (Spring 1961), 371–87.

[71] *Transactions of the New York Academy of Sciences*, (series 2) 23 (4) (1961), 386–96.

[72] *Discovery*, 23 (5) (May 1962), 30–5. Reprinted in Edmund Leach, *Genesis as Myth and Other Essays* (London: Jonathan Cape, 1969).

Garden of Eden, and the story of Cain and Abel. Leach generously states that 'this approach to myth analysis derives originally from the techniques of structural linguistics associated with the name of Roman Jakobson, but is more immediately due to Claude Lévi-Strauss . . . '.[73]

Although some of his writings were known to individual anthropologists, it might be said that Lévi-Strauss made his official entry into British anthropological circles when the Association of Social Anthropologists (ASA) held a seminar in June 1964 in Cambridge to examine his writings on myth analysis and totemism. This seminar actually originated in the Spring of 1963 when members of ASA meeting in Oxford decided to devote a future session to this genre of his writings, and consequently invited certain persons, notably Mary Douglas, K. O. L. Burridge, Michael Mendelson, Peter Worsley, and Robin Fox, to prepare papers. Subsequently, Edmund Leach was invited to serve as the seminar convener in Cambridge, and, seeing his role as 'strictly catalytic', he circulated to participants copies of an English translation of 'La Geste d'Asdiwal' produced by Nicholas Mann. In *The Structural Study of Myth and Totemism* edited by Leach,[74] this translation of the Asdiwal essay appeared as the head piece followed by the contributions of the above mentioned invited authors, plus a new piece containing Nur Yalman's observations on Lévi-Strauss's first major volume on Amerindian myths, *Le Cru et le Cuit*, which was published in Paris in the autumn of 1964, and had therefore not been available at the time of the Cambridge discussions.[75]

Leach himself recognised retrospectively in print in 1982 that there had been some kind of watershed and change of direction in his subject matter and theoretical concerns. This second phase of his writings roughly stretched from the early sixties to the eighties.

Although Leach expressed critical attitudes towards Lévi-Strauss's writings on kinship, there are many Lévi-Straussian contributions by which he was fascinated, and which he deeply admired, such as Lévi-Strauss's formulations about 'savage' thought,[76] his techniques of decoding myth, and his demonstration of 'transformational' analysis.

In fact, Leach's little Fontana volume entitled *Lévi-Strauss* in 1970, written at a time when some differences had already crystallised between them, is a challenging and fascinating piece of writing to deconstruct. It was translated

---

[73] Leach, *Genesis as Myth*, p. 11.

[74] *The Structural Study of Myth and Totemism*, ed. Edmund Leach, (London: Tavistock Publications, 1967).

[75] Claude Lévi-Strauss, *Mythologiques I: Le Cru et le Cuit* (Paris, 1964).

[76] 'The *Savage Mind* taken as a whole is an entrancing book. The exploration of the way we (the Primitives and the Civilized alike) use different kinds of languages for purposes of classification, and of the way that the categories which relate to social (cultural) space are interwoven with the categories which relate to natural space is packed with immensely stimulating ideas.' Leach, *Lévi-Strauss*, p. 9.

into six languages and ran to three editions. Although critical of Lévi-Strauss's shallow fieldwork, and his reliance on dubious documents, it would seem that Leach on the whole did appreciate Lévi-Strauss's complicated explorations of the thought logic of South American mythology, and was much impressed with his demonstration of homologous and transformational relations on many registers and dimensions. Lévi-Strauss's ingenious decoding attempts stimulated Leach, who already had semiotic leanings, to experiment with similar analyses. Thus it is transparent in chapter 4 ('the Structure of Myth') of *Lévi-Strauss*, where Leach sets out to instruct the reader about Lévi-Strauss's approach to myth, that he cannot resist the temptation to make an authorial substitution and to play at 'Leach imitating Lévi-Strauss'.[77] He gives his own analysis in the Lévi-Straussian mode of interconnected Greek myths (e.g. 'Kadmos, Europe, and the Dragon', 'Minos and the Minotaur', 'Theseus, Ariadne and the Minotaur', and others such as the Oedipus cycle), and suggests the plausibility of Lévi-Strauss's central thesis that the function of mythology is to exhibit publicly, though in disguise, unconscious, existential paradoxes; and that myths deal with irresolvable contradictions that we hide from consciousness because their implications run directly counter to the fundamentals of human morality. Leach's own illustrations reveal that a matrix is formed by the oppositions between the relative positions of human beings and deities and animals, that 'the polarity Nature: Culture, Gods: Men . . . affirms that the relationship between gods and men is one of ambiguous and unstable alliance—exemplified by marriage, followed by feud, followed by marriage accompanied by poisoned marriage gifts'.[78] Such myth messages were congenial to Leach's own independently generated ideas on ambiguous and ambivalent liminal entities and on the nearness of sinning and creativeness. Leach draws a major message from the whole set of Greek stories he analyses: 'If society is to go on, daughters must be disloyal to their parents and sons must destroy (replace) their fathers.'[79] No doubt this message was in accord with his own personal declaration that at some stage a pupil will have to repudiate his own teacher if he is to be creative himself.

One can point to many other affinities between Leach's sense of metaphorical and metonymical logic and many Lévi-Straussian analogies, but Leach was much more cautious than Lévi-Strauss, and modestly agnostic, when it came to the issue of universal trends in the structural patterning of thought categories and other cultural phenomena. He certainly avoided grand pronouncements about the fundamental properties of the human mind, the collective unconscious of the human mind, and underlying relations of an algebraic kind objectively embedded in human thought.

[77] Leach, *Lévi-Strauss*, p. 80.
[78] Ibid., p. 72.
[79] Ibid., p. 80.

Nevertheless, a great deal of his own actual analysis of verbal categories, of myths, of representations in art form and so on did depend on his reliance on binary categories, their contrasts and intersections, and the affective load carried by the overlaps as well as interstices between them. He made liberal use of the Euler diagram to discuss taboo. In certain of his essays he also relied on the tripartite schema of Van Gennep (separation, limnial phase, aggregation) as a general structural pattern applicable to the phenomena at hand (although he would simultaneously insist on understanding the context in which the schema was employed).

It is in certain elaborations and applications of this theoretical bent that we witness the distinctive ways in which Leach's perspective on the work of social anthropology differed from that of Lévi-Strauss. It was in his notable and remarkable essays focused on Biblical materials, early Christian doctrines, and art that Leach demonstrates his own brand of virtuosity. These essays contain transformational analyses of thought structures and symbolic complexes together with their dialectical linkage within the larger social contexts and existential concerns of the people who generated and deployed them.

8. The Comparativist Stance: Us and Them

Leach was trenchantly committed to the view that modern anthropology is as much about 'us' as it is about 'them'. He was also vociferous that 'there is no class of "primitive societies" which can be contrasted with "modern socie-ties" as "static" is to "dynamic"'.[80] This is one of the issues on which he registered his dissent from Lévi-Strauss's distinction between the premodern 'cold societies', resistant to change, and the modern 'hot societies', continu-ously volatile and changing.

Human beings are generative beings and they have always been in tension with their environment. Other peoples, whether of the past or in the present, are like us in certain features, a principle common feature being similarities in linguistic structure. 'Neanderthal man, despite his strange appearance, was a human being like ourselves, a rational creature operating with language in the two crucial domains of metonymy and metaphor.' To an audience of archaeologists, Leach enunciated his 'universalist' position thus: 'Human beings on the Australian continent some 40,000 years ago were rational men like ourselves, for their ancestors had needed to design sea-borne rafts and to exercise forethought.'[81]

[80] Leach, 'Masquerade . . .'.
[81] Leach, 'View from the Bridge', p. 167.

If the people an anthropologist studies in the field are people like us in the senses mentioned above, then their culture can be viewed as a transformation of ours and ours of theirs. We thus arrive at a point where we have to introduce a conception favoured by Leach in the second phase of his theorising, namely 'transformational transcription'. In the context of viewing culture as a 'text', he associates transformational relations in the ways linguists like Jakobson and Chomsky used the term. (Leach ultimately associated transformation with 'mathematical' manipulations, and in his later writings resorted to that label to encompass quite a number of his structuralist demonstrations.)

Thus Leach's firm repudiation of evolutionism in its crude nineteenth-century form, and of the quest for 'the ultimate primitive who is "quite different" from civilized man', was linked to his commitment to a comparative method which looked for 'cross-cultural schema' and transcriptions that spanned both the alleged 'primitive societies' and the modern 'civilized societies.' 'My own prejudices go all the other way. The data of ethnography are interesting to me because they so often seem directly relevant to my own allegedly civilized experiences. It is not only the differences between Europeans and Trobrianders which interests me, it is their similarities.'[82] He demonstrated the fruit of this comparativist view when he juxtaposed high Christian theology with 'primitive' materials allegedly documenting ignorance of the facts of physiological paternity in his famous essay on 'Virgin Birth', which he delivered as the Henry Myers Lecture in 1966.[83] Each schema compared entailed fitting pieces of ethnographic evidence that came from a single context to form a pattern; this contextual stipulation separates the structuralist comparative method from the snippets-of-evidence prodigality of Frazer.

Leach's essay was in large part directed at Melford Spiro who had in a 1966 essay criticised an interpretation Leach had made in 1961,[84] in discussing the beliefs and attitudes of the Tully River Blacks concerning sex as reported by Roth in 1903.[85] Roth had concluded that his informants were ignorant of any causal connection between copulation and pregnancy.[86] Spiro had declared himself to be personally persuaded that Roth's statements must mean that the aborigines in question were ignorant of physiological paternity, and had asked 'by what evidence or from what inference can it be concluded that . . . the statements mean what Leach claims they mean?'[87] And Leach

---

[82] Edmund Leach, 'Virgin Birth'. The Henry Myers Lecture 1966. Reprinted in Edmund Leach, *Genesis as Myth and Other Essays* (London, Jonathan Cape, 1969), p. 97.
[83] *Genesis as Myth and Other Essays*, pp. 85–112.
[84] E. R. Leach, 'Golden Bough or Golden Twig?' *Daedalus*, 90, no. 2 (Spring 1961), 371–87.
[85] W. E. Roth, *Superstition, Magic and Medicine*, N. Queensland Ethnographic Bulletin. 5 (Brisbane: Vaughan, 1903).
[86] Leach quotes from his 1961 essay, see 'Virgin Birth', p. 87.
[87] Ibid., p. 87.

accordingly replies, 'What is really at issue is the technique of anthropological comparison which depends in turn upon the kind of "meaning" which we are prepared to attribute to ethnographical evidence.'[88] The merit of his essay, he declares, 'lies in its method'.[89] Leach sets out his method of inference and comparison which he later in the essay identified as 'structuralist' à la Lévi-Strauss, and contrasts it with the neo-Tylorean perspective, which Frazer further distorted and which Spiro himself now espouses.

Of Spiro's method Leach said: 'He believes that explanation consists of postulating causes and ultimate origins for the facts under observation.'[90] And his neo-Tylorean naivete consists in not simply taking an ethnographer's report that 'members of X tribe believe that . . . ' as an orthodoxy, a dogma; Spiro and all neo-Tyloreans 'desperately want to believe that dogma and ritual must correspond to the inner psychological attitudes of the actors concerned'.[91] By way of illustration he gave a witty account of a Church of England marriage service.

Leach charged that a long line of distinguished anthropologists, which includes Frazer and Malinowski as well as Professor Spiro, were 'positively eager to believe that the aborigines were ignorant' while at the same time displaying 'an extreme reluctance to believe that the products of aboriginal thought can be structured in a logical way'.[92] Leach's explanation either anticipates or aligns itself with the early formulations of the critiques of colonialism,[93] and is in advance of some of the later neo-Marxist and 'post-modern' commentary.

The Frazer–Hartland generation of anthropologists were guilty of adopting two mutually inconsistent attitudes to these stories. Where they come from present-day 'primitive' people they are obviously survivals from their earlier primitive stage of ignorance. But the theology of the 'higher religions' manifesting similar patterns was not amenable to anthropological investigation at all: the five volumes of Hartland devoted to the discussions of Virgin birth contain scarcely a single reference to Christianity, and the corresponding volumes of *The Golden Bough* by Frazer 'make no attempt to fit the details of Christian theology into a cross-cultural schema which includes "primitive" materials'.[94]

---

[88] Ibid., p. 88.
[89] Ibid., p. 86.
[90] Ibid., p. 88.
[91] Ibid.
[92] Ibid., pp. 91–2.
[93] I have in mind here such texts as those written by Hymes, and Talal Assad.
[94] 'Virgin Birth', p. 95.

9. The Structural Analysis of Biblical Narratives

Leach found in the Bible a treasure house of narratives, which he construed to be of a mythical nature, and which he found eminently suitable for his kind of structuralist analysis. Fully realising that he was taking a risk in dealing with Old Testament and New Testament texts which had been subject to a long tradition of commentary by Jewish and Christian scholars, he made a serious effort not only to familiarise himself in detail with the Bible translated into English, but also to study commentarial works of scholars dealing with issues pertinent to his own analysis and interpretation. He was also sensibly aware that his approach to the Bible as a unitary mythological text amenable to his kind of structuralist analysis was at variance with that of the Biblical scholars who sought to distinguish different textual genres and to identify in the texts what portions were 'historical' and what portions were not. He took care to say that he was by no means rejecting these scholarly pursuits or trying to prove them right or wrong. He was doing his own thing, and consequently set out his method of procedure and making inferences and establishing patterns. He was offering a new way of reading the Bible.[95]

Leach recognises that historians of the Bible and theologians of Christianity and Judaism may present a formidable obstacle on the basis of their specialist knowledge of interpolations and the 'historical' intentionalities of those whose compositions constituted the Bible. He makes a spirited defence of his approach: 'I take it for granted that none of the stories recorded in the Bible, either in the Old Testament or in the New, are all [*sic*] likely to be true as history. In its present form the Bible is a much edited compendium of a great variety of ancient documents derived from many sources, but the end product is a body of mythology, a sacred tale, not a history book.'[96] Leach is aware that 'all scholarly opinion recognizes that the present recension of the books of the Old Testament is an assemblage of very varied writings which was finally edited and made fully canonical only around 100 BC. Likewise all agree that the purportedly "early" works in the collection contain numerous interpolations which have been inserted from time to time by later editors in the interests of consistency or with a view to providing traditional support for a disputed point of political or religious doctrine.'[97]

---

[95] Leach himself has mentioned that the distinguished Judaic scholar J. Neusner had commented favourably on his writings in *The Talmud as Anthropology*, Annual Samuel Friedland Lecture (The Jewish Theological Seminary of America, 1979).

[96] Leach, 'Why did Moses have a Sister?' in Edmund Leach and D. Alan Aycock, eds. *Structuralist Interpretations of Biblical Myth*, (Cambridge University Press, 1983), p. 35. This piece was first delivered as The Royal Anthropological Institute Huxley Lecture for 1980.

[97] Edmund Leach, 'The Legitimacy of Solomon: Some Structural Aspects of Old Testament History', *European Journal of Sociology*, VII (1966), 58–101. It was reprinted in Edmund Leach, *Genesis as Myth and Other Essays* (London, Jonathan Cape, 1969), pp. 25–83. All references here are to this second publication, p. 34.

Since the time of the assemblage, however, the stories of the Old Testament have retained the same structures despite the changing fashions of theology, and Leach argues that he is not concerned with questions of truth in historiographical terms or of Jewish or Christian theology, but with 'patterns or structures in the record as we now have it, and this record has been substantially unchanged over a very long period. To assess these structures we do not need to know how particular stories came to assume their present form nor the dates at which they were written.'[98] Thus he takes the structuralist stand that he is doing comparison not in terms of content but in terms of structures, and that materials and stories that may share little content may well share 'similarities' and 'differences' of structure of a more abstract kind. These structural identities and differences include inversions, transformations, and contradictions. So, in sum, Leach bases his analysis 'on a presumption that the whole of the text as we now have it *regardless of the varying historical origins of its component parts* may properly be treated as a unity'.[99]

'The Legitimacy of Solomon' was first published in 1966 and is, in my view, the best essay on Biblical narratives in the structuralist mode composed by Leach. It illustrates well the way in which Leach extracted structural patterns and existential dilemmas from Old Testament materials.

Leach makes a fundamental point of method and interpretation in this essay, which he would try to implement and demonstrate in this as well as subsequent treatments of the Bible and early Christianity: 'we may compare one myth with another and note the varying positions and mutual relations of the various elements concerned *but we cannot go further without referring back to the total ethnographic context to which the myth refers*' (emphasis added).[100] Leach expounds the 'total ethnographic context' in certain Biblical materials in terms of postulating the normative categories relating to tribal segmentation, then mapping these segments onto territory as spatial allocations, and then playing these against the references to alleged actual marriages and sex relations and to political manoeuvres, and other practical realities on the ground. The myths reflect in their own terms the tensions, contradictions, manipulations and fudging that this complex dynamic generates. The relations between these levels are not direct and one to one, but are dialectical interplays that are context-sensitive and open-ended, and exhibit themes and issues deeply embedded in Jewish culture.

Leach states that his 'purpose is to demonstrate that the Biblical story of the succession of Solomon to the throne of Israel is a myth which "mediates" a

---

[98] 'The Legitimacy of Solomon', p. 33.
[99] Ibid., p. 45.
[100] Ibid., p. 30.

major contradiction. The Old Testament as a whole asserts that the Jewish
political title to the land of Palestine is a direct gift from God to the descendants of Israel (Jacob). This provides the fundamental basis for Jewish endogamy—the Jews should be a people of pure blood and pure religion, living in
isolation in their Promised Land. But interwoven with this theological dogma
there is a less idealized form of tradition which represents the population of
ancient Palestine as a mixture of many peoples over whom the Jews have
asserted political dominance by right of conquest. The Jews and their "foreign" neighbours intermarry freely. The synthesis achieved by the story of
Solomon is such that by a kind of dramatic trick the reader is persuaded that
the second of these descriptions, which is morally bad, exemplifies the first
description, which is morally good.'[101]

In a nutshell, the irresolvable problems engendered in Jewish Biblical
history can also be seen as an agreement with the following elementary
formulas of general significance. A taboo against incest coupled with a rule
of exogamy provides a basis for forming marriage alliances between
antagonistic groups within a single political community. Furthermore, it is
the nature of real political communities that they consist of self-discriminated
groups which are at any point in time either mutually antagonistic or in
alliance. A rule of endogamy provides a basis for expressing the unitary
solidarity of a religious community, the chosen people of God. In real life
the religious communities and the political communities seldom coincide.
There is a total incompatibility between a rule of endogamy and the recognition that society consists of politically antagonistic groups allied by
marriage.

When one reflects upon all Leach's essays on Biblical narratives one notes
with interest his assertions that they embody and convey religious truths or
'metaphysical truths' and not other kinds of truth, 'historical' or 'scientific'.
Religious truths are presented in terms of a 'mytho-logic'. Leach seems to
have concluded in the latter part of his career that if most religions are
concerned with the mediation between omnipotent deity in heaven and human
beings on earth, or between the supernatural realm and this world, then all the
interesting actions—the puzzles, the paradoxes and their attempted solutions,
the transformational operations that result in a change of state—lie primarily
at the level of this mediation. A virtually omnipresent human preoccupation is
the transformational nexus between life-death-rebirth or resurrection, including the passage of the dead to ancesterhood and their regeneration in successor
generations. The religious truths that in fact surface in the Biblical materials
revolve around liminal states and interstitial spaces, and with special beings
who are simultaneously kings and prophets, saints and sinners, mediators and

---

[101] 'The Legitimacy of Solomon', p. 40.

tricksters. The Bible affirms the role of the wilderness and the value of the reclusive life for having special experiences and acquiring special energies. It is from that space and regime that the prophet emerges to preach the message and perform heroic acts, even miracles. The religious truths also seem to focus on the dialectics of sexuality and procreation, incest taboos and marriage rules, and their observance and transgression, and on the tensions between endogamy and exogamy—all of which have implications for the maintenance of ancestry and group boundaries and personal identity. It also seems that religious narratives suggest in the face of official rules that the creative powers of foundational patriarchal leaders are linked to their breaking those rules (as seen from the unorthodox marriages of Moses and Joseph). Lastly, Leach's establishing the immense importance and necessity of female figures in the Biblical narratives, despite the male orientation of the edited canonical version, must be of interest and congenial to feminist writers on early and later Christianity, as well as on comparative religions.

10. Anthropology of Art and Architecture

Leach had always on the side been interested in the objects and artefacts of the so-called 'premodern'/'primitive' societies which had simultaneously aesthetic and religious/ritual and practical significances, and which in any case must be understood in the contexts of their use. The practice of removing objects from their contexts of production and use and placing them in museums for viewing as exhibits was an issue on which he had acerbic things to say. He was an advocate of informed ways of assembling museum objects that gave the alien viewer a sense of their multivalent attributes and the contexts in which they were originally deployed.[102] He was particularly interested in Melanesian objects, especially those from the Sepik River region, and from the Trobriands,[103] and in

---

[102] See E. R. Leach, 'Aesthetics' in *The Institutions of Primitive Society. A Series of Broadcast Talks* by E. E. Evans-Pritchard, Raymond Firth, Edmund Leach, *et al.* (Oxford, Blackwell, 1954), pp. 25–38. Reprinted as 'Art in Cultural Context' in *Cultural and Social Anthropology. Selected Readings*, ed. Peter B. Hammond (New York, Macmillan, 1964), pp. 344–50.

[103] The fine collection of Sepik artefacts collected by Gregory Bateson was deposited in the Haddon Museum at Cambridge University, and was much appreciated. Anthony Forge, a pupil of Leach later studied Sepik artefacts and became an authority on them. Leach was very interested in the artistic, aesthetic, and textual researches of Giancarlo Scoditti, who did fieldwork in Kitava in the Trobriands. He was particularly taken with a wood carving of Monikiniki (snake figure) in Scoditti's collection. Malinowski had recognised Monikiniki as being in some sense the mythical founder of Kula, but had not recorded the relevant mythology. Leach had urged Scoditti to present the mythology he had recorded together with the iconographic decoding of the carving illustrated with photographs. I am grateful to Giancarlo for providing me with some correspondence written by Leach on this matter.

Hindu and Buddhist iconography.[104] He very much cherished his election as a Trustee of the British Museum.

It was, however, when he was engaged in his structuralist analysis of Biblical narratives and Christian art and movements that Leach, who had a discriminating visual faculty and had a phenomenal visual memory, began systematically to examine and reveal the relationships among doctrinal cosmologies, their institutional realisations, and their visual and tactile representations in Art and Architecture. As previously underscored, Leach was irresistibly drawn to experimenting with and testing new ideas on anthropological materials and to making interdisciplinary connections.

I recommend two essays by Leach which portray his structuralist interpretations and anthropological perspectives on art and architecture, namely 'Melchisedech and the emperor: icons of subversion and orthodoxy',[105] and 'Michelangelo's Genesis: A structuralist interpretation of the Sistine Chapel ceiling'.[106]

It is the latter essay, that I shall consider here. 'Michelangelo's Genesis' had a long run on the lecture circuit originating as an illustrated lecture given at the Slade School of Art in University College London, on 9 February 1977; a version without illustrations (a mishap due to a printers' strike) was published in *The Times Literary Supplement* on 18 March of that year. Much revised versions of the lecture were subsequently given to a variety of anthropological/history of art audiences in widely dispersed localities including Vancouver, Cambridge, London, and Sydney. The final version printed in *Semiotica* (1985), together with eighteen plates of the panels of the Sistine Chapel, was based on a lecture given to an Indiana University audience in Bloomington in October 1984 as one of the Patten Foundation lectures.

Leach's topic is the patterning of the iconography in the principal pictures on the ceiling of the Chapel. He is humbly aware that there is a vast bibliography of writings relating to Michelangelo and many treatises by art historians devoted to describing, commenting, and interpreting the panels. But

---

[104] In a quite early essay Leach included in his exposition the significance of iconographic features in Hindu–Buddhist sculpture: see Edmund Leach, 'Pulleyar and the Lord Buddha: an aspect of religious syncretism in Ceylon', *Psychoanalysis and the Psychoanalytic Review* 49, no. 2 (Summer 1962), 81–102.

[105] Edmund Leach, 'Melchisedech and the emperor: icons of subversion and orthodoxy' Presidential Address of the Royal Anthropological Institute 1973, and published in *Structuralist Interpretations of Biblical Myth*, ed. Edmund Leach and D. Alan Aycock, (Cambridge, Cambridge University Press, 1983), ch. 4, pp. 67–88.

[106] Edmund Leach: 'Michelangelo's Genesis: Structural Comments on the Paintings of the Sistine Chapel Ceiling', *The Times Literary Supplement*, 18 March 1978. Revised version in *Semiotica* (December 1985). Two other notable essays which cannot be treated here are: Edmund Leach, 'The Gatekeepers of Heaven: Anthropological Aspects of Grandiose Architecture', *Albuquerque Journal of Anthropological Research*, 39, no. 3 (1983), 243–64; Edmund Leach and Revd John Drury, *The Great Windows of King's College Chapel*. (Published by King's College Chapel, 1988).

he is proposing that his structuralist mode of analysis has something to offer that has been missed out by most of the art historians.[107]

Obviously Michelangelo had to some extent intentionally evolved a design of the artistic project he was about to execute; and he was to some extent constrained by the materials he had to work with, by the existing structure of the Chapel, by the wishes and requirements of his patrons, the principal one being the Pope, by the Biblical Treatment of his artistic theme, by prior and current art styles, and so on. So what is it that Leach thinks his theory and method of structuralism can reveal that is special to it?

> Michelangelo was working within a long established artistic convention which is manifested in a whole series of quite explicit cross-references from the Old Testament to the New through the ordering of the designs. However, when he molded that convention to fit in with the particular requirements of the total logic of his complicated overall design, it seems very likely that he did not fully understand, at a conscious level, just what he was doing. He did what he did partly because that was how the jigsaw puzzle worked out, but also because that was somehow how it had to be. My purpose is to show you, at least in part, just why it had to be like that.
>
> It is this kind of part-conscious, part-unconscious, subliminal logic that the structuralist is looking for because *he* believes that the structure of such a logic will help us to understand something of significance about the nature of aesthetics and of the operation of human minds in general.[108]

Leach focuses in this essay on the nine main panels and the four corner panels of the Sistine Chapel ceiling. I can only convey briefly his interpretive method and some of the main points he makes and leave it to the interested reader to study closely the eighteen plates and one figure in the original essay.

> Notice at once that the nine center panels are arranged in alternation small-large-small-large. This was dictated in part by the physical form of the roof. But, besides having to adjust his overall composition to the peculiarities of the shape of the vaulting Michelangelo also took account of the various uses of the floor space below.
>
> As it is today the screen which separates the ante-chapel from the chapel proper comes under Panel 7 'Noah's Sacrifice' but the screen was originally closer to the altar and stood directly beneath the border between Panel 5 'The Creation of Eve' and Panel 6 'The Fall'.
>
> This detail is important because it meant that the distinction between the Chapel proper (at the Altar end), which was reserved for the Pope and the

---

[107] Leach mentions that a paper by the art historian, S. Sinding-Larsen ('A Re-reading of the Sistine Ceiling' in *Acta ad Archaeologiam et Artum Historiam Pertinentia*, vol. iv, 143–57, Rome: Institutum romanum Novegiae, 1969) has conclusions 'that dovetail in very well with those of my own account which relies on a quite different technique of analysis'. He encountered this paper a good while after he had produced his first version, and therefore finds the coincidence of views reassuring.

[108] 'Michelangelo's Genesis', p. 4.

Cardinals, and the Ante-Chapel, which was sometimes open to aristocratic laity, is marked in the ceiling as the distinction between Sacred and Profane.

All the main panels to the West of the screen (as it then was) show God in his role as Creator; all the main panels to the East of the screen towards the door, show sinful man without God. Directly over and to the East of the screen is the crisis of the Fall, the boundary between this World of Suffering and the Other World of Paradise. It is relevant that in medieval churches the screen separating the nave from the choir was commonly fronted by a crucifix and known as the 'rood-screen' on that account.

The general structure of the iconography is as follows. Panels 1, 2, and 3 show God in the Cosmos without Man. Panels 4, 5, and 6 show the Garden of Eden Story in which God and Man are together in Paradise. Panels 7, 8, and 9 relate to the story of Noah where sinful Man is in this World separated from God. Thus the middle triad mediates the two extremes. This mediation pattern is repeated in various symmetries.

Throughout his explication of the panels Leach probes the logic of their arrangement as triads. Invoking his favourite Euler diagram, he focuses in particular on the intersecting boundary between two opposed categories as the mediating and creative and ambiguous betwixt and between component. Thus the middle panel in the triadic arrangement of panels, and again the middle part within a panel, are focused on as special zones of the sacred, the sites of ritual action, and the locus of intermediaries who combine opposite values, or who are generative in producing the paired polarities.

Leach identifies the manner in which different episodes and persons in the Genesis account are elided and fused in some of the panels. He next shows that the panels simultaneously cross-reference Old Testament episodes with New Testament ones, and that there is both a prefiguration of events to come from the Old to the New as well as an inversion in the meaning from negative fall of man to positive redemption of man through Christ.

> It is only quite recently that the critics have noticed that for an ordinary lay observer the sequence is back to front, Creation in reverse. Entering by the door at the East end we start with Man alone in his corruption and are led back step by step to assimilation with God. The unstated text for the whole composition is the passage from St. Paul: 'As in Adam all die; so also in Christ shall all men be made alive'.
>
> This Old Testament/New Testament inversion is reiterated all the way through. The key points for our understanding of this fact have already been mentioned. First, Eve, whose creation has pride of place at the Center, is also the Virgin Mary, the second Eve, the 'Church of my Salvation', just as Adam is also the second Adam, Christ the Redeemer. But furthermore, where one might expect a Crucifix above and in front of the rood screen, we in fact encounter a cruciform Tree of Life around which is coiled the Serpent of the Garden of Eden. Of that more in a moment.[109]

---

[109] 'Michelangelo's Genesis', pp. 20–1.

It is in Panel 6 that

> the key ambiguity comes, as it should, at the center in the form of the
> Serpent/Tempter coiled around the Tree of Life and in that of the Tree itself.
> There are really two serpents; one faces the still innocent Eve and *grasps* her
> by the hand; the other is the arm of God, the Biblical Cherubim who drives
> out the sinners from the Paradise Garden armed with a flaming sword which
> turned every way, to keep the way of the tree of 'life'.
>
> But the two serpents combined to provide yet another key symbol. There
> was a medieval tradition that the crucifix on which Christ died to redeem our
> sins was cut from the Tree of Life that grew in the Garden of Eden. Here, in
> the picture, the Serpent, the Cherubim and the Tree are combined in a
> cruciform image which stands, let us remember, above and just in front of
> the rood screen. This device of the double headed serpent forming a cross is
> repeated in the corner panel to the right of the altar.[110]
>
> The text for this [latter] picture [of the double-headed serpent forming a
> cross] comes from Exodus. The Israelites wandering in the Wilderness
> complain to God who punishes them for their lack of faith by sending a
> plague of serpents. Moses appeals to God. God instructs Moses to set up a
> brazen serpent with the promise that those who gaze upon this seemingly
> idolatrous figure will be be cured. Michelangelo depicts this scene using a
> long established convention. Moses does not appear. The saved and damned
> are separated, the saved being on the altar side, to the left of the picture. As
> before, the serpent is two headed though here it is an explicit symbol of
> salvation instead of an explicit symbol of damnation. In this case the
> crucifix-serpent is lit by the glory of God shining from the divine light of
> Panel 1 immediately above.
>
> The association between the story of *The Brazen Serpent* and the
> Crucifixion has direct biblical sanction. It comes in St. John's Gospel:
> 'And as Moses lifted up the serpent in the wilderness even so must the
> Son of Man be lifted up: that whosoever believeth in him should not perish
> but have eternal life'. That much the orthodox critics have noticed, but they
> have not paid any attention to the consquential feedback for our under-
> standing of the corresponding imagery in Panel 6 which, as we have seen,
> puts the Crucifix in the Garden of Eden. The implication is surely plain. As
> we proceed from the altar towards the door the Serpent in the Tree of Life
> stands for damnation through Adam; as we reverse our steps and move from
> the door to the altar the same image is symbolic of Christ on the Cross of
> Death and stands for salvation through Christ.[111]

Leach deals with a number of other inversions, but the summary implication
of all of them is that 'at a grand scale level, the Old Testament message
concerning the Creation and the Fall, that appears in the panels when read in
sequence from altar to door, should be inverted and read as a New Testament

---

[110] Ibid., pp. 21–2.
[111] Ibid., p. 25.

message of Redemption through the Crucifixion and the Eucharist when the same panels are read from door to altar'.[112]

The New Testament meaning, he claims, is ordinarily the direct converse of the manifest Old Testament meaning, and this argument rests on the 'mytho-logic' uncovered by his structuralist reading. Modern orthodox scholarship tends to be scornful of ambiguity, 'yet many practicing artists would themselves maintain that all artistic statement is ambiguous'.[113]

'Michelangelo's Genesis' is perhaps Leach's most ambitious attempt on the anthropology of art. He boldly ventures into a field that is considered the province of art historians, and while acknowledging their scholarship and contributions, he proffers his own 'structuralist' analysis of an artistic production as capable of bringing to light certain features unconsidered or unseen by most of them. The essay attempts to demonstrate the systematic nature of the structuralist method he espoused and developed, and the imaginative revelation of the powerful, creative, and transformative role of ambiguous in-between middle terms in triadic arrangements. It has to be admitted that some art historians have been critical of his venturing into their domain, and that by and large most of them, as well as most anthropologists, have not engaged with his efforts in this direction. I personally think that this is to be deplored.

11. The Work of Sustaining Institutions

Provost of King's College

Edmund Leach was elected a Fellow of King's College in 1960; he was elected Provost of King's in 1966. 'Though still relatively new to the College, his election as Provost in 1966 came as no surprise. It fitted the mood of the times, a mood for change.'[114]

We may recall that Mao's Cultural Revolution had begun in 1966 (and raged for a decade) in China. By the late sixties student activism and radical politics including demonstrations against nuclear weapons were in ferment both in Europe and in the United States. May 1968 saw the militant student uprising in Paris; soon afterwards in the United States the repudiation of the Vietnam War and opposition to conscription came to a boil. It is possible that taking cognisance of the Cultural Revolution in China, and seeing signs of impending student militant politics, Leach may have used the Reith Lectures delivered in 1967 as a platform to talk of necessary change in Britain and the need for scientists and policy makers to act creatively and responsibly. In *A*

---

[112] 'Michelangelo's Genesis', p. 27.
[113] 'Michelangelo's Genesis', p. 28.
[114] Hugh-Jones, *Edmund Leach*, p. 31.

Runaway World?[115] Leach upbraided the older generation for having failed to create a viable world for young people to live in; he linked youthful disorder to a breakdown of family life, and urged a reform in the current educational system, the proper task of which is to impart genuinely creative and relevant knowledge to face the challenges of a world propelled by technological revolution. By the late sixties, many students in Cambridge wanted representation in college councils and were advocating withdrawal from financial involvements in South Africa.

How did Leach as head of a famous House deal with its affairs during the twelve years of his tenure? Let me quote parts of an account of Leach's performance by Stephen Hugh-Jones, who having been an undergraduate at King's, was thereafter a doctoral student under Leach's direction, and later a Fellow of King's, throughout Leach's years as Provost (1966–79):

> The stage was set for a rethinking of the College and changes there were — the Hall was turned back to front, the servery became a self-servery, the high table was made low, and English not Latin became the Provost's language in Chapel. More significantly it was under his Provostship that King's, after years of discussion and contention, finally decided to admit women as undergraduates and Fellows. Edmund took personal pleasure in the fact that, despite the wrangles, the final vote was approved *nem con* at the congregation on 21 February 1970.[116]
>
> The admission of women went hand in hand with another change in the social make up of the College, an increasing number of students from state schools, the result of an admissions policy inaugurated by Provost Annan and championed by Edmund and his ex-student and colleague [physical anthropologist] Alan Bilsborough. The students' relations with this Provost were respectful rather than close; they admired him but did not know him well. These were also years of student militancy and here, rather to the surprise of many, especially the students themselves, the same man who, in his Reith Lectures, had seemed to advocate greater permissiveness and the ceding of power from the old to the young, now seemed to play a cautious and often rather conservative role.
>
> An enthusiastic supporter of another major change, student representation on the College council and other administrative bodies, he was rather less enthusiastic about the targets and manner of their other demands and protests. Though a rebel himself, when confronted by other rebels his conservatism came to the fore. For Edmund they simply did not go about it all in the right kind of way nor behave in the manner that he thought students ought. With students in mind he expressed his views as follows — 'the whole system of things and people which surrounds us coerces us to be

---

[115] Leach, *A Runaway World?*

[116] Both Leach and Hugh-Jones are in error regarding this historic occasion. The Minutes of the King's College Council state that 'at an ordinary congregation held on 27 May 1969' the motion for the admission of women was carried with 'Ayes 48 and the Provost, Noes 5, Abstentions 6'.

conformist; even if you want to be a rebel you will still have to go about things in a conventional way if you are to gain recognition and not to be rated insane'.

An active and efficient administrator, he took pleasure in 'making things work'. He certainly liked power but it was not power over people that he wanted but the power to put his ideas and plans into effect and then watch them run. This mechanic's interest in systems fitted with his anthropologist's interest in people and their institutions. In the machinations of College affairs he was neither autocratic nor devious and he knew how to delegate.

The years of his Provostship coincided with his emergence as a man of public affairs, the holder of numerous appointments, and with a gradual transition from young Turk to an Establishment figure. As Chairman of its Needs Committee he played an important role during his period on the General Board. A tough, independent and determined administrator with a good strategic mind, he championed the need for long term planning within the University and helped to push through a number of structural reforms, most notably the grouping of the Arts faculties into Inter-faculty Committees in line with the Sciences.[117]

Edmund retired from the Anthropology Department in 1978 and from the Provostship the year after and became an elder statesman, full of wise council and ever ready to back and encourage new projects and initiatives. Apart from a truly splendid farewell feast in the Hall, marked by his memorable speech about himself as a 'dying god', he went out of his way to avoid all forms of memorial, festschrift and the like.[118]

Aside from his acts of generosity towards research students through the Esperanza Trust (of which more shortly), and from his own private funds, Leach made some gifts to King's. He transferred to the College his quite substantial house and garden at Storey's Way, and had willed half the proceeds of the sale of his valuable library for making long overdue improvements to the library of the College.

Fellow and president of the Royal Anthropological Institute
'The Institute is very close to my heart' (Leach)

The following notice of Leach's passing away composed by Adrian C. Mayer appeared in *Anthropology Today*:

Professor Sir Edmund Leach, born in 1910, died in Cambridge on 6 January 1989. An Obituary will be published shortly in A.T.: but Fellows and Members of the Royal Anthropological Institute owe a special debt to Edmund which should be separately expressed.

From the time when he was first elected to the Council in 1946, Edmund

---

[117] Hugh-Jones, *Edmund Leach*, pp. 31–2.
[118] Ibid., p. 34.

was one of the most active supporters of the Institute, seeing the help he gave it as being part of his more general advocacy of anthropology in the world at large. During the late 1950s and 1960s, he took a leading part in moves to enlarge the Fellowship and reorganize the Institute's publications. But his greatest challenge came in 1971, when his Presidency coincided with the Institute's loss of its premises in Bedford Square and with a low point in its finances. It was characteristic of his commitment that he agreed to serve an extended four-year term, by the end of which the Institute's affairs had started to turn, under the long-term objectives set out by the Development Committee he had formed in 1972. Thereafter, Edmund continued as an active Vice-President, attending most Council meetings—at which his contributions were, as might be expected, imaginative and controversial as well as helpful.

It will be a cause of great satisfaction to his colleagues to know that he lived to see the Institute attain most of its objectives for which he had worked, often through the generous support of the Esperanza Trust, of which he was the donor and principal trustee. Without its help, the purchase of the Institute's premises would have been jeopardized, the development of A.T. put at risk, and many of its academic initiatives weakened. That the Institute has been able to respond to a changing world has to an important degree been due to Edmund's initiative and practical support.[119]

The RAI published (as its *Occasional Paper* no. 42) 'a near-complete bibliography of his publications over the fifty years of his career, as a tribute to its former President and as a working tool for scholars . . . The first item in the bibliography is a letter to *The Times* published in 1935 about reforms in China; the last (apart from posthumous publications) is an anonymous leaflet on the Great Windows of King's College Chapel, Cambridge, co-authored with the Dean of King's.'[120] Among other things, the Preface to the Bibliography written by the then President of the RAI, Eric Sunderland, says: 'he established and generously endowed the Esperanza Trust for Anthropological Research, and he continued to be intimately involved in its affairs, which included assisting in the purchase of the Institute's current premises, its launching and sustaining of *Anthropology Today*, and myriad other matters of concern to anthropology generally, under the umbrella of the RAI'.[121]

The Esperanza Trust was named after the sugar factory, La Esperanza, on the estates of Hermanos Leach in the Argentinian province of Jujuy, and was funded from money Leach had inherited from its sale. A statement by the RAI says 'According to the Founder's wish, the Trust gives unobtrusive support to the Institute's work in many ways as well as funding the Leach/RAI Fellowships'.[122]

---

[119] *Anthropology Today*, 5, no. 1 (February 1989), 1. The obituary written by Chris Fuller and Jonathan Parry 'Petulant inconsistency? The intellectual achievement of Edmund Leach' was published in *Anthropology Today*, 5, no. 3 (June 1989), 11–14.
[120] Publication notice of the RAI Distribution Centre, Letchworth.
[121] *Edmund Leach: A Bibliography*, p. 1.
[122] Edmund Leach served as Chair of the Esperanza Fund until his death. Audrey Richards was one of the Trustees (among others), and after her retirement Jean la Fontaine replaced her, and after Leach's death, became Chair.

As Mayer and Sunderland have already intimated, Leach made other benefactions to the Institute: a small collection of antique Chinese pottery was given to it to auction; and he left half the proceeds of the sale of his valuable library to it. Leach effectively used his financial and administrative skills to help the Institute regain its vitality. He also no less importantly vigorously urged and led the launching, as a supplement to the *Journal*, of another publication, *Anthropology Today,* which would deal with contemporary issues and new intellectual and artistic pursuits that would appeal to a wider reading public than the professionals. He saw the relevance of giving more visibility to ongoing studies on race relations, refugee studies, studies of feminist issues, and ongoing efforts in visual anthropology, including the burst of ethnographic and other documentary films.

His own concern with the state of racial prejudice and race relations in Britain is reflected in 'Noah's Second Son. A Lady Day Sermon at King's College, Cambridge', published in *Anthropology Today*.[123] The second son is of course Ham, whose descendants were condemned to be 'servants of servants unto his brethren', also by extension 'black' skinned. Leach condemns the notion that people can be sorted into exclusive 'racial categories'. Although he does refer critically to 'apartheid' in South Africa, and other perhaps softer versions of it in India (the caste system) and in Israel where 'racist prejudice' prevails, his main message is 'let us worry about our own society' in Britain. Discussion of this issue is timely because 'If "race" is now a matter of public debate it is because things are changing rather than because they are standing still.' The important changes taking place in Britain are linked with greater opportunities in education: 'the many defects of our present system of attitudes are not immutable. If we fully understand that fact we must not be complacent but we need not despair.'[124]

12. Retirement, Retrospection, and Final Illness

After relinquishing his positions as Professor of Anthropology in 1978 and, a year later, as Provost of King's College, Leach continued to be active and productive for another eight or nine years until poor health drained away his energies and incapacitated him.

Celia and Edmund went to live outside Cambridge in the village of Barrington. 'The Birk' consisted of a simple cottage, and a functional study and compact library. Its marvellous feature was the large garden and orchard, and beyond it many acres of woods kept as a natural reserve.

In retirement, Leach remained quite busy until the end of 1988 not only attending seminars and meetings both in Cambridge and London, but also

---

[123] *Anthropology Today*, 4, no. 4 (August 1988).
[124] Ibid., p. 5.

lecturing abroad especially in the United States. For example, in the Fall of 1979, accompanied by Celia, he spent a term at Cornell University as a Senior Fellow of the Andrew Dixon White Center for the Humanities, and visited some universities to give lectures (including Harvard). He contributed the position paper entitled 'Past/Present: Continuity or Discontinuity' to the Second Annual Symposium on Historical Linguistics and Philology held at the University of Michigan, April 1982;[125] he contributed to the Harvey Lecture Series at the University of New Mexico (1983),[126] and the Patten Foundation Lectures at Indiana University (1984–5).[127] Earlier in 1983 Leach served as the President of XV Pacific Science Congress held at Dunedin, New Zealand, and delivered the address 'Ocean of Opportunity'.[128] In the same year, he participated as the discussant for a symposium entitled 'Text, Play, Story', organised by The American Ethnological Society (11–14 February 1983) in Baton Rouge, Louisiana. The symposium was planned to coincide with the Mardi Gras in New Orleans.[129]

A conference entitled 'Symbolism Through Time' supported by the Wenner-Gren Foundation Anthropological Research was held in the city of Fez, Morocco from January 13–20 1986. Edmund Leach contributed a paper entitled 'Aryan Invasions over Four Millenia', which was published in a volume edited by Emiko Ohnuki-Tierney, *Culture Through Time. Anthropological Approaches*.[130] The volume was posthumously dedicated by the editor 'to Edmund Leach, a towering intellect and a modest man'.

Leach made his last visit to the United States to present 'Masquerade: The Presentation of the Self in Holi-day Life' at the Tenth Anniversary celebration of the Department of Anthropology at The Johns Hopkins University, and at Harvard University in April 1986.

A cursory look at the list of his publications after retirement between the

[125] This was published in the *Journal of Historical Linguistics and Philology*, 1, no. 1 (1983), 70–87.

[126] The lecture entitled 'The Gate Keepers of Heaven: Anthropological Aspects of Grandiose Architecture' was published in the *Albuquerque Journal of Anthropological Research*, 39, no. 3 (1983), 243–64.

[127] The titles of the two Patten lectures were 'Semiotics, Ethnology, and the Limits of Human Understanding'; and 'Michelangelo's Genesis: A Structuralist Interpretation of the Sistine Chapel Ceiling' which was later published in *Semiotica*, 56, nos. 1/2, pp. 1–30.

[128] A revised version of this address was published in *Pacific Viewpoint*, 24, no. 2 (1983), 99–111.

[129] The Proceedings were published as follows: *Text, Play, Story: The Construction and Reconstruction of Self and Society*; Stuart Plattner, Proceedings Editor, Edward B. Bruner, Editor and Symposium Organiser; Washington, DC: The American Ethnological Society, 1984. Edmund Leach's comments as discussant appear under the title 'Conclusion. Further Thoughts on the Realm of Folly', pp. 356–64.

[130] Stanford, California: Stanford University Press, 1990. Leach's essay appears on pp. 227–45.

years of 1978–88 as given in the Royal Anthropological Institute *Biblio-graphy*[131] shows the enormous number of pieces he wrote especially in the form of book reviews, an activity in which he assiduously engaged, and enjoyed, throughout his career.

In the last years of his life, Leach was engaged in an activity, even a pastime, which he obviously enjoyed. The man who cared not for a commemorative festschrift from his past students, colleagues, and friends, who was embarrassed by praise and preferred argument, attempted to set the record straight about his social and family background, his career, his experiences as well as his prejudices, in a mode of writing and speaking that combined humour and irreverence, frankness and a near-breaking of academic etiquette. Informative, and in places unconventional, the essay 'Glimpses of the Unmentionable in the History of British Social Anthropology' was written for the *Annual Review of Anthropology* (1984).[132] He turned the 'traditional' invitation by the *Review* to eminent professors emeriti and emiritae magisterially to reminisce about their careers into a polemical and experimental exercise in the sociology of knowledge. The essay featured an innovative and controversial thesis concerning the link between the theorising of some eminent anthropologists and their social class and nationality.

Edmund Leach passed away on 6 January 1989. He had not wanted a memorial service for the same reason he had not wanted a festschrift to commemorate his retirement in 1978. But there was a funeral service at King's College Chapel at which the College's famed angelic choir sang for him.

The high points of the service, besides the singing of the choir, were 'the Address', given by Stephen Hugh-Jones; and 'the Reading' by Dadie (G. H. W.) Rylands of John Donne's poem

> Death, be not proud, though some have called thee
> Mighty and dreadful, for thou art not so . . .

At the end of the service, there was a solemn and moving procession from the Chapel, round the front court to the gateway, in this order (which Leach would have anticipated): coffin, family, Provost, Vice-Provost, participants in the service, and Fellows in significant order. An observer noted that above the buildings the setting sun and rising full moon coincided.

After the cremation, tea was served in the College Hall to all the guests.

STANLEY J. TAMBIAH
Harvard University

Note. I thank Michael Herzfeld for valuable editorial assistance.

---

[131] *Edmund Leach: A Bibliography*, op. cit.
[132] *Annual Review*, 13 (1984), 1–23.

TONY LLOYD

Antony Charles Lloyd
1916–1994

TONY LLOYD was born on 15 July 1916 into a Hampstead family that was part of the Fabian circle. His brother and sister survive him. He would have hated to mention any connections, but it will prove relevant that Tawney was a sort of uncle, G. D. H. Cole lived next door and the Fabians holidayed together: the Lloyds and Bernard Shaw might be found staying with the Webbs. H. G. Wells and Maynard Keynes were visitors. Later Tony's mother would talk of the Bloomsbury set in the same kind of hilarious terms that Tony used in his own story-telling. There is a tale that in 1919–20, Sydney Webb, told his two assistants, one of whom was Tony's father, the political scientist Charles Mostyn Lloyd, that one or other of them must stand for Parliament. Both refused, so the matter was decided by the toss of a coin. C. M. Lloyd stayed where he was. The loser, who stood for Parliament, was Clement Attlee. C. M. Lloyd was a colleague of Laski and Beveridge in the London School of Economics. He was foreign editor and, later, temporary editor of the *New Statesman*. He did not however forget his classical scholarship, but reviewed translations from the Loeb Classical Library for that journal. The Latin spelling of his son's name, Antony, was due to his insistence.

Tony Lloyd would also not have drawn attention to the fact that he had a private schooling. After The Hall in Hampstead, he went on to Shrewsbury, celebrated at the time for its production of classical scholars. According to one story, the choice of private schooling was due to his mother, who is remembered by some as a strong and independent character in her own right. But it was his father, not his mother who influenced Tony.

He went on to Balliol with an exhibition, to read the combination of Classics and Philosophy known as Greats. At his first tutorial, he was told to read a book in German for the next tutorial. The young Lloyd replied, 'But I don't read German.' His tutor looked at him in astonishment and said, 'But

Proceedings of the British Academy, **97**, 347–355. © The British Academy 1998.

there is a fortnight until the next tutorial, Mr Lloyd.' Lloyd thoroughly approved of this attitude and his resulting command of German was to stand him in good stead more than once. He obtained a half-blue for chess, coxed the Balliol second boat, and later engaged in fencing and squash.

After Oxford, he was appointed Assistant Lecturer in Philosophy at Edinburgh, a post which he held until 1946. But his tenure was interrupted by the war. He joined the Queen's Own Hussars, but again the social prestige of the regiment cannot have weighed with him enough to prevent him missing dinner with his Colonel by falling asleep in the bath. He was subsequently transferred. The Italian campaign, in which he was a tank commander, enabled him to learn Italian and his German became useful at a time when German troops were surrendering. He claimed that one captive had been too polite to evade capture, because the signorina had served the spaghetti.

With the war over, in 1946 he was appointed Lecturer in the Department of Logic at St Andrews. His mother was now widowed. After a while, she came to join him and he cooked for her. Cooking eventually became an enthusiasm, but in early days guests have differing memories, one recalling a formal meal, served, slightly cold, by a maid in full attire.

His young colleagues in St Andrews very much admired him. One remembers him as a living Socrates, a challenger of the status quo and a rebel. It was scholastic logic that was being taught when he arrived. He headed a campaign, along with Pat Henderson, who had translated Tarski, and other young Turks including Jonathan Cohen (later FBA), to get Bertrand Russell's logic onto the syllabus. In this, after an initial rebuff, he succeeded.

He persuaded Ian Kidd (now FBA) to deliver his first paper, which Lloyd then tore to shreds. Kidd said, 'I'm sorry you didn't like my paper.' Lloyd looked uncomprehending and replied, 'I liked it very much.' He liked nothing so much as a paper which he thought merited vigorous attack. This could be intimidating to those who did not know him and it sometimes intimidated even his seniors. Beginning with hesitations, he would wind himself up into a torrent of criticism, with quick turns of the head, sometimes finishing with loud bursts of laughter. Some misconstrued this as anger, but in fact it was excitability. If anyone pointed out a mistake in his own reasoning, he would stop at once and acknowledge it with a perfect equanimity which had been missing a moment earlier. His vigorous manner animated his private conversations, as well as his public performances, and his friends were never bored.

His teaching manner at St Andrews was entirely different. One former student, later a colleague, remembers him with gratitude as his best teacher there. He lectured on Logic and on Plato, speaking slowly and clearly, leaving no gaps in explanation, but encouraging interruption and discussion. He once said he would like to be remembered as a teacher.

In 1957, he moved to become Professor in the Liverpool Philosophy Department. He stayed first in a hotel, or, as he would say, *an* hotel, then with his mother in a large, dark, and draughty Victorian house, full of old furniture not unlike his later retirement flat. At times there were festoons of electric cables. Neither of them seemed to notice the Spartan character of the surroundings.

He was a hands off professor, not an organiser of the department. Still less was he willing to take part in University business. He once replied to a University questionnaire that he had no staff members, but he did have five colleagues, and that is how he saw his role. It was his policy to put straight into the waste-paper basket any letters from the University starting with the word 'if'. Letters after 1979 at many universities, of course, would start, 'if we were to implement a 25% cut, . . . '. Other letters from the University administration would survive unanswered until out of date. This was a principled neglect, not a matter of accident; he regarded it as good administration. The University did not penalise him or his department, but, on the contrary, admired his other intellectual gifts. Examiners' meetings were equally innocent of organisation, and not because of any lack of interest on his part in the exact mark each student should receive. This approach did not stop him being in demand as an external examiner because of his unusual range of knowledge.

He did not consider Ethics to be a philosophical subject, as he informed the colleague he appointed to teach the subject before interviewing him. Nor did he have any interest in Philosophy of Religion, or in religion itself, despite his mother's strong religious commitment. But he nonetheless supported these two subjects in his own department. He once advocated a double increment in pay for one of these colleagues with the line, 'although he does not do a proper academic subject, . . . ' Extreme differences in views on ethics, religion, or politics did not necessarily stand in the way of close friendship with him. His philosophical interests were clearly circumscribed, but at the same time they extended into areas far outside those of his philosophical contemporaries. He enjoyed reading Hegel as others might enjoy reading poetry and he was interested in Sartre and Existentialism. The most striking and fruitful example was his concern with Neoplatonism.

He had already published his blockbusting two-part article on Neoplatonic and Aristotelian Logic in 1955–6, two years before his translation to Liverpool. But once in Liverpool, he collaborated with a major Neoplatonist scholar of a very different stripe, who was head of the Classics Department, A. H. Armstrong. Hilary Armstrong, who was elected a Fellow of the Academy in 1970, is known for the best English translation of Plotinus to date. His interest in Neoplatonism was utterly different from Lloyd's, being scholarly and devotional, not that of an analytic philosopher. But he very much appreciated the cooperation Lloyd offered from an uncompromisingly different viewpoint and he persuaded Lloyd to contribute a major article on the later Neoplatonists to the volume he was editing, *The Cambridge History of Later Greek and Early Medieval Philosophy* (1967). This volume was largely written by members of the Liverpool Faculty.

Liverpool was then, and has remained, an important centre for the study of Ancient Philosophy. During Lloyd's time, the Classics Department had H. J. Blumenthal and, as Armstrong's successor, A. A. Long, the History Department H. Liebeschuetz and another subsequent Fellow of the Academy, R. A. Markus, the Philosophy Department Pamela Huby and Howard Robinson. Lloyd also employed as an assistant lecturer from time to time a future President of the British Academy, Anthony Kenny. Gillian and Stephen Clark came after Lloyd left. In 1982, Lloyd started with Blumenthal a series of international conferences at Liverpool on Neoplatonism, which has continued.

He used to invite a small selection of his colleagues for philosophical discussion to his home, where he would serve an excellent wine in beautiful glasses. Sometimes the author chosen for discussion was a classic, for example Spinoza, but often a modern philosopher, Mackie, Wiggins, or Davidson. He had a gift for reducing complex argument to essentials and he reacted vehemently to anything he took to be rhetoric disguising a lack of supporting argument.

There were also fortnightly meetings on Ancient Philosophy with the Manchester departments of Greek and Philosophy, which included for a time C. Lejewski and later George Kerferd and Gordon Neal. The meetings of 1980–1 under Kerferd and Long led to an edition and translation of a work familiar, when it was first suggested, only to Lloyd, Ptolemy *On the Kriterion*.

In the 1980s, he started visiting seminars at the Institute of Classical Studies in London, especially those on the Peripatetic and Neoplatonist commentators on Aristotle, and he was accompanied by up to four members of the Liverpool group. Already at the end of the 1960s, he had visited an Institute seminar in London on Stoicism given by the young A. A. Long. Now in the 1980s, Lloyd encouraged the relevant member of his own department to come and made that financially possible. He would arrive with a set of handwritten exercise books from which he could reel off references to exactly which Neoplatonists had said what and where. He was very diffident, however about inflicting information on colleagues. Some of the most abstruse information was prefaced with an, 'as you know'. More often, he would make rapid allusions to diverse material, as if it was well known to everybody. To get the benefit of his encyclopaedic knowledge, it was necessary to insist on ignorance and then the exercise books would be deployed and the full set of references given. Someone should have been there while he was writing too, to insist on their own ignorance. Not always, but too often, in his writing, one can see that he does not want to tire the reader with information that everyone, in his view, must surely have and the references become fewer as the paragraphs progress towards their end. At his home, besides the exercise books he had a drum of index cards with further handwriting. These records will shortly be available in the Archives of King's College, London. After his retirement to Hove, Lloyd continued to come to London seminars, including now Mario Mignucci's seminars at King's College on Ancient Logic.

After the seminars, he liked a good drink in a pub before proceeding to a convivial restaurant. He probably liked the pub the better of the two. These occasions were much enjoyed by all, but being a bachelor himself, he probably spent most time with fellow bachelors. In conversation he had a rich supply of anecdotes, told often at his own expense. He was a notable raconteur. His willingness to celebrate his own mistakes may have encouraged him in pursuing some hobbies at which he was less than expert. His interest in gardening and in electrical repairs were combined, when in mowing the lawn, he severed the television cables for his and the other flats in the house and sought to repair them with Sellotape. Among other exploits, he bought a lawnmower that didn't work, but on taking it back to the shop where he believed he had bought it, found the owner denied all knowledge of him. (In another version, on reporting his new lawnmower stolen, he returned to find it in his shed.) While trying to repair a light fixture in his flat, he accidentally poked a hole through the ceiling into the WC of the flat upstairs and was threatened with a call to the police. When he went away for any period of time, he would leave his silver with the bank, but often on return had great difficulty in establishing his identity. He was asked to leave a wine-tasting at Woolworths for spitting out the wine into the washing up liquid. To his friends he would have a different story to tell almost every evening they met.

Philosophy and Ancient Philosophy were by no means his only interest. His hobbies were many and various. He started in childhood with a huge butterfly collection. Another thing he collected was Victorian watercolours. He came eventually to love both opera and cooking and compared the two, saying he could read recipes as musicians read scores. He collected French wines and the quality of his wine and cooking is remembered as compensating for the coldness of the rooms. He was widely read in English, French, and Russian fiction of the nineteenth century, although he knew the Russian only in translation, and he had a large collection of nineteenth-century novels, including first editions. He liked French literature best, especially Flaubert and Stendahl. His favourite novel in German was Fontane's *Effi Briest*, his favourite English novelist Trollope. Two professors of English thought he could well have held a chair in their subject. He enjoyed long visits, either alone or staying with his brother, to Italy, France, and Austria, being fluent in all the relevant languages. He also enjoyed, in the spirit of exploration, two academic visits to the USA, one in the 1960s to Lawrence, Kansas, and one to join A. A. Long, after Long had left Liverpool for Berkeley.

Two very different enthusiasms were chatting in working men's pubs and watching soccer. He always went into the public bar, never the lounge or the saloon, and that in the days when entry into the wrong bar could, in some pubs, produce total silence. But he was very well known and liked. A televised soccer match could bring a philosophical conversation to an end almost in mid-sentence. His reputation as a scholar was not the centre of his own perspective and it may have pleased him that the last two hobbies he shared with the common man, although he himself was a very uncommon man. In some ways, he seemed rather old fashioned, with his formal dress and his nineteenth-century pronunciation of Latin.

For all his sociability, he avoided discussing emotional matters, even with close friends, being rather a private man. Music was a great solace to him. One of his friends conjectures that this deterred him from indulging his great love of music in company, lest his reaction should be on public display. For the same reason, he left his own retirement party early, leaving the guests to finish the eating and drinking. He was not a self-publicist, nor a publicist of any kind. When the main annual UK philosophy conference was held in Liverpool in 1968, it was not at Lloyd's instigation, but at the Vice-Chancellor's. Lloyd gave the shortest Presidential address ever and left the stage. He was probably pleased to be elected a Senior Fellow of the British Academy in 1992, but he could not bring himself to tell his brother what the letter was to which he was replying with an acceptance. He did, however react appreciatively to the celebration in Balliol of a then forthcoming Festschrift of 1991, *Aristotle and the Later Tradition, Oxford Studies in Ancient Philosophy* (suppl. vol., ed. Henry Blumenthal and Howard Robinson). This contains a bibliography of his writings on Ancient Philosophy.

He has been described as a Labour Party Leninist in the mould of the Webbs. Among his papers there are some lectures of a syndicalist stripe, but there is no hint of where or when he might have delivered them. Apart from this and from some canvassing for the Labour Party, described in the usual hilarious terms, his political views seem to have influenced his private, rather than his public life. His preference for the working man's bar has been mentioned. He was also against property ownership and that influenced his choice of Hove as a place to retire, because there was a lot of property to rent. He believed in the redistribution of wealth and he also held that the University should play a role in regard to the plight of poor people in Liverpool, considering itself part of the working-class community within which it was located. Yet he confided these intensely held views only to his closest friends and appears not to have tried to persuade the University itself. He was perhaps too private a person and there may be a further key to his inaction in a remark made to a friend that it was no use trying to live up to the life that his father had lived. Certainly, he spoke of his father and his father's work only in a serious tone, never with the high frivolity with which he described much of his own experience. And he regarded his academic life (a life very different from that of today's academic, or of most academics then) as, politically, a self-indulgence.

He made close friendships with people of extremely different political views from his own and he thought it important not to influence the political thinking of students. One student with similar views to his own only discovered this link long after he had ceased being a student.

He found writing difficult and some of his writing is elliptical. This is not so much true of earlier writing, but it is true of the last book, which sums up his insights into Neoplatonism, *The Anatomy of Neoplatonism* (1990). The book contains most valuable insights and would have to be read by all specialists at the graduate level or above, but could not be recommended to those not already well versed in the subject.

In his articles, Lloyd had a gift for drawing attention to topics that had been neglected by recent Philosophy: the idea of individuals as bundles of qualities, the idea of self-awareness, the idea of thought that does not involve propositions, the character of tenses in verbs and the idea that the cause is greater than the effect. His articles on the last four subjects appeared in 1964, 1969–70, 1970, and 1976 and are much more readable than the later book. The first topic was covered only in passing in his densely packed two-part article of 1955–6, but was very well documented.

He contributed articles also in Modern Philosophy, but his work in Ancient Philosophy started with three articles on Plato in 1952–3. He was able in 1955 to take on the daunting task of reviewing a History of Ancient Logic. In 1955–6, he made his name with his two-part article in the first volume of the new journal *Phronesis*, 'Neoplatonic Logic and Aristotelian Logic'. His fluency in German was already proving its value. Not only was Neoplatonism not being studied by English-speaking philosophers, but neither was the German literature. He knew the work of Heinze and Faust and was able to correct the views of Praechter, Prantl, and Erdmann. In his 1955–6 article, he gave an account *inter alia* of the Neoplatonist Porphyry, who in opposition to his own teacher Plotinus, made Aristotle's Logic an indispensible part of Western philosophical education. Lloyd's has been called the best attempt to reconstruct a coherent Porphyry.

But Lloyd had what has been called a love–hate relationship with Neoplatonism. He was more at home with analytical minds like his own: the Stoics, Aristotle and the Aristotelian, Alexander of Aphrodisias, or Porphyry, insofar as Porphyry revived Aristotle's Logic. In Plato he felt there was a lack of argued substantiation. In 1970–1, Lloyd published two articles partly or wholly on Stoic grammatical theory. In one, delivered to the Academy, he drew attention to the Stoic treatment of the tenses and aspects of verbs. In the other, he showed how the Stoics' parts of speech related to their metaphysical categories. In 1978, he published an article that must have pleased him particularly, because it brought some of his closest interests together. He drew attention to a fascinating debate between the Stoics and their Aristotelian adversary, Alexander, on a subject that was made prominent in the twentieth century by Bertrand Russell. The question is what is meant by a statement like, 'Socrates walks'. Does it imply the present existence of Socrates? If so, what are we to make of, 'Socrates is dead'? The question has wider implications for the meaning of declarative statements and of names in general. The moves of the rival ancient Schools are highly ingenious, but the report of them is tucked away where others had not noticed it in Alexander's *Commentary on Aristotle's Prior Analytics* (*Commentaria in Aristotelem Graeca*, vol. 2, part 1, p. 402, lines 1–405, 16). Lloyd's article, 'Definite propositions and the concept of reference', appeared in J. Brunschwig, ed. *Les Stoiciens et leur logique* and it shows, perhaps better than any other, what Lloyd found so interesting about later Greek Logic.

In 1981, Lloyd published a short, but important monograph, *Form and Universal in Aristotle*. He showed that the ancient commentators on Aristotle took him to believe in individual, as opposed to universal, forms. Moreover, repeating a claim already made in *Mind* in 1970, he argued, convincingly, against the then current orthodoxy, that this was indeed Aristotle's view. More controversially, he argued that Aristotle was interpreted, and interpreted rightly, as thinking universals are never objective things, as forms are, but exist only in the mind. And he took Aristotelian individual forms to be individuals in their own right, rather than owing their individuality to something else.

So far Lloyd's interest in ancient Grammar and Logic involved him in no particular conflict, but the later Neoplatonists were harder for him to stomach. Curiously, in his *Cambridge History* chapter of 1970, he doubted (p. 276) whether the Neoplatonists would have anything interesting to say on the Philosophy of Physics and he never investigated this subject. Yet he might have found it less uncongenial than some of the Neoplatonists' attempts to combine Logic with their higher Metaphysics or what he found still more infuriating, their misunderstanding of certain logical matters. He further explains in his *Phronesis* article of 1955 (p. 58) that one cannot look to the Neoplatonists, as one can to the Stoics, for advances in Formal Logic. They cannot be credited with a single theorem. What one can investigate is their Logic in a wider sense, sometimes called Philosophical Logic. But even this was a strain for Lloyd, when he came to later figures. He does not think very highly in his *Anatomy* of Proclus, for example, even though he is willing here and elsewhere patiently to expound him. But he is not always complimentary about the earlier Aristotelian School either. At one point (p. 23), he says: 'It is perhaps an unexpected pleasure to be able to report that this inept tale initiated by the two leading Peripatetics since Theophrastus was not repeated by any Neoplatonist known to us on this subject.' (For these purposes Lloyd was counting Themistius as well as Alexander as a Peripatetic.)

Lloyd's coming to terms with the Neoplatonists is marked by his changed attitude to their mysticism. In 1970, in the *Cambridge History*, he discussed the highest kind of mystical union, which for Neoplatonists is a negation of thought and consciousness. He comments: 'this seems to belong to some Indian mysticism but to have no place in what counts as philosophy in Europe'. By the time of *Anatomy*, he sees the mysticism as very relevant to the Logic after all. Admittedly, he is talking about a lower level of mystical experience, but its relevance had not previously been acknowledged. He describes (p. 126) Neoplatonism as idealist and says that the Neoplatonist hypostases, or levels of reality, are experiences, or types of consciousness. So the element of personal experience is needed to complement the philosophical system. The Neoplatonic genus (p. 166), in striking contrast to Aristotle's, is a mystical experience. Logical structure thus requires mystical support, but also mysticism would lose its philosophical interest were it not for the logical structure. Every real thing (p. 182–3) is a thinking. Accordingly, Lloyd is scholar enough to devote two chapters of the book to a mysticism which he surely found deeply uncongenial. He would not have wanted a Neoplatonist heaven of serene non-propositional contemplation, much less one that lay beyond all thinking, but rather a heaven which included fierce argumentation about propositions, alongside many other delights and distractions.

Curiously enough, he did in conversation appeal to Neoplatonist ideas in attacking Wittgenstein's treatment of thought as closely tied to language. Uncongenial as Neoplatonism may have been in some ways, he used it as a corrective to what he saw as superficial in Wittgensteinianism. Lloyd found in Plotinus, though not in Proclus, a distinction between thought which involved whole propositions and thought which involved only a single concept. Plotinus also talked of grasping the entire intelligible world as a whole. He considered that the highest mystical experience was beyond words and thinking. It would involve silence; words would be useless. Better for the portrayal of some experience would be the Egyptian hieroglyphs, which were not words, but pictorial symbols. The Wittgensteinians, he complained (though this would not have been true of many of them), ignored thinking by means of images and also ignored the idea of grasping something whole.

His written output was more important than its volume might suggest. His lasting legacy resides in the large number of interesting topics from later Greek Philosophy, which had been ignored because they were buried in texts which other philosophers were not reading. Again and again, he unearthed them and revealed their true interest.

RICHARD SORABJI
King's College, London

Note. I want to thank the many friends of Tony Lloyd who gave me information: Hilary Armstrong, Jonathan Barnes, Henry Blumenthal, Peter Brunt, Jonathan Cohen, John Dillon, Raymond Frey, Peter Heath, Paul Helm, Michael Hinton, Pamela Huby, Tony Kenny, George Kerferd, Ian Kidd, Elizabeth Lloyd, Oliver Lloyd, Tony Long, Howard Robinson, Bob Sharples, and Lucas Siorvanes.

SETON LLOYD

Seton Howard Frederick Lloyd
1902–1996

SETON LLOYD died on 7 January 1996 at the age of ninety-three. His long and varied archaeological career of forty years divided naturally into four almost equal phases, each of markedly different character, and was succeeded by an extended period of retirement during which he remained active and involved until very latterly. Beginning in Egypt in 1929, he moved to Iraq in 1930, where his archaeological skills were developed by his participation in the grand scale excavations of the Oriental Institute, Chicago, on the Diyala river. From 1939 to 1949 he held the Iraqi Government appointment of Technical Adviser to the General Directorate of Antiquities, a position which kept him largely in Iraq during the War where he suffered inevitable interruptions from the upheavals of those years. In 1949 he was appointed Director of the recently founded British Institute of Archaeology at Ankara, thus shifting the scene of his activities to Turkey, where he remained in post for twelve years. On return to England, he was an obvious choice to succeed Professor Max Mallowan as Professor of Western Asiatic Archaeology at the Institute of Archaeology, University of London, a post which he held from 1962 until his retirement in 1969. His knowledge of Near Eastern Archaeology, in the shaping of which he had himself played a significant part, was thus unrivalled and survives in many meticulous academic publications as well as more readable works for a wider public.

The course of Lloyd's personal life and career is well documented by himself in his delightful and informal memoir, *The Interval*, so named from a quotation from the philosopher George Santayana.

There is no cure for birth and death but to enjoy the interval . . .

Those who read it can be left in little doubt but that Lloyd enjoyed his active and successful Interval. He was born in 1902 into a substantial Quaker

Proceedings of the British Academy, **97**, 359–377. © The British Academy 1998.

background of well known names, Howards, Cadburys, Frys, Foxes, Gurneys, Barclays, whose family ramifications gave him widespread circles of kinsmen. He was the second child in a family of eight (in a background of large families), and grew up in Edgbaston. His father, a director of the firm Allbright and Wilson, was handicapped by deafness and seems to have been a somewhat remote figure, and it is to his mother Florence (*née* Armstrong) that he refers as a more formative influence. In his memoir he mentions many childhood illnesses, among them polio, but the only visible trace of this in later life was a somewhat immobile face. He was educated at Uppingham.

On leaving school in 1920, he was articled to a firm of Birmingham architects, also attending classes at the Central Municipal School of Art. Subsequently he transferred to London in 1923 and completed his training at the Architectural Association, qualifying as an ARIBA in 1926. Thus his natural aptitude for drawing was trained into fine architectural draughtsmanship, which was to be an important tool in his later, unexpected career. He completed his training with two years as assistant to Sir Edwin Lutyens, and in 1928 set up a small architectural practice with two friends. A career as architect might have been expected to follow, but in fact only a single house in England was designed and built by him in his professional capacity, a pleasant residence for Charles Seltman on the north edge of Dartmoor at Whiddon Down, with a fine view of Cawsand Beacon. Nevertheless it is clear that his years of training were invaluable to him later.

Lloyd's entirely fortuitous entry into archaeology was brought about by a sudden turn in personal relationships, the irony of which was later appreciated by the main participants. Lloyd and his architect friend Brian O'Rorke were both interested in the same young lady. O'Rorke was contracted to join an archaeological expedition in Egypt as advisory architect, but on his becoming engaged and subsequently married to the young lady in question, Lloyd replaced him as member of the expedition. The sequel to this occurred in the following generation, when Lloyd's son John married O'Rorke's daughter Tessa.

Thus it was in 1929 that Lloyd joined the Egyptian Exploration Society's excavations at El Amarna in middle Egypt, then under the direction of the Dutch archaeologist Henri Frankfort. It was a momentous meeting for Lloyd, who later always referred to Frankfort as a formative intellectual influence on his life. As the expedition architect, Lloyd was occupied with planning buildings and drawing objects as he gained his first experience of life on a dig at this rather untypical site with its single period occupation and no stratigraphy. A surviving relic from his time at El Amarna is the model of an Egyptian XVIIIth Dynasty mansion for which he drew the plans. This is still on display in the Egypt Museum in Cairo.

However, the decisive event of the season (for Lloyd at any rate) was not strictly archaeological but the visit to the site of Professor J. H. Breasted with Mr and Mrs J. D. Rockefeller. It transpired that they had come to head-hunt Frankfort to lead the projected expedition to Iraq to be mounted by the Oriental Institute, Chicago. Frankfort accepted but stipulated that he wished to have Lloyd as his advisory architect. So Lloyd was signed up as a member of that magnificently conceived and generously funded project, which was to occupy the next eight years of his life (1930–7). This established him in his archaeological career, and gave him thorough training in quintessentially Mesopotamian conditions. He emerged from the experience as a master of stratigraphic, mud-brick excavation.

He arrived in Iraq in the autumn of 1929 knowing little of the country and its archaeology. Preparations for the projected excavations on the Diyala river were not yet ready, so he had a chance to visit excavations then in progress: Jordan at Warka, Watelin at Kish, Woolley at Ur, and later Campbell Thompson with Mallowan and Hamilton at Kuyunjik. Until the Diyala expedition could be mounted, Frankfort took his team by way of induction for a winter season at Khorsabad, where the Oriental Institute, Chicago, had recently opened excavation. Lloyd found himself in a small but goodly company of outstanding personalities whose names were to become famous in Near Eastern Archaeology: besides Frankfort himself there was Gordon Loud, Thorkild Jacobsen, and Pierre Delougaz. Lloyd's first attempt at excavating mud-brick was unsatisfactory. After he had struggled for some time without perceptible results, Delougaz pointed out to him that he was simply digging into the excellent masonry of the thick city-wall, and proceeded to give Lloyd his first lesson in wall-tracing.

It fell to Lloyd as dig architect to design and build the excavation house at Tell Asmar on the Diyala, already identified from inscribed bricks as the site of ancient Eshnunna. This lay some forty miles east of Baghdad in total desert, well away even from any water source, so the practical difficulties were considerable. The lavish scale on which he was encouraged to build was not solely for the purpose of indulgence but more a practical necessity to provide tolerable living conditions for a substantial team to work many months each year in those inhospitable conditions. His account of the task is typically entertaining, and the house was built, a palatial complex with a towered gatehouse and three courtyards for workrooms, services, and living quarters. The running water for seven bathrooms and eleven lavatories had to be trucked in from ten miles away. Generators supplied electricity. Today only the ruins are visible.

The Iraq Expedition of the Oriental Institute, Chicago, conducted six seasons of excavation from this base, digging for three to four months each year over the winter from November or December to March. At the end of the first season Lloyd was given a proper contract of employment for the duration of the expedition by the Oriental Institute, and thus became one of the key members of the enterprise. The unoccupied part of the year left him free to travel widely in the Middle East and Greece on his way to and from England, and to get to know archaeological colleagues and to familiarise himself with their excavations. He records particularly visiting Crete with John Pendelbury, whom he had known from El Amarna, and also staying at the excavation house of the Oriental Institute's North Syrian expedition at Rihaniya in the Amuq, where he got to know McEwan, Braidwood, and Haines. On his return to England in the summer of 1931 he became engaged to Joan Elizabeth Firminger, whom he married the following year in the South of France. Thereafter she accompanied him each year to the Diyala, but the marriage was not to be a success and they were divorced in 1935.

The work of the Iraq Expedition on the Diyala sites can be seen as a fine team effort by able individuals coordinated by the genius of Frankfort. Each man took responsibility for the excavation and publication of his alloted site(s), but clearly all benefited from collaboration. Tell Asmar was excavated by Frankfort, with Lloyd as architect and Jacobsen as epigraphist, while from the second season on, Delougaz conducted operations at Khafaje from a secondary base. Frankfort did two seasons at Ishchali with Jacobsen, 1934/5 and 1935/6, and Lloyd himself had two seasons alone at Tell Agrab, 1935/6 and 1936/7.

At Tell Asmar Lloyd took over the main responsibility for the major excavated buildings, principally the Palace of the Rulers and the adjoining Temple of 'Gimilsin' (Šu-Sin) in the seasons 1930/1 and 1931/2, and the Northern Palace area including the Abu Temple in the seasons 1931/2–1934/5, while at Tell Agrab in the last two seasons he excavated the Temple of Shara. Also at Tell Asmar he conducted soundings in search of the known main temple E-Sikil, which was never found, and to locate the main city wall.

The Palace of the Rulers had to be excavated down through numerous rebuildings of the Old Babylonian period to the original foundation under the Third Dynasty of Ur. The excavations produced a wealth of epigraphic material, building inscriptions, *in situ* or not, stamped bricks, and other inscribed objects. These permitted a reconstruction of the list of rulers by Jacobsen and the construction of a chronology against which the various building phases could be dated with relative precision. The original foundation proved to be a square temple with *Breitraum* cella approached on a straight axis through a courtyard, built and dedicated by the ruler Ituria for his overlord Šu-Sin of Ur. Obliquely to this, Ituria's son Ilušu-iliya as an independent ruler built his palace. Lloyd's reconstruction of the complex drawn in 1932 was the first of his many such drawings and is well known.

The Abu Temple was first identified in 1932 as a small single-shrine building of the Akkadian period lying just below the surface under an eroded corner of the Northern Palace. In the first such operation which he conducted, Lloyd traced the phases of this temple down through Early Dynastic III to the large square temple of Early Dynastic II, then through successive archaic phases of Early Dynastic I to a small irregular Protoliterate shrine, the earliest building on the site. The most dramatic find of this temple sequence was the hoard of statues found buried beside the altar in one of the shrines of the square temple (ED II). This group of twenty-one statues, mostly men with long hair and beards painted black with bitumen, standing in attitudes of prayer, is one of the most striking finds in the whole of Mesopotamian archaeology, and the two largest figures especially, one male and one female, with their huge, staring, inlaid eyes, unforgettably symbolise the spirit of this archaic period. It was while excavating this temple that Lloyd improvised a simple technique of taking vertical photographs of excavations from above by suspending a camera from kites, an adaptation which has been much copied by his successors.

At an outlying mound, Tell Agrab, Lloyd initiated a survey, then excavated on his own for two seasons with fifty workmen. Relying on a combination of observation and reasoning, he began work immediately above the high altar of the main sanctuary of what turned out to be the Shara Temple. The surviving part of this very large temple was well preserved, and interesting enough for its reconstructable plan but especially for its extraordinarily complete inventory of temple equipment. Among the prize pieces were some fine sculpture and copper figurines including a model chariot driven by a man and drawn by four onagers.

As if the labours of their four month winter–spring season on the Diyala sites were not enough, Jacobsen and Lloyd initiated a subsidiary project arising from the team's links with the excavations at Khorsabad. After the 1931/2 season, Jacobsen while staying at Khorsabad, visited the ruins at the village of Jerwan usually referred to by earlier travellers as a 'causeway', 'bridge', or 'dam', and the rock sculptures and inscriptions of Sennacherib at Bavian, where the river Gomel flows out of the hills into the plain. Having obtained a permit, Lloyd and Jacobsen worked at Jerwan for four weeks in the spring 1933 respectively as surveyor and epigraphist and at the same season in 1934 they worked at Bavian. The combination of survey of the physical remains and the establishment of the texts of the accompanying inscriptions enabled them to show for the first time that these two sites represented two stages of Sennacherib's project to tap the waters of the river Gomel and take them by canal across country to augment the waters of the river Khosr and thus ensure a better water supply for his new capital of Nineveh. The ruins at Jerwan could be shown to be a massive aqueduct carrying waters of the Gomel canal over one of the Gomel's tributary wadis. This collaboration of Lloyd and Jacobsen was a fine piece of work, which was to receive a rapid and exemplary publication.

Frankfort, as leader of the Iraq Expedition, ensured that time and funds were secured for post-excavation work, which seems to have been something of a novelty in those days. The chief members of the expedition were based in London, and the Expedition maintained an office in Sicilian Avenue where drawings and materials could be prepared for publication. Lloyd himself spent much of the disengaged part of each year working here. The first result was the appearance of his and Jacobsen's *Sennacherib's Aqueduct at Jerwan* (OIP 24; Chicago 1935), published the year after the project's completion, so Lloyd early established the pattern of prompt publication which he was to maintain throughout his career. He also found time in these years to write the first of his many general books on Mesopotamian archaeology, *Mesopotamia: excavations on Sumerian sites* (Lovat Dickson and Thompson, London, 1936), a succinct account of the archaeological work being conducted at that time on sites of the third millennium BC and earlier.

The death of Breasted led to the withdrawal of Oriental Institute funding and the end of the expedition at least for Frankfort and his team, who conducted their seventh and last season working at Khafaje and Tell Agrab over the winter 1936/7. (A different expedition funded by the University Museum, Pennsylvania, and the American School of Oriental Research was able to conduct two further campaigns at Khafaje in the spring 1937 and over the winter 1937/8). Lloyd's seven and a half years with the Iraq Expedition had transformed him from a young architect of uncertain direction to an established archaeologist with deep experience of stratigraphic archaeology on Mesopotamian sites in a well-funded project. He was not to remain long without archaeological employment, but he was never again to enjoy such generous funding and the large-scale activity which this permitted. It was a story of riches to rags, but he was always sufficiently adaptable to tailor his projects to his resources and to produce valuable results with restricted budgets.

While still working in London on processing Diyala material, he was invited by Professor John Garstang to join his projected excavations at Yümük Tepe, Mersin, in Cilicia. He worked there for two winter seasons, autumn 1937 to spring 1938 and the same period 1938/9, after which the excavations were interrupted by the outbreak of war. This employment brought Lloyd for the first time to Turkey and its archaeology and history, and formed a connection which was to last for most of his life. It also gave him experience of a more varied archaeology than the single period El Amarna or the Diyala mud-brick stratigraphy. This modestly funded operation consisted essentially of a stratigraphic step-trench cut down the north-east side of the mound. But for its time and with its limited resources, the excavation gained a remarkable archaeological sequence from the Iron and Bronze Ages back through the Chalcolithic to the Neolithic. Significant architectural remains were recovered for the Late Bronze Age (level VII), the Chalcolithic (level XVI) and the Neolithic (level XXVI). This was accompanied by a fine sequence of pottery. Lloyd was later to speak of the extraordinary interest attaching to the results of this excavation.

After his first Mersin season, he planned and conducted his ground-breaking Sinjar survey, assisted by his friend Gerald Reitlinger and with financial assistance from Garstang. Before beginning this, he made a journey through the extreme south-eastern towns of Turkey, from Malatya, through Diyarbakir as far as Mardin. This was by no means easy in those days, for the area was a military zone requiring special permission to enter and continual police checks. He published a short account of this trip.

His aim in undertaking the Sinjar survey was to fill in the archaeological blank between Assyria on the Tigris and the settlement of the Khabur, at that time recently surveyed and excavated by Max Mallowan. In this he was conspicuously successful. The southern watershed of Jebel Sinjar and its eastward extension up to the Tigris as it slopes away into the Jezirah has at periods in the past supported very substantial settlement, and is a crucial marginal zone through which ran a fluctuating line marking the limits of successful rainfall agriculture. The level plain is thickly dotted with tells of all periods: Lloyd noted that from one central point over two hundred are visible. In his three week survey, he visited and plotted seventy-eight sites on the map, identifying recognisable periods of occupation and describing the salient features of the more distinctive.

It is a measure of his success in this previously little known area that a substantial number of the sites which he first identified have subsequently been excavated with notable results. Actually he himself was first in the field, the following year after his second season at Mersin. From 20 May to 8 June 1939 he conducted soundings on behalf of the Iraqi Department of Antiquities at two of the prehistoric sites which he had recorded. At Grai Resh he excavated a well-preserved Uruk private house, and at Tell Khoshi, apparently on the city wall, an Akkadian shrine with Early Dynastic predecessor. Others have since followed in his footsteps, and successful excavations have been conducted at Eski Mosul, Tell Thalathat, Tell Hawa, Tell al Rimah, Tell Taya, and Yarim Tepe. Again Lloyd was involved in placing a new area on the archaeological map.

He seems to have been unusually fortunate throughout his career, unlike many archaeologists, in that new openings always appeared when needed. While at Mersin in the spring of 1939, he was invited by the Iraqi Directorate of Antiquities to take up the post of Archaeological Adviser, which he accepted with effect from October of that year, a momentous decision indeed.

Lloyd was to view the War, which broke out at about the same time as he arrived in Iraq, from a Baghdad and Middle Eastern perspective. This appointment in Baghdad which he held through the War years into the post-war period for nearly ten years (1939–49) was the second phase of his career. The excavations in these years with which his name is associated are those of Uqair (1940–1), Hassuna (1943–4), and Eridu (1947–8), all conducted in collaboration with Fuad Safar, with whom he formed a close friendship. He also gave general guidance to the excavations conducted by Taha Baqir at Aqar Quf (1942–5) and Tell Harmal (1945).

These years could not but be punctuated by the alarums of war. From spring 1940 for one year Lloyd was seconded to Jerusalem to work in the British Public Relations Office. During this time he began writing his book *Twin Rivers*, a concise history of Iraq, designed to supply the need for such a book. On his return to Baghdad in 1941 he was almost at once caught up in the events of the pro-Axis Rashid Ali *coup d'état*, which resulted in all British residents who had not been evacuated being besieged in the British Embassy with very little food for an entire month (May 1941). Fortunately the coup collapsed, the pro-British government was reinstated, and Iraq was occupied by British forces. Lloyd took up residence in a fine old Ottoman house on the Tigris at the South Gate, which served as a centre for political activities in support of the occupation. He played his part in these along with his official archaeological duties. Throughout this time he was very much at the centre of British society in Baghdad and was regularly deputised to escort visiting dignitaries to the Museum, meeting in the course of this 'a curious variety of people'. One visitor, in April 1943, less curious but more welcome, was Sergeant Ulrica Hyde of the Royal Army Service Corps, who, stationed in Cairo, had accompanied a convoy to Baghdad. Her meeting with Lloyd led to their marriage in Cairo in February 1944, and a life-long match. Ulrica Hyde, always known as Hydie, was an artist and sculptor and had trained at the Royal College of Art before joining the army for the War. Those who knew her remember her as a very remarkable and lovable personality, with a passionate devotion to animals, everything from horses and salukis to birds, praying mantises, and stick insects. Indeed she was seldom without one or more exotic pets, often about her person. The Lloyds' son John was born in Jerusalem in May 1945 and their daughter Clare after their move to Turkey in September 1949.

The excavations conducted in Iraq by Lloyd with Safar and Baqir were all important in their own ways. At Tell Uqair, he uncovered a small but well-preserved Protoliterate temple on a platform. The walls were preserved to two metres and he was able to enter the temple through its own still standing doors. The shrine was virtually intact. The walls were painted and the altar decorated with leopards. Preservation or recording of these was extremely taxing. With this temple Lloyd had found a preserved platform temple like those postulated though not preserved at Khafaje and Ubaid but earlier.

Tell Hassuna took the history of Mesopotamian settlement back to its beginnings. Excavating down in two linked soundings to virgin soil through fifteen levels, the excavators encountered Ubaid and Halaf pottery, ending with a type, observed before only in Nineveh level I, now named *Hassuna* from this, the type site. The Hassuna sequence produced successive levels of *pisé*-built houses down to a first 'camp-site' level of hearths, pots, and burials. Lloyd's attempt to estimate the age of the earliest settlement by depth of archaeological deposit, which suggested *c*.5000 BC, was later triumphantly substantiated by carbon-14 tests.

With the sites of Aqar Quf and Tell Harmal Lloyd seems to have taken less of an initiative and confined himself more to his advisory role. Both in any case were much more conventional excavations than he was used to, hardly ground-breaking though by no means without importance. Lying on the western and eastern edges of Baghdad respectively, the one was the Middle Babylonian Kassite capital city Dur Kurigalzu, and the other a small Old Babylonian walled city Šaduppum, the westernmost of the Diyala sites.

With Eridu, however, Lloyd was again very much in the business of pushing back the frontiers of the knowledge of Mesopotamian prehistory to ever earlier levels. Previously excavated by Taylor in 1854, Campbell Thompson in 1918 and Hall in 1919, the ancient site had not yielded particularly notable results. Lloyd however, with his knowledge of Khafaje, Ubaid, and Uqair behind him, came to Eridu with a clear idea of what he wanted to know and where to seek it. Probing beneath the southern corner of the Ur III ziggurat he soon located a recognisable temple (level VI) well filled with Ubaid pottery. This was embedded in five distinct casings of brickwork (levels V–I), identified as successive enlargements of the temple platform ending with the outermost, faced in stone and dating to the Protoliterate period. Examining the substructure of his Ubaid temple Lloyd found himself 'involved in the familiar task of examining one temple after another right down to the deepest levels . . .'. In fact he recovered plans of a further eleven successive temples (VII–XVII) down to presumed virgin soil passing through various phases of Ubaid back to Hajji Mohammed ware, of which an earlier and previously unknown version was named 'Eridu ware'. Again Lloyd was associated with the writing of new pages of Mesopotamian prehistory, and in particular it was he who was able to draw together the evidence of early temple cultures from the Diyala and southern and central Mesopotamia. Due to contemporary work at Tepe Gawra in the north, he was also able to point to early pottery links between north and south.

Life in post-war Baghdad seems to have passed pleasantly for the Lloyd family. They had now taken over the greater part of the South Gate house.

Baghdad high society was clearly very open. The Prime Minister Nuri es-Said was accustomed to drop in unannounced to Lloyd's office. Lloyd was also entrusted with the job of inducting the ill-fated young King Feisal into archaeology at weekly meetings. For recreation there was riding and shooting. Home leave in post-war Britain by contrast must have seemed bleak (Lloyd had only had one spell of leave during the War). On the sudden death of her mother in 1947, Hydie Lloyd returned to England to settle family affairs, and it was at this time that she bought the lovely old mill-house Woolstone Lodge, immediately below the Uffington White Horse on the Berkshire downs. It was to be their home base, then family home for the rest of their lives.

After the War, plans were being made to reopen the British Schools of Archaeology abroad in Rome, Athens, Jerusalem, and Iraq, and further plans were made to found a new one in Turkey. Garstang, who had resumed excavations at Mersin in 1946 and 1947 was the moving spirit behind this, and the School—or 'Institute' as was preferred for reasons of translation into Turkish—was opened in 1948. Garstang agreed to act as Director for its inaugural year, 1948, but wrote to Lloyd informing him of developments and inviting him to Ankara to see if he were interested in the post for the following year. A combination of reasons suggested to Lloyd that his stint of almost ten years as Archaeological Adviser in Baghdad had run its course, and he therefore accepted. In March 1949, the Lloyds moved into the 'rather awful little house in the suburb called Yeni Şehir' (in Meşrutiyet Caddesi), where the Institute began. In March the following year they were able to move it into more commodious premises nearby at Bayındır Sokak, where they stayed for seven years, moving the Institute in 1957 to the then half-built house in Tahran Caddesi (the second half was built in 1962 after Lloyd's retirement from the Directorship).

So began the next phase of Lloyd's life, his twelve years in Turkey. The move from Iraq involved for him a sharp reduction in salary, accommodation, and archaeological budget. There were compensations, however, and both Lloyds came to love Turkey, its archaeology and its history as they had previously loved the very different present and past of Iraq. Certainly Turkey of the immediate post-war years was very different from the Turkey of today. Atatürk's capital of Ankara was not yet thirty years old, Turkey's modern road system was barely on the drawing-board, and clearly much old Ottoman charm and remote, backward poverty remained untouched. In spite of the then difficulties of transport, the Lloyds were assiduous in getting to know their new country and travelled widely at a time when travelling was still a (sometimes disagreeable) adventure. Lloyd's archaeological work took them to the south-east, south, west, and later north-east, and family holidays to the Aegean and south coast. Altogether there seems to have been little of Turkey which Lloyd did not get to know.

Then there was the matter of reading himself into the archaeology of his new sphere, known to him up to that point only from his two seasons at Mersin before the War. He moved rapidly and within six months of his arrival in Ankara was able to select an extremely significant piece of work with minuscule funding, his Polatlı sounding, undertaken in August 1949. The true measure of the decline in archaeological resources to which Lloyd had to adjust, became clear: from the lavish operations of the Oriental Institute on the Diyala, he had worked through the fluctuating finances of the Iraqi Department of Antiquities and come at last to the parsimonious provision of the British Institute of Archaeology at Ankara, which for his first field season was able to offer him only £100.

Lloyd however had the experience and resource to be able to maximise the effectiveness of the grant. When invited by the Director General of Antiquities, Dr Hamit Koşay to undertake work at Polatlı near Gordion, where a high *höyük* on the outskirts of the town was being quarried away for brick-making, Lloyd immediately spotted the potential for obtaining an important stratigraphical sequence for central Anatolia within his financial constraints. He collaborated with Nuri Gökçe, Director of Ankara Museum, who was able to match his £100 with an equivalent sum from the Turkish Ministry. With this they were able to work a three-week season.

Excavation was facilitated by the vertical cutting or 'cliffs' left by the quarriers. Also the locals were prepared to remove, and even pay for, the excavated spoil, a unique experience for Lloyd of being able to sell his dump. Ingeniously excavating a series of five separate sondages, he was able to splice together the results, obtaining a sequence of thirty-one levels spanning almost the entire Bronze Age. With this went an excellent pottery sequence which served to draw together the then known sequences from Troy through central Anatolia to Cilicia. Typical village architecture was found in most levels. The results of the season were published with characteristic meticulousness in *Anatolian Studies*, 1 (1951).

For Lloyd's second season in 1950 funds still would not run to proper excavation. Seeking a useful project he conceived a survey of the site of Harran, in which he was assisted by William Brice. This was a site which Lloyd had been unable to visit on his 1938 journey through the cities of the south-east Turkish frontier. The fruits of this three-week survey, also published in *Anatolian Studies*, 1 (1951), included a site plan by Brice and a plan and elevations of the medieval *kale* by Lloyd, also of a basilican church in the north sector. The publication of the topography and surface monuments of this great historic site was a significant step and well worth the three weeks of the July heat.

For the following season, 1951, there were sufficient funds for a modest excavation, again in collaboration with Nuri Gökçe. The team began at Aşağı

Yarımca near Harran, where three years earlier, a stele with Cuneiform inscription had been found. When the source of the stele proved to be a much later Sabian building, excavations were moved to Sultantepe, a very high *höyük* between Harran and Urfa. A rainwater gully high up on the southwest side had washed out some basalt Assyrian column bases, so excavation began here. It soon became clear that massive Assyrian walls and pavements were projecting all round the north end of the *höyük* some 7 metres below the summit, the remains of a huge building or buildings which had occupied this summit in Assyrian times. These eroded remains were traced around the north end of the *höyük* by trenching down from above, and as luck would have it, the excavators in the course of this four-week season hit a pile of Assyrian tablets stacked against a wall surrounded by a semi-circle of pithoi. A further six-week season was required the following year to complete the removal of the more than 400 tablets and investigate their archaeological context. Unfortunately the excavators were forced to conclude that there was little more that could be done to reveal this Assyrian citadel without a systematic removal and recording of the 7 metres of Hellenistic and Roman occupation, which a trial trench had shown to be particularly barren. Clearly this was out of the question from all points of view, not least the financial, and after the second season the site was regretfully abandoned. It still awaits the attentions of a better provided or more ruthless excavator. The prize of the Sultantepe archive however remains: a provincial library of Assyrian religious and literary texts of the later seventh century BC.

The following season, 1953, with funds still needing to be husbanded, a further survey was decided. Having been captivated by Seljuk civilisation, Lloyd selected the great harbour castle of Alanya for investigation. The survey itself was conducted by Lloyd while his collaborator Storm Rice worked on the inscriptions. This season produced the book *Alanya* (published by the British Institute of Archaeology at Ankara in 1958), which contains some of Lloyd's finest architectural drawings and is in general a model of its kind.

By 1954 the Institute was at last able to fund a full-scale archaeological excavation. The site chosen was Beycesultan in the area of James Mellaart's Southern Turkey survey, a large double mound on the upper reaches of the Meander River near Çivril. It was clearly a major site, located in a little-known area, which might be expected to throw light on the Arzawa lands known from the Hittite records, and archaeologically to bridge the gap between the sites and cultures of the interior and those of the western coastlands. The surface pottery suggested a good Bronze Age range but nothing later. Its six seasons of excavation, 1954–9, fulfilled the hopes up to a point: the architecture was dramatic and the pottery sequence unusually rich. If one senses a certain disappointment with the results, this is due to the dearth of other finds, above all of any written documents. This total absence of any indication of writing in the big and important buildings of the Middle and Late Bronze Age remains extraordinary, and is perhaps to be explained by the supposition that it may have been committed to wood or other perishables rather than the clay tablets produced by Boğazköy and other Hittite sites. Nevertheless Beycesultan remains a type site for the Bronze Age of the south-west and a still unsurpassed link between the interior and the coast.

It was to turn out a very different site from anything encountered before by Lloyd, and he admitted that it was probably the most difficult excavation he ever undertook. Unlike the comparatively straightforward mud-brick architecture of which Lloyd was now an acknowledged master, this most Anatolian of sites employed timber on a massive scale in its building. Even the biggest buildings were timber-frame constructions, usually on stone rubble foundations and with panels of mud-brick filling in the open parts of the frame. The resulting inflammability of such structures produced a different degree of ruination, which, combined with collapsed upper floors, made for a highly complicated archaeological deposit. This demanded all Lloyd's experience, skill, and patience to disentangle, but in the end his work was entirely successful.

Of the buildings recovered, the larger excavation on the east mount exposed a Late Bronze Age group of megaron-type houses (level III) and below these the Middle Bronze burnt palace (level V). The former were very substantial buildings with two streets. One complex included easily recognisable stables, while another abutted an extraordinary 'wine shop' and 'bar', where a number of human skeletons lying in disorder suggested nothing so much as a gruesome terminal party. The Burnt Palace, a vast construction with prodigious amounts of timber, could certainly be characterised as a political and administrative centre. Though burnt with great ferocity, it was largely empty of objects which implies that its occupants had time to evacuate it. Lloyd's reconstruction of the building is something of a classic.

On the west mound the most notable buildings were the remarkable series of shrines excavated in two areas out on the city wall (trench R), and in the deep sounding (trench SX). The former yielded an extraordinary Late Bronze double shrine with temple furnishings largely intact including weird terra cotta 'horns'. This building lay over an early Middle Bronze shrine. In the deep sounding below levels of Early Bronze I houses, another extraordinary sequence of double shrines of the Early Bronze II levels was revealed. The sondage continued on down through Early Bronze III to twenty levels of the Chalco/Neolithic and virgin soil. Lloyd's reconstructions of these shrines are often reprinted.

Lloyd's direction of the British Institute of Archaeology at Ankara carried it virtually from its beginning to a fully grown establishment. Its early success amply justified Garstang's wisdom in locating it as the first foreign archaeological mission in Ankara, where all others, French, German, Dutch, American, remained Istanbul-based. Garstang's choice of Lloyd as Director was equally well judged. Official recognition of his work came his way. He had already been awarded the OBE in 1948, while still Technical Adviser in Baghdad, and in 1958 as Director in Ankara he was awarded the CBE. In 1955 he was elected Fellow of the British Academy.

Lloyd twice moved the Institute to better premises: from Meşrutiyet Caddesi to Bayındır Sokak, then to Tahran Caddesi. The Lloyd family lived in the Bayındır Sokak Institute, but with the move to Tahran Caddesi, the Council encouraged the family to rent a separate flat, a separation which Lloyd later judged 'a disaster'. With children being educated in England, the Lloyd's migration became an increasing strain. On the academic and social side in those years the Institute prospered, and the roll of its fellows and scholars is full of names who then or subsequently became prominent in Anatolian archaeology and elsewhere: Michael Gough, Basil Hennessy, James Mellaart, John Evans, Charles Burney, David Stronach to name but a few. With many of these the Lloyds formed enduring friendships.

In particular Michael Gough with his wife Mary were prominent in the Institute and with their own projects, and Michael himself was to succeed Lloyd as Director. James Mellaart, Institute Scholar, 1951–4, and Fellow, 1955, initiated his South Anatolian survey which led to commencement of excavations at Beycesultan, where he acted as Assistant, then Field Director to Lloyd throughout. He was given the new Institute appointment of Assistant Director in 1959. Charles Burney, Institute Scholar 1954–5, and Joint Fellow, 1957–8, conducted (on bicycle) a North Anatolian survey in the years 1954–7, which extended from the Bosphorus to the Armenian Highlands, concentrating in the last two years on the then little known Urartian sites. Lloyd's interest in Urartu was aroused, and in 1958 with Burney and R. D. Barnett he took the opportunity to visit the main sites around Lake Van and those located by Burney's survey. He hoped to inaugurate excavations, but since the whole area east of the Euphrates was still a military zone, the time was not yet ripe.

The latter part of Lloyd's tenure was overshadowed by the 'Dorak Affair'. In 1958 Mellaart reported having been shown a treasure in Izmir with an alleged provenance from the village of Dorak. With the agreement of Lloyd and other Institute members, Mellaart's drawings of this treasure were revised and published in the *Illustrated London News*, 29 November 1959. No trace of the treasure has ever subsequently been seen, but the Turkish press, amid growing disquiet at the ever increasing international trade in stolen antiquities, chose to make it the centrepiece of a public outcry. This dogged Lloyd's last years in post and continued to vex his successor, but he with typical loyalty and generosity stoutly defended Mellaart at the time and later.

In 1961 Lloyd resigned from the Directorship of the Institute. For over 30 years, ever since his first entry into archaeology, he had been permanently based abroad, in Iraq, then Turkey. Since the advent of his family, and the education of his children in England, his family life had suffered from constant migration and separations. He felt quite reasonably that he had earned some home life. So he withdrew to the idyllic surroundings of Woolstone Lodge, where, as one can sense from his memoirs he revelled in some well-deserved domesticity. In 1960 he and Hydie had adopted a Polish boy, Josef Levandowski, who became their second son. Lloyd worked steadily on his publications and Hydie on her sculpture. But Cincinnatus was soon called from his plough.

In 1961 Professor (later Sir) Max Mallowan was awarded a Senior Research Fellowship at All Souls and relinquished his post as Professor of Western Asiatic Archaeology at the Institute of Archaeology, University of London. Lloyd was induced, not without hesitation, to apply for the post and was duly appointed, taking up the position in October 1962. He held it for seven years up to his retirement in 1969 at the age of 67. It was the last phase of his professional career, and the Institute, like all who had secured Lloyd's services before, benefited greatly.

For him this represented a return from Anatolia to Mesopotamia. He had never taught in an academic context before and approached the experience with some diffidence. But he need not have worried. His qualities of patience and thoroughness allied to his deep knowledge of the Mesopotamian past saw him through any initial difficulties. And what a tale he had to tell, drawing on his own twenty years in the Mesopotamian field, supplemented by his extensive research on behalf of his already numerous publications.

His years at the Institute are remembered as a golden period of Western Asiatic archaeology there by those, including the present writer, who were students under him. He had as colleagues in the Western Asia Department Peter Parr, who had recently succeeded Dame Kathleen Kenyon, to teach the archaeology of the Levant, and James Mellaart, appointed at Lloyd's own initiative shortly after his arrival, for Anatolian archaeology. Barbara Parker (later Lady Mallowan) backed up his Mesopotamian courses with her own on art and seals, and Rachel Maxwell Hyslop gave courses on metallurgy. Late in his tenure Lloyd introduced the BA Course in the Archaeology of Western Asia, though this did not begin to be taught until after his retirement.

As Professor at the Institute of Archaeology he was able, indeed expected, to conduct an excavation, and at this point the possibility of an Urartian excavation dormant since 1958, became a reality. In 1964, with Charles Burney and others, he spent a season of survey in order to choose a site. The sites in the province of Van identified by Burney were now pre-empted by Turkish archaeologists, but Lloyd and Burney were given the relatively unknown province of Muş to survey. There they selected at Lloyd's insistence a rocky hilltop site on the upper Murat Su (south branch of the Euphrates), named after the local village Kayalıdere. The survey was much disturbed, but in the end not interrupted, by John Lloyd's falling ill with typhoid. He had to be nursed by Hydie in the primitive hotel in Muş until well enough to be moved to Erzurum and finally Ankara.

An initial season of excavation at Kayalıdere by Lloyd and Burney was conducted in 1965. All the Lloyd family except Joe were present, as was also Dominique Collon, Hydie's niece, who had taken the postgraduate diploma under Lloyd at the Institute of Archaeology the previous year. John Lloyd, now a student following his father's footsteps at the Architectural Association, served as architect, and produced fine drawings in good Lloyd tradition. The season lived up to or exceeded expectations. All the regular features of Urartian civilisation were present at this small provincial fortress: a square temple of well-dressed masonry, magazines with huge storage pithoi, rock-cut tombs, and a rich collection of bronzes both military gear and furniture decoration. Altogether it was very promising and held out the hope of further seasons of successful excavation. But it was not to be. Difficulties over the excavation permit which had occurred in 1965 were even more serious in 1966, which under the circumstances was perhaps a blessing in disguise. While the excavation team were waiting for the permit, in August 1966 a major earthquake destroyed the local town Varto and severely damaged the village of Kayalıdere including the school-house which had served as dig-house for the expedition. The permit was never given, and Lloyd relinquished control of the expedition funds to Burney, who transferred operations to Urartian north-west Iran. So ended Lloyd's last dig.

Intermittent reference has been made above to Lloyd's publications, which deserve consideration in their own right. They naturally divide into his formal excavation reports, both preliminary and final, and his more popular writings for general readership. Both were of a high quality. A full bibliography compiled by Dr Dominique Collon was printed in *Iraq*, 44 (1982), 221–4, a volume dedicated to Lloyd in honour of his eightieth birthday. Even to this list a few items have to be added: 1981, the long-delayed final publication *Eridu* (with Fuad Safar and Mohammed Ali Mustafa); 1986, his memoir *The Interval* (self published, in collaboration with D. Collon); 1987, 'Palaces of the Second Millennium BC' (*Anadolu*, 21 [1978/80]—*Festschrift Akurgal*); 1989, *Ancient Turkey. A traveller's history of Anatolia* (British Museum Publications). Characteristic of his excavation reports were his own drawings, plans, sections, and reconstructions executed in his beautiful and elegant style and illustrating with great clarity the way he knew exactly what he had been doing in excavating. His combination of the roles of excavator and architect was central to his achievements, and while other archaeologists have also combined the two skills, it may safely be judged that Lloyd was in the first rank.

His earliest dig reports were of course those from the Diyala, appearing as Oriental Institute Publications, and like the excavations themselves large-scale, grand, and generous. The first *Sennacherib's Aqueduct at Jerwan* (1935, in collaboration with Thorkild Jacobsen) exactly exemplifies Lloyd's ability to conceive, execute and encapsulate in a beautiful book a given piece of work. The other Diyala volumes on which he collaborated are also models of their kind: the Tell Asmar Palace and Temple with Frankfort (1940); and the Diyala Pre-Sargonid Temples with Delougaz (1942). These were prepared as part of the post-excavation work during the non-excavating part of the year. Only the Diyala Private Houses and Graves (with Delougaz, 1967) was substantially deferred by events.

As with his excavations, his dig reports after parting from the Oriental Institute were less lavish, but no less meticulous. Reports on his Sinjar work appeared in early numbers of *Iraq*, inaugurating a long but intermittent connection with that journal. The wartime excavations of Uqair and Hassuna were reported in wartime in the *Journal of Near Eastern Studies*, and the post-war Eridu in the rather problematic early numbers of *Sumer*. His move to Turkey naturally transferred his allegiance to the new *Anatolian Studies*, where Polatlı, Harran, Sultantepe, and the six seasons of Beycesultan are all reported, as was later Kayalıdere. Beycesultan warranted three volumes of final report, published in collaboration with Mellaart by the British Institute of Archaeology at Ankara. Alanya as noted was treated in an elegant monograph.

In his more general publications, Lloyd served both Iraq and Turkey well, and a number of his books ran into republished and revised editions, as well as being translated into several languages. During his years in Iraq he began early with *Mesopotamia: excavations on Sumerian sites* (1936), continued by *Ruined Cities of Iraq* (1942), *Twin Rivers: a brief history of Iraq* (1943), and *Foundations in the Dust: a story of Mesopotamian Excavation* (1947), and retrospectively *The Archaeology of Mesopotamia* (1974). For Turkey he swiftly produced the Pelican *Early Anatolia* (1956), then *Early Highland Peoples of Anatolia* (1967), and very retrospectively *Ancient Turkey: a traveller's history of Anatolia* (1989), of which the paperback edition appeared when he was 91. *Mounds of the Near East* (1963, the published form of his Rhind Lectures, Edinburgh, 1962), bridged his experience in both countries. Most general of all, ranging well beyond his own personal experience, was the Thames and Hudson *Art of the Ancient Near East* (1961). If one may pick out from these books the contributions of special and enduring value, one would probably settle on *Foundations in the Dust, Early Anatolia*, and *Mounds of the Near East*.

Besides his Rhind Lectures, other notable lectures by Lloyd were published in journals: 'Bronze Age Architecture in Anatolia' (Reckitt Archaeological Lecture, *Proceedings of the British Academy*, 49 [1963]); 'Anatolia: an archaeological renaissance' (Inaugural lecture, *Institute of Archaeology Bulletin*, 5 [1965]); 'Twenty-five years of British Archaeology in Turkey' (25th Anniversary of the British Institute of Archaeology at Ankara, *Anatolian Studies*, 24 [1974]). 'Aspects of Mesopotamian Architecture' (First Bonham Carter Memorial Lecture, 1975), unfortunately remained unpublished by his own wish.

During his Professorship at the Institute of Archaeology and after his retirement Lloyd remained active in the affairs of the British Institute of Archaeology at Ankara. He served as Honorary Secretary from 1962 to 1972 and in 1975 was elected President, serving until 1981, and subsequently as Honorary Vice-President until his death. He was also President of the British School of Archaeology in Iraq, 1979–82 and subsequently Honorary Vice-President.

Lloyd came to archaeology with his architect's training allied to a fine drawing hand and a natural conscientious thoroughness. He learned his archaeology in the grand theatre of the Diyala excavations. His understanding of buildings enabled him to master rapidly the techniques of stratigraphic digging as well as to record and reconstruct for publication what he found. It was these aspects of archaeology which interested him and at which he was to excel. His excavations are remembered for the recovery of a series of remarkable buildings: the palace and temples at Tell Asmar, the Shara Temple at Tell Agrab, Sennacherib's aqueduct, the Ubaid, Uqair, and Eridu temples as examples of early religious continuity in Mesopotamia, and the Bronze Age palaces and shrines of Beycesultan. His interests and skills are also well illustrated by his surveys of the medieval standing remains of Harran and Alanya, and indeed by his article on the Safvet Paşa Yalı at Kanlıca, the residence before its destruction by fire of James Mellaart's father-in-law (*Anatolian Studies*, 7 [1957]). His more purely stratigraphic excavations include Hassuna and the small-scale but highly informative Polatlı, sounding. At Sultantepe he was unable to reach significantly the tantalisingly glimpsed Neo-Assyrian buildings but by good fortune hit the jackpot of the library of tablets.

Lloyd's excavations were aimed at carefully chosen targets. They were, as has been emphasised, modestly funded after the initial phase, and never employed a very extensive staff. It is notable, however, and doubtless says something about the man, how many successful collaborations he conducted. The big, multi-disciplinary excavation teams only really began to come in after Lloyd had withdrawn from the field. His publications contain many sly references to the relative inappropriateness of rigorous and dogmatic British archaeological methods to Near Eastern conditions. As for the 'New Archaeology', Lloyd regarded it with somewhat diffident scepticism, excusing himself on the grounds of being old-fashioned, an attitude which looks quite defensible from the standpoint of today. His name is associated with the addition of many new areas to the archaeological map of the Ancient near East from the Diyala through Upper Mesopotamia to the Anatolian plateau. His record of publication was impeccable, and unlike so many of his profession he left no backlog of unpublished material. Indeed while there were among his contemporaries more extrovert and flamboyant figures than he, the body of work which he bequeathed compares favourably with theirs.

Seton Lloyd was a tall, imposing figure, who always dressed well. He united an outward reticence, even diffidence, with a pleasing, dry humour. His life-long passion for shooting may nowadays seem to sit rather uneasily with his love of natural beauty, but this was not an uncommon combination in his generation. He was very happy in his marriage to Hydie, who shared his love of travel and out-of-the-way places. Indeed his last book, *Ancient Turkey*, is dedicated to her as his 'travelling companion'. Sadly she predeceased him, dying in 1987. The atmosphere which they created in the beautiful setting of Woolstone Lodge remains a happy memory for all who knew it.

J. D. HAWKINS
Fellow of the Academy

DONALD MACKINNON   *Laird Parker*

Donald MacKenzie MacKinnon
1913–1994

IN A MOMENT OF INSPIRED JUDGEMENT—which is not the unvarying characteristic of academic committees—the Electors to the Norris-Hulse Chair of Divinity in the University of Cambridge invited Donald MacKinnon to move from the Regius Chair of Moral Philosophy in the University of Aberdeen to the Faculty of Divinity in Cambridge. The Fellows of Corpus Christi College shared the wisdom of the Electors, and MacKinnon joined the fellowship in 1960.

The Cambridge Faculty of Divinity at that time included Geoffrey Lampe and C. F. D. Moule, matched in stature in Moral Sciences by the elusive genius of John Wisdom. There was also a vibrancy and vigour in public debate on matters of faith and ethics. The rigour of the terms in which the debate was carried on was much enhanced by the powerful contributions of the new Norris-Hulse Professor. The Cambridge Faculty of Theology Lecture series were astonishingly successful, both as delivered to large attentive audiences, and in the published form of books such as *Objections to Christian Belief*. For good or for ill, much that has happened within the churches in this country, and to the place of theology within them can be traced back to that projection by the Cambridge Faculty of academic and scholarly debate into the public arena.

I start here for two reasons: the first is to underline the point that Donald MacKinnon was a theologian and philosopher whose engagement with those disciplines was a matter of mind and heart and soul. He did not have the detachment of the middle-aged Hume which allowed the latter his own self-created myth of testing the boundaries of scepticism from 6 a.m. till noon and turning easily to the distractions of backgammon in the evening. MacKinnon's probing of the boundaries of belief was an imperative of his own engagement with belief rather than an academic or pedagogic exercise. The second reason is that there is a sense in which a great deal of MacKinnon's intellectual

Proceedings of the British Academy, **97**, 381–389. © The British Academy 1998.

development can be seen as a preparation for the Cambridge which he—a layman and a philosopher appointed to a senior Chair of Divinity—found in 1960.

None of this is to imply 'all intellectual work and no play', for this particular Jack was anything but dull. The intellectual seriousness made the wit, the smile (which unrolled from the eyes upward to the forehead and then downwards to the mouth), and the shared delight in academic gossip all the richer as part of the greater harmony. The *persona* was of course grand and at times eccentric, but what held the respective audiences entranced was the combination of intellectual passion and the spirit of enquiry which is in constant tension with truth and reality. The pressures which this produced were often concealed from others, but never from his wife Lois to whom therefore his colleagues and his pupils owe so much.

Donald MacKinnon was born on 27 August 1913 in Oban, Scotland. He was always pleased to be thought of as a highlander, and although by no means a political nationalist was sharply conscious of much that makes Scotland culturally different from England. However, not one to be pigeon-holed in this or other contexts, he was tendentiously capable of substituting 'North Britain' for 'Scotland' should there be more hot air than that particular balloon could stand. He was an only child and his father held the significant and distinctive position of Procurator Fiscal for Argyll. The wider family is still involved in the practice of law in Oban and the West Highlands. That area of Scotland clearly remained 'home' for him, for he and his wife kept a cottage, Tigh Grianach, near Oban, for many years until his eventual retirement to Aberdeen in 1978. Living strands of these roots are to be found in the regard with which he was held by fellow highlanders as diverse in interests as the Gaelic poets Sorley MacLean and Ian Crichton Smith on the one hand, and the former Lord Chancellor, Lord MacKay of Clashfern, on the other.

His early schooling at Cargilfield School, Edinburgh was followed by a scholarship to Winchester. He always spoke warmly of his time at Winchester, where the atmosphere of intellectual challenge and freedom which he found suited his talents well. It was during his schooldays that he became a communicant member of the Anglican Church. The importance of this for MacKinnon was very great indeed in a whole variety of ways. Most significantly, though perhaps most unobtrusively, it gave him a liturgical discipline which was the context of most of his intellectual work. It is arguable that the more austere patterns of worship in the Church of Scotland might not have served him equally well. On the other hand, his membership of the Anglican communion was held within the Scottish Episcopal Church. Being in that specific sense outside the Established Church be it of Scotland or England brought its own perspectives upon which he remarked from time to time. Earlier *Who's Who* entries used mischievously to allude to this by listing under the heading *Clubs* 'the Scottish Episcopal Church' and 'the Labour Party'.

His education continued as a scholar of New College, Oxford, and early success came with the award of the John Locke Scholarship, which appropriately, albeit accidentally, marks well one key strand of his thinking. He attached great importance to Locke's distinction between primary and secondary qualities, seeing there early insistence upon the attachment of an empiricist epistemology to a realist ontology. For all the attractions of forms of idealism, whether in metaphysics, ethics or even the philosophy of history, an engagement with the world experienced in empirical form lay very near the core of MacKinnon's approach to both philosophical and theological questions. For example, he remained an admirer of H. H. Price whom he invited to deliver the highly successful series of Gifford Lectures in Aberdeen, which were in due course published as *Belief.* Equally he was known to comment on Collingwood whom he much admired, that, nonetheless, Collingwood's work on the empirical remains of Roman antiquity, was an indirect counterweight to his seminal but idealistically inclined *Idea of History.*

(This empirically inclined perspective on the philosophy of history informed MacKinnon's later engagement with the theological implications of the later dominance of Bultmann's theology over New Testament scholarship, and I shall return to this issue in due course.) Following Greats and further theological study, MacKinnon spent a year as an Assistant Lecturer in Moral Philosophy in the University of Edinburgh (1936–7). It is typical of his own way of marking out his intellectual tributes as well as debts that he always referred to this post as 'Assistant to A. E. Taylor'.

Within the year he was recalled to Oxford to a Fellowship at Keble where he taught an extraordinary number of the generation of philosophers who dominated British philosophy in the second half of this century. Each, doubtless have their own impressions of him, as he had of them. He recounted, for example the story of one student, who arrived in Oxford in the later years of the war. The student in question, who in later life held senior positions in the British academic firmament, had through his family history a more direct understanding of the impact of war in mainland Europe than most of his teachers. His approach to writing philosophy tutorial papers belligerently rejected the conventions of Oxford of that time. He was passed from tutor to tutor in the hope that some intellectual modus vivendi might be found. Eventually Donald was asked to take him on. After reading the first essay submitted, Donald avoided the trap of trying to do the impossible and chart a steady line in discussion from the student's starting point to the topic as set. He simply remarked how interesting the essay was, but that it could not be accepted as a contribution to the philosophical topic set and handed it back with a note of the subject for next week. Apparently the same limited engagement took place for a further two tutorials. However, 'in the fourth week', as Donald recalled with evident excitement, 'he cracked, and produced a first class piece of work'. The student in question was Ernest Gellner.

Donald's kindness to students took many different forms and found its own manners of expression in Oxford, Aberdeen, and Cambridge. Professor Ronald Hepburn, for example, pays tribute to the risk which MacKinnon took in giving him an appointment as his Assistant after what MacKinnon referred to as 'an abortive year in Divinity', and before what was the usual route of an established record in graduate study. Others recount with astonishment his ability to recognise and recall personal details about students from distant years, sometimes briefly encountered, and to make a chance meeting in the street a sharing of common memories.

It was during his years at Keble that some of the many stories of his occasional unconventional behaviour took root. His eccentricities then, as later in Aberdeen and Cambridge, even by Oxbridge standards gave him an early and distinctive place in British intellectual life. Like many a good myth a grain of fact could occasionally be divined, but that was not the point. They represented how colleagues and students came to see and want to remember Donald MacKinnon. Basically, everybody remembers him and comes to believe that they were present on one or other of the occasions which give rise to the rich vein of MacKinnon folklore. The latter like each good *perikope* has several contenders for empirical origin. By changing the variables each story could transfer easily either forwards or backwards in time between Oxford, Aberdeen, and Cambridge. Thus one finds former Cabinet members, Peers of the Realm, school teachers, civil servants, parsons, doctors, Bishops, and captains of industry alike able—indeed eager—to share a common inheritance of MacKinnonia. The stories however are always told with affection and indeed respect, because whatever the level of conscious articulation, there was amongst the least philosophical, and even the most this-worldly, an awareness of intellectual and spiritual depth.

In 1947 MacKinnon accepted the Regius Chair in Moral Philosophy in the University of Aberdeen. It was in one sense a going home, a return to his native land. As with all such translations there was much gain but some losses. Intellectually the pattern of work was very different—large first year classes, in the Scottish tradition, and fewer honours and postgraduate students. The local community took him to their heart with the unostentatious acceptance, characteristic of the place, that Professors from Oxford might well be a bit different—some, of course, more different than others. The locals all knew him, from the waitress in the coffee shop in 1987 who recognised him from the daily morning queue in the baker shop thirty years before, to the newspaper delivery man whose respect and genuine fondness took him to Donald's funeral in 1994. My own first sighting of Donald MacKinnon is probably not untypical. I went as an eleven-year-old boy to a packed 'Any Questions' type evening in the local church hall. One of the panel amongst the local worthies was this large shambling man who sat on the end of the panel in the second chair on the left of the chairman. He was introduced as 'Professor of Moral Philosophy' with slight stress on the word 'Moral'. During the evening he appeared to read a book, feel the need to count his pocket change several times, make copious notes to which he did not refer, sharpen a pencil with an open razor blade, but at the same time dominate the discussion by sheer intellectual power and engagement of the emotions. There was no doubt that this was the great MacKinnon, as even an unsophisticated eleven-year-old could tell.

The division of responsibilities required a teaching focus defined by the title of the Chair and in this respect, there was the loss of the wide teaching remit of an Oxford Tutor. The compensations, however, included the podium afforded by the first year moral philosophy class which included the few who would continue the study of philosophy for a further three years, but also the many (amounting even in those days to a further one hundred or so) who comprised the curious volunteers, the reluctant conscripts and possibly a few of the intellectually halt and lame. This was indeed a challenge and MacKinnon responded magnificently. The conscripts were enthralled, and the halt and the lame learned to exercise their intellectual talents in ways not thought possible.

His contribution to the intellectual life of the University and city also took significant indirect forms. One of the most remarkable of these was the array of seminal thinkers, in addition to H. H. Price, who in MacKinnon's time gave Gifford Lectures in Aberdeen—including, for example, Gabriel Marcel, John Wisdom, Michael Polanyi, and Paul Tillich.

During that period (1947 to 1960), which contained some darker moments, MacKinnon gave himself, perhaps too generously, to public presentations, to conferences, seminars, and meetings of a non-academic as well as professional academic nature. He was politically as well as ecclesiastically engaged. This is evident from papers and broadcasts of the time, as well as later publications which drew upon them, for example in his iconoclastic Gore Memorial Lecture in Westminster Abbey, *The Stripping of the Altars* (1968), and in his Boutwood Lectures in Corpus Christi College, Cambridge, *Creon and Antigone: Ethical problems of Nuclear Warfare* (1981).

His central philosophical work of that period *A Study in Ethical Theory* (1957), provided an intellectual structure which defined at that time the position from which he carried out his duties as Regius Professor of Moral Philosophy. The book was reasonably well noticed by his peers and contemporaries, but there was not a natural location for it on the map of moral philosophy which was at the time being sketched out by Richard Hare and others who were more directly influenced by the rather more constrained picture of the intellectual arena allowed by the aftermath of Ayer's *Language, Truth and Logic*. The shape of the book was an evaluation of the contrasting consequences for ethical argument of utilitarian and Kantian approaches. As such the work had greater emphasis on historical perspectives than tended to be fashionable in the nineteen-fifties, although it was certainly a contribution to moral philosophy rather than the history of moral philosophy more narrowly defined. The elusive and now wholly successful final section dealing with the relation between religion and ethics was a forerunner to much, later, illumination. However, one most important legacy to be discerned in later writings is his respect for the Utilitarian insistence that human happiness cannot be wholly divorced from empirically describable states of affairs including social conditions. This grounding of our account of what is good in the empirical world, however, was tempered by his preoccupation with the Kantian emphasis that morality has ultimately to relate to what is good in itself, rather than be wholly preoccupied with what is a means to some further end.

The move to Cambridge brought with it congenial colleagues in the Faculty of Divinity to which he now belonged and for many who taught and enquired there over the next fifteen years at the centre of memory and intellectual formation lay the D Society. This met regularly in the MacKinnons' home in Parker Street and undoubtedly benefited as much from the informal discussion which followed over tea as from the more formal seminar which preceded that. Donald MacKinnon was of course in one of his natural elements on those Wednesday afternoons and although it was predictable that he would open the discussion after the paper, it was not equally predictable what form his contribution would take—be it anecdote, mischievous memory, a detailed critique based on seemingly vast multi-lingual reading, or an evident enthusiasm and admiration for a particularly fine academic *tour de force*. This last was not distributed lavishly but I particularly remember such a response to a paper by Mary Hesse. This illustrates well another of his characteristics—a capacity to appreciate to the full the creative use of expert knowledge and scholarship. This gave him what was then a less than wholly fashionable appreciation of the qualities of the type of scholarship and qualities of learning of those theologians whom he met through his regular invited participation in the Castelli Colloquia in Rome.

These were the qualities which he recognised in the scholarly work of, for example, Geoffrey Lampe, although he was equally enthusiastic about his joint authorship with Lampe of a series of articles brought together in 1966 in *The Resurrection*, a book with a readership much wider than the collectivity of professional theologians. This typifies the expression in Cambridge of his wish to see wider, but informed debate of the central elements of Christian belief. Over the years he had broadcast regularly on what was then called the Third

Programme, and some of his best contributions were reprinted along with his Gore Memorial Lecture in *The Stripping of the Altars* (1968), for example 'Authority and Freedom in the Church', 'Is Ecumenism a Power Game?', and 'The Controversial Bishop Bell'. His arrival in Cambridge preceded the publicity surrounding the publication of John Robinson's *Honest to God* (1963), which achieved a degree of notoriety because John Robinson happened also to be the Bishop of Woolwich. There was much in that book which was commonplace in academic theology and which was more lightweight than Robinson's more considered writings on New Testament themes. However, although he was not above pointing this out, there is no doubt that MacKinnon relished this wider arena for theological discussion which Robinson had helped create. His most penetrating offering to this wider discussion was his contribution, 'Moral Objections', to the Cambridge lecture series and book *Objections to Christian Belief.* There was one clear sense in which he dominated Cambridge theology for the next decade or more: there were certainly those who expressed exasperation at his style, but there could be none there who were unaware of his intellectual presence.

A string of pupils and junior colleagues have moved to senior academic and ecclesiastical posts in the United Kingdom and overseas. His intellectual achievements are in part to be seen in the stimulus which, through them, he has given to the variety of fields in which they have chosen to work. The possibility of such second order influence, however, is always premised upon first order contributions and what is distinctive about Donald MacKinnon is the number of intellectual fronts upon which he advanced as it seemed, simultaneously.

There is a sense in which in any attempt to list or give separate mention to these is to dismember what in reality was a living whole. For example, his preoccupation with the debate between realism and anti-realism certainly took root in the fundamental questions of the nature and existence of God. Consideration of that, however, was linked to his exploration of Aristotle's views on Primary Substance, which in turn was of immense significance for his evaluation of the Christological debates of the first four centuries AD.

Likewise his often illustrated commitment to the importance of poet, playwright, and novelist in the European tradition of philosophical and theological reflection had wide ramifications. Thus Sophocles' Oedipus was a source of revelation and insight into the ethical and psychological character of self-knowledge, rather than simply a literary example of 'what oft was thought'. Nor was MacKinnon's treatment of Creon and Antigone in his Boutwood Lectures of 1981 anything less than an interweaving of the literary, the political, the moral, and the theological, in a probing meditation upon the implications of the nuclear deterrent.

The latter was an issue which had weighed upon him from the first realisation of its implications. This gave an incisive edge to his participation in the wider discussion of political power and its basis. He deeply appreciated the invitation to deliver the fifth Martin Wight Memorial Lecture at the LSE, recalling as it did for him and others the stimulus and excitement of the group which Wight led and to which MacKinnon belonged in the 1960s, and which was the womb which gave birth to a volume of essays well-titled *Diplomatic Investigations*. His interest in the concept of as well as the exercise of power, played a significant part in his reflections upon the churches of his time, and he could be especially fierce in his distaste for ecclesiastical self-regard and the political dangers of allying an absolutist theology with secular power. Nonetheless, his disdain for what Caiaphas represented went hand in hand with an appreciation of the responsibilities of ecclesiastical as well as political office. Proximate to his consideration of these issues and underlying the particular thread which he wove through a series of inter-connected but different theological and philosophical questions, was his refusal to share any intellectually flawed dismissal of the problems associated with the concept of evil.

Whether in the discussion of the nature of political power, or of the relationship between moral and religious belief, in his preference for the concept of natural law, rather than the more fashionable natural rights as a basis for political order, or in his interpretation of theological accounts of incarnation and salvation, his insistence upon the reality of evil gave his writing a tension and a depth of consequence to MacKinnon himself as well as his readers.

It made his contribution more difficult to assimilate than those who could do passable imitations of his occasionally exaggerated syllables sometimes realised. For him it left his thinking and the written expression of it in more fragmented form than, I believe, he would have wished. He constantly stressed the importance of the particular and the individual and set his face against the possibility of the grand over-arching theory. He had absorbed the later Wittgenstein in part through John Wisdom. He saw the importance of the individual example, assembled with others as reminders; in the end he was more in sympathy with Aristotle than Plato, and quite centrally his Christology was based upon the historical particularity of the incarnation.

His most consistent attempt to articulate his central concerns is to be found in his Gifford Lectures of 1965 and 1966, published in 1974 under the title *The Problem of Metaphysics*. There, it is fair to say that it is the manner of the journey rather than the arrival which is the central contribution of this book, and the same may legitimately be said of the legacy of Donald MacKinnon. Thus there is no single MacKinnon contribution, and out of the plethora of insights and explorations I quote one, not as representing the total oeuvre, for my point is that that is not how MacKinnon worked, but rather as exemplifying the manner in which one pupil responds to his teacher:

It is when one allows one's attention to fasten upon the sorts of exploration of the human reality that we have here reviewed that we come to recognise the paradox that, while in one way a proper respect for the irreducibility of the tragic inhibits metaphysical construction, in another the sort of commentary on human life, which one finds in the tragedies here reviewed and the parables analysed, makes one in the end discontented with any sort of naturalism. It is as if we are constrained in pondering the extremities of human life to acknowledge the transcendent as the only alternative to the kind of trivialisation which would empty of significance the sorts of experience with which we have been concerned. (*The Problem of Metaphysics*, p. 145.)

As will be evident from the foregoing, Donald MacKinnon neither sought nor expected the recognition of social or political elites. However, his election as a Fellow of the British Academy in 1978 gave him evident satisfaction and pleasure.

STEWART SUTHERLAND
Fellow of the Academy

KENNETH MUIR

Kenneth Arthur Muir
1907–1996

KENNETH MUIR was one of the most eminent Shakespearean scholars and critics of our time. As editor of five of the plays and author of a large number of books and essays on the plays and poems, he is read all over the world. His beautiful speaking of poetry and the lucid and witty presentation of his learning inspired lecture audiences at home and abroad. He generously promoted the work of others, not least as editor of *Shakespeare Survey* and as the first Chairman and later the President of the International Shakespeare Association. His own work was not limited to Shakespeare: the subjects of his more than fifty books and his almost innumerable articles range from Wyatt, through Renaissance and Romantic writers, to modern poetry and fiction. His range also extended beyond the confines of the English language, to translations of Racine and Corneille and of Golden Age Spanish drama. His zest and industry remained undiminished until shortly before his death, and in terms of publication he was as productive in the twenty years after his retirement from the King Alfred Chair of English Literature in the University of Liverpool as he had been during the forty-five years of his uncommonly active professional life in York, Leeds, and Liverpool. As the fell sergeant Death moves more swiftly than publishers, new essays by him are still appearing, more than a year after his death. The latest of these is a counter-blast to what he saw as 'Base Uses' of Shakespeare: characteristic of a scholar and man who, in the words of Ernst Honigmann, the recipient of the Festschrift to which this essay was contributed, was 'an immense force on the side of sanity and goodness (I can think of no other word) in an increasingly wicked world'.

In the autobiography which he left for posthumous publication Kenneth Muir presented the story of his life under three headings: 'Politics', 'Theatre', 'Academic', in that order. In an earlier and shorter version of the autobiography which he deposited with the University soon after his retirement, a 'Theatre'

Proceedings of the British Academy, **97**, 393–409. © The British Academy 1998.

section comes first, and yet the conclusion to the entire manuscript establishes a different order of preference:

> Although I hope to be remembered for some time as the editor of several of Shakespeare's plays and of *Shakespeare Survey*, as the author of several sound and sober books on Shakespeare, as the biographer of Sir Thomas Wyatt, and as the lucky discoverer of some splendid new poems of his, I believe that the English Department at Liverpool, one of the best and perhaps the happiest, is the best thing I have helped to create.

As all this indicates, the various categories under which his activities could be classified were not separate and discrete but mutually supportive. In this interdependency rests the unique quality of his achievements. The Preface to what is perhaps his most widely read work of criticism, *Shakespeare's Tragic Sequence* (1972), characteristically states: 'I have, perhaps, learnt more from performances of the tragedies than from the critics, and more still from those amateur groups with which I have been associated in one capacity or another.' When retiring from his Liverpool Chair, he welcomed the opportunity to close his academic and theatrical career in one symbolic gesture by appearing as Prospero in a production of *The Tempest*, directed by a young member of his Department. When, in October 1995, he wrote to Tony Blair to congratulate him on his speech to the Labour Party conference, he also felt bound to point out that a reference to the great writers of the past which Blair had made might be open to misinterpretation.[1] 'I know from personal experience', he wrote, 'that the writings of Shakespeare, Milton, Blake, Dickens and many others can inspire rather than hinder one's political activity.' In *King Lear*, which he edited for the Arden Shakespeare (1952), the lines closest to his heart were Gloucester's discovery of social justice: 'So distribution should undo excess / And each man have enough'; and in a late essay on 'Dissident Poets' (1991) he praised Shelley for escaping, in *The Mask of Anarchy*, from mere abstraction and for presenting Freedom 'in concrete terms of bread, clothes and fire, as well as justice, peace and love'. A committed socialist throughout his life, he saw no difficulty in combining practical politics with literary scholarship. In day-to-day terms it meant correcting proofs while crossing the Mersey between committee meetings in Liverpool University and in Birkenhead Town Hall. On a deeper level it meant that, whether acting as an academic leader, a politician, or a literary critic, he was impelled by the same basic convictions, humane rather than doctrinaire. He was always proud of an early (1947) essay of his, on Marx discovering in lines from *Timon of Athens* the meaning of the cash-nexus—even though he also felt that the fact that the

---

[1] Blair had insisted 'I want us to be a young country again . . . not resting on our past glories.' Those included some of the world's 'finest literature, art, and poetry', but while 'we are proud of our history . . . its weight hangs heavy upon us'. (Leader's speech, Labour Party Annual Conference, 1995.)

essay had appeared in a Marxist journal nearly cost him his appointment to the King Alfred Chair. He never lost his belief in literature as the vehicle of truth and in the discipline of literary criticism as its servant—a belief that reached through Matthew Arnold and Shelley right back to Sidney's *Apology for Poetry*. The keystones of this belief remained those set down in his Liverpool Inaugural lecture, 'The Study of Literature' (1952): the proper end of criticism, informed by scholarship, is to demonstrate that 'if the immediate function of literature is delight, the ultimate end is nothing less than the Good Life or the Greater Glory of God'. Muir remained untouched by the theoretical approaches which came to dominate much of English Studies in the 1970s, 80s and 90s. In a world of relativity and deconstruction, he knew what truth was and what goodness was. If this made his work in these decades seem old-fashioned, it also gave it a wholeness and strength which appeal, and last, beyond fashion.

Characteristically, Kenneth Muir did not include a 'Personal' section in his autobiographical manuscript, although in the last few months of his life he planned, but did not write, a section on 'those I have loved'. He valued love and friendship, and would write as it were professionally of these phenomena: of, for example, how Shelley in *The Defence of Poetry* argues that 'poetry by stimulating the imagination increases our capacity to love' ('Shelley's Magnanimity', 1981). But, naturally reticent, and in keeping with an austerity of demeanour which, unless one knew him well, belied his own very real capacity for love and friendship, he would not write of personal relations. A reader of his autobiography would barely know that he married Mary Ewen in 1936 and would find no reference to the birth of a daughter, Katherine (1943), and a son, David (1951). The marriage was one of true minds; and he was deeply bereft by the death of Mary from leukaemia in 1975, followed by Katherine's death from the same illness, and only some six months after it had been diagnosed, in 1981. Ten years later he wrote a poem of emotion recollected in tranquillity—a poem which was not for publication at the time, but which may be cited here as evidence that the outward stoicism with which he faced his losses co-existed with profound inward grief, and that the sympathetic imagination was a fact of his life, not just a literary topic:

The Missing Snapshot

Ten years ago—a memory buried deep,
Now disinterred—your terminal disease
Gained a remission, offering fruitless hope.

You walked me off my feet along the steep
And gravelly paths, in a mild Indian summer,
Above the Pembroke sands, until we reached

A neolithic grave. At your request,
Pretending I was dead, I lay outstretched,
Arms crossed upon my chest with shuttered eyes.

The final photograph you took of me—
Entitled (and a camera never lies)—
'Grave portrait of a prehistoric man'.

But when they scanned (at last) all your effects—
Selected records, photos, diaries, notes—
They never found the print or negative.

Doubtless you feared this photo of your father,
After his spurious death once more alive,
Would leave an after-load of suffering,

Because he knew how brief was your reprieve.

Kenneth Muir was born in the parish of St James's, Hatcham, south-east London, in a house in the New Cross Road that was later to be destroyed in the blitz. Years later he was thrilled to discover that his birthplace was only a mile or so from the tavern where Marlowe was stabbed to death. He was proud to say that he came of a long line of naval officers. His grandfather, George William Muir, had served with great distinction in the Crimean war at the age of seventeen and his grandmother was thought to be the granddaughter of the Dr Thomas who was called (too late) to attend Byron in his last illness. His uncle, Arthur Thomas Muir, commanded the *Niger*, one of the first gunboats to be torpedoed in World War I. Kenneth Muir's father, Robert Douglas Muir (1869–1914), had been educated at the Royal Naval College, studied medicine in London and Brussels, and settled as a general practitioner in the New Cross area. His marriage, in 1899, to Edith Mary Barnes, who taught in the Sunday School where he was superintendent, was initially regarded by the Muir family as something of a mésalliance: she was the daughter of the manager of a brewery—a fact that was to be concealed from the children, who were always told that he was 'a carpenter, like St Joseph'. But the family soon came to appreciate the remarkable intelligence and energy of the young woman who, on marriage, gave up the independence of a 'New Woman' (she was the buyer for a London dress store and went to Paris every year to study the fashions) and re-trained to become her husband's dispenser and book-keeper. When he died of diabetes at the age of 45, leaving her with four young children, she coped courageously in severely reduced circumstances; and each of the children—of whom Kenneth was the third—was enabled to develop his or her own talents. Grace ended up as Vice-Principal of a College of Further Education, Douglas as an actor, and Alec as Chief Constable of County Durham.

Kenneth Muir was seven when his father died, and he remembered him chiefly as a devout Christian who presided daily at family prayers and a stern disciplinarian who did not spare the cane. His own first prize at school, at the age of eleven, was for his knowledge of the Bible. In later years he came to feel that his father had acted 'as a conscience, a superego' throughout his life: 'It makes me feel guilty when I am not working. It drives me to work more than I should, and seldom to relax.' But he also came to discover that his father had been a member of two literary societies and the leading spirit in an all-male group that met monthly to read plays, mostly Shakespeare's but also Goldsmith's and Sheridan's; and he always knew that his love of Shakespeare began from the pocket editions his father used. Eventually, this love was to be developed at school, but only after some years of considerable misery.

In 1917 Kenneth Muir entered Epsom College, a boarding school for the sons of doctors, where he was to spend the next nine years. Earlier, he had been taught at home, by a governess who could no longer be afforded after the death of his father, and then in a local day school from which he mainly remembered a 'seedy' Latin master who taught the boys a pronunciation they had afterwards to unlearn. This was only one of his handicaps at Epsom. Holding a free place—a scholarship reserved for the sons of deceased doctors—he was looked down on by the sons of Harley Street consultants: 'To lose a father was regarded as tasteless.' Skinny, bookish, and bad at games, he met contempt in a school that valued physical prowess. In the Spartan regime that prevailed he suffered from chilblains and frostbite, and he was always to remember how, on two occasions, his hands were so swollen that the sleeves of his jacket had to be slit before he could undress. Most of all he remembered his otherness as a budding socialist in what was virtually an all-Tory environment. Years later, when his name first appeared in *Who's Who* and he received a letter from the then headmaster of his old school, asking him to become a fundraiser, he wrote back: 'Dear Sir, I am one of your failures.'

A failure in terms of the school's ethos, he was nonetheless an academic success, with School Certificate examination results good enough to gain him an offer of free medical education at University College Hospital. As this seemed the only way into higher education, he began to study for First MB but, though doing well in science subjects, he was desolate without the Arts and so transferred after a term to History, English Literature, French and Latin and, on the strength of his Higher Certificate results, gained a place, but not a scholarship, to read English at St Edmund Hall, Oxford. A bequest from his father's partner enabled him to take up the place. The last three years at Epsom had been happy: he had won prizes for verse-speaking and for debating and had been allowed to subscribe to *The Daily Herald*. The most formative experiences had been in the school's play-reading and acting society, run by an imaginative English master and known as 'The Mermaid Tavern'. Under its auspices he took part in readings of plays, from *Gammer Gurton's Needle* to *Arms and the Man*, and played the lead in productions of *The Way of the World*, *Venice Preserved*, *The Rivals*, Hardy's *Queen of Cornwall*, *Doctor Faustus* and *Macbeth*. And in the holidays he would spend twopence on the fare from home to the Old Vic and five pence on a gallery seat, from which he admired Ion Swinley as Hamlet and Othello and in later seasons saw the young Gielgud as Hamlet, Richard II, Malvolio, and Antony, and Edith Evans as the Shrew and Rosalind.

He came up to Oxford as a devout Shavian, soon after the General Strike; but in his undergraduate years, he used to say, politics was less important than poetry. Much of his study of literature was extra-curricular, since English literature, as understood by the examinations system, ended in 1880. In the late 1920s Muir and his contemporaries were reading Lawrence, Joyce, Yeats, and Eliot, but when M. R. Ridley offered a course on modern poetry, he talked of Brooke, Flecker, and Bridges; and when the Professor of Poetry, H. W. Garrod, ventured into the modern field, he also chose to speak on Brooke, together with Bridges and Humbert Wolfe. Muir found some lectures brilliant—notably those given by C. S. Lewis, F. P. Wilson, and Brett Smith—but the rest of the teaching, as well as the syllabus, uninspiring. He graduated in 1929 with Second Class Honours, brought down in his Finals by his dislike of Anglo-Saxon when taught as a purely linguistic subject. Barred from the opportunity of doing research, he proceeded to take the Diploma in Education, which he later regarded as a blessing in disguise, both because he discovered that he loved teaching and because the course itself was not very demanding and left him plenty of time to read in Bodley, to begin to write his own poetry, and to act. As a graduate he was free to take part in performances at John Masefield's private theatre at Boar's Hill where earlier, in the autumn of 1928, he had been invited to play Antipholus of Syracuse in *The Comedy of Errors* because, Mrs Masefield wrote, 'we have heard so much of your speaking of verse'. The production nearly came to grief, when it was discovered at the last minute that undergraduates were allowed to act only in OUDS or College productions. But Mrs Masefield successfully appealed to the Vice-Chancellor for a special relaxation of the rule, and Kenneth Muir always treasured the note he received from Masefield after the last performance, thanking him in the words of Marvell for 'daring the prelate's rage'. In his last Oxford year, 1929–30, he acted at Boar's Hill in dramatisations of *The Iliad* and of Blake's *Jerusalem* (Book 4) and took the part of Satan in a rare performance of Blake's play *The Ghost of Abel*; and he was one of three finalists in the Oxford Recitations, run by Masefield to encourage verse-speaking, with his fellow-poets Binyon and Bottomley as judges.

Appointed in 1930—mainly, he believed, on the strength of a reference from John Masefield, by then Poet Laureate—to a lectureship at St John's College, York, an Anglican Training College for Teachers, Muir began an academic career deeply committed to teaching and theatre, to poetry and politics. His convictions made for an uneasy relationship with the College Principal who tried on three separate occasions to sack him—the last time for encouraging students to come to his study to discuss religion, literature, and politics. On each occasion the sacking was rescinded on the insistence of the chairman of the College governors, Archbishop William Temple, who was a regular and enthusiastic attender of Muir's Shakespeare productions. Meanwhile, like so many of his contemporaries in the 1930s, Muir was driven to take an active part in politics by events at home and abroad: by the great Depression and unemployment; by the Japanese invasion of Manchuria and the Italian invasion of Abyssinia, by the rise of Hitler and the persecution of the Jews. He read and was influenced by Auden and Spender; and he read *Christianity and Social Revolution*, a volume of essays to which Christians and Marxists had contributed, and was influenced particularly by the work of John Macmurray and Karl Polanyi. These two were the intellectual leaders of a group entitled The Christian Left, which he joined; and this led to an invitation to join a smaller splinter group who met monthly in London to discuss the future of socialism and the possibility of a reconciliation between Christianity and Marxism. He helped to edit a printed news sheet of the Christian Left which appeared at irregular intervals and included the great theologian Niebuhr among its contributors, and also to publish a number of cyclostyled pamphlets, on subjects such as working-class consciousness and the historical roots of British socialism.

It was a heady time to be a young intellectual and poet: not so much a dawn in which it was bliss to be alive as a dusk in which the encroaching darkness, of present miseries and wars to come, was shot through with the will to hope. It is reflected in the epigraph—Hotspur's 'I tell you, my lord fool, out of this nettle, danger, we pluck this flower, safety'—of Kenneth Muir's first book, a collection of poems entitled *The Nettle and the Flower* and published by Oxford University Press in 1933. And it is reflected in the assertion which ends the long poem that gave the volume its title:

> We need not fear the sorrow and the pain,
> we need not shrink from all that life may bring,
> from the harsh nettle we may pluck the flower,
> ignore the thorn and gather up the rose.

Blake, Shelley, and Keats, rather than Auden, are the young poet's masters; and the flower plucked is not Hotspur's 'safety' but a Romantic vision of how

> All the sharp fragments of the broken mirror
> of life, are unified to form a glass,
> wherein we see the beauty that outlasts Time—
> the perfect vision of immortal art!

Resounding with echoes of past poets, the volume proclaims poetry as the salvation of the present. 'Poetry leads!' (that is, over 'philosophy', 'Church' and 'science') he exclaims in a poem addressed to Sean O'Loughlin, an Oxford friend with whom he was exchanging weekly letters in which each of them set out his ideas on each of Shakespeare's plays, in chronological order. Muir continued to publish his poetry in periodicals and in a volume, *Jonah and the Whale* (1935), where verses of his accompanied a wood-engraving by Gertrud Hermes. But the next major publication, in joint authorship with O'Loughlin and the result of their correspondence, was also his first venture into Shakespeare criticism: *The Voyage to Illyria* (1937). In its sensitive attention to Shakespeare's poetry, it foreshadows his later work. In their preoccupation with imagery, the authors have learned from Caroline Spurgeon and the early writings of G. Wilson Knight. But, as a work of the 1930s, the book is also strangely old-fashioned, reading the sequence of plays and poems in a Dowdenesque fashion as revelations of Shakespeare's inner life: an approach which Muir—but not O'Loughlin—was to denounce in the Preface to the second edition (1970).

In real life during these York years he was approaching Shakespeare in quite a different way, via the theatre. He directed two or three student productions at St John's College and—in a period that he was to remember as a kind of Golden Age—joined the York Settlement Community Players, with whom he played Orsino in *Twelfth Night*, the Ghost in *Hamlet*, and Agamemnon in *Troilus and Cressida*. He co-directed the last two and *King Lear*, as well as more modern drama: Ibsen's *Rosmersholm* and Lenormand's *Shadow of Evil* (in his own translation). As it happened, this activity also became his way into university employment, as Bonamy Dobrée, Professor of English Literature at Leeds, came to see the production of *Troilus and Cressida* and suggested that Muir apply for a lectureship in his department. He was duly appointed—luckily, he was to say later, *The Voyage to Illyria* had not yet appeared—and moved to Leeds in 1937. He had married Mary Ewen, a fellow socialist and teacher, in the previous year, and the salary-cut implied by the move (since the University would not give him credit for the seven years at St John's) was a serious matter. But his desire for a more academic environment prevailed. He and Mary bought a cookery book which had 100 recipes for sixpenny meals for two people, and he began to review eight novels a month for *The Yorkshire Post*, thus increasing his earnings by more than 50 per cent.

At the time, English Literature at Leeds was a very small unit. With Bonamy Dobrée, who remained Head of the Department throughout the 14 years Muir spent there, and whom he never ceased admiring, there were only two lecturers: Wilfred Childe and Douglas Jefferson. For part of the war years, as Dobrée went off to train artillery officers and to work for the Army Bureau of Current Affairs, and as Jefferson was called up, there were only Childe and Muir to cover the entire syllabus. And Muir had to combine lecturing to undergraduates with war work, first as officer in charge of the War Room, North East Regional Control, where his job was to train a dozen or so telephonists, clerks, and teleprinter operators to dispatch fire-engines, ambulances, and rescue parties from one town to another during an air raid, and then in a Report Centre where he gave unappreciated lectures to army units.

After the war, the teaching staff expanded, with notable appointments of Harold Fisch, Arnold Kettle, and G. Wilson Knight. Kenneth Muir formed important and lasting friendships with each of these new colleagues. Leeds was an exciting centre for English studies. Drama flourished, too. It had been understood that one of Muir's functions at Leeds would be to direct for the students' dramatic society; on arrival he took over a production of *All for Love*, and later he directed *The Importance of being Earnest*, *Heartbreak House*, his own translation of *The Trojan Women*, and *Coriolanus*. He never really approved of modern dress productions of Shakespeare, but for this, mid-war, *Coriolanus* there was a desperate shortage of men for the battle scenes. So Volumnia and Virgilia listened to bulletins of the battles (in Shakespeare's words) on the six o'clock news, Coriolanus became a fascist dictator and the Tribunes were Labour politicians. When the students decided to direct their own productions, Muir became involved in the staff dramatic society and took a series of leading roles, among them Vershinin in *Three Sisters*, Cusins in *Major Barbara*, Rakitin in *A Month in the Country*, Mirabel in *The Way of the World*, Holofernes in *Love's Labour's Lost*, and Gloucester in a historic *King Lear* with Wilson Knight as Lear. Knight himself directed several productions, and one of the most successful was of Racine's *Athalie* in a translation by Muir. Its fame eventually reached the ears of Eric Bentley, who asked Muir, by this time in the University of Liverpool, to translate five of Racine's plays for Hill and Wang's Dramabooks. He translated the remaining four plays while serving as Dean of the Faculty of Arts. *Five Plays of Racine* (1960) has to compete, in this country, with the later Penguin translation, but is still a standard text in the United States. He liked to say that these translations gave him 'some compensation for not having been able to write viable poetic drama', and in the last two decades of his life he was to produce, in collaboration with Ann Mackenzie, some brilliant translations of Calderon.

Scholarly writing, and not poetic drama, came out of the Leeds years, once the lightening of the wartime teaching-load made research possible. During his last year at York he had written a study of Keats for which he had not found a publisher; parts of it were published many years later, in a volume of essays by members of the Liverpool English Department which he edited, entitled *John Keats: A Reassessment* (1958). He had also begun a book on the University Wits, which was interrupted by the war. This was set aside because, by the time he was able to return to research, he had been offered contracts to edit the poems of Sir Thomas Wyatt for the New Muses Library and *Macbeth* for the 'New' Arden. These commissions, to which was soon added the Arden *King Lear*, were to make his name as a scholar; and they were earned by his earlier work. He attributed the invitation to edit Wyatt to

Dobrée's patronage and literary connections; but Una Ellis-Fermor, General Editor of the Arden Shakespeare, sought him out as the author of *Voyage to Illyria* and—possibly more importantly—of an article on 'The Future of Shakespeare' in *Penguin New Writing* of July 1946. In this he had laid out a programme for what needed to be done in Shakespeare studies, personally prophetic insofar as it asks for 'an exhaustive study of Shakespeare's use of his sources', but above all demonstrating a close familiarity with, and stringent appraisal of, the state of Shakespeare scholarship at the time. The article had also attracted the attention of Allardyce Nicoll, who asked him to contribute a Retrospect on Shakespeare criticism to *Shakespeare Survey 4*, and thus began a lifelong association with that journal and with Nicoll's two other foundations, the Shakespeare Institute at Stratford-upon-Avon and the biennial International Shakespeare Conference held there. Muir was eventually to succeed Nicoll as editor of *Survey* and, after being responsible for fifteen annual volumes, to hand the editorship on to Stanley Wells.

Editing Wyatt was a case of teaching himself basic research skills on the job—a situation almost unimaginable nowadays, when a doctorate and the book that comes out of the thesis are virtually mandatory qualifications for the humblest post in higher education. He had to learn to read sixteenth-century handwriting and, besides, had only nine months for his work on the manuscripts. As always, he met the deadline. The resulting volume, *Collected Poems of Sir Thomas Wyatt*, was published in 1949, revised for a second impression, and then reprinted several times, despite Muir's pleas to the publishers to be allowed to make corrections and revisions and, after 1960, to incorporate the unpublished Wyatt poems which he had discovered in the Blage manuscript in the library of Trinity College, Dublin, and which he felt made it academically disreputable to call the Muses edition 'Collected'. Instead, he published the Blage manuscript poems through the Liverpool University Press (1961) and incorporated them in the new *Collected Poems of Sir Thomas Wyatt* which he co-edited with Patricia Thomson, for the same Press (1969). By that time he had also shed new light on the historical and personal context of the poems in a volume, *Life and Letters of Sir Thomas Wyatt*, published in the 'Liverpool Texts and Studies' series (1963). With the tact and humility of the true scholar he lets Wyatt speak for himself. Details of texts and attributions may continue to be debated, but Muir's lasting contribution is not only to have made a remarkable addition to the corpus of English Renaissance poetry but also to have made it once and for all impossible to dismiss the poetry of Wyatt as 'drab age verse', the way C. S. Lewis did in the *Oxford History of English Literature in the Sixteenth Century*.

Editing Shakespeare was less of a start from scratch, more congenial and also more likely to bring academic rewards, as indeed Muir's *Macbeth* and *King Lear* did, and justifiably so, when they appeared as the first and third of the 'New' Arden Shakespeares in, respectively, 1951 and 1952. Spoiled for choice, as we now are, between competing multi-volume editions, each play text fully annotated and supplied with prefaces and appendices discussing the text, sources, stage history, critical fortunes, and other aspects, we may not always appreciate the impact of those editions in the 1950s. The 'New' Ardens had initially been meant to be simply revised versions of the Arden Shakespeare: the early instructions to editors were to preserve the form of each original page, which meant that only minimal alterations could be made in the text, and that new material in the commentary had to be of precisely the same length as any passage deleted. This soon proved unworkable but Muir, undoubtedly the most deadline-conscious of the editors, probably suffered the most from changing guidelines, as what had begun as a revision became a new edition. Nevertheless, and from within a work-schedule where sabbaticals were unheard of, he produced—on time, of course—two editions which have established themselves as classics, have been repeatedly reprinted and, if superseded in some respects by newer editions, will continue to be referred to. Not, perhaps, so much for the textual scholarship—Muir, for example, refused to consider the possibility of the Quarto and the Folio texts of *King Lear* having independent authority, and insisted on the legitimacy of a con-flated text—as for the commentary, enriched by his work on the sources. Generations of students also owe much to the informative and critically balanced introductions to the texts. By the time he wrote them, he had abandoned the biographical approach of *The Voyage to Illyria* and in the introduction to *King Lear* he finds it 'intolerable' to suppose 'that Shakespeare had experienced the suffering that is at the heart of *King Lear*'. He had founded his critical position, which he would retain for the rest of his life, on Keats's assertion of Shakespeare's 'negative capability'. At the same time, the ultimate optimism of *The Nettle and the Flower* informs the view of *King Lear* on which he would insist throughout his later writings, against the pessimism of the 1960s—when, in Jan Kott's *Shakespeare Our Contemporary* and Peter Brook's famous RSC production, the play became Shakespeare's *Endgame*—and against cultural materialist readings of more recent decades. With typical sanity and directness he states in his introduction that, if there is something gratuitous about the death of Cordelia, it 'does not mean that the gods kill us for their sport; it means simply that they do not intervene to prevent us from killing each other'.

In 1951 Kenneth Muir applied for, and was appointed to, the King Alfred Chair of English Literature in the University of Liverpool. He felt the time had come, he used to say, 'to run my own show'. But uprooting himself from Leeds, where he was singularly happy in his friends, in his colleagues, and in his municipal and theatrical activities, was not easy. By 1951 he had become a senior lecturer, a city councillor and chairman of the Leeds City Labour Party as well as the Leeds Fabian Society, and had just ceased being the editor of a weekly newspaper. The years in which he had built his academic career had also been thronged with political activity. He had moved, via the Christian Left, into active membership of the Labour Party. Its Leeds secretary, Len Williams, was also the editor of the *Leeds Weekly Citizen*, the oldest surviving Labour Party paper, founded in 1911. When Williams denounced him for writing reviews for the conservative *Yorkshire Post*, Muir took this as an oblique invitation to write for the *Citizen*, and over the next twelve years he wrote some thousand (unpaid) articles, mostly of a thousand words each. Under his own name he wrote literary articles on practically every English writer, countering complaints from readers who thought literature was 'bourgeois' by concentrating on the political views of the writers discussed, or their Yorkshire connections. Writing on non-literary topics, he used a variety of pseudonyms, male and female. This enabled him to engage in dialectics: on controversial matters he would put forward opinions under one name and attack them under another. On one occasion five of these pseudonyms as well as he himself were all invited to address a local society in successive weeks: he accepted in his own person and got friends in different parts of the country to post polite refusals from the rest. Party politics, which had been suspended during the war, were resumed in 1945, and in the local elections Muir was returned as one of the Labour candidates for the Harehills ward. At much the same time, and though desperately busy electioneering for the General Election, he allowed himself to be persuaded to take over the editorship of the *Leeds Weekly Citizen*. Once the election had brought Labour into power, he set about trying to make the *Citizen* a more interesting paper, one which put issues under debate instead of merely churning out the party line. He published articles by Hugh Gaitskell and Hugh Dalton and roped in his friends from the Christian Left to write for the paper, but even so the main burden of filling the columns fell on himself. Thriving under pressure that would have overwhelmed most others, he persisted for four and a half years until, in the run-up to the 1950 election, the board of trustees of the paper instructed him to avoid all criticism of the government and to adopt a less 'intellectual' attitude. He resigned in protest against such censorship, not without a sense of relief. All the while he had also been heavily engaged in council work, not least as chairman of the Primary and Secondary Education Subcommittees. One of his tasks in this capacity was to explain the implementation of the 1944 Education Act to meetings of parents. In complete sincerity he would tell his audiences that in future every child—whether he or she went to a Grammar, Secondary Modern, or Technical School—would receive an education appropriate to age and ability. The gradual realisation that this was not happening turned him into an advocate of comprehensive education and left a nagging sense of guilt towards those crowds of parents he felt he had misled.

'It seems inevitable', Muir wrote in his 1991 essay on 'Dissident Poets', 'for Angry Young Men to move right as they get older and settle down.' He cannot have had himself in mind, partly because from the very beginning his socialism was more compassionate than angry, but mainly because, as he became a Professor and settled down in a Victorian house in Birkenhead, he certainly did not move right. Nor did his political activity cease. He was duly elected chairman of the constituency Labour Party and was for many years a member of its executive committee. For a while he was chairman of the Wirral Fabian Society. Within three years of moving to Birkenhead he was elected a councillor for Grange ward, and he spent thirteen years on the education committee. They were, though, often contentious, and ended with his resignation on a matter of principle. Altogether he found being a borough councillor in Birkenhead rather different from being a city councillor in Leeds: he felt, in his own words, that 'the bosses regarded a professor with suspicion, as a possible threat to their power'.

As a professor, heading the Liverpool English Department for 23 years, Kenneth Muir relished power: not for its own sake but because it enabled him to get things done. In the 1950s there were still not that many professors about, and the title conferred authority, which he exercised for the good of his department. Before long, he was also Dean of the Faculty of Arts—then a Faculty of thirty departments, including not only the Humanities and Ancient and Modern Languages but also Architecture and Civic Design, Social Science, Psychology, Political Theory, Economics, Geography, and even Education. He chaired endless meetings with brisk efficiency, while also carrying a full teaching-load and writing books and articles. Frustrated by the Faculty's resistance to his proposals for reform, he began but—perhaps fortunately—did not complete, a detective story entitled Death of a Dean. (He was himself an avid reader of detective fiction and an addict of television's Maigret series in the 1960s.) The reason why he abandoned it, he would say, was that he could not imagine any of his colleagues as potential murderers. Indeed, though he was a thorn in the flesh of the more conservative of those colleagues, he was also regarded with a great deal of affection, as no one could doubt his idealism and absolute integrity. There was much mutual respect between him and his Vice-Chancellor, Sir James Mountford. Muir dedicated to Mountford *The Life and Letters of Sir Thomas Wyatt* which he wrote during his deanship; and Mountford dubbed as 'paramuiral' a series of interdisciplinary courses which Muir had introduced to bridge the gap between Arts and Sciences at a time when there was much concern about the 'Two Cultures'. By the time he retired, there were not many responsible University offices which he had not held. He was Public Orator for four years, and of the forty-three orations he had to compose, the ones most congenial were for Harold Wilson (then Prime Minister) and for a great fellow-Shakespearean and friend, Muriel Bradbrook.

He was for years chairman of the Library Committee and of the Board of Extramural Studies—both areas close to his heart. As so often, his reform plans—such as the proposal for a 'Birkbeck of the North' for part-time adult students— were ahead of his time. His activities reached outside the University, both through teaching—he was a draw on extramural courses and always ready to give lectures to schools—and through committee-work, on the Joint Matriculation Board, the School's Council and the Postgraduate Awards Committee of the Department of Education and Science.

In the midst of all this activity, and drawing benefit from his refusal to regard academia as an ivory tower, there was his own department, where he ruled by example rather than by decree. There was democracy, if you were around to take part in it: departmental meetings would begin at 12.15, and if your class overran, you were likely on arrival to find the chairman donning his hat and coat for an ineluctable 12.30 departure for staff-house lunch. There was a work-ethic based on the assumption that teaching and researching into literature were the most important and enjoyable things anyone could do—an assumption which made for a quality culture long before the term had been invented. In consequence there was little bureaucracy and much intellectual democracy: freedom for even the most junior member of staff to be listened to in the exchange of ideas, and to be encouraged to publish. There was occasionally a somewhat edgy relationship between representatives of English Literature and of English Language—debates about the place of Old English in the syllabus, and about the amount of Literature a Language student should read, which echoed back to Muir's Leeds days and to his own undergraduate experience—but these were amicably resolved, especially after Simeon Potter, famous linguist, had been succeeded as Language Professor by Jimmy Cross, who wrote on Anglo-Saxon literature. In the 1960s and 1970s the Department steadily expanded—when Muir retired there were five times as many students graduating each year as when he was appointed—and there was a good deal of movement in and out of staff. Happily a core of those whom he had joined in 1951 remained, among them Kenneth Allott with whom, as another 1930s poet turned literary scholar, he had much in common, and Miriam Allott who, a scholar and editor in her own right, completed after his death her husband's work on Matthew Arnold and in due course succeeded him in the A. C. Bradley Chair of English Literature. Muir was proud to say that his Department was a seedbed for professors: of his appointees, G. K. Hunter went to a foundation chair at Warwick, Ernest Schanzer to Munich, Norman Sherry to Lancaster, Inga-Stina Ewbank to Bedford College, London. He was also proud to have replaced these with a group of bright young graduates whom he rightly saw as future academic leaders: Vincent Newey, Nick Shrimpton, Hermione Lee, Janet Montefiori, Ann Thompson, Nick Grene. And a particular source of joy and pride into his retirement was to see first one and then another distinguished Shakespearean scholar appointed to the succession of the King

Alfred Chair: first his friend of many years, Philip Edwards, followed on his retirement by Jonathan Bate.

The example that Kenneth Muir set before his colleagues might nowadays be termed 'time-management': every letter replied to by return of post, every deadline met, every interstice of time between scheduled engagements used for essential reading, writing, and proof-correcting. These, though, were only the outward symptoms of the deep-seated devotion to scholarship which manifested itself in a prodigious output of publications during the Liverpool years (a period which includes his retirement, since the University allotted him a room to which he resorted, crossing the Mersey daily, until the last month of his life). In the early years his main work was on Shakespeare's sources, gathering what was known and adding new evidence of indebtednesses, echoes, and borrowings. As one discovery after another was chronicled in *Notes and Queries*, that journal came to be known affectionately in the Department as 'Old Muir's Almanac'. The resulting book, published in 1957, bore the title *Shakespeare's Sources* I, as it dealt only with the comedies and tragedies and he intended to deal with the histories in a second volume. But the urgent need (which Muir had demonstrated ten years earlier, in his *Penguin New Writing* article) to extend and complete our knowledge of Shakespeare's sources was now being served by the publication of Geoffrey Bullough's monumental eight-volume collection of *Narrative and Dramatic Sources of Shakespeare* (1957–75); and more pressing tasks intervened. When Muir's *The Sources of Shakespeare's Plays* appeared in 1977, it was not a second volume but a source study of all the plays, incorporating the first volume. Bullough's work remains an invaluable reference and research tool, and Muir's takes its place beside it as managing in a single volume to give a comprehensive view of Shakespeare's use of his source material. In its demonstration of the extent of Shakespeare's reading and of the complex ways in which that reading is transmuted in the texts, it remains the *Road to Xanadu* of Shakespeare studies.

Faced with the range and abundance of Muir's writings in the Liverpool years, one is forced to generalise; but in order to do so adequately one would need his own ability to be both comprehensive and trenchant. For his strength as a scholar and critic lay not in startling originality but in wisdom and sanity, in judicious balance, and in a pellucid prose that holds the reader by its flair for the precise, illuminating phrase. The source of that strength, it seems, was in a central wholeness where all he had read and done came together and nothing was lost. Past experience—not least the sheer fluency that *The Leeds Citizen* had forced upon him—conditioned present achievement. It gave him, as reviewers of his books tended to say, an extraordinary and catholic breadth of approach and an ability to cross-refer between different fields of knowledge. Most particularly, his experience of acting and directing fed directly into both his textual and his critical work. He wrote on dramatic texts from a constant awareness that they are, above all, plays for the stage. From playing the Cardinal in a student production of *Women Beware Women* in 1967 grew an interest in Middleton which produced both an edition of *Three Plays of Middleton* (1975) and a number of essays that were to form the core of *Shakespeare: Contrasts and Controversies* (1985). He felt strongly about the value of this kind of interaction in his approach to Shakespeare. Not only did his York productions of *Macbeth* and *King Lear* lead naturally to the Arden editions of those plays, but when he edited the Oxford *Troilus and Cressida* in the early 1980s, he was both re-living his own Leeds production of that play nearly forty years earlier and drawing on accumulated textual expertise (which included editing the Signet *Richard II* and the New Penguin *Othello* in the 1960s). His involvement—at Epsom, Oxford, York, Leeds, and Liverpool—in productions of five of Shakespeare's comedies was, he felt, what prompted the writing of *Shakespeare's Comic Sequence* (1979). Similarly, his enjoyment of professional productions of Restoration comedy came together with long-term memories of playing Mirabel in *The Way of the World*, to inform his book, *The Comedy of Manners* (1970), where he can assert from first-hand experience that 'no dramatist has equalled Congreve in the creation of character by diction and rhythm'.

The wholeness of his work could also be traced to an unshakeable belief in the value of English Studies as a discipline and in his own place within it. This is not to say that he was self-sufficient: he was always ready generously to consider the opinions of others and could treat with a blend of wise tolerance and deadpan irony even those he regarded as belonging to the lunatic fringe—as in his book on *Shakespeare's Sonnets* (1979). But it gave a confidence which enabled him to continue building on his own insights, so that lectures grew into books, and one book spawned another. Lectures on *The Two Noble Kinsmen* and *Edward III*, together with writings on *Pericles*, grew into the book on *Shakespeare as Collaborator* (1960), which planted the challenge to write on the uniqueness of Shakespeare in *Shakespeare the Professional* (1973) and *The Singularity of Shakespeare* (1977). Having launched, in his British Academy Shakespeare Lecture of 1958, his famous dictum that there is no such thing as Shakespearean Tragedy, only Shakespeare's tragedies, he proceeded to expand it in various publications, culminating in *Shakespeare's Tragic Sequence* (1972), which was almost bound to find its counterpart in *Shakespeare's Comic Sequence* (1979).

Kenneth Muir was naturally unostentatious, but he was quietly proud of his achievements and not afraid to show his enjoyment of the honours bestowed on him: the honorary doctorates from the Universities of Rouen and Dijon, the presidency of the International Shakespeare Association, and in particular the Fellowship of the British Academy, to which he was elected in 1970. He was a regular attender of Academy meetings and chaired many of the annual

Shakespeare Lectures with customary wit and elegance. He was himself a superb lecturer and—foreign audiences often showing their appreciation more volubly than British ones—enjoyed receiving standing ovations in the United States, which he visited many times from 1948 onwards, and in most countries in Europe. His work was his life, and it was not always easy for him to remember that not everybody lived at his level: when Mary, his wife, was in hospital after the birth of their son and asked him to bring her something to read, he brought a copy of his just-published edition of *Macbeth*. His utter lack of guile or malice won him loyal friends at every level, social and intellectual, but he enjoyed nothing so much as a friendly gossip with fellow-Shakespeareans from all over the world at the International Shakespeare Conferences. These have been held at the Shakespeare Institute in Stratford-upon-Avon every other year since 1947, and Kenneth Muir did not miss a single one since he was first invited by Allardyce Nicoll, in 1949, to join what was then a small and select group. The sudden onset of his mortal illness happened just before the 1996 Conference, but he would go to Stratford, though barely able to speak. The paper he had prepared had to be delivered by Philip Edwards, but he would attend it and every other occasion, including theatre performances, during the Conference. He cut the cake to celebrate the fiftieth birthday of *Shakespeare Survey*. Within a few weeks he was gone, leaving the rest of us feeling that we 'shall never see so much, nor live so long'.

INGA-STINA EWBANK
University of Leeds

Note. There is a selective bibliography of Kenneth Muir's writings, 1937–79, in the book of essays in his honour, *Shakespeare's Styles*, ed. Philip Edwards, Inga-Stina Ewbank, and G. K. Hunter (Cambridge, 1980). A more comprehensive bibliography will appear in his Autobiography, forthcoming from Liverpool University Press.

In preparing this Memoir I have been able to draw on the manuscript autobiography and other papers left to me by direction in Kenneth Muir's will. For information and help I am very grateful to Professor Philip Edwards and Professor Stanley Wells. If there are any mistakes, the responsibility is mine.

STUART PIGGOTT

Stuart Piggott
1910–1996

STUART PIGGOTT was born on 28 May 1910, the grandson of the schoolmaster at Childrey, four miles from Uffington, at that time in Berkshire, and a mile from West Challow where he ended his days. Piggott's father was also a school-master and in 1910, at the age of 36, he was a master at Churcher's College, Petersfield. Known affectionately as 'The Captain' to the boys, he had married a Welshwoman, a Phillips, from Breconshire. In this pedigree must have lain the source of Piggott's distinguished good looks and his startlingly original, mercurial mind. There were no brothers or sisters and the focus of familial contact lay with his paternal grandparents and aunts living, as Piggotts had lived since at least the early seventeenth century, under the hooves of the Uffington White Horse.

This sense of place and belonging was clearly, to all who knew him, close to the core of Stuart Piggott's being. Tracing his ancestry in a *Retrospect* published in 1983,[1] he emphasised how 'Piggotts have been around in Marcham, Hatford and West Challow and the families had died out or slipped quietly downhill to the status of farm labourer or, at best, small peasant farmers. My great-grandfather was one of these, in Uffington . . . and my grandfather at the age of 10 was taken up to the last of the traditional festive "scourings" in 1857 by Thomas Hughes . . . who wrote up the event in *The Scouring of the White Horse* and who recorded the scourers as "singing a rambling sort of ditty, with a fol-de-rol chorus":

> The awld White Horse wants zettin to rights
> And the Squire hev promised good cheer
> Zo we'll gee un a scrape to kip un in zhape
> And a'll last for many a year.

[1] 'Archaeological Retrospect 5', *Antiquity*, LVII (1983), 28–37.

Proceedings of the British Academy, **97**, 413–442. © The British Academy 1998.

> A was made a lang lang time ago
> Wi a good dale o' labour and paines
> By King Alfred the Great when he spwiled their consate
> And caddled they wosbirds the Danes.'

Before he was twenty Piggott was to publish a rather different cultural and chronological attribution for this unique chalk hillside carving. But the salient aspects of his approach to life and study are set out here very clearly. He believed in the laying on of hands and the transmission of tradition. He was a great democrat and deplored snobbery of any kind.

In 1918 Piggott entered Churcher's College where he appears to have had a relatively undistinguished career. In the *Retrospect* he says 'I suppose I was reasonably intelligent but I was idle, wayward and capricious, exerting myself only on subjects that interested me, and acquiring a detestation of alternative activities such as compulsory games, sports and the OTC.' Lack of interest in maths and science led to his failure to attain part of his School Certificate which led to his non-qualification for university entrance. Nevertheless, a number of his masters at Churcher's had (in those happier pre-national curriculum days!) imparted to him an eclectic baggage of interests—Biblical textual criticism, Indo-European philology, botany, and the history of art and architecture. Furthermore Petersfield, with its bookshop (and Stuart could never long resist a bookshop) provided something of a *salon* of artists, journalists, and writers to whom he was introduced and from whom he absorbed much of the 'business' side of academic life: writing to set length, book production processes, illustration techniques.

This informal and extramural education created the perfect background for his career as it was to develop. By the age of fourteen he had produced, in a school exercise book, *The Prehistoric Remains at Petersfield* which wedded pretty creditable drawings of flint implements to what Piggott himself called an 'embarrassingly awful' text; he had already sent some of those drawings to Reginald Smith, at that time Keeper of British Prehistory at the British Museum, whence he had received an encouraging and useful reply. Increasingly during his summer holidays Piggott had been devoting himself to more and more seriously directed fieldwork. Between the ages of sixteen and eighteen he was to spend a good deal of time looking at, and drawing, plans of earthworks on Butser Hill, just south of Petersfield.[2] By assiduous sherd collection, he located a Roman-British settlement site there; a note appeared in the parish magazine which, picked up by a local newspaper, thus came to the attention of O. G. S. Crawford. Crawford was a key figure in British archaeology at this time. 'Possessed with the divine impatience of the pioneer' (as Wheeler described him)[3] he had, in

---

[2] Ultimately published in *Antiquity*, IV (1930), 187–200.
[3] R. E. M. Wheeler, *Alms for Oblivion* (1966), 155.

1921, been made chief of the Ordnance Survey's newly founded Archaeology Division and was, with extraordinary energy, compiling their index of sites and find-spots in Britain. A great publicist, in 1927 he founded the journal *Antiquity* which was to form an important outlet for Piggott's early work. Crawford immediately recognised Piggott's qualities and they became fast friends as Piggott devilled for him, checking references, and the accuracy of their location on maps.

A further important figure in Piggott's development was a family friend. George Heywood Sumner had retired in middle age to Hampshire from a quite prominent position in the Arts and Crafts Movement, associated first with Morris and latterly with the 'populist' wing that included Walter Crane and W. A. S. Benson. In 1902 he set up house at Cuckoo Hill near South Gorley and exercised a consuming interest, for his last forty years, in the antiquities of Dorset and Hampshire. He became a close friend of Dr J. P. Williams-Freeman of Weyhill whom Piggott knew from the Petersfield connection. Both men were at the forefront of that style of landscape archaeology founded in a deep love of the countryside that surrounded them, and an intimate knowledge of its contours and natural cover. Sumner's unique contribution was his development of a wonderfully evocative illustrative style, gentle, humorous and supremely decorative, yet also rigorous and precise, that adorns his beautiful volumes, published by the Chiswick Press, *The Ancient Earthworks of Cranborne Chase* (1913) and *The Ancient Earthworks of the New Forest* (1917). A glance at Piggott's early drawings will reveal the homage that he paid to Sumner's artistic vision.

Piggott published his first note in the *Antiquaries Journal* for 1927 on the excavation of some Iron-Age pits at Knighton Hill, near Compton Beauchamp, about five miles from Childrey. In this same year he published papers on place-name evidence[4] and on Berkshire mummers plays[5] which demonstrate the breadth of his early interest in 'his country'. Kipling, of whose pastoral poetry Stuart was very fond, had summed all this up a quarter of a century before:

> God gave all men all earth to love,
>   But since our hearts are small,
> Ordained for each one spot should prove
>   Belovèd over all;
> That, as He watched Creation's birth,
>   So we, in godlike mood,
> May of our love create our earth
>   And see that it is good.
>   ('Sussex', 1902)

and had enshrined in poems such as 'Puck's Song'[6] the model of such landscape-historical cum archaeological affection.

---

[4] *Antiquity*, I (1927), 478–9.
[5] *Folklore*, XXXIX (1927), 271–81.
[6] R. Kipling, *Puck of Pook's Hill* (1906).

Piggott's first lengthy analytical article was published in 1930.[7] It sum-
marises fieldwork conducted between the ages of sixteen and eighteen on
Butser Hill (above) which he had clearly discussed with Williams-Freeman
and O. G. S. Crawford; the illustrations were drawn from RAF air photographs
(to which Crawford must have guided him). His own beautiful maps and plans
were founded on Heywood Sumner's approach, but executed with greater
restraint, and running to an altogether greater depth of landscape detail. A
major force in landscape archaeological analysis had clearly arrived.

But we leap ahead. Piggott's frequent visits to Berkshire had brought him
into contact with the museum at Reading and its curator, W. A. Smallcombe,
who offered him, on leaving school at seventeen, a post as assistant 'at a
nominal salary'—which Piggott recalls in his 1985 *Retrospect* as ten shillings
(50p) a week. His duties encompassed everything from the classification of
wild flowers (in which, we have already seen, he had some capacity even if he
had to 'sweat it out with Bentham and Hooker') to archaeology itself. Here
another formative experience awaited, for, living at Boxford, a few miles from
Reading, was Harold Peake—the co-author with Herbert Fleure of 'The
Corridors of Time' series of books that covered broad archaeological issues
across the whole of the Old World; *The Origins of Agriculture* had just
appeared in 1926. Peake was also a highly original honorary curator at
Newbury Museum; giving each century of prehistory equal presentation in
his displays, he offered a genuine sense of time to his public. The story was
told[8] that when a school inspector spoke of things that had happened 'very
long ago', a Newbury child interjected, 'Oh but that was quite lately, in the La
Tène period.' Such exuberance also acted host to some archaeological eccentricities, but Piggott, quite able to see his way through that, took good
advantage of the 'open-house' kept by the Peakes at Boxford. Peake, at that
time President of the Royal Anthropological Institute, was instrumental in
appointing Vere Gordon Childe, who had just taken up the first appointment
as Abercromby Professor of Archaeology at Edinburgh, as Honorary Librarian
of the Institute in a design to create a new focus for scientific, interdisciplinary
archaeology—away from the Society of Antiquaries with its baggage-train of
incunabula and heraldry. Significantly Abercromby's endowment of the Chair
in Edinburgh arose out of an essentially similar dispute with the Society of
Antiquaries of Scotland. Archaeology was changing shape and size rapidly and
Piggott was, unorthodoxly but nevertheless precisely, placed to take advantage
of this.

Another important figure of the old school who was to influence Piggott at
this time was Dr Eliot Curwen. He and his son E. Cecil Curwen had been

[7] *Antiquity*, IV (1930), 187–220.
[8] H. Peake and H. J. Fleure, *Times and Places*, Corridors of Time, X (1956), iii.

discovering and mapping the landscape archaeology of the South Downs since before the First World War. They had recognised, in some instances for the first time, the enclosures and traces of flint-mine shafts pertaining to the Neolithic, the earliest period of farming prehistory in Britain. Their work had been of the keenest interest to O. G. S. Crawford whose research in Wiltshire and Dorset had focused on similar objectives. Piggott, using his time at Reading to maximum advantage, had meanwhile found his way into the study of Neolithic pottery particularly through a series of pit-finds located by the Thames at Pangbourne and at Caversham, the former including a rare type of burial with an intact pot of what Piggott was later to term the Abingdon style. He published these finds in 1928[9] and it was his interest and energetic expertise in the analysis of Neolithic pottery that impelled the Curwens to invite Piggott to participate in their excavation of the Neolithic 'causewayed enclosure' at The Trundle in 1928, an excavation which in turn reflected on what had been done since 1925 by Alexander Keiller at Windmill Hill near Avebury in Wiltshire.

Piggott, in company with his father, who was a friend of the Curwens, excavated at The Trundle in 1928 and 1930. Clearly during this period his authority and the breadth of experience were burgeoning and by 1930 he was laying out the trenches at The Trundle according to the new precepts of order and precision that he had encountered during a visit to the excavations at Windmill Hill. At The Trundle Piggott also met for the first time two Cambridge men, Charles Phillips, at that time teaching history, and Grahame Clark, conducting research on the Mesolithic of Britain at Peterhouse. Both men were to play an important role in Piggott's future development. Thenceforth they were to meet regularly in London and Cambridge and were to form an important axis for change.

In 1927 the Royal Commission on the Ancient and Historical Monuments of Wales had disappeared under a cloud, or perhaps 'pall of smoke' would be a more accurate expression, when R. E. M. Wheeler from his position as late Keeper at the National Museum of Wales had conducted a quite devastating review of the *Inventory for Pembrokeshire* (in *Antiquity*, 1927). The review (which still makes the flesh of Secretaries of Royal Commissions creep) brought about the resignation of the Secretary of the Welsh Royal Commission and the appointment of W. J. Hemp, a member of the Ancient Monuments Inspectorate at that time, in his place. Through the intercession of O. G. S. Crawford, Hemp offered Piggott the post of 'typist' (later investigator) with RCAHMW. This would almost certainly have been a disaster (indeed Piggott would not have accepted the appointment) except that RCAHMW

---

[9] 'Neolithic pottery and other remains from Pangbourne, Berks and Caversham, Oxon', *Proc. Prehist. Soc. E. Anglia*, VI (1928), Pt. I, 30–9.

was headquartered, at that time, in London, thus placing him, at this delicate stage of his career, close to the centre of affairs. As he himself later put it (*Retrospect*, 31) 'I found . . . that I was not temperamentally a fieldworker, and realised that, with no academic qualifications, my only hope of recognition would be through publications of adequate standard.'

Piggott's self-assessment is at fault in at least one regard. Nobody who worked with him, or who reads the reports of his excavations or survey fieldwork, can conclude other than that he had a natural fieldworker's eye. That he was not happy in the Welsh Commission cannot be gainsaid. This was due however, it may be suggested, to the humiliating mean-mindedness of the old-style Government service, from which Piggott's personality had little inborn defence; to an innate lack of sympathy between himself and Hemp (whom Piggott regarded as a snob) and to an inability to love the north Welsh landscape of Anglesey and Caernarvon where he was asked to work. Nowhere is this lack of sympathy with a non-lowland landscape made more explicit than in a short poem written much later in thanks to Cyril and Aileen Fox for a short sojourn spent with them in Exeter in the late 1940s.

> Warm west winds in an Exeter garden
> Far from Scotland's Calvinist gloom
> Ere my Celtic arteries harden
> While the snowdrops are still in bloom
> How I gasp for it, eagerly grasp for it
> A spring resurrection from winter's tomb.
>
> Talks Dobunnic, and walks Dumnonian
> Crucks and mirror-style, chamfrein and bowl
> Façade and pediment (quite Summersonian)
> Each one blowing his own trumpet scroll.
> Hint of the sun in it, glint of the fun in it
> A light-hearted banquet for reason and soul.

As neat a parody as one could wish of his friend and neighbour John Betjeman, and a delightful acknowledgement of hospitality, but with clear overtones of alienation in Edinburgh's grey winter.

But the time was not wasted; indeed the years 1929–32 were frenetic in their activity. Besides, as always, fulfilling his duties fully and conscientiously, Piggott was now crucially positioning himself in the newly emergent discipline of archaeology. It was during this period that he undertook his first major research project—a study of British Neolithic pottery—following the Reading and The Trundle experience. He already had access to the Windmill Hill material excavated by Keiller, and Thurlow Leeds's material from Abingdon, Oxfordshire. He visited collections all over England, in the Isle of Man, in Cardiff, and in Edinburgh (where he discussed the subject in some depth with Gordon Childe). In 1932, his first major research paper—drawn hurriedly from him by a request from Wheeler (who knew a good thing when he saw it) appeared in the *Archaeological Journal* which Wheeler was editing.[10]

This paper exhibits a quite astounding process of maturation by a man still only twenty years old. His links with Peake, and with Childe, had been exploited and consolidated as he identified the European antecedents of Neo-lithic pottery style; he drew on the 'Western' bowl styles and the North/Central European corded wares to indicate fundamental divisions in the British record, then skilfully manipulated the British evidence to indicate its regional variety. With time, of course, he was to take this analysis much further. In the same number Childe, now well in the saddle as Abercromby Professor in Edinburgh, contributed a complementary article on the European background of the mat-erial[11] and important links were forged at this time, the future value of which Piggott could not have known. In this same year he also published a paper[12] in which he trailed quite another area of interest that was to exercise considerable influence over him for the next forty years—neatly set in the context of his home country. The Uffington White Horse had long been either dismissed as a non-antiquity (for example, by Stukeley) or, following the line propounded by Thomas Hughes, was seen to be of Anglo-Saxon date. Piggott took up an earlier suggestion of prehistoric Iron Age date by documenting and demonstrating this likelihood on the basis of Iron Age decorated coins and metalwork. Iron Age decorated metalwork was to form a key interest for Piggott in the future.

With almost papal *chutzpah* (if the notion can be forgiven) Grahame Clark, Piggott, and Christopher Hawkes, according to more than one of them, decided that the known prehistoric world (in Britain) should be divided between them. Clark already deeply entrenched (literally at Peacock's Farm) in the Mesolithic laid incontrovertible claim to that quarter. Hawkes was clearly devoted to the Iron Age and Late Bronze Age 'which left the Neolithic and Earlier Bronze Age to Piggott'. To what extent this was always a joke and to what extent it *became* a joke is unclear; one suspects that, at the time, Piggott may have felt a little insecure in the face of these colleagues' impeccable academic creden-tials. A little gamesmanship, natural enough among twenty year olds running the same course, may have been taking place and his relationship with the two in the future, while always friendly, was sometimes guarded in a manner not wholly accounted for by his innate shyness.

But Piggott and Clark had one serious piece of business to attend to before they set off on their 'predestined' separate paths. The 'Old Guard'—among them Reginald Smith, Reid Moir, Miles Burkitt, and Leslie Armstrong—

---

[10] 'The Neolithic pottery of the British Isles', *Archaeol. Journ.* LXXXVIII (1931), 67–158.
[11] V. G. Childe, 'The Continental Affinities of British Neolithic Pottery', *Archaeol. Journ.* LXXXVIII (1931), 37–66.
[12] 'The Uffington White Horse', *Antiquity*, V (1931), 37–46.

controlled many of the linkages of 'the profession' as it stood. Their interest focused upon the Old Stone Age where some of their ideas were very questionable, notably those of Reid Moir on the exaggerated antiquity of Man in East Anglia based upon a false reading as 'worked flints' of stones that had been shaped by natural forces and were associated with very early stratified deposits—the 'eoliths'.[13] Reginald Smith had, rather perversely, interpreted A. E. Peake's excavated evidence of 1914[14] from the flint-mine complex at Grimes Graves clearly against Peake's own views; solely on the basis of flint implement typology Smith saw the mines as Palaeolithic (Old Stone Age) in date. From 1920 to 1939 A. Leslie Armstrong[15] conducted a long series of excavations to confirm that Palaeolithic date, by flint tool typology as well as other evidence. All the excavational evidence at Grimes indicated, to the uncommitted mind, a Neolithic date, as did all the evidence from all other excavated mines in Britain and in Europe.

It was on this weak point that Clark and Piggott decided to focus their attack,[16] demolishing the unstable structure of the evidence as previously built. It was the first torpedo in British archaeology, understandably launched jointly, and with very considerable courage. Published by the young Turks in the somewhat older Turk's journal, it caused a considerable *furore* in archaeological circles at the time. A major blow had been delivered to the hierarchy as it stood; more were to follow.

In 1932 London saw the first meeting of the resurrected International Congress for Prehistoric and Protohistoric Sciences. Childe and Hawkes were the prime movers with Sir Charles Peers, president of the Society of Antiquaries, presiding. The old was brought face to face with the new. The *gravitas* of international authority lay in the hands of Childe (aged 40), Hawkes (27), Clark (25), and Piggott (22). Piggott had given a paper on the chronology of British long barrows (published in S. Piggott, 'The relative chronology of British Long Barrows', *Proceedings of the First International Congress for Prehistoric and Protohistoric Sciences*, 1932) which demonstrates both the island-wide grasp of his material and the speed with which he was generating his wider expertise in Neolithic studies. Keiller provided one focus of the conference when his house at 4 Charles Street, Berkeley Square, was opened as a meeting place for the conference with material from his work at Windmill Hill on display.

---

[13] J. Reid Moir, *The Antiquity of Man in East Anglia* (Cambridge, 1927).

[14] A. E. Peake, *et al. Report on the Excavations of Grimes Graves, Weeting, Norfolk* March–May 1914, Prehist. Soc. of East Anglia (1915).

[15] A. L. Armstrong, 'The Grimes Graves Problem in the Light of Recent Researches', *Proc. Prehist. Soc. East Anglia*, V (1926), 91–136.

[16] J. G. D. Clark and S. Piggott, 'The Age of the British Flint Mines', *Antiquity*, VII (1933), 166–83.

Alexander Keiller is the next figure to exercise a major influence on Piggott's life. In 1925 when he took on the excavations at Windmill Hill, Keiller was 35 years old. He was a member of the Dundee family that had made a considerable fortune by the manufacture of confectionery and, of course, marmalade. He found little to attract him to the family business and prior to the First World War established a motor-car firm in London which fostered in him an interest in fast cars, precision instruments, and technical drawing. He learned to fly in 1909 and by the early 1920s he was expressing greater and grander interest in field archaeology in Britain, undertaking a detailed survey of stone circles in Aberdeenshire (where the family estate, at Morven, was located). In 1923 he corresponded with O. G. S. Crawford about their mutual interest in flying and aerial photography. The two Scots, 'borrowing' a DH9 aircraft from the De Havilland aviation company, and using captured German camera equipment, embarked upon the 'Wessex from the Air' project. This was the first archaeological survey of a region from the air, financed by Keiller and executed in the summer of 1924, and published in 1928 by the Oxford University Press in large format.[17]

Today their photographs evoke a landscape long gone, apparently illuminated by a brighter sun; the number of new discoveries, and new perceptions was quite staggering. Avebury figures prominently and the proposal to erect a Marconi radio mast on Windmill Hill, a low eminence just north-west of Avebury, where many Neolithic finds had been made, prompted Keiller to purchase the site and to commence excavations in 1925. At first he secured the assistance of H. St George Gray, one of General Pitt-Rivers' original assistants in his seminal series of excavations on Cranborne Chase in the 1890s and now curator at Taunton Museum. A laying-on of hands indeed, and it is difficult to picture the mercurial, impulsive man of affairs working well in harness with the older archaeologist from a quite different background. By 1927 Keiller felt able to take on the direction of work himself.

By 1928 Piggott had met Keiller in connection with his study of Neolithic pottery—for which Windmill Hill was already providing the most fertile source available. After the 1932 Congress (above) Piggott came to know Keiller well and one recognises, perhaps, the mutual friend Crawford working steadily in the background. Certainly in due course Crawford was to write to Piggott, 'Keiller is erratic and sometimes infuriating, but he is a genuine enthusiast and really loves archaeology . . . I have a feeling that you and K *will* work well together. . . . K is open to ideas.' If any man could work courteously but firmly according to his own lights, carry the moment of tension with a happily chosen quip and be assured in his production of ideas in an easily digestible format, it was Stuart Piggott.

---

[17] O. G. S. Crawford and A. Keiller, *Wessex from the Air* (Oxford, 1928).

By 1933 Piggott was asked by Crawford, with Charles Drew, Curator of the Dorset County Museum, to excavate one of the Thickthorn Down Long Barrows in north-west Dorset. Keiller volunteered to do (his beloved) survey work. Piggott took his entire annual leave (four weeks) from RCAHMW to work on the site. This, Piggott's first set-piece major excavation, was published in 1936 in the second volume of the *Proceedings of the Prehistoric Society*.[18] The excavation took place over two months and used W. E. V. Young, the invaluable Windmill Hill foreman, as well as local workmen. In the excavation report, an exemplary model, Piggott—for it is largely Piggott— sets out previous work on similar sites, the objectives of the excavation and then a succinct statement of results with excellent drawings and photographs; as nice a piece of business as could be concluded in two months of an English summer. But not in one month, and when Hemp visited towards the end of the four weeks he was asked for further leave of absence because 'as always, the work took longer than we had anticipated' (*Retrospect*). Hemp refused the request 'out of hand' and, if he sensed that which I sense at this distance in time, I am not sure he can entirely be blamed—he was no stranger to excavation himself having been responsible for two chambered tomb excavations in Anglesey. A crisis was thus created, an entirely fortunate one for Piggott.

Keiller 'after a short silence' offered Piggott full-time employment as his general assistant with principal responsibility for excavations, now due to begin at Avebury itself, as well as other initiatives, keeping abreast of which would require a man of Piggott's sweep of understanding. One idea that Stuart recollected was Keiller's proposal to use a Zeppelin dirigible to carry out an air photographic survey of a large tract of England—as he put it to Stuart 'It's so slow and so large you could plot sites straight on six inch maps—and it's even got a *bar*!' Other ideas were more practicable if, perhaps, less glamorous. Following the lead of W. F. Grimes and others, Keiller had since the 1920s been fascinated by the prospect of identifying the geographical origin of stone axes by examining their petrology. In 1936 he, together with Piggott and Drew, established the Sub-committee of the South-Western Group of Museums and Art Galleries on the Petrological Identification of Stone Axes. Keiller was chairman and Piggott secretary with F. S. Wallis as petrologist. The organisation is still at work today with over 1500 implements sectioned and a corresponding contribution to knowledge attained.[19]

Keiller had also, in 1924, acquired a considerable quantity of William

---

[18] C. D. Drew and S. Piggott, 'The Excavation of Long Barrow 163a on Thickthorn Down, Dorset', *Proc. Prehist. Soc.* II (1936), 77–96.
[19] W. F. Grimes, 'The history of implement petrology in Britain', in T. H. McK. Clough and W. A. Cummins, eds., *Stone Axe Studies*, CBA Research Rep. 23 (1979), 1–4.

Stukeley's papers from his descendants. Piggott's introduction to this source-material had important results in the future; in 1934 he used the content of the papers to demonstrate to Keiller that limited excavation might locate the course of the West Kennet Avenue and expand knowledge of the stone circles within the earthwork enclosure at Avebury itself—a notion sweetly judged to appeal to Keiller's enthusiasm. The result was five major seasons of excavation in the Avebury area from 1934 to 1939 in which the basis of our knowledge of the monument today was completely laid. More than that, however, was to follow. As Piggott relates[20] 'I was hardly prepared for the plan which he suddenly propounded to me late one night in the Red Lion at Avebury. He had decided . . . to acquire the whole of the land on which the main monument of Avebury lay and as much of the West Kennet Avenue as possible; to devote himself to its excavation and judicious restoration and as there was the possibility . . . of ultimately acquiring the Manor House as well, of leaving London and transferring his library, drawing offices and museum to Avebury as an archaeological institute (the Morven Institute) to carry out this task.'

All this was done and must have kept Piggott well occupied, the work continuing until the very eve of the Second World War. Yet Piggott's professional development was gaining apace in stature and quality alongside these events.

1935 was the year when the keys finally passed from the Old to the New Guard in British Archaeology. The courageous publication of the paper on 'The Age of British Flint Mines' in 1933 had dealt a considerable blow; the need now was for a publication dedicated to prehistory, partly in Britain but also in Europe, where the interest of younger prehistorians was turning now to the later periods of prehistory. The plan, conceived by Grahame Clark, was to take over the Society controlling the premier journal of British prehistory—the *Proceedings of the Prehistoric Society of East Anglia* and to re-launch it as *'The Proceedings of the Prehistoric Society'*. In 1934 Piggott offered a paper to the former journal, which was accepted, on 'The mutual relations of the British Neolithic ceramics'[21] which clearly indicated the way things were going. In 1935 a referendum of members was held and then, inevitably, a crucial meeting, which some of the Old Guard saw fit not to attend, and fast car journeys from Wessex and Cambridge to Norwich were in order to 'put infantry on the ground'. How Piggott must have enjoyed driving Keiller's MG Midget that 200 miles, as he long afterwards enjoyed driving his own MG until some time after his retirement. In the nature of British revolutions, this was a relatively bloodless affair which, however, gave birth to one of the most

[20] I. F. Smith, 'Alexander Keiller 1889–1955' *Windmill Hill and Avebury: Excavations by Alexander Keiller 1925–39* (Oxford, 1965), xix–xxii.
[21] *Proc. Prehist. Soc. East Ang.* VII, Part III (1934), 373–81.

successful learned societies that still flourishes today—Grahame Clark became its editor (and continued in the role for thirty-five years). The membership of 420 rose by 59 at its first AGM; it now stands at well over 2,000.

Meanwhile papers continued to appear in the journals—on Stukeley (a note on Anna Stukeley's account of the Uffington White Horse),[22] on Neolithic pottery from a number of sites, on long barrows, and on the excavations at Avebury with one notable collaboration with S. Hazzledine Warren, Grahame Clark, *et al.* on the Archaeology of the submerged land-surface of the Essex coast.[23] This last paper, with its interdisciplinary content, its focus on documentation and its extraction of the maximum from unattractive and difficult evidence set in its geo- and eco-archaeological environment, tells us that we have entered the modern archaeological world. Piggott played, of course, only a part, but a prominent part it was, and his contribution defining the late Neolithic Grooved Ware style shows his burgeoning authority in this diagnostic feature of the Neolithic period.

In 1935 Piggott produced a first book, modest in size but not in scope, and firmly based on the Childean approach, *The Progress of Early Man* (in the 'How-and-why' series edited by Gerald Bullett). The book is, above all, attractively written and leads the reader to an accessible appreciation of what prehistoric archaeology is about, while displaying very considerable reading and erudition. The influences of Harold Peake are there to be seen, as well as Piggott's own unique sense of 'the past in the present'. 'Inside . . . [the Prae Wood Iron Age Oppidum of the Catuvellauni near St Albans, Hertfordshire] . . . among other remains, cobbled roads have been found with cart ruts, which are the same width apart as the modern gauge of 4ft $8^1/_2$ in. The standard width is evidently extremely ancient, for it appears as early as the New Stone Age in the Mediterranean.' The fascination with wheeled vehicles (and not just fast motor cars!) was with him, we shall see, a lifetime later.

By 1936, over and above his growing responsibilities at Avebury, Piggott was called upon to conduct the rescue excavation of a long barrow threatened by house-building at Holdenhurst near Christchurch, Hants.[24] Now, at last, Piggott was alone running his own full-scale excavation which for any excavator is the moment of test. With a budget of £30 Piggott mounted an irreproachable sampling exercise that covered all the statistical possibilities of the barrow. He sets out a very modern looking research strategy and part of the flanking ditches of the barrow were excavated. The report, published within a year, is well illustrated, brief, and very much to the point, with a pottery report

---

[22] *Antiquity*, VIII (1935), 230.

[23] *Proc. Prehist. Soc.* II, 2 (1936), 178–210.

[24] 'The Excavations of a Long Barrow in Holdenhurst parish, near Christchurch, Hants', *Proc. Prehist. Soc.* III, 1 (1937), 1–14.

by Piggott. It set a pattern followed in successive reports of writing up very soon after the digging season finished (during the following winter) which meant that every aspect of the work was entirely fresh in his memory. It also meant, of course, that no backlog of report writing ever arose—an aspect of Stuart's career that is scarcely paralleled.

It was also in 1936 that Keiller took the important step of proposing Piggott for Fellowship of the Society of Antiquaries, at the age of 25. His youth, as well, perhaps, as his recent association with 'the young Turkish tendency', together with the distrust with which Keiller himself was viewed in some antiquarian quarters, led to his exclusion by blackball. Stuart told the story that he had been enjoined to meet Keiller after the election, at the Ritz, just a step away along Piccadilly, in order to celebrate. Upon the bad news being communicated, Keiller, predictably, exploded with a Scots roar 'I'll give them black balls! Waiter! A bottle of champagne and caviar!' Piggott was elected a Fellow on 4 February 1937. He was elected a Fellow of the Society of Antiquaries of Scotland in the following year.

In 1935 Piggott entered for the postgraduate Diploma in Archaeology, a one year course in the Institute of Archaeology in London founded the year before by the Wheelers, in order to gain some formal qualification. There, with Wheeler daily arriving stylishly in his grey Lancia, as Stuart gently puts it in the *Retrospect* he was 'one of the few who heard Wheeler lecture on the lower Palaeolithic'. 'After I had attended a couple of times he begged me not to appear again, but "mug it up myself".' Piggott did this 'with the help of friends' and obtained the Diploma in 1936 (he was eventually to be made a Fellow of University College London, in 1985). One of those friends, a fellow student whom he had met earlier on Curwen's excavations at The Trundle, was Cecily Margaret Preston, the daughter of a wealthy ironmaster; now 24 years old, she had, through a childhood interest in Roman coinage, come into contact with the Wheelers and learnt the excavator's trade on their technically path-breaking excavations at Verulamium in the early 1930s. Although born in Kent, she had conceived a great affection for the downland of Wessex which drew the two together. Stuart and Peggy were married on 12 November 1936 and moved to Priory Farm, Rockbourne in Hampshire, an early nineteenth century Gothic Revival house, the delights of which they proceeded steadily to enhance. Both were highly accomplished excavators and dedicated archaeologists but complementing talents also existed; Peggy was, by all accounts, an awful cook, while Stuart was fascinated by the art. Indeed the story goes that as a very young boy Stuart had been confined to bed with scarlet fever with strict medical instruction to eschew nourishment. His mother suggested that an egg, lightly boiled, might be in order, to be told that he was content, sublimating his appetite by reading recipe books.

In 1936–7 Piggott carried out the research for his second major contribution to prehistoric studies. His familiarity with the early antiquaries working in

Wessex, and with the museums of the region, together with his enlivened interest in broader European connections fostered by Peake and his contacts at the 1932 Congress—including of course Childe—all conspired to interest him in the series of apparently rich metalwork-bearing graves relating to the southern British Early Bronze Age. 'The Early Bronze Age in Wessex'[25] is an enquiry and argument of such complexity and such erudition, packed with ideas, that it is fair to say that it is still now, after his death, a controversial paper. Still much quoted, it is a seminal example, alongside Childe's own analysis of the *Linearbandkeramik* cultures of Central Europe, of the historico-cultural approach to prehistory.

By 1938, of course, the gravity of the political situation in Europe was apparent to everybody. Piggott had, anyway, been tiring of the Keiller auto-cracy; his marriage had made this insupportable and he left Keiller's full-time employment in 1937, although he went on assisting Keiller on an *ad hoc* basis until 1939. In a manner that many today might find surprising, Government, at that time of immense stress, agreed a programme, not inexpensive, of excavation of ancient monuments in advance of urgent defence works. Stuart and Peggy found themselves excavating round barrows on Crichel Down, Dorset.[26] This particular land requisition was, on its disposal after the war, to create political history. Far more important, arguably, was the extraordinary find of a trepanned skull of Early Bronze Age date to which Piggott gave major prominence in a paper drawing on the British and European parallels for this practice.[27]

By early 1938 the Piggotts' reputation as freelance excavators was highly regarded. They worked at Little Woodbury with Gerhard Bersu in both 1938 and 1939, Stuart building a series of models to illustrate the structural develop-ment of the site as well as assisting Bersu through the unfamiliar process of publication in Britain. Also in 1938, the investigation of a group of burial mounds at Sutton Hoo near Woodbridge, Suffolk, had commenced. Preliminary work in 1938 had made it clear that the mounds represented an Anglo-Saxon cemetery of considerable importance, and in 1939 the excavation of the largest mound was begun under the auspices of Ipswich Museum. When the indications of an unrobbed *in situ* ship burial became evident, the Office of Works was notified and, war-time works being under way in the vicinity, the excavation was taken over by The Office and Charles Phillips was asked to assume direction. In July and August of that year both Peggy and Stuart were prominent members of a team of experts brought in to expedite, in the most difficult circumstances, the excavation of a royal East-Anglian ship burial that contained probably the

---

[25] *Proc. Prehist. Soc.* IV (1938), 52–106.
[26] Published ultimately in the *Archaeologia*, jointly with C. M. Piggott, XX (1944), 47–80.
[27] 'A Trepanned Skull of the Beaker Culture from Dorset and the Practice of Trepanning in Prehistoric Europe', *Proc. Prehist. Soc.* VI, 1 (1940), 112–32.

richest and most interesting furniture known to British archaeology. Of course any such heroic episode will create its own tradition of stories and Stuart's was almost too often told to be retold here: the retrieval of the great golden and bejewelled purse mount and belt buckles, the problems with security that enjoined secrecy and the need to retain the finds on the person at all times despite the need for relaxation at the local pub. There they met with the standard scepticism of all British workmen contemplating the work of others, so seemingly similar to their own but conducted for longer hours and for less money. 'Found any gold yet, then?' came the enquiry, and one can see Stuart lifting his head with a smile and saying 'Oh yes, my pockets are full of it' — in the certain knowledge that they wouldn't believe him.

But September 1939 saw an end to all this, as the global imperative brought a new direction to Piggott's life. The beginning of the war found him serving with a Light Anti-Aircraft battery stationed at Longford Castle $2\frac{1}{2}$ miles north-west of Fordingbridge. The battery had been raised by the Earl of Radnor, and Piggott became a clerk in the Battery Office (it was here that the Crichel Down report was written up). In early 1941 Glyn Daniel, working at that time with aerial photographic intelligence was asked by his CO about other archaeologists 'at a loose end'. He quickly traced Piggott, who was soon offered a commission in the Intelligence Corps and ultimately, after a period at Medmenham, near Marlow, was detailed, with two junior officers, to set up an air photographic interpretation unit for transfer to the Far Eastern theatre.

Eventually late in 1941 Piggott left on the 'horseshoe' run to India, first to Shannon (where, delayed for a week, he was able to paint and sketch) and then on to Lisbon, Freetown, Lagos, Leopoldville, Kampala, Khartoum, and Cairo. In Cairo the parlous state of affairs at Singapore, and the Japanese invasion of Burma in mid-December, led to delay, which facilitated informal study of Islamic architecture among the city's mosques, although the National Museum of Antiquities was closed (only five months later Rommel was to be hammering at the gateway to the Nile Delta). After some delay Piggott joined Glyn Daniel (later to be Disney Professor at Cambridge) and Terence Powell (later to be Professor at Liverpool) and other officers in Delhi to form the Central Photographic Interpretation Section within which Stuart was the senior Army representative in a combined operations office under Daniel's command.

After some time, as Army and Air Force representatives, Daniel and Piggott were detailed to attend an Anglo-American conference on aerial photographic interpretation in Algiers in the summer of 1943. Difficult relations between British and American commands after the head-banging of the 'Torch' episode meant that the conference was cancelled so that the two were delayed in Cairo—by now fairly relaxed in its distance from the sterner aspects of the war. Daniel was taken ill and unable to fly so that the two, as

Daniel puts it[28] ' . . . spent a very pleasant few days in Cairo, went out again to
the pyramids and ate and drank surprisingly well. One night after a very good
dinner at the St James's Restaurant we were so delighted with the local
Egyptian wine . . . that we found ourselves unsteadily walking home singing
"Vinicole et Viticole, let the tide of victory roll" — two putative professors in
splendid form!' The Cairo episode was a wonderful opportunity for relaxation
and almost certainly the episode that cemented a friendship that lasted until
Glyn's death in 1986. Daniel suggests that it was Stuart who prompted him to
try his hand at detective fiction which he did with not inconsiderable success.

After several weeks, with the Algiers meeting in the air, passage was
offered to Malta and the two spent two 'blissful' days inspecting megalithic
monuments and rock-cut tombs on the island, several spattered with bits of
German and Italian aircraft. In August 1943 when the first convoy with
wine aboard reached the island, Piggott and Daniel were still there, and
after a 'good evening', Daniel tells us, Piggott added a poem to a collection
of war-time poetry he had been writing. The two did eventually reach
Algiers — an abortive mission that led to an initial, rather abrasive, episode
with Wheeler who, preparing himself for the rigours of Sicily, had,
wrongly, and like many another 'sharp-end' soldier, little regard for carefully garnered intelligence.

Fire among the Ruins — 1942–45 was eventually published by the Oxford
University Press in 1948. The motive:

> Come with me, sharing my walk in the ruins,
> the unloved walk I have made so many times,
> must make again and must make for how long
> for how long —
> in a ruined world in an unending sunset
> where underfoot the ground is treacherous, slipping
> in the unseen bog, the scree or the silent river . . .
>   'The Fire'[29]

Piggott's sense of the past in the present is nowhere, perhaps, better illustrated
than by a verse written on his ack-ack battery in Wiltshire:

> Watching the platoon
> boil tea on fires made in
> the forsaken courtyard
> switching the wireless
> to a febrile croon.
>
> I had not forgotten
> barbarian hearths blackening
> proud pavements in Verulam

---

[28] G. E. Daniel, *Some Small Harvest* (London, 1986), 159.
[29] *Fire Among the Ruins — 1942–45*, (Oxford, 1948): 'The Fire', 7–9.

when Rome had crumbled
Goth ridden, rotten . . .
'Soldier Making Tea'[30]

His sense of loss while separated from his wife and the English countryside is
best captured in these lines written in India:

> . . . with half the earth, and all a maniac war
> to separate me from you.

> How we two
> shared in our love of England! Whether the creeks and flats
> by Orford or by Cley, or whether the land
> where England ends, and Wales begins in hills,
> and Craswall Abbey never will be found.
> And how we knew, and, God! how well we loved
> the downland; from the Purbeck to the Thames,
> from Frome to Chichester in the western wind
> that ever sweeps Blewburton, the menacing calm
> in Kingley Vale, the evening night aslant
> on Alton Priors below the Knap Hill steeps:
> sun on the sea and bright on Upwey Down,
> and then the Knoll from Toyd and our own valley!
> 'Letter from India (for C.M.P.)'[31]

In India, Piggott, who always fully acknowledged the very privileged
conditions of his war service, was nevertheless frustrated by the imposed break
in his professional career and its development. A partial solution was however
to hand. Within a month of life in Delhi he had found the Central Asian
Museum and had obtained permission to work on its reserve collections there
when off-duty—a project he published in *Antiquity* in 1943.[32]

In April 1944 Wheeler, after delaying until after the Salerno landings on
the mainland of Italy, accepted appointment as the Director General of the
Archaeological Survey of India and later sought Piggott's release from 'the
women's work of air photographic service', in order that he could be allocated
to the Survey's staff. Fortunately the Army vetoed the idea—as Piggott and
Wheeler would have, almost certainly, composed a volatile cocktail, the
excellent qualities of both being polar expressions of the same dedication.
Nevertheless, and more importantly, Piggott was truly bitten by the Indian
archaeological bug and conducted considerable correspondence with Childe, in
Edinburgh and Seton Lloyd in Baghdad to mitigate the isolation of his
research. Most importantly the work gave Piggott the vital view of Europe
from the outside, and against its Eurasian background, that was to become such

---

[30] *Fire Among the Ruins*, 'Soldier Making Tea', 9–10.
[31] *Fire Among the Ruins*, 'Letter from India (for C.M.P.)', 16–19.
[32] 'The Hissar Sequence—the Indian evidence', *Antiquity*, XVII (1943), 169–82.

an important component of his future perceptions. His book, *Prehistoric India*, was published in 1950.

In 1945 Lieutenant Colonel Piggott was shipped home to Britain to await demobilisation. This must have represented an unenviable juncture of his life—no job, no formal qualifications, yet with a body of experience and a bibliography that matched the performance of any senior scholar. He returned to Peggy and the house at Rockbourne. Already his collection of paintings was beginning to take shape. Eric Gill, Paul Nash (a wonderful lithograph of the West Kennet Avenue entitled 'Landscape of the Megaliths' stunned any visitor to Stuart's sitting room) and a number of John Pipers and Graham Sutherlands all spoke of his interest in the combined effect of Man and Nature on the southern English landscape while Augustus John and a Ben Nicolson reflected the spareness of Stuart's aesthetic, if not of his personality. India had not left him aesthetically unscathed and a series of Indian objets d'art accompanied him back to this country. These did not include, however, the base-metal teapot manufactured in Birmingham that was shown to him as a monastery's greatest treasure, on a visit to Tibet while taking a period of furlough in India—a story used to effect in lectures on prehistoric exchange.

During her grass-widowhood Peggy had met Austin Lane Poole, President of St John's College, Oxford who suggested a way through one of the obstacles that faced Piggott on his return. Through his good offices Stuart was permitted to enrol for a B.Litt. (with minimum period of residence) in the Modern History Faculty—to present a thesis on William Stukeley. We know that some of this work was already behind him, but the availability of Bodley's Library accelerated the process so that he was able to submit his thesis in the spring of 1947. The University was, in due course, to offer him an honorary D.Litt.

By that time Vere Gordon Childe had been offered the post of Director of the Institute of Archaeology in London and had accepted it. His post in Edinburgh, part-funded by the Abercromby bequest, had thus become open. Piggott always made it very clear that he had no expectations of this post, although anyone with the perception of hindsight can see that the situation was otherwise. He was the obvious candidate for a Chair distinguished by its unorthodoxy, its internationalism, and its humanity. In late 1946, therefore, Piggott received a letter from the Secretary of the University of Edinburgh asking him to accept the Abercromby Chair. Nobody who knew him can doubt his surprise, but for all his modesty there was not the least surprise among his peers at the time. He accepted the post and was driven the four hundred miles north by Vere Gordon Childe. Childe, notoriously, never had any clear idea of the rules of the road, and it is perhaps a matter of great good fortune that our story does not close at this juncture. Stuart told a delightful story about Childe's *Schlossenberg Kultur* which as an external examiner during the year before his take-over, he encountered in students' scripts and which caused him puzzlement and, characteristically, humility. He had not previously heard of this culture—he questioned widely to conclude that the only possible explanation was the uninitiate's interpretation of Childe's very strong accent and the 'slash-and-burn cultures' of the earlier Neolithic!

With few prejudices Piggott entered post in September 1947. Peggy and he took a flat in Gloucester Place in the New Town of Edinburgh but retained the Rockbourne house for use in the vacations. His welcome to Scotland was relatively warm. His predecessor had been an eccentric, 'difficult' man; here was new blood. In 1947 he was immediately warranted as a Commissioner of the RCAHMS and remained so until 1976. The Office of Works was to invite Stuart and Peggy to excavate sites, and they were quick to assess the nature of the problems in Scotland and to make a deliberate decision to concentrate their efforts differentially, he concentrating on earlier prehistory and she on later.

As a Commissioner, Stuart was an important influence in the re-seeding of RCAHMS after the fallow years of the War. He, then, and throughout his time, encouraged standards of drawing and presentation which have stood RCAHMS in good stead until the present day. The inclusion of elevational and axiometric drawings was something that he had researched (and practised) himself in order to allow greater accessibility to technical drawing standards by a wider lay public. These influences are quite evident in the Stirlingshire and Peeblesshire *Inventories*. In the case of the Roxburghshire *Inventory* he was a tower of strength, assisting staff in site analysis which led directly to Peggy's important excavations at Hownam Rings and Hayhope Knowe, the results of which are only now being re-thought by a new generation of archaeologists. Indeed he wrote substantial parts of the text of the volume. Piggott himself was also increasingly interested by the architecture he saw around him in Scotland; he was a major force in directing the interests of RCAHMS into vernacular recording (barely covered, if at all, by the Royal Warrant at that time) which, again, has been a strong influence that has been sustained.

In 1948 Stuart was invited by The Office of Works to excavate and interpret the site in its guardianship at Cairnpapple Hill, West Lothian. The excavation is an important one because it shows Piggott, for the first time, operating in an excavational environment totally foreign to his own chalk and related soils. Unfamiliar it may have been but there is no sign of this either in the archive of his work nor in the published account.[33] The excavation introduced a new standard to Scotland at that time which was effectively taken up within five years by others. In this particular instance Stuart's customary rapidity in submitting his report actually 'beat the clock' and some delay in the journal's publication resulted in the report appearing in the volume assigned to the year before the excavation took place. During this time he produced

---

[33] *Proc. Soc. Antiq. Scot.* LXXXII (1947–8), 68–123.

another important short book *British Prehistory* (Oxford, 1949), in the Home University Library Series edited by the autocratic Gilbert Murray—another extremely effective popularising text for the layman.

But what of the University and the archaeology courses? In the *Retrospect* Piggott recalls that 'Constructing and teaching single-handed an appropriate course presented problems. Childe had constructed an unworkable B.Sc. which I quickly converted into an Honours MA.' All of this harks back to the decision by the University of Edinburgh that Abercromby's bequest should not be amended to provide a full professorial salary. Childe had suffered under this predicament and, likewise, so did Piggott until the mid-fifties. One way of addressing this problem was Piggott's acquisition of R. J. C. Atkinson as an assistant. Meanwhile he began to teach a fully European prehistory course 'filling the gaps in my own knowledge before instructing others even more ignorant'. Having no model of teaching for himself, he developed his own—a teaching style that I knew at its fullest and others knew in earlier circumstances. 'He was an excellent teacher and had both the power to fascinate and intrigue his audience; and to show a real concern for them, his students; he was always ready to help when they were keen to learn and also readily took on the role of *pater familias* when some sorrow or disaster struck any one of them' writes Anne Ross, a student of the 1950s and I, as a student of the sixties, can aver that his teaching commitment never left him. Known to generations of students as 'Piggins' (because of his fussy precise mannerisms?) he was always a well-liked and admired teacher. His predilection for the most magnificent waistcoats also earnt him the less attractive, but always affectionate, 'Toad' after the expansive but vulnerable character created by Kenneth Grahame. But it is also true that Stuart never suffered fools easily. Students who did not follow him quickly would be lost. They had to be enthusiastic and conscientious, or Stuart himself lost interest, and never very far from Stuart's elbow was a 'black dog', what he termed '*accidia et anhedonia*', easily set loose by the failure of others to live up to his high expectations for them, releasing all his own capacity for self-doubt.

Piggott's productiveness in the 1950s and 1960s was prodigious. After the publication of Cairnpapple he undertook the excavation, in company with his war-time friend Terence Powell, of three chambered cairns at Cairnholy in Galloway on behalf of The Office of Works.[34] After Cairnpapple and Cairnholy he continued work in Scotland excavating at Torwoodlee hill fort and 'broch' in Selkirkshire,[35] and with Peggy, at Castle Law, Glencorse, Midlothian, and at Craigs Quarry near Dirleton, East Lothian.[36] Through all this effort he maintained his interest in the Southern English Neolithic. He wrote an

[34] *Proc. Soc. Antiq. Scot.* LXXXIII (1948–9), 103–61.
[35] *Proc. Soc. Antiq. Scot.* LXXXV (1950–1), 92–117.
[36] *Proc. Soc. Antiq. Scot.* LXXXVI (1951–2), 191–6.

analysis of the available evidence from Stonehenge and excavated there in 1950 with his new lecturer R. J. C. Atkinson and with J. F. S. Stone. The publication of this short season of excavation of two Aubrey Holes (and one of the earliest radiocarbon assays for a British archaeological site) stimulated Brian O'Neil, at that time Chief Inspector of Ancient Monuments, to project the major series of excavations at Stonehenge undertaken by Atkinson and Piggott in 1953, 1956, 1958, and 1964. But at the same time his interests were expanding in other directions. Study of Iron Age metalwork—firedogs, swords, and scabbards, the Torrs chamfrein which led ultimately to a seminal paper on the Scottish Iron Age grew—first in the context of Pictish studies, as an account of the archaeology in F. T. Wainwright's '*The Problem of the Picts*' and later, in 1966, his seminal analysis of the Scottish Iron Age formed the core of A. L. F. Rivet's *The Iron Age in Northern Britain* ('A Scheme for the Scottish Iron Age', 1–16). In 1952 and 1953 Piggott was again excavating sites among the Clava group of cairns and ring cairns, and at Braidwood Fort, Midlothian. The excavation of the West Kennet long barrow followed in 1955–6. Piggott's excavation career was by no means over at this juncture; he was to excavate, jointly with Derek Simpson, the stone circle at Croft Moraig in Perthshire in 1965,[37] and finally in 1972 his work at Dalladies, Angus, in association with Trevor Watkins, published, in 1974.[38]

This extraordinary output has to be set against his many contributions to public service. He was a member for many years of both the English and Scottish Ancient Monuments Boards. He was a Trustee of the British Museum from 1968 to 1974 and of the National Museum of Antiquities of Scotland 1954–77. He was President of the Prehistoric Society 1963–6, President of the Society of Antiquaries of Scotland from 1967 to 1971 and its secretary for foreign correspondence from 1950 to 1966, and a Vice-President of the Society of Antiquaries of London from 1955 to 1958. We have already seen his contribution as a Commissioner of the Royal Commission on the Ancient and Historic Monuments of Scotland.

Alongside this activity Piggott was quickly building his department into one of only two departments teaching a single honours undergraduate degree in the early 1950s, and a highly effective one at that. Richard Atkinson's appointment in 1950 was an essential part of this process and by 1956, when Atkinson moved to Cardiff to inaugurate the Department and Chair there (and a third department), a cohesive academic structure had been built in Edinburgh. Indeed in 1955 Piggott was offered the Directorship of the Institute of Archaeology in London. He firmly refused it, however, as he eschewed all distractions from real scholarly output, but most particularly the distractions

---

[37] Published in *Proc. Prehist. Soc.* XXXVII, Pt. 1 (1971), 1–15.
[38] *Proc. Soc. Antiq. Scot.* CIV (1971–2), 23–47.

associated with administration, and what is nowadays called management. Indeed he used, gleefully, to claim that he never opened brown envelopes, only blue or white ones.

Following Cairnholy, the Office of Works engaged him, with Atkinson, also a skilled excavator, on a series of excavations in the south of England, at Wayland's Smithy (a stone-built chambered tomb set beside the Berkshire Ridgeway in his heart-land) and, as we have seen, at West Kennet long barrow which was published as a monograph by the Ministry of Works (*The West Kennet Long Barrow—Excavations 1955–56* (HMSO, 1962). In 1956 with Atkinson as principal he undertook the most recent major campaign of excavation at Stonehenge (published in 1996 after Atkinson's death). After Stonehenge (and there is no doubt that the non-publication of this site, as well as that at Wayland's Smithy in Berkshire by his partner, cast a shadow for Piggott) he withdrew from excavation to a considerable extent.

Publications flowed. By 1950 he had published his first major work (finished in 1948) (*William Stukeley—An Eighteenth Century Antiquary*, Oxford, 1950), a work of profound scholarship, and, characteristically, sympathy with his great predecessor. By 1951 he had finished his grand survey of the British Neolithic. 'Vultures' as he always called it (a reference to an alleged misprint on the title page in galley), *Neolithic Cultures of the British Isles* (Cambridge, 1954) is still the only inclusive survey of the period and the only start-point for any student of the period. Regrettably Cambridge University Press dealt with the book in a leisurely fashion, so that its appearance in 1954 coincided with the first impact (tentative as it was) of the radiocarbon revolution. Proving, as it did, that all his dates were wrong, it made little impact upon his thesis—simply showing that everything he had suggested had taken longer to happen, with the sequence broadly still secure.

By 1954 Stuart's and Peggy's marriage was at an end. There is no point in minimising the impact that this had upon Stuart. In material terms it led to the disruption and loss of the Rockbourne house and his move from Gloucester Place to a smaller flat in Great King Street, also in the New Town. Stuart was fortunate enough to possess, and to find, friends in Edinburgh who matched his own interests and with whom he could find solace. Stewart and Alison Sanderson, living at that time in the New Town, became very firm friends and by the mid 1950s he had begun to share a delight with them in his old interest in cooking—for Stuart was always a most attentive and capable host. In the early 1960s he began to participate in the column that Stewart Sanderson offered to *The Scotsman* entitled *Off the Beeton Track*. The example of such punning set Stuart, in one of his pieces, to write, ' "If you are a good scholar", I said to my hostess as we were having a cosy chat in the kitchen before dinner, "you go back to the original sauces." ' A subtle mixture of wit and knowledge then led through to a discussion of the deeper origin of sauces (and the sources of sauces), finally providing a sauce recipe comprising 'nothing more than *foie gras*, olive oil, red wine and a grating of nutmeg'. To eat *chez* Piggott was always to enjoy much laughter, good company, archaeological and non-archaeological, and wonderful food and drink. Even a trip to the loo was memorable, confronted as one was with a collage of newspaper cuttings, (Piggott Wins Against All Odds, Piggott Trounced Again—different Piggott of course but he always followed his namesake's career with interest), jostling with his certificates of membership of the Order of Mark Twain (twice) and other memorabilia.

With Atkinson's departure Piggott was joined in 1957 by Charles Thomas and then slowly, with the Robbins revolution, numbers, hard fought for, began to increase until by 1977 Stuart was supported by three staff, Dr Trevor Watkins, David Ridgway, and myself. Working together with David Talbot Rice (Watson Gordon Professor of Fine Art) a post in Classical Archaeology had also been created which, upon Anthony Snodgrass's elevation to the Chair in Cambridge, passed to James Coulton. All of his colleagues felt the impact of Stuart's academic leadership and example and all felt his constant encouragement to develop new ideas, seek to prove them by recourse to the evidence available, retrieve the evidence by field research if the evidence was not available, and to publish, always to publish, the result.

But once again we leap too far ahead, for from 1955 we enter probably the most internationally active and intellectually productive years of Piggott's life—a period heralded by his election as a Fellow of the British Academy in 1953 and the award of a D.Litt.Hum. by the University of Columbia in 1954. In 1958 he produced *Scotland Before History*, set off with haunting illustrations by Keith Henderson. The book was the first survey of Scottish prehistory since Childe's foundatory work of 1935[39] incorporating all the new information, much of it of his own collection since that date. This volume was closely followed by one of the best popular introductions to archaeology, published in 1959, *Approach to Archaeology*. The book shows again immensely catholic knowledge as it draws excerpts from all over the Old World. The book grew from a lecture course given to future teachers of history in the Moray House Teacher Training College in Edinburgh (what a splendid idea!)—and, of course, was a 'topping out' of Stuart's regular appearances on the panel of 'Animal Vegetable Mineral?'—the very seriously successful TV show that went out between 1953 and 1959 to the strains of the Prelude from Bach's Violin Sonata No. 6 in E major. Both Glyn Daniel, the chairman of the show, and Mortimer Wheeler became national figures, but Piggott, a regular contributor, very much the 'straight man' to Wheeler's and Daniel's splendid fireworks, did not court that. *AVM?* was, by far, the most successful

---

[39] V. G. Childe, *The Prehistory of Scotland* (1935).

archaeological exposition ever to have been seen on British television, one senses that it contributed not a little to Piggott's growing confidence during this period.

In 1957 O. G. S. Crawford died suddenly and Glyn Daniel took over the editorship of *Antiquity*. He wrote in his autobiography[40] that he wanted Stuart to share the editorship with him but Stuart would not do so. Nevertheless, 'I have spoken to Stuart Piggott on matters relating to *Antiquity* almost every week from 1957 until the present day.' Here was indeed the binding cord of that friendship that began in the War years. Ruth and Glyn Daniel, with their love of good food and travel, were constant companions for Stuart in summers spent in various parts of Europe. Stuart travelled widely in France and Iberia, Scandinavia and Germany, and jointly directed with John Ward Perkins the survey of the monuments of prehistoric Malta sponsored by the Inter-University Council for Higher Education Overseas. A joint Edinburgh–Cambridge (Piggott–Daniel) student field visit to the Lipari islands forms a memorable highlight in a number of careers. All this, of course, was the fabric of Piggott's rapidly burgeoning knowledge of European archaeology, carefully crafted into his lecture courses in Edinburgh. In 1962 he gave six lectures to the Society of Antiquaries of Scotland comprising the Rhind Lecture series for that year that were to form the foundation of his magnum opus (in my view) *Ancient Europe* published in 1965.

In 1963, however, Piggott produced two extraordinarily important pieces of work that must be singled out for their significance in his, and British Archaeology's, development. The first was his Presidential Address to the Prehistoric Society, that he had helped to found in 1935, in which he sets out a passionate plea for the maintenance and enhancement of standards. 'I . . . do not want to see an anticlimax, and a tolerance of shoddy work, merely because the problems are now more complex and the subject so much more difficult. The very difficulties should serve as a challenge and they are not diminished by trying to persuade ourselves that they do not exist.' It is to be hoped that British Archaeology has risen to this challenge. Stuart, however, never an optimist, perceived very strongly the danger of declining standards and, towards the end of his life, felt their actual presence. His words have for all of us in the discipline of field archaeology an extraordinary relevance today.

Also in 1963 as a tribute to his friend of long standing, Cyril Fox, he produced his beautifully written, elegantly constructed model for the Beaker Culture of Britain—an astonishing feat of insight which reveals par excellence Piggott's ability to sweep a broad horizon with photographic recollection and then to synthesise the mass of accumulated data clearly, concisely, and convincingly. At a stroke Piggott brought Beaker studies from Abercromby's

[40] G. E. Daniel, *Some Small Harvest* (1986), p. 229.

study of 1912 very much into the modern world. Simultaneously, of course, he paid tribute to that eminent founder of the Edinburgh Chair. Since 1963 successive attempts to reanalyse the Beaker pottery of Britain have never been as wholly convincing, and none have the sweep of 'Abercromby and After'.[41]

Ancient Europe—from the beginnings of Agriculture to Classical Antiquity (Edinburgh, 1965), dedicated 'To my pupils, past and present', is an equally remarkable synthesis but, of course, on an altogether wider canvas. The apparatus of the book alone, its index, bibliography and annotations are substantial achievements. The aim of the body of the book is to 'place barbarian Europe in . . . its rightful place, as the necessary precursor and subsequent contemporary of the ancient civilised world'.[42] The book is firmly aligned on an historico-cultural approach, with links to the historic and recent era firmly indicated. All variation is between innovating and non-innovating societies defined by standard Childean cultural models. Piggott ends the book[43] in a manner that makes his approach abundantly clear 'But there is one most moving work of art from the ancient world into which one could read an epitome of the final situation, the great silver birthday-present dish of Theodosius I of 388 AD. The emperor sits flanked by the youths of his barbarian guard . . . bewildered boys look out, away from the Byzantine World, beyond the Barbarian Europe that was theirs, and into that of the Middle Ages, and of our own time.'

Travel in Europe, particularly now in eastern Europe, continued and Piggott was honoured everywhere as a distinguished guest. His excursions with, and in support of, Ruth Tringham were a notable feature of the early sixties and led to her own synthesis of the Neolithic of Eastern Europe published in 1971.[44] With other close friends Terence Powell, Nancy Sandars, and John Cowen he also travelled widely—notably to the Caucasus in 1966 and, in 1968, to Poland, Moscow, Leningrad (as then was), and Kiev. He was an active member of the British Academy's Overseas Policy Committee from 1969 to 1981 and in 1971 he went to Moscow as its emissary to negotiate formal exchanges of archaeologists between the two countries.

The stream of published work did not falter. In 1965 he produced the Neolithic and Bronze Age chapter for Volume 1.1 of the *Victoria County History of Wiltshire*, his final statement on the earlier prehistory of Wessex and reassessing his own seminal contribution of 1938. In 1968 he produced an

---

[41] I. LL. Foster and L. Alexander, eds., *Culture and Environment. Essays in Honour of Sir Cyril Fox* (1963), 53–92.
[42] *Ancient Europe*, p. 21.
[43] Ibid., p. 264.
[44] R. J. Tringham, *Hunters, Fishers and Farmers of Eastern Europe, 6000–3000BC* (London, 1971).

entertaining yet vastly learned volume, the sixty-third in the *Ancient Peoples and Places* series edited by Glyn Daniel for Thames & Hudson, entitled *The Druids*. In the volume he considers the evidence for Druids as they existed in their European Celtic *milieu*, their description within contemporary written sources, and thence to their re-invention in the sixteenth century and the flourishing of the spurious (or, at least, quite separate) tradition to this day.

In 1968 Stuart received a spontaneous tribute from those 'pupils' to whom he had dedicated *Ancient Europe*. The *Festschrift* was edited by John Coles and Derek Simpson. *Studies in Ancient Europe—Essays presented to Stuart Piggott* (Leicester, 1968) was 'a mark of respect and affection by [seventeen] former pupils and colleagues who have benefited from Stuart Piggott's scholarship and friendship in the past . . . '

From 1967–70 Piggott served as President of the Council of British Archaeology. On demitting office he gave a valedictory address,[45] an address which follows on from the concerns about standards set before the Prehistoric Society in 1963 (above) to a point where these concerns are much graver and reveal the degree of Piggott's concern for the welfare of archaeology as he approached the age of sixty. Piggott, with the heights of *AVM?* behind him, inveighs in his address against the trivialisation of archaeology, against falling standards and against fundamentally unsuitable governmental structures that he saw as exercising an unfortunate influence upon its proper development and practice. This visionary address of 1970 makes arresting reading twenty-five years later when many of the issues to which he animadverts are still now at the centre of our attention.

In 1972 Piggott was appointed CBE. (He appears in his investiture photograph[46] to be less than quite comfortable in top-hat and tails.) On the occasion of his sixty-fifth birthday a more formal celebration edited by Vincent Megaw was made: (*To illustrate the monuments—Essays on archaeology presented to Stuart Piggott* (London, 1976)). With thirty-four contributions by scholars from all over the world, many of them close friends, it was prefaced by a tribute from his old friend John Betjeman, now Poet Laureate, who characteristically harked back to former days

> . . . 'When church was still the usual place for marriages
> And carriage-lamps were only used for carriages.
>
> How pleased your parents were in their retirement
> The garden and yourself their chief requirement.
> Your father, now his teaching days were over,
> Back in his native Berkshire lived in clover.
> Your cheerful mother loyally concealed

---

[45] *Annual Report*, Council for British Archaeology, XX (1970).
[46] G. E. Daniel, *Some Small Harvest* (London, 1986), facing p. 320.

Her inward harkening for Petersfield.
For Hampshire Downs were the first Downs you saw
And Heywood Sumner taught you there to draw . . . .

. . . St. Mary, Uffington . . . .
. . . To us the Church, I'm glad that I survive
To greet you, Stuart, now you're sixty-five.

Stuart retired in June 1977 to the cottage at West Challow, that he had inherited almost ten years before from his two maiden aunts whom he had supported in their latter years, and where he spent the rest of his life; the Department of Speculative and Preventive Archaeology, University of West Challow, as he would entitle it on mischievous postcards. For there is no doubt that Piggott found unattractive and often plainly unreadable much of the archaeological theory that increasingly dominated the subject in the latter years of his academic tenure, and there was little prospect that he would come to terms with it in retirement. He thought much of it pretentious in tone and feeble in capacity and there he would stand. While standing there, however, he would continue to produce publications of extraordinary quality. In the year after his retirement Stuart had given the Walter Neurath Memorial Lecture on the subject *Antiquity Depicted—Aspects of Archaeological Illustration*—a discourse upon the history and nature of the depiction of archaeological material and sites, produced by Thames & Hudson as a very attractive little book.

One of his first tasks on taking over the cottage at West Challow was to construct an extension that rivalled the cottage itself in size, in order to accommodate his enormous library. Many of the books and most of the host of offprints arranged in labelled cardboard boxes had been gifted to him from almost every imaginable source creating a unique research resource now, at least partly, permanently available to scholarship in the Ashmolean Museum and the Institute of Archaeology in Oxford.

By 1983 he had produced a volume of major importance following his life-long interest in wheeled vehicles which he saw as a key issue in the emergence of a European identity, as well, of course, as a fundamental cultural stimulant throughout the whole of the Old World. *The Earliest Wheeled Transport*, was published by Thames & Hudson, and was recognised by the award of the Gold Medal of the Society of Antiquaries of London and by the award of an Honorary D.Litt. by the University of Edinburgh in 1984. He was to extend this survey by a second volume *Wagon, Chariot and Carriage* published in 1992. Before this Piggott filled the void that still existed between his own work on William Stukeley (which he had revised and extensively enlarged in 1985) and the volume published by Sir Thomas Kendrick in 1950,[47] covering the

---

[47] T. D. Kendrick, *British Antiquity* (London, 1950).

emergence of the British antiquarian tradition up to the end of the sixteenth century. *Ancient Britain and the Antiquarian Imagination* published in 1989 contains all the characteristics that one expects of his writing—elegance, precision, conciseness, and incisiveness.

In 1987 Stuart was elected President of the Wiltshire Archaeological and Natural History Society a tenure that he shared with Peggy (now Guido) who was a vice president from 1984. They both died in office sharing this most appropriate homecoming. From 1991 Piggott's health began seriously to fail and as his sight became affected so his ability to read was curtailed. Unfailing consideration and his hospitable instinct never left him but the brilliant glow of his zest for life was dimmed. In 1993 he was awarded the Grahame Clark Medal of the British Academy and he went on producing items for publication until 1995. Stuart died on 23 September 1996. To the very end his was always an amazingly acute understanding which was a valuable and a valued sounding board for younger scholars, and he retained a phenomenal breadth of know-ledge within what appeared to be an unimpaired memory, as well as a some-times gentle, sometimes not so gentle, wit and a delight in gossip. He also, to the end, remained, in his modesty, reticence, and willingness to please and to help others, a very natural gentleman.

Any final assessment of Stuart Piggott's career will have to wait some years or even decades for a proper evaluation. It has been said, within Scotland, that he never fully played his part in the development of Scottish archaeology; the record as only partly set out in this memoir shows that view to be entirely mistaken. From 1947 until his retirement from the Abercromby (to Stuart always 'the Applecrumble') Chair in 1977 he served both research and public archaeology in Scotland with dedication and enthusiasm. He undertook the effective creation of a thriving archaeology department in the University of Edinburgh ultimately of international renown, together with an Honours degree that was in design and content second to none, producing a stream of graduates and postgraduates who have in turn served the enhancement of the subject in Scotland and all over the world. His own revolutionary work upon the Neolithic and Iron Age of Scotland is perfectly matched by that of one of his postgraduate students, John Coles, who gave a modern foundation to Scottish Bronze Age Studies[48] in which Piggott took great pride. He was, of course, a long-term member of both major public bodies in Scotland's archaeology and was President of the Society of Antiquaries of Scotland (in a reforming presidency). He conducted at least seven major excavations in Scotland and exercised a guiding influence over many others. He wrote and edited two major works of synthesis on Scottish archaeology as well as pursuing his international career.

[48] *Proc. Soc. Antiq. Scot.* XCIII (1959–60), 16–134; XCVII (1963–4), 82–156 and CI (1968–9), 1–110.

He was, however, customarily frank in declaring that his *Urheimat* and his heart lay elsewhere and Scots, understandably, find this difficult to understand. But it was so, and he made no bones about it; it is quite irrelevant to the issue, and there is no doubt that Piggott served his adopted home well. The suggestion that he did not found 'a School of Scottish Archaeology' would have been met with a clap of that deep bass laughter that those who knew him delighted in. Stuart's love for his own 'fair country' was of an intensity that scorned national loyalties of any sort—and he entertained a deep suspicion of any who proclaimed them. Piggott regarded himself as truly a European; if there was to be any division between himself and the universality of mankind. He would have been appalled by the very notion of a School of Scottish (or English, or British) archaeology.

But did Stuart Piggott not produce a 'school', a human legacy, of any kind? Indeed he did. He, together with Hawkes perhaps, brought the school of pragmatic historico-cultural archaeology to its highest current level of attainment. Like taxes, and death itself, this school has always been with us since the foundation of archaeology as a discipline and I suggest that it will always be with us. It was upon this platform that Piggott, with his profound historical and humanistic insights, found himself comfortable. If asked why he did not exercise his considerable influence to further the interests of that 'school' and its adherents he, I think, would have replied that he saw it as neither necessary, on the one part, nor, indeed, entirely proper, on the other, so to do. But Piggott's other major contribution lay on the altogether broader canvas of the history and development of human ideas where as a scholar of astounding breadth of experience and erudition he offered archaeology its proper place in the broader development of thought from the fifteenth to the nineteenth century; and it is difficult to see, among his contemporaries, who could have accomplished this to such all-inclusive and such readable effect.

In the last analysis, however, Stuart Piggott's influence upon his students and colleagues was a very personal one. To know him was to understand his straightforward appreciation of the vulnerability of the evidence with which he dealt. He argued archaeology as a study of humanity with his own peculiarly enlightened view of that objective. If students followed that inspirational lead they could be guaranteed the 'fun' of which Stuart so often spoke. It was Stuart's ability to impart that sense of 'fun' that made him such a very effective communicator to the public, both through the written word and, with his distinctive beaky nose and splendid waistcoats, directly through television—when gently led to the ring by Glyn Daniel. It is that personal impact that led me, days after his death, to write that 'to many Stuart Piggott's death will be a personal bereavement' and I have been astonished how many people have responded positively to that spontaneous remark. He, himself, quoted John Aubrey (1626–97) with reference to his own career, again with characteristic modesty:

> Surely my starres impelled me to be an Antiquary, I have the strangest luck at it, that things drop into my lap.

If Stuart had been born today I would like to think that they still could.

Stuart was, by his own request, cremated *simpliciter* in Oxford on 30 September 1996.

ROGER MERCER
Royal Commission on the Ancient
and Historical Monuments of Scotland

Note. I should like to acknowledge with considerable gratitude the assistance of the following in the composition of the above memoir: Christine Allan, RCAHMS; Fionna Ashmore, Society of Antiquaries of Scotland; Dr Sara Champion, Southampton; Dr Christopher Chippindale, University of Cambridge; Dr Ros Cleal, Avebury Museum; Professor John Coles, Thorverton, Devon; John Dunbar (former Secretary RCAHMS); Dai Morgan Evans, Society of Antiquaries of London; Richard Feachem, Bow Street, Cardiganshire; Lady Aileen Fox, Exeter; Frances Healy, Charlbury, Oxfordshire; Duncan and Kay McArdle, Alford, Aberdeenshire; Diana Murray RCAHMS; Dr Graham Ritchie RCAHMS; Dr Anne Ross, Bow Street, Cardiganshire; Stewart and Alison Sanderson, Primsidemill, Yetholm, Roxburghshire; Kenneth Steer (former Secretary RCAHMS); Nicholas Thomas, Bristol.

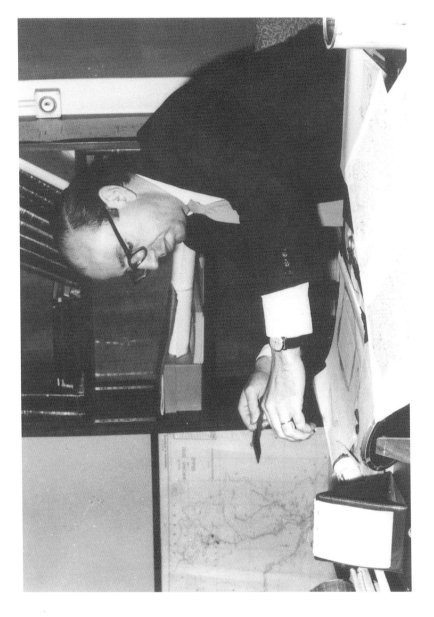

EDMOND SOLLBERGER

Edmond Sollberger
1920–1989

EDMOND SOLLBERGER[1] was born on 12 October 1920, in Istanbul, where his father was an accountant. He was Swiss by birth, his family origin being in Wynigen in the Canton of Berne, French speaking, and Roman Catholic by upbringing. He received his early education in Istanbul, in the *Collège religieux français*, a rather monastic establishment run by friars, concerning which he had some very mixed memories, and strange stories. His early years in Istanbul set him on a career in which his command of languages played an important part, a working knowledge of Turkish and modern Greek being a useful legacy of this time, to which he was able later to add a practical knowledge of Arabic.

He completed his schooling in Istanbul in 1939, and received his further education at the University of Geneva, first in the faculty of *Sciences économiques et sociales* from 1940 to 1941, but mainly in the faculty of *Lettres* from 1941 to 1945, where he studied general linguistics together with English and Spanish. During this period he had the curious experience in vacation time of passing by train between Geneva and Istanbul through Nazi occupied territory.

At Geneva he benefited from training in general linguistics under Henri Frei in the department established by Ferdinand de Saussure. De Saussure had died in 1913, and his first two successors in the Chair, his former pupils Charles Bally and Albert Sechehaye, who together had edited and published notes of his lectures as the influential *Cours de linguistic générale* (1916), were themselves succeeded by their pupil Frei. Sollberger was thus trained in a sound tradition, which in addition to historical philology, included a pioneering understanding of structural linguistics (the study of 'a language as a coherent structure and a

---

[1] Obituary notices have been published by Paul Garelli in *Revue d'assyriologie*, 84 (1990), 97–9 and Christopher Walker in *Archiv für Orientforschung*, 35 (1988), 258–60 [the date of the latter is correct, the journal being out of pace with actual years].

Proceedings of the British Academy, **97**, 445–463. © The British Academy 1998.

homogeneous system').[2] As long ago as 1878, de Saussure had published his *Mémoire sur le système primitif des voyelles dans les langues indo-européennes* (dated 1879), but the existence of the sounds postulated by him in Proto-Indo-European had only been confirmed as recently as 1927 by the recognition by J. Kurylowicz of the character of the ḫ in the recently deciphered cuneiform 'Hittite',[3] so reference to this would probably have been part of the course. The excellence of the training in this sector is demonstrated by the career of another pupil of de Saussure, Antoine Meillet, whose work in the field of Indo-European comparative linguistics is still valued. Sollberger spoke of an exercise in which the students were required to translate a given passage into Proto-Indo-European. The main benefit of his linguistic training at Geneva was however the clear view of language in general which prepared him to study an individual specimen without being bound by the traditional frame of classical grammar.

Being thus prepared, he chose Sumerian as the subject of his doctoral dissertation, apart from Egyptian the oldest recorded language and one with no known cognates ancient or modern. He had already done preliminary reading at Geneva in the general field of Assyriology, and had found that books which he wished to consult were often out to someone else. It was only later, when he met Dr Paul Garelli, that he found that they had been contemporaries at the University of Geneva, studying in different faculties, unknown to each other, and had each had the same experience of finding library books missing from the shelf. They found also indeed that they were both 'Stambouliotes', having passed their early years in expatriate families based in Istanbul, factors leading to a particularly close friendship.

Apart from early essays at systematising Sumerian grammar, some of them very brief, by P. Haupt, S. Langdon, F. Delitzsch, and B. Meissner, the most substantial attempts at the time when Sollberger took up the study were those of Arno Poebel, *Grundzüge der sumerischen Grammatik* in 1923,[4] Cyril J. Gadd, 'The Sumerian Language' in his *A Sumerian Reading Book* in 1924,[5] and Anton Deimel, *Šumerische Grammatik der archaistischen Texte mit Übungsstücken zum Selbstunterricht* also in 1924,[6] with a revised and augmented edition in 1939. The Sumerian language was written (though not spoken) during some two millennia, and both Poebel and Gadd drew material from various periods, some from the third, much from the second, and also

---

[2] Quoting the definition of S. Potter, *Language in the Modern World* (rev. edn., London, 1975), p. 195.

[3] 'ə indoeuropéen et ḫ hittite', *Symbolae grammaticae in honorem J. Roswadowski* (Krakow, 1927), I, pp. 95–104.

[4] (Rostock).

[5] (Oxford), pp. 14–42.

[6] *Orentalia* (Rome), os, 9–13.

some from student texts of the first millennium BC. Deimel on the other hand, as his title indicated, took his evidence largely from texts of the third millennium BC, when Sumerian was still a spoken language. In the foreword to his 1924 *Grammatik* he observes that he is not attempting a historical grammar, but that he will base his conclusions on the oldest accessible material, that of the time of Urukagina, ruler of Lagash, with his contemporaries and immediate predecessors. In archaeological terms this was the latter part of the Early Dynastic period, the time before the conquest of southern Mesopotamia by Sargon, the Semitic speaking ruler of Akkad, in about 2370 BC. Deimel had seen therefore that it made sense to concentrate on a body of material belonging to a limited time and area,[7] and before it was greatly influenced by Akkadian, though in practice he included reading examples (*Übungen*) from later in the third millennium. Deimel was a pupil of J. N. Strassmaier (1846–1919), who had spent years copying texts, mostly of the Neo-Babylonian and Achaemenian periods, in the British Museum, and must have observed the value of detailed study of a coherent group of evidence. He considered that it was not sensible to spend time on works of synthesis until large numbers of texts had been published,[8] and Deimel (1865–1954) in choosing to work on a particular group of texts for his grammar was possibly influenced by this view. In this respect Deimel's method was closer in thinking to the strictly defined approach of the Geneva school, and this may have played a part in Sollberger's decision to go to him at the Pontifical Biblical Institute in Rome for his first steps in what he called the *voie périlleuse* of Sumerology, and under Deimel he passed *inoubliables semaines* in 1947. He chose much the same material as Deimel to work on, limiting it to the royal inscriptions of Lagash from the period before Sargon, and confining himself strictly to this corpus. With impeccable application he copied afresh all of the known texts, over 300 in number, visiting most of the Museums involved, including the British Museum in the summer of 1947, and the Imperial Ottoman Museum in Istanbul in 1951, where he was able to stay with his parents. His resulting *Corpus des inscriptions ' royales' présargoniques de Lagaš*, not published until 1956, entirely written out in his own clear hand, including the title page, remains a work of permanent value. This material formed the basis first for his paper 'Etudes de linguistique sumerienne' which appeared in 1950 appropriately in the *Cahiers Ferdinand de Saussure*,[9] and included an attempt to define the phonemes of Sumerian, but definitively in 1952 in his *Le Système verbal dans les inscriptions*

---

[7] This point was recognised by Poebel himself not long after (*The Sumerian Prefix Forms e- and i- in the Time of the Earlier Princes of Lagaš* [Assyriological Studies, 2] (Chicago, 1931), pp. 1–2).

[8] E. A. Wallis Budge, *The Rise and Progress of Assyriology* (London, 1924), p. 228.

[9] 9 (1950), 51–88.

' *royales*' *présargoniques de Lagaš: contribution à la grammaire suméri-enne.*[10] Both the *Système verbal*, involving complicated diacritics, and the *Corpus* are in their different ways fine examples of book production, something in which he took pride, and in his contacts with the press he established a firm friendship with the proprietress, Madame E. Droz. Sollberger acknowledged a great debt to Frei, to him *le Maître*, citing several of his publications in the Bibliography of the *Système verbal*, and in 1971 contributing a paper to his Festschrift.[11] In 1961 he rounded off these studies, so to speak, with his paper 'Le syllabaire présargonique de Lagaš',[12] in which he carefully analysed the phonetic values of the signs on the basis of their usage in the texts in his *Corpus* and other contemporary texts.

In 1949 he had been appointed *Assistant d'archéologie* in the Musée d'art et d'histoire at Geneva and completed his thesis while serving in that post. Also in 1949 he married Ariane Zender from Geneva, thereby going against Deimel's advice that if he wished to pursue an academic career the best thing would be for him either to become a Roman Catholic priest or to marry an heiress. In the event he chose better than Deimel had advised, and throughout his married life he had wonderful support from Ariane, who, according to the dedication in his *Système verbal*, had seen his studies as *non une rivale mais une alliée*, and who together with him offered generous hospitality to friends and visiting colleagues at Putney and then Richmond.

While he was working on his thesis, the two volumes of Adam Falkenstein's *Grammatik der Sprache Gudeas von Lagaš* appeared in 1949 and 1950. In this Falkenstein also limited himself to a well defined group of texts, about a century and a half later than the latest of those dealt with by Sollberger, who was able to visit him in Heidelberg in 1952, and to discuss his manuscript, at that time almost ready for the press. Falkenstein had served as one of the referees of his thesis, and subsequently devoted a lengthy review to it,[13] thereby recognising its importance.

It was part of the procedure that a candidate for the degree of Doctor of Letters at Geneva should publish his dissertation, and in doing this, Sollberger was bound to come up against the traditional European approach to the study of language. The great advances of the nineteenth century in language study, mainly in Europe, had centred very much on the Indo-European group. The native languages of most European scholars belonged to this group, most of them had studied Latin and usually Greek not only at school but also at university level, and those who took up Semitic languages found that with

[10] Librairie E. Droz, Genève.
[11] Genre et nombre en Sumérien', *Cahiers Ferdinand de Saussure*, 26 (1969) [= *Mélanges H. Frei* (1971)], 151–60.
[12] *Zeitschrift für Assyriologie*, 54 (1961), 1–50.
[13] *Archiv für Orientforschung*, 18 (1957–8), 89–96.

some modifications similar grammatical categories could be applied to them. The great Hebraist Wilhelm Gesenius who set the main lines of the future study of the Semitic languages had training in classics, and it is possible to see Carl Brockelmann's *Grundriss der vergleichenden Grammatik der semitischen Sprachen* (Berlin, 1908–13) as part of the process of publishing grammars and handbooks by the so-called Neo-grammarian school, most of whom worked in the Indo-European field.[14] Equally, L. H. Gray, primarily an Iranologist, could later produce a serviceable *Introduction to Semitic Comparative Linguistics* (Columbia University Press; New York, 1934).

It is clear that the Department of de Saussure and his successors at Geneva took full account of this tradition, but when methods had to be developed for studying strange languages, often known only orally, such as those of the Indian tribes of the United States,[15] it became clear that traditional categories were not enough. Different languages had distinct structures, so the linguist's approach would be to analyse Sumerian in terms of its own structures, with appropriate new terminology, rather than treating it as a rather peculiar form of an Indo-European language such as Latin.

This meant that many scholars did not accept his approach, bearing out perhaps what Igor M. Diakonoff referred to as 'a joke well known among Assyriologists that there are as many Sumerian languages as there are Sumerologists'.[16] In his Preface Sollberger states the intention of his volume to be to study Sumerian in the light of the principles of general linguistics, and to furnish a description of Sumerian which would be of use in the field of general linguistics. He does not claim that it will be of use to Sumerologists, though the writer remembers a beginning student in the 1950s telling him that he had found it more helpful for learning Sumerian than the existing standard works. In subsequent years there has been a recognition that each language should be studied in its own terms, though to what extent Sollberger's work contributed to this is not clear. In 1965, Thorkild Jacobsen, who gave a quite different analysis of the Sumerian verb, also accepted that the analysis should be 'one not imposed upon the language from outside but inherent in its own structure'.[17]

---

[14] See e.g. W. P. Lehman, *Historical Linguistics* (3rd edn., London and New York, 1992), p. 33.

[15] Sollberger cited for instance F. Boas, *Handbook of American Indian Languages*, I (Washington, 1911) in his bibliography (*Système verbal*, p. 11).

[16] In S. J. Lieberman (ed.), *Sumerological Studies in Honor of Thorkild Jacobsen on his Seventieth Birthday* [Assyriological Studies 20] (Chicago, 1976), p. 99; cited in part in M. L. Thomsen, *The Sumerian Language* [Mesopotamia 10] (Copenhagen, 1984), p. 11.

[17] 'About the Sumerian Verb' in H. G. Güterbock and Thorkild Jacobsen (eds), *Studies in Honor of Benno Landsberger on his Seventy-Fifth Birthday* [Assyriological Studies, 16] (Chicago, 1965). pp. 71–102 at 71, n. 2 = Jacobsen, *Towards the Image of Tammuz and Other Essays* (Cambridge, Mass., 1970), p. 431, n. 2. In this Jacobsen modestly acknowledged that his suggestions could be 'no more than subjective guesswork' but at the same time he believed that the guesses were educated and systematic (*Studies*, p. 71, n. 1 = *Image*, p. 430, n. 1).

It is perhaps significant that until Sollberger took up his post at the British Museum there was no copy of the *Système verbal* in the Library of the Department of Western Asiatic Anitiquities.

At a dinner organised in 1963 by Samuel Noah Kramer to honour Cyril J. Gadd on the occasion of the publication of their joint work *Ur Excavations Texts*, VI, *Literary and Religious Texts*, 1,[18] both Kramer and Sollberger spoke. Kramer's speech was mostly about Gadd, but in the course of it he referred to Sollberger, by then a good friend, as someone who had come on the scene in a rather unusual way. No one in the Assyriological field had heard of him until in the years following the war he began consulting a number of foreign scholars, Kramer among them, mostly by letter, on points concerning the Sumerian language. When the results of his studies began to appear, particularly the *Système verbal*, Kramer said that he was initially rather suspicious, but that when he came to examine the details carefully he had to admit that he could find nothing incorrect. This was in fact a significant admission from a man who, as a pupil of Arno Poebel, had learned Sumerian in a different way. Poebel, himself a former theological student who had entered the field of cuneiform studies under Hermann Hilprecht, used traditional terminology, though he recognised that Sumerian was a language totally different from those usually studied, and was trying to find new ways of dealing with it.[19] Kramer had actually thought that Sollberger had been unwise to publish his volume,[20] but nevertheless he elsewhere described him as 'one of the leading young Sumerologists'.[21] In the context of differing opinions among Sumerologists, Kramer referred to Jacobsen as a friendly 'adversary'.

Though Sollberger had not started as a specialist in ancient times, his knowledge of Sumerian now placed him in that category, and in 1952, the year in which the *Système verbal* was published, and for which he was awarded the degree of Doctor of Letters at the University, he was promoted to *Conservateur d'archéologie* in the Geneva Museum, in 1958 to *Conservateur principal*, and in the following year *Directeur ad interim* while Pierre Bouffard, the Director, was serving as *Conseillier administratif* of the City of Geneva. Also from 1956 he served as *Privat-Docent* for Sumerian and Akkadian in the Faculty of Letters of the University of Geneva. The five years during which he held this parallel teaching post were too short for foreign

---

[18] Gadd had copied the tablets before the war, and he invited Kramer to collaborate with him in writing the introduction, see S. N. Kramer, *In the World of Sumer. An Autobiography* (Detroit, 1986), pp. 214–15.

[19] I owe this view of Poebel's work to Dr Claus Wilcke.

[20] An opinion expressed to Dr J. E. Curtis.

[21] *In the World of Sumer*, p. 216. It is worth noting that the *Système verbal* was reprinted in Germany in 1972.

students to come to him, but his single pupil Françoise Bruschweiler succeeded him in this university post and has made valuable contributions.

The year 1960 was a time of important decisions for him. Though he had received rapid promotion in the Geneva Museum, and was likely to be appointed Director in due course, he became increasingly frustrated by the limited extent of the material for him to work on in the collections, and his comparative isolation from the main stream of Assyriology. He was one of the leading international experts on Sumerian and had also by this time mastered the better known Akkadian, and had by 1951 catalogued all the cuneiform texts in the Museum,[22] many of them collected, and some already published, by Alfred Boissier. He had also, as a faithful curator, published the guide *Antiquités orientales (Salles 14–15)* [Guides illustrés 6] (Geneva, 1958), as well as a series of Museum oriented articles, including notes on recent acquisitions of his department, most of them from the time when he was the head.[23] He was later on able to surprise his colleagues with unexpected knowledge arising from his work on these collections, such as his ability to read Palmyrene. He had moreover more or less exhausted the cuneiform material of particular interest in Swiss collections with the publication of 'Inscriptions votives babyloniennes conservées dans les collections suisses'.[24] During this time he published a substantial article 'Sur la chronologie des rois d'Ur et quelques problèmes connexes',[25] proposing a closely argued chronology for the latter part of the third millennium, including particularly the Third Dynasty of Ur, to well into the second millennium BC, including the parallel line of rulers (ensis) of Lagash, sometimes known as the 'Second Dynasty of Lagash', one of whom was the great Gudea, not included in any king list, but important because of the large number of inscriptions from their time. He did not assign absolute dates in his resulting 'Synopsis chronologique', but provided data which readers could apply according to their adherence to the possible alternative high, middle, low, or very low chronologies variously proposed for the late third and early

---

[22] 'The Cuneiform Collection in Geneva', *Journal of Cuneiform Studies*, 5 (1951), 18–20, amounting to about 850 items. Before his appointment to the staff he had already published some pre-Sargonic texts in 'Documents cunéiformes au Musée d'Art et d'Histoire', *Genava* 26 (1948), 48–72; and subsequently another tablet (jointly with I. J. Gelb), 'The First Legal Document from the Later Old Assyrian Period', *Journal of Near Eastern Studies*, 16 (1957), 163–75.

[23] 'Récents accroissements des collections de l'Asie occidentale', *Les Musées de Genéve*, 8, 2 (1951); 'Trois terres cuites mésopotamiennes', Ibid. 9. 5 (1952); 'Nouvelles acquisitions. L'offrande du chevreau', Ibid. 11. 3 (1954); 'Statuettes de Syrie et du Liban', Ibid. 13. 4 (1956); 'Un bas-relief phénicien', Ibid. NS. 1. 1. (1960; and in the section 'Genève' under 'Altorientalische Altertümer in Museen und Privatsammlungen', *Archiv für Orientforschung*, 17 (1954–6), 187–9, 409–10.

[24] *Genava*, NS, 2 (1954), 237–44.

[25] *Archiv für Orientforschung*, 17 (1954–6), 10–48.

second millennia BC. He favoured the high chronology throughout his career, but was flexible in his application of it, later on accepting the policy of the British Museum and the *Cambridge Ancient History* in using the middle chronology. His paper remains an important contribution to a continuing debate, and has not been superseded.[26]

At the end of 1954 he had received a twelve months leave of absence and a grant from the *Fonds national suisse de la Recherche scientifique* so that he and Ariane could make a study visit to the United States. While there he was based at Yale, but was also able to examine tablets in the Metropolitan Museum, the Harvard Semitic Museum, The University Museum in Philadelphia, the Oriental Institute of the University of Chicago, Princeton Theological Seminary, Hartford Theological Seminary, and other collections. This visit gave him the opportunity to meet and discuss these texts with Benno Landsberger, Samuel N. Kramer, Thorkild Jacobsen, Ignace J. Gelb, Vaughan E. Crawford, Ferris J. Stephens, as well as with Albrecht Goetze, William M. Laffan Professor of Assyriology and Babylonian Literature at Yale, his academic host.[27]

In late 1956 and early 1957 he was granted leave to participate as *Mitarbeitendes Gast* in the German excavations under Heinrich Lenzen at Warka, ancient Uruk, renewing his contact with Falkenstein who was the official epigraphist of the expedition,[28] and taking the opportunity also to study texts in the Iraq Museum.[29] He became well known to those specialists who had not met him before when he organised the ninth Rencontre assyriologique internationale at the Musée d'art et d'histoire in Geneva in June 1960, choosing the topic very appropriate to his expertise, *Aspects du contact suméro-akkadien*, and editing the proceedings as a valuable contribution to a much debated subject.[30]

In the same year, 1960, he received an invitation from Richard D. Barnett to come to London and join the staff of the British Museum. When he was making the decision about this, he was actually in hospital following a serious operation, and was also considering an invitation to take up a chair at the

---

[26] Concerning one of the crucial points D. O. Edzard has most recently commented that 'The chronological relation of the "Second Dynasty of Lagaš" to the Third Dynasty of Ur has not yet been settled' (*Gudea and his Dynasty* [The Royal Inscriptions of Mesopotamia. Early Periods, 3. 1] (Toronto, 1997), p. 3.

[27] 'Selected Texts from American Collections', *Journal of Cuneiform Studies*, 10 (1956), 11–31; and see *The Business and Administrative Correspondence under the Kings of Ur* (1966), p. x and tablet index on pp. 9–11.

[28] H. Lenzen, *et al.*, *XV. vorläufige Bericht über die von dem Deutschen Archäologischen Institut und der Deutschen Orient-Gesellschaft aus Mitteln der Deutschen Forschungsgemeinschaft* (Berlin, 1959), p. 5.

[29] His article 'On Two Early Lagaš Inscriptions in the Iraq Museum', *Sumer*, 13 (1957), 61–4 was a product of this visit.

[30] In *Genava*, 8 (1960), 241–314.

University of Geneva. He was a determined anglophile, however, and the lure of the largest collection of cuneiform texts in the world tipped the balance in favour of the British Museum, and he later described how he wrote his letter of acceptance from his hospital bed, the effort causing perspiration to pour off him. A year later he was invited by Albrecht Goetze to take up the post of Curator of the Babylonian Collection at Yale, due to become vacant in 1962 through the retirement of Ferris J. Stephens, but by then he was well established in London, and the position was filled by William W. Hallo.

When Cyril Gadd (1893–1969),[31] the last Keeper of Egyptian and Assyrian Antiquities in the British Museum, retired in 1955 to take up the Chair of Ancient Semitic Languages and Civilizations in the School of Oriental and African Studies of the University of London, his former department was divided into Egyptian Antiquities and Western Asiatic Antiquities under I. E. S. Edwards and R. D. Barnett respectively. In 1955 Richard Barnett[32] had only one academic colleague, Donald J. Wiseman, on the establishment of his department, joined by the writer in 1959. He succeeded in obtaining the appointment in May 1960 of a cuneiformist, Dr R. F. G. Sweet subsequently of Toronto, to fill the post vacated by Gadd in 1955, but for domestic reasons Dr Sweet had had to withdraw a month later. Barnett was therefore still looking for a replacement for Gadd, and, when in 1960 Gadd retired from the University and after some delay his Chair was divided into two, one for Assyriology and one for Semitic Languages, and in February 1961 Donald Wiseman was appointed to the former and Dr J. B. Segal to the latter, the posts to be taken up in October, Barnett found that he would be without a cuneiform specialist. He knew and liked Sollberger from the time of his first visit to copy texts for his *Corpus*, had seen him in action as he ran the Rencontre assyriologique in Geneva, and had recently had contact with him when he had been again in the British Museum working on texts, at which time the vacancy had actually been touched on. The invitation to come to London was issued with the agreement of the Director Sir Frank Francis, and was to entail Sollberger obtaining British Nationality, the necessary preliminary to 'establishment', in Civil Service terminology. He was appointed to the staff in September 1960, but partly for reasons of health, was not able to take up his post until March 1961. Barnett gave him to understand that he was likely to succeed him as Keeper of the Department, probably in 1969 when he hoped himself to succeed Seton Lloyd as Professor of Near Eastern Archaeology at the University of London. This was a reasonable expectation in the situation at the time, but in the event, Barnett was not appointed to the University Chair, so Sollberger had five more years to wait, and when the time came he had some uncomfortable

---

[31] Obituary, *PBA*, 56 (1972), 363–402.
[32] Obituary, *PBA*, 76 (1986), 321–45.

moments since his candidacy for the Keepership took place under the regime of Sir John Pope-Hennessy, who later in his retirement speech claimed as one of his achievements as Director of the Museum, that he had put an end to the idea that the most appropriate candidate for a Keepership would normally be an existing senior member of the department in question.

Edmond Sollberger and his wife Ariane with their two young daughters Nicole and Josette moved to London in 1961, living temporarily in Kensington but settling in a pleasant flat in Putney, and moving some years later to a house in Richmond, and subsequently to another, also in Richmond. In each home he and Ariane offered generous hospitality, and his study was a model of order and the location in which he prepared much of his careful and accurate published work.

In the Museum he had the rank of Temporary Assistant Keeper I, and outside he was coopted for subsequent election to the Council and Executive Committee of the British School of Archaeology in Iraq, and also to the Council of Management of the British Institute of Archaeology at Ankara, and in the same year, 1961, he became a Corresponding Member of the German Archaeological Institute.

One of his colleagues in the Museum was Dr Hugo H. Figulla, also a cuneiformist, who had been working in the department for some years, but was never, to his chagrin, more than an unestablished supernumerary member of the staff. He was moreover in his seventy-fifth year by 1960, and decided to retire at the age of seventy-eight in early 1964.[33]

In the Museum Sollberger took over the administration of the tablet collections from Donald Wiseman, overlapping with him for six months, and himself preparing two volumes in the series *Cuneiform Texts from Babylonian Tablets in the British Museum* by editing copies made long before by Theophilus Goldridge Pinches,[34] of whom he wrote that his 'immense services to Assyriology are not always fully realized'. Pinches had been a member of the Museum staff, but had sided with Hormuzd Rassam in a dispute with Wallis Budge and as a result had been obliged to leave the service of the Trustees. Many of his accurate copies of cuneiform texts in the Museum had lain unpublished for over half a century, and Sollberger was determined to do him belated justice. He later edited another group of Pinches copies of texts not in the British Museum in *The Pinches Manuscript* in the Italian series *Materiali per il vocabulario neosumerico*, V (Rome, 1978). This manuscript had been

---

[33] He continued to work for many years beyond the normal retirement age, because as a refugee from Nazi Germany he had been treated initially as an enemy alien in wartime Britain, and was only able to buy a house for his (second) wife and son late in life, and needed to pay off the mortgage.

[34] *Cuneiform Texts*, 44, *Miscellaneous Texts* (1963), and 45, *Old-Babylonian Business Documents* (1964).

passed to him in 1958 by Ernst Weidner, and in the following year he had drawn attention to one text in it of particular interest because it referred to the ruler of Byblos (*ku-ub-la*) in the late third millennium BC, the earliest reference then known.[35] He also himself copied tablets for volume 50 of the British Museum *Cuneiform Texts* series, *Pre-Sargonic and Sargonic Economic Texts* (1972). The series had been initiated in 1896 by Wallis Budge, and over the years many of the volumes had gone out of print, and he readily took up the policy of Richard Barnett of reprinting earlier volumes, completing this when he himself became Keeper with volumes 34 to 41, 42 (1959) having been the first post-war volume, prepared by H. H. Figulla.

He was also instrumental in arranging for Dr Paul Garelli to publish a volume, VI (1975), in the series *Cuneiform Texts from Cappadocian Tablets in the British Museum*,[36] Garelli having previously published a substantial number of Cappadocian texts in the Geneva Museum,[37] which he had worked on there in Sollberger's time as curator.

Having come to the British home of the excavations of Sir Leonard Woolley at Ur, and having contributed a characteristically systematic annotated list of the early inscriptions from that site to the Woolley Memorial Volume,[38] he prepared a volume of copies of texts with full Descriptive Catalogue in the series *Ur Excavations Texts*, VIII, *Royal Inscriptions*, II (1965), thereby providing a supplement to the volume, *Ur Excavations Texts*, I, *Royal Inscriptions*, published by Gadd and Leon Legrain in 1928.

Another product of his early years at the British Museum was his article 'Graeco-Babyloniaca', published in 1962.[39] In this he took up some further early copies by Pinches of a number of Sumerian and Akkadian tablets inscribed in cuneiform on the obverse with the same text transliterated into Greek characters on the reverse. Pinches had published some of these in 1902,[40] and others have taken up this material subsequently and made modifications,[41] but Sollberger performed a useful service in bringing it forward for attention.

Richard Barnett was very conscientious in seeking to provide introductory publications on the collections of his department, and against some mild resistance he persuaded Sollberger to write a popular booklet on *The Babylonian Legend of the Flood* (1962).[42] In this he amused himself by giving all the

---

[35] 'Byblos sous les rois d'Ur', *Archiv für Orientforschung*, 19 (1959–60), 120–2; the text being *Pinches Manuscript*, no. 111.

[36] This completed the publication of this class of texts in the British Museum, *CCT*, I–IV (1921–7) having been by Sydney Smith, and V (1956) by Smith and D. J. Wiseman.

[37] *Revue d'assyriologie*, 59 (1965), 19–48: 60 (1966), 93–121.

[38] 'Notes on the Early Inscriptions from Ur and el-'Obēd', *Iraq*, 22 (1960), 69–89.

[39] *Iraq*, 24 (1962), 63–72.

[40] *Proceedings of the Society of Biblical Archaeology*, 24 (1902), 108–19.

[41] Most recently M. J. Geller, 'The Last Wedge', *ZA* 87 (1997), 43–95, at 68–85 (re-edition of the texts), and 68–85 (copies).

[42] 2nd edn., 1966; 3rd edn., 1971.

quotations from the text of the Gilgamesh Epic in the idiosyncratic translation
into archaising English hexameters by Reginald Campbell Thompson, and by
indicating the pronunciation of the four short vowels in Akkadian, *a*, *e*, *i*, and
u, by explaining that they should sound like the *u* respectively in English
'buck', 'bury', 'business' and 'bull'. He delighted in demonstrating that he
knew more peculiar things about the English language than most native
English speakers, as when he used the word 'glabrous' in an article in
reference to an inscribed surface on a statue, assuming, rightly, that most of
us would have to look it up.

Among other Museum tasks, which included standing in for Barnett in his
absences, he carried out some rearrangement of the Babylonian Room of the
department. This was in the days when such work was undertaken with the
help of a Museum carpenter and painter, any labels being put out to a jobbing
printer. The project was completed in 1963, in time for the twelfth Rencontre
assyriologique internationale which took place in London in July of that year.

In this period he also completed a volume which he had begun in Geneva,
The Business and Administrative Correspondence under the Kings of Ur
(1966), the first in a new series, *Texts from Cuneiform Sources*, of which he
was a joint editor. In this he transliterated and translated over 370 texts, many
of them previously unpublished, and provided an Introduction and a lengthy
Glossary (100 pages) occupying half the volume, giving useful lexical data
from this body of texts, one of the stated intentions of the Series being to
'facilitate the work of the [Chicago Assyrian] Dictionary staff'.[43] This glossary
has very innovative qualities, treating the Sumerian words as elements of
language, and not simply as a graphemic system, and has to be consulted
constantly by every scholar working with materials of the period of the Third
Dynasty of Ur.[44]

In December 1966, having completed the necessary period of residence, he
obtained British Nationality, and following the formality of a Civil Service
Commission competition in which he was successful, he was established in the
Museum in the grade Assistant Keeper I in July 1967.

At the beginning of January 1970, following energetic lobbying by Barnett,
he was promoted to Deputy Keeper, and following the death of Cyril Gadd in
1969 he was appointed to succeed him as one of the three editors of the revised
edition of the *Cambridge Ancient History*, the others being I. E. S. Edwards
and N. G. L. Hammond. He had helped the two surviving editors with the final
preparation of Volume I, Part 2, which appeared in 1971, and was a full editor

---

[43] *TCS*, I, p. vii. The preparation of a vocabulary for a set body of texts by the specialist
dealing with them, as a contribution towards a major language dictionary, was something
advocated by Sir Alan Gardiner in the light of his experience with the Egyptian *Wörterbuch*
in Berlin (*Ancient Egyptian Onomastica* (Oxford, 1947), I, pp. xix–xx).
[44] I am indebted to Dr Claus Wilcke for this assessment.

for Volume II, Parts 1 (1973) and 2 (1975), though for these he was largely dealing with contributions commissioned by Gadd. With Volume III the choice of contributors was in his own hands and since he was responsible for the whole of Western Asia considerable work was involved. He had seen however how Gadd's last years had been almost taken over by the heavy burden of editing other people's contributions, and was careful to keep his involvement within bounds. Various delays meant that Volume III, Part 1 did not appear until 1982 and Part 2 not until 1991 when C. B. F. Walker saw the work commissioned by him, with a few additions, to completion.

In his *Corpus* he had referred to the standard work of the great master François Thureau-Dangin, *Die sumerischen und akkadischen Königsinschriften*,[45] which included transliterations and translations of many of the texts he was dealing with, but which was naturally rather out of date. In his Preface he says 'La refonte complète de *SAK* par A. Falkenstein étant imminente, je n'ai joint à mes copies ni transcriptions ni traductions', depending on what Falkenstein had told him. When asked in the early 1960s for his definition of the word 'imminente' (used in 1956) he smiled ruefully and saw the funny side. In 1971 he partially supplied the gap when in collaboration with Jean-Robert Kupper he published the very convenient volume *Inscriptions royales Sumériennes et Akkadiennes* which gave new translations (Sumerian by him and Akkadian by Kupper) of about a third of the inscriptions dealt with by Thureau-Dangin with more recently discovered texts together with brief notes and a sixty-page 'Répertoire des noms propres'. This was the third volume of a new series, *Littératures anciennes du proche-orient*, published under the aegis of the École Biblique of Jerusalem by the Éditions du Cerf, who had been associated previously in the production of the Jerusalem Bible. For this series, which it was proposed would cover material in all ancient near eastern languages, he had been Editor-in-Charge (*Directeur*) of Sumerian texts since 1966, and was arranging that other volumes would follow.[46] In this volume, he agreed to use the middle chronology, while stating that he favoured the high one, and also denied himself his preference for the writing Sur- instead of Ur- in personal names such as Ur-Nammu, for which following Pinches and Poebel he would have preferred Sur-Nammu.[47]

He also participated with Dietz Otto Edzard and Gertrud Farber in the preparation of a basic reference work, *Die Orts- und Gewässernamen der*

---

[45] Vorderasiatische Bibliothek, 1. 1 (Leipzig, 1907), referred to as *SAK*.

[46] It had been intended that the important inscriptions of Gudea of Lagash would form a separate volume in the series, the translations to be supplied by Falkenstein. Sadly he died in 1966 at the early age of sixty and this did not take place.

[47] He repeated his defence of this reading in his note 'Sur-Nanše' in *Revue d'assyriologie*, 79 (1985), 87–8.

präsargonischen und sargonischen Zeit (Weisbaden, 1977) in the series *Réper-toire Géographique des Textes Cunéiformes*, 1.[48]

He had a clear hand both in copying cuneiform signs, but also in writing Romanised script, as he had shown in his *Corpus*. When he was invited by the volume editor of the Pontifical Biblical Institute to prepare an introductory grammar of Sumerian, he proposed that he would write it out entirely by hand. He suggested the title *A Sumerian Primer*, but other commitments kept him from carrying this out.

Richard Barnett was due to reach his sixty-fifth birthday in 1974, and after the element of uncertainty already mentioned Sollberger was successful in the competition for the Keepership and took up the post at the beginning of February 1974. His appointment had been confirmed in October 1973, very soon after his election in July 1973 to Fellowship of the British Academy. At this time, in addition to other roles, he was also serving on the editorial board of the *Cahiers Ferdinand de Saussure*.

His new duties in the Museum inevitably meant that he had to deal with more administration than had been involved with the tablet collection, which he now delegated to Christopher Walker. He gave full support to the continua-tion of the *Catalogue of Babylonian Tablets*, which had been initiated under Barnett with the publication of the first volume by H. H. Figulla in 1961, taking up from the Catalogue of Assyrian tablets prepared long before by Carl Bezold (1889–99) and Leonard W. King (1914), and continued with the preparation of three volumes largely on the collections from Abu Habbah, ancient Sippar, by Erle Leichty of Philadelphia.

He introduced an orderly and indeed rigid system of filing his papers, something he would not entrust to anyone else, and could always put his hand on any document he needed. In his period as Keeper he was able to see a new Syrian and an Ivories gallery arranged, and two other temporary galleries in what was known as the 'Instant Scheme' for Iran and Anatolia, in space (originally occupied by the Ethnographic collections and briefly by the Tut-ankh-Amun exhibition) where the floors would eventually need strength-ening. The need to strengthen these floors (above the King's Library) caused him particular frustration with one Iranian antiquity, a column base from Persepolis, acquired by Barnett from the Oriental Institute of the University of Chicago in exchange for two Assyrian reliefs, which was too heavy even for the north-east staircase landing, and involved him in prolonged paper exchanges with Works Services, culminating in its placing in a basement gallery,[49] far away from anything else Iranian. This gave him a thorough baptism into the cares of office.

---

[48] W. Röllig (ed.), Beihefte zum Tübinger Atlas des Vorderen Orients, B, 7/1.
[49] Where it still remains in late 1997.

He made some selective acquisitions of antiquities for the Museum, but the most important was of the British share of material excavated at Tell ed-Duweir, ancient Lachish, reckoned at that time at about 50,000 pieces but subsequently at nearer 17,000, purchased in 1980 from the Institute of Archaeology of the University of London. The British Museum collection of Palestinian antiquities had always been rather meagre, so this acquisition of material excavated between 1932 and 1938 by a British expedition under James Starcky, opened the possibility of a very much improved permanent exhibition of Levantine, including Palestinian, antiquities in due course.[50] At the beginning of his Keepership he recommended to the Trustees that the Museum give financial support to outside excavators without any expectation of receiving antiquities in return. He was able to see this policy established, and British Museum support for Near Eastern excavations became a regular procedure.

Soon after his promotion to the Keepership he was elected Chairman of the British Museum branch of the First Division Association, the union of the senior academic staff, and in this capacity he was involved in some rather tough sessions with Sir John Pope-Hennessy in his early years as Keeper.

In 1977 he was invited by the Rector of the University of Rome and the Director General of Antiquities of Syria to serve on an International Committee for the Study of the Texts from Ebla, and attended the first meeting of this body in January 1978 in Rome. The site known as Tell Mardikh about 35 miles south-west of Aleppo had been selected for excavation in 1964 by a team from the University of Rome under Dr Paolo Matthiae. Inscriptions found during the excavations showed that it could be identified with the city of Ebla, already well known from Babylonian and Assyrian cuneiform inscriptions of the late third and early second millennia BC (more usually as Ibla in previous history writing). It came to particular prominence in the public eye with the discovery in 1974 and 1975 of an archive of cuneiform tablets of the 24th–23rd centuries BC, inscribed in Sumerian and Akkadian, but also in the local language, usually known now as Eblaite or Eblaic, classified by many as West Semitic, but considered by Sollberger to be 'West-Akkadian'.[51] Very soon there was extensive speculation about the significance of these texts, and particularly concerning any relationships with the Old Testament. As a result of this there was disagreement between the Director of the expedition and the official Epigraphist, and the Director established the International Committee with the aim of assuring the systematic publication of the texts.[52] For this purpose a

---

[50] A gallery in an advanced stage of preparation in 1997. [Opened in July 1998].

[51] *Administrative Texts Chiefly Concerning Textiles* [Archivi Reali di Ebla. Testi, VIII] (Rome, 1986), p. 1.

[52] The members of the Committee were P. Matthiae (Italy; Chairman), A. Archi (Italy), G. Buccellati (USA), D. O. Edzard (Germany), P. Fronzaroli (Italy), P. Garelli (France), H. Klengel (Germany), J.-R. Kupper (Belgium), F. Rashid (Iraq), E. Sollberger (UK).

series *Archivi Reali di Ebla. Testi* was established, with a periodical *Studi Eblaiti* for preliminary and parallel material.[53] Members of the Committee undertook themselves to deal with groups of texts, and Sollberger characteristically took on material which resulted in his volume *Administrative Texts Chiefly Concerning Textiles* which appeared some years later, and for which he studied the texts in Aleppo in September 1981. In 1980 he contributed a paper on 'The So-called Treaty Between Ebla and "Ashur"' to the *Studi*,[54] in which he argued that the crucial place-name in this text, read in the first publication as Ashur, the capital of the important early kingdom of Assyria (in which case a treaty with so distant a place would be of considerable interest) could not be read more precisely than as A-bar-sal, an unidentified location, throwing a different light on the text. In this article he did not claim to have understood the text fully, but aimed to bring sobriety to the atmosphere of speculation.[55]

In 1979 he was involved in the establishment of another important publication project, *The Royal Inscriptions of Mesopotamia,* based in Toronto. This series, initiated by Professor A. Kirk Grayson, aimed at providing a kind of 'Loeb' edition of all the texts in this category, with transliteration on the left, and translation on the right-hand page. Sollberger was designated Editor-in-Chief, a recognition of his international academic standing, and also Editor-in-Charge of the Sumerian Section. In this capacity he lectured in Toronto at the launch of the project.

In 1981 he played a prominent part in instigating and, jointly with the British School of Archaeology in Iraq, arranging the twenty-ninth Rencontre assyriologique international, due to take place in July 1982 in London. He served as Chairman of the planning committee until he was most unfortunately struck down by a serious stroke, and was obliged to take six months sick leave, at first in hospital and then at home, almost completely isolated from contact with colleagues and friends. He was much missed at the Rencontre, at which he would have been one of the leading hosts, and only the very closest friends were able to visit him during the period of the congress. He had a strong constitution, having recovered successfully on a previous occasion from an accident when a motor vehicle knocked him down in Great Russell Street, and now, with very considerable resilience, he largely recovered and was able to return to the Museum in Autumn 1982, at first on half time, but after a month and a half on full time again. At this time the Trustees were bringing in a policy of retirement at 60 for heads of departments, and since in October 1982

---

[53] A separate series, *Materiali epigrafici di Ebla*, was established under the editorship of Giovanni Pettinato in Naples.

[54] *Studi Eblaiti*, 3 (1980), 129–55.

[55] The disagreement continues, G. Pettinato still calling this text a Treaty between Ebla and Ashur (*Ebla. A New Look at History* (trans. C. F. Richardson; Baltimore and London, 1991), pp. 229–37).

he had reached the age of 62, he decided to retire at the end of March 1983. At first after his illness he found that his memory of the values of cuneiform signs had gone, but in the course of the following months this returned and he was able to resume academic work, and in retirement he completed his study of the textile texts from Ebla, and returned to the Museum on a casual basis to work on a catalogue of inscribed clay cones ('nails'). His Ebla textile texts volume inevitably fell somewhat short of his normal high standard, but a re-edition of the same texts[56] has itself come in for severe criticism.[57]

He was always more interested in what might be called the practical down-to-earth side of ancient times, the history, economy etc., giving little attention to literature, religious or otherwise.[58] In this respect he was in sympathy with Ignace J. Gelb who, in his paper 'The Philadelphia Onion Archive',[59] concluded by saying, 'I have chosen this lowly topic as a modest expression of protest against such esoteric and, in the present state of our knowledge, seemingly fruitless pursuits as those devoted to the study of the resurrection of Tammuz and of the Sumerian beliefs in afterlife. This is not a question of the relative importance of studies devoted to grammar, lexicon, or material culture as against those dealing with theological or metaphysical matters. The question is simply that of priorities. As all man's ideas about things divine are human, it is my firm belief that we shall never know what was the nectar of the gods until we learn what was the daily bread of the people.' In this spirit Sollberger in his paper 'Ur-III Society: Some Unanswered Questions', delivered at the eighteenth Rencontre assyriologique at Munich in 1970,[60] pointed out that for a period rich in documents 'our texts inform us on one hand about the extraordinary, and not the trivial; on the other hand about the accidental but not the essential'. He then discusssed the many details of the socio-political organisation of the Empire of the Third Dynasty of Ur which could not be learned from the texts but concluded that he was 'not a pessimist' and that he liked to 'believe that one day most, if not all, of our questions may be reasonably answered. For this, we shall of course need a systematic study of all available textual sources, trying first to understand the texts without colouring them by interpretations and speculations based on outside, and often

---

[56] G. Pettinato, *Testi amministrativi di Ebla. Archivio L. 2752* [Materiali epigrafici di Ebla 5] (Rome, 1996).

[57] F. Pomponio, *Bibliotheca Orientalis*, 54 (1997), coll. 397–9.

[58] Though in his article 'The Rulers of Lagaš (*Journal of Cuneiform Studies*, 21 (1967) [Festschrift for Albrecht Goetze], 279–91) he dealt with a text which he suggested might be a 'politico-satirical work written by the Lagaš scribe in answer to the author(s) of the Sumerian Ling List who had ignored the rulers of Lagaš'.

[59] In Assyriological Studies, 16 (n. 17 above), pp. 57–62.

[60] D. O. Edzard, *Gesellschaftsklassen im Alten Zweistromland und in den angrenzenden Gebieten—XVIII. Rencontre assyriologique internationale, München, 29. Juni bis 2. Juli 1970* [Bayerische akademie der Wissenschaften: Phil.-Hist. Kl. Abh., N.F. 75] (Munich, 1972), pp. 185–9.

far-fetched, comparisons. It will be a long and sometimes tedious task, but the rewards are tempting. Perhaps students ought to be encouraged to try and digest that *indigesta moles* rather than speculate on cosmic philosophies. But this is, after all, only my personal attitude, for, while I do not want to re-open here a famous debate, I must confess that I have always sided with the Onions.'

He showed the same down-to-earth approach when in his introductory paper 'The Temple in Babylonia' to the twentieth Rencontre assyriologique at Leiden in 1972,[61] he pointed out as a warning in the interpretation of evidence that, apart from a staircase at the side, the main sitting room of his house in Richmond had the same ground plan as a Babylonian temple.[62] There are many typically illuminating observations in this paper, some arising from the detached view he brought from his unusual academic entry to the field of Assyriology. On the usage of the Sumerian words *é*, 'house' (and 'temple'), and *é-gal*, 'big house' (and 'palace') for example, and the Akkadian counter-parts *bītum*, 'house; temple', and *ekallu*, 'palace', he comments that 'the Akkadian language does not seem to perceive the semantic relation of *é-gal* to *é*, most probably because at the time of the first contact between the two languages and cultures *é-gal* had already become a frozen syntagm which simply meant "palace" and no longer, analytically, "big house"'. This may be a rather trivial point, and perhaps one answering a question not many would think to ask, but it is something that his background in linguistics enabled him to notice.[63]

Though brought up as a Roman Catholic he became more or less agnostic, but he was careful not to undermine the faith of others. When his daughters were preparing for confirmation in the Anglican Church, he took trouble to walk from the Museum to the area of Regent's Street to obtain good quality Prayer Books for them. He was in fact a good walker, the British Museum to Sadlers Wells Theatre and back (about 3 miles) being a typical lunch hour expedition. In his early years at the Museum he was a frequent participant in the group of colleagues and visiting scholars working in the Students' Room who went outside to lunch, sometimes to one of the local pubs, and on one occasion a group of seven or eight over to Regent's Street under his direction to a café offering remarkable cream pastries. A favourite destination when the group was smaller was an Italian diner near Holborn underground station where the mature waitress was always pleased to see him in particular, and would wait anxiously to see whether he approved of the sausage, egg, and

---

[61] [F. R. Kraus (ed.),] *Le temple et le culte* (Leiden, 1975), pp. 31–4.

[62] This remark, which greatly amused the audience, was not included in the published version of his paper.

[63] It is incidentally, of course, a point which could interest Hebraists in connection with the derivation of Hebrew *hêkāl*, 'palace; temple'; though not an aspect he would have had in mind.

chips, or whatever it happened to be. She was less concerned about the others of the party. In later years, when he was seeking to be more abstemious, he favoured small sandwich bars of the kind where the clients sit on round stools fixed to the floor and often face mirrors placed round the walls to give the impression of greater space.

Sollberger was a man of robust prejudices. He was a faithful user of Daniel Jones's *English Pronouncing Dictionary* which went through many editions following its first publication in 1917, and he made regular use of his copy of the 1947 edition. Jones sometimes gives alternative pronunciations of a word, and Sollberger would defend the pronunciations he favoured with energy and wit. He was a staunch conservative politically, and a regular reader of *The Times* newspaper, with its 'easy disposable' sections which ended up in the refuse bin at the railway station. He admired people who would 'stick to their guns', and when an opposition politician said that free school milk should be abolished, and actually carried this out in office, he quoted it with approval.

He was an entertaining, witty, and erudite companion and a firm friend, and it was a cause of great sadness to his family and friends that he was cut off at a comparatively early age. He was honoured in a memorial issue of the *Revue d'assyriologie*,[64] which contained an obituary notice by his old friend Paul Garelli, and a bibliography by his Museum colleague Christopher Walker, and a number of articles by former friends and colleagues. He has left a valuable body of work as a legacy, and his name will have a honoured place in the history of the subject.

TERENCE C. MITCHELL
British Museum

Note. I am indebted for help of various kinds in the preparation of this notice to Mrs Ariane Sollberger as well as to others, notably Françoise Bruschweiler, John Curtis, Paul Garelli, Richard Hudson, Christopher Walker, and Claus Wilcke.

---

[64] Volume 84, part 2 (1990).

ERIC STOKES

Eric Thomas Stokes
1924–1981

ERIC STOKES was born on 10 July 1924 in Hampstead, London into a Cockney working-class environment. His father, Walter John Stokes, had fought in the Rifle Brigade in the First World War and had been severely traumatised. After the War he was only able to take casual jobs. Eric Stokes's mother, Winifred came from a Welsh Baptist family. Her religious beliefs and love of poetry, strongly influenced the young Stokes. He won a scholarship to Holloway School and received an uneventful education until the outbreak of war, when his school was evacuated from London and he was sent to Towcester, Northamptonshire. Boarded in village houses, Stokes was thrown together with Frank King (MA Christ's College, Cambridge; Headmaster, Highbury Grove School, 1955), the history master of Holloway School, who was a formative influence on his intellectual life and later took him to visit Cambridge. T. E. Lawrence's *Seven Pillars of Wisdom*, which King recommended to Stokes, seems to have awakened an early interest in travel. As a boy, Stokes had spent much time wandering around London streets and churches which also gave him a strong sense of the lived past. During the War he sometimes hitch-hiked to the capital with friends to observe the bomb damage at first hand. He always retained his affection for London and, in later years, he sometimes took his graduate students on long rambles from one Wren church to the next on the way from King's Cross Station to the India Office Library on the South Bank.

In December 1941 Stokes won an Exhibition to Christ's College, Cambridge to read History.[1] The life of the University was severely disrupted by war but Stokes developed a life-long interest in the History of Political Thought, which was already a major subject in the Historical Tripos. Michael Oakeshott, the philosopher and political theorist, had been a Fellow and College Lecturer at Gonville and Gaius College and was a member of the

[1] Cambridge University *Reporter*, 24 Dec. 1941.

Proceedings of the British Academy, **97**, 467–498. © The British Academy 1998.

History Faculty until 1940. He was to take up this position again in 1947, by which time Stokes had himself returned to Cambridge. Herbert Butterfield was also lecturing in the Faculty and had begun his campaign to return political philosophy and religion to a central place in the analysis of historical change.

In the meantime, however, Stokes was 'tossed casually by war half-way across the globe and brigaded willy-nilly with men of diverse Commonwealth nations and races'.[2] In 1943 he was called up as an officer cadet and sent by a long and circuitous sea route to India. Avoiding U-boats, his troopship zig-zagged across the Atlantic before passing through the Mediterranean and Arabian seas. Two thirds of the soldiers on board were suffering from dysentery and sunburn by the time their boat finally docked in Bombay in the spring of 1944.

Eric Stokes's years in India from 1944–6 were the formative influence on his view of the world. He found his later periods in Malaya and Africa challenging, but it was India to which he was most attached and where he felt most at home. His experience there taught him the 'conviction, or if you will, illusion . . . that part of the total meaning of things was to be discovered in this encounter with the world outside the European continent',[3] espe-cially as this experience lay 'beyond the confines of urban, industrial civilisation'.[4] In the spring of 1944, he reported as an officer cadet trainee to the Cadet Wing, School of Artillery, India Command at Deolali near Bombay.[5] Later in the year he moved for further training to Ambala in the Punjab. Stokes was commissioned as a Lieutenant in the Royal Artillery and finally, in early 1945, allotted to the 30th Indian Mountain Artillery Regiment. He spent the first half of 1945 in a Reinforcement Camp for South-East Asia Command at an unidentified location 'east of the Brahma-putra'.[6] He never set foot in Burma during wartime because the dramatic Japanese surrender intervened.

Mountain artillery units were still an essential fighting arm in the difficult terrain of southern Asia. Yet the spirit of Stokes's new unit seemed to hearken back to the days of Kipling's 'Barrack-room Ballads' and the struggles of martial races on the mountainous rim of India. The Colonel under whom he was to serve was reputed to be 'very horsey', disliking 'stinking mechanical vehicles'.[7] Stokes used to remark ironically that in the 1940s, when the rest of

---

[2] 'The Voice of the Hooligan. Kipling and the Commonwealth Experience' in N. McKen-drick (ed.), *Historical Perspectives. Studies in English thought and Society in honour of J. H. Plumb* (London, 1974), p. 286.

[3] Ibid.

[4] Ibid., p. 287.

[5] E. T. Stokes [ETS] to Jessie Muirhead [JM], 1 Aug. 1944.

[6] ETS to JM, 21 May 1945

[7] ETS to JM, 21 May 1945.

the world was engaged in a death-struggle which was resolved by mass air-bombardment and nuclear warfare, the Indian authorities were still apparently more concerned with uprisings on the North-West Frontier. Pathan millenarian leaders seemed to bulk as large in their strategy as Adolf Hitler or Marshal Tojo.

Stokes was trained by his martinet unit commander as a connoisseur of the pack mules and small horses which pulled the Mountain Artillery over the Indian ranges. He learned that white mules were always to be purchased in preference to brown ones and that the bruising inflicted by falling off them was mild by comparison with the abuse that he received from his superior officers when he did so. He was wary of the mules, which frequently bit or kicked him. But he wrote to his sister, Jessie Muirhead, that he preferred working with the animals alongside Indian troops to the brittle and formal life of the officers' mess.

Eric Stokes's early contacts with Indians made him much more open with his Indian colleagues and graduate students of later days than many of his peers. In 1944 he wrote from India of his pleasure of meeting Indians on equal terms as compared with 'the mercenary servility which is the normal rule here'.[8] He was always prepared to chide and joke with them in a manner which initially startled, but ultimately charmed even the most prickly members of the Indian intelligentsia whom he later encountered. Here the Subaltern of Mountain Artillery was perhaps of some service to the later historian of India. In one respect, though, Stokes did not put his Indian experiences to the service of his academic scholarship. He learned a considerable amount of Urdu in the Army. His notes for artillery manoeuvres are written in Romanised Urdu, and he received friendly letters from his Indian NCOs in the language.[9] When he began to work on Indian social history in the 1970s, he never built on this proficiency in spoken Urdu. Perhaps the hiatus had been too long, or the Arabic script was too daunting.

Relatively few of Stokes's letters to his family during these years contain general comments about the situation in south Asia. He records his life as a rigid and often tedious routine, enlivened by games of chess and second rate-American films. To ease the boredom, which was not broken until the unit was ready for action in the very month that the atomic bomb was dropped, he made observations of the tropical night-sky and distantly admired the grace of Indian women during early morning rides around the military stations. His sister sent him *The New Statesman* and *Penguin New Writing* which sustained his strong political and literary interests.

Occasionally Stokes's broader reflections broke through the circumstantial

---

[8] ETS to JM, 1 Oct. 1944.
[9] Letter in romanised Urdu to ETS in London from an Indian NCO (illegible), 1946.

detail of these letters. Visiting Bombay, he was struck by the wealth of Malabar Hill, home of the local elite, and compared it with the poverty of the 'depressed classes or untouchables, the biggest blot on Indian life and a crying condemnation of the caste system which perpetuates it'.[10] He felt the hostility of the residents of the major towns to the British, now clinging to their great south Asian Empire by their finger tips. Walking through the Indian neighbourhoods of Calcutta in his uniform, he realised with 'what cold hatred the politically conscious people (clerks, etc.) regarded me' and felt 'rather like a Nazi officer must have felt, walking along a Paris Boulevard'.[11] Visiting Calcutta University's History Department he fell into strenuous debate with its lecturers, trying to persuade them that 'we English weren't such blackguards as they tended to think'.[12] Stokes remained ambivalent about the British Empire, being born into it and yet criticising it from the inside. He remarked that his Calcutta opponents were rational men who could see both sides of the argument. They could hardly be expected to view the British dispassionately. In an abject failure of colonial rule, 'two million peasants had died a mere two years ago'[13] during the great Bengal famine of 1943.

Stokes was in Delhi, on leave from Ambala, during the visit of the Cabinet Mission in April 1946. This was the British delegation which failed to bring about a final compromise between the Indian National Congress and the Muslim League, and so paved the way for the Partition of August 1947. At this time he recorded his sympathy for the Hindus in a striking manner. Deploring the preponderance of Muslim buildings in Delhi, he wrote 'From the beginning out here I have been more attracted towards Hinduism than Islam, which I instinctively regard as something alien to India.'[14] He recognised that Hindus and Muslims had lived together in reasonable harmony for a thousand years, and that a considerable exchange of values and practices had taken place. Contemporary communal hatreds were, he thought, not so much a consequence of British policies of divide-and-rule, but resulted instead from 'a growing knowledge of and realisation of the past . . . The Hindu is become growingly aware of the devastation of his culture which the Muslims carried out. There is hardly a Hindu temple of any age or note in the whole of the north Indian plain.' These thoughts about Indian religion mirrored quite directly the ideology of the emergent Hindu right wing.

Eric Stokes's early views on Indian religion are also intriguing on a personal level. He recorded his preference for friendship with Muslims. His own strong, but rather abstract Christian convictions might have been expected

---

[10] ETS to JM, 15 Dec. 1944.
[11] ETS to JM, 24 June 1945.
[12] Ibid.
[13] Ibid.
[14] ETS to JM, 3 April 1946.

to find a sympathetic echo in Islam, as with many Britons who disliked what they took to be the 'idolatry' of Hinduism. But here we begin to glimpse the attraction to paradox and ambiguity which was an important component of his attitudes. Having read some of the Hindu scriptures in translation, Hinduism itself appeared to him to be a congenial religion of paradox and diversity. Complex to the end, he finished the letter to his sister about Delhi's architecture by wondering if he had been too harsh about Muslim culture.

Caste divisions also seemed to be a critical feature of Indian life to Stokes at this time. On an earlier visit to Bombay, Stokes had speculated that there was a good chance that 'when the British bayonets left India' the wealthy Parsi Zoroastrian community of Bombay might be subject to 'a scourge greater than the pogroms of the Middle Ages' from a revolution of the untouchables.[15] His attitudes mirrored the conventional British view that Indian society was irrevocably split on the lines of caste and religion and that the Raj was the only thing that lay between India and anarchy. That view was at least plausible in the last two years of British rule.

The young British officer's casual observation of the strong communal divisions which permeated the Indian Army confirmed these judgements of racial essence. Stokes noted that the Mountain Artillery regiments took the pick of Indian troops, especially 'Sikhs and [Muslim] Punjabis. The former are definitely more clever, but the Punjabis are easily the most lovable.'[16] He also wrote that he had intervened in a dispute between a Muslim Sanitary Havildar and a Hindu Gurkha soldier who complained that his food had been polluted by the Muslim.[17] In Malaya in the following year, he complained that his Ahir troops were to be replaced with Dogras (Kashmiri Hindus). The Ahirs (pastoralists and peasants from north India) 'are not soldiers by instinct, and hence need a lot of supervision' but 'they were very likeable individually'.[18]

When, in the early 1960s, Stokes first began to write on Indian social as opposed to intellectual history, he still thought of castes and religions as concrete and sharply defined social units. His later experience of the African 'tribe' had already raised many questions for him about the ultimate value of these colonial social categories. But the early analyses of the Rebellion of 1857 tend to describe the castes as the major actors.[19] In the 1970s, however, he was to be influenced at Cambridge by the social anthropology of Edmund Leach and Stanley Tambiah, which held that castes were not the hard-edged entities that Stokes had once thought. Close reading of British Indian revenue and

[15] ETS to JM, 15 Dec. 1944.
[16] ETS to JM, 15 Dec. 1944.
[17] ETS to JM, 8 May 1945.
[18] ETS to JM, 8 Feb. 1946.
[19] Eric Stokes, *The Peasant and the Raj. Studies in agrarian society and peasant rebellion in colonial India* (Cambridge, 1978), preface; cf. pp. 140–84.

rent-rate reports of the nineteenth century was to convince him that factions and interests within broad caste groups were the most important units of analysis.[20] In this respect, he was to quietly move from the colonial to the post-colonial in his own thinking.

Meanwhile, in India Command, Stokes noted what he regarded as the ominous failure of the Army to recognise Victory in Asia Day (15 August 1945). He speculated that units such as his, which had recently finished their training, would be used to reoccupy the former south-east Asian territories of the British Empire. In the event, his unit left Bangalore on 21 September 1945 and carried out occupation duties near Rangoon and Bangkok. It was finally stationed in Malaya for a brief period in early 1946. Here its main duty was to disband the Indian National Army, the force which had been raised by the nationalist leader, Subhas Chandra Bose, to fight alongside the Japanese against the British.

Stokes's first introduction to Malaya, where he and his wife were later to spend five years, was not auspicious. The country had been wrecked by warfare; rations and commodities were hard to come by. Stokes also felt the people of the Far East were 'inscrutable' and never imagined forming the links with them which he believed he had developed with Indians.[21] Yet he thought that he had had a 'very easy war' and had missed 'very sticky' fighting on the Burma Front by the 'skin of his teeth'.[22] Writing from the Royal Artillery Mess in Peshawar on 22 July 1946, he remarked that, despite the heat of the North-West Frontier, he would have preferred India to the grim England of 1946, but Cambridge would probably not keep open his place unless he returned for the Michaelmas Term 1946.

Another consideration dampened Stokes's interest in going home. A confirmed democrat of twenty one years of age in the days of Attlee's popular government, he nevertheless wrote that he would find it a great wrench to break with 'a society where relations are still unmarred by twisted views of equality' which prevailed in the West.[23] Dealing with Indian troops, who looked to the British officer for their welfare and happiness created 'a very happy, idyllic relationship' so different from the 'national and class struggles' of Europe. Such romantic and paternalist attitudes had been essential to the British Empire and explain why so many of its servants found it difficult to live in post-war Britain, preferring Africa or Australasia. In Eric Stokes's case, they also chimed with his continuing interests in Michael Oakeshott's ideas,

---

[20] Eric Stokes, *The Peasant and the Raj. Studies in agrarian society and peasant rebellion in colonial India* (Cambridge, 1978), preface; cf. pp. 140–84.

[21] ETS to JM, 8 Feb. 1946.

[22] ETS to JM, 15 Aug. 1945.

[23] ETS to JM, 8 Feb. 1946.

the role of Victorian idealist philosophy in the British Empire and the poetry of Tennyson or Kipling.

Demobilised under an early release scheme, Stokes returned to Christ's for the Michaelmas Term 1946 along with so many other members of the wartime generation. History teaching at Christ's had been galvanised by the arrival there as Fellow of J. H. Plumb, who had worked in intelligence during the War. Stokes was to take Plumb's special subject in Part II of the Tripos and was also supervised by Anthony Steel, the medieval historian. The moral and intellectual life of the University had been transformed more broadly by the return of hundreds of mature and experienced men and women. Acutely aware of the loss of life and promise they had witnessed, they were determined to make every moment count.

Stokes pursued his academic interests in British History and the History of political theory. He was inspired by Plumb's lectures on the eighteenth century and Pevsner's on English architecture, besides following the lectures of David Knowles, Michael Postan, Helen Cam, John Saltmarsh, and Edward Miller. His growing interest in the peasantry, in sharp contrast to his concerns in intellectual history, was also galvanised by reading Marc Bloch's studies of France.

The returning 1946 year included Charles Parkin, whom Stokes had met in India (Fellow and College Lecturer, Clare College, 1948–83) and Frank Spooner (Fellow, 1951–7, later Professor of Economic History at Durham, 1966–85) who became close friends of his. Parkin was another enthusiast for the History of Political Thought and later wrote on Edmund Burke. Other contemporaries and later correspondents were 'Bill' E. T. Williams (later Warden of Rhodes House, Oxford), James Mossman (later Foreign Office Intelligence and foreign affairs journalist) and Kenneth Ballhatchet (later Professor of History at SOAS, London University). Christie Eliezer, a Tamil mathematician from Sri Lanka was also a close friend with whom Stokes was to serve in Malaya. All these men helped develop his historical interests. The letters written between them over the next two decades ranged over politics, religion, and current affairs. Almost Victorian in tone, they are testimony to high-minded ideals of scholarship and service and to a day-to-day literary stylishness, which are now difficult to reproduce.

Two other important developments occurred at this period. In 1947 Eric Stokes, who had always been of a questioning but spiritual frame of mind, was confirmed as an Anglican Christian in Christ's College Chapel. The officiating priest was Canon I. T. Ramsey, an important influence on Stokes's religious life. About this time, he met Florence Mary Lee, then a student teacher at Homerton College, whom he married in 1949. They were to bring up their four daughters in Malaya and Rhodesia.

After graduation in 1949, Stokes's experience of India and interest in the history of political thought drew him, by a stroke of cleverness, to combine two fields that were to become very significant in post-War Cambridge: extra-European history and the history of political thought. He began to work on the influence of James Mill and the British utilitarians on the government of the East India Company. This work was finally presented as a Ph.D. thesis in 1952 and was published as *The English Utilitarians and India* in 1959. His supervisor in this work was Dr. T. G. P. Spear (graduate of St Catharine's College and Bursar of Selwyn), formerly of the Government of India Information Service in Delhi, who had returned to Selwyn College as Fellow and Bursar after Independence. Spear proved an enthusiastic but somewhat distant supervisor (apparently he did not finally read the thesis in full until after it had been examined in late 1952).[24] Spear's own interests in eighteenth- and early nineteenth-century Delhi fitted well with those of Stokes. One of Stokes's examiners was to be C. H. Philips (later Director of SOAS and Vice-Chancellor of London University), an expert on the history of the East India Company. Philips also proved to be a strong supporter of Stokes throughout his career.

The opportunities for university teaching in straitened post-war Britain were limited. By 1950 Stokes had decided he was unlikely to secure a position in Britain. Now married, he began to look for academic posts overseas. This attracted him because he was acutely aware of the importance of training a generation of local people to occupy positions of responsibility, now that British rule in Asia was ending. At this period, lecturers' posts in the Empire were still dispensed by the Inter-University Board for Higher Education which worked closely with the Colonial Office. Stokes went to London for an interview in answer to an advertisement for a history post in the Caribbean. Instead, on arrival, he was sent down the corridor to the door marked 'Malaya', where he secured a lectureship in the new University of Malaya in Singapore.

The Federation of Malaya (present-day Malaysia and Singapore) to which Eric and Florence Stokes embarked in the middle of 1950 was a different place from the devastated society which he had briefly visited four years before. The region was now beginning to embark upon the long economic boom which was to make it the world's most dynamic economic region. The old colonial society patterned on the Indian model with its huge bungalows, lush gardens, and innumerable servants had been destroyed by Japanese occupation and the horrors of internment in Changi Gaol. It had given way to a more modest, and less racially segregated expatriate community of middle-class people with restricted incomes of whom the Stokes were typical. In the University, European, Malay, and Chinese staff and students lived together. The Chinese element was dominant among the undergraduates, accounting for 564 out of the 859 students in 1951–2. Malay men were better represented on the Arts

---

[24] P. Spear to ETS, 21 Feb. 1953.

side, though Malay women were notable by their absence throughout the University.[25]

Government policy, too, had changed quite rapidly immediately before the Stokeses' arrival, reflecting Britain's need to cling on in an area of great strategic and economic importance. It was only recently that the authorities had decided to transform the venerable Raffles College, an undergraduate teaching institution, and an associated medical college into the University of Malaya, which was to have advanced English-medium teaching and research facilities.[26] The developmental aspects of colonial rule were to be stressed in what John Lonsdale has called 'the imperialism of the welfare state'. The new History Department taught British, European, and Commonwealth history (all of which Stokes tried his hand at). But Malcolm MacDonald, who was both High Commissioner and Chancellor of the University, along with some of his officials, believed that a sense of common Malayan identity should also be fostered.[27] Malayan and Chinese literature and some south and south-east Asian history made its appearance in the advanced classes at the University.

Although in retrospective comparison with central Africa, south-east Asia was a relatively open and progressive colonial society, the British authorities faced serious unrest. One local correspondent informed Stokes before he set sail in late 1950 that there were now a dozen murders a day in the Federation.[28] He added that it was unsafe to travel beyond Johore Baru a few miles away from Singapore, and that the population 'though not pro-Bandit . . . was certainly not pro-British' and that the authorities were totally incompetent. Soon after the Stokeses arrived in Singapore, they found the city paralysed and in flames following the so-called Maria Hertogh riots (11–13 December 1950).[29]

Further riots and disturbances followed in the next two years as the Malayan Communist Party mobilised for war against the British. Their insurgency was only brought to an end by the vigorous and authoritarian rule of General Sir Gerald Templer, who instituted the scheme of protected villages to seal off the Chinese squatter farmers from Communist infiltration.

---

[25] Student Statistics, *Magazine of the Students Union. University of Malaya, 1950–52 edn.*, p. 120.
[26] Edwin Lee and Tan Tai Yong, *Beyond Degrees. The making of the National University of Singapore* (Singapore, 1996), pp. 81–95; cf. minute, 9 Jan. 1948, 'Higher education salaries, Malaya' Colonial Office Records, 117/160/1, Public Record Office, London.
[27] Foreword, *Magazine of the Students' Union, University of Malaya, 1950–2 edn.*).
[28] D. Fryer to ETS, 27 May 1950.
[29] *Singapore, An illustrated history, 1941–1984* (Information Division, Ministry of Culture, Singapore, 1984), pp. 132–3. Maria Hertogh was a Dutch Catholic girl who had been brought up during the war by a Muslim family. Following a law suit over her custody, she was sent to a Catholic orphanage, an event which sparked off mass protests during which eighteen people were killed, signalling growing tension between the colony's different ethnic and religious groups.

In the rich Chinese commercial city of Singapore, these problems seemed relatively distant, the disturbances concentrated up-country in the rubber estates. Living in the protected environment of the University of Malaya, the Stokeses encountered a few radical activists such as James Puthucheary, who was later imprisoned by the authorities. Letters from students and colleagues in other parts of the colony, however, spoke of the tense situation. On the occasion of one riot, the students came to the campus armed with hockey sticks to protect their white teachers from molestation. As a former officer, Stokes joined the local Volunteer Corps. He appears to have believed that the best way to defeat Communist insurgency was to continue the 'Asia for the Asians policy' which had been announced by Malcolm MacDonald.[30] Stokes's natural contacts among indigenous intellectuals included people such as Eunice Thio, a lecturer in History, who believed in nationalist political activity, but was hostile to Communist radicalism.[31] More rapidly than most expatriates, including academics, Stokes had begun to believe in managed, but quite brisk decolonisation.

Stokes's attitudes to Malayan political issues had formed rapidly, and, as in India, he was well ahead of official and expatriate thinking. Yet his ideas were still tinged with idealistic paternalism. In a talk for University Staff he delivered in November 1952 he discussed the 'Basis of a Malayan Nation'. A nation, he wrote anticipating Benedict Anderson's main thesis, was a 'modern community' acutely aware of its own special identity which was created by economic structure and the 'intercommunication of ideas'. Malayan society was a 'frontier society' whose 'main cluster of roots went back less than three generations'.[32]

In Malaya, Stokes argued, the sense of 'Malayaness' was initially developed amongst a new class, the upwardly mobile Chinese and Indian immigrants. The problem for Malaya, he thought, was that this middle class mobilisation against the British had opened up a divide not only between the commercial elites, the Malayan peasants and Chinese squatters, but even between the Chinese bourgeoisie and the old Malayan official class.[33] In these conditions 'ancient race prejudice' could flourish as it had done in India where the modern hatred of the Hindu moneylender 'rallied the ancient hostility of religion' to fight on its side and bring about Partition.

In India, though, there was a central administration and a core of nationhood which was strong enough for the British to devolve power to and ready to fight militant Communism. That was not so in Malaya or south-east Asia as a whole.[34] The British still had one final task in presiding over the emergence of

---

[30] Stokes to unidentified correspondent, 25 May 1952.
[31] E. Thio to Stokes, 20 Feb. 1953.
[32] 'Malayan Students compared with others, ISS Conference 1952', MS.
[33] 'Basis of a Malay Nation', MS, Nov. 1952.
[34] 'Malaya and the Colonial Question in Asia', 1954, MS.

a new, democratic Malaya. A successful outcome had become more likely, he told an Adult Education Class in 1953, as new Chinese immigration had ceased during the War and the new Malay-born Chinese elite was disenchanted with the Communist government in China. Yet racial antagonisms were still so strong that an independent Singapore might have to be created.[35] Here Stokes anticipated events nearly a decade ahead, when Singapore finally split from the newly independent Malaysia.

Nevertheless, in 1953 Stokes thought that there was still the basis for a democratic Malay nation which included Singapore. The prospects were brighter than in other Asian societies whose 'hopeless poverty makes freedom meaningless'. It depended largely on how the predominantly Chinese middle class conducted itself. The middle class would need to compromise internally between different races. More important, he thought, it would need to turn its back on its 'gross materialism', which had been intensified by western secularism, and improve its 'moral conduct' through social provision and community development. The British government also had a role here, he thought. It had a duty to do nothing to promote communalism politically. It should not, for instance, institute separate communal electorates as it had done in India. Instead, working with the trade unions it should promote social welfare. It must 'prepare the administration for the transfer of power by ensuring that now Asians of high quality are given training'.[36]

In a small way Stokes attempted to put these ideals into action in his own sphere of authority. Soon after he arrived, he had noticed that the staff's indigenous servants were housed in cramped and unventilated quarters. He intervened with the University authorities to improve their conditions, though embarrassingly it transpired that they preferred their old quarters to the new, custom-built accommodation created for them. Still the officer of sepoys, he also wanted to provide entertainments and Christmas boxes for members of the subordinate staff to 'improve the general spirit of relationships among us'.[37]

Biography is easier when the subject retains a straightforward and predictable moral or political position throughout his life. Fundamentally, Stokes probably did remain the Christian idealist revealed by many of his letters. But his intellect was always attracted to paradox and humour and he was constantly on the lookout for an occasion to tease, amuse, or shock his audience. While believing strongly in the historical influence of ideas, he would still sometimes take up a surprisingly materialist, even cynical position. Less than two years after his lecture on the need for a moral basis of Malay nationhood, we find him addressing a pious British Council 'Conference on

[35] 'Political Disunity; the historical background', MS.
[36] Ibid.
[37] 'not sent', 1951

Commonwealth Studies' and arguing that the Commonwealth bond was ultimately based on commercial interest, and nothing more. There was a message here. Britain's 'shrewd commercial instinct' had 'preserved her from those dangerous delusions of power and prestige which have misled other colonial powers'. He presumably had the imminent French defeat at Dien Bien Phu in mind.[38]

Stokes's desire to shock people from current orthodoxies or pieties mirrored his historian's opinion about the complexity of historical causation. He felt that neither idealogical nor economic interpretations of historical events could possibly be sufficient on their own. As he wrote in a Singapore student magazine, monocausal arguments necessarily moved out of the realm of historical explanation into that of political ideology.[39]

In general, though, it was the problems of building up a young history department, writing lectures to cover much of modern history and taking up once again the history of the English utilitarians in India that occupied Stokes in Malaya. On campus at least, relations between the races were quite good, with Muslims, Chinese, Eurasians and Europeans, working and living side by side. Stokes was distantly impressed by the energy and bravura of its head, C. N. Parkinson, a historian of Asian trade, best known, of course, for Parkinson's Law. Stokes also encouraged students and younger members of the Department to move away from European political History to studies of the local Chinese and Malay communities. Wang Gungwu, one of his students and later friends in the Malayan and Singapore university system, was later to make major contributions to the historical sociology of pre-colonial and colonial south-east Asia which took up in detail some of the issues to which Stokes had briefly alluded in his talks and unpublished papers.[40]

Yet while Stokes himself wrote history about Britain, India, and central Africa, he published nothing significant about south-east Asia. His only historical exploration of the region was contained in lectures on the Malay princes and indirect rule, a form of government which he wrote about more fully in the case of Africa. Why was this? The main reason was certainly that he had not finished revising his doctoral thesis for publication. He also seems to have accepted the common Raj attitude that south-east Asia was really a poor man's India. In an unusually savage review of John Bastin, *The Native Policies of Sir Stamford Raffles in Java and Sumatra* (Oxford, 1957) in the journal *History*, he asserted that Sir Stamford Raffles was 'not a man of settled principle but . . . a mecurial opportunist', who derived anything that was

---

[38] 'Malaya and the Colonial Question in Asia', MS.
[39] 'Can History be Objective?, *Magazine of the Students Union, University of Malaya. Sessions 1950–51 and 1951–2*, pp. 56–65.
[40] Wang Gungwu to ETS, 1 July 1952.

important in his programmes from Indian precedents, which Bastin had supposedly ignored. Bastin responded negatively to this attack, and with some justice.[41] Ironically, the historiography of south-east Asia began to develop quite quickly about the time of Stokes's departure and he unwittingly made some contribution to its development.

By 1954, Stokes was, according to his letters to Charles Parkin, beginning to feel a sense of drift in his life in the University of Malaya. The Ph.D. thesis was passed but not yet published. Cambridge University Press committed an error of judgement by stating that it did not publish dissertations when Percival Spear showed the final draft to them in 1953.[42] In the meantime, Stokes had neither the leisure nor the inclination to continue the modifications to the thesis which Spear had proposed.

The situation in Malaya was also changing. The Communists had been defeated, but the Malays had emerged in a very strong position. What Stokes had called 'the Gamble on Independence'[43] was in train and he may have felt that the future for expatriate academics was less rosy than it had been. Most important, the education of the Stokeses' two children was a looming problem. While educational standards were good in the Federation, many of the British residents, still scarred by memories of Japanese occupation and Communist violence, sent their children home.

Moving out of the colonial into the domestic university world, Stokes was appointed to a lectureship in History at the University of Bristol where he spent the years 1955–6. Stokes found his new colleagues pleasant, but he never really adjusted to the large civic university after the intimacy and novelty of Malaya or the traditions of Cambridge. By comparison with anthropology departments, British university history departments were still disinclined to teach overseas history, even of the constitutional and ideological sort which Stokes then practised.

Distant temporarily from the colonial frontier, Stokes had time in Bristol to consider the relationship between his recent experiences and the political thought which still preoccupied him. He was naturally attracted to the organic understanding of state and society of which Burke was the leading British proponent. He rejected abstract rights theories of the European and socialist tradition. But in view of his experiences of colonial war and repression, he worried about where the state and individual rights fitted into Burke's scheme. Was the expansion of Europe with its injustices, slaughter, and expropriation of native peoples 'natural' in the Burkean sense? 'Do you, like Burke, throw a decent veil over the beginning of states?'[44] How was the day-to-day repression

[41] John Bastin to ETS, 29 July 1958 and clipping.
[42] P. Spear to ETS, 21 Feb. 1953.
[43] MSS, 1954.
[44] ETS to Charles Parkin, 23 May 1956.

of the colonial state in Cyprus, Malaya, Kenya (and very shortly Suez) to be reconciled with the idea that power was a gift from God to the rulers?

The contemporary study of political ideas in Britain seemed to have little to say on such matters. 'What in your view', he asked Parkin, 'is the relationship of the academic study of historical ideas to our own political situation?'[45] Ultimately, Stokes must have answered himself. Direct action in their appropriate spheres by educated men, inspired by the best of both the liberal and the organic traditions, was the most that could be hoped for. Besides, Stokes was suffering 'regret and nostalgia over leaving Malaya'. Among other things, return to England had checked his fuller acceptance of Christianity and revived some long-standing problems he had about belief in the Divinity of Christ. He sometimes depicted himself as more of a deist or unitarian than an orthodox Christian.[46] He also began to 'feel deeply that I am not fitted for the life of an academic recluse . . . I would like to make some contribution to the awful African problem.'[47] It was this thought that went back with him to the colonial frontier in Salisbury, Southern Rhodesia.

Despite his staleness with the work and the place, it was during his period in Bristol that Stokes completed most of the revisions to his Ph.D. thesis which was to be published in 1959 as *The English Utilitarians and India*. The work has been called 'a minor classic in the History of Political Thought' (F. Rosen),[48] and it was received with extremely favourable reviews. One reason for this was its literary quality. It won Stokes a 'Silver Pen Award, 1955–9' from the 'Journal Fund' of New Jersey in the same group as Henry Kissinger, Samuel Huntington, George Kennan, and Ralf Dahrendorf. It also appeared at the right time. Twelve years after Indian Independence, the British were beginning to consider their former south Asian Empire with greater objectivity. Spurred by the centenary of the Mutiny-Rebellion of 1857, Indians were also beginning to reassess the so-called Age of Reform of the 1830s which was thought to have been a prelude to the Rebellion. Most important, the book appeared to show political ideas in action and analyse the first major western attempt to modernise the 'Third World'. It attracted American interest at a time when Americans were in the grip of modernisation theory and beginning self-consciously to take up the 'White Man's burden'.

Inevitably, for a classic nearly forty years old, *The English Utilitarians* has suffered as much emulation as refutation over the years. The metaphor Stokes applied to Robinson and Gallagher's *Africa and the Victorians* applies as well to his own book. Like some ancient and scarred African bull elephant, tusks

[45] ETS to Parkin, Boxing Day 1956.
[46] Ibid.
[47] ETS to Parkin, 25 May 1956, not sent?
[48] F. Rosen, 'Eric Stokes and the English Utilitarians' forthcoming.

splintered, one-eyed, carcass bristling with embedded spears, it still crashes on through the bush. Of the main contentions it contained, the great importance of evangelical thought on the government of Britain and its empire in the first half of the nineteenth century has been continuously vindicated. If anything, Boyd Hilton's *The Age of Atonement* (Cambridge, 1989) and continuing work by Andrew Porter show this theme being extended and developed.

By contrast, the role of utilitarianism in Indian government and Indian revenue systems has appeared to dwindle over time. The earliest line of attack on this idea was from historians of the Indian localities. These scholars showed either that Indian social structures reproduced themselves underneath the turmoil of land-revenue settlements, blunting or rendering insignificant British policy initiatives, or that the British themselves were prevented by their lack of money and knowledge of the country from effecting much change. Yet here some of Stokes's argument can be preserved. The detailed work of Peter Penner[49] has shown that men of the R. M. Bird and James Thomason school of revenue administration did actually put the 'levelling' doctrines of net-produce rent theory into practice in some districts of northern India. Later work on the history of agrarian Punjab also suggested that broadly utilitarian and evangelical ideas were important, and were acted upon by officials such as Robert Cust and Robert Montgomery.

Another, and more recent line of critique has been directed at Stokes's reading of the domestic context of utilitarian ideas. Lynn Zastoupil has argued that Stokes associated John Stuart Mill too easily with James Mill's position on Indian government. Zastoupil argues that the Younger Mill moved much closer in his views to Burke and the organic tradition which valued the customs and language of subject peoples.[50] F. Rosen has likewise argued that Stokes relied overmuch on Elie Halevy's view of the utilitarian tradition.[51] This led him to over-emphasise its authoritarian implications and ignore the extent to which both James Mill and Jeremy Bentham drew rigid limits to the exercise of state power by their repeated insistence on the need for representative government.

This still leaves us with the problem of locating the ideological basis of the clear authoritarian and interventionist tone of Indian government after 1818. The answer may lie in the inheritance of the era of Lord Wellesley, whose aggressive aristocratic paternalism, inspired individuals such as Charles Metcalfe without benefit of utilitarianism. Yet Stokes's arguments may still have some force. For instance, C. E. Trevelyan, a key figure in Lord William Bentinck's 'Age of Reform', was nearer to the model of a utilitarian evangelical

[49] Peter Penner, *The Patronage Bureaucracy in North India. The Robert M. Bird and James Thomason School, 1820–70* (Delhi, 1986).
[50] Lynn Zastoupil, *John Stuart Mill and India* (Stanford, 1994).
[51] F. Rosen, 'Stokes and Utilitarians'.

and in both India and Ireland, his commitment to representative government was very weak. Controversies such as this demonstrate that it is the capacity of *The English Utilitarians and India* to continue to raise historical questions which marks it out as a seminal work on the history of British government and India.

Before the book's long and somewhat painful gestation was completed, Stokes himself had been translated to another field of imperial crisis. In 1956 the British Government decided to extend its policy of developing higher education to central Africa and founded the University College of Rhodesia and Nyasaland at Salisbury. Roland Oliver having rejected the Chair of History, the authorities offered it to Stokes, who accepted. But the posting was a difficult one. Florence Stokes remembers that arriving in Rhodesia in 1957 was like 'landing on the moon', a far cry from the cosmopolitanism of Singapore. The journey on the Union Castle Line to South Africa was followed by a three days' train journey up into the High Veld, a reminder of the continuing social and political dependence of central Africa on the huge white bastion to the south. Though the new Principal, Walter Adams (later Director of LSE), met the Stokeses off the train, the University house they occupied was at that time four miles outside Salisbury in deep elephant grass with no telephone or public transport.

These practical problems were dwarfed by political and social ones. This was the period shortly before the acrimonious breakup of the Central African Federation into black and white dominated national units. In Southern Rhodesia the power of the new generation of white settlers who had fled post-war Britain or who were seeking a new beginning outside South Africa was visibly growing.[52] Racial attitudes were much harsher than they had been in Malaya and black people were treated with barely concealed contempt. Initially, there were no black members of staff at the College. Black students had to pay fees for education beyond the age of eleven unless they were in mission schools while white students had their education free. Blacks were subject to rigorous pass laws which meant, for instance, that the Stokeses' African servants were unable to bring their wives or husbands to stay in the white township, although the law allowed this in the University enclave to which the Stokeses later moved.

Not the least distasteful feature of Rhodesia was that white neighbours in their first housing colony snooped on each other and informed the police of fraternisation with the blacks. African nationalism was rigidly controlled in the colony, but white political activity in sympathy with African aspirations was already growing and was strongly represented among the young British and South African teachers on the Campus. Lecturers from the University who carried out extra-mural classes in the black suburb of Harare, including Stokes,

---

[52] See, e.g., Anthony Verrier, *The Road to Zimbabwe, 1890–1980* (London, 1986).

were regularly tailed by police agents. Shortly before Stokes left the Campus in 1963, one of his politically active colleagues in the History Department, Terence Ranger, was deported from the colony by the government of Sir Roy Welensky as white Southern Rhodesia slipped towards the inglorious interlude of UDI and white domination.

As Professor responsible for the future of a major department of a new university, Stokes's attitude was more cautious than that of his activist colleagues. His position was that 'the true British political tradition was the spirit and practice of representative government'. Democracy was still a distant ideal in central Africa because of the great gap in education between rich and poor. But representative government was not, and educated Africans should be rapidly 'admitted to a share of political power' as representatives of all Africans.[53] Elsewhere he justified this position by arguing that the genius of the British political tradition was not that of the abstract European Rights of Man, but of 'representative rather than democratic government'.[54] It was uniquely suited to the type of political gradualism which was needed in central Africa: 'the European is required to enter into close relations with the African, to wrench him from his tribal society, to congregate him in factories and towns, to look to him as a market, to instruct him in western tastes and values . . . For in such attunement lies the preordained harmony where interest and morality coincide.' While Stokes saw this modernisation process as inevitable, he was not sanguine about its results and regretted the rapid destruction of old beliefs and communities.

Stokes's attitudes were not informed only by his reading of political thought. As in Malaya, he was fearful that either a too fast or a too slow advance towards the goal of full representative government would pitch the country into the hands of Communist radicals. He disliked doctrinaire socialism both because it was godless and because it overrode individual rights. On this—and on this alone—he was at one with the Salisbury white oligarchy. He gave several talks to the African Broadcasting Studios. One of these (15 September 1960) was a subtle intervention in the official campaign to counter Communist influence among the black population. He argued that Communist rule in Russia did not mean equality, as some black nationalists were arguing. Instead, the Soviet Government 'deliberately kept wages low and the shops half empty of foodstuffs and household goods in order that Russia might have the world's largest standing army and such expensive toys as rockets to the moon'. The Communist danger was quite real because Africa was 'ripe for the totalitarian messianism of the Right (e.g., Egypt) or the Left'.[55]

---

[53] ETS to Editor, *Evening Standard*, Salisbury, 1 Dec. 1959.
[54] 'The Meaning of Democracy. Another View', MS, apparently published in the *Central African Examiner*, a journal which catered to 'the less-unprogressive white intelligentsia' of Salisbury (Dr Richard Brown, personal communication).
[55] 'Political Messianism in Africa', *The Central African Examiner*, 17 Dec. 1960, p. 20; cf. 'Alarums-and-Excursions', ibid., Dec. 1962, pp. 25–6.

On the other hand, the University College of Rhodesia and Nyasaland was a place of considerable intellectual buoyancy, expanding its numbers of history lecturers. As Professor, Eric Stokes had to lecture across an even wider range of medieval and modern history than had been the case in Singapore. His witty, irreverent side relished the 'delightful, music-hall comedy feel to life' as panjandrum in a new but very remote college.[56] More interesting, it had been in the previous fifteen years that African history had come of age as an academic discipline in African, British, and American universities. Basil Davison's *Old Africa Rediscovered* (1960) and *Black Mother* had given the subject visibility, though Stokes thought that they were somewhat sentimental.[57]

The 'scientific' historical work, however, had been done by Roland Oliver (London) G. P. Murdock (Yale) and many historians in South African Universities. In Salisbury itself, Terence Ranger was taking the lead in charting the history of black experience under colonialism. A British historian from Christ's, Richard Brown set himself to study the pre-colonial societies of central Africa. Clyde Mitchell, head of anthropology (later Professor in Manchester and Oxford) was also a powerful force in departmental politics and, as a friend of Stokes and successor to Gluckman, a firm supporter of cooperation between anthropology and history.[58] In this he was aided by Jaap van Velsen (author of *The Politics of Kinship. A Study in Social Manipulation among the Lakeside Tonga of Nyasaland* (Manchester, 1964). The ancient historian, C. R. Whittaker, was another who nudged the department towards the study of a broad social history.

With the *English Utilitarians* a recently published critical success, it was not to be expected that Stokes would give up his interest in the influence of ideas on historical change or his Indian concerns. But he devoted some of his time to the history of Zambezian Africa and the government of South Africa. The focus on smaller administrative units, tribal structures and even popular resistance was slowly to move his Indian work, too, in a different direction. He and his colleagues recognised that 'the prevalent trend in historical writing is unquestionably affected by the rise of African nationalism and the belief in the need for examining the African past with renewed sympathy and insight'.[59]

A powerful influence here was the Rhodes-Livingstone Institute which, through the work of the anthropologist, Max Gluckman, and others had brought central Africa into the forefront of anthropological theory. During Stokes's time, two seminal conferences were held. The first, the Leverhulme History Conference (Salisbury, September 1960) brought together historians

---

[56] ETS to Parkin, 2 July 1957.
[57] 'East Africa', MS.
[58] Personal communication from Dr C. R. Whittaker, 9 January 1997.
[59] ETS, review of A. J. Hanna, *The Story of Rhodesia and Nyasaland* (London, 1960) MS, 17 Aug. 1960.

and anthropologists, including African intellectuals. Another at Lusaka in September 1963 was devoted to the new African social and political history. Some of the papers at this meeting drew on oral history techniques which were being pioneered at this time by Jan Vansina. Others considered novel topics such as the role of spirit medium cults. The historical role of these cults in the formation of African kingdoms and their resistance to European invasion was highlighted by their contemporary importance in African nationalist movements.

Terence Ranger and Richard Brown were in the forefront of this work, but a new generation of indigenous male and female history graduates of Stokes's department, such as Mutumba Mainga and Lishoma Muuka (later of the Zambian Ministry of Foreign Affairs) also made one of their first appearances before white academic audiences at this meeting.[60] To Terence Ranger's delight, Stokes had put him in charge of the first History Honours Group of students out of which Mutumba Mainga and several other future Ph.D.s were drawn.[61] In addition to the new African history, a major influence on all the participants in these meetings was the school of British social anthropology. The references in the papers to 'segmentary states' and 'acephalous societies' distantly echo the seminal work of Edward Evans Pritchard. A more direct influence in Salisbury were the South African based anthropologists, Max Gluckman, Meyer Fortes (later Stokes's colleague at Cambridge), and Audrey Richards.

As in politics, so in academic matters, Stokes was a liberal rather than a radical. He approved of the new central African 'school of sociological [i.e. anthropological] history', but seemed to echo Ronald Robinson in arguing that it was 'deficient in analysis' and was condemned to mere antiquarianism unless it elucidated broad, comparative issues.[62] This was to be a theme in Stokes's later Indian historical writing. On the one hand, he always insisted on full primary documentation. For instance, writing some years before to Parkin who felt that appropriate 'historical explanation' had no necessary connection with primary documentary evidence, Stokes asserted that 'without original sources, there is no feel of history'.[63] On the other hand, he believed that all history was essentially comparative history. The comparative element for Stokes was generally supplied by the structures and policies of colonial administrators, even at the level of local administration. In his Cambridge years, he seemed to accept some of Geoffrey Elton's critique of 'soft', social history topics.

[60] 'Zambesian History', MS.
[61] Personal communication from Professor Ranger, 8 Jan. 1997.
[62] 'Zambesian History', p. 4.
[63] Parkin to ETS, 9 Dec. 1949.

Though he took up anthropological taxonomies of kingdoms and states, Stokes was critical of the concept of culture, which he thought meaningless as an analytical term. In later years he viewed with puzzlement the headlong rush in American studies of India towards what he regarded as essentialising 'ethnohistory'. He had little time for gender studies, believed there were iron limits to the worth of the history of mentalities and paid strangely little attention to religion in his own work. Stokes, however, was in no sense an academic conservative. He always received novel intellectual positions with the fascination of the student of thought. His critique of them was pointed, but rarely dismissive.

In these circumstances, it is not surprising that Stokes's contribution to African historiography was to be largely in examining the micro-structures of central African colonial administration and the taxonomy of the more solidly founded African kingdoms. The book he edited with Richard Brown, *The Zambezian Past* (1966), which issued from the Lusaka Conference, contained a part introduction and two articles by Stokes. This work, like much of what was done in the University College, had arisen out of the need to teach undergraduate special subjects to whites and Africans in Central African History[64] and to assign archivally-based projects to advanced students.

Stokes believed that he was the only member of the department who did not really 'come off' as an African historian as such. He felt he had spent too much time finishing off his Indian work and running up the successive 'impasses', as he thought, of Milnerism and Indirect Rule. Neither of these produced much published work for him. Milnerism came to nothing because Milner himself seemed *sui generis* in British imperial history, an authoritarian failure who was of little significance compared with the idealist school of Lionel Curtis. Despite copious note-taking, Indirect Rule also seemed a dead fruit, with Lord Lugard himself already having said all that needed to be said.

It was Roland Oliver who pointed Stokes to the issue of the British pacification of central Africa. Stokes, therefore, began to research and write on the fall of Yao power on Lake Malawi and the attenuated survival under British paramountcy of King Lewanika's Barotse kingdom in the far west of the Zambezian Valley. In a retrospective comment of 1974 he argued that these essays were 'period pieces'. Because of their emphasis on the paramount importance of British motives and policies, he felt they defied the trend of Africanisation. This was then running strongly and reached its apogee as far as Barotseland was concerned in Gwyn Prins's, *The Hidden Hippopotomus* (1982).

Even in 1960, however, Stokes believed that it was 'important to preserve the truth that there had actually been a historical phenomenon called imperialism and that European motives and actions still deserved continued study'.[65] That

---

[64] 'History as taught and written at UCRN, 1957–63', *Rhodesian History*, 5, 1974, 1–3.
[65] 'History as taught', ibid.

view has been amply endorsed more recently. For African historians were to come to realise in the following twenty years that to account for African resistance and African social forms, from spirit cults to 'tribes', still required a steady concentration on the nature of European power which moulded them and provided the conditions in which they could reproduce themselves.

Stokes's two essays in *The Zambezian Past* and his contribution to the volume's introduction marks the transition between his early work on the political theory of empire and his later articles on Indian social history. Indeed, until Stokes and T. R. Metcalf began to work on social change in the north Indian regions in the 1960s, there was nothing remotely resembling this style of work in modern Indian historiography. In *The Zambezian Past*, Stokes is happy to concede the importance of African agency. The centralised states of pre-colonial Africa had the capacity and sometimes the will to resist European invasion. Similarly, decentralised or 'acephalous' polities also often threw up long standing resistance movements, he argued. By contrast, it was semi-centralised but segmentary kingdoms which, with their internal divisions, were easy prey to the white conquerors. He later applied some of these arguments to nineteenth-century India.

But such historical sociology could only go so far, Stokes asserted. Purposive European imperialism had also to be taken into account. Analysing Sir Harry Johnston's destruction of the Malawi kingdoms between 1893 and 1903, Stokes noted the practical constraints within which British conquest operated. Given considerable military and political resources, Lord Lugard could afford to crush indigenous resistance quickly in northern Nigeria but then totally recast native authority in the form of 'indirect rule'. The model, Stokes believed, was the Indian experience of Lord Dalhousie's period which Lugard quoted. And the key was not so much the Indian native states, but the operation of British authority in the so-called non-regulation provinces.[66] In Malawi, Johnston had no such resources. Paradoxically, he therefore set himself to systematically subvert African authority and effect a piecemeal, but complete conquest.[67] Yet even these practical constraints were not the whole story. Johnston himself was a protégé of the 'aggressive' modernising imperialism of Joseph Chamberlain and the British politicians of the 1890s.

In these essays and other papers, Stokes tried to reach behind the formal distinction between direct and indirect rule. He also sought to distance himself somewhat both from the 'Africanist' theories of his Salisbury colleagues and from the view that 'local crises' explained British policy in its entirety. This

[66] 'Indirect Rule: expediency or ideology', MS.
[67] E. T. Stokes and R. Brown (eds.), *The Zambezian Past. Studies in Central African History* (Manchester, 1966), pp. 352–75.

view had been powerfully reinforced by Robinson and Gallagher two years earlier in their *Africa and the Victorians*.

Sometime before completing his Zambezian work, Stokes had already made one final general statement on the role of ideas in the British Empire of the later nineteenth century. His inaugural lecture given in the University College of Rhodesia and Nyasaland in 1960 was published as *The Political Ideas of English Imperialism*. Thirty-eight pages in length, it stands as sketch for a volume on the intellectual history of the British Empire of the later nineteenth century which he never published. He did, however, do a considerable amount of work on state papers in the UK and Africa and published several preliminary articles which were facilitated by a Rockefeller grant which he received in the late 1950s.

Stokes's inaugural in Rhodesia is particularly illuminating because it is much more self-reflective than *The English Utilitarians* and it ranges over the whole of imperial history rather than focusing on India alone. It begins with a defence of intellectual history or political thought, as he calls it, against the tendency to dismiss ideology as a force in political history which was in full spate with the 'Namierite deluge' of the 1950s and 1960s. Even if Herbert Butterfield's strictures on Namier's view of the eighteenth century lacked force (and they probably did not), Stokes argued, one could not 'take the mind out of the history' of the later nineteenth century when 'classes open to intellectual influences had a much closer hold on political power'.[68] Despite this rejection of Namierism, Stokes remained fascinated at some level by the notion of political faction and the politics of rational economic man. He was to see the heresy emerge once again in the so-called Cambridge school of Indian political history of Anil Seal and John Gallagher ten years later and often quixotically denounced his own earlier work on ideology as the history of 'one clerk talking to another'. Yet it was this capacity to tack between the politics of ideology and those of practical reason which made Stokes such an interesting historian.

In the *Political Ideas of English Imperialism* Stokes was also reacting against the highly abstract and academic history of political theory represented by the tradition of Bradley, Hobhouse, Sidgwick, and others whose reflections on politics had been removed from the active world of politics to 'the quiet of the College cloister'. His stress on the need to contextualise the work of prominent thinkers in wider and deeper currents of thought echoed the approach of Michael Oakeshott and anticipated, in a minor way, the approach of Quentin Skinner.

In his inaugural lecture, Stokes tried to demonstrate the influence of the idealist thought of T. H. Green and S. R. Bosanquet on imperial ideology. It

[68] *The Political Ideas of English Imperialism* (Salisbury, 1963), p. 7.

was ironic, he argued, that most of those latter-day Hegelians who articulated the notion of state and society as organic entities girded by sentiment and tradition were liberals in politics, uneasy about imperial expansion (this was, indeed, a description of his own views). Idealist thought was, nevertheless, an important influence on figures such as Lionel Curtis and the Round Table group who, before the First World War, had sought to refound the British Empire on an ideal of trusteeship and insist on the moral basis of imperial power. Aspects of this line of thought were later taken up by Stokes's Ph.D. student, Clive Dewey, who discerned idealist strains in the later nineteenth century discourse among British Indian officials on the ideal of 'village community' and the paternalist traditions of the Punjab Commission.[69]

Stokes also provided some clues as to how he would have developed the history of Utilitarian and 'liberal imperialist' tradition which had been analysed in the *English Utilitarians*. This tradition, more calculating and devoid of sentiment than the idealist one, but equally prone to accept the use of force in the interests of progress was propelled into the later nineteenth century by thinkers such as James FitzJames Stephen and Lords Cromer and Milner who applied the 'policy of thorough' to African government. Stokes saw this tradition bifurcating towards, on the one hand, the ideology of the 'high imperialism' of the 1890s and 1900s, and towards the scientific, eugenicist, and authoritarian socialism of the Webbs and other radicals, on the other. Both these traditions subscribed to national efficiency, though the earlier utilitarian emphasis on the individual being was now supplanted by an emphasis on the individual race.

Two other features of the inaugural lecture were of interest. First, Stokes revealed his deep sympathy with Rudyard Kipling, a topic to which he was to return in his inaugural lecture in Cambridge in 1974. He resented the tendency of the post-war anti-imperialist age to denounce Kipling as a mediocre artist and a mindless chauvinist. In both these lectures he sought to show, as more recent and level-headed literary critics have done, that Kipling's views on race and empire were both more nuanced and more ambiguous than superficial readings suggest. Britain's Empire in this reading was as evanescent as all other despotisms; East did ultimately meet West, but in ways neither intended.

In Rhodesia in 1961 Stokes gave a series of talks on the meaning of University education, alerted to the topic by the teething troubles of the new African universities and colleges. He was also conscious of the debate raging in Britain associated with C. P. Snow's (another Christ's man) thesis about the 'two cultures'. Stokes's theme was the need to support humane teaching and learning in an era when the demand in both advanced and developing societies was for

---

[69] See, especially, C. J. Dewey, *Anglo-Indian Attitudes. The mind of the Indian Civil Service* (London, 1993), pp. 7–10.

technocrats and specialists.[70] He turned back to Sir Walter Moberley's, *The Crisis of the University* (1947) which also argued against over-specialisation. Stokes thought that one great advantage of the University College of Rhodesia and Nyasaland was that it was still intimate enough to remain a community of learning. Stokes also drew upon Cardinal Newman's *On the Scope and Nature of University Education* to argue that 'while liberal knowledge must be morally neutral', each scholar or scientist must comprehend this learning in the light of 'private belief and faith'. The student need not be ashamed to hold fast to 'instinctive truths and elemental loves', even though he dimly perceived their true rationality. Ten years before in Singapore Stokes had argued that the western intellectual tradition derived its dynamism precisely from its rootedness in the security of 'moral and religious agency'.[71] The problem was that the ancient faiths of Asia were being subverted or abandoned, freeing the intellect as a pure principle of power. The danger of the divorce of reason from morality also faced the new African societies. Here again, in Salisbury, the influence of Christian idealism broke surface from under the calm of Stokes's rationalism.

More mundane educational issues, however, divided members of the Salisbury staff. The University College's high admission standards had the inevitable effect of keeping African participation at a minimum. Opinion was divided between those members of staff who argued for a reduction of standards to promote racial integration of the student body and others who felt that this was wrong and that high academic standards were the best gift for London University to bequeath to its African offshoots.[72] While tending to the latter view, Stokes's combination of humour and moral seriousness as Chairman of the Faculty of Arts and Social Sciences averted a damaging personal rift in the midst of these passionate arguments. The issue was later resolved by the institution of a pre-A-level course for African students, funded and taught by the University.

Stokes summed up his lived experience of nationalism in India, south-east Asia, and Africa when he wrote for a Rhodesia talk 'a democracy cannot hold down another community against its will . . . a prolonged effort at coercion drives the nationalist movement into the hands of the extremists, so that the final solution is always worse than the one which might have been obtained by negotiation at the beginning'.[73] To today's audience this may seem self-evident; to the Salisbury audience of 1962, it was far from so. Milnerism fitted here too. Stokes interpreted Milner as a late embodiment of that utilitarian tradition, welfare-orientated but authoritarian, whose first experiments had

[70] 'The first year at the University', MS.
[71] 'Malayan Students', MS.
[72] Personal communication from Professor Terence Ranger, 19 March 1997.
[73] 'Nationalism', MS.

been carried out in India in the 1830s. Milner's austere 'priest-like' devotion to duty and the state both attracted and repelled Stokes.[74] Milner argued that the Boer Republics were hangovers of the medieval world trying to impede the development of the modern. But it was in his time, Stokes thought, that the 'ideal of imperialism' (a term Stokes used in a specific sense) was 'tested and defeated'. The High Commissioner had forgotten the limitations to state action that did not rest on the popular will.

This, however, was not a lesson that had been learned by the white ruling class in Southern Rhodesia. Though Stokes had greatly enjoyed his years at Salisbury and regarded them as a period of service to the broader ideal of a racially blind Commonwealth, he had already begun to look for positions in British universities which were poised to expand once again. In 1960 for instance, he was in discussion with University College London about a Readership there[75] and had also been approached by J. S. Galbraith about a position in the University of California. By 1963 he was determined to return to Britain.

Political uncertainty in Africa was a major concern. It was clear to Stokes that the racial tensions of central and southern Africa could not be resolved without major conflagrations now that Kenya, Uganda, Nyasaland, and Northern Rhodesia were independent, majority-ruled republics, while the white Rhodesian expatriates clung resolutely to power in Salisbury. The University College, founded to create a cohesive multi-racial ruling elite for central Africa as a whole could not possibly work when nationalism and racism were tearing apart the political environment in which it had developed. As Stokes wrote to Sir Alexander Carr-Saunders (Director of the London School of Economics, 1937–56, Vice-Chancellor, London University) of the deportation by the Federal Government of Terence Ranger, who was regarded as a dangerous radical, 'Terry's expulsion has merely brought to a head the long-gathering crisis. With the Rhodesian Front Victory, the impending break-up of the Federation, and our unpopularity in the [African-ruled] North, the College is now looking into the mouth of that dark tunnel through which, as you expressively said to me, it needs must pass.'[76]

Stokes's attitude to the College's Principal, Walter Adams was ambivalent, but he certainly doubted the wisdom of Adams's 'Napoleonic principle: when in doubt expand'. This was because 'a University cannot operate like a resistance movement and must be in an effective working relationship with the Government of the day',[77] a view that also divided him from his more radical younger colleagues.[78] The real tragedy, according to Stokes, was that

---

[74] 'Milner and Southern Africa', MS.

[75] Ifor Evans to ETS, 5 Jan. 1960.

[76] ETS to Sir Alexander Carr-Saunders, duplicate, 25 Jan. 1963.

[77] Ibid.

[78] Personal communication from Dr C. R. Whittaker, 9 Jan. 1997.

'the multi-racial ideal on which the College was founded has been rejected—at least in the political sense—by black and white alike'.[79] The College Council remained, apart from one silent African, completely white and, in effect, dominated by the Salisbury European members. The student body was still overwhelmingly white. The result was the spread of a 'quiet despair about the future' among the staff.

The danger Stokes saw was of the fragmentation of university education in central and East Africa into a devalued system in the black north, cut off from its London links, and an embattled white core in Salisbury. The solution which Stokes (and Ranger) proposed was that the College at Lusaka (Northern Rhodesia–Zambia) should be taken into direct communication with London University once the Federation broke up in order to preserve its quality of education. Stokes also felt that the rapid development of a law school in Salisbury might help to recruit able young Africans and preserve 'the British conception of higher education in central Africa'.[80] In the event, 'quiet despair' was to be a more appropriate emotion; all the institutions in contention would be battered by economic collapse and revolutionary war in the 1970s.

The Stokeses' decision to return to the UK was also determined by family concerns. The perennial problems of securing a good education for four daughters loomed again. In 1963, therefore, Stokes applied for the position of Lecturer in History at the University of Cambridge and was appointed as a University Lecturer in Colonial Studies from 1 October 1963 to the retiring age.[81] Since he had left the University in 1949, he had kept in close touch with it through his friend Charles Parkin, besides entertaining visiting luminaries such as Ronald Robinson.

Cambridge was unusual among British universities at this time in that its History Faculty regarded Commonwealth and 'extra-European' history as a staple of undergraduate teaching. To the older generation of historians of the Commonwealth and Empire such as Nicholas Mansergh and E. E. Rich was now added the dynamic pair of Robinson and Gallagher, whose *Africa and the Victorians* Stokes had both welcomed and critiqued several years before. It was Rich, however, a historian of Canada and Master of St Catharine's College, who proved Stokes's strongest supporter and it was to Rich's College that he returned in the Michaelmas Term of 1963. Stokes followed Oliver MacDonagh as Director of Studies in History and went through the usual *cursus honorum* of College office and committees. Such committees were particularly active as the College engaged in a large and contentious rebuilding programme, expanded its Fellowship and, ultimately, admitted women.

Stokes, though sceptical and impish in his attitude to established authority,

[79] ETS to Carr-Saunders, 25 Jan. 1963, p. 2.
[80] 'A Law School and the Future of Higher Education in Central Africa', draft MS., 1962–3?
[81] *Reporter*, 31 July 1963, p. 2071.

had always venerated the ideal of Cambridge from afar, 'the sense of generation on generation, the beauty of ancient buildings, the grace of ceremony, the
peace of College courts' as he saw it from Singapore in 1952.[82] Now
ensconced in the Fenland town struggling to slough off, in the early 1960s,
its Victorian carapace, the romance tarnished somewhat.

Stokes kept in touch with his Rhodesian colleagues, particularly during the
events which followed the Unilateral Declaration of Independence in 1965. He
continued to be involved in Asian and African issues at the national level as a
result of his membership of the Inter-University Council for Higher Education
(1972–9), the Indian Committee of the British Council, the Cambridge Living-
stone Trust and membership of the Governing Body of the School of Oriental
and African Studies. His many research and lecture trips to India also kept him
abreast of events in the Subcontinent, and on one of these, in 1977, he became
an Honorary D.Litt. of the University of Mysore.

Yet Stokes's life undoubtedly became more sedate and domestic than it
had been in the colonies. A moderate reformer as ever, he was more favourable
than most of his peers to demands for student representation and an end to
formal dining in college halls. With four academic daughters and a resolute
wife, he resented the manner in which female guests were excluded from high
table and women were denied access to the older colleges. Even at the height
of the generally tame student demonstrations which marked the Vietnam era in
Cambridge, he urged the Governing Body of St Catharine's 'not to hate the
undergraduate'. On the other hand, he was no libertarian. He was hostile to the
casual sexual permissiveness which was another feature of this period, believing that it damaged family life, which he greatly valued.

Stokes was elected in 1970 to the Smuts Chair of Commonwealth History
in succession to Professor P. N. Mansergh and in 1977 he became Chairman of
the History Faculty. His main concern in College and Faculty committees was
to promote talent and work for some change in the rather hidebound Historical
Tripos. The fact that Stokes was a proficient political theorist greatly aided his
attempts to promote extra-European history, as 'intellectual historians' then
regarded themselves as the elite of the Cambridge Faculty. Stokes attracted an
international body of graduate students who mostly worked with him on Indian
agrarian issues in contrast to the so-called 'Cambridge school' of political
historians of India grouped around Anil Seal and John Gallagher. Several of
these went on to make major contributions to Indian agrarian history through
the sort of detailed studies of rent, revenue, and demographic change which he
had pioneered.[83] As a supervisor, Stokes was supportive and kind, but

[82] 'Malayan Students' MS., 1952, p. 2.
[83] e.g., Professor Ernest Chew, Dr Clive Dewey, Dr Neil C. Charlesworth, Dr Ratnalekha
Ray, Dr Chittabrata Palit, Dr Simon Commander, Dr Peter Musgrave, Professor Sugata Bose,
Professor Sumit Guha. Dr Susan B. Bayly, however, turned towards the study of religion.

definitely of the old school in that he viewed the writing of a dissertation as the personal act of a mature scholar, not as an exercise in teaching, or 'training', as the rubric now has it. His graduate students appreciated their visits to the Stokeses' house in south Cambridge. For many of them, their strongest memories of Eric Stokes were of his impish humour and capacity to puncture academic pomposity even while chairing meetings in Commonwealth History.

At Cambridge, Eric Stokes's intellectual life developed in two main directions which had already been foreshadowed in Malaya and Africa, towards theories of imperialism and Indian social history. Lecturing for the Part I Tripos paper, the 'Expansion of Europe' and the new paper he had helped to establish, 'The West and the "Third World" since the First World War', he tried to maintain the broad overview of imperial ideology and practice which had informed *The English Utilitarians*. Much of his intellectual effort here was spent in responding to Robinson and Gallagher's challenge to the field, while reserving a space for the intellectual history of empire. He expanded the critique of *Africa and the Victorians* which he had published in Rhodesia[84] in a series of articles and lectures. This was the most acute and also the most sympathetic of the large number of reviews, comments, and even multi-volume works attempting to turn back their 'historiographical revolution'. Ronald Robinson admitted as much when he remarked 'Old Stokey, was the only one who ever really understood us'.

While he certainly drew on earlier responses of Colin Newbury and David Fieldhouse, Stokes anticipated practically every lineament of the critique of *Africa and the Victorians* which the field later painfully developed. Essentially, his argument was that their emphasis on the supreme importance of the British occupation of Egypt in triggering the Partition of Africa was overdone. The French were already seeking to advance in West Africa as early as 1878, while the movement forward of chartered companies, individual entrepreneurs, anti-slavers, and others could not be reduced to the Egyptian question.

Whereas Robinson and Gallagher's understanding of contemporary Suez and South African crises in the 1940s and 1950s shaped their view of the Scramble for Africa, Stokes's personal experience of the working of sub-imperial agents and colonial capital in south-east Asia and Africa gave him a more complex view of that history. It was ironic, he thought, that despite Robinson and Gallagher's apparent emphasis on African agency, they reduced central Africa to a passive victim of colonial expansion from north and south, while the Muslim *jihads* of French West Africa became, for them, epiphenomena of European expansion.

It is notable also that, rather than tackling the Robinson and Gallagher

---

[84] 'Historical Association of Rhodesia and Nyasaland', 1963.

thesis at the level of the ideology of empire, he chided their apparent diminution of the economic factor in British territorial expansion. Lenin and Hobson continued to play a (reduced) part in Stokes's scheme, while they had been rejected with derision by Robinson and Gallagher. European capitalism did change its form about 1900, Stokes thought, but Lenin's view of 'imperialism the highest stage of capitalism' had to be understood as an argument directed more to developments in European government and finance than African and Asian ones. If one read what Lenin really wrote about Africa during the period of the Scramble, it was much the same as what Robinson and Gallagher said, he concluded mischievously.[85]

Stokes genuinely admired Robinson and Gallagher, the 'great artificers' of the new imperial history, and he always eschewed the point scoring and idle comparisons between the virtues of the Smuts Professor, the Beit Professor, and the Vere Harmsworth Professor, which some of their less stellar followers indulged in. It was remarkable indeed that all this talent was circulating between Oxford and Cambridge in the same short span of years. Normally dull seminars on 'imperial and Commonwealth history' at the two places were temporarily galvanised by Stokes's iconoclasm and the ironic detachment of Robinson or Gallagher. But one reason why Stokes admired his comperes was that they had 'turned the field' by a single stroke of insight. Since the *English Utilitarians*, he had felt himself unable to do that, once gloomily remarking that scholars produce only two truly original books, if they are lucky, one impelled by the hunger of youth, the other by intimations of mortality.

Stokes's difficulty was that the complexity of his understanding of history was in absolute antithesis to his view that the field responded to the one brilliant idea. In the circumstances, he could not have found a more difficult terrain to work on than Indian agrarian history of the early nineteenth century. It is easy to see why the topic appealed to him, of course. Indigenous resistance had become a scholarly industry and Stokes was highly responsive to the interest in resistance of the clever young Indians who now came to study Ph.D.s under him in increasing numbers. Stokes's early essays on the Mutiny–Rebellion of 1857 referred back to the work done by his Africanist colleagues on the link between 'primary' anti-colonial resistance and later 'proto-nationalist' movements. With Mau Mau ten years behind, the Vietnamese revolution in its final bloody stages, and peasant revolutions breaking out in Latin America, western capitalism seemed about to bury itself in the mud of peasant resistance. This was a romantic delusion, as we now know, but compelling at the time.

Stokes also felt the pull of British and European historiography and, more

---

[85] E. T. Stokes, 'Late nineteenth-century colonial expansion and the attack on the theory of economic imperialism: a case of mistaken identity?', *Historical Journal*, 12, 2 (1969), 285–301.

circumspectly, anthropology. The agrarian history of M. M. Postan, Joan Thirsk, and Eric Hobsbawm was mirrored in Europe by the grand syntheses of Fernand Braudel and Emmanuel le Roy Ladurie. Indian anthropology and history now seemed set on an upward path in Europe, north America, and India. More practically, the Indian rebellion of 1857 was a topic that could be mined for sources in Cambridge itself and had considerable potential for undergraduate and graduate research in the University.

Stokes was elected a Fellow of the British Academy in 1980, but, sadly, was unable to attend any meetings. He died tragically young at the age of fifty-six. It is difficult to know whether he would have produced the other 'big book' on agrarian history or ventured back into the terrain of the history of imperial ideas. The two volumes of essays on Indian agrarian history, *The Peasant and the Raj* (Cambridge, 1978) and *The Peasant Armed* (New Delhi, 1986) are considerable achievements in their own right, if inevitably unfinished and difficult for non-specialists to penetrate. His own work and that of his colleagues on African political systems and resistance movements made it clear to him how primitive Indian agrarian historiography was even in the early 1960s when he was searching for a new topic. A simplistic argument that the 1857 Rebellion was merely a mutiny was confronted by the equally simplistic view that it was the 'first war of independence'. The Marxist argument, that the 'landlords' betrayed the people to the British in the course of the struggle, seemed complex by comparison.

Using the detailed British records of the Rebellion and the official rent-rate and land-revenue settlement reports of the 1870s and 1880s, Stokes began to show how the particular forms of the pre-existing Indian political systems combined with the impact of British agrarian taxation to create very different outcomes in different parts of north India. This was very much the work of a 'splitter' rather than a 'lumper'. He distanced himself from the view promoted at that time by T. R. Metcalf, *The Aftermath of Revolt* (Berkeley, 1966) that the Rebellion was determined by the degree of penetration of indigenous capitalism in the form of the moneylender or *bania*. Instead, he found that the weight of land-revenue and access to commercial opportunities was a more accurate 'predictor' of the propensity to rebel than were the depredations of the moneylender. He also retreated from his own early view that simple caste affiliations were the mainspring of revolt.

Much of this work was very austere; its generalisations were delicately moulded and never exaggerated. One Indian historian, Gyanendra Pandey, argued that this was constraining empirical history, unable to take seriously the reality of popular resistance and revolt.[86] More recently, Rajat Ray has

---

[86] G. Pandey, 'A view of the observable. A positivist "understanding" of agrarian society and political protest in colonial India', *Journal of Peasant Studies*, 7 (1979–80), 375–83.

implied that Stokes underplayed the element of 'traditional patriotism' and by inference religious feeling in the Rebellion.[87] Both views have some truth in them. Stokes made little use of indigenous sources (even in translation) and he steered clear of religion and culture as an issue in his analysis. It is noteworthy that only one of the ninety or more undergraduate long essays that he assigned for his Cambridge documentary-based Special Subject on 1857 in the early 1970s concerned religion and ideology. Most of these student papers were set as detailed district or subdivisional studies of tenurial forms, such as he was carrying out himself.

This was partly because Stokes had become suspicious of the tendency of the contemporary American 'ethnohistory' to reify 'culture' as a social given. His wary but admiring relationship with British social anthropology did not extend to French structuralism or American debates about historical meta-narratives. Indeed, he specifically warned one of his graduate students not to waste time reading about the anthropology of religion. His views may also have reflected the hard, positivistic stance taken by both the right and the left in Cambridge at that time, with Geoffrey Elton lauding the mythical historian who entered the archives with a mind like a *tabula rasa*, while Peter Laslett urged his followers to retool with statistics or be relegated. Yet Stokes's stance remains a puzzle, given his own stated conviction that religion was the fundamental aspect of human experience. The result was that it seemed in Stokes's later historical writings that Europeans continued to have ideology and religion (though he now saw these as largely ineffectual in practice), while Asians or Africans merely had tenurial systems and the structures of everyday economic life.

The only break in a socio-economic history as dead-level as the great north Indian plain itself were the first two remarkable chapters of his posthumous work, *The Peasant Armed* which deal with the British and Indian soldiers of the Bengal Army, and subjectively drew on his experience as a young man in the Indian Mountain Artillery. The stylistic excellence of this work was reminiscent of the articles on literature and empire which he regularly wrote for the *Times Literary Supplement*, to finance new dresses for his daughters, or so he claimed, and his inaugural lecture 'Kipling: the Voice of the Hooligan', published in the Festschrift for J. H. Plumb. This imaginative piece of writing played on the tension between the sense of an idealised agrarian past and the onset of modern industrialisation in Kipling's work, especially *Kim*. Stokes argued that the agrarian historian was trying to do something similar in his

---

[87] R. K. Ray, 'Race, Religion and Realm. The political theory of "the Reigning India Crusade"', in Mushirul Hasan and Narayani Gupta (eds.), *India's Colonial Encounter. Essays in Memory of Eric Stokes* (Delhi, 1993), pp. 133–82.

attempt to capture the reality of that past before its memory was entirely eclipsed.

Eric Stokes regarded all his work on the agrarian history of India as provisional, and often said so. When he died of lung cancer on 5 February 1981 (never having smoked a cigarette in his life), his work on the Mutiny book was palpably incomplete. Whether he would ever have attempted to reintegrate the history of political thought with economic and social history, and the history of the British colonisers with that of indigenous society, remains unclear. My view is that paradox, scepticism, and a fundamental honesty about the limits of historical explanation would always have impeded him from bundling up his ideas on this subject in an appropriately dramatic form. He was also acutely aware that there is a right time for an idea in the development of historiography. The high tide of 'area studies' and local history in the 1970s had swept himself and many others into the creeks of the Ganges, the Jumna or the Limpopo, as he once memorably put it. But the tide was now receding and there was a danger that a whole generation of historians would be beached on the sands of these distant rivers.

Eric Stokes's work and teaching on Britain, India, and Africa nevertheless remain a vital intellectual influence in universities throughout the world, not least in India and Africa themselves. His own life and writings also stand as a memorial to a time now only forty years past, but seemingly of the deepest antiquity, when educated, middle-class Britons played a significant, and some-times, as in Stokes's case, humane role on the World Stage.

C. A. BAYLY
Fellow of the Academy

Note. I am deeply grateful to Mrs Florence Stokes for making this memoir possible by patiently answering my many questions and by supplying me with Professor Stokes's correspondence and papers. Mrs Jessie Muirhead kindly made available ETS letters from India 1944–6. Others who have provided invaluable help are Professor Frank Spooner, Professor Terence Ranger and Dr C. R. Whittaker, and Dr Richard Brown. I have benefited from the comments of Dr S. B. Bayly, Dr John Lonsdale, Dr N. Gupta, Dr T. N. Harper, Dr John Thompson, and Professor Lynn Zastoupil. Manuscript references are to the Stokes papers except when otherwise indicated.

DALE TRENDALL   *La Trobe University*

Arthur Dale Trendall
1909–1995

A. D. (DALE) TRENDALL was one of the foremost historians of classical art of
the twentieth century. He was not only the leading authority on the red-figured
vases produced during the fifth and fourth centuries BC in the Greek colonies
and native towns of south Italy and Sicily, but a scholar who had a profound
influence on the humanities in general, and classical studies in particular, in
Australia and New Zealand for more than half a century.

He was born on 28 March 1909, in Glenmore (Auckland), New Zealand, of
parents who had migrated from England. His father, Arthur Dale Trendall,
taught woodworking and technical drawing. His mother, Iza Whaley Uttley-
Todd, was also a teacher and seems to have had a profound influence upon her
son's character. It was from her that he derived his great love of Gilbert and
Sullivan, which he knew by heart and was fond of quoting. And it is significant
that his first book, *Paestan Pottery*, is dedicated to her alone. His uncle,
Charles Uttley-Todd, was involved in the building of the new Australian
capital, Canberra. It was, therefore, not inappropriate that Dale himself was
later to accept a university appointment in Canberra, and to be concerned with
the development of that city, as a member, from 1958 to 1967, of the National
Capital Planning Committee.

Under his parents' influence he began to develop that quickness of observation, those powers of memory and of concentration to which he owed his
later remarkable achievements. In 1912 his parents visited England for a year:
late in life he claimed to remember the devastation at Messina still visible after
the catastrophic earthquake of 1908, and to recall being taken to see a great
aunt who had been born on the day of the battle of Waterloo. However, the
family returned to New Zealand before the outbreak of the First World War,
and moved to the rural hamlet of Howick (now part of the city of Auckland),
where they remained until 1916 when they moved into Auckland proper so that

Proceedings of the British Academy, **97**, 501–517. © The British Academy 1998.

Dale could begin his schooling. He remembered fondly those idyllic years at Howick: at the back of the house a stream meandered through a large paddock; there was an orchard and a dairy; the family kept a cow, chickens, and ducks; transport was horse-drawn.

As a boy Dale spent ten years (1916–25) at King's College in Auckland, which at that time, as he once remarked, was more concerned to turn out young gentlemen than potential scholars. Nevertheless, it is only fair to say that his outstanding intellectual ability was recognised by his teachers, and encouraged; and Dale maintained his association with King's until the end of his life. During these years he regularly received prizes for proficiency in Languages and Literature, as well as Mathematics and Science, and he won the Stuckey Prize for English Literature in 1925. He was Dux of the school in 1924 and 1925, and in his final year a school prefect; and his headmaster prophesied 'a brilliant future'. His earliest literary work, now sadly lost, dates from this time. It was entitled *The Furniture and Appurtenances of Heaven as Revealed to Wondering Mortals through the Medium of Hymns A & M*, and included, for example, a section on heavenly timepieces (as in 'Lord, her watch Thy Church is keeping'). It was prefaced by a limerick:

> A missionary maid named O'Brien,
> Sang Hymns A and M to a lion,
> Of the maiden there's some,
> In the lion's tumtum,
> But she's mainly an angel in Zion.

Even now I have a vivid memory of Dale reciting these lines with relish, a bright twinkle in his eye and a puckish grin on his face.

It was during these years at King's (in fact 1920) that he fell seriously ill from peritonitis after a burst appendix. He had to endure a considerable period of convalescence; but during his enforced leisure he read voraciously. This was the foundation of his extraordinary knowledge of the byways of English literature in the nineteenth and early twentieth century, as well as of classic detective fiction. This interest remained strong throughout his life, and there were few occasions later that did not call forth a favourite quotation, often from Saki, Kai Lung, or the Good Duke Alfred. At this time too he developed an abiding interest in stamps and coins (an interest that found expression in the 1930s in a few short pieces on archaeology on stamps for *Gibbons' Stamp Monthly*, and in the early 1960s in Canberra when he was a member of the Advisory Committee on Decimalisation).

In 1926, having won a University of New Zealand Entrance Scholarship, he began his studies at the University of Otago (then part of the University of New Zealand) in Dunedin. He lived at Selwyn College, and his experiences there were probably significant for his later career as Master of University House in Canberra. He chose Dunedin (rather than Auckland) at the instigation of his parents who felt that he should begin to be more self-reliant. At first he intended to major in mathematics, but he had been able to learn Latin at King's College and his incipient interest in classics was fostered by the inspiring teaching of Professor T. D. Adams. Adams possessed a mellifluous voice, and a manner of presentation and delivery that was matched in Dale's experience only by the Cambridge philosopher F. M. Cornford. These lectures, which also introduced him to Greek art, produced a lasting impression, and immediately brought about his decision to follow a career in classics. But more fundamentally Adams provided a conception of classical studies that was not confined to language and literature, but all embracing; and a model of a sensitive and kindly scholar. This debt to Adams was acknowledged in 1938 in the dedication of his second book, *Frühitaliotische Vasen*.[1] Trendall completed his BA in 1928, and in the following year he gained his MA (NZ), with First Class Honours in Latin. He was awarded the James Clark Prize for Greek in 1928, and for Latin in 1929.[2]

For a young New Zealander in the 1920s, with a keen mind and a desire to pursue a career in classical studies, England was clearly the next step. However, he returned to King's College in Auckland to teach for a year before taking up, in 1931, a University of New Zealand travelling scholarship which enabled him to proceed to England. There he briefly rented accommodation in London (Gordon Square) before moving to Trinity College in Cambridge where he gained a Studentship (£200 per annum). He was excused the first two years of the Classical Tripos on the strength of his previous work in New Zealand, and graduated in 1933 with a starred First (one of only six that year) and distinction in classical archaeology. During these years he attended lectures by A. E. Housman (whose scholarship he admired but whose style he found very dry), A. B. Cook (whose classical knowledge he found encyclopaedic), A. W. Lawrence, and C. T. Seltman. But he was most impressed by the lectures of the philosopher F. M. Cornford and the historian M. Charlesworth. During his Cambridge years his supervisor was A. S. F. Gow, for whom he developed a considerable admiration, although he never forgot Gow's remark, overheard as Dale was leaving after his first interview: 'Another damned colonial!' Yet it was Gow who first introduced him to the Oxford scholar J. D. Beazley, the eminent classical archaeologist, whose approach to the study of Greek vases was to be inspirational for the young scholar.

In later years Dale would occasionally delight friends, especially young friends, with anecdotes from his own student days in Cambridge. One incident

[1] See also L. S. Adams, *Thomas Dagger Adams, A Memoir* (1954), pp. 26–7.
[2] *King's Collegian*, 29/1 (1930) 7.

that comes readily to mind occurred at an afternoon tea at the home of Charles Seltman. Among the guests was a certain Prudence Wilkinson, one of the outspoken young women of the time, and soon to marry F. L. Lucas (see that interesting work *From Olympus to the Styx*, dedicated 'To Each Other'). During a lull in the conversation and the rattle of teacups, Miss Wilkinson was heard to remark: 'Don't you think, Mr Seltman, that the average man's appreciation of the Parthenon sculptures is entirely due to latent homosexuality?'

During the first long vacation (1932) at Cambridge Dale travelled in Italy, partly to learn Italian, partly to see the archaeological sites. He was much impressed by the remains of the Greek cities, most especially the unspoiled beauty of Paestum. This experience, combined with the influence of J. D. Beazley, led to his decision to devote his life to the red-figure pottery produced by the Greek inhabitants of South Italy and Sicily. It was a subject that he pursued with absolute devotion and undimmed enthusiasm for more than 60 years. He once remarked to me that he had 20,000 loves, and they were all vases.

But his decision to study this relatively neglected area of Greek pottery was courageous. At that time, partly through the outstanding work of Humfry Payne, Greek art of the Archaic period was very much in vogue, and South Italian vases were not appreciated, but deemed to be 'late' and 'colonial'. As Dale himself later observed, the general attitude was 'rather like Virgil's advice to Dante in regard to the lost souls outside the gate of Hell: "non ragionam di lor, ma guarda e passa"'.[3] Like his contemporary and friend T. J. Dunbabin, who had gone from Sydney to Oxford, Dale felt a sympathy for the vibrancy and novelty of colonial Greek culture in Magna Graecia, and so he persevered, though he certainly felt at times that he was working nearly alone:

> my colonial upbringing had perhaps given me a slight prejudice in favour of the Western Greek colonists and it enabled me to view some of their problems, as well as their attitude to the motherland, with a more sympa-thetic eye, and perhaps with even a greater understanding, than my English colleagues, who tended to look upon the ancient Greek world very much through the eyes of the Athenians rather than those of the Syracusans or Tarentines.[4]

But the problem for the young student was not only scholarly prejudice, but also the sheer amount of material, and the task was to prove more formidable than he at first realised. From the middle of the fifth century until the early third century BC certain of the Greek colonies and native centres in Magna Graecia produced pottery painted in the red-figure technique with

[3] A. D. Trendall and Alexander Cambitoglou, *The Red-figured Vases of Apulia* (Oxford, 1982), p. 1036.
[4] Address on the occasion of the conferring of the degree of Doctor of Letters at La Trobe University, 16 Dec. 1991.

scenes drawn from myth and everyday life. These vases represent not only a significant example of the artistic sensibility of the Western Greeks, but a fundamental source for many aspects of Greek and native culture, from religion, burial customs, and the theatre, to warfare, costume, and jewellery. The output was large. Today, well over 20,000 such vases survive, scattered in museums and private collections from Trondheim in the northern hemisphere to Dunedin in the southern, and many more appear each year through regular or illicit excavations. Furthermore, in the early 1930s serious scholarship devoted to South Italian red-figure vases was not extensive, and most vases remained unpublished, often gathering dust in museum basements (his work, as he once remarked, fell into the category of 'dirty' rather than 'dirt' archaeology). The great German archaeologist Adolph Furtwängler had recognised one group of early South Italian vases which he thought had been made by immigrant Athenian potters at Thurii. In Italy, G. Patroni and P. Ducati had made some progress in differentiating the principal local fabrics of Apulia, Lucania, and Campania, and Patroni had postulated the existence of a fabric at Paestum. In England the work of J. D. Beazley, though principally concerned with Athenian vase-painting, provided useful notes, especially on the initial phases of Lucanian and Apulian, and E. M. W. Tillyard's publication in 1923 of the Hope vases represented a considerable step forward in distinguishing local South Italian from imported Athenian red-figure. But most significant was an article published in 1929 by one of Beazley's students, Miss Noël Moon (later Mrs Walter Oakeshott), on the early phases of South Italian pottery. It was the work of Beazley and of Moon, in particular, that provided the immediate stimulus to Dale's research, and it was a debt that he readily acknowledged.[5]

At the beginning of his career he set himself the task of identifying the five principal local red-figure styles, which we now recognise as Apulian, Lucanian, Campanian, Paestan, and Sicilian; of defining the chronological development of painted pottery in South Italy during the Classical period; and of attributing, through a careful stylistic analysis, the many thousands of vases to painters and groups. If today the basic classification has been established, this is mainly Trendall's achievement. But it was not at first easy to decide where to begin.

His first article appeared in 1934 in the *Journal of Hellenic Studies*. It dealt with an Early Apulian volute-krater that had been found in a large tomb at Ceglie near Bari in 1898, but had remained unpublished. Much of the short piece is taken up with iconographic matters, but already style has a place: following an opinion of Beazley, the vase is placed between the Painter of the

[5] See 'Beazley and Early South Italian Vase Painting', in D. Kurtz, ed., *Beazley and Oxford* (1985), pp. 31–41.

Berlin Dancing Girl and the followers of the Sisyphus Painter, about 410 or a
little later, and the mainstream of Early Apulian production is located at
Taranto.

After completing his studies in Cambridge, Dale received the Charles
Walston Studentship which enabled him to profit from a year spent in Greece.
But Italy had captured his imagination, so he moved to the British School at
Rome for two years as Rome Scholar in Classical Studies. His topic of research
was the red-figure pottery of South Italy, in particular the 'style presumed to be
Paestan'. He finally chose this topic as a starting-point because the number of
Paestan vases was relatively small, most were to be found in the museums of
Naples and Madrid, and comparatively little research had been carried out.
Moreover, Paestan was recognised to have a certain importance in providing
the only two South Italian vase-painters who signed their work—Asteas and
Python; the style was relatively homogeneous; and the mythological subjects
were of considerable interest. A preliminary article in the *Journal of Hellenic
Studies* for 1935 broke new ground by attempting to outline the early phase of
Paestan before the main production of Asteas and Python. This was followed
the next year by his first book, *Paestan Pottery*, printed under the auspices of
the British School. Here, for the first time, the fabric was studied as a whole:
all Paestan red-figure vases then known, some 400, were collected and organised into painters and groups on the basis of a thorough stylistic analysis using
the Morellian method as it had been adapted to painted Greek vases by
Beazley. It was a methodology that he was to employ in all his publications.
Some fifty years later Dale returned to the study of Paestan pottery, completing,
as he felt, the cycle of his research. *The Red-figured Vases of Paestum*,
published in 1987, again by the British School at Rome, is a much more
elaborate work than its predecessor, incorporating almost 2000 vases, which
are, however, catalogued and discussed in the same sensitive manner, and with
the same clarity and thoroughness. But this is not merely an enlargement of its
predecessor: new perspectives on the development of Paestan are revealed,
particularly the presence of a new artist, the Aphrodite Painter, whose vases
reveal a strong Apulian character and suggest that the artist may have moved
about 330 from Taranto or thereabouts to Paestum.

The publication of *Paestan Pottery* brought Dale both a Fellowship (1937)
at Trinity College, where he had been a Student and Research Scholar, and a
Litt.D. from the University of New Zealand (Beazley was the assessor), the
degree which, along with his later Cambridge Litt.D., he most valued. He did
not, however, return immediately to Cambridge, for upon the resignation of
Ellis Waterhouse in June, 1936, he was appointed Librarian of the British
School at Rome, a position that he held for the next two years. His duties
involved a considerable reorganisation of the Library, but he also found time to
give lectures at the British School, the German Archaeological Institute, and

the American Academy, and to take students around the monuments of Rome and the ruins of Pompeii and Paestum, demonstrating his desire to impart something of his own fascination with the remains of classical civilisation. During the summer months he travelled extensively not only in southern Italy but on visits to museums elsewhere in Europe (Berlin, Vienna, Leningrad, Moscow). The immediate result of this activity was *Frühitaliotische Vasen*, a volume in the prestigious series *Bilder griechischer Vasen* (edited by J. D. Beazley and Paul Jacobsthal), a long essay really in which he set forth his thoughts on the early phases of Lucanian and Apulian red-figure. When the series was reprinted in the early 1970s, he insisted on revising the work, which he did while propped up in bed after a debilitating fall.

These years passed in Italy during his young manhood left an indelible impression. They not only consolidated his feeling for the country and its people, but gave him a love of good Italian food and wine (among his favourite Roman restaurants were 'Fagiano' near the Column of Marcus Aurelius, and later 'Da Giggetto' in the old Jewish quarter), and later during his Mastership he took particular care with the cuisine and the wine cellar at University House in Canberra, and even instituted a periodic Wine Symposium. These years also gave him an enduring love of Italian opera, for he heard such singers as Beniamino Gigli, Giacomo Lauri-Volpi, and Maria Caniglia in their prime; and often in later life he could be heard humming an aria as he made cold coffee for the mid-morning break in his flat at La Trobe University or walked rapidly to the mailroom.

Finally, in 1938, he resigned the post of Librarian and left Rome to take up his Fellowship in Cambridge. He might have spent his academic career there, but in the following year he was offered the opportunity of a free trip by boat to New Zealand and a visit to his parents after seven years absence. In August, while in Auckland, he unexpectedly received an invitation to apply for the Chair of Greek in the University of Sydney, which had been recently vacated by J. Enoch Powell, who had returned to England at the approach of war in Europe. He accepted the invitation, and thus, at the outbreak of the Second World War, Dale was established in Sydney. He found a suitable flat on the second floor of a building at no. 2, Penshurst Avenue, Neutral Bay, with a beautiful view over Sydney Harbour. The flat provided two bedrooms as well as a study, dining-room, and sitting-room, so he persuaded his parents to leave New Zealand in 1940 and join him in Sydney. Every weekday he would take a ferry at 8 a.m. across the Harbour, then a tram in order to arrive at the university for his first Greek class at 9 a.m.

Early in 1941, however, with the Japanese threat growing, Trendall and three other academics ('men of the professor type') from the University of Sydney (T. G. Room, Professor of Mathematics; R. J. Lyons, Senior Lecturer in Mathematics; and A. P. Treweek, Lecturer in Greek) were approached by a representative of the Chief of the Australian General Staff to see if they would be willing to help with the decoding of Japanese signals. The group got together informally to study available books on cryptography and to work on Japanese diplomatic messages supplied by the Army. During this period they succeeded in breaking the Japanese LA-code, a low-grade code used for consular messages. Room, Lyons, and Treweek moved to Melbourne the same year to join the Signals Intelligence Organisation set up by Captain Eric Nave. Trendall was transferred early in 1942, and proved to be exceptionally gifted as a cryptographer. He headed a small group working out of Victoria Barracks in St Kilda Road, a group that specialised in decrypting Japanese diplomatic signals. In later years, however, he was very reticent about this period of his life, and he was very reluctant to talk about his own accomplishments.[6]

The end of the war brought a return to regular university teaching, not just of Greek, for in 1948 the University of Sydney was persuaded to establish the first Department of Archaeology in Australia. Trendall was appointed Professor of Archaeology while retaining the Chair of Greek. In developing courses in both classical and near eastern archaeology he had the assistance of J. R. Stewart, a specialist in the archaeology of Cyprus, whom he had managed to persuade to come to Sydney in 1946 as a Teaching Fellow in History, and who was now transferred to the new department as Senior Lecturer. Trendall and Stewart had, one suspects, rather different ideas on the subject of archaeology, and both were determined individuals, but though they may have had their differences, they remained friendly until Stewart's untimely death in 1962.[7] Certainly, the new programme produced some outstanding graduates: one of the first was J. B. Hennessy, who was to continue the Australian activities in Cyprus, and eventually to succeed Stewart in the Edwin Cuthbert Hall Chair of Middle Eastern Archaeology at Sydney. On the Classical side Dale's finest pupil during these Sydney years was undoubtedly Martin Frederiksen, who went on to a distinguished career as an ancient historian at Oxford, and whose early death in 1980 he felt very deeply. Another favourite pupil of this Sydney period was Alicia Totolos, who moved to London and became the first Secretary of the Institute of Classical Studies, welcoming over the years many Commonwealth scholars 'with an openness and warmth . . . typically Australian'.[8]

---

[6] See David Jenkins, *Battle Surface! Japan's Submarine War Against Australia, 1942–44* (Sydney, 1992), pp. 42–3, 157–9.

[7] On Stewart, see R. S. Merrillees, 'Professor James R. Stewart: A Biographical Lecture', in C. A. Hope and J. K. Zimmer, eds., *Essays on Australian Contributions to the Archaeology of the Ancient Near East* (Melbourne, 1983), pp. 33–51.

[8] Address by J. R. Green at the National Gallery of Victoria, Melbourne, on 5 August 1997, launching the international appeal in aid of the A. D. Trendall Research Centre for Ancient Mediterranean Studies.

In his teaching, as in his research, Dale's passionate involvement in the study of the Classical world found an outlet. His lectures on Greek art, which were delivered three times a week and were open to all comers, were inspiring and came to enjoy a legendary renown. As one former evening student at the University of Sydney recently recalled, 'What Professor Trendall had that no other lecturer of that time seemed to have was passion. . . . If Professor Trendall had chosen to hold his lectures at midnight in the rain in the Quadrangle, he would have drawn a crowd.'[9] Even after he left teaching in Sydney for administration in Canberra, he did not lose his enjoyment in communicating his enthusiasms to both scholar and layman. Occasionally he was persuaded to give a series of lectures on Greek and Roman art: for the Department of Fine Arts at the University of Melbourne, for example, or for the Australian National University, in 1956, when there was standing-room only in the theatre and long and spontaneous applause after the last lecture, as appreciative letters to the local newspaper at the time noted.

The new courses in archaeology in Sydney after 1948 were designed to make as much use as possible of the objects in the Nicholson Museum. This museum justly bears the name of Sir Charles Nicholson, Vice-Provost and then Provost of the University of Sydney from 1854 to 1862, who donated his sizable collection of Mediterranean antiquities to the university in the enlightened belief that it would have greater impact in fostering an interest in the Classical world in Australia than in England, where such collections were not uncommon at the time. In addition to his other responsibilities, Dale was honorary curator of the Nicholson Museum, and from 1946 to 1951, with the assistance of Stewart, he concentrated upon the improvement of the display by the acquisition of new cases and the installation of better lighting, and more particularly upon increasing the number and variety of the holdings through judicious acquisitions. An Association of Friends of the Nicholson Museum was formed in 1946 'with the aims of stimulating a wider interest in the Museum and of providing additional funds for the purchase of suitable antiquities'.[10] In the years after the war it was possible to build up the collections with material not only from excavations in Cyprus and the Near East, but with many important classical objects that were obtained in Europe, relatively inexpensively, as old collections were broken up: in 1946, for example, a superb Attic Late Geometric krater from the Dipylon Workshop, and vases from the Cowdray collection; in 1947 a Chalcidian neck-amphora and three other vases from the collection of Sir Herbert Cook at Doughty House (Richmond); in 1951 the collection of Roman glass that had belonged to Professor A. B. Cook of Cambridge; and, of course, major examples of South Italian red-figure pottery (often with the help of Noël Moon). The aim was not

---

[9] *The Gazette*, University of Sydney (Dec. 1992).
[10] A. D. Trendall, 'The Nicholson Museum', *Art and Australia* (Dec. 1967), 533.

to develop a public gallery but representative collections that would be used in the teaching of the different ancient Mediterranean cultures. Many are the Australian students who have benefited from this vision.

Obviously, the years of world war had interrupted Dale's research into South Italian pottery. In fact, after 1939, when he arrived in Sydney, he was not able to return to Europe until the end of 1950, although he did visit New Zealand in 1947 (when he discovered a lost red-figured cup by Douris in the Canterbury Museum in Christchurch),[11] and again in August 1949, when he stayed at Selwyn College in Dunedin while studying the Greek pottery in the Otago Museum. Not only was travel difficult, but few new publications were available. In later life he was somewhat sensitive about this 'lost' decade in his scholarly achievement. Yet the period was by no means unfruitful, for not only did he prepare a guide to the casts of Greek and Roman sculpture in the Nicholson Museum (now the only witness to that collection), but he edited and partly wrote the basic Handbook to the museum. Moreover, the second edition of this Handbook, produced in 1948 in collaboration with J. R. Stewart, was well received internationally, providing an excellent introduction to the art and archaeology of the Near East and the Classical World.

Late in 1950 Dale was free, however, to return to a war-ravaged Europe. In December he was in Rome, staying at the British School, now under the able direction of J. B. Ward-Perkins, whom he had met in the 1930s and who remained a life-long friend. His presence in Rome and the completed reinstallation of the vases in Sala VIII of the Museo Gregoriano Etrusco led to the invitation to publish the South Italian and Etruscan red-figure vases in the Vatican. The resulting catalogue, written in elegant Italian, appeared in two monumental volumes in 1953 and 1955:[12] not only does it provide a definitive classification, but its introductory sections on the various styles may still be consulted with great profit. At this time he was also concerned about a possible move from Sydney to Cambridge, for he was among those being considered for the Chair of Archaeology, recently vacated by A. W. Lawrence. In the event, the Electors chose Jocelyn Toynbee. This was not a great disappointment, for Dale was in fact reluctant to leave Sydney, partly because he had devoted much effort to building up Classical art and archaeology there, but also because his parents were now aged and his mother particularly in poor health.

This first post-war trip lasted until January, 1952, and was the longest of any he undertook, involving visits to sites and museums in Greece, the Near East, North Africa, as well as collections in England, France, and America, for

[11] His satisfaction at this unexpected discovery is expressed in 'Attic Vases in Australia and New Zealand', *Journal of Hellenic Studies*, 71 (1951), 178–93 at 186.
[12] A. D. Trendall, *Vasi antichi dipinti del Vaticano: Vasi italioti ed etruschi a figure rosse*, vols. I–II (Città del Vaticano, 1953–5).

he was very aware of the gaps in his knowledge. From this time until increasing age brought a halt to his travels in 1990 he made annual pilgrimages to Europe, with frequent visits to the United States. Indeed, he estimated that he had travelled some 25 times around the world. And in Italy he came to be referred to as 'archeologo volante' and 'rondine d'inverno'. These journeys often lasted three or four months, normally somewhere between October and May, so that he could avoid the heat of an Australian summer and, in later years, also avoid the beginning of the academic year in March. They were stimulated not only by a love of travel, but also by a strongly-held belief that it was imperative to examine, at first hand, as many vases as possible, and that to rely, particularly in matters of style, solely on photographs or illustrations was inadequate and potentially misleading.

For many years he sojourned regularly in London, enjoying the hospitality of the Principal of London University, Sir Douglas Logan, and of Lady Logan at their residence in Gordon Square. He developed a warm friendship with T. B. L. Webster, and his admiration for the scholar and the man will be evident to all who read the summary of the memorial lecture he gave in December, 1974.[13] Their mutual concern with Greek drama led to their collaboration on *Illustrations of Greek Drama*, published in 1971, a work that examined pictures on Archaic and Classical vases that seemed to illustrate (but not 'represent') moments in Greek plays. Although not pioneering, the book helped to spawn a lively (and continuing) debate on the possible influence of drama on representations in Greek art. Trendall was also a fervent supporter of Webster's brainchild, the Institute of Classical Studies, and over the years he is said to have given some twenty lectures and seminars at the Institute, presenting his latest researches and new South Italian vases.

In October, 1953, he was invited to become the first Master of University House at the Australian National University in Canberra. This was an inspired choice, but it is not entirely clear why he accepted. He had served as Acting Vice-Chancellor during that year with considerable aplomb, and he seems to have acquired a certain taste for administration. He seems also to have felt that he had achieved his main goals at Sydney University, and, after fifteen years in Sydney, he perhaps realised that he needed a different challenge and a change of scene (especially after his mother's death early in 1954). In any event he took up his new position in April of the following year. The task before him was formidable. University House had been newly built to be the graduate residence of the university, to provide a centre for university staff and to represent, in a sense, the university to the general community in Canberra. 'The Master, in short, had to be a distinguished scholar and man of affairs, an

---

[13] 'T. B. L. Webster Memorial Lecture', *Bulletin of the Institute of Classical Studies*, 21 (1974), 1–2.

official public relations officer and the proprietor of what, in law, was a common boarding house.'[14] It is perhaps not surprising that he should have been successful in juggling the diverse demands of his new position, for at Sydney from 1947 to 1950 he had acted as Dean of the Faculty of Arts and Chairman of the Professorial Board, while still teaching his normal complement of courses. Dale remained for fifteen years as Master of University House, and with his urbanity, cultivated taste and 'fine Italian hand', guided the fledgling institution through the difficult early years and gave it a distinctive style which, despite many forced changes, has not entirely disappeared.

His position as Master, and as Deputy Vice-Chancellor (1958–64) of the Australian National University, brought him to the notice of many influential people, foremost of whom was the Prime Minister, R. G. Menzies. These relationships in turn led to new responsibilities. For example, in 1961 he was appointed Chairman of the Interim Council of what was to become (1964) the Australian Institute of Aboriginal (later Aboriginal and Torres Strait Islander) Studies, and he continued in this position until 1966, thus playing a prominent role in its early development. Again, in 1955 he served on the three-member Royal Commission instituted to examine the discontent at the University of Tasmania. The final report of the Commission criticised in diplomatic language the governance of the university, and made important recommendations, though unfortunately these were only implemented in part. Had they been fully instituted subsequent events (including the dismissal of the Professor of Philosophy, S. S. Orr, which precipitated one of the most extraordinary cases in Australian academic history) might have been handled very differently.[15] But perhaps Trendall's most significant influence was felt in the formulation of educational policy, particularly in the area of Higher Education, an influence achieved both informally through his friendship with Menzies and formally through his membership, from 1959 to 1970, of the Australian Universities Commission.

Since he felt keenly the need for an Australian equivalent of the British Academy, which would represent the humanities to the Commonwealth Government and to the community generally, he was prominent, as a Foundation Fellow and inaugural Chairman, in the establishment of the Australian Humanities Research Council, which in 1969 became the Australian Academy of the Humanities. Indeed, he delivered the Inaugural Address at the first annual meeting of the Research Council in November, 1957, and again in May, 1979, to commemorate the first decade of the Academy.

[14] Francis West, *University House, Portrait of an Institution* (Canberra, 1980), p. 21.
[15] See Richard Davis, *Open to Talent: The Centenary History of the University of Tasmania, 1890–1990* (1990), esp. chapter 5. For the Orr case, see most recently C. Pybus, *Gross Moral Turpitude* (1993).

Despite the heavy demands of academic administration Trendall found time to continue his research. When he began his study of South Italian red-figure in the 1930s he concentrated upon Paestan, numerically the smallest of the local South Italian fabrics, but during the 1950s and 1960s he moved on to the larger and more complex task of differentiating the red-figure pottery of Lucania, Sicily, and Campania, and of identifying the individual painters. A series of articles devoted to particular artists culminated in two volumes that have become the *locus classicus* on the subject. *The Red-figured Vases of Lucania, Campania and Sicily* was published at Oxford in 1967, with supplementary volumes appearing in 1970, 1973, and 1983. Though based, in the case of Lucanian, upon the preliminary work of Noël Moon and, in the case of Campanian, upon a fundamental article by J. D. Beazley, these volumes go far beyond what had previously been attempted: the basic development of painted pottery in the three regions over some 150 years is set forth and analysed through the study of some 6500 vases and 250 painters or stylistic groups.

The work of Beazley on Athenian black- and red-figure vases, and of Trendall on the comparable South Italian red-figure inevitably suggests a comparison. Although Trendall readily adopted Beazley's methodology for the study of figured vases, the resulting monographs are rather different. Beazley's major catalogues are austere, with little explanation provided and no illustrations; and his detailed comments must be sought elsewhere, in his basic articles and general books. Trendall's principal publications include similar lists of vases arranged according to painters and stylistic groups, but each catalogue is preceded by a general commentary, often lengthy, on typical features of style, and on interesting points in the iconography or vase shapes. Since there are always copious illustrations, the reader is readily able to gain some understanding of the characteristics of a painter or group, and of the reasons for Trendall's attributions.

He also took on at this time the arduous task of preparing approximately every three years a report on recent archaeological activity in South Italy and Sicily for the British publication *Archaeological Reports*. The first instalment appeared in 1955, the last in 1973. These reports remain important sources for excavations that have been only partially published or not published at all. Dale was very pleased when Martin Fredericksen agreed to carry on the series.

His friendship with (Sir) Joseph Burke, the first Herald Professor of Fine Art in the University of Melbourne, gave him an introduction to (Sir) Daryl Lindsay, Director of the National Gallery of Victoria from 1941 to 1955, and to Lindsay's successor, Dr Eric Westbrook. With Lindsay's support the Trustees of the munificent Felton Bequest were persuaded to devote considerable funds to the creation of a representative collection of Greek vases of high quality.[16] The first two vases, which arrived in 1956, were outstanding choices:

---

[16] For Trendall's role, see Ursula Hoff, *Art Bulletin of Victoria*, 36 (1995), 61.

an Attic black-figure amphora near in style to the great master Exekias; and a Chalcidian black-figure psykter-amphora, a unique piece, that remains the finest Greek vase in Australia. As Honorary Consultant of the National Gallery from 1956 to 1992 Trendall oversaw the continued growth of this distinguished collection of vases and wrote the popular guide. He had, of course, always believed in the necessity of establishing collections of Classical antiquities as an important aid in promoting an understanding of ancient Mediterranean culture, particularly in Australia and New Zealand, which were geographically far from the centres of Classical civilisation, and he was ever on the lookout for opportunities. In 1948, for example, he had been largely responsible for the acquisition by the Otago Museum in Dunedin of a large part of the A. B. Cook collection. And when in 1957 Canterbury University College (now the University of Canterbury) in Christchurch received a gift of Greek vases in memory of James Logie, who had been Registrar, Trendall was consulted over the purchase, and invited to write the catalogue, which eventually appeared in 1971 as *Greek Vases in the Logie Collection*. Today some eleven universities in Australia have teaching collections of Classical antiquities: they are a tribute to Trendall's astute advice and judicious encouragement.[17]

In March, 1969, Dale retired as Master of University House. He had lived in Canberra for fifteen years, just as he had spent fifteen years in Sydney. He had foreseen for some time that, for economic reasons, changes would be necessary in the running of University House, changes which would be more easily instituted by a new Master. Moreover, he wished to devote all his remaining years and energy to scholarship, free from administrative obliga-tions. He considered retirement to England or Italy, where he would be closer to colleagues and collections, but he felt that he could do more in the Antipodes, where he had after all been born, to further the development of Classical studies. Thus when he was invited to become the first Resident Fellow at La Trobe University, a university newly established at Bundoora on the northern outskirts of Melbourne, he accepted. His 'retirement' at La Trobe was to last more than a quarter of a century. As Resident Fellow of the university he was given a flat that he had a hand in designing on the top floor of the south wing of Menzies College. This flat provided living quarters for himself, and room for the great personal library and photographic archive (some 40,000 photographs at the time of his death), which he had assiduously accumulated over a working lifetime as an essential tool of his research (eventually bequeathed to the university as the basis for a research centre). It also provided a small balcony or solarium where after the day's work he

---

[17] An account of these university collections is given by Trendall himself in *Twenty Years of Progress in Classical Archaeology* (Sydney, 1979).

would often sit talking with friends over a glass of sherry, or watching the glorious sunsets or the grey herons nesting in the great gum nearby.

Though he occasionally chaired a committee, provided advice to the university authorities, or gave a course of lectures or a graduation address, these years were notable principally for his scholarly accomplishments. A steady stream of books and articles appeared. After his definitive study of Lucanian, Campanian, and Sicilian red-figure, he turned his attention to the vase production of ancient Taras (Taranto) and Apulia, the last and most prolific of the South Italian fabrics. In this he was fortunate to have the collaboration of Alexander Cambitoglou, who had first met Trendall in 1951 and took up a post at the University of Sydney in 1961 with Trendall's encouragement. In this same year they published a joint study of the earlier phases of Apulian, entitled *Apulian Red-figured Vase-painters of the Plain Style*, but this was to prove only a preliminary to the main work, *The Red-figured Vases of Apulia*, which was issued by the Clarendon Press in 1978 and 1982. In three volumes, incorporating some 1300 pages and 400 plates, perhaps 10,000 vases are assembled and attributed to about 370 painters and groups, thereby providing the first comprehensive treatment of the subject. But as with Trendall's earlier works its usefulness does not cease with this classification, for the volumes are a treasure of knowledge, accumulated over many decades, on the style, subjects, shapes, and chronology of the red-figure vases of Apulia. It is certainly a *'monumentum aere perennius'*, unparalleled in the archaeology of Magna Graecia. When one examines these volumes, it is hard to believe that any individual will ever study as many South Italian vases as Trendall, or 'know' them so thoroughly.

The final decade of his scholarly activity was given over to two supplements (1983 and 1991–2) to the main volumes on Apulian pottery, to a work on Greek red-figure fish-plates, and most usefully to a popular handbook (*Red Figure Vases of South Italy and Sicily*, 1989), in which he attempted to condense a lifetime's research.

But it would be wrong to believe that his influence during his years at La Trobe University was confined solely, or even most significantly, to his scholarship, for he made friends readily, especially among the young, and his door gave entry to a new and wonderful world to many students of the university and particularly to residents of Menzies College. Those who ventured into his lair discovered someone not only distinguished in his chosen field but deeply cultured and humane, with a lightning wit; someone too who was genuinely young at heart and concerned about their problems. Thus he was consulted as some wise, old uncle, and his influence on many young lives was quite profound. And in his last illness it was particularly these young friends who provided the most support. In the late 1980s he developed diabetes, which affected his eyesight. He endured two operations, but his sight did not improve. Late in 1992 he began to have a problem with his heart, which was stabilised, but increasing frailty eventually forced him to move into a home for the aged. He was much assisted during this difficult time by an old friend, Dr Kel Semmens, and through the devoted assistance of two other friends he continued to come to La Trobe two or three days a week to answer correspondence. In 1995 he suffered a number of small strokes, and died on 13 November. He never married.

Trendall was a man of medium height, with thinning hair, fine and silvery, in later life. All his movements were quick, his eyes sparkled with intelligence, and a mischievous smile often lit up his face. He could be demanding, and he could put his scholarly opinions eloquently and passionately. To some he could seem at times intimidating, but to those who knew him well he was a man of great charm and humanity. As John Boardman has remarked: 'his company and conversation shimmered with his delight in his work and in the world around him'.[18] In addition to his sharp mind, he possessed a slightly perverse sense of humour, which not infrequently emerged in his writing. For example, in one of his major works, *The Red-figured Vases of Campania, Lucania and Sicily*, page 569, after dealing with a dreary series of Campanian red-figure vases ornamented entirely with female heads, he remarks: 'The pink-cheeked faces which decorate these vases . . . are among the last manifestations of the r.f. style and point to the fulfilment of Katisha's prophecy in the *Mikado*:

> Thy doom is nigh
> Pink cheek, bright eye.'

There are many stories recounted that exemplify his quick and subtle wit. One of the most famous concerns an occasion during his years in Canberra, when he was asked to provide a name with a classical flavour for the new police-boat that was about to be launched on Lake Burley Griffin. Without hesitation he suggested 'Platypus', which was enthusiastically accepted as a very suitable Australian name. He did not, however, mention that the literal meaning of the Greek word, 'flatfoot', was no less appropriate. On another occasion, some time during the 1960s, after dinner at University House, a small group was discussing a suitable motto for the new (and costly) National Library, an enterprise that had been realised largely through the efforts of Sir Harold White and Sir Archibald Grenfell Price. During the conversation Trendall was heard to remark: 'alba, sed non sine pretio'.

He possessed a strong sense of duty and an unusual power of concentration and discipline. Even in later years he would rise early and work until five or six in the evening, often seven days a week. He was punctilious about answering any letters (and he did this by hand) as soon as possible—something that was

---

[18] Obituary in *The Independent*, 25 Nov. 1995.

not always easy given the number (the record in my time was some fifty items in one day), and his replies to queries about vases sometimes amounted almost to mini disquisitions.

Many honours, academic and public, came to him during a long life. In 1976 he was made a Companion of the Order of Australia (AC), the highest honour that his adopted country can bestow. In England he was elected Fellow of the Society of Antiquaries in 1939, and in 1968 Fellow of the British Academy,[19] of which he was awarded the Kenyon Medal in 1983. In Italy, too, his work was recognised. He was made a Commendatore dell'Ordine al Merito of Italy (1965), and also Commendatore dell'Ordine di S. Gregorio Magno (1956), a signal honour from the Vatican to someone who was not Catholic. He was particularly proud that, in 1973, he was elected a Foreign Member of the Accademia dei Lincei, and a Corresponding Member (later Honorary Fellow) of the Pontificia Accademia Romana di Archeologia. In 1971 he received the Galileo Galilei Prize from Italian Rotary, a gold statuette by Emilio Greco, which he later donated to the National Gallery of Victoria.

Dale Trendall believed absolutely in the value and joy of knowledge, and in the sharing of that knowledge with all who would listen. He was as much at home with the brash undergraduate as with the eminent scholar.

IAN McPHEE
La Trobe University

Note. Dale Trendall very deliberately left few personal papers, so this brief memoir is largely based upon our discussions during the last twenty years of his life. But I am especially grateful to Miss M. K. Steven and to Sir John Boardman for their comments. I am also indebted for recollections to the following: Ruth Carington Smith, Bill Grainger, Dick Green, Elizabeth Pemberton, Con Slump, Alicia Totolos. For his years in Rome, I have consulted: T. P. Wiseman, *A Short History of the British School at Rome* (1990), and the *Reports* of the British School for the years 1933–9. For his Canberra years, see Francis West, *University House: Portrait of an Institution* (1980).

[19] He was elected an Ordinary Fellow of the Academy, at a time when scholars from Commonwealth countries were still eligible.

VERONICA WEDGWOOD

Cicely Veronica Wedgwood
1910–1997

FEW BRITISH HISTORIANS IN THE TWENTIETH CENTURY have commanded so wide a readership as Dame Veronica Wedgwood and few have enjoyed so fully the admiration of both the general reader and the academic community—even though some of the latter were slow to recognise her true quality. All through her working life she wrote out of an intense enthusiasm for her subject and a compelling desire to communicate it to as broad a public as possible. Her love of it was kindled by her first history lesson (how many of us can say that?). 'I was six', she recalled; 'a world of inexhaustible possibilities opened before me—real people, real things that had really happened to them.' On the walk home from school that day she was frustrated at failing to get her nurse to share her passionate interest in Caradoc's confrontation with Caesar.[1]

Her next major discovery was that the past was accessible through the actual words written or spoken by men and women long departed, and through their records of their transactions, some preserved in printed books, many still awaiting the excitement of discovery in archives. Original sources possessed a unique excitement for her; even in earliest adolescence a vast History of England was taking shape in a growing pile of pencil-written 200-page pads. She took so much pleasure in self-expression, and wrote so swiftly and naturally that she was clearly born to be a writer; three novels and a play were among her early juvenilia. But she found her real *métier* in making sense of the immediate records of the past, and much as she enjoyed telling a story it was more satisfying to her, from quite an early age, when it was a true story about real people. Later, when she had polished her literary skill to a

---

[1] 'The velvet study', in *History and Hope: The Collected Essays of C. V. Wedgwood* (1987), p. 12.

*Proceedings of the British Academy, * **97**, 521–534. © The British Academy 1998.

pitch rare indeed among modern historians, narrative remained her supreme
gift, and it has won many readers to a love of history. Conrad Russell has
recorded how, at the age of eight, he took her *William the Silent* from his
parents' bookshelves—the first history book he had ever read—and found that
once embarked on it he could not put it down.[2] Sir Roy Strong and John
Morrill too have testified to the part that her books played in awaking a passion
for history in them.

Cicely Veronica Wedgwood was born on 20 July 1910 at Stocksfield in
Northumberland. Her father, Sir Ralph Wedgwood Bt, was for sixteen years
chief general manager of the London and North Eastern Railway. She must
have been one of the last survivors of those proprietary days to hold a free
railway pass, which was a blessing to impecunious student history societies, to
whose invitations to lecture she responded generously. Her mother Iris
(*née* Pawson) was a novelist and travel-writer, and she was the great-
great-great-granddaughter of Josiah Wedgwood the potter; her brother was
deputy chairman of the family firm until 1966. Hers was a rich cultural background. Ralph Vaughan Williams was her father's cousin and dedicated his
London Symphony to him, and she herself formed an enduring love of music
and opera. History was in her genes, as well as the urge to write, for her
uncle Josiah Wedgwood MP (later Baron Wedgwood) found time among his
multifarious activities and interests to play the chief part in founding the
official *History of Parliament* and to write its first two published volumes.
Veronica helped him with that work, and later made one of her rare
departures from early modern history, art, and literature in order to write
his biography.

She grew up in London, and after early years at Norland Place School in
Holland Park Avenue she was educated privately by governesses under the
loving and enlightened supervision of her parents. She became particularly
devoted to one governess, a Swiss lady who nurtured not only her love of
history but her natural skill in languages. She thought of herself in retrospect as
'a cross, difficult, lumpish child',[3] but a child whose father sought to curb her
runaway pen by advising her to write history, and for whom a birthday present
of Gibbon's *Decline and Fall* proved to be an intellectual landmark, was no
ordinary pupil. In due course, after short spells at the Sorbonne in Paris and
with a German family in Bonn, she went up to Lady Margaret Hall, Oxford,
where she graduated with first class honours in Modern History. Unusually she
opted to submit a BA thesis, and it sealed her success. A. L. Rowse was one of
her tutors, and he remembered her as his first outstanding pupil. It is interesting
to speculate on where her next steps might have taken her if it had been as

[2] Conrad Russell, 'C. V. Wedgwood', broadcast talk on BBC Radio Three, 8 August 1995.
[3] 'The velvet study', p. 14.

normal then as it is now to proceed from a distinguished first degree to supervised research directed at a higher one. She would probably not have taken that course, for her vocation was to become a writer rather than a teacher, and for the kind of writing she had in mind, scholarly and disciplined though it was, the formal training of a D.Phil. was not necessary. Then and later an academic career was open to her, but she decided against it. She wanted more independence than a heavy and regular load of teaching would have allowed her; and for all her gift for friendship she was at the core a reserved and private person whom the collegiate life might not have suited. She did some tutoring at Somerville, but she soon left Oxford and went to live in Bloomsbury.

Literary work with a flexible time-table went better with her commitment as a writer than fixed hours of lectures, seminars, and tutorials would have done, but she worked very hard all the same. She undertook various editorial tasks for Jonathan Cape, but her main employment was with Lady Rhondda's weekly periodical *Time and Tide*. The volatile Lady Rhondda, who exhausted her personal fortune in keeping it afloat, was a notoriously difficult person to work for, and Veronica was dismayed at being designated her successor when she died in 1958. She strove very hard, though in the end unsuccessfully, to keep the debt-ridden paper going. But though she wrote many pieces for *Time and Tide* and devoted considerable time to it, she can never have thought of it as her main occupation. Only four years after graduating she published *Strafford*, her first book—and that was after a considerable amount of rewriting under the guidance of J. E. (later Professor Sir John) Neale, who gave her much valued advice on its structure. *Strafford* had an immediate success both with professional historians and with the broad reading public, and it deserved it, for it was not only beautifully written, with a profound sympathy for its subject, but it was based on a wider range of sources than any previous biographer had used, including the important Fitzwilliam manuscripts. The book was essentially a vindication of a man towards whom the whig historians had shown a hostile bias; Veronica responded warmly to Strafford's undoubted idealism, his strong affections and loyalties, his belief in order and authority when both were being unworthily undermined, and his devotion to the hard work of administration amidst a regime in which 'the Lady Mora' too often held sway. But she gradually came to see that she had taken him too much at his own valuation. Partly because of the new accessibility after the last war of many unpublished Wentworth family papers, and partly through the work of her fellow-historians J. P. Cooper, Hugh Kearney, and Gerald Aylmer, she came to appreciate that she had underestimated the scale on which Strafford had enriched himself in the public service, the unscrupulous nature of the means whereby he had done so, and the ruthlessness with which he had pursued and brought down his political opponents. With typical intellectual honesty she decided to revise her whole appraisal of him. It was not only fresh documentary evidence, convincing new work by fellow-scholars and a maturer knowledge of the ways of the world that led her to so. During the quarter century between the writing of her first book and of her second, the world experienced most of what was worst of both fascist and communist dictatorship, and most westerners (hard-line ideologues excepted) adopted a far more critical stance towards unbridled self-aggrandisement, a cavalier attitude to due legal process, and the sacrifice of the rights of individuals to the supposed interests of the state. There were many refugees in England after the war, the victims of totalitarianism, and Veronica took a strong interest in their plight. She helped many of them privately, and from 1950 served on a committee 'to inquire into cases of deprivation of British citizenship'.

So when *Thomas Wentworth First Earl of Strafford 1593–1641: A Revaluation* appeared in 1961 it was not so much a revision as a new book, despite its incorporation of much from the earlier one. As well as being considerably longer, it is more nuanced, better-balanced, and surer-footed amongst the tangles and intrigues of Caroline politics. Strafford emerges as an altogether more complex and interesting figure than in the first version, his failings faithfully acknowledged but his finer qualities and ideals justly appraised. His worst faults, as she sees them, were his inordinate ambition and his lack of judgement in human relationships; his final tragedy was to a great extent of his own making. In the latter respect he had much in common with his master, about whom she was to write so affectingly in *The Trial of Charles I.* Her concluding assessment of Strafford is no less moving, as well as penetrating, and it crowns one of the classic biographies of an early modern statesman.

Both *Strafford* and *Thomas Wentworth* were dedicated 'To A. H. P.', in the latter case to his memory. He was Veronica's maternal grandfather, Albert Henry Pawson, 'whose love, wisdom and knowledge [she wrote in the later book] had surrounded my childhood'. 'Understandest thou what thou readest?' he had asked her teasingly when she first immersed herself in Gibbon.[4] It is good that he lived long enough to be abundantly answered.

Only three years after *Strafford*, and when still only twenty-eight years old, she published one of her longest and most ambitious books, *The Thirty Years War*. It was and always will be a daunting subject—daunting in the inescapable density of its detail, in the complexity of its diplomatic history and its military campaigns, above all in the mass and variety of sources that need to be mastered if the treatment of it is to have any claim to authority and originality, as Veronica's most decidedly has. She possessed the linguistic equipment, as well as the scholar's judgement and the sheer industry required, for she was

---

[4] 'The velvet study', p. 16.

fluent in French and German and could read Spanish, Italian, Dutch, and Swedish. She achieved not only an original and independent synthesis, but she presented the war (or wars) with a structural lucidity and a narrative gift for which two generations of students and teachers have blessed her. She has been criticised for seeing the war as 'essentially a German conflict' and underplaying the involvement of the Scandinavian and western powers, and also for overstating its ultimately negative character: 'the outstanding example in European history of meaningless conflict', she called it in conclusion.[5] Perhaps her view of it was darkened by the looming shadow of another German war. At any rate the critic whom I have cited described her book as nevertheless a classic, and so it is.

Only a year after the publication of *The Thirty Years War* she fulfilled a commission to contribute a short biography of *Oliver Cromwell* to the Brief Lives series. Its modest scale precluded any real originality, but it was well done, and worth the revision and augmentation to which she treated it for a new edition in 1973. Her main labour during the darker years of the Second World War was devoted to *William the Silent* (1944), which ranks as one of her major (as well as most popular) achievements and won her the James Tait Black prize. It remains as exciting as the youthful Conrad Russell found it, and it does full justice to a heroic subject. It is grounded in a thorough knowledge of the complex politics of Spain, the Low Countries and western Europe generally, and it has introduced thousands of English-speaking readers to the story of the revolt of the Netherlands. Although it is inevitably subject to the limitations of a biographical approach to so large a historical theme, its narrative drive is as strong as in any of her works. Occasionally, as in *Strafford*, its very real eloquence tips over into eulogy (at least for this reader), and though William was a far less flawed character than Wentworth, the even finer studies that were still to come would be the more compelling for their relative restraint.

Veronica was by this time much in demand as a reviewer, and this and her editorial work were not the only demands on her time, for she was a skilled translator. Her English version of Karl Brandi's massive *The Emperor Charles V* appeared in 1939, and that of Elias Canetti's *Die Blendung*, likewise translated from the German, and published in England as *Auto-da-Fé*, in 1946. In the latter year she also brought out *Velvet Studies: Essays on Historical and Other Subjects*. She was a most polished essayist, whether on the scale of a brief editorial or a full-blown article. Some of these pieces, perhaps most memorably 'Cavalier poetry and Cavalier politics', reflected her strong interest in seventeenth-century literature, especially where it inter-

---

[5] Geoffrey Parker, *The Thirty Years War* (1984), pp. xv, 216–17; C. V. Wedgwood, *The Thirty Years War* (1938), p. 526.

reacted with contemporary political issues. Others like 'Two painters' (Van Dyck and William Dobson) bore witness to her abiding love of the fine arts, which early visits with her father or maternal grandfather to the great art collections in continental Europe had awoken, and which the many hours she spent in the National Gallery and other great collections at home and abroad had constantly kept alive. At least three substantial articles signalled a preoccupation with the English Civil War, for she was already laying the foundations of her major work on the Great Rebellion. She garnered a later harvest of essays and addresses in *Truth and Opinion* (1960), and she republished what she wanted to save of both collections, along with some later articles and talks, in *History and Hope* (1987). Some of these papers convey an idea of her qualities as a lecturer: lucid, shapely, beautifully turned, with an easy command of the listener's attention, but modest and unrhetorical. A few contain some of her rare and brief snatches of autobiography, and some of the most absorbing are those in which she speaks of her own craft. One of the most memorable of the latter is 'A sense of the past', which originated in 1957 as the first Leslie Stephen Lecture (at Cambridge) to be given by a woman.

Meanwhile in 1949 she contributed a short book on *Richelieu and the French Monarchy* to the Teach Yourself History series edited by her old tutor and now close friend A. L. Rowse, and in the following year a survey of *Seventeenth Century English Literature* to the Oxford University Press's Home University Library. The former was a typically stimulating and judicious text for students of all ages, the latter a triumph of lucid compression that at the same time succeeds in communicating some of her own enthusiasms. She was publishing a book a year at this stage, for *The Last of the Radicals*, her biography of her uncle Josiah, came out in 1951, and *Montrose* (in the Brief Lives series) in 1952. Both are written with affection, but in *Montrose* she resists any temptation to over-romanticise a temptingly romantic subject and places the man and his exploits firmly in their historic context.

By this time she had won not only a national but an international reputation. *William the Silent* was translated into Swedish in 1946, French and Dutch in 1947 and German somewhat later. With characteristic generosity she donated her early royalties to the relief of Dutch victims of the German occupation, and Queen Juliana admitted her to the Order of Orange Nassau in 1946. *The Thirty Years War* was also widely translated and enjoyed a particular success in Germany, whence she received the Goethe Medal in 1958. At home she was elected a Fellow of the Royal Society of Literature in 1947. Her standing in both literary and historical circles was bringing her not only recognition but responsibilities, which she shouldered gladly and always took seriously. The hard work that she did for the English Centre of International PEN led to her being made its President from 1951 to 1957. She was also President of the English Association in 1955–6, and of the Society of

Authors from 1972 to 1977. For twenty-five years, starting in 1953, she was a member of the Royal Commission on Historical Manuscripts. She served with a special enjoyment two terms as a Trustee of the National Gallery, from 1962 to 1968 and from 1969 to 1976, and she was on the Advisory Committee of the Victoria and Albert Museum from 1960 to 1969.

She was appointed CBE in 1956, and she became Dame Veronica when she was raised to DBE in 1968. Her public honours were crowned when she was admitted to the Order of Merit in 1969, and she was its senior non-royal member when she died. Lady Margaret Hall made her an Honorary Fellow in 1962, and in the same year she accepted an appointment as Special Lecturer in University College London. Only the British Academy was conspicuously slow in recognising her achievement, for it did not elect her a Fellow until 1975. An attempt to explain (though not to excuse) that delay will be made shortly. Recognition in the United States was signalled, though not for the first time, by her membership from 1953 to 1968 of the Institute of Advanced Studies at Princeton, which offered her blessed spells of uninterrupted research and writing. In America she was also elected an honorary member of the Academy of Arts and Letters, the Academy of Arts and Sciences, the American Historical Society, and the American Philosophical Society. Harvard and Oxford are among the many universities on both sides of the Atlantic which conferred honorary degrees on her.

In 1955 she published the first instalment of what she probably intended to be her magnum opus, though she was far too modest to use such a term about her own work. She planned to write at least three volumes with the general title of *The Great Rebellion*, spanning the whole period of upheaval in Britain from the initial Scottish revolt to the Restoration. The first volume was called *The King's Peace 1637–1641*, and it displays her artistry at its height. It begins with a memorable picture of Charles I's dominions and peoples on the eve of the troubles, and of the king and the minister who strove to rule them. It is not the sort of account that a professional social or political historian would have written, but it is valid (as well as vivid) in its own right. The book is dedicated to G. M. Trevelyan and it is written in his tradition, combining strict scholarship with a keen awareness of the interests of the general reader, though Veronica excels him here in literary grace, while probing the sources at least as deeply. Her narrative flair takes wing with the National Covenant and the Scottish wars, and the dramatis personae of 1640–1 are superbly delineated.

Three years later came the second volume in the work, *The King's War 1641–1647*, a fully worthy successor to the first, and incidentally by some way her longest book. It was ahead of its time in the skill and care with which it counterpointed English and Scottish history; Veronica would have been amused by the current insistence that Britain was involved in 'a war of three kingdoms', as though this was a new discovery. She showed as sure a touch in describing military campaigns and battles as in unfolding the political developments, but that came as no surprise. She had long enjoyed walking over battlefields and reconstructing for herself the manoeuvres of armies over them, and as early as 1945 she had written a perceptive paper on 'The Strategy of the Great Civil War'.[6] I vividly remember taking part with her and Norman Gibbs in a BBC radio feature of the early 1960s on the battle of Marston Moor, in which we recorded our descriptions together on the field itself and then discussed the engagement and its consequences in the studio. Her knowledge and judgement in matters military were impressive, but it is her imaginative grasp of what it was like to come to push of pike or sustain a cavalry charge that carries the reader through the detailed story of the wars.

In the reviews of these two volumes, many academic historians as well as literary critics recognised their high artistry and their true scholarship. Yet in academic circles generally they were received with a certain reservation. Veronica's way of writing history was out of fashion in academe during most of her writing career. University historians in Britain, continental Europe, and America mostly felt their main task to be to search for comprehensive explanations of large-scale developments which transcended the personal and the contingent, and the kind of explanation that they most favoured was the economic. What Veronica, with centuries of precedent to justify her, called the Great Rebellion had become the English Revolution, and it was almost a dogma that real revolutions are by definition social revolutions. For a generation and more after the Second World War, Marx's model of historical causation was immensely influential, and even those who reacted against Marx tended to proffer an alternative that was equally deterministic: witness the controversy in the English-speaking world as to whether the driving force behind the English Revolution lay in the rising gentry or the declining gentry. There was also a cult of the quantifiable—'cliometrics' or 'serial history'— which yielded and continues to yield valuable results, but becomes excessive when it depreciates the study of historical phenonema which cannot be precisely measured. Another powerful influence was that of the *Annales* school, with its emphasis on structures and trends rather than particular events, its concentration on the *longue durée*, and its elevation of analysis over narrative. No serious historian, least of all Veronica, would deny that the contributors to *Annales* widened the scope of historical enquiry very significantly, or that the major works of Fernand Braudel and Emmanuel Le Roy Ladurie, to name only two, are masterpieces. But the school's relegation of traditional political narrative to an inferior category of *histoire événementielle* was a typical piece of Gallic intellectual arrogance, and in late years there has been a wholesome reaction against it. So there has against a less reputable assumption, mainly unspoken, that professional (i.e. academic) historians should communicate in a

[6] Reprinted in *History and Hope*, pp. 122–5.

language and vocabulary intelligible only to their fellow-workers at the coal-face of specialised research, or at least only to serious students. A certain tendency to look down on 'fine writing' is, one hopes, a thing of the past.

Veronica was of course fully aware of the great debates over historical causation and over the historian's proper task, and she was by no means indifferent to them. For a while after graduating she was a member of R. H. Tawney's economic history seminar at the Institute of Historical Research. Of theories of history, she wrote in 1946,

> I have had many, even for some years the theory that in the interests of scholarship it is wrong to write history comprehensible to the ordinary reader, since all history so written must necessarily be modified and therefore incorrect. This was I think too much against my nature to have held me long.[7]

We can only be thankful that she had the strength of mind to follow her bent and practise her craft in the manner for which she was supremely gifted. History for her could never be just the preserve of specialists, because a knowledge of the past is something to be desired by all readers with an intelligent interest in the human condition. What moved her most to write was a desire to convey her own feeling and excitement over past events to those who had not the time or the skill to gather their knowledge of them, as she did, from the original sources, and to convey it in the form of a narrative. Most people who read history for pleasure and instruction have come to love the subject through books of the kind at which she excelled; some knowledge of *what* happened in the past normally precedes a deeper curiosity as to *why* it happened, and how it fits into a larger pattern of historical development. But she was very much more than a *vulgarisatrice*, and she was not always given due credit for the thoroughness with which she studied her sources or the many new insights she derived from them.

She never claimed that her own manner of writing history was superior to that of others, or that it answered all the questions that a reader might put to the past. Questions of long-term causation and *les grands courants de l'histoire universelle* were not her *métier*, but she did not consider them unimportant. Her understandable revulsion against the dogmatism and bad manners that some academic historians were displaying in the so-called gentry controversy led her to pass over the interesting social and regional differences in the pattern of allegiance in the Civil War; indeed she is distinctly thin on the question of why people of all ranks chose to side with king or parliament, or did their best to avoid committing themselves. But her own justification of her method deserves to be read, in the introductions to both *The King's Peace* and *The*

---

[7] *History and Hope*, p. 16.

King's War and in the memorable essay on 'The sense of the past', written while working on the latter, in which she discusses the historian's 'attempt to make the imaginative leap from our own epoch to an earlier one'.[8] She credits the Romantics from Sir Walter Scott onward with a largely new attempt to bring the reader inside the minds of people in an earlier age, with all its differences of mindcast and physical circumstance, and to present the events that befell them with all the immediacy that they themselves experienced. She herself set out to tell the story of the Great Rebellion 'in such a way as to bring out the hourly urgency and confusion through which contemporaries lived', without posterity's knowledge of what was going to happen next.[9] Rather than focus on underlying causes, she preferred 'to give full importance and value to the admitted motives and the illusions of the men of the seventeenth century', aiming 'to restore their immediacy of experience'.[10] She admitted that this approach had its limitations, but she saw drawbacks in the methods of her critics:

> Before history can be put into a coherent perspective it is often necessary to clear away the misinterpretations and the half-knowledge by which contemporaries lived. But the application of modern methods of research, together with modern knowledge and prejudice, can make the past merely the subject of our own analytical ingenuity or our own illusions. With scholarly precision we can build up theories as to why and how things happened which are convincing to us, which may even be true, but which those who lived through the epoch would neither recognise nor accept. It is legitimate for the historian to pierce the surface and bring to light motives and influences not known at the time; but it is equally legitimate to accept the motives and explanations which satisfied contemporaries. The two methods produce different results, but each result may be a fair answer to the particular question that has been asked. They become misleading only if either is accepted as the whole truth.[11]

She would not concede that her method totally neglected the historian's duty of explanation. 'A narrative history, a description of what happened and *how* it happened', she contended, 'often answers the question of *why* it happened.'[12]

One of the great virtues of her mature work was its impartiality. She wrote with such sympathetic understanding of what motivated the leading figures on both sides in the Civil War that although her own inclinations lay towards the parliament's cause there was quite a widespread popular assumption that she was at heart a royalist. She was aware of this, and it mildly irritated her. But she had such an acute sense of the tragedy of the king's fate in the aftermath of the Civil War that the story of his trial and execution took on a life of its own

---

[8] *History and Hope*, p. 416.
[9] C. V. Wedgwood, *The King's War 1641–1647* (1958), p. 11.
[10] C. V. Wedgwood, *The King's Peace 1637–1641* (1955), p. 16.
[11] Ibid., p. 15.
[12] Wedgwood, *The King's War*, p. 11.

for her, and she decided to devote a separate book to it. *The Trial of Charles I*
appeared in 1964, and it is hard to regret her decision, for nothing of hers is
more beautifully written or finer in its insights into character.

I have devoted considerable space to her writings on the Civil War period,
because although she never completed *The Great Rebellion*, what she did write
of it (including *The Trial*) has a strong claim to be her finest work, and it
prompted her to reflect and write about her craft as a historian as no previous
undertaking had done. It is a matter for profound regret that she did not carry
the story of the Interregnum to its conclusion, and one can only speculate on
the reasons for her failure to do so. It can hardly have been the mixed reception
of the first two volumes by some academic reviewers, for she was too strong-
minded to be seriously discouraged by criticism, and the response by the
public to which she mainly addressed herself was enthusiastic. It is even
less likely that she found the world of the 1650s uncongenial, for when she
was chosen to give the first Neale Lecture at University College London in
1970 she took as her subject 'Oliver Cromwell and the Elizabethan inheritance',[13] and not long after she revised and augmented her short life of the
Protector. A brief piece on *Milton and His World*, published in 1969, was also
sympathetically concerned with the 1650s.

It may be that when she tried to pick up the threads of *The Great Rebellion*
she found that her separate publication of *The Trial of Charles I* presented her
with problems of presentation, since she would have to tell a considerable part
of her story twice, but her introduction to *The Trial* shows that when she wrote it
she still fully intended to carry the main work through to the Restoration. She
was, however, repelled by the acrimony with which academic historians continued to wrangle over the causes and significance of the English Revolution,
and her reluctance to become involved probably helped to put her off continuing her great project until the dust had settled somewhat. She had many other
calls on her time to distract her, and she had no reason in her fifties to doubt that
she had many more years of full intellectual vigour ahead of her. In addition to
all she was doing for various organisations devoted to the interests of writers in
general and historians in particular, she was much in demand as a lecturer.
Between publishing *The King's Peace* and *The Trial of Charles I*, she gave
the 1956 presidential address to the English Association (on 'Literature and
the historian'), the 1957 Fairclough Lecture in Leicester University (on 'The
common man in the Great Civil War'), the Leslie Stephen Lecture of the same
year and the six Clark Lectures of the following one, all in Cambridge, the
Northcliffe Lectures in University College London not long after, and the
Foundation Lecture of 1963 in Birkbeck College (on 'History and hope'). All
these had to be prepared for publication; how many other talks she gave—

---

[13] Reprinted in *History and Hope*, pp. 317–35.

unpaid of course—to branches of the Historical Association and to historical societies in both British and American universities is past reckoning, for she generously accepted invitations whenever she could.

It was in this period too that she virtually rewrote *Strafford* as *Thomas Wentworth . . . A Revaluation*. She revised her Clark Lectures for publication by the Cambridge University Press in 1960 as *Poetry and Politics under the Stuarts*, and it is one of the most engaging and illuminating of her shorter books. Its subject is the poetry inspired by public events and public figures, and it is almost as much concerned with the popular verse of the broadsheet ballads as with the polite literature of the court and the country houses. It opened up the study of the Caroline court masques and courtly verse as a key to the mentality of Charles I's government in the 1630s, a topic that has since become something of a growth industry, and without exaggerating their significance (as some since have done) concluded that their adulation and artifice did help to close the king's mind to the harsh political realities that were soon to confront him. Veronica was also ahead of the field in recognising the remarkable talents of Marchamont Nedham, and she made an interesting case that popular balladry declined in quality in the later seventeenth century, just when sophisticated political satire entered upon a brilliant age.

History and literature were for her inseparable subjects, and the history of painting was interlinked with them. In 1967 she published a short book on *The World of Rubens, 1577–1640*, and she followed it eight years later with an expanded version of her Walter Neurath Memorial Lecture at Birkbeck College, on *The Political Career of Peter Paul Rubens*. Rubens spent lengthy periods at the court of Charles I in the role not only of an artist but of a diplomat.

Apart from another public lecture, on *The English Civil War in Perspective* (1978), only one more book was to come from her, though she published a revised edition of *The Trial of Charles I* in 1980. After an unwonted pause in her output she decided to write a concise history of the world, an undertaking which proved even more onerous than she had anticipated. She managed to complete the first half of it, extending to the mid-sixteenth century, and it appeared in 1984 as *The Spoils of Time*. I confess that I have not read it, so I would certainly not wish to imply any judgement of it, but many readers must share my regret that she took on this very demanding project before she completed *The Great Rebellion*. One would give so much to read what she had to say about the Putney debates, and the rule of the Rump, and the conquest of Ireland, and the character of the Cromwellian Protectorate, and the experience of the royalists in defeat, and the commotions which culminated in the Restoration. As it was, she completed neither that work nor her history of the world, for by the mid-1980s a cruel crippling of her intellectual powers was beginning to put research and writing beyond her capacity.

It is matter for gratitude that she remained herself during a decade and more in which the academic world fully caught up with the wider reading public in recognising her outstanding merit as a writer and a scholar. This was registered through a succession of honorary degrees, through her belated election to our Fellowship, and by the publication of a Festschrift in 1986. The contributors to *For Veronica Wedgwood These: Studies in Seventeenth-Century History* included historians as diverse (and in some cases as opposed!) as Christopher Hill, J. H. Hexter, A. L. Rowse, Maurice Ashley, Ivan Roots, and Roger Lockyer, while essays by Sir Roy Strong and Oliver Millar bear witness to her standing in the history of art. It ends with a valuable bibliography by Jaqueline Hope-Wallace.

None of these honours made the slightest difference to the innate modesty, indeed the true humility, with which Veronica faced the world. She was a quietly devout Christian, and the beauty with which she read the lessons in her parish church is well remembered. She was never narrowly tied to her own subject—if a combination of world history, literature, and art could ever be narrow! She loved reading outside her own field, poetry especially, and music and opera were part of her life. She also much enjoyed cooking, for she was a charming hostess as well as a delightful guest. She had many friends, and she made more by her personal generosity to people in need, whether refugees or fellow-writers fallen on hard times. For many years she shared a house in St John's Wood with the critic Philip Hope-Wallace and his sister Jaqueline, and after Philip's death in 1979 Jaqueline remained her companion for the rest of her life. They had a flat in London, but spent more and more of their time at the cottage that they shared near Alfriston in Sussex.

It was a tragedy that Alzheimer's disease caused her fine mind to lose its powers far ahead of her strong physical constitution. She lost not only the capacity to read and to work, but after a time even the ability to speak. The devoted care that Jaqueline Hope-Wallace gave her all through those silent years is beyond her friends' praise, but more than one of them has remarked that sufferers from her illness retain certain essential traits of character even when their cognitive powers are disabled. Enough remained of Veronica's grace of mind, her inner serenity, and her capacity for affection to make her circumscribed life bearable both for her and her devoted companion, whom (perhaps alone of those near to her) she never ceased to recognise.

It is surely not fanciful to see this nobility of character shining through in her books. They are permeated by her response to all that is generous and magnanimous, her compassion for history's victims, and her sympathy in judging the failings of those (such as Charles I and Strafford) whom her honesty compels her to reckon responsible for their own fates. It is doubtful whether any other British historian in her time has awoken a taste for serious history in so many readers who might not otherwise have come to the subject.

Yet she always practised her craft with rigour, and it seems not inappropriate to end by quoting what she had to say on the vexed old question of whether history is an art or a science: 'All sciences are devoted to the quest for truth; truth can neither be apprehended nor communicated without art. History therefore is an art, like all the other sciences.'[14]

AUSTIN WOOLRYCH
Fellow of the Academy

Note. For information and comments I am greatly indebted to Miss Jaqueline Hope-Wallace, Mr Richard Ollard, Lady Wedgwood (Dr Pamela Tudor-Craig), and Dr John Morrill. I have also drawn freely on the obituaries in the national newspapers.

[14] 'Art, truth and history' (1958), in *History and Hope*, p. 261.